Business and Administrative
Communication

Fourth Edition

Business and Administrative
Communication

Kitty O. Locker
The Ohio State University

Irwin
McGraw-Hill

Boston, Massachusetts   Burr Ridge, Illinois   Dubuque, Iowa
Madison, Wisconsin   New York, New York   San Francisco, California   St. Louis, Missouri

Irwin/McGraw-Hill

A Division of The **McGraw·Hill** *Companies*

BUSINESS AND ADMINISTRATIVE COMMUNICATION

This book is printed on acid-free paper.

2 3 4 5 6 7 8 9 0 VNH VNH 9 1 0 9 8 (US Edition)
  2 3 4 5 6 7 8 9 0 VNH VNH 9 1 0 9 8   (International Edition)

ISBN 0-256-22057-3

Publisher: *Craig S. Beytien*
Sponsoring editor: *Karen Mellon*
Developmental editor: *Catherine Schwent*
Marketing manager: *Ellen Cleary*
Senior project manager: *Mary Conzachi*
Production supervisor: *Dina Genovese*
Designer: *Larry J. Cope*
Cover illustrator: *Electronic Publishing Services, Inc.*
Compositor: *Carlisle Communications, Ltd.*
Typeface: *10.5/12 Palatino*
Printer: *Von Hoffmann Press, Inc.*

Library of Congress Cataloging-in-Publication Data

Locker, Kitty O.
   Business and administrative communication / Kitty O. Locker. —
4th ed.
      p.   cm.
   Includes index.
   ISBN 0-256-22057-3
   1. Businesss communication. 2. Communication in management.
I. Title.
HF5718.L63   1998
651.7—dc21   97–10359

http://www.mhhe.com

To my husband, Bob Mills, with love

About the Author

Kitty O. Locker is an Associate Professor of English at The Ohio State University in Columbus, Ohio, where she teaches courses in business and technical discourse and in research methods. She has taught as Assistant Professor at Texas A&M University and the University of Illinois.

She has also written *The Irwin Business Communication Handbook: Writing and Speaking in Business Classes* (1993), coauthored *Business Writing Cases and Problems* (1980, 1984, 1987), and co-edited *Conducting Research in Business Communication* (1988). She has twice received the Alpha Kappa Psi award for Distinguished Publication in Business Communication: for her article " 'Sir, This Will Never Do': Model Dunning Letters 1592–1873" and for her article " 'As Per Your Request': A History of Business Jargon." In 1992 she received the Association for Business Communication's Outstanding Researcher Award.

Her research in progress includes work on the effect of commenting styles on student attitudes and performance, collaborative writing in the classroom and the workplace, and the emer-

gence of bureaucratic writing in the correspondence of the British East India Company from 1600 to 1800.

Her consulting work includes conducting tutorials and short courses in business, technical, and administrative writing for employees of Ross Products Division of Abbott Laboratories, Franklin County, the Ohio Civil Service Employees Association, AT&T, the American Medical Association, Western Electric, the Illinois Department of Central Management Services, the Illinois Department of Transportation, the A. E. Staley Company, Flo-Con, the Police Executive Leadership College, and the Firemen's Institute. She developed a complete writing improvement program for Joseph T. Ryerson, the nation's largest steel materials service center.

She has served as the Interim Editor of *The Bulletin of the Association for Business Communication* and, in 1994–95, as President of the Association for Business Communication (ABC). She is currently editor of ABC's *Journal of Business Communication*.

1333 Burr Ridge Parkway
Burr Ridge, IL. 60521-6489

September 19, 1997   *Irwin/McGraw-Hill*
                                     A Division of The McGraw-Hill Companies

Dear Student:

Business and Administrative Communication (BAC) takes the mystery out of writing and speaking effectively.

As you read,

- Use the Chapter Outline to preview what you'll learn. Check your understanding with the Summary of Key Points at the end of the chapter.

- Note the terms in boldface type and their definitions. In later chapters, the linked chain icon identifies the page where the term is first defined.

- Use items in the lists when you prepare your assignments or review for tests.

- Use the examples, especially the paired examples of effective and ineffective communication, as models to help you draft and revise. Comments in red ink signal problems in an example; comments in blue ink note things done well.

The side columns offer anecdotes and examples that show the principles in the text at work in a variety of business and administrative situations. Some readers like to read all the sidebars first, then come back to read the chapter. Other readers prefer to take a break from the page to read the sidebar. The logos identify the kind of example:

 International examples show how to apply or modify the principles when you communicate with international audiences.

 Ethical and Legal examples alert you to ethical decisions and legal implications of business and administrative communication.

 Technology examples show how technology can help create better messages and how technological changes affect the way people produce, transmit, and interpret business messages.

September 19, 1997
Page 2

On-the-Job examples show the principles in the text at work.

Sidebar Classics are oldies but goodies--still relevant to today's business world.

Just-for-Fun anecdotes show the lighter side of business communication. Skip them if you're in a hurry, or read them just for enjoyment.

When you prepare an assignment,

- Review the analysis questions in Chapter 1. Some assignments have "Hints" to help probe the problem. Some of the longer assignments have preliminary assignments analyzing the audience or developing reader benefits or subject lines. Use these to practice portions of longer documents.

- If you're writing a letter or memo, read the sample problems in Chapters 7, 8, and 9 with a detailed analysis, strong and weak solutions, and a discussion of the solutions to see how to apply the principles in this book to your own writing.

- Remember that most problems are open-ended, requiring original, critical thinking. Many of the problems are deliberately written in negative, ineffective language. You'll need to reword sentences, reorganize information, and think through the situation to produce the best possible solution to the business problem.

- Learn as much as you can about what's happening in business. The knowledge will not only help you develop reader benefits and provide examples but also make you an even more impressive candidate in job interviews.

Business and Administrative Communication can help you develop the communication skills required for success in Workforce 2000. Have a good term--and a good career!

Cordially,

Kitty O. Locker

Kitty O. Locker
locker.1@osu.edu

1333 Burr Ridge Parkway
Burr Ridge, IL 60521-6489

September 19, 1997   *Irwin/McGraw-Hill*

*A Division of The **McGraw·Hill** Companies*

Dear Professor:

Business and Administrative Communication (BAC) can make your job teaching business communication just a little bit easier.

You'll find that this edition of BAC is as flexible, specific, interesting, comprehensive, and up-to-date as its predecessors. The features teachers and students find so useful have been retained: the anecdotes and examples, the easy-to-follow lists, the integrated coverage of ethics and international business communication, the analyses of sample problems, the wealth of in-class exercises and out-of-class assignments. But a good thing has become even better. This edition of BAC is the most effective teaching tool yet.

Major Changes in the Fourth Edition

Seven major changes make the text even more useful:

- Greater emphasis on e-mail prepares students to "hit the ground running" when they use e-mail on the job. Students will find specific advice about e-mail in four chapters and e-mail assignments in many chapters.

- Coverage of the Web allows students to play with one of the most enjoyable forms of business communication. Students get advice about screen design, examples of Web pages, and Web problems in several chapters.

- Categorization of problems into "Getting Started," "E-Mail Assignments," "Communicating at Work" (problems for your students with jobs), "Web Assignments," and "Letter/Memo/Report Assignments" enables you to draw from the diversity of channels available to today's business communicators.

- More coverage on tone helps students be confident but not arrogant, subordinate but not cringing.

- New and expanded chapter opening statements by business people keep the text up-to-date.

- Citations under the sidebars build credibility.

- Communication theory moves to an appendix, since many students have already covered this material in earlier communication classes.

September 19, 1997
Page 2

Features Retained

BAC retains the features that made the third edition the number one book in business communication:

- **BAC is flexible.** Choose the chapters that best fit your course and your students. Choose from in-class exercises, messages to revise, problems with hints, and cases presented as they'd arise in the workplace. Many problems offer several options: small group discussions, individual writing, group writing, or oral presentations.

- **BAC is specific.** BAC provides specific strategies, specific guidelines, specific examples. BAC takes the mystery out of creating effective messages.

- **BAC is interesting.** Anecdotes from a variety of fields show business communication at work. The lively side columns from *The Wall Street Journal* and a host of other sources keep students turning pages and provide insights into the workplace that business students demand.

- **BAC is comprehensive.** BAC includes international communication, ethics, collaborative writing, organizational cultures, graphs, and technology as well as traditional concerns such as style and organization. Assignments allow students to deal with international audiences or to cope with ethical dilemmas.

- **BAC is up-to-date.** The fourth edition of BAC incorporates the latest research and practice so that you and your students stay on the cutting edge.

Supplements

The stimulating, user-friendly supplement package has been one of the major reasons that BAC is so popular. You can get the supplements in an Instructor's Resource Box with separate file folders for each chapter so that you can add your own notes and handouts.

The Instructor's Resource Box contains

- **Answers to all exercises, an overview and difficulty rating for each problem, and, for 40 of the problems in the book, a detailed analysis, discussion and quiz questions, and a good solution.** Even if you rarely use an *Instructor's Manual,* you may want to check for answers to unusual exercises, such as which age group is most likely to have moved in the last year.

- **Fifty transparencies** with examples to critique and key points to use in lectures and discussions.

- **Additional transparency masters** with ready-to-duplicate examples and lecture points.

September 19, 1997
Page 3

- **Additional exercises and cases** for diagnostic and readiness tests, grammar and style, and for letters, memos, and reports.

- **PowerPoint electronic acetates** to enliven your classes.

- **Lesson plans and class activities for each chapter.** You'll find discussion guides for transparencies, activities to reinforce chapter materials and prepare students for assignments, and handouts for group work, peer editing, and other activities.

- **Sample syllabi** for courses with different emphases and approaches.

- **A test bank** with 1,200 test items with answers and a difficulty rating for each. The test bank is also available on computer disks so that you can generate your own tests and quizzes.

- **Effective writing software** with seven lessons on building better grammar skills. Lessons cover mood and voice, tense, case, agreement and reference, modifiers, connectives, and punctuation. The software is available bundled with BAC.

- **A CD-ROM** with handouts, e-mail assignments, and materials you can use to create your own individual presentations.

Continuing the Conversation

You can get more information about teaching business communication from the meetings and publications of The Association for Business Communication (ABC). Contact

Professor Robert J. Myers, Executive Director
Association for Business Communication
Baruch College--CUNY
Department of Speech
17 Lexington Avenue
New York, NY 10010
Voice: 212-387-1340; Fax: 212-387-1655; E-mail: 70511.753@compuserve.com

This edition incorporates the feedback I've received from instructors who used earlier editions. Tell me about your own success stories teaching *Business and Administrative Communication*. I look forward to hearing from you!

Cordially,

Kitty O. Locker
locker.1@osu.edu

Acknowledgments

All writing is in some sense collaborative. This book in particular builds upon the ideas and advice of teachers, students, and researchers. The people who share their ideas in conferences and publications enrich not only this book but also business communication as a field.

Several people reviewed the third edition, suggesting what to change and what to keep. Additional reviewers commented on drafts of the fourth edition, helping me further improve the book. I thank all of these reviewers for their attention to detail and their promptness! The people whose names I have been given are

Yvonne Merrill, *University of Arizona*
Jean E. Perry, *University of Southern California*
Elizabeth Jenkins, *Pennsylvania State University*
Maxine B. Hart, *Baylor University*
Vanessa D. Arnold, *University of Mississippi*
Barbara Hagler, *Southern Illinois University*
Jeanette Ritzenthaler, *New Hampshire College*
Sherilyn K. Zeigler, *Hawaii Pacific University*
Dona Vasa, *University of Nebraska-Lincoln*
Barry Lawler, *Oregon State University*
Kelly Searsmith, *University of Illinois*
Andrew Cantrell, *University of Illinois*
Mark Hartstein, *University of Illinois*
Linda M. LaDuc, *University of Massachusetts, Amherst*

The following people commented on specific aspects of the book or helped me with specific needs:

Bill Allen, *University of LaVerne*
Donna Kienzler, *Iowa State University*
Peter Hadorn, *Virginia Commonwealth University*
Susan Isaacs, *Community College of Philadelphia*

Michael D. Mahler, *Montana State University*
Frederick K. Moss, *University of Wisconsin—Waukesha*

Many of the teachers and students who used the third edition have taken the time to tell me about their experiences with the book. I am especially grateful to the professors whose students shared their evaluations of the text with me:

Jaye Bausser, *The Ohio State University*
Cheryl Glenn, *Oregon State University*
Elaine Hage, *Forsythe Technical Community College*
Paula R. Kaiser, *University of North Carolina at Greensboro*
Sherry Sherrill, *Forsyth Technical Community College*
Bonnie Thames Yarbrough, *University of North Carolina at Greensboro*

In addition, the book continues to benefit from people who advised me on earlier editions:

Vanessa Arnold, *University of Mississippi*
Lynn Ashford, *Alabama State University*
Dennis Barbour, *Purdue University—Calumet*
Carole Bhakar, *The University of Manitoba*
Sallye Benoit, *Nicholls State University*
Raymond W. Beswick, *formerly of Synerude, Ltd.*
Vincent Brown, *Battelle Memorial Institute*
John Bryan, *University of Cincinnati*
Janice Burke, *South Suburban College of Cook County*
John Carr, *The Ohio State University*
Brendan G. Coleman, *Mankato State University*
Moira E. W. Dempsy, *Oregon State University*
Gladys DeVane, *Indiana University*
Jose A. Duran, *Riverside Community College*
Dorothy J. Dykman, *Point Loma Nazarene College*
Mary Ann Firmin, *Oregon State University*
W. Clark Ford, *Middle Tennessee State University*
Robert D. Gieselman, *University of Illinois*

Robert Haight, *Kalamazoo Valley Community College*
Les Hanson, *Red River Community College, Canada*
Maxine Hart, *Baylor University*
Charles Hebert, *The University of South Carolina*
Paulette Henry, *Howard University*
Carlton Holte, *California State University, Sacramento*
Glenda Hudson, *California State University, Bakersfield*
Elizabeth Huettman, *Cornell University*
Daphne A. Jameson, *Cornell University*
Joy Kidwell, *Oregon State University*
Susan E. Kiner, *Cornell University*
Keith Kroll, *Kalamazoo Valley Community College*
Milton Kukon, *Southern Vermont College*
Suzanne Lambert, *Broward Community College*
Gordon Lee, *University of Tennessee*
Andrea A. Lunsford, *The Ohio State University*
John T. Maguire, *University of Illinois*
Iris Washburn Mauney, *High Point College*
Jayne Moneysmith, *Kent State University–Stark*
Evelyn Morris, *Mesa Community College*
Frank P. Nemecek, Jr., *Wayne State University*
Florence M. Petrofes, *University of Texas at El Paso*
Virginia Polanski, *Stonehill College*
Kathryn C. Rentz, *University of Cincinnati*
Frank Smith, *Harper College*
Pamela Smith, *Florida Atlantic University*
Judith A. Swartley, *Lehigh University*
Mel Tarnowski, *Macomb Community College*
Linda Travis, *Ferris State University*
Donna Vasa, *University of Nebraska*
David A. Victor, *Eastern Michigan University*
George Walters, *Emporia State University*
Judy West, *University of Tennessee-Chattanooga*
Rosemary Wilson, *Washtenaw Community College*

I'm pleased to know that the book has worked so well for so many people and appreciative of suggestions for ways to make it even more useful in this edition. I especially want to thank the students who have allowed me to use their letters and memos, whether or not they allowed me to use their real names in the text.

I am grateful to all the business people who were willing to interrupt busy schedules to write the chapter-opening statements for this book. The companies where I have done research and consulting work have given me insights into the problems and procedures of business and administrative communication. Special acknowledgment is due Joseph T. Ryerson & Son, Inc., which hired me to create the Writing Skills Program that ultimately became the first draft of this book. And I thank the organizations that permitted me to reproduce their documents in this book and in the transparency masters.

Paula Weston did library research and helped with proofreading; Gianna Marsella and Andrea Williams made innumerable phone calls to schedule the interviews. The book continues to incorporate the contributions of Bennis Blue, Susan Carlson, Kathy Casto, Jane Greer, Ruth Ann Hendrickson, Scott Miller, and Carole Clark Papper to earlier editions.

My publisher, Irwin/McGraw-Hill, continues to provide strong editorial and staff support. I am particularly grateful to Karen Mellon for her creative problem solving, patience, and encouragement, to Jenny Boxell and Harriet Stockanes for taking care of necessary details, and to Larry Cope, and Mary Conzachi, for the appearance of the book.

And, finally, I thank my husband, Robert S. Mills, who continues to provide a sounding board for ideas, encouragement, a keen eye for typos, and, when deadlines are tight (as they continue to be, even on this fourth edition), weekly or nightly rides to Federal Express.

Contents in Brief

Table of Contents

PART 2
LETTERS AND MEMOS   143

The Building Blocks of Effective Messages

CHAPTER 1

Business Communication, Management, and Success

Chapter Outline

An Inside Perspective:
Business Communication, Management, and Success

Andrew Drysdale, Communications Director
Boise Cascade Corporation

Andrew Drysdale has practiced, counseled, and taught business communication for more than 20 years. He helps people develop effective communication strategies and materials that support business objectives.
Boise Cascade is a major forest products company based in Boise, Idaho, that makes paper and wood products and distributes building products and office supplies. The company owns and manages over 2 million acres of forests in the United States that provide much of the wood and wood fiber required to make these wood and paper products.

Business people communicate with a variety of individuals and groups every day. At Boise Cascade, these important audiences include employees, shareholders, government officials, customers, community leaders, the news media, suppliers, and anyone else in a position to help or hinder our work or our business operating environment. Consistently effective communication, based on trustworthy behavior, is essential to developing the understanding and support among these audiences that result in their contributing to our success. The ability to communicate well is becoming an increasingly valued competence in the business world.

In business we communicate for only one reason: to influence someone to think or behave in a particular way. For example, managers want to influence employees to understand, support, and work for business goals such as increasing productivity, sales, profits, and quality while reducing costs. People in sales and marketing want to influence customers to purchase our products and services. Company officials want to influence investors to buy our stock.

To influence any audience, we must understand and relate to their interests and needs. We must get to know them, establish mutually beneficial working relationships, and communicate in ways we've learned will most likely resonate favorably with them.

Typically, effective communication is based on face-to-face interaction between people working to establish and maintain mutual trust and understanding.

This interpersonal communication is often supported by the appropriate written, spoken, and broadcast communication material. Memos, newsletters, news releases, speeches, videotapes, and other media must be designed to clearly convey messages that support the interpersonal communications that precede or follow. However, when we rely solely on these media, no matter how well crafted, we lose the ability that interpersonal communication provides to gauge if and how people respond to our communication. Essentially, we confuse merely disseminating information with interactive communication.

To increase the chances for success of any important business activity, develop a communication plan at the outset. The plan's goal should be influencing the desired thinking and behavior of all the people necessary to the activity's success. The plan should articulate a clear purpose, the desired outcomes, and the messages and methods that will work best with audiences you need to reach. Without this kind of planned communication, the success of the activity and of the people involved is jeopardized unnecessarily.

Business communication affects a company's bottom line directly and indirectly. Done well, communication helps us avoid costs and make the most of opportunities. For example, it can help determine whether a regulator grants a flexible operating permit, a customer buys our product, or an employee is motivated to do his or her best work.

Anyone can enhance his or her business career by demonstrating the communication skills that are increasingly necessary for businesses and business people to succeed. Take the time to master these skills and make them an important part of what you have to offer an employer.

Andrew Drysdale, October 24, 1996

Visit Boise Cascade's Web site: http://www.bc.com

"Communication skills . . . are increasingly necessary for businesses and business people to succeed."

Andrew Drysdale, Boise Cascade

Business depends on communication. People must communicate to plan products, hire, train, and motivate workers; coordinate manufacturing and delivery; persuade customers to buy; and bill them for the sale. Indeed, for many businesses and nonprofit and government organizations, the "product" is information or services rather than something tangible. And information and services are created and delivered by communication. In every organization, communication is the way people get their points across and get work done.

Communication takes many forms: face-to-face or phone conversations, informal meetings, e-mail messages, letters, memos, and reports. All of these methods are **verbal communication,** or communication that uses words. **Nonverbal communication** does not use words. Pictures, computer graphics, and company logos are nonverbal. Interpersonal nonverbal signals include smiles, who sits where at a meeting, the size of an office, and how long someone keeps a visitor waiting.

COMMUNICATION ABILITY = PROMOTABILITY

Even in your first job, you'll communicate. You'll read information; you'll listen to instructions; you'll ask questions; you may solve problems with other workers in teams. In a manufacturing company, hourly workers travel to a potential customer to make oral sales presentations. In an insurance company, clerks answer customers' letters. Even "entry-level" jobs require high-level skills in reasoning, mathematics, and communicating.[1]

As you rise in an organization, high-level skills, including the ability to speak and write well, determine how fast and how far you go. As Joyce Cochenour, an administrator at Allstate Insurance, points out,

> If you want to stay at the entry level . . . you really don't have to write much. If you want promotions, on the other hand, writing becomes important. If you want to get into management positions, you're going to have to speak in front of groups and do some writing.[2]

Anne Faircloth of *Fortune* advises,

Learn how to talk the walk—and write it as well. . . .[T]echnical prowess won't get you to the top unless you can express yourself in written and spoken words to a variety of audiences—customers, colleagues, analysts, journalists, and many more.[3]

When several candidates for a promotion all have good technical skills, differences in communication skills may decide who gets the job. Ben Ordover explains his practice as a division president at CBS:

Many people climbing the corporate ladder are very good. When faced with a hard choice between candidates, I used writing ability as the deciding factor. Sometimes a candidate's writing was the only skill that separated him or her from the competition.[4]

"I'll Never Have to Write Because . . ."

Some students aren't convinced that they will need to write well to succeed professionally. They may think that a secretary or technical writer will do their writing, that they can use form letters if they do have to write, that only technical skills matter, or that they'll call rather than write. Each of these claims is fundamentally flawed.

Claim 1: "Secretaries or Technical Writers Will Do All My Writing."

Downsizing and voice mail have cut support staffs from 10 to 30% nationwide. Of the secretaries who remain, 71% are administrative assistants whose duties are managerial, not clerical.[5] As a result, most workers in business and government today draft and revise their own letters, memos, and reports at desktop computers or terminals. You'll be responsible for correct spelling, mechanics, and format as well as organization, logic, audience analysis, or tone.

In high-tech companies, materials that go to the general public or to the government may be edited or even written by technical writers. Even in organizations with a large staff of technical writers, however, engineers and computer programmers still write their own internal proposals and reports and their own letters. And virtually every business expects its accountants, sales representatives, and managers to do their own writing.

Claim 2: "I'll Use Form Letters When I Need to Write."

A **form letter** is a prewritten fill-in-the-blank letter designed to fit standard situations. The writer can personalize a form letter by having it individually typed with the recipient's name and address. Sometimes form letters have several different paragraphs from which the writer can choose, depending on the circumstances. Using a form letter is OK if it's a good letter, but some of the letters currently in use are dreadful. (See Figure 1.5 later in this chapter for an example of one bad form letter.)

Even good form letters cover only routine situations. The higher you rise in your organization, the more frequently you'll face situations that aren't routine, that demand creative solutions. If you develop the skills necessary for good writing and original thinking, you're far more likely to realize your potential and reach your career goals.

Quality in Communication*

Communication is an essential function—just as human resources, sales, etc. are essential.

[At Wausau,] we start with selecting people with good communication skills. We use formal training provided by our writers and editors, our education staff, and even outside university professors. We also coach people within the company in communication techniques. Good communication has become part of the culture of the organization.

*Quoted from Jim Van Eyck, phone interview with the author, December 6, 1993.

Legal Implications of Business Writing*

Letters and memos create legal obligations for organizations.

When a lawsuit is filed against an organization, the lawyers for the plaintiffs have the right to subpoena documents written by employees of the organization. These documents may then be used as evidence that an employer fired an employee without adequate notice or that a company knew about a safety defect but did nothing to correct it.

Organizations whose actions are irresponsible or negligent deserve to be condemned by their own words. But a careless writer can create obligations that the writer does not intend and that the organization does not mean to assume.

Careful writers and speakers think about the larger social context in which their words may be read. What might those words mean to other people in your field? What might they mean to a judge and jury?

*Based on Elizabeth A. McCord, "The Business Writer, The Law, and Routine Business Communication: A Legal and Rhetorical Analysis," *Journal of Business and Technical Communication* 5.2 (April 1991): 173–99.

Claim 3: "I'm Being Hired as an Accountant, Not a Writer."

Your technical skill in accounting or computer science or marketing may get you your first job. The ability to speak and write effectively may help you keep it. The inability to write is the main reason that Big Six accounting firms fire new hires.[6] In response to the need for better writing by accountants, the province of Manitoba has instituted a writing competency exam as part of its licensing procedure for accountants. In the United States, the Uniform CPA Examination began in 1994 to evaluate candidates on six aspects of writing ability—organization, conciseness, clarity, use of standard English, responsiveness to the question, and appropriateness for the reader—as well as on technical knowledge of accountancy.[7] At Ernst and Young, performance appraisals rate CPAs' abilities in five areas, one of which is writing working papers and reports.[8]

Almost every entry-level professional or managerial job requires you to write e-mail messages, speak to small groups, and write some paper documents. Many people in business and government routinely write from 10 pages of letters and memos a week to, in some cases, 20 to 30 pages a day. And that doesn't count the dozens of e-mail messages workers write and receive. The Air Force estimates that it produces 500 million pages of writing a year.[9] Most professionals find that the higher they go, the more they write. Margot Northey found that 80% of the partners in the Big Six accounting firms wrote memos every day; 67% wrote reports or notes to a financial statement and 93% wrote letters to clients *at least* once a week.[10]

Claim 4: "I'll Just Pick Up the Phone."

Most people in organizations say they spend more time talking and listening than they do reading and writing. But no organization depends exclusively on oral communication. People in organizations put things in writing to make themselves visible, to create a record, to convey complex data, to make things convenient for the reader, to save money, and to convey their own messages more effectively.

"If it isn't in writing," says a manager at one company, "it didn't happen." Writing is an essential way to make yourself visible, to let your accomplishments be known.

Written memos and reports document what was said and done and the reasons for decisions. Carefully written memos and reports enable a company to use its earlier experience without having to reinvent the wheel every time a new set of people tackles a recurring problem. Written documents also allow individuals and companies to protect themselves. If there is no written record, chaos—and expensive lawsuits—may result.

Written channels (including graphics) are better than oral ones for conveying numbers and complex information. Written channels are less expensive than oral ones for reaching large groups of people or transmitting information over long distances. Writing may also be more convenient for the recipient. To talk, both people must be free at the same time. This is rarely the case in business. Only 12% of business phone calls find the intended receiver in the office on the first try.[11] When you send a letter or memo, the recipient can read it when it's most convenient. Even more important, the reader can proceed at a convenient pace, skimming easier or less important sections and rereading difficult or key sections. Written documents become even more important in international business. Talking on the phone requires immediate comprehension. Reading a fax or telex is easier for a manager doing business in a language other than his or her native language.

Finally, putting a message in writing makes it easier to present your ideas in the most effective way, even in difficult situations. We've all had the experience of fumbling for words, only to think of the perfect words to make a point after it was all over. Writing, because it can be revised, gives us the second chance we may need to achieve the effect we want.

The Managerial Functions of Communication

According to Henry Mintzberg, managers have three basic jobs: to collect and convey information, to make decisions, and to promote interpersonal unity.[12] Every one of those jobs is carried out through communication. Managers collect relevant information from conversations, the grapevine, phone calls, memos, reports, databases, and the Internet. They convey information and decisions to other people inside or outside the organization through meetings, speeches, press releases, videos, memos, letters, and reports. Managers motivate organizational members in speeches, memos, conversations at lunch and over coffee, bulletin boards, and through "management by walking around."

Effective managers are able to use a wide variety of media and strategies to communicate. They know how to interpret comments from informal channels such as the company grapevine; they can speak effectively in small groups and in formal presentations; they write well.

Communication—oral, nonverbal, and written—goes to both internal and external audiences. **Internal audiences** (Figure 1.1) are other people in the same organization: subordinates, superiors, peers. **External audiences** (Figure 1.2) are people outside the organization: customers, suppliers, unions, stockholders, potential employees, government agencies, the press, and the general public.

The Importance of Listening, Speaking, and Interpersonal Communication

Informal listening, speaking, and working in groups are just as important as writing formal documents and giving formal oral presentations. As a newcomer in an organization, you'll need to listen to others both to find out what you're supposed to do and to learn about the organization's values and culture. Informal chitchat, both about yesterday's game and about what's happening at work, connects you to the **grapevine,** an informal source of company information. You may be asked to speak to small groups, either inside or outside your organization.[13] Networking with others in your office and in town and working with others in workgroups will be crucial to your success.

These skills remain important as you climb the corporate ladder. In fact, a study of 15 executives judged good performers by their companies showed that these executives spent most of their time in informal contact with other people. They asked questions; they joked; they schmoozed; they nudged people toward the direction they wanted them to go. These informal discussions and meetings took 76% of these executives' work time. The resulting interactions with thousands of employees and outsiders enabled them to promote their agendas.[14]

Listening at Pillsbury*

Top managers in some companies are isolated. Pillsbury managers avoid that problem by encouraging anonymous phone calls.

Pillsbury employees can sound off to a recording machine. Another company provides verbatim anonymous transcripts. Pillsbury's CEO gets them all.

Some comments report problems: delayed pension benefits or expense reimbursements.

Many comments suggest ideas or provide genuinely useful knowledge. One caller suggests a new topping for Pillsbury's frozen pizza. Another notes that the time clock in Eden Prairie, Minnesota, was five minutes fast. Still another notes that a certain retail product isn't on the local grocery store shelf.

Some comments support managers' decisions. Dozens of employees phoned in to applaud the action of one manager in shutting down a plant during a snowstorm.

Pillsbury's managers listen. And as a result, in small, important ways, the company is changing the way it does business.

*Based on Thomas Petzinger, Jr., "Two Executives Cook Up Way to Make Pillsbury Listen," *The Wall Street Journal,* September 27, 1996, B1.

Figure 1.1

The Internal Audiences of the Sales Manager—West

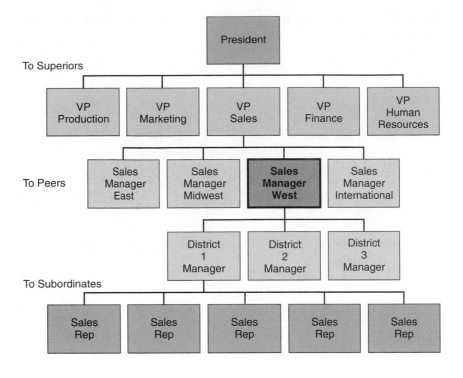

Figure 1.2

The Organization's External Audiences

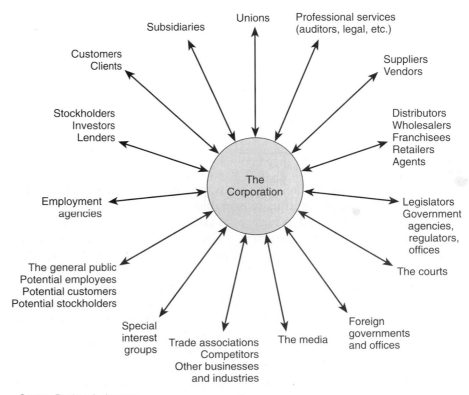

Source: Daphne A. Jameson

The Documents That Writers in Organizations Write

People in organizations produce a large variety of documents. Donald Skarzenski, Manager of Marketing Communication at Cadre Technologies, lists the items he produces:

> Those of us who make our living in business and technical writing create product overviews, sales guides, brochures, press releases, configuration guides, product announcements, data sheets, business plans, newsletters, magazine articles, user's manuals, reference guides, proposals, specifications, marketing plans, advertising copy, and more.[15]

The most common documents written by accounting practitioners, according to Rebekah Maupin, are

> proposals, progress reports, audit reports, financial reports, audit programs, and instructions and procedures.[16]

Figures 1.3 and 1.4 list a few of the documents produced at Joseph T. Ryerson & Son. Ryerson, a subsidiary of a Fortune 500 company, has 25 plants across the United States; it fabricates and sells steel, aluminum, and plastics to a wide variety of industrial clients.

All of the documents in Figures 1.3 and 1.4 have one or more of the **three basic purposes of organizational writing:** to inform, to request or persuade, and to build goodwill. When you **inform,** you explain something or tell readers something. When you **request or persuade,** you want the reader to act. The word *request* suggests that the action will be easy or routine; *persuade* suggests that you will have to motivate and convince the reader to act. When you **build goodwill,** you create a good image of yourself and of your organization—the kind of image that makes people want to do business with you.

Most messages have multiple purposes. When you answer a question, you're informing, but you also want to build goodwill by suggesting that you're competent and perceptive and that your answer is correct and complete. In a claims adjustment, whether your answer is *yes* or *no,* you want to suggest that the reader's claim has been given careful consideration and that the decision is fair, businesslike, and justified. In a policy and procedure bulletin, the writer wants to suggest that the policy will help the organization and the reader. Without goodwill, the reader might think that the organization was hung up on red tape, or that it was trying to play Big Brother to employees. People are more likely to follow procedures if they feel that the policies are fair and the procedures reasonable.

Two of the documents listed in Figure 1.4 package the same information in different ways for different audiences. The 10-K report filed with the Securities and Exchange Commission (SEC) and the annual report distributed to stockholders contain essentially the same information, but differing purposes and differing audiences create two distinct documents. The 10-K report is informative, designed merely to show that the company is complying with SEC regulations. The annual report, in contrast, has multiple purposes and audiences. Its primary purpose is to convince stockholders that the company is a good investment and a good corporate citizen. Annual reports will also be read by employees, stockbrokers, potential stockholders, and job applicants, so the firm creates a report that is persuasive and builds goodwill as well as presenting information.

Figure 1.3   **Internal Documents Produced in One Organization**

Document	Description of Document	Purpose(s) of Document
Transmittal	Memo accompanying document, telling why it's being forwarded to the receiver	Inform; persuade reader to read document; build image and goodwill
Monthly or quarterly report	Report summarizing profitability, productivity, and problems during period. Used to plan activity for next month or quarter	Inform; build image and goodwill (report is accurate, complete; writer understands company)
Policy and procedure bulletin	Statement of company policies and instructions (e.g., how to enter orders, how to run fire drills, etc.)	Inform; build image and goodwill (procedures are reasonable)
Request to deviate from policy and procedure bulletin	Persuasive memo arguing that another approach is better for a specific situation than the standard approach	Persuade; build image and goodwill (request is reasonable; writer seeks good of company)
Performance appraisal	Evaluation of an employee's performance, with recommended areas for improvement or recommendation for promotion	Inform; persuade employee to improve
Memo of congratulations	Congratulations to employees who have won awards, been promoted, or earned community recognition	Build goodwill

Figure 1.4   **External Documents Produced in One Organization**

Document	Description of Document	Purpose(s) of Document
Quotation	Letter giving price for a specific product, fabrication, or service	Inform; build goodwill (price is reasonable)
Claims adjustment	Letter granting or denying customer request to be given credit for defective goods	Inform; build goodwill
Job description	Description of qualifications and duties of each job, used for performance appraisals, setting salaries, and for hiring	Inform; persuade good candidates to apply; build goodwill (job duties match level, pay)
10-K report	Report filed with the Securities and Exchange Commission detailing financial information	Inform
Annual report	Report to stockholders summarizing financial information for year	Inform; persuade stockholders to retain stock and others to buy; build goodwill (company is a good corporate citizen)
Thank-you letter	Letter to suppliers, customers, or other people who have helped individuals or the company	Build goodwill

The Cost of Correspondence

Writing costs money. In 1996, according to the Dartnell Institute, a short one-page business letter cost between $13.60 and $20.52, depending on how it was produced.[17] Dartnell's estimates assume that an executive dictates a letter in 10 minutes. But a consultant who surveyed employees in seven industries found that most of them spent 54 minutes planning, composing, and revising a one-page letter.[18] Her respondents, then, each spent over $84 at 1996 prices to create a one-page letter. One company in Minneapolis writes 3,000 original letters a day. If each of those letters is written in slightly less than an hour, it spends at least $252,000 a day just on outgoing correspondence.

In many organizations, all external documents must be approved before they go out. A document may **cycle** from writer to superior to writer to another superior to writer again 3 or 4 or even 11 times before it is finally approved. The cycling process increases the cost of correspondence.

Longer documents can involve large teams of people and take months to write. An engineering firm that relies on military contracts for its business calculates that it spends $500,000 to put together an average proposal and $1 million to write a large proposal.[19]

Good communication is worth every minute it takes and every penny it costs. In fact, in a survey conducted by the International Association of Business Communicators, CEOs said that communication yielded a 235% return on investment.[20]

THE COSTS OF POOR CORRESPONDENCE

When writing isn't as good as it could be, you and your organization pay a price in wasted time, wasted efforts, and lost goodwill.

Wasted Time

Bad writing takes longer to read. Studies show that up to 97% of our reading time is taken not in moving our eyes across the page but in trying to understand what we're reading. How quickly we can do this is determined by the difficulty of the subject matter and by the document's organization and writing style.

Second, bad writing may need to be rewritten. Many managers find that a disproportionate amount of their time is taken trying to explain to subordinates how to revise a document.

Third, ineffective writing may obscure ideas so that discussions and decisions are needlessly drawn out. People inside an organization may disagree on the best course, and the various publics with which organizations communicate may have different interests and values. But if a proposal is clear, at least everyone will be talking about the same proposed changes, so that differences can be recognized and resolved more quickly.

Fourth, unclear or incomplete messages may require the reader to ask for more information. A reader who has to supplement the memo with questions interrupts the writer. If the writer is out of the office when the reader stops by or calls, even more time is wasted, for the reader can't act until the answer arrives.

Wasted Efforts

Ineffective messages don't get results. A reader who has to guess what the writer means may guess wrong. A reader who finds a letter or memo unconvincing or insulting simply won't do what the message asks. In 1986, Frank Grazian said that between 15% and 30% of business and government letters and memos were written only because the first document didn't do the job.[21]

One company sent out past-due bills with the following language:

> Per our conversation, enclosed are two copies of the above-mentioned invoice.
> Please review and advise. Sincerely, . . .

The company wanted money, not advice, but it didn't say so. The company had to write third and fourth reminders. It waited for its money, lost interest on it—and kept writing letters.

The Cost of Confused, Overstuffed Corporate Writing*

A few years ago an oil company chemicals unit spent a bundle reinventing from scratch a selective pesticide one of its own researchers had found five years before; he'd buried the news 25 pages deep in a hopeless gumbo of report prose that no one apparently could get through. Another, luckier company accidentally stumbled on a similar in-house report about a new production process just before it began building a plant using the older, costlier way. . . .

Fuzzy building instructions have added hundreds of thousands of dollars to building costs. And a single hyphen omitted by a supervisor at a government-run nuclear installation may hold the cost record for punctuation goofs. He ordered rods of radioactive material cut into "10 foot long lengths"; he got 10 pieces, each a foot long, instead of the 10-foot lengths required. The loss was so great it was classified [as secret by the federal government].

*Quoted from William E. Blundell, "Confused, Overstuffed Corporate Writing Often Costs Firms Much Time—and Money," *The Wall Street Journal,* August 21, 1980, 21.

Lost Goodwill

Whatever the literal content of the words, every letter, memo, or report serves either to build or to undermine the image the reader has of the writer.

The form letter printed in Figure 1.5 failed because it was stuffy and selfish. Four different customers called to complain about it. When you think how often you are annoyed by something—a TV commercial, a rude clerk—but how rarely you call or write the company to complain, you can imagine the ill will this letter generated.

As the comments in red show, several things are wrong with the letter in Figure 1.5.

1. **The language is stiff and legalistic.** Note the obsolete (and sexist) "Gentlemen:" "Please be advised," "herein," and "expedite."
2. **The tone is selfish.** The letter is written from the writer's point of view; there are no benefits for the reader. (The writer says there are, but, without a shred of evidence, the claim isn't convincing.)
3. **The main point is buried** in the middle of the long first paragraph. The middle is the least emphatic part of a paragraph.
4. **The request is vague.** How many references does the supplier want? Are only vendor references OK, or would other credit references, like banks, work too? Is the name of the reference enough, or is it necessary also to specify the line of credit, the average balance, the current balance, the years credit has been established, or other information? What "additional financial information" does the supplier want? Annual reports? Bank balance? Tax returns? The request sounds like an invasion of privacy, not a reasonable business practice.
5. **Words are misused** (*herein* for *therein*), suggesting either an ignorant writer or one who doesn't care enough about the subject and the reader to use the right word.

CRITERIA FOR EFFECTIVE MESSAGES

Good business and administrative writing meets five basic criteria: it's clear, complete, and correct; it saves the reader's time; and it builds goodwill.

1. **It's clear.** The meaning the reader gets is the meaning the writer intended. The reader doesn't have to guess.
2. **It's complete.** All of the reader's questions are answered. The reader has enough information to evaluate the message and act on it.
3. **It's correct.** All of the information in the message is accurate. The message is free from errors in punctuation, spelling, grammar, word order, and sentence structure.
4. **It saves the reader's time.** The style, organization, and visual impact of the message help the reader to read, understand, and act on the information as quickly as possible.
5. **It builds goodwill.** The message presents a positive image of the writer and his or her organization. It treats the reader as a person, not a number. It cements a good relationship between the writer and the reader.

Whether a messages meets these five criteria depends on **the interactions among the writer, the audience, the purposes of the message, and the situation.** No single set of words will work in all possible situations.

A Form Letter that Annoyed Customers   **Figure 1.5**

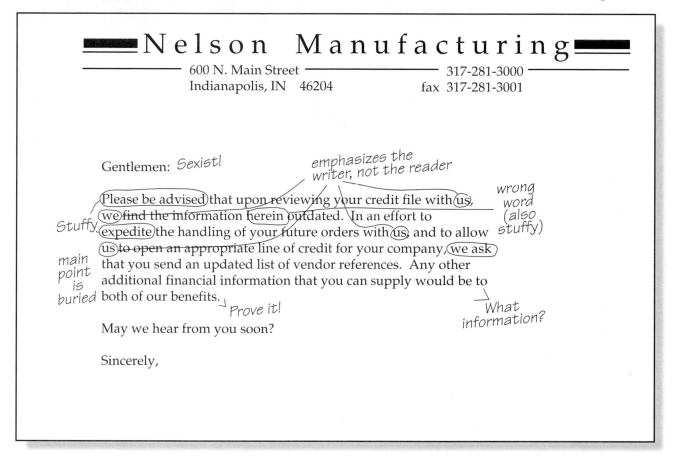

BENEFITS OF IMPROVING CORRESPONDENCE

Better writing helps you to

- **Save time.** Reduce reading time, since comprehension is easier. Eliminate the time now taken to rewrite badly written materials. Reduce the time taken asking writers "What did you mean?"
- **Make your efforts more effective.** Increase the number of requests that are answered positively and promptly—on the first request. Present your points—to other people in your organization; to clients, customers, and suppliers; to government agencies; to the public—more forcefully.
- **Communicate your points more clearly.** Reduce the misunderstandings that occur when the reader has to supply missing or unclear information. Make the issues clear, so that disagreements can surface and be resolved more quickly.
- **Build goodwill.** Build a positive image of your organization. Build an image of yourself as a knowledgeable, intelligent, capable person.

TRENDS IN BUSINESS AND ADMINISTRATIVE COMMUNICATION

Both business and business communication are changing. Ten trends in business, government, and nonprofit organizations affect business and administrative communication: a focus on quality and customers' needs,

MBNA issues Visas and Mastercards for affinity groups. Between 1991 and 1996, total return on its common stock climbed 602%, compared with 216% for the S&P 500. MBNA's success is based on concern for customers. In concrete terms, that means reaching goals—like answering the phone within two rings at least 98.5% of the time.

Customer Service Pays*

When heavy rains made it impossible to use a crane to install a residential air conditioner, De Mar Plumbing, Heating & Air Conditioning hired a helicopter. Though the cost was $400 more than the installation budget, the company stuck to its original bid.

The company videotaped the installation and gave a copy of the tape to the customer. The customer showed the tape at his New Year's Eve party. A resulting sale yielded a profit of $2,400—a return on investment of 600%.

*Based on Phaedra Hise, "Pushing the Customer Service Envelope," *Inc.*, July 1993, 24.

entrepreneurship and outsourcing, teams, diversity, international competition and opportunities, technology, legal and ethical concerns, balancing work and family, the end of the job, and the rapid rate of change.

Focus on Quality and Customers' Needs

Successful companies make money by offering high-quality products and services that their customers want. Aladan Corp., founded in 1986 in Dothan, Alabama, has cornered nearly 20% of the world market in latex examination gloves by providing a quality product quickly at a low price.[22] Chris Zane's Cycles has grown 25% a year in New Haven, Connecticut, by offering free lifetime service and a cellular phone with the bicycles he sells, gourmet coffee while bikes are serviced, a toll-free number, and 90-day price guarantees.[23]

While flexible, responsive companies have been growing, many of the giant US companies that relied on their large market share for continued profits have gone through painful downsizing. Xerox Corporation, for example, once figured that because the service department earned a profit, it didn't matter that its copiers broke down and had to be serviced. But people wanted copiers that didn't break down and turned to Japanese copiers.[24] Xerox has been able to reinvent itself. Now, more companies are "benchmarking": comparing themselves to the best in their industries. The best companies are working to be even better. Chevron created "process masters" to help spread best practices from one plant to another. A new way of cleaning pipes developed in one refinery now saves $1 million every time a refinery needs cleaning.[25]

Focusing on what customers want may lead a business to redefine itself. Business Interiors sold office furniture in Irving, Texas. The CEO said, "Forget what we sell, let's ask customers what they want and organize ourselves around that." Now the company provides a wide range of products and services—including computer-aided design for offices and office buildings.[26]

Communication is at the center of the focus on quality and customers' needs. Brainstorming and group problem solving are essential to develop more efficient ways to do things. Then the good ideas have to be communicated throughout the company. Innovators need to be recognized. And only by listening to what customers say—and listening to the silences that may accompany their actions—can an organization know what its customers really want.

Entrepreneurship and Outsourcing

In 1995, nearly 13 million Americans were self-employed and working full-time at home.[27] That figure doesn't count the small business owners whose companies have grown beyond the owner's home or garage. Entrepreneurship is so popular that many business schools now offer courses, internships, or whole programs in starting and running a business.

Some established companies are trying to match the success and growth rate of start-ups by nurturing an entrepreneurial spirit within their organizations. Innovators who work within organizations are sometimes called **intrapreneurs.** Researchers at 3M can spend 15% of their time working on ideas that don't need management approval; Post-it Notes and the Scotch-Brite Never Rust wool soap pad are two products that came out of 3M's "skunk works." Thermo Electron lets managers "spin out" promising new businesses. Xerox employees write business proposals competing for corporate funds to develop new technologies.[28]

Some businesses have been forced to become entrepreneurial because of outsourcing. **Outsourcing** means going outside the company for products and services that once were made by the company's employees. The people who are now Corsair Communications Inc. were jettisoned in December 1994 by the California-based defense contractor for whom they'd worked most of their professional lives. Instead of automatically getting assignments and pay, they had to propose products and find customers. Eighteen months later, the company is succeeding—in large part because CEO Mary Ann Byrnes has changed the corporate culture.[29]

Entrepreneurs have to handle all the communication in the organization: hiring, training, motivating, and evaluating employees; responding to customer complaints; drafting surveys; writing business plans; making presentations to venture capitalists.

Outsourcing makes communication more difficult—and more important—than it was when jobs were done in-house. It's harder to ask questions, since people are no longer down the hall. And it's easier for problems to turn into major ones. Some companies now are creating a "Chief Resource Officer" to monitor contracts with vendors so that lines of communication will be clear.

Teams

To produce quality products while cutting costs and prices, more and more companies are relying on cross-functional teams. A team of 10 middle managers from various departments at the North Island Naval Depot improved the process of manufacturing replacement parts for fighter planes. They cut the time needed to manufacture and deliver a part by 42% and have saved the Navy—and thus taxpayers—$1.7 million in a year and a half.[30] Teams at Dettmers Industries in Stuart, Florida, make a product in 80 hours—down from 140 hours three years ago. Though employees earn more—sometimes much more—than workers in comparable local industries, the company's labor costs have remained steady, while sales are up 50% and profit margins are twice the industry standard.[31]

The prevalence of teams puts a premium on learning to identify and solve problems, to share leadership, to work *with* other people rather than merely delegating work *to* other people, to resolve conflicts constructively, and to motivate everyone to do his or her best job.

Have Customer, Will Travel*

How does a travel agent make a profit when schedules are available free on the Web? Gary Hoover prospers by giving travelers more than just tickets.

At his Travelfest stores in Austin, Texas, customers can pick up visa applications, check the *Hotel and Travel Index*, and buy books, videos, maps, luggage, and water purifiers. A "learning center" offers 20 classes every month, from Spanish to overcoming the fear of flying.

Much of the information is free. The travel supplies bring in about 20% of revenues—but more than 20% of profits. And these goods and services bring in people planning to travel—so that Hoover's 88 employees can sell them tickets, too.

*Based on John Case and Jerry Useem, "Six Characters in Search of a Strategy," *Inc.*, March 1996, 50.

Diversity

Teams put a premium on being able to work with other people—even if they come from different backgrounds.

Women, people of color, and immigrants have always been part of the US workforce. But for most of our country's history, they were relegated to clerical, domestic, or menial jobs. Even when men from working-class families began to get college degrees in large numbers after World War II, and large numbers of women and minorities entered the professions in the 60s and 70s, only a few made it into management. Now, US businesses realize that barriers to promotion hurt the bottom line as well as individuals. Success depends on using the brains and commitment as well as the hands and muscles of every worker.

In the last decade, we have also become aware of other sources of diversity beyond those of gender and race: age, religion, class, regional differences, sexual orientation, physical disabilities. Helping each worker reach his or her potential requires more flexibility from managers as well as more knowledge about intercultural communication. And it's crucial to help workers from different backgrounds understand each other—especially when continuing layoffs make many workers fear that increased opportunities for someone else will come only at a cost to themselves.

Treating readers with respect has always been a principle of good business and administrative communication. The emphasis on diversity simply makes it an economic mandate as well.

International Competition and Opportunities

More and more of the products we buy—from ballpoint pens to clothing to cars—are made overseas. Even if a company does not try to sell outside the United States, it must still compete with all the international companies that sell products in North America.

But the international market offers opportunities as well as competition. Otis sells 80% of its elevators internationally. Casa Herrera, a South Los Angeles maker of food-processing equipment, sells not only in the United States but also in the United Kingdom, China, and even the Middle East. Cannondale, a bicycle manufacturer in Georgetown, Connecticut, does 37% of its sales in Europe and invoices customers in 13 currencies.[32]

Even workers who stay within the United States may have international bosses. Honda makes Accords in Ohio; Toyota makes Camrys in Kentucky; Mazda has a plant in Michigan. Meanwhile, Ford builds a "world car" in Belgium and Missouri with parts from Ohio, Mexico, Germany, France, and Belgium.[33]

All the challenges of communicating in one culture and country increase exponentially when people communicate across cultures and countries. Succeeding in a global market requires **intercultural competence,** the ability to communicate sensitively with people from other cultures and countries, based on an understanding of cultural differences.

Technology

Changes in technology support and drive changes in other areas. Intranets—Web pages just for employees—give everyone in an organization access to information. To save the Waterville, Maine, ballet company, a retired Marine colonel assembled a nationwide board of directors that met every other night on the Internet. Fax, e-mail, pagers, and text typewriter (TTY) telephones enable deaf and other hearing-impaired employees to fill a variety of jobs.[34]

Levi's Web page builds brand loyalty.

Technology helps organizations save money. FedEx cut the cost of checking on delivery status from $5 a package to only 5 cents by letting customers ask electronically on their own PCs. Total savings are estimated at $2 million a year. Aetna insurance company saves $6 million a year by replacing paper insurance manuals with documents that exist only online. A health insurance company uses desktop publishing to create benefits booklets for its customers. The savings: only 5 days—not 45—are needed to produce new booklets, a huge backlog is eliminated, and the company saves $350,000 in postal costs alone. Fingerhut sends customers with children a birthday flyer with toys appropriate for the child's age and sex and a personalized message—complete with the child's name and birth month. Fingerhut's mail order sales have grown every year—up to 14%—even during the recession.[35]

Virtual reality, whose early uses have been primarily for war and other games, shows promise of other applications. When the 1995 Bosnian peace talks threatened to bog down on the width of a corridor through the Bosnian–Serb territory, a virtual reality mapping program let American negotiators take Serbian President Slobodan Milosevic on a virtual flight over

How Private Are E-Mail and Voice Mail?*

They aren't private at all.

In 1996, in an e-mail to his boss, a man described another superior as a "back-stabbing bastard." Superiors saw a printout of the message, read all the writer's e-mail, and fired him. A US District Court ruled that the company had the right to read employees' e-mail and act on it.

Both e-mail and voice mail messages can be reproduced and sent (without your knowledge) to audiences you never planned on.

What's the solution? Assume anything you put on e-mail and voice mail can be read and heard by everyone. If you must be indiscreet, do it in person—not on something that will be stored.

*Based on Raju Narisetti, "Work Week," *The Wall Street Journal,* March 19, 1996, A1, and Frances A. McMorris, "Is Voice Mail Private? Don't Bet on It," *The Wall Street Journal,* February 28, 1995, B1.

the area. The program helped settle details as small as on which side of a particular road a border would fall.[36]

Modems, faxes, and videophones allow employees to work at home rather than commute to a central office. Fax and e-mail make it easy to communicate across oceans and time zones. Teleconferencing makes it possible for people on different continents to have a meeting—complete with visual aids—without leaving their hometowns.

Technological change carries costs. Technology makes it easier for companies to monitor employees—even when they're out of the office. While technology creates new jobs, it eliminates old ones, requiring employees to retrain. Acquiring technology and helping workers master it requires an enormous capital investment. Learning to use new-generation software and improved hardware takes time and may be especially frustrating for people who were perfectly happy with the old software. And the very ease of storing information and sending messages means that managers have more information and more messages to process. **Information overload** occurs when messages arrive faster than the human receiver can handle them. In the information age, time management depends in part on being able to identify which messages are important so that one isn't buried in trivia.

The technology of office communication also affects the way people interpret messages. Readers expect all documents to be well designed and error free—even though not everyone has access to a laser printer or even to a computer. Fax technology leads people to expect documents instantly, even though the work and thinking required to produce the document still take time.

Legal and Ethical Concerns

Legal fees cost US businesses hundreds of thousands of dollars. The price of many simple items, such as ladders, is inflated greatly by the built-in reserve to protect the manufacturer against lawsuits. Companies are finding that clear, open communication can reduce lawsuits by giving all the parties a chance to shape policies and by clarifying exactly what is and isn't being proposed.

Ethical concerns don't carry the same clear dollar cost as legal fees. But over the last 20 years, Ivan Boesky's insider trading, Beechnut's allowing fake apple juice to be sold in its baby food, Watergate, the savings and loan debacle, and experiments suggesting that many business people and business students were willing to commit fraud[37] have left many consumers with a deep distrust of both business and government. To regain public trust and to avoid further regulation, business and government must both act ethically and convince the public that they are doing so.

To help clients encourage good people to do the right thing, KPMG Peat Marwick, a Big Six accounting firm, offers an "ethics audit" to increase discussion of ethical issues in the workplace and identify places where an organization's system may break down.[38]

Language, graphics, and document design—basic parts of any business document—can be ethical or manipulative. Persuasion and gaining compliance—activities at the heart of business and organizational life—can be done with respect or contempt for customers, co-workers, and subordinates.

Ethical concerns start with telling the truth and offering good value for money. Organizations must be concerned about broader ethical issues as well: being good environmental citizens, offering a good workplace for their employees, contributing to the needs of the communities in which they operate.

Balancing Work and Family

The Wall Street Journal now runs a regular column on Work and Family. One staff writer notes,

> The whole notion of work has changed. Though America remains a productive and work-oriented society, work is just a part of life. People crave more balance.[39]

It's not just women who want more time with their families: men are also turning down promotions and even quitting jobs. In 1995, Jeffrey Stiefler resigned as president of American Express and William Galston resigned as domestic-policy advisor to President Clinton. Both men took less time-consuming jobs that allow them to spend more time with their children. Two research studies named a "lack of balance between work and personal life" one of the top six reasons new managers fail and one of the top five reasons relocations fail. In contrast, Xerox and First Tennessee National Corp. are among companies who have found that taking workers' family needs into consideration produces clear gains in productivity and customer service.[40]

Balancing work and family requires using ways other than physical presence to demonstrate one's commitment to and enthusiasm for organizational goals. It may require negotiating conflicts with other workers who have different family situations or who raised children years ago when fewer companies were family-friendly. The downside of this trend is that sometimes work and family life are not so much balanced as blurred. Lori D. Lewis, Hewlett-Packard's Worldwide Reseller Channel Manager for Disk Drives, reports that she approves prices on a cellular phone on the ski slopes.[41] This flexibility is necessary in an age of downsizing and doing business in many time zones, but it means that she, like many managers, is essentially on call all the time.

The End of the Job

In traditional jobs, people did what they were told to do. Now, they do whatever needs to be done. As one man explains,

> [At the old company,] my work could be represented by a small circle labeled "Me" inside of a much larger one labeled "Not Me." At Corsair, a third circle, nearly as large as the first, is inserted between the other two, and it is labeled, "Maybe Me."[42]

With flatter organizations, workers are doing a much wider variety of tasks. Teams of hourly workers at Weyerhaeuser visit customers in the United States and in Japan to see the demands that high-speed printing makes on their newsprint. When they come back from a trip, they make presentations for two or three weeks to co-workers at the plant.[43]

Your parents may have worked for the same company all their lives. You may do that, too, but you have to be prepared to job hunt—not only when you finish your degree, but also throughout your career. That means continuing to learn—keeping up with new technologies, new economic and political realities, new ways of interacting with people.

Rate of Change

Rapid change is a constant in business and government today. Change means that what worked yesterday may not work today, let alone tomorrow. But change is stressful. Many people, especially those who have felt battered by changes in the workplace, fear that more change will further erode their positions. Even when change promises improvements, people have to work to learn new skills, new habits, and new attitudes.

Just a Deadline. No Directions.*

School assignments are spelled out, sometimes even in writing. In the workplace, workers are less likely to get details about what a document should include. The transition can be disorienting. One intern reported, "I was less prepared than I thought. . . . I was so used to professors basically telling you what they want from you that I expected to be, if not taught, then told, what exactly it was that they wanted these brochures to accomplish. . . . They have not taken the time to discuss it—they just put things on my desk with only a short note telling me when they needed it done. No directions or comments were included."

*Intern's quotation from Chris M. Anson and L. Lee Forsberg, "Moving Beyond the Academic Community," *Written Communication* 7.3 (April 1990): 211.

Jack Welch, CEO of General Electric, is widely acknowledged as the leading master of corporate change in our time. He says,

> You've got to be on the cutting edge of change. You can't simply maintain the status quo, because somebody's always coming from another country with another product, or consumer tastes change, or the cost structure does, or there's a technology breakthrough. If you're not fast and adaptable, you're vulnerable. This is true for every segment of every business in every country in the world.[44]

Rapid change means that no college course or executive MBA program can teach you everything you need to know for the rest of your working life. You'll need to remain open to new ideas. And you'll need to view situations and options critically, so that you can evaluate new conditions to see whether they demand a new response. But the skills you learn can stand you in good stead for the rest of your life: critical thinking, computer savvy, problem solving, and the ability to write, to speak, and to work well with other people.

UNDERSTANDING AND ANALYZING BUSINESS COMMUNICATION SITUATIONS

Sometimes your boss will tell you to write a memo or make a presentation. Sometimes you'll receive a message that demands a response. Sometimes you'll need to write a document to get information or action or to showcase something you've done.

As Andrew Drysdale of Boise Cascade notes, it's a misconception to think that communication requires little forethought or effort. The best communicators are conscious of the context in which they communicate; they're aware of options.

Ask yourself the following questions:

- **What's at stake—to whom?** Think not only about your own needs but also about the concerns your boss and your readers will have. Your message will be most effective if you think of the entire organizational context—and the larger context of shareholders, customers, and regulators. When the stakes are high, you'll need to take into account people's emotional feelings as well as objective facts.
- **Should you send a message?** Sometimes, especially when you're new on the job, silence is the most tactful response. But be alert for opportunities to learn, to influence, to make your case. You can use communication to build your career.
- **What channel should you use?** Paper documents and presentations are formal and give you considerable control over the message. E-mail, phone calls, and stopping by someone's office are less formal. Oral channels are better for group decision making, allow misunderstandings to be cleared up more quickly, and seem more personal. Sometimes you may need more than one message, in more than one channel.
- **What should you say?** Content for a message may not be obvious. How detailed should you be? Should you repeat information that the audience already knows? The answers will depend on the kind of document, your purposes, audiences, and the corporate culture. And you'll have to figure these things out for yourself, without detailed instructions.
- **How should you say it?** How you arrange your ideas—what comes first, second, and last—and the words you use shape the audience's response to what you say.

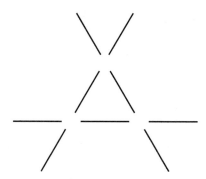

Figure 1.6

Creative problem solving will help you find good solutions. In this puzzle, move 4 lines to form 5 triangles.

How to Solve Business Communication Problems

When you're faced with a business communication problem, you need to develop a solution that will both **solve the organizational problem and meet the psychological needs of the people involved.** The strategies in this section will help you solve the problems in this book. Almost all of these strategies can also be applied to problems you encounter on the job.

- **Understand the situation.** What are the facts? What can you infer from the information you're given? What additional information might be helpful? Where could you get it?
- **Use the six questions for analysis below to analyze your audience, your purposes, and the situation.** Try to imagine yourself in the situation, just as you might use the script of a play to imagine what kind of people the characters are. The fuller an image you can create, the better.
- **Brainstorm solutions.** In all but the very simplest problems, there are *several* possible solutions. The first one you think of may not be best. Consciously develop several solutions. Then measure them against your audience and purposes: Which solution is likely to work best?
- **If you want to add or change information, get permission first.** You can add facts or information to the problems in this book only if the information (1) is realistic, (2) is consistent with the way real organizations work, and (3) does not change the point of the problem. If you have any questions about ideas you want to use, *ask your instructor.* He or she can tell you *before* you write the message.

    Sometimes you may want to use a condition that is neither specified in the problem nor true in the real world. For example, you may want to assume you're sending a letter in April even though you're really writing it in October. Change facts *only with your instructor's approval.*

    When you use this book to create messages on the job, you can't change facts. That is, if it's October, you can't pretend that it's April just because it may be easier to think of reader benefits for that time of year. But it may be possible to change habits that your company has fallen into, especially if they no longer serve a purpose. Check with your supervisor to make sure that your departure from company practice is acceptable.

Use this process to create good messages:[45]

    Answer the six questions for analysis on pg. 22.
    Organize your information to fit your audiences, your purposes, and the situation.
    Make your document visually inviting.
    Revise your draft to create a friendly, businesslike, positive style.
    Edit your draft for standard English; double-check names and numbers.
    Use the response you get to plan future messages.

Succeeding Against the Odds*

I developed my communication skills as a technique of survival. I was born in poverty and spent two years on the welfare rolls, and I learned early that I had to communicate or die. And so I talked my way out of poverty—I communicated my way to the top. . . .

I read and re-read books on self-improvement, success and communication. The most important lesson I learned from these books is what I call "other focusing." This means, among other things, that if we want to communicate with employees, managers, and even competitors we must ask ourselves not what we want but what they want.

This rule made me a millionaire. For the only way I got to where I am today was by persuading thousands of blacks and whites, some of whom were very prejudiced, that the only way they could get what they wanted was by helping me get what I wanted. All the law and prophecy of communication theory can be found in that formula.

*John H. Johnson, owner and publisher of *Ebony* magazine, quoted in Gloria Gordon, "EXCEL Award Winner John H. Johnson Communicates Success," *IABC Communication World* 6, no. 6 (May 1989): 18–19.

Answer the Six Questions for Analysis.

Be sure that you can answer the following six questions before you begin composing your message.

1. **Who is (are) your audience(s)? What characteristics of your audience(s) are relevant to this particular message? If you are writing or speaking to more than one person, how do the people in your audience differ?**

   How much does your audience know about your topic? How will they respond to your message? Some characteristics of your readers will be irrelevant; focus on ones that matter *for this message.* Whenever you write to several people or to a group (like a memo to all employees), try to identify the economic, cultural, or situational differences that may affect how various subgroups may respond to what you have to say.

2. **What are your purposes in writing?**

   What must this message do to solve the organizational problem? What must it do to meet your own needs? What do you want your readers to do? to think or feel? List all your purposes, major and minor. Specify *exactly* what you want your reader to know or think or do. Specify *exactly* what kind of image of yourself and of your organization you want to project.

   Even in a simple message, you may have several related purposes: to announce a new policy, to make readers aware of the policy's provisions and requirements and to have them feel that the policy is a good one, that the organization cares about its employees, and that you are a competent writer and manager.

3. **What information must your message include?**

   Make a list of the points that must be included; check your draft to make sure you include them all. If you're not sure whether a particular fact must be included, ask your instructor or your boss.

   To include information without emphasizing it, put it in the middle of a paragraph or document and present it as briefly as possible.

4. **How can you build support for your position? What reasons or reader benefits will your reader find convincing?**

   Brainstorm to develop reasons for your decision, the logic behind your argument, and possible benefits to readers if they do as you ask. Reasons and reader benefits do not have to be monetary. Making the reader's job easier or more pleasant is a good reader benefit. In an informative or persuasive message, identify at least five reader benefits. In your message, use those that you can develop most easily and most effectively.

   Be sure the benefits are adapted to your reader. Many people do not identify closely with their companies; the fact that the company benefits from a policy will help the reader only if the saving or profit is passed directly on to the employees. That is rarely the case: savings and profits are often eaten up by returns to stockholders, bonuses to executives, and investments in plants and equipment or in research and development.

5. **What objection(s) can you expect your reader(s) to have? What negative elements of your message must you deemphasize or overcome?**

   Some negative elements can only be deemphasized. Others can be overcome. Be creative: is there any advantage associated with (even though not caused by) the negative? Can you rephrase or redefine the negative to make the reader see it differently?

6. **What aspects of the total situation may affect reader response? The economy? The time of year? Morale in the organization? The relationship between the reader and writer? Any special circumstances?**

Communication skills paved the way from welfare to riches for John H. Johnson, owner and publisher of *Ebony* magazine.

Readers may like you or resent you. You may be younger or older than the people you're writing to. The organization may be prosperous or going through hard times; it may have just been reorganized or may be stable. All these different situations will affect what you say and how you say it.

Think about the news, the economy, the weather. Think about the general business and regulatory climate, especially as it affects the organization specified in the problem. Use the real world as much as possible. Think about interest rates, business conditions, and the economy. Is the industry in which the problem is set doing well? Is the government agency in which the problem is set enjoying general support? Think about the time of year. If it's fall when you write, is your business in a seasonal slowdown after a busy summer? Gearing up for the Christmas shopping rush? Or going along at a steady pace unaffected by seasons?

To answer these questions, draw on your experience, your courses, and your common sense. You may want to talk to other students or read *The Wall Street Journal* or look at a company's annual report. Sometimes you may even want to phone a local business person to get information. For instance, if you needed more information to think of reader benefits for a problem set in a bank, you could call a local banker to find out what services it offers customers and what its rates are for loans.

Organize Your Information to Fit Your Audiences, Your Purposes, and the Situation.

You'll learn several different psychological patterns of organization later in this book. For now, remember these three basic principles:

1. Put good news first.
2. In general, put the main point or question first. In the subject line or first paragraph, make it clear that you're writing about something that is important to the reader.
3. Disregard point 2 and approach the subject indirectly when you must persuade a reluctant reader.

Make Your Document Visually Inviting.

A well-designed document is easier to read and builds goodwill. To make a document visually attractive

- Use subject lines to orient the reader quickly.
- Use headings to group related ideas.
- Use lists and indented sections to emphasize subpoints and examples.
- Number points that must be followed in sequence.
- Use short paragraphs—usually six typed lines or fewer.

If you plan these design elements before you begin composing, you'll save time and the final document will probably be better.

The best physical form for a document depends on how it will be used. For example, a document that will be updated frequently needs to be in a loose-leaf binder, so the reader can easily throw away old pages and insert new ones.

Revise Your Draft to Create a Friendly, Businesslike, Positive Style.

In addition to being an organizational member or a consumer, your reader has feelings just as you do. Writing that keeps the reader in mind uses **you-attitude.** Read your message over as if you were in your reader's shoes. How would you feel if *you* received it?

Good business and administrative writing is both friendly and business-like. If you're too stiff, you put extra distance between your reader and yourself. If you try to be too chummy, you'll sound unprofessional. When you write to strangers, use simple, everyday words and make your message as personal and friendly as possible. When you write to friends, remember that your message will be filed and read by people you've never even heard of: avoid slang, clichés, and "in" jokes.

Sometimes you must mention limitations, drawbacks, or other negative elements, but don't dwell on them. People will respond better to you and your organization if you seem confident. Expect success, not failure. If you don't believe that what you're writing about is a good idea, why should they?

You emphasize the positive when you

- Put positive information first, give it more space, or set it off visually in an indented list.
- Eliminate negative words whenever possible.
- Focus on what is possible, not what is impossible.

Edit Your Draft for Standard English; Double-Check Names and Numbers.

Business people care about correctness in spelling, grammar, and punctuation. If your grasp of mechanics is fuzzy, if standard English is not your native dialect, or if English is not your native language, you'll need to memorize rules and perhaps find a good book or a tutor to help you. Even software spelling and grammar checkers require the writer to make decisions. If you know how to write correctly but rarely take the time to do so, now is the time to begin to edit and proofread to eliminate careless errors. Correctness in usage, punctuation, and grammar is covered in Appendix B.

Always proofread your document before you send it out. Double-check the reader's name, any numbers, and the first and last paragraphs.

Use the Response You Get to Plan Future Messages.

Evaluate the **feedback,** or response, you get. The real test of any message is "Did you get what you wanted, when you wanted it?" If the answer is *no,* then the message has failed—even if the grammar is perfect, the words elegant, the approach creative, the document stunningly attractive. If the message fails, you need to find out why.

Analyze your successes, too. You know you've succeeded when you get the results you want, both in terms of objective, concrete actions and in terms of image and goodwill. You want to know *why* your message worked. Often, you'll find that the principles in this book explain the results you get. If your results are different, why? There has to be a reason, and if you can find what it is, you'll be more successful more often.

SUMMARY OF KEY POINTS

- Communication helps organizations and the people in them achieve their goals. The ability to write and speak well becomes increasingly important as you rise in an organization.
- People put things in writing to create a record, to convey complex data, to make things convenient for the reader, to save money, and to convey their own messages more effectively.
- **Internal documents** go to people inside the organization. **External documents** go to audiences outside: clients, customers, suppliers, stockholders, the government, the media, the general public.
- The three basic purposes of business and administrative communication are **to inform, to request or persuade, and to build goodwill.** Most messages have more than one purpose.
- A one-page business letter that took 10 minutes to dictate cost between $13.60 and $20.52 in 1996. Poor writing costs even more since it wastes time, wastes effort, and jeopardizes goodwill.
- Good business and administrative writing meets five basic criteria: it's **clear, complete,** and **correct;** it **saves the reader's time;** and it **builds goodwill.**
- To evaluate a specific document, we must know the interactions among the writer, the reader(s), the purposes of the message, and the situation. No single set of words will work for all readers in all situations.
- Ten trends affecting business and administrative communication are a focus on quality and customers' needs, entrepreneurship and outsourcing, teams, diversity, international competition and opportunities, technology, legal and ethical concerns, balancing work and family, the end of the job, and the rapid rate of change.
- To understand business communication situations, ask the following questions:

  - What's at stake—to whom?
  - Should you send a message?
  - What channel should you use?
  - What should you say?
  - How should you say it?

- The following process helps create effective messages:

  - Answer the six questions for analysis on the next page.

- Organize your information to fit your audiences, your purposes, and the situation.
- Make your document visually inviting.
- Revise your draft to create a friendly, businesslike, positive style.
- Edit your draft for standard English; double-check names and numbers.
- Use the response you get to plan future messages.

- Use these six questions to analyze business communication problems:

  1. Who is (are) your audience(s)? What characteristics are relevant to this particular message? If you are writing to more than one reader, how do the readers differ?
  2. What are your purposes in writing?
  3. What information must your message include?
  4. How can you build support for your position? What reasons or reader benefits will your reader find convincing?
  5. What objection(s) can you expect your reader(s) to have? What negative elements of your message must you deemphasize or overcome?
  6. What aspects of the total situation may affect reader response? the economy? the time of year? morale in the organization? the relationship between the reader and writer? any special circumstances?

- A solution to a business communication problem must both solve the organizational problem and meet the needs of the writer or speaker, the organization, and the audience.

Exercises and Problems
For Chapter 1

GETTING STARTED

1–1   Letters for Discussion—Landscape Plants

Your nursery sells plants not only in your store but also by mail order. Today you've received a letter from Pat Sykes, complaining that the plants (in a $572 order) did not arrive in a satisfactory condition. "All of them were dry and wilted. One came out by the roots when I took it out of the box. Please send me a replacement shipment immediately."

The following letters are possible approaches to answering this complaint. How well does each message meet the needs of the reader, the writer, and the organization? Is the message clear, complete, and correct? Does it save the reader's time? Does it build goodwill?

1.

> Dear Sir:
>
> I checked to see what could have caused the defective shipment you received. After ruling out problems in transit, I discovered that your order was packed by a new worker who didn't understand the need to water plants thoroughly before they are shipped. We have fired the worker, so you can be assured that this will not happen again.
>
> Although it will cost our company several hundred dollars, we will send you a replacement shipment.
>
> Let me know if the new shipment arrives safely. We trust that you will not complain again.

2.

> Dear Pat:
>
> Sorry we screwed up that order. Sending plants across country is a risky business. Some of them just can't take the strain. (Some days I can't take the strain myself!) We'll send you some more plants sometime next week and we'll credit your account for $372.

3.

> Dear Mr. Smith:
>
> I'm sorry you aren't happy with your plants, but it isn't our fault. The box clearly says, "Open and water immediately." If you had done that, the plants would have been fine. And anybody who is going to buy plants should know that a little care is needed. If you pull by the leaves, you will pull the roots out. Since you don't know how to handle plants, I'm sending you a copy of our brochure, "How to Care for Your Plants." Please read it carefully so that you will know how to avoid disappointment in the future.
>
> We look forward to your future orders.

4.

> Dear Ms. Sykes:
>
> Your letter of the 5th has come to the attention of the undersigned.
>
> According to your letter, your invoice #47420 arrived in an unsatisfactory condition. Please be advised that it is our policy to make adjustments as per the Terms and Conditions listed on the reverse side of our Acknowledgement of Order. If you will read that document, you will find the following:
>
>> " . . . if you intend to assert any claim against us on this account, you shall make an exception on your receipt to the carrier and shall, within 30 days after the receipt of any such goods, furnish us detailed written information as to any damage."
>
> Your letter of the 5th does not describe the alleged damage in sufficient detail. Furthermore, the delivery receipt contains no indication of any exception. If you expect to receive an adjustment, you must comply with our terms and see that the necessary documents reach the undersigned by the close of the business day on the 20th of the month.

5.

> Dear Pat Sykes:
>
> You'll get a replacement shipment of the perennials you ordered next week.
>
> Your plants are watered carefully before shipment and packed in specially designed cardboard containers. But if the weather is unusually warm, or if the truck is delayed, small root balls may dry out. Perhaps this happened with your plants. Plants with small root balls are easier to transplant, so they do better in your yard.
>
> The violas, digitalis, aquilegias, and hostas you ordered are long-blooming perennials that will get even prettier each year. Enjoy your garden!

1–2   Memos for Discussion—Announcing a Web Page

The Acme Corporation has just posted its first Web page. Ed Zeplin in Management Information Systems (MIS), who has created the page, wants employees to know about it.

The following memos are possible approaches. How well does each message meet the needs of the reader, the writer, and the organization? Is the message clear, complete, and correct? Does it save the reader's time? Does it build goodwill?

1.

> To: All Employees
>
> From: L. Ed Zeplin, MIS   *LEZ*
>
> Subject: It's Ready!
>
> I am happy to tell you that my work is done. Two months ago the CEO finally agreed to fund a Web page for Acme, and now the work of designing and coding is done. At last, Acme has joined the 20th century (just when it's ending).
>
> I wanted all of you to know about Acme's page. (Actually it's over 40 pages.) Now maybe the computerphobes out there will realize that you really do need to learn how to use this stuff. Sign up for the next training session! The job you save may be my own.
>
> If you have questions, please do not hesitate to contact me.

2.

> To: All Employees with Computers
>
> From: L. Ed Zeplin, MIS   *LEZ*
>
> Subject: Web Page
>
> Check out the company Web page at http://www.server.acme.com/homepage.html

3.

> To: All Employees
>
> From: L. Ed Zeplin, MIS   *LEZ*
>
> Subject: Visit Our Web Page
>
> Our Web pages are finally operational. The 43 pages take 460 MB on the server and were created using HoT MetaL, a program designed to support HTML creation. Though the graphics are sizeable and complex, interlacing and code specifying the pixel size serve to minimize download time. Standard HTML coding is enhanced with forms, Java animation, automatic counters, and tracking packages to ascertain who visits our site.
>
> The site content was determined by conducting a survey of other corporate Web sites to become cognizant of the pages made available by our competitors and other companies. The address of our Web page is http://www.server/acme/com/homepage.html. It is believed that this site will support and enhance our marketing and advertising efforts, improving our outreach to desirable demographic and psychographic marketing groups.

4.

> To: All Employees
>
> From: L. Ed Zeplin, MIS   *LEZ*
>
> Subject: Web Page Shows Acme Products to the World, Offers Tips to Consumers,
>   and Tells Prospective Employees about Job Possibilities
>
> Since last Friday, Acme's been on the World Wide Web. If you have a computer with
> Netscape, check out the page at http://www.server.acme.com/homepage.html. You
> can't view the page if you don't have a computer or if you're still using a Mac SE or
> a 286.
>
> I have included pages on our products, tips for consumers, and job openings at
> Acme in the hope of making our page useful and interesting. Content is the number
> one thing that brings people back, but I've included some snazzy graphics, too.
>
> When I asked people for ideas for the company pages, almost nobody responded.
> But if seeing the page inspires you, let me know what else you'd like. I'll try to fit it
> into my busy schedule.
>
> So check it out. But don't spend too much time on the Web: you need to get your
> work done, too!

5.

> To: All Employees
>
> From: L. Ed Zeplin, MIS   *LEZ*
>
> Subject: How to Access Acme's Web Page
>
> Tell your customers that Acme is now on the Web:
>   http://www.server.acme.com/homepage.html
>
> Our Home page has links to our mission statement, product information, the com-
> pany history, our annual report, job openings, and tips for customers. Visitors can
> choose the page(s) that interest them. E-mail links let potential customers and job-
> seekers contact us directly.
>
> Web pages offer another way for us to bring our story to the public. Our major com-
> petitors have Web pages; now we do, too. Other companies have found that Web
> pages increase sales, often reaching customers far from our normal sales and distri-
> bution channels. Our advertisements and packaging will feature our Web address.
> And people who check out our Web page can learn even more about our commit-
> ment to quality, protecting the environment, and meeting customer needs.
>
> If you'd like to learn more about how to use the Web or how to create Web pages for
> your unit, sign up for one of our workshops. "Introduction to the Web" will be of-
> fered September 25 from 2–3 pm and October 5th from 4–5 pm. "Authoring Web
> Pages" will be offered October 10th from 8am to noon. All workshops meet in Room
> 203. To sign up, send me an e-mail message (zeplin.1@acme.com) or stop by my of-
> fice in Room 205.
>
> If you have comments on Acme's Web pages or suggestions for making them even
> better, just let me know.

1–3 Discussing Strengths

Introduce yourself to a small group of other students. Identify three of your strengths that might interest an employer. These can be ex-perience, knowledge, or personality traits (like enthusiasm).

1–4 Analyzing Audience and Purpose

In both 1–6 and 1–7, below, you're writing about yourself. How do differences in audi-ence and purpose affect what you say and how you say it?

In both 1–7 and 1–8, below, you're writing about your writing. How do differences in audience and purpose affect what you say and how you say it?

COMMUNICATING AT WORK

1–5 Understanding the Role of Communication in Your Organization

Interview your supervisor to learn about the kinds and purposes of communication in your organization. Your questions could include the following:

- What channels of communication (e.g., memos, e-mail, presentations) are most important in this organization?
- What documents or presentations do you create? Are they designed to inform, to persuade, to build goodwill—or to do all three?
- What documents or presentations do you receive? Are they designed to inform, to persuade, to build goodwill—or to do all three?
- Who are your most important audiences within the organization?

- Who are our most important external audiences?
- What are the challenges of communicating in this organization?
- What kinds of documents and presentations does the organization prefer?

As Your Instructor Directs,
  a. Share your results with a small group of students.
  b. Present your results in a memo to your instructor.
  c. Join with a group of students to make a group presentation to the class.

MEMO ASSIGNMENTS

1–6 Introducing Yourself to Your Instructor

Write a memo (at least 1½ pages long) intro-ducing yourself to your instructor. Include the following topics:

Background: Where did you grow up? What have you done in terms of school, extracurricular activities, jobs, and family life?
Interests: What are you interested in? What do you like to do? What do you like to think about and talk about?
Achievements: What achievements have given you the greatest personal satisfaction? List at least five. Include things that gave *you* a real sense of accomplishment and pride, whether or not they're the sort of thing you'd list on a résumé.

Goals: What do you hope to accomplish this term? Where would you like to be professionally and personally five years from now?

Use complete memo format with appropriate headings. (See Appendix A for examples of memo format.) Use a conversational writing style; check your draft to polish the style and edit for mechanical and grammatical correct-ness. A good memo will enable your instructor to see you as an individual. Use specific de-tails to make your memo vivid and interest-ing. Remember that one of your purposes is to interest your reader!

1–7   Introducing Yourself to Your Collaborative Writing Group

Write a memo (at least 1½ pages long) introducing yourself to the other students in your collaborative writing group. Include the following topics:

Background: What is your major? What special areas of knowledge do you have? What have you done in terms of school, extracurricular activities, jobs, and family life?

Previous experience in groups: What groups have you worked in before? Are you usually a leader, a follower, or a bit of both? Are you interested in a quality product? In maintaining harmony in the group? In working efficiently? What do you like most about working in groups? What do you like least?

Work and composing style: Do you like to talk out ideas while they're in a rough stage or work them out on paper before you discuss them? Would you rather have a complete outline before you start writing or just a general idea? Do you want to have a detailed schedule of everything that has to be done and who will do it, or would you rather "go with the flow"? Do you work best under pressure, or do you want to have assignments ready well before the due date?

Areas of expertise: What can you contribute to the group in terms of knowledge and skills? Are you good at brainstorming ideas? Researching? Designing charts? Writing? Editing? Word processing? Managing the flow of work? Maintaining group cohesion?

Goals for collaborative assignments: What do you hope to accomplish this term? Where does this course fit into your priorities?

Use complete memo format with appropriate headings. (See Appendix A for examples of memo format.) Use a conversational writing style; edit your final draft for mechanical and grammatical correctness. A good memo will enable others in your group to see you as an individual. Use details to make your memo vivid and interesting. Remember that one of your purposes is to make your readers look forward to working with you!

1–8   Describing Your Experiences in and Goals for Writing

Write a memo (at least 1½ pages long) to your instructor describing the experiences you've had writing and what you'd like to learn about writing during this course.

Answer several of the following questions:

- What memories do you have of writing? What made writing fun or frightening in the past?
- What have you been taught about writing? List the topics, rules, and advice you remember.
- What kinds of writing have you done in school? How long have the papers been?
- How has your school writing been evaluated? Did the instructor mark or comment on mechanics and grammar? Style? Organization? Logic? Content? Audience analysis and adaptation? Have you gotten extended comments on your papers? Have instructors in different classes had the same standards, or have you changed aspects of your writing for different classes?
- What voluntary writing have you done—journals, poems, stories, essays? Has this writing been just for you, or has some of it been shared or published?
- Have you ever written on a job or in a student or volunteer organization? Have you ever typed other people's writing? What have these experiences led you to think about real-world writing?
- What do you see as your current strengths and weaknesses in writing skills? What skills do you think you'll need in the future? What kinds of writing do you expect to do after you graduate?

Use complete memo format with appropriate headings. (See Appendix A for examples of memo format.) Use a conversational writing style; edit your final draft for mechanical and grammatical correctness.

Building Goodwill

Chapter Outline

An Inside Perspective:
Building Goodwill

Stephen Kyo Kaczmarek, Staff Development and Information Coordinator
Franklin County Board of Commissioners

Steve Kaczmarek provides training programs to more than 1,300 county employees and produces speeches, news releases, a monthly newsletter, and specialty publications. He created the county's 50-page Web site, manages the annual employee recognition ceremony, and assists with special events such as charity fundraisers, news conferences, and child-parent shadowing days at county agencies. Located in the center of Ohio and home to the state's capital, Franklin County has a population of more than one million people.

Writing and speaking from the audience's point of view is critical in my job. Whether I'm announcing a new training program, responding to a constituent inquiry, or answering questions from the news media, I use you-attitude and positive emphasis to better serve my audience. For instance, many of our training programs are voluntary, which means I must "promote" them so employees sign up. By showing employees the benefits of attending—and writing with their interests in mind—I usually get a healthy response. I used the same approach during a food drive. Ultimately, our employees not only met our target for food and money but even went over our goal by $25,000.

Honesty is essential in all forms of communication, but nowhere is communication more closely scrutinized for truth than when working with the media. The worst thing a communications professional can do is lie or misrepresent the truth. Why? In addition to the obvious ethical problems, lying damages a professional's credibility. Once that is lost, the media will not trust what that pro-fessional says, making him or her ineffective. Building trust is an integral part of building goodwill.

With more than one million people in Franklin County, the Commissioners work hard to meet the many needs of constituents. Their effort includes respecting the diversity of both the workforce and customers. To that end, the Commissioners have built into their strategic plan components which recognize the value of diversity, and I have provided training to employees in diversity awareness, sexual harassment awareness, and business communication to address the Commissioners' goals. We've learned much, including the notion that building goodwill means more than simply choosing the right word for the right situation—it includes respecting others' ideas, values and points of view. It also means recognizing the many facets of diversity, such as age, race, gender, physical challenge, and socioeconomic status. We strive to be inclusive when we communicate, which helps us build goodwill.

Stephen Kaczmarek, March 3, 1997

Visit Franklin County's Web site: http://www.co.franklin.oh.us

"Whether I'm announcing a new training program, responding to a constituent inquiry, or answering questions from the news media, I use you-attitude and positive emphasis to better serve my audience."

Steve Kaczmarek, Franklin County Board of Commissioners

Goodwill smooths the challenges of business and administration. You-attitude, positive emphasis, and bias-free language are three ways to help build goodwill. Writing that shows **you-attitude** speaks from the reader's point of view, not selfishly from the writer's. **Positive emphasis** means focusing on the positive rather than the negative aspects of a situation. **Bias-free language** is language that does not discriminate against people on the basis of sex, physical condition, race, age, or any other category. All three help you achieve your purposes and make your messages friendlier, more persuasive, and more humane. They suggest that you care not just about money but also about your readers and their needs and interests.

You-Attitude

According to Professor Francis W. Weeks, former Executive Director of the Association for Business Communication, the most prevalent problem in business communication is that writers think only of themselves and their problems, not about the reader. Putting what you want to say in you-attitude is a crucial step both in thinking about the reader's needs and in communicating your concern to the reader.

How to Create You-Attitude

You-attitude is a style of writing that looks at things from the reader's point of view, emphasizing what the reader wants to know, respecting the reader's intelligence, and protecting the reader's ego.

To apply you-attitude, use the following six techniques:

1. Focus not on what you do for the reader, but on what the reader receives or can do. In positive or neutral situations, stress what the reader wants to know.
2. Refer to the reader's request or order specifically.
3. Don't talk about your own feelings unless you're sure the reader wants to know how you feel.
4. Don't tell readers how they feel or will react.
5. In positive situations, use *you* more often than *I*. Use *we* when it includes the reader.
6. In negative situations, avoid the word *you*. Protect the reader's ego. Use passive verbs and impersonal expressions to avoid assigning blame.

As we look at examples of these techniques, note that many of the you-attitude revisions are *longer* than the sentences lacking you-attitude. You-attitude sentences have *more* information, so they are often longer. They are not wordy. **Wordiness** means having more words than the meaning requires. We can add information and still keep the writing tight.

1. Focus Not on What You Do for the Reader, But on What the Reader Receives or Can Do. In Positive or Neutral Situations, Stress What the Reader Wants to Know.

Readers want to know how they benefit or are affected. When you provide this information, you make your message more complete and more interesting.

Lacks you-attitude:	I have negotiated an agreement with Apex Rent-a-Car that gives you a discount on rental cars.
You-attitude:	As a Sunstrand employee, you can now get a 20% discount when you rent a car from Apex.

The first sentence focuses on what the writer does, not on what the reader receives. Any sentence that focuses on the writer's work or generosity lacks you-attitude, even if the sentence contains the word *you*. Instead of focusing on what we are giving the reader, focus on what the reader can now do.

Lacks you-attitude:	We are shipping your order of September 21 this afternoon.
You-attitude:	The two dozen Corning Ware starter sets you ordered will be shipped this afternoon and should reach you by September 28.

The reader is less interested in when we shipped the order than in when it will arrive. Note that the phrase "should reach you by" leaves room for variations in delivery schedules. If you can't be exact, give your reader the information you do have: "A UPS shipment from California to Texas normally takes three days." If you have absolutely no idea, give the reader the name of the carrier, so the reader knows whom to contact if the order doesn't arrive promptly.

2. Refer to the Reader's Request or Order Specifically.

When you write about the reader's request, order, or policy, refer to it specifically, not as a generic *your order* or *your policy*. If your reader is an individual or a small business, it's friendly to specify the content of the order; if you're writing to a company with which you do a great deal of business, give the invoice or purchase order number.

Lacks you-attitude:	Your order . . .
You-attitude (to individual):	The desk chair you ordered . . .
You-attitude (to a large store):	Your invoice #783329 . . .

3. Don't Talk about Your Own Feelings Unless You Know the Reader Wants to Know How You Feel.

In most business situations, your feelings are irrelevant and should be omitted.

Lacks you-attitude:	We are happy to extend you a credit line of $5,000.
You-attitude:	You can now charge up to $5,000 on your American Express card.

The reader doesn't care whether you're happy, bored stiff at granting a routine application, or worried about granting so much to someone who barely qualifies. All the reader cares about is the situation from his or her point of view.

It *is* appropriate to talk about your own emotions in a message of congratulations or condolence.

> You-attitude: Congratulations on your promotion to district manager! I was really pleased to read about it.

In internal memos, it may be appropriate to comment that a project has been gratifying or frustrating. In the letter of transmittal that accompanies a report, it is permissible to talk about your feelings about doing the work. But even other readers in your own organization are primarily interested in their own concerns, not in your feelings.

4. Don't Tell Readers How They Feel or Will React.

It's distancing to have someone else tell us how we feel—especially if the writer is wrong. Avoid statements about the reader's feelings or reactions.

> Lacks you-attitude: You'll be happy to hear that Open Grip Walkway Channels meet OSHA requirements.
>
> You-attitude: Open Grip Walkway Channels meet OSHA requirements.

Maybe the reader expects that anything you sell would meet government regulations (OSHA—the Occupational Safety and Health Administration—is a federal agency). The reader may even be disappointed if he or she expected higher standards. Simply explain the situation or describe a product's features; don't predict the reader's response.

When you have good news for the reader, simply give the good news.

> Lacks you-attitude: You'll be happy to hear that your scholarship has been renewed.
>
> You-attitude: Congratulations! Your scholarship has been renewed.

5. In Positive Situations, Use You More Often than I. Use We When It Includes the Reader.

Whenever possible, focus on the reader, not you or your company.

> Lacks you-attitude: We provide health insurance to all employees.
>
> You-attitude: You receive health insurance as a full-time Procter & Gamble employee.

Most readers are tolerant of the word *I* in e-mail messages, which seem like conversation. Edit paper documents to use *I* rarely if at all. *I* suggests that you're concerned about personal issues, not about the organization's problems, needs, and opportunities. *We* works well when it includes the reader. Avoid *we* if it excludes the reader (as it would in a letter to a customer or supplier or as it might in a memo about what *we* in management want *you* to do).

6. In Negative Situations, Avoid the Word You. Protect the Reader's Ego. Use Passive Verbs and Impersonal Expressions to Avoid Assigning Blame.

In negative situations, the word *you* will attack or insult the reader, so avoid it. One alternative is to use a noun for a group of which the reader is a part instead of *you* so readers don't feel that they're singled out for bad news.

> Lacks you-attitude: You must get approval from the Director before you publish any articles or memoirs based on your work in the agency.
>
> You-attitude: Agency personnel must get approval from the Director to publish any articles or memoirs based on their work at the agency.

Two more strategies are to use passive verbs and impersonal expressions to avoid blaming the reader. **Passive verbs** describe the action performed on something, without necessarily saying who did it. (See Chapter 4 for a full discussion of passive verbs.) **Impersonal expressions** omit people and talk only about things.

In most cases, active verbs are better. But when your reader is at fault, passive verbs may be useful to avoid assigning blame.

Normally, writing is most lively when it's about people—and most interesting to readers when it's about them. When you have to report a mistake or bad news, however, you can protect the reader's ego by using an impersonal expression, one in which things, not people, do the acting.

Lacks you-attitude: You made no allowance for inflation in your estimate.
You-attitude (passive):   No allowance for inflation has been made in this estimate.
You-attitude (impersonal): This estimate makes no allowance for inflation.

A purist might say that impersonal expressions are illogical: an estimate, for example, is inanimate and can't "make" anything. In the pragmatic world of business writing, however, impersonal expressions often help you convey criticism tactfully.

You-Attitude beyond the Sentence Level

Good messages apply you-attitude beyond the sentence level by using content and organization as well as style to build goodwill.

To create goodwill with content,

- Be complete. When you have lots of information to give, consider putting some details in an appendix, which may be read later.
- Anticipate and answer questions the reader is likely to have.
- When you include information the reader didn't ask for, show why it is important.
- Show readers how the subject of your message affects them.

To organize information to build goodwill,

- Put information readers are most interested in first.
- Arrange information to meet your reader's needs, not yours.
- Use headings and lists so that the reader can find key points quickly.

Consider the letter in Figure 2.1. As the red marginal notes indicate, many individual sentences in this letter lack you-attitude. The last sentence in paragraph 1 sounds both harsh and defensive; the close is selfish. The language is stiff and filled with outdated jargon. Perhaps the most serious problem is that the fact most interesting to the reader is buried in the middle of the first paragraph. Since we have good news for the reader, we should put that information first.

Fixing individual sentences could improve the letter. However, it really needs to be totally rewritten. Figure 2.2 shows a possible revision.

The revision starts with good news and specifies the amount of credit. Using the company's name makes the letter more specific and builds goodwill by linking the company name to the good news. The negative statement about bills is put in the middle paragraph. The phrasing is changed to put "2 ten, net 30" in everyday language; the 2% saving is presented as a benefit, a point that was lost in the original. Instead of a selfish close, the last paragraph now focuses on benefits to the reader.

You-Attitude with International Audiences

When you communicate with international audiences, look at the world from their point of view.

The United States is in the middle of most of the maps sold in the United States. It isn't in the middle of maps sold elsewhere in the world.

The United States clings to a measurement system that has been abandoned by most of the world. When you write for international audiences, use the metric system.

Even pronouns and direction words need attention. *We* may not feel inclusive to readers with different assumptions and backgrounds. *Here* won't mean the same thing to a reader in Bonn as it does to one in Boulder.

Figure 2.1   **A Letter Lacking You-Attitude**

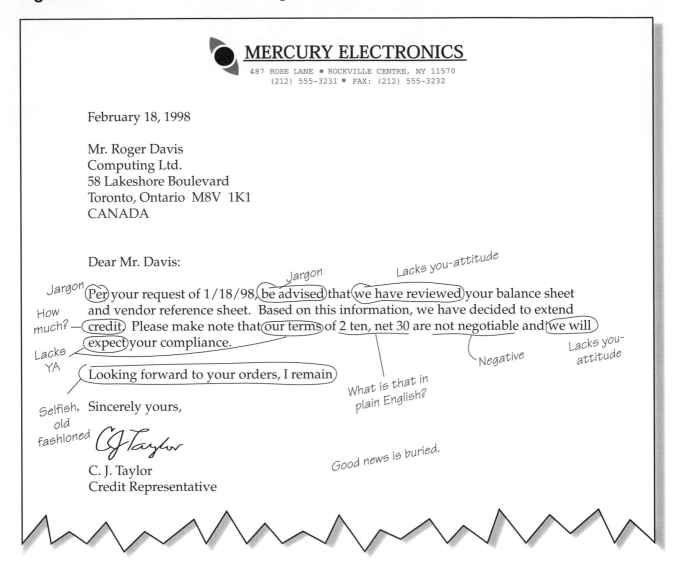

POSITIVE EMPHASIS

Some negatives are necessary. When you have bad news to give the reader—announcements of layoffs, product defects and recalls, price increases—straightforward negatives build credibility. Sometimes negatives are needed to make people take a problem seriously. Wall Data improved the reliability of its computer programs when it eliminated the term *bugs* and used instead the term *failures*. In some messages, such as disciplinary notices and negative performance appraisals, your purpose is to deliver a rebuke with no alternative. Even here, avoid insults or global attacks on the reader's integrity or sanity. Being honest about the drawbacks of a job reduces turnover. And sometimes negatives create a "reverse psychology" that makes people look favorably at your product. Rent-a-Wreck is thriving. (The cars really don't look so bad.)[1]

But in most situations, it's better to be positive. Annette N. Shelby and N. Lamar Reinsch, Jr., found that business people responded more positively to positive rather than to negative language and were more likely to say they would act on a positively worded request.[2] Martin Seligman's research for

A Letter Revised to Improve You-Attitude   **Figure 2.2**

MERCURY ELECTRONICS

487 ROSE LANE ● ROCKVILLE CENTRE, NY 11570
(212) 555-3231 ● FAX: (212) 555-3232

February 18, 1998

Mr. Roger Davis
Computing Ltd.
58 Lakeshore Boulevard
Toronto, Ontario M8V 1K1
CANADA

Good News in
¶ 1

Dear Mr. Davis:

← *Specific*   ← *Company name*

Yes, you can have a credit line of $10,000 with Mercury Electronics.

Bills are due within 30 days of invoices; you can save 2% by paying within ten days.

"2 ten,
net 30"
in plain
English

Presented as benefit

Whether you need standard boards or custom-designed wiring, at Mercury you can get the high-quality parts you need to make the products your customers want.

Sincerely,

C J Taylor

Last ¶ written from
reader's point of view

C. J. Taylor
Credit Representative

Met Life found that optimistic salespeople sold 37% more insurance than pessimistic colleagues. As a result, Met Life began hiring optimists even when they failed to meet the company's other criteria. These "unqualified" optimists outsold pessimists 21% in their first year and 57% the next.[3]

How to Create Positive Emphasis

You can deemphasize negative information by using the following five techniques:

1. Avoid negative words and words with negative connotations.
2. State information positively. Focus on what the reader can do rather than on what you won't or can't let the reader do.
3. Justify negative information by giving a reason or linking it to a reader benefit.
4. If the negative is truly unimportant, omit it.
5. Bury the negative information and present it compactly.

Now, let's see how to apply each of these techniques.

Figure 2.3

Negative Words to Avoid

afraid	error	lacking	trivial
anxious	except	loss	trouble
avoid	fail	some mis- words:	wait
bad	fault	misfortune	weakness
careless	fear	mistake	worry
damage	hesitate	missing	wrong
delay	ignorant	neglect	many un- words:
delinquent	ignore	never	unclear
deny	impossible	no	unfair
difficulty	many in- words:	not	unfortunate
some dis- words:	inadequate	objection	unfortunately
disapprove	incomplete	problem	unpleasant
dishonest	inconvenient	reject	unreasonable
dissatisfied	insincere	sorry	unreliable
eliminate	injury	terrible	unsure

The Wait From This Point*

Visit Disney World, and you'll stand in line for the most popular rides. Helpful signs tell you how long the wait will be from various points in line. If you're not ready to wait that long, you leave.

If you do stay in line, you'll be pleasantly surprised: the line will move faster than advertised.

The signs deliberately overstate the wait. Recently, the sign at the Indiana Jones Adventure ride advised a wait of 25 minutes. It actually took less than 20.

"It's part of the psychology," says Tony Baxter, Vice President of Conceptual Development at Disney's imagineering unit.

*Based on Jeff Rowe, "Waiting in Line Is All Part of the Amusement at Theme Parks," *Columbus Dispatch*, June 14, 1996, 1C.

1. *Avoid Negative Words and Words with Negative Connotations.*

Figure 2.3 lists some common negative words. If you find one of these words in a draft, try to substitute a more positive word. When you must use a negative, use the *least negative* term that will convey your meaning.

The following examples show how to replace negative words with positive words.

Negative:	We have failed to finish taking inventory.
Better:	We haven't finished taking inventory.
Still better:	We will be finished taking inventory Friday.

Negative:	If you can't understand this explanation, feel free to call me.
Better:	If you have further questions, just call me.
Still better:	Omit the sentence.

If a sentence has two negatives, substitute one positive term.

Negative:	Never fail to back up your disks.
Better:	Always back up your disks.

When you must use a negative term, use the least negative word that is accurate.

Negative:	Your balance of $835 is delinquent.
Better:	Your balance of $835 is past due.

Getting rid of negatives has the added benefit of making what you write easier to understand. Sentences with three or more negatives are very hard to understand.[4]

Beware of **hidden negatives:** words that are not negative in themselves but become negative in context. *But* and *however* indicate a shift, so, after a positive statement, they are negative. *I hope* and *I trust that* suggest that you aren't sure. *Patience* may sound like a virtue, but it is a necessary virtue only when things are slow. Even positives about a service or product may backfire if they suggest that in the past the service or product was bad.

Negative:	I hope this is the information you wanted. [Implication: I'm not sure.]
Better:	Enclosed is a brochure about road repairs scheduled for 1999–2001.
Still better:	The brochure contains a list of all roads and bridges scheduled for repair during 1999–2001. Call Gwen Wong at 555-3245 for specific dates when work will start and stop and for alternate routes.

Negative:	Please be patient as we switch to the automated system. [Implication: You can expect problems.]
Better:	If you have questions during our transition to the automated system, call Melissa Morgan.
Still better:	You'll be able to get information instantly about any house on the market when the automated system is in place. If you have questions during the transition, call Melissa Morgan.

Negative:	Now Crispy Crunch tastes better. [Implication: it used to taste terrible.]
Better:	Now Crispy Crunch tastes even better.

Removing negatives does not mean being arrogant or pushy.

Negative:	I hope that you are satisfied enough to place future orders.
Arrogant:	I look forward to receiving all of your future business.
Better:	Call Mercury whenever you need transistors.

When you eliminate negative words, be sure to maintain accuracy. Words that are exact opposites will usually not be accurate. Instead, use specifics to be both positive and accurate.

Negative:	The exercycle is not guaranteed for life.
Not true:	The exercycle is guaranteed for life.
True:	The exercycle is guaranteed for 10 years.

Negative:	Customers under 60 are not eligible for the Prime Time discount.
Not true:	You must be over 60 to be eligible for the Prime Time discount.
True:	If you're 60 or older, you can save 10% on all your purchases with RightWay's Prime Time discount.

Legal phrases also have negative connotations for most readers and should be avoided whenever possible. The idea will sound more positive if you use normal English.

Negative:	If your account is still delinquent, a second, legal notice will be sent to you informing you that cancellation of your policy will occur 30 days after the date of the legal notice if we do not receive your check.
Better:	Even if your check is lost in the mail and never reaches us, you still have a 30-day grace period. If you do get a second notice, you will know that your payment hasn't reached us. To keep your account in good standing, stop payment on the first check and send a second one.

2. State Information Positively. Focus on What the Reader Can Do Rather Than on What You Won't or Can't Let the Reader Do.

Sometimes positive emphasis is a matter of the way you present something: Is the glass half empty or half full? Sometimes it's a matter of eliminating double negatives. When there are limits, or some options are closed, focus on the alternatives that remain.

Negative:	We will not allow you to charge more than $1,500 on your VISA account.
Better:	You can charge $1,500 on your new VISA card.
or:	Your new VISA card gives you $1,500 in credit that you can use at thousands of stores nationwide.

As you focus on what will happen, **check for you-attitude.** In the last example, "We will allow you to charge $1,500" would be positive, but it lacks you-attitude.

When you have a benefit and a requirement the reader must meet to get the benefit, the sentence is usually more positive if you put the benefit first.

A Layoff by Any Other Name*

Companies trying to put a positive spin on layoffs have come up with a variety of euphemisms. They really don't fool anybody, and the companies look foolish at best, dishonest at worst.
   Here are some of the terms:

   Bank of America: Release of resources.
   Bell Labs: Involuntary separation from payroll.
   Clifford of Vermont: Digital Equipment Career-change opportunity.
   Harris Bank of Chicago: Rightsizing the bank. . . .
   Newsweek: Reduction in force (RIF). . . .
   Procter & Gamble: Strengthening global effectiveness. . . .
   Stouffer Foods Corp.: Schedule adjustments. . . .
   Wal-Mart: Normal payroll adjustment.
   Corporation: Involuntary severance. . . .
   Sometimes, it's better to just be negative.

*Based on William Lutz, "The New Doublespeak," in "Hit the Road, Jack," *Newsweek*, August 12, 1996, 57.

Negative:	You will not qualify for the student membership rate of $25 a year unless you are a full-time student.
Better:	You get all the benefits of membership for only $25 a year if you're a full-time student.

Truth Can Be Spoken in Different Ways*

One Iranian told a fable of an ancient king who had an ominous dream. In the dream the king saw himself aged and afflicted, with decaying and falling teeth. Calling together his court astrologers for an interpretation, the shaken king heard the first say, "Your Majesty, I regret to tell you that the interpretation must be bad. The dream means that you will die within a year." In a rage the king threw the brash astrologer out of his court and turned to the second man.

The second astrologer said, "Your Majesty, it is good news, the very best. It means that all your programs and projects will live on after you, and all your sons and daughters will survive you." The king, who was old and knew he might die soon, nevertheless was pleased with this interpretation and richly rewarded the astrologer.

*Quoted from John P. Fieg and John G. Blair, *There Is a Difference: 12 Intercultural Perspectives* (Washington, DC: Meridian House International, 1975), 83.

3. *Justify Negative Information by Giving a Reason or Linking It to a Reader Benefit.*

A reason can help your reader see that the information is necessary; a benefit can suggest that the negative aspect is outweighed by positive factors. Be careful, however, to make the logic behind your reason clear and to leave no loopholes.

Negative:	We cannot sell computer disks in lots of less than 10.
Loophole:	To keep down packaging costs and to help you save on shipping and handling costs, we sell computer disks in lots of 10 or more.

Suppose the customer says, "I'll pay the extra shipping and handling. Send me seven." If you can't or won't sell in lots of less than 10, you need to write:

Better:	To keep down packaging costs and to help customers save on shipping and handling costs, we sell computer disks only in lots of 10 or more.

If you link the negative element to a benefit, be sure it is a benefit the reader will acknowledge. Avoid telling people that you're doing things "for their own good." They may have a different notion of what their own good is. You may think you're doing customers a favor by limiting their credit so they don't get in over their heads and go bankrupt. They may think they'd be better off with more credit so they could expand in hopes of making more sales and more profits.

4. *If the Negative Is Truly Unimportant, Omit It.*

Omit negatives only when

- The reader does not need the information to make a decision.
- You have already given the reader the information and he or she has access to the previous communication.
- The information is trivial.

The following examples suggest the kind of negatives you can omit:

Negative:	A one-year subscription to *PC Magazine* is $49.97. That rate is not as low as the rates charged for some magazines.
Better:	A one-year subscription to *PC Magazine* is $49.97.
Still better:	A one-year subscription to *PC Magazine* is $49.97. You save 43% off the newsstand price of $87.78.

Negative:	If you are not satisfied with Interstate Fidelity Insurance, you do not have to renew your policy.
Better:	Omit the sentence.

5. *Bury the Negative Information and Present It Compactly.*

The beginning and end are always positions of emphasis. Use these positions for ideas you want to emphasize. Put negatives in the middle of a paragraph rather than in the first or last sentence and in the middle of the message rather than in the first or last paragraphs.

When a letter or memo runs several pages, remember that the bottom of the first page is also a position of emphasis, even if it is in the middle of a paragraph, because of the extra white space of the bottom margin. (The first page gets more attention because it is on top and the reader's eye may catch lines of the message even when he or she isn't consciously reading it; the tops and bottoms of subsequent pages don't get this extra attention.) If possible, avoid placing negative information at the bottom of the first page.

Giving a topic lots of space emphasizes it. Therefore, you can deemphasize negative information by giving it as little space as possible. Give negative information only once in your message. Don't list negatives vertically on the page since lists take space and emphasize material.

How to Apologize

When you are at fault, you may build goodwill by admitting that fact forthrightly. Apologies are a special kind of negative and call for slightly different rules.

- **No explicit apology is necessary if the error is small and if you are correcting the mistake.**

  Negative: I'm sorry the clerk did not credit your account properly.
  Better: Your statement has been corrected to include your payment of $263.75.

- **Do not apologize when you are not at fault.**

  When you have done everything you can and when a delay or problem is due to circumstances beyond your control, you aren't at fault and don't need to apologize. It may be appropriate to include an explanation so the reader knows you weren't negligent. If the news is bad, put the explanation first. If you have good news for the reader, put it before your explanation.

  Negative: I'm sorry that I could not answer your question sooner. I had to wait until the sales figures for the second quarter were in.
  Better: We needed the sales figures for the second quarter to answer
  (neutral or   your question. Now that they're in, I can tell you that . . .
  bad news)
  Better: The new advertising campaign is a success. The sales figures
  (good news)   for the second quarter are finally in, and they show that . . .

  If the delay or problem is long or large, it is good you-attitude to ask the reader whether he or she wants to confirm the original plan or make different arrangements.

  Negative: I'm sorry that the chairs will not be ready by August 25 as promised.
  Better: Due to a strike against the manufacturer, the desk chairs you ordered will not be ready until November. Do you want to keep that order, or would you like to look at the models available from other suppliers?

- **When you apologize, do it early, briefly, and sincerely.**

  Apologize only once, early in the message. Let the reader move on to other, more positive information.

  Even if major trouble or inconvenience has resulted from your error, you don't need to go on about all the horrible things that happened. The reader already knows this negative information, and you can omit it. Instead, focus on what you have done to correct the situation.

  If you don't know whether or not any inconvenience has resulted, don't raise the issue at all.

Positive Emphasis in Canada*

In the United States, ask someone "How are you?" and you'll probably get the standard response: "Fine, thank you" or even "Terrific!" In Canada, the standard response is "Not bad."

The words that create goodwill vary from culture to culture. Canadians—like people in Great Britain, New Zealand, and other Commonwealth countries—tend to understate and downplay. As a result, positive emphasis will be a bit less positive than it would be in the United States.

You-attitude takes precedence over every other principle: use the language that works for your audience.

*Based on Margot Northey, personal communication, October 28, 1993, Montreal, Canada, and Roger Graves, "U.S.–Canadian Correspondence as Intercultural Communication," Association for Business Communication Annual Convention, New Orleans, LA, November 4–8, 1992.

Negative:	I'm sorry I didn't answer your letter sooner. I hope that my delay hasn't inconvenienced you.
Better:	I'm sorry I didn't answer your letter sooner.

**A Soft Answer
Turneth Away
Lawsuits***

Lawyers usually tell
individuals and companies
not to admit liability, lest the
admission become evidence
in a lawsuit for damages.

But one soft drink company
found that sincere apologies
satisfied people, so they
didn't sue.

The company had a spate
of complaints about exploding
bottles. But instead of giving
people a form to fill out and
saying, "Contact our risk
department," service
representatives were told to
empathize and apologize.

The company's liability
expenses went down $2
million in a year.

*Based on Cynthia Crossen, "The
Simple Apology after Poor Service
Is in Very Sorry State," *The Wall
Street Journal,* November 29,
1990, B8.

TONE, POWER, AND POLITENESS

Tone is the implied attitude of the writer toward the reader. If the words of a document seem condescending or rude, tone is a problem. Tone is tricky because it interacts with power: the words that might seem friendly from a superior to a subordinate may seem uppity if used by the subordinate to the superior. Norms for politeness are cultural and generational. Language that is acceptable within one group may be unacceptable if used by someone outside the group.

The desirable tone for business writing is businesslike but not stiff, friendly but not phony, confident but not arrogant, polite but not groveling. The following guidelines will help you achieve the tone you want.

- **Use courtesy titles for people outside your organization whom you don't know well.** Most US organizations use first names for everyone, whatever their age or rank. But many people don't like being called by their first names by people they don't know or by someone much younger. When you talk or write to people outside your organization, use first names only if you've established a personal relationship. If you don't know someone well, use a courtesy title:

Dear Mr. Reynolds:
Dear Ms. Lee:

- **Be aware of the power implications of the words you use.** "Thank you for your cooperation" is generous coming from a superior to a subordinate; it's not appropriate in a message to your superior.

Different ways of asking for action carry different levels of politeness.[5]

Order: (lowest politeness)	Turn in your time card by Monday.
Polite order: (midlevel politeness)	Please turn in your time card by Monday.
Indirect request: (higher politeness)	Time cards should be turned in by Monday.
Question: (highest politeness)	Would you be able to turn in your time card by Monday?

Generally, you need less politeness when you're asking for something small, routine, or to the reader's benefit. You need more politeness if you're asking for something that will inconvenience the reader and help you more than the person who does the action.

Higher levels of politeness may be unclear. In some cases, a question may seem like a request for information to which it's acceptable to answer, "No, I can't." In other cases, it will be an order, simply phrased in polite terms.

Generally, requests sound friendliest when they use conversational language.

Poor tone:	Return the draft with any changes by next Tuesday.
Better tone:	Let me know by Tuesday whether you'd like any changes in the draft.

- **When the stakes are low, be straightforward.** Messages that "beat around the bush" sound pompous and defensive.

Poor tone:	Distribution of the low-fat plain granola may be limited in your area. May we suggest that you discuss this matter with your store manager.
Better tone:	Our low-fat granola is so popular that there isn't enough to go around. We're expanding production to meet the demand. Ask your store manager to keep putting in orders, so that your grocery is on the list of stores that will get supplies when they become available.
or	Store managers decide what to stock. If your store has stopped carrying our low-fat granola, the store manager has stopped ordering it. Talk to the manager. Managers try to meet customer needs, so if you say something you're more likely to get what you want.

■ **When you must give bad news, consider hedging your statement.** John Hagge and Charles Kostelnick have shown that auditors' suggestion letters rarely say directly that firms are using unacceptable accounting practices. Instead, they use three strategies to be more diplomatic: specifying the time ("currently, the records are quite informal"), limiting statements ("it appears," "it seems"), and using impersonal statements that do not specify who caused a problem or who will perform an action.[6]

REDUCING BIAS IN BUSINESS COMMUNICATION

Bias-free language is language that does not discriminate against people on the basis of sex, physical condition, race, age, or any other category. Using bias-free language and visuals is a good idea for at least five reasons. First, organizations that treat people fairly should use language that treats people fairly. A second reason for using bias-free language and visuals is to remove a potential barrier to the images people create of themselves. A steady diet of sexist language encourages women to have low aspirations, to seek jobs rather than careers, to think that middle management is as high as they can go. Pictures in ads, college catalogs, and annual reports that omit people in wheelchairs and people of color make it more difficult for those who have traditionally been pushed to the margins to participate in the center of society. A third reason to use bias-free language and visuals is that the law is increasingly intolerant of biased documents and hostile work environments. The fourth reason is that bias-free language and visuals are profitable. Treating each group with respect and understanding is essential to win loyalty and business. The fifth reason to use bias-free language and visuals, and perhaps the most important, is that they're fairer and friendlier.

Everything we do in good business communication attempts to build goodwill. Bias-free language and visuals help sustain the goodwill we work so hard to create.

Check to be sure that your language is nonsexist, nonracist, and nonagist. When you talk about people with disabilities or diseases, talk about the people, not the condition. When you produce newsletters or other documents with photos and illustrations, choose a sampling of the whole population, not just part of it.

Making Language Nonsexist

Nonsexist language treats both sexes neutrally. Check to be sure that your writing is free from sexism in four areas: words and phrases, job titles, courtesy titles, and pronouns.

Figure 2.4   **Getting Rid of Sexist Terms and Phrases**

Instead of	Use	Because
The girl at the front desk	The woman's name or job title: "Ms. Browning," "Rosa," "the receptionist"	Call female employees *women* just as you call male employees *men*. When you talk about a specific woman, use her name, just as you use a man's name to talk about a specific man.
The ladies on our staff	The women on our staff	Use parallel terms for males and females. Therefore, use *ladies* only if you refer to the males on your staff as *gentlemen*. Few businesses do, since social distinctions are rarely at issue.
Manpower Manhours Manning	Personnel Hours or worker hours Staffing	The power in business today comes from both women and men. If you have to correspond with the US Department of Labor's Division of Manpower Administration, you are stuck with the term. When you talk about other organizations, however, use nonsexist alternatives.
Managers and their wives	Managers and their guests	Managers may be female; not everyone is married.

Words and Phrases

If you find any of the terms in the first column in Figure 2.4 in your writing or your company's documents, replace them with terms from the second column.

Not every word containing *man* is sexist. For example, *manager* is not sexist. The word comes from the Latin *manus* meaning *hand;* it has nothing to do with maleness.

Avoid terms that assume that everyone is married or is heterosexual.

Biased: You and your husband or wife are cordially invited to the dinner.
Better: You and your guest are cordially invited to the dinner.

Job Titles

Use neutral titles which do not imply that a job is held only by men or only by women. Many job titles are already neutral: *accountant, banker, doctor, engineer, inspector, manager, nurse, pilot, secretary, technician,* to name a few. Other titles reflect gender stereotypes and need to be changed.

If you need a substitute for a traditional word, check the US Department of Labor's *Job Title Revisions to Eliminate Sex- and Age-Referent Language* from the Dictionary of Occupational Titles, 4th ed., 1991.

Instead of	Use
Businessman	A specific title: executive, accountant, department head, owner of a small business, men and women in business, business person
Chairman	Chair, chairperson, moderator
Foreman	Supervisor (from *Job Title Revisions*)
Salesman	Salesperson, sales representative
Waitress	Server
Woman lawyer	Lawyer
Workman	Worker, employee. Or use a specific title: crane operator, bricklayer, etc.

Courtesy Titles

Memos normally use first and last names without courtesy titles. Letters, however, require courtesy titles in the salutation *unless* you're on a first-name basis with your reader. (See Appendix A for examples of memo and letter formats.)

Ms. in Any Language*

Other countries are also developing nonsexist courtesy titles for women.

- ■ When you know your reader's name and gender, use courtesy titles that do not indicate marital status: *Mr.* for men and *Ms.* for women. There are, however, two exceptions:

  1. If the woman has a professional title, use that title if you would use it for a man.

     Dr. Kristen Sorenson is our new company physician.

     The Rev. Elizabeth Townsley gave the invocation.

  2. If the woman prefers to be addressed as *Mrs.* or *Miss,* use the title she prefers rather than *Ms.* (You-attitude takes precedence over nonsexist language: address the reader as she—or he—prefers to be addressed.)

     To find out if a woman prefers a traditional title,

     a. Check the signature block in previous correspondence. If a woman types her name as *(Miss) Elaine Anderson* or *(Mrs.) Kay Royster,* use the title she designates.

     b. Notice the title a woman uses in introducing herself on the phone. If she says, "This is Robin Stine," use *Ms.* when you write to her. If she says, "I'm Mrs. Stine," use the title she specifies.

     c. Check your company directory. In some organizations, women who prefer traditional titles can list them with their names.

     d. When you're writing job letters or crucial correspondence, call the company and ask the receptionist which title your reader prefers.

Ms. is particularly useful when you do not know what a woman's marital status is. However, even when you happen to know that a woman is married or single, **you still use *Ms.* unless you know that she prefers another title.**

In addition to using parallel courtesy titles, use parallel forms for names.

United States
Miss
Mrs.
Ms.

France
Mademoiselle (Mlle.)
Madame (Mme.)
Mad.

Spain
Seniorita (Srta.)
Senora (Sra.)
Sa.

Denmark
Frøken
Fru
Fr.

Japan
San
San
San

*Based on Mary Ritchie Key, *Male/Female Language* (Metuchen, NJ: Scarecrow Press, 1975), 50, and John C. Condon and Fathi Yousef, *An Introduction to Intercultural Communication* (Indianapolis: Bobbs-Merrill, 1975), 50.

Not Parallel	**Parallel**
Members of the committee will be Mr. Jones, Mr. Yacone, and Lisa.	Members of the committee will be Mr. Jones, Mr. Yacone, and Ms. Melton.
	or
	Members of the committee will be Irving, Ted, and Lisa.

- ■ When you know your reader's name but not the gender, either

  1. Call the company and ask the receptionist, or

  2. Use the reader's full name in the salutation:

     Dear Chris Crowell:

     Dear J. C. Meath:

- ■ When you know neither the reader's name nor gender, you have three options:

  1. Use the reader's position or job title:

     Dear Loan Officer:

     Dear Registrar:

  2. Use a general group to which your reader belongs:

     Dear Investor:

     Dear Admissions Committee:

     Terms that are meant to be positive (*Dear Careful Shopper:* or *Dear Concerned Citizen:*) may backfire if readers see them as manipulative flattery.

Although many people claim to dislike *Dear Friend:* as a salutation in a form letter, research shows that letters using it bring in a higher response than letters with no salutation.

3. Use a letter format that omits the salutation. The AMS Simplified letter format (see Appendix A) includes the inside address and uses a subject line but omits the salutation and complimentary close.

SUBJECT: RECOMMENDATION FOR BEN WANDELL

Pronouns

When you write about a specific person, use the appropriate gender pronouns:

In his speech, John Jones said that . . .
In her speech, Judy Jones said that . . .

When you are not writing about a specific person, but about anyone who may be in a given job or position, traditional gender pronouns are sexist.

Sexist: a. Each supervisor must certify that the time sheet for his department is correct.

Sexist: b. When the nurse fills out the accident report form, she should send one copy to the Central Division Office.

There are four ways to eliminate sexist generic pronouns: use plurals, use second-person *you*, revise the sentence to omit the pronoun, and use pronoun pairs. Whenever you have a choice of two or more ways to make a phrase or sentence nonsexist, choose the alternative that is the smoothest and least conspicuous.

The following examples use these methods to revise sentences *a* and *b* above.

1. Use plural nouns and pronouns.

Nonsexist: a. Supervisors must certify that the time sheets for their departments are correct.

Note: When you use plural nouns and pronouns, other words in the sentence may need to be made plural too. In the example above, plural supervisors have plural time sheets and departments.

Avoid mixing singular nouns and plural pronouns.

Nonsexist but   a. Each supervisor must certify that the time sheet for
lacks agreement: their department is correct.

Since *supervisor* is singular, it is incorrect to use the plural *their* to refer to it. The resulting lack of agreement is becoming acceptable orally but is not yet acceptable to many readers in writing. Instead, use one of the four grammatically correct ways to make the sentence nonsexist.

2. Use *you*.

Nonsexist: a.   You must certify that the time sheet for your department is correct.

Nonsexist: b.   When you fill out an accident report form, send one copy to the Central Division Office.

You is particularly good for instructions and statements of the responsibilities of someone in a given position. Using *you* also frequently shortens sentences, since you write "Send one copy" instead of "You should send one copy." It also makes your writing more direct.

3. Substitute an article (*a*, *an*, or *the*) for the pronoun, or revise the sentence so that the pronoun is unnecessary.

Nonsexist: a.   The supervisor must certify that the time sheet for the department is correct.

Nonsexist: b.   The nurse will
1. Fill out the accident report form.
2. Send one copy of the form to the Central Division Office.

4. When you must focus on the action of an individual, use pronoun pairs.

Nonsexist: a.   The supervisor must certify that the time sheet for his or her department is correct.

Nonsexist: b.   When the nurse fills out the accident report form, he or she should send one copy to the Central Division Office.

Making Language Nonracist and Nonagist

Language is **nonracist** and **nonagist** when it treats all races and ages fairly, avoiding negative stereotypes of any group. Use these guidelines to check for bias in documents you write or edit:

- **Give someone's race or age only if it is relevant to your story.** When you do mention these characteristics, give them for everyone in your story—not just the non-Caucasian, non-young-to-middle-aged adults you mention.
- **Refer to a group by the term it prefers. As preferences change, change your usage.** Fifty years ago, *Negro* was preferred as a more dignified term than *colored* for African Americans. As times changed, *Black* and *African American* replaced it. Surveys in the mid-1990s showed that almost half of blacks aged 40 and older preferred *black*, but those 18 to 39 preferred *African American*.[7]

   Oriental has now been replaced by *Asian*.

   The term *Latino* is the most acceptable group term to refer to Mexican Americans, Cuban Americans, Puerto Ricans, Dominicans, Brazilianos, and other people with Central and Latin American backgrounds. (*Latina* is the term for an individual woman.) Better still is to refer to the precise group. The differences among various Latino groups are at least as great as the differences among Italian Americans, Irish Americans, Armenian Americans, and others descended from various European groups.

   Eskimo is a negative label. A better term is *Inuit*, which means *the people*.

   Older people and *mature customers* are more generally accepted terms than *Senior Citizens* or *Golden Agers*.
- **Avoid terms that suggest that competent people are unusual.** The statement "She is an intelligent black woman" suggests that the writer expects most black women to be stupid. "He is an asset to his race" suggests that excellence in the race is rare. "He is a spry 70-year-old" suggests that the writer is amazed that anyone that old can still move.

Talking about People with Disabilities and Diseases

A disability is a physical, mental, sensory, or emotional impairment that interferes with the major tasks of daily living. One in six people in the United States has a disability; the number of people with disabilities will rise as the population ages.[8]

Attempts To Create a Unisex Pronoun*

For over 140 years, people have attempted to coin a unisex pronoun. None of the attempts has been successful.

Date	*he* or *she*	*his* or *her*	*him* or *her*
1850	ne	nis	nim
1884	le	lis	lim
1938	se	sim	sis
1970	ve	vis	ver
1977	e	e's	em
1988	ala	alis	alum

*Based on Dennis E. Baron, "The Epicene Pronoun: The Word That Failed," *American Speech* 56 (1981): 83–97, and Ellen Graham, "Business Bulletin," *The Wall Street Journal*, December 29, 1988, A1.

Use positive emphasis and people-first language to focus on people and their potential, not their disabilities.

Follow these guidelines when you discuss people with disabilities or diseases:

- **Use *people-first* language to focus on the person, not the condition.** **People-first language** names the person first, then adds the condition. Use it instead of traditional adjectives used as nouns that imply the condition defines the person.

Instead of	Use	Because
The mentally retarded	People with mental retardation	The condition does not define the person or his or her potential
Cancer patients	People being treated for cancer	

- **Avoid negative terms, unless the audience prefers them.** You-attitude takes precedence over positive emphasis: use the term a group prefers. People who lost their hearing as infants, children, or young adults often prefer to be called *deaf*. But people who lose their hearing as older adults often prefer to be called *hard of hearing*, even when their hearing loss is just as great as that of someone who identifies as part of deaf culture.

    Just as people in a single ethnic group may prefer different labels based on generational or cultural divides, so differences exist within the disability community. Using the right term requires keeping up with changing preferences. If your target audience is smaller than the whole group, use the term preferred by that audience, even if the group as a whole prefers another term.

    Some negative terms, however, are never appropriate. Negative terms such as *afflicted*, *suffering from*, and *struck down* also suggest an outdated view of any illness as a sign of divine punishment.

Instead of	Use	Because
Confined to a wheelchair	Uses a wheelchair	Wheelchairs enable people to escape confinement.
AIDS victim	Person with AIDS	Someone can have a disease without being victimized by it.
Abnormal	Atypical	People with disabilities are atypical but not necessarily abnormal.

Choosing Bias-Free Photos and Illustrations

When you produce a document with photographs or illustrations, check the visuals for possible bias. Do they show people of both sexes and all races? Is there a sprinkling of various kinds of people (younger and older, people using wheelchairs, etc.)? It's OK to have individual pictures that have just one sex or one race; the photos as a whole do not need to show exactly 50% men and 50% women. But the general impression should suggest that diversity is welcome and normal.

Check relationships and authority figures as well as numbers. If all the men appear in business suits and the women in maids' uniforms, the pictures are sexist even if an equal number of men and women are pictured. If the only blacks and Latinos pictured are factory workers, the photos support racism even when an equal number of people from each race are shown.

In 1996, as Marilyn Dyrud has shown, only 22% of the images of humans in clip art files were women, and most of those showed women in traditional roles. An even smaller percent pictured members of minority groups.[9] Don't use biased clip art or stock photos: create your own bias-free illustrations.

SUMMARY OF KEY POINTS

- **You-attitude** is a style of writing that looks at things from the reader's point of view, emphasizing what the reader wants to know, respecting the reader's intelligence, and protecting the reader's ego.
  1. Focus not on what you do for the reader, but on what the reader receives or can do. In positive or neutral situations, stress what the reader wants to know.
  2. Refer to the reader's request or order specifically.
  3. Don't talk about your own feelings unless you're sure the reader wants to know how you feel.
  4. Don't tell readers how they feel or will react.
  5. In positive situations, use *you* more often than *I*. Use *we* when it includes the reader.
  6. In negative situations, avoid the word *you*. Protect the reader's ego. Use passive verbs and impersonal expressions to avoid assigning blame.
- Apply you-attitude beyond the sentence level by using organization and content as well as style to build goodwill.
- **Positive emphasis** means focusing on the positive rather than the negative aspects of a situation.
  1. Avoid negative words and words with negative connotations.
  2. State information positively. Focus on what the reader can do rather than on what you won't or can't let the reader do.
  3. Justify negative information by giving a reason or linking it to a reader benefit.
  4. If the negative is truly unimportant, omit it.
  5. Bury the negative information and present it compactly.
- The desirable tone for business writing is businesslike but not stiff, friendly but not phony, confident but not arrogant, polite but not groveling. The following guidelines will help you achieve the tone you want.
  - Use courtesy titles for people outside your organization whom you don't know well.
  - Be aware of the power implications of the words you use.
  - When the stakes are low, be straightforward.
  - When you must give bad news, consider hedging your statement.
- Writing should be free from sexism in four areas: words and phrases, job titles, courtesy titles, and pronouns.

R-E-S-P-E-C-T*

Most major airlines and hotel chains provide disability training to employees. . . . I recognize when someone has been trained—to offer me a Braille menu, use my name when addressing me, or take a moment to orient me to a new environment. What I appreciate even more, though, is . . . simple, common courtesy.

I don't care how many pages in an employee manual somewhere are devoted to . . . the dos and don'ts of interacting with someone who is deaf, blind, or mentally retarded. Among hundreds of experiences in airports and hotels, the one distinction that separates the (mostly) pleasing from the (occasionally) painful in my encounters has been the honest friendliness and respect with which I have or have not been treated.

Ask me where I'd like to sit, whether I need help getting there, and what other kinds of help I need.

Please, assume that I know more about my disability than anyone else ever could.

Respect me as you do any other customer who is paying for the same service, and have the grace to apologize if something does go wrong.

Too many companies, it seems to me, are busy shaking in their boots over the imagined high cost of accommodating people with disabilities when, in many instances, a good old-fashioned refresher course in manners would cover most bases.

*Quoted from Deborah Kendrick, "Disabled Resent Being Patronized," *Columbus Dispatch*, July 21, 1996, 3B.

- *Ms.* is the nonsexist courtesy title for women. Whether or not you know a woman's marital status, use *Ms. unless* the woman has a professional title or unless you know that she prefers a traditional title.
- Traditional pronouns are sexist when they refer to a class of people, not to specific individuals. Four ways to make the sentence nonsexist are to use plurals, to use *you*, to revise the sentence to omit the pronoun, and to use pronoun pairs.
- Bias-free language is fair and friendly; it complies with the law. It includes all readers; it helps to sustain goodwill.
- Check to be sure that your language is nonsexist, nonracist, and nonagist. When you talk about people with disabilities or diseases, talk about the people, not the condition. When you produce newsletters or other documents with photos and illustrations, choose a sampling of the whole population, not just part of it.

Exercises and Problems For Chapter 2

GETTING STARTED

2–1   Evaluating the Ethics of Positive Emphasis

The first term in each line below is negative; the second is a positive term that is sometimes substituted for it. Which of the positive terms seem ethical? Which seem unethical? Briefly explain your choices.

home equity loan	second mortgage
tax	user fee
tax increase	revenue enhancement
nervousness	adrenaline
problem	challenge
price increase	price change

2–2   Using Passives and Impersonal Expressions to Improve You-Attitude and Positive Emphasis

Revise each of these sentences to improve you-attitude and positive emphasis, first using a passive verb, then using an impersonal expression (one in which things, not people, do the action). Are both revisions equally good? Why or why not?

1. You did not send us your check.

2. You did not include all the necessary information in your letter.

3. By failing to build a fence around your pool, you have allowed your property to violate city regulations against health hazards.

2–3   Focusing on the Positive

Revise each of the following sentences to focus on the options that remain, not those that are closed off.

1. As a first-year employee, you are not eligible for dental insurance.

2. I will be out of the country October 25 to November 10 and will not be able to meet with you then.

3. You will not get your first magazine for at least four weeks.

2–4   Identifying Hidden Negatives

Identify the hidden negatives in the following sentences and revise to eliminate them. In some cases, you may need to add information to revise the sentence effectively.

1. This publication is designed to explain how your company can start a recycling program.
2. I hope you find the information in this brochure beneficial to you and a valuable reference as you plan your move.
3. In thinking about your role in our group, I remember two occasions where you contributed something.

2–5   Improving You-Attitude and Positive Emphasis

Revise these sentences to improve you-attitude and positive emphasis. Eliminate any awkward phrasing. In some cases, you may need to add information to revise the sentence effectively.

1. It will be necessary for you to submit Form PR-47 before you can be reimbursed for your travel expenses.
2. Starting next month, the company will offer you a choice of three HMOs.
3. I'm sorry you were worried. I'm happy to tell you that your request to change health plans arrived by the deadline.
4. A penalty of $100 in addition to the annual fee is automatically assessed for late applications postmarked March 2 or later. No penalty will be charged if you bring the application and fee to our office by March 1.
5. After hours of hard work, I have negotiated a new employee benefit for you.
6. I was Treasurer of the Accounting Club. Of course, we didn't have much money so I didn't have much responsibility, but I was able to put into practice principles I learned in the classroom.
7. In this workshop, you will learn how to manage subordinates more effectively.
8. We are pleased to send you a copy of "Investing in Stocks," which you requested. We hope you call us when you are ready for more information or to purchase stocks.
9. If you have any problems using your e-mail account, I will be glad to try to explain it so that you can understand.
10. If you submitted a travel request, as you claim, we have failed to receive it.

2–6   Improving You-Attitude and Positive Emphasis

Revise these sentences to improve you-attitude and positive emphasis. Eliminate any awkward phrasing. In some cases, you may need to add information to revise the sentence effectively.

1. No subcontractor shall be employed without the previous consent of the Director.
2. I am delighted to tell you that we have chosen you as one of our summer interns. We hope you will like working here.
3. I have worked each summer for the last six years in my family's business. Perhaps because the owners were my parents, I was given some real assignments—not just the usual gofer and clerical work that most high school and college students do.
4. After the performance review, Jane Ross from Human Resources will meet individually with you and with other managers to help you identify ways to work on two or three of your major shortcomings.
5. Your comments on the survey are completely confidential. Nothing you write can ever be used against you in any way.
6. Don't worry about getting your story in the next newsletter. It isn't filled up, so I didn't have to delay your story till next month.
7. You will pay $30 more if you wait till after October 1 to register for the conference.
8. If you have any problems doing double-sided printing, I will be happy to try to help you.
9. Since the questionnaire is lengthy and time-consuming, you may not want to complete it right now. It is OK to set it aside and even take it home, as long as you don't keep it more than two weeks.
10. If you sent in a check with your order, as you claim, we have failed to receive it.

2–7   Revising Sexist Job Titles

Suggest nonsexist alternatives for each of the following:

cleaning lady	mailman
congressman	night watchman
garbage man	repairman
male nurse	salesman
mail boy	waitress

2–8   Eliminating Biased Language

Explain the source of bias in each of the following and revise to remove the bias.

1. We recommend hiring Jim Renker and Elizabeth Shuman. Both were very successful summer interns. Jim drafted the report on using rap music in ads, and Elizabeth really improved the looks of the office.
2. All sales associates and their wives are invited to the picnic.
3. Although he is blind, Mr. Morin is an excellent group leader.
4. Unlike many blacks, Yvonne has extensive experience designing Web pages.
5. Chris Renker
   Pacific Perspectives
   6300 West Coronado Blvd.
   Los Angeles, CA
   Gentlemen:
6. Enrique Torres has very good people skills for a man.
7. *Parenting 2000* shows you how to persuade your husband to do his share of child care chores.
8. Mr. Paez, Mr. O'Connor, and Tonya will represent our office at the convention.
9. Sue Corcoran celebrates her 50th birthday today. Stop by her cubicle at noon to get a piece of cake and to help us sing "The Old Grey Mare Just Ain't What She Used to Be."
10. Because older customers tend to be really picky, we will need to give a lot of details in our ads.

E-MAIL MESSAGES

2–9   Advising a Hasty Subordinate

Three days ago, one of your subordinates forwarded to everyone in the office a bit of e-mail humor he'd received from a friend. Titled "You know you're Southern when . . . ," the message poked fun at Southern speech, attitudes, and lifestyles. Today you get this message from your subordinate:

> Subject: Should I Apologize?
>
> I'm getting flamed left and right because of the Southern message. I thought it was funny, but some people just can't take a joke. So far I've tried not to respond to the flames, figuring that would just make things worse. But now I'm wondering if I should apologize. What do you think?

Answer the message.

2–10   Responding to a Complaint

You're Director of Corporate Communications; the employee newsletter is produced by your office. Today you get this e-mail message from Caroline Huber:

> Subject: Complaint about Sexist Language
>
> The article about the "Help Desk" says that Martina Luna and I "are the key customer service representatives 'manning' the desk." I don't MAN anything! I WORK.

Respond to Caroline. And send a message to your staff, reminding them to edit newsletter stories as well as external documents to replace biased language.

COMMUNICATING AT WORK

2–11   Evaluating You-Attitude and Positive Emphasis in Documents that Cross Your Desk

Identify three sentences that use (or should use) you-attitude and positive emphasis. If the sentences are good, write them down or attach a copy of the document(s) marking the sentence(s) in the margin. If the sentences need work, provide both the original sentence and a possible revision.

As Your Instructor Directs,
   a. Turn in the sentences and revisions.
   b. Share the sentences and revisions with the class in a brief oral presentation.
   c. Discuss the sentences and revisions with a group of students. What patterns do you see?

MEMO ASSIGNMENT

2–12   Answering an Inquiry about Photos

You've just been named Vice President for Diversity, the first person in your organization to hold this position. Today, you receive this memo from Sheila Lathan, who edits the employee newsletter.

As Your Instructor Directs,
   a. Work in a small group with other students to come up with a recommendation for Sheila.

   b. Write a memo responding to her.
   c. Write an article for the employee newsletter about the photo policy you recommend and how it relates to the company's concern for diversity.

Subject: Photos in the Employee Newsletter

Please tell me what to do about photos in the monthly employee newsletter. I'm concerned that almost no single issue represents the diversity of employees we have here.

As you know, our layout allows two visuals each month. One of those is always the employee of the month (EM). In the last year, most of those have been male and all but two have been white. What makes it worse is that people want photos that make them look good. You may remember that Ron Olmos was the EM two months ago; in the photo he wanted me to use, you can't tell that he's in a wheelchair. Often the EM is the only photo; the other visual is often a graph of sales or something relating to quality.

Even if the second visual is another photo, it may not look balanced in terms of gender and race. After all, 62% of our employees are men, and 78% are white. Should the pictures try to represent those percentages? The leadership positions (both in management and in the union) are even more heavily male and white. Should we run pictures of people doing important things, and risk continuing the imbalance?

I guess I could use more visuals, but then there wouldn't be room for as many stories—and people really like to see their names in print. Plus, giving people information about company activities and sales is important to maintaining goodwill. A bigger newsletter would be one way to have more visuals and keep the content, but with the cost-cutting measures we're under, that doesn't look likely.

What should I do?

CHAPTER 3

Adapting Your Message to Your Audience

Chapter Outline

Adapting Your Message to Your Audience

Theresa E. Potter, Director of Marketing
Glory Foods

Theresa Potter identifies channels and innovative strategies to reach consumers. Her marketing plans include advertising, public relations, and promotional events. Located in Columbus, Ohio, Glory Foods markets 22 heat-and-eat southern-style products including greens, blackeyed peas, cornbread and muffin mixes, hot sauce, and peppered vinegar.

Analyzing audiences is exactly the same for marketing and writing: you have to identify who the audiences and decision makers are, what motivates them, and how to reach them.

We use both qualitative and quantitative research to learn about our target markets. For example, focus groups showed us that men are increasingly becoming decision makers for food purchases. We also learned that there are distinct differences between northern and southern consumers. We're using this information to decide which new products to pursue and how to reach current users and nonusers effectively.

I use my knowledge about the audience to develop a marketing plan. The plan is discussed internally with Glory's national sales manager, sales representatives, and president. Then the plan is presented to Glory Foods food brokers and retail buyers for their input. Each presentation is based on the audience. What will they want to know? What questions will they have? Does the plan need changes?

Our ads are based on what we know about our audiences. Convenience is the first thing people care about; taste is a strong second. Consumers perceive that canned products have a longer shelf life than fresh or even frozen foods. A key selling point for Glory Foods is taste. Customers continue to state that these products taste like they prepared them from scratch with fresh foods; they don't have the typical canned aftertaste.

Ads, like other messages, are most effective when they're adapted to the audience. Glory custom-tailors its advertising messages for each market. Our radio ads start and end with a jingle, *Just about the Best*, with gospel singers singing the praise of Glory Foods. In the middle of this "donut," an instrumental version of the jingle continues. Over this background music, a local DJ records a 20-second announcement, using a specific script we've written for that city.

Promotional events and in-store demonstrations still prove to be the most effective way to get people to first try Glory products. We participate in Black Expos, Southern Women's Shows, and consumer trade shows. Consumers are astonished at how good the products taste, and they spread the word to friends and family.

Theresa E. Potter, January 27, 1997

Call Glory Foods at 614-252-2042

"[Y]ou have to identify who the audiences and decision makers are, what motivates them, and how to reach them."

Theresa E. Potter, Glory Foods

Multiple Audiences for an Industry Report*

The federal government planned to change regulations affecting a consumer product. A consortium of manufacturers wanted to influence the regulations, so it hired a consulting company to write a report on how various changes would affect manufacturing, safety, and cost. The consortium was both the consultants' initial audience and a gatekeeper. If it didn't like the report, it wouldn't send it on to the federal government.

The primary audience was the federal government, which would set the regulations. Within this audience were economists, engineers, and policymakers.

Secondary audiences included the general public, other manufacturers of the product, and competitors and potential clients of the consulting company.

Industry reviewers emerged as a watchdog audience. They read drafts of the report and commented on it. Although they had no direct power over this report, their goodwill was important for the consulting company's image—and its future contracts. Their comments were the ones that authors took most seriously as they revised their drafts.

*Based on Vincent J. Brown, "Facing Multiple Audiences in Engineering and R&D Writing: The Social Context of a Technical Report," Journal of Technical Writing and Communication, 24, no. 1 (1994): 67–75.

Knowing who you're talking to is fundamental to the success of any message. You need to identify your audiences, understand their motivations, and know how to reach them.

IDENTIFYING YOUR AUDIENCES

The first step in analyzing your audience is to decide who your audience is. In an organizational setting, the person to whom a letter or memo is addressed is not necessarily the most important audience. Indeed, you may need to consider five separate audiences.[1]

1. The **initial audience** is the first audience to get your message. Sometimes the initial audience tells you to write the message.
2. A **gatekeeper** has the power to stop your message instead of sending it on to other audiences. The gatekeeper therefore controls whether your message even gets to the primary audience. Sometimes the supervisor who assigns the message is also the gatekeeper; sometimes the gatekeeper is higher in the organization. In some cases, gatekeepers may exist outside the organization.
3. The **primary audience** will decide whether to accept your recommendations or will act on the basis of your message. You must reach the primary audience to fulfill your purposes in any message.
4. The **secondary audience** may be asked to comment on your message or to implement your ideas after they've been approved. Secondary audiences also include lawyers who may use your message—perhaps years later—as evidence of your organization's culture and practices.
5. A **watchdog audience,** though it does not have the power to stop the message and will not act directly on it, has political, social, or economic power. The watchdog pays close attention to the transaction between you and the primary audience and may base future actions on its evaluation of your message.

As the following examples show, one person can be part of two audiences. Frequently, a supervisor is both the initial audience and the gatekeeper. Sometimes the initial audience is also the primary audience who will act on the message.

Dawn is an assistant account executive in an ad agency. Her boss asks her to write a proposal for a marketing plan for a new product the agency's client is introducing. Her **primary audience** is the executive committee of the client company, who will decide whether to adopt the plan. The **secondary audience** includes the marketing staff of the client company, who will be asked for comments on the plan, as well as the artists, writers, and media buyers who will carry out details of the plan if it is adopted. Her boss, who must approve the plan before it is submitted to the client, is both the **initial audience** and the **gatekeeper.**

Joe works in the data processing unit of a bank. He must write a monthly progress report describing his work. This month, he has worked on implementing a centralized system for handling customers' checks. His boss is **both a primary and an initial**

Tyron Ricketts is a veejay for VIVA TV in Germany. The music and ads look and sound like MTV, but the veejays speak German. VIVA's blend of local and international teen culture fits its audience and has made the network a success.

audience. His boss will write a performance appraisal evaluating his work, so Joe wants to present his own efforts positively. The boss may also include paragraphs from Joe's progress report in a memo to the president of the bank, who wants to know when the bugs in the system will be worked out. The president is thus also a **primary audience.** The **secondary audience** includes the bank's customer service representatives, who must answer customer questions and deal with complaints about the new system, and sales representatives from the computer company that sold the hardware to the bank, who want to be sure that bank personnel are able to use the equipment effectively.

WAYS TO ANALYZE YOUR AUDIENCE

The most important tools in audience analysis are common sense and empathy. **Empathy** is the ability to put yourself in someone else's shoes, to feel with that person. Empathy requires that one not be self-centered. In all probability, the audience is *not* just like you. Use what you know about people and about organizations to predict likely responses.

Analyzing Individuals

When you write or speak to people in your own organizations and in other organizations you work closely with, you may be able to analyze your audience as individuals. You may already know your audience; it will usually be easy to get additional information by talking to members of your audience, talking to people who know your audience, and observing your audience.

The **Myers-Briggs Type Indicator** uses four dimensions to identify ways that people differ.[2] One of these is well known: introvert-extravert. Introverts get their energy from within; extraverts are energized by interacting with other people. The other three dimensions in the Myers-Briggs scale are sensing-intuitive, thinking-feeling, and perceiving-judging. Sensing-intuitive

Figure 3.1   **Using Myers-Briggs Types in Persuasive Messages**

If Your Audience Is	Use This Strategy	Because
An Introvert	Write a memo and let the reader think about your proposal before responding.	Introverts prefer to think before they speak. Written documents give them the time they need to think through a proposal carefully.
An Extravert	Try out your idea orally, in an informal setting.	Extraverts like to think on their feet. They are energized by people; they'd rather talk than write.
A Sensing Type	Present your reasoning step by step. Get all your facts exactly right.	Sensing types usually reach conclusions step by step. They want to know why something is important, but they trust their own experience more than someone else's say-so. They're good at facts and expect others to be, too.
An Intuitive Type	Present the big picture first. Stress the innovative, creative aspects of your proposal.	Intuitive types like solving problems and being creative. They can be impatient with details.
A Thinking Type	Use logic, not emotion, to persuade. Show that your proposal is fair, even if some people may be hurt by it.	Thinking types make decisions based on logic and abstract principles. They are often uncomfortable with emotion.
A Feeling Type	Show that your proposal meets the emotional needs of people as well as the dollars-and-cents needs of the organization.	Feeling types are very aware of other people and their feelings. They are sympathetic and like harmony.
A Perceiving Type	Show that you've considered all the alternatives. Ask for a decision by a specific date.	Perceiving types want to be sure they've considered all the options. They may postpone coming to closure.
A Judging Type	Present your request quickly.	Judging types are comfortable making quick decisions. They like to come to closure so they can move on to something else.

Based on Isabel Briggs Myers, "Effects of Each Preference in Work Situations," *Introduction to Type* (Palo Alto, CA: Consulting Psychologists Press, 1962, 1980).

measures the way someone gets information. Sensing types gather information through their senses. Intuitive types see relationships. Thinking-feeling measures the way someone makes decisions. Thinking types use objective logic to reach decisions. Feeling types make decisions that feel "right," without necessarily being able to define the path they took to make the decision. Judging-perception measures the degree of certainty someone needs. Judging types like closure. Perceptive types like possibilities.

The poles on each of these scales represent a preference, just as we have a preference for using either our right or our left hand to write. If necessary, we can use the opposite style, but we have less practice in it and use it less easily.

You can find out your own personality type by taking the Myers-Briggs Type Indicator at your college's counseling center or student services office. Some businesses administer the Myers-Briggs Type Indicator to all employees. Even when you don't have official results, you can often make accurate guesses about someone's type by close observation.

As Figure 3.1 suggests, you'll be most persuasive if you play to your audience's strengths. Indeed, many of the general principles of business communication reflect the types most common among managers. Putting the main point up front satisfies the needs of judging types, and some 75% of US managers are judging. Giving logical reasons satisfies the needs of the nearly 80% of US managers who are thinking types.[3]

Analyzing the Organizational Culture and the Discourse Community

Be sensitive to the culture in which your audiences work and the discourse community of which they are a part. An **organization's culture** is its values, attitudes, and philosophies. An organization's culture is revealed verbally in the organization's myths, stories, and heroes and nonverbally in the allocation of space, money, and power. A **discourse community** is a group of people who share assumptions about what channels, formats, and styles to use for communication, what topics to discuss and how to discuss them, and what constitutes evidence.

In an organization that values equality and individualism, you can write directly to the CEO and address him or her as a colleague. In other companies, you'd be expected to follow a chain of command. Even if you know the name of the real decision maker, you'd be expected to send your message through your boss—and to be deferential to your superiors. Some organizations prize short messages; some expect long, thorough documents. Some cultures expect people to float trial balloons; others prefer that people work out all the details before they propose a change. Messages that are consistent with the organization's culture have a greater chance of succeeding.

Every organization—businesses, government agencies, nonprofit organizations, even colleges—has a culture. An organization's culture is constructed by the people who found and change the organization.

You can begin to analyze an organization's culture by asking the following questions:

- Is the organization tall or flat? Are there lots of levels between the CEO and the lowest worker, or only a few?
- How do people get ahead? Are the organization's rewards based on seniority, education, being well liked, making technical discoveries, or serving customers? Are rewards available only to a few top people, or is everyone expected to succeed?
- Does the organization value diversity or homogeneity? Does it value independence and creativity or being a team player and following orders? What stories do people tell? Who are the organization's heroes and villains?
- How important are friendship and sociability? To what extent do workers agree on goals, and how intently do they pursue them?
- How formal are behavior, language, and dress?
- What are the organization's goals? Making money? Serving customers and clients? Advancing knowledge? Contributing to the community?

Organizations, like nations, can have subcultures. For example, manufacturing and marketing may represent different subcultures in the same organization: they may dress differently and have different values.

To analyze an organization's discourse community, ask the following questions:

- What channels, formats, and styles are preferred for communication?
- What do people talk about? What topics are not discussed?
- What kind of and how much evidence is needed to be convincing?

A discourse community may be limited to a few people in an organization. However, some discourse communities span an entire organization or even everyone in the same field in the nation or the world. You will be a member

They Looked at the Audience and Saw Themselves*

Before a bank took a survey of its customers, employees were asked to describe the bank's typical customer.

The CEO answered: "About 60, upper-income, community leader."
The middle managers said: "About 40, with grown children. On the way up; good, solid citizen."
The tellers said: "Twenties or thirties, newly married, just starting out. Lots of energy and drive."

According to the survey, the typical customer was in the mid-30s, had been married a few years, earned $20,000 a year, had 1½ cars and 2 children.

People looked at customers but saw only themselves.

*Based on Ray Considine and Murray Raphel, *The Great Brain Robbery* (Pasadena, CA: The Great Brain Robbery, 1981), 68–69.

Micromarketing at Target*

The Target store on Phoenix's eastern edge sells prayer candles, but no child-toting bicycle trailers. The Target store 15 minutes away in Scottsdale, Ariz., sells the trailers but no portable heaters; those can be found 20 minutes south in Mesa. . . .

Target is a master at what retailers call "micromarketing"—a consumer-driven technology-packed strategy to tailor merchandise at each store to the preferences of its patrons. . . .

The watershed event came from Target's success at selling team-logo athletic apparel in the same markets where their fans lived. That business grew from almost nothing in 1991 to $100 million [in 1994]. . . .

The industry adage that "retail is detail" is ever more true in micromarketing. In practice, attending to details for Target means carrying local favorite Jays potato chips in Chicago but stocking Saguaro brand chips in Phoenix. It also means sending more one-piece bathing suits to its stores on Florida's western coast, where the crowd is older, while packing off extra bikinis to the younger patrons of that state's eastern stores.

*Quoted from Gregory A. Patterson, "Different Strokes: Target 'Micromarkets' Its Way to Success; No 2 Stores Are Alike," The Wall Street Journal, May 31, 1995, A1, A9.

of several overlapping discourse communities. Succeeding in a job—whether it's flipping burgers or balancing books, managing a *Fortune* 500 company or running a hospital—requires becoming part of a discourse community. In your college courses, you learn what questions to ask about accounting systems or marketing plans; you learn what kinds of evidence you should use to prove that a landscape plan should include perennials or that a company should sell its products in Europe.

Different organizations may represent different discourse communities, even when they hire people from the same disciplines. Lawyers in one state agency may see the documents they write as dry, factual, and unimportant, with the real emphasis on oral arguments in negotiations or trials. Lawyers at another agency may see themselves writing multipurposed, compelling documents designed not only to carry the weight of litigation but also to enhance the organization's image in the eyes of its various publics.[4] FedEx sales representatives court large customers with frequent phone calls; UPS workers send a bid and let that speak for itself—an approach consistent with UPS's culture of humility and modesty.[5]

Analyzing Members of Groups

In many organizational situations, you'll analyze your audience not as individuals but as members of a group: "taxpayers who must be notified that they owe more income tax," "customers living in the northeast side of the city," or "employees with small children." Focus on what group members have in common. Although generalizations won't be true for all members of the group, generalization is necessary when you must appeal to a large group of people with one message. In some cases, no research is necessary: it's easy to guess the attitudes of people who must be told they owe more taxes. In other cases, databases may yield useful information. In still other cases, you may want to do original research.

If you know where your audience lives, databases enable you to map demographic and psychographic profiles of customers or employees. **Demographic** characteristics are measurable features that can be counted objectively: age, sex, race, religion, education level, income, and so on. Sometimes demographic information is irrelevant; sometimes it's important. Does education matter? Well, the fact that the reader has a degree from Eastern State rather than from Harvard probably doesn't matter, but how much the reader knows about accounting may. Does age matter? Sometimes. "Generational marketing" is helping manufacturers design and market products. Ford divides consumers into six generations. Then it develops vehicles to meet the profile of each group.[6] But other marketers are finding that age alone is inadequate to sell to the "mature market."[7]

Psychographic characteristics are qualitative rather than quantitative: values, beliefs, goals, and lifestyles. Many marketers use the Values and Life Styles profiles (VALS) developed by the SRI research firm in California. VALS profiles divide US buyers into nine categories, including Believers, the conservative middle class who "have benefited by the rules of the game"; Strivers, conspicuous consumers who don't have lots of money but who want to be in style; Fulfilleds, ambitious, hardworking, comfort-loving people who "control nearly 50% of the buying power" in the United States; and Actualizers, highly educated people who are interested in conservation, the environment, and inner growth.[8] Knowing what your audience finds important allows you to organize information in a way that seems natural to your audience and to choose appeals that the audience will find persuasive.

Kids & Cul-de-Sacs   **American Dreams**   **Smalltown Downtown**

Boomtown Singles   **Hispanic Mix**   **Shotguns & Pickups**

Money & Brains   **Golden Ponds**   **Mobility Blues**

Claritas, Inc., combines demographic and psychographic data to identify the ZIP codes that are most likely to have one of 62 lifestyle clusters.

Another market research firm, Claritas Inc., combines demographic and psychographic data to identify the ZIP codes that are most likely to have one of 62 lifestyle clusters, including "Furs and Station Wagons" (wealthy suburbanites with teenagers), "Blue Chip Blues" (upscale blue-collar families), "New Melting Pot" (recent middle-class immigrants and singles), or "Shotguns and Pickups" (rural blue-collar workers and families).[9]

Often it's useful for a company to identify customer segments. Taco Bell identified two groups of high-potential customers: *penny pinchers*, who visit Taco Bell frequently but don't spend much on a visit, and *speed freaks*, who are more interested in convenience than price. To attract these consumers, Taco Bell lowered prices on its core menu items and reengineered its production, cutting wait time by 71%. These changes tripled sales and—even with lower prices—raised profits $20 million.[10]

Big audiences or expensive projects may justify the cost of focus groups, interviews, and questionnaires. **Focus groups** are small groups (usually no more than 12 people) who come in to talk with a skilled leader about a potential product. In an **interview,** the researcher talks to one person at a time. **Ques-**

tionnaires or **surveys** are less expensive because they can be filled out by many people at the same time. Chapter 14 discusses these and other research methods.

CHOOSING CHANNELS TO REACH YOUR AUDIENCE

Communication channels vary in speed, accuracy of transmission, cost, number of messages carried, number of people reached, efficiency, and ability to promote goodwill. Depending on the audience, your purposes, and the situation, one channel may be better than another.

Sometimes your channel choice is determined by the audience. Even in 1996, one company still posted announcements and job openings on bulletin boards because the mail staff, cleaning people, and some clerical workers didn't have computers and so couldn't check e-mail.[11] Even people who have access to the same channels may prefer different ones. When a university updated its employee benefits manual, the computer scientists and librarians wanted the information online. Faculty wanted to be able to read the information on paper. Maintenance workers and carpenters wanted to get answers on voice mail.[12]

The bigger your audience, the more complicated channel choice becomes, since few channels reach everyone in your target audience. When possible, use multiple channels. For example, print ads and customer service materials should contain not only 800 numbers but also street or e-mail addresses so that people who don't like to make phone calls or who have hearing impairments can contact the company.

USING AUDIENCE ANALYSIS TO ADAPT YOUR MESSAGE

If you know your audience well and if you use words well, much of your audience analysis and adaptation will be unconscious. If you don't know your audience or if the message is very important, take the time to analyze your audience formally and to revise your draft with your analysis in mind.

As you answer these questions for a specific reader, think about the organizational culture in which your reader works. At every point, your reader's reaction is affected not only by his or her personal feelings and preferences but also by the political environment of the organization, the economy, and current events.

1. What Will the Reader's Initial Reaction Be to the Message?

a. Will the reader see this message as highly important?
   Readers will read and act on messages they see as important to their own careers; they may ignore messages that seem unimportant to them.
   When the reader may see your message as unimportant, you need to

   - In a subject line or first paragraph, show your reader that this message is important and relevant.
   - Make the action as easy as possible.
   - Suggest a realistic deadline for action.
   - Keep the message as short as possible.

b. How will the fact that the message is from you affect the reader's reaction to the words you use?
   The reader's experience with you, your organization, and the subject you're writing about shapes the way the reader responds to this new message. Someone who thinks well of you and your organization will be prepared to receive your message favorably; someone who thinks poorly

of you and the organization will be quick to find fault with what you say and the way you say it.

When you must write to a reader who has negative feelings about your organization, your position, or you personally, you need to

- Make a special effort to avoid phrases that could seem parental, arrogant, rude, hostile, or uncaring.
- Use positive emphasis (➤ p. 39) to counteract the natural tendency to sound defensive.
- Develop logic and reader benefits fully.

2. How Much Information Does the Reader Need?

a. How much does the reader already know about this subject?

It's easy to overestimate the knowledge an audience has. People outside your own immediate unit may not really know what it is you do. Even people who once worked in your unit may have forgotten specific details now that their daily work is in management. People outside your organization won't know how *your* organization does things.

When some of your information is new to the reader, you need to

- Make a special effort to be clear. Define terms, explain concepts, use examples.
- Link new information to old information that the reader already knows.
- Use paragraphs and headings to break up new information into related chunks, so that the information is easier to digest.
- Test a draft of your document with your reader or a subset of your intended audience to see whether the audience can understand and use what you've written.

b. Is the reader's knowledge based on reading? Personal experience?

Things we have learned directly, through personal observation and experience, always seem more real and more true than things we've learned indirectly or from books. Other people may see our experience as an exception, an aberration, or a fluke; we see it as the best guide of what to expect in the future.

If you're trying to change a reader's understanding of a policy or organization, you need to

- Acknowledge the reader's initial understanding early in the message.
- Use examples as well as theory or statistics to show the difference between short-term and long-term effects, or to show that the reader's experience is not universal.
- Allow the reader to save face by suggesting that changed circumstances call for new attitudes or action.

c. What aspects of the subject does the reader need to be aware of to appreciate your points?

When the reader must think of background or old information to appreciate your points, you can

- Preface information with "As you know" or "As you may remember" to avoid suggesting that you think the reader does not know what you're saying.
- Put old or obvious information in a subordinate clause.
- If the background information or reminder is long, put it in a separate section with an appropriate heading or in an attachment to your letter or memo.

How to Find Rich People*

Lots of marketers would like to sell products and services to rich people. But how do you find them?

Tom Stanley looks for business-to-business ads in trade journals. Full-page ads indicate solid companies owned by people who buy cars, insurance, and financial services. Best of all, because the ad is designed to sell, it will have the company's name, address, and phone number.

Rock and Dirt, for example, lists new and used earth-moving and mining equipment. Stanley pointed out a full-page ad selling reconditioned diesel engines. If a sales representative drives to the company, Stanley says, "You will probably visit a plant, and you will probably meet a man who does not wear a suit. He may look like someone that does not have money, but it is likely that this prospect will turn out to be a great client."

*Based on Thomas J. Stanley, *Selling to the Affluent* (Homewood, IL: Business One Irwin, 1991), 55–59.

The Audiences for a CPA Audit Report*

An audit report may be used by at least five different audiences:

The client, who may resent any report that isn't fully favorable.
Bankers, investors, and creditors, who make decisions based on audit reports and who may hold the CPA financially responsible for the report with a "third-party" lawsuit.
Colleagues, who use the reports, but who may have different ethical or theoretical positions.
Attorneys, who will use the reports as evidence for or against the CPA if a suit is filed.
The AICPA (American Institute of Certified Public Accountants), which sets the standards for accounting reports.
Good audit reports meet the needs and overcome the possible objections of all of these audiences.

*Based on Aletha S. Hendrickson, "How to Appear Reliable without Being Liable: C.P.A. Writing in its Rhetorical Context," *Worlds of Writing: Teaching and Learning in Different Discourse Communities,* ed. Carolyn Matalene (New York: Random House, 1989), 323.

3. What Obstacles Must You Overcome?

a. Is your reader opposed to what you have to say?

Readers who have already made up their minds are highly resistant to change. When you must write to readers who oppose what you have to say, you need to

- Start your message with any areas of agreement or common ground that you share with your reader.
- Make a special effort to be clear and unambiguous. Points that might be clear to a neutral reader can be misread by someone with a chip on his or her shoulder.
- Make a special effort to avoid inflammatory statements.
- Limit your statement or request to the smallest possible area. If parts of your message could be delivered later, postpone them.
- Show that your solution is the best solution currently available, even though it isn't perfect.

b. Will it be easy for the reader to do as you ask?

Everyone has a set of ideas and habits and a mental self-image. If we're asked to do something that violates any of those, we first have to be persuaded to change our attitudes or habits or self-image—a change we're reluctant to make.

When your request is time-consuming, complicated, or physically or psychologically difficult, you need to

- Make the action as easy as possible. Provide a form that can be filled out quickly; provide a stamped, self-addressed envelope if you are writing to someone in another organization.
- Break down actions into a list, so the reader can check off each step as it is completed.
- Show that what you ask is consistent with some aspect of what the reader believes.
- Show how the reader (not just you or your organization) will benefit when the action is completed.

4. What Positive Aspects Can You Emphasize?

a. From the reader's point of view, what are the benefits of what you have to say?

Benefits help persuade the reader that your ideas are good ones. Make the most of the good points inherent in the message you want to convey.

- Put good news in the first paragraph.
- Use reader benefits that go beyond the basic good news of the first paragraph.

b. What experiences, interests, goals, and values do you share with the reader?

A sense of solidarity with someone can be an even more powerful reason to agree than the content of the message itself. Always use all the ethical strategies that are available to win support for your ideas.

When the message will be read by only one reader, or by readers who all share the same experiences, interests, goals, and values, you can

- Consider using a vivid anecdote to remind the reader of what you share. The details of the anecdote should be interesting or new; otherwise, you may seem to be lecturing the reader.

Before their redesign, Olathe Lanes East and West looked alike. But Easts customers bowl to relax while Wests customers bowl to compete. Now a food court with soothing curves is the center of the East facility, with bowling lanes attached. At West, lanes still dominate, decorated with energetic triangles.

- Make a special effort to make your writing style friendly and informal.
- Use a salutation and close that remind readers of their membership in this formal or informal group.

5. What Expectations Does the Reader Have about the Appropriate Language, Structure, and Form for Messages?

a. What style of writing does the reader prefer?

Good writers adapt their style to suit the reader's preferences. A reader who sees contractions as too informal needs a different style from one who sees traditional business writing as too stuffy. As you write,

- Use what you know about your reader to choose a more or less distant, more or less friendly style.
- Use the reader's first name in the salutation only if you use that name when you talk to him or her in person or on the phone.

b. Are there "red flag" words that may distract the reader?

If a term has a special meaning to a reader, you don't have time to convince the reader that the term is broader or more neutral than his or her understanding. When you need agreement or approval, you should

- Avoid terms that carry emotional charges for many readers: for example, *criminal, un-American, feminist, fundamentalist, liberal.*
- Use your previous experience with an individual reader to replace any terms that have particular meanings for him or her.

c. How much detail does the reader want?

A message that does not give the reader the amount of or kind of detail he or she wants may fail. When you know your readers, ask them how much detail they want. When you write to readers you do not know well, you can

- Provide all the detail the reader needs to understand and act on your message.
- Group chunks of information under headings so that the reader can go directly to the parts of the message that he or she finds most interesting and relevant.

Rx for Profits*

Mr. Ost owns three of the smallest drugstores you ever saw, all located in the most bombed-out and burned-out section of [Philadelphia]. But he is doing $5 million of business a year, more than twice the average drugstore rate. . . .

[H]e noticed an assistant labeling a prescription by typewriter instead of by computer. She was translating it, she explained, because to many Spanish-speaking customers, English labels were gibberish. Afraid of confusing dosage, some wouldn't take their medicine.

With a few lines of programming code, Mr. Ost expanded a simple commitment to service into a powerful marketing weapon. He loaded some 1,000 common regimens in Spanish, any of which could be printed instead of the English equivalent with a single keystroke. Business took off. . . .

When an Asian influx hit, he leaped forward again, labeling in Vietnamese. Soon he was writing 400 prescriptions a day at his second location—half in English, 30% in Spanish and 20% in Vietnamese.

*Quoted from Thomas Petzinger, Jr., "Druggist's Simple Rx: Speak the Language of Your Customers," *The Wall Street Journal*, June 16, 1995, B1.

- Imitate similar documents to the same audience. If they have succeeded, you're probably safe in using the same level of detail that they do.

d. Does the reader prefer a direct or indirect structure?

Individual personality or cultural background may lead a reader to prefer a particular kind of structure. You'll be more effective if you use the structure and organization your reader prefers.

e. Does the reader have expectations about formal elements such as length, visuals, or footnotes?

A document that meets the reader's expectations about length, number of visuals, and footnote format is more likely to succeed. If you can't meet those expectations, you need to

- Revise your document carefully. Be sure that a shorter-than-usual document covers the essential points; be sure that a longer-than-usual document is free from wordiness and repetition.
- Check with the reader to see whether the standards are flexible.
- Pretest the message on a subset of your audience to see if the format enhances or interferes with comprehension and action.

6. How Will the Reader Use the Document?

a. Under what physical conditions will the reader use the document?

Reading a document in a quiet office calls for no special care. But suppose the reader will be reading your message on the train commuting home, or on a ladder as he or she attempts to follow instructions. Then the physical preparation of the document can make it easier or harder to use.

When the reader will use your document outside an office,

- Use lots of white space.
- Make the document small enough to hold in one hand.
- Number items so the reader can find his or her place after an interruption.
- Consider using plastic to protect the document.

b. Will the reader use the document as a general reference? As a specific guide? As the basis for a lawsuit?

Understanding how your audience will use the document will enable you to choose the best pattern of organization and the best level of detail. A great deal of detail is needed in an Environmental Protection Agency Inspection Report that will be used to determine whether to bring suit against a company for violating pollution control regulations. A memo within a company urging the adoption of pollution control equipment would need less information. Different information would be needed for instructions by the manufacturer of the equipment explaining how to install and maintain it.

If the document will serve as a general reference,

- Use a subject line to aid in filing and retrieval. If the document is online, consider using several key words to make it easy to find the document in a database search program.
- Use headings within the document so that readers can skim it.
- Give the office as well as the person to contact so that the reader can get in touch with the appropriate person some time from now.
- Spell out details that may be obvious now but might be forgotten in six months or a year.

If the document will be a detailed guide or contain instructions,

- Check to be sure that all the steps are in chronological order.
- Number steps or provide check-off boxes so that readers can easily see which steps they've completed.
- Group steps into five to seven subprocesses if there are many individual steps.
- Put any warnings at the beginning of the document; then repeat them just before the specific step to which they apply.

If the document will be used as the basis for a lawsuit,

- Give specific observations with dates and exact measurements as well as any inferences you've drawn from those observations.
- Give a full report with all the information you have. The lawyer can then decide which parts of the information to use in preparing the case.

c. Will the document be filed?

In contemporary organizations, everything of importance will be filed. When you know that your message will be filed,

- Use a specific subject line.
- Specify details that may be forgotten six months or a year from now.
- Check both the draft and the final typed copy for accuracy, completeness, and friendliness.

READER BENEFITS

Reader benefits are benefits or advantages that the reader gets by using your services, buying your products, following your policies, or adopting your ideas. Reader benefits are important in both informative and persuasive messages. In informative messages, reader benefits give reasons to comply with the policies you announce and suggest that the policies are good ones. In persuasive messages, reader benefits give reasons to act and help overcome reader resistance.

Characteristics of Good Reader Benefits

Good reader benefits are adapted to the audience, are based on intrinsic rather than extrinsic advantages, are supported by clear logic and are explained in adequate detail, and are phrased in you-attitude. Each of these criteria suggests a technique for writing good reader benefits.

1. Adapt Reader Benefits to the Audience.

What one reader sees as an advantage may be unimportant to a second reader and a drawback to a third. When you write to different audiences, you may need to stress different reader benefits.

Suppose that you manufacture a product and want to persuade dealers to carry it. The features you may cite in ads directed toward customers—stylish colors, sleek lines, convenience, durability, good price—won't convince dealers. Shelf space is at a premium, and no dealer carries all the models of all the brands available for any given product. Why should the dealer stock your product? To be persuasive, talk about the features that are benefits from the dealer's point of view: turnover, profit margin, the national advertising campaign that will build customer awareness and interest, the special store displays you offer that will draw attention to the product.

Different Benefits for Different Audiences*

Fluoride toothpaste sells for its decay prevention benefits in Germany, Holland, and Denmark with the basic US marketing and advertising strategy; but in England, France, and Italy, the cosmetic claims for toothpaste are more important, and the US strategy does not work.

Volvo . . . has emphasized economy, durability, and safety in America; status and leisure in France; performance in Germany; and safety in Switzerland. Price is considered to be a critical variable to Mexican consumers, but quality is of more importance to Venezuelans.

Closing [a $100,000 life insurance sale to a Chinese-American, the sales rep] stressed that Met Life was a venerable 119 years old—a standard pitch to Chinese-Americans. . . . It probably worked better than Snoopy, the "Peanuts" character used in the insurer's mainstream ads. Says Ruben Lopez, Met Life's marketing director for special projects, "The Chinese aren't going to buy life insurance from a dog."

*Quoted from Robert F. Roth, *International Marketing Communications* (Chicago: Crain, 1982), 296–97; David A. Ricks, *Big Business Blunders* (Homewood, IL: Dow Jones-Irwin, 1983), 60; and "Tapping into a Blossoming Asian Market," *Newsweek*, September 7, 1987, 47.

Figure 3.2   **Extrinsic and Intrinsic Rewards**

Activity	Extrinsic Reward	Intrinsic Reward
Making a sale	Getting a commission	Pleasure in convincing someone; pride in using your talents to think of a strategy and execute it
Turning in a suggestion to a company suggestion system	Getting a monetary reward when the suggestion is implemented	Solving a problem at work; making the work environment a little more pleasant
Writing a report that solves an organizational problem	Getting praise, a good performance appraisal, and maybe a raise	Pleasure in having an effect on an organization; pride in using your skills to solve problems; solving the problem itself

The Wall Street Journal wanted subscribers to renew their subscriptions for two more years rather than just for one. The cost of the second year was 66% of the cost of the first year. The mailing admitted that renewing for two years would tie up the money but presented the cost of the second year as "a 34% tax-free return on your money." The benefit was highly appropriate for an audience concerned about returns on investments and aware of the risk that normally accompanies high returns. *Garbage* magazine urged subscribers to respond to the first renewal notice to save the paper that an additional mailing would take. This logic was appropriate for an audience concerned about the disposal of solid waste.

2. Base Reader Benefits on Intrinsic Rather than Extrinsic Benefits.

Intrinsic benefits come automatically from using a product or doing something. **Extrinsic benefits** are "added on." Someone in power decides to give them; they do not necessarily come from using the product or doing the action. Figure 3.2 gives examples of extrinsic and intrinsic rewards for three activities.

Intrinsic rewards or benefits are better than extrinsic benefits for two reasons:

1. There just aren't enough extrinsic rewards for everything you want people to do. You can't give a prize to every customer every time he or she places an order or to every subordinate who does what he or she is supposed to do.
2. Research shows that extrinsic rewards may actually make people *less* satisfied with the products they buy or the procedures they follow.

In a groundbreaking study of professional employees, Frederick Herzberg found that the things people said they liked about their jobs were all *intrinsic* rewards—pride in achievement, an enjoyment of the work itself, responsibility. Extrinsic features—pay, company policy—were sometimes mentioned as things people disliked, but they were never cited as things that motivated or satisfied them. People who made a lot of money still did not mention salary as a good point about the job or the organization.[13] The 1993 class of the Harvard business school ranked salary seventh in reasons for choosing a job. Job content and level of responsibility ranked first and second. In 1996, 46% of people surveyed in a Harris poll said "success" meant family and/or children, not money.[14]

A number of psychological experiments show that extrinsic rewards (pay, in most of the experiments) actually reduce intrinsic motivation. Subjects who are paid for their performance spend less time on the assigned task and seem less willing to do it than other subjects performing the same tasks without external rewards.[15] The more interesting the task, the more likely this negative correlation is to occur. This research suggests that you'll motivate subordinates more effectively by stressing the intrinsic benefits of following policies and adopting proposals.

3. Prove Reader Benefits with Clear Logic and Explain Them in Adequate Detail.

A reader benefit is a claim or assertion that the reader will benefit if he or she does something. Convincing the reader, therefore, involves two steps: making sure that the benefit really will occur, and explaining it to the reader.

If the logic behind a claimed reader benefit is faulty or inaccurate, there's no way to make that particular reader benefit convincing. Revise the benefit to make it logical.

Faulty logic:	Using a computer will enable you to write letters, memos, and reports much more quickly.
Analysis:	If you've never used a computer, in the short run it will take you *longer* to create a document using a computer than it would to type it. Even after you know how to use a computer and its software, the real time savings comes when a document incorporates parts of previous documents or goes through several revisions. Creating a first draft from scratch will still take planning and careful composing; the time savings may or may not be significant.
Revised reader benefit:	Using a computer allows you to revise and edit a document more easily. It eliminates retyping as a separate step and reduces the time needed to proofread revisions. It allows you to move the text around on the page to create the best layout.

If the logic is sound, making that logic evident to the reader is a matter of providing enough evidence and showing how the evidence proves the claim that there will be a benefit. Always provide enough detail to be vivid and concrete. You'll need more detail in the following situations:

a. The reader may not have thought of the benefit before.
b. The benefit depends on the difference between the long run and the short run.
c. The reader will be hard to persuade, and you need detail to make the benefit vivid and emotionally convincing.

Does the following statement have enough detail?

You'll save money by using our shop-at-home service.

Readers always believe their own experiences. Readers who have never used a shop-at-home service may think, "If somebody else does my shopping for me, I'll have to pay that person. I'll save money by doing it myself." They aren't likely to think of savings from not having to pay for gas and parking, from having less car wear and tear, and from not losing the time it would take to travel to several different stores to get the selection you offer. Readers who already use shop-at-home services may believe you if they compare your items and services with another company's to see that your cost is lower. Even then, you could make saving money seem more forceful and more vivid by telling readers how much they could save and mentioning some of the ways they could use your service.

4. Phrase Reader Benefits in You-Attitude.

If reader benefits aren't in you-attitude (⚬ p. 34), they'll sound selfish and won't be as effective as they could be. A Xerox letter selling copiers with strong you-attitude as well as reader benefits got a far bigger response than did an alternate version with reader benefits but no you-attitude.[16] It doesn't matter how you phrase reader benefits while you're brainstorming and developing them, but in your final draft, check to be sure that you've used you-attitude.

> Lacks you-attitude: We have the lowest prices in town.
> You-attitude: At Havlichek Cars, you get the best deal in town.

How to Identify and Develop Reader Benefits

Brainstorm lots of reader benefits—perhaps twice as many as you'll need for the final letter or memo. Then you can choose the ones that are most effective for that audience, or that you can develop most easily. The first benefit you think of may not be the best. It's a lot easier to discard a so-so reader benefit when you have better ones to use in its place.

Sometimes reader benefits will be easy to think of and to explain. When they are harder to identify or to develop, use the following steps to identify and then develop good reader benefits.

1. Identify the feelings, fears, and needs that may motivate your reader.
2. Identify the objective features of your product or policy that could meet the needs you've identified.
3. Show how the reader can meet his or her needs with the features of the policy or product.

1. Identify the Feelings, Fears, and Needs That May Motivate Your Reader.

One of the best-known analyses of needs is Abraham H. Maslow's hierarchy of needs.[17] Physiological needs are the most basic, followed by needs for safety and security, for love and a sense of belonging, for esteem and recognition, and finally for self-actualization or self-fulfillment. All of us go back and forth between higher- and lower-level needs. Whenever lower-level needs make themselves felt, they usually take priority.

Maslow's model is a good starting place to identify the feelings, fears, and needs that may motivate your audience. Figure 3.3 shows organizational motivators for each of the levels in Maslow's hierarchy. Often a product or idea can meet needs on several levels. Focus on the ones that audience analysis suggests are most relevant for your audience, but remember that even the best analysis may not reveal all of a reader's needs. For example, a well-paid manager may be worried about security needs if her spouse has lost his job or if the couple is supporting kids in college or an elderly parent.

2. Identify the Features of Your Product or Policy That Could Meet the Needs You've Identified.

Sometimes just listing the reader's needs makes it obvious which feature meets that need. Sometimes several features together meet the need. Try to think of all of them.

Suppose that you want to persuade people to come to the restaurant you manage. It's true that everybody needs to eat, but telling people they can satisfy their hunger needs won't persuade them to come to your restaurant rather than going somewhere else or eating at home. Depending on what features your restaurant offered, you could appeal to one or more of the following subgroups:

Managing Millions for the Super-Rich*

When families of "significant wealth" (up to $100 million to invest) choose an investment advisor, whether the advisor can generate a high rate of return isn't important. What matters more, according to a survey of 3,400 wealthy individuals, is confidentiality. Also important, say the money managers whose clients have millions to invest, are personal attention, trust, and comfort.

*Based on William E. Sheeline, "Selling Advice to the Super-Rich," *Fortune*, July 29, 1992, 56–61.

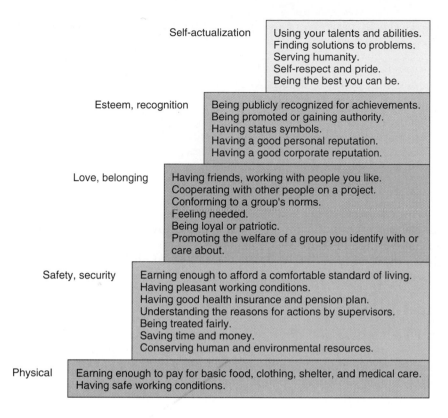

Figure 3.3

Organizational Motivations for Maslow's Hierarchy of Needs

Subgroup	Features to Meet the Subgroup's Needs
People who work outside the home	A quick lunch; a relaxing place to take clients or colleagues
Parents with small children	High chairs, child-size portions, and things to keep the kids entertained while they wait for their order
People who eat out a lot	Variety both in food and in decor
People on tight budgets	Economical food; a place where they don't need to tip (cafeteria or fast-food)
People on special diets	Low-sodium and low-calorie dishes; vegetarian food; kosher food
People to whom eating out is part of an evening's entertainment	Music or a floor show; elegant surroundings; reservations so they can get to a show or event after dinner; late hours so they can come to dinner after a show or game

To develop your benefits, think about the details of each one. If your selling point is your relaxing atmosphere, think about the specific details that make the restaurant relaxing. If your strong point is elegant dining, think about all the details that contribute to that elegance. Sometimes you may think of features that do not meet any particular need but are still good benefits. In a sales letter for a restaurant, you might also want to mention the nonsmoking section, your free coatroom, the fact that you're close to a freeway or offer free parking or a drive-up window, and how fast your service is.

Whenever you're writing to customers or clients about features that are not unique to your organization, it's wise to present both benefits of the features themselves and benefits of dealing with your company. If you talk about the benefits of dining in a relaxed atmosphere but don't mention your own restaurant, people may go somewhere else!

3. Show How the Reader Can Meet His or Her Needs with the Features of the Policy or Product.

Features alone rarely motivate readers. Instead, link the feature to the readers' needs—and provide details to make the benefit vivid!

Weak: We have placemats with riddles.
Better: Answering all the riddles on Monical's special placemats will keep the kids happy till your pizza comes. If they don't have time to finish (and they may not, since your pizza will be ready so quickly), just take the riddles home—or answer them on your next visit.

Make your reader benefits specific.

Weak: You get quick service.
Better: If you only have an hour for lunch, try our Business Buffet. Within minutes, you can choose from a variety of main dishes, vegetables, and a make-your-own-sandwich-and-salad bar. You'll have a lunch that's as light or filling as you want, with time to enjoy it—and still be back to the office on time.

Why Reader Benefits Work

Reader benefits improve both the attitudes and the behavior of the people you work with and write to. They make people view you more positively; they make it easier for you to accomplish your goals.

Expectancy theory says most people try to do their best only when they believe they can succeed and when they want the rewards that success brings. Reader benefits tell or remind readers that they can do the job and that success will be rewarded.[18] Thus they help overcome two problems that reduce motivation: people may not think of all the possible benefits, and they may not understand the relationships among efforts, performance, and rewards.[19]

WRITING OR SPEAKING TO MULTIPLE AUDIENCES WITH DIFFERENT NEEDS

Many business and administrative messages go not to a single person but to a larger audience. When the members of your audience share the same interests and the same level of knowledge, you can use the principles outlined above for individual readers or for members of homogenous groups. But often different members of the audience have different needs.

Rachel Spilka has shown that talking to readers both inside and outside the organization helped corporate engineers adapt their documents successfully. Talking to readers and reviewers helped writers involve readers in the planning process, understand the social and political relationships among readers, and negotiate conflicts orally rather than depending solely on the document. These writers were then able to think about content as well as about organization and style, appeal to common grounds (such as reducing waste or increasing productivity) that several readers shared, and reduce the number of revisions needed before documents were approved.[20]

When it is not possible to meet everyone's needs, meet the needs of gatekeepers and decision makers first.

Content and choice of details

- Provide an overview or executive summary for readers who want just the main points.
- In the body of the document, provide enough detail for decision makers and for anyone else who could veto your proposal.

Play to the Primary Audience*

When an architect gave the Worthington City Council its first official look recently at plans for developing 45 acres at the site of the United Methodist Children's Home on High St., council President John Coleman didn't mince words on which audience the architect should be playing to.

As Rick Morse juggled the plans on an easel, Coleman suggested he move to the other side, because he was blocking the council's view.

"If I stand on the other side, the audience can't see," Morse said.

"They're not going to vote," Coleman said. "You can set your own priorities."

*Quoted from Carol Ann Lease, "Behind the Screens," *The Columbus Dispatch*, July 29, 1987, E1.

- If the decision makers don't need details that other audiences will want, provide those details in appendixes—statistical tabulations, earlier reports, and so forth.

Organizing the document

- Use headings and a table of contents so readers can turn to the portions that interest them.
- Organize your message based on the decision makers' attitudes toward it.

Level of formality

- Avoid personal pronouns. *You* ceases to have a specific meaning when several different audiences use a document.
- If both internal and external audiences will use a document, use a slightly more formal style than you would in an internal document.
- Use a more formal style when your write to international audiences.

Use of technical terms and theory

- In the body of the document, assume the degree of knowledge that decision makers will have.
- Put background information and theory under separate headings. Then readers can use the headings and the table of contents to read or skip these sections, as their knowledge dictates.
- If decision makers will have more knowledge than other audiences, provide a glossary of terms. Early in the document, let readers know that the glossary exists.

SUMMARY OF KEY POINTS

- The **primary audience** will make a decision or act on the basis of your message. The **secondary audience** may be asked by the primary audience to comment on your message or to implement your ideas after they've been approved. The **initial audience** routes the message to other audiences and may assign the message. A **gatekeeper** controls whether the message gets to the primary audience. A **watchdog audience** has political, social, or economic power and may base future actions on its evaluation of your message.
- Common sense and empathy are crucial to good audience analysis.
- The following questions provide a framework for audience analysis:

    1. What will the reader's initial reaction be to the message?
    2. How much information does the reader need?
    3. What obstacles must you overcome?
    4. What positive aspects can you emphasize?
    5. What expectations does the reader have about the appropriate language or format for messages?
    6. How will the reader use the document?

- **Reader benefits** are benefits or advantages that the reader gets by using the writer's services, buying the writer's products, following the writer's policies, or adopting the writer's ideas. Reader benefits can exist for policies and ideas as well as for goods and services. Reader benefits tell readers that they can do the job and that success will be rewarded.
- Good reader benefits are adapted to the audience, based on **intrinsic** rather than **extrinsic** advantages, supported by clear logic and explained in adequate detail, and phrased in you-attitude. Extrinsic benefits simply aren't available to reward every desired behavior; further, they reduce the satisfaction in doing something for its own sake.

How Would Marketers Categorize You?

Wondering how marketers would categorize you? On the Web, you can take the VALS 2 survey at
   http//future.sri.com/VALS/
survey.html
   If you're Japanese, check
   http://future.sri.com/VALS/
jvals.html
   For a description of VALS 2, with snapshots of how companies use it in marketing, check
   http://future.sri.com/vals/
vals.description.html

- To create reader benefits,

  1. Identify the feelings, fears, and needs that may motivate your reader.
  2. Identify the objective features of your product or policy that could meet the needs you've identified.
  3. Show how the reader can meet his or her needs with the features of the policy or product.

- When you write to multiple audiences, use the primary audience to determine level of detail, organization, level of formality, and use of technical terms and theory.

Exercises and Problems For Chapter 3

GETTING STARTED

3–1   Identifying Audiences

In each of the following situations, label the audiences as initial, gatekeeper, primary, secondary, or watchdog.

1. Russell is seeking venture capital so that he can expand his business of offering soccer camps to youngsters. He's met an investment banker whose clients regularly hear presentations from business people seeking capital. The investment banker decides who will get a slot on the program, based on a comprehensive audit of each company's records and business plan.

2. Maria has created a Web page for her travel agency. She hopes to sell tickets for both leisure and business travel.

3. Carolyn is marketing auto loans. She knows that many car buyers choose one of the financing options presented by the car dealership, so she wants to persuade dealers to include her company in the options they offer.

4. Paul works for the mayor's office in a big city. As part of a citywide cost-cutting measure, a blue-ribbon panel has recommended requiring employees who work more than 40 hours in a week to take compensatory time off rather than being paid overtime. The only exceptions will be the police and fire departments. The mayor asks Paul to prepare a proposal for the city council, which will vote on whether to implement the change. Before they vote, council members will hear from (1) citizens, who will have an opportunity to read the proposal and communicate their opinions to the city council; (2) mayors' offices in other cities, who may be asked about their experiences; (3) union representatives, who may be concerned about the reduction in income that will come if the proposal is implemented; (4) department heads, whose ability to schedule work might be limited if the proposal passes; and (5) the blue-ribbon panel and good- government lobbying groups. Council members come up for reelection in six months.

5. John is a college professor who is applying to the American Free Enterprise Foundation to fund research he wants to do. The Director of the Foundation reads all proposals to determine that they fit the foundations's criteria and then funnels them to experts for opinions. Two experts read each proposal, summarize it for the selection committee, and rank it against the other proposals they have read. The selection committee will vote on which proposals to fund and whether to fund them fully or at a reduced rate.

3–2   Choosing a Channel to Reach a Specific Audience

Suppose that your business, government agency, or nonprofit group had a product, service, or program targeted for each of the following audiences. What would be the best channel(s) to reach people in that group in your city? Would that channel reach all group members?

a. Renters.
b. African American owners of small businesses.
c. People who use wheelchairs.
d. Teenagers who work part time while attending school.

e. Competitive athletes.
f. Parents whose children play soccer.
g. Hispanics.
h. People willing to work part time.
i. Financial planners.
j. Hunters.

3–3   Identifying and Developing Reader Benefits

Listed here are several things an organization might like its employees to do.

1. Use less paper.
2. Attend a brown-bag lunch to discuss ways to improve products or services.
3. Become more physically fit.
4. Volunteer for community organizations.
5. Ease a new hire's transition into the unit.

As Your Instructor Directs,

a. Identify the motives or needs that might be met by each of the activities.
b. Take each need or motive and develop it as a reader benefit in a full paragraph. Use additional paragraphs for the other needs met by the activity. Remember to use you-attitude!

3–4   Identifying Objections and Reader Benefits

Think of an organization you know something about, and answer the following questions for it.

1. Your organization is thinking of creating a training video. What objections might people have? What benefits could videos offer your organization? Who would be easiest to convince?
2. The advisory council of State College recommends that business faculty members have three-month internships with local organizations to learn material. What objections might people in your organization have to bringing in faculty interns? What benefits might

your organization receive? Who would be easiest to convince?
3. Your organization is thinking of expanding or creating a Web site. What fears or objections might people have? What benefits might your organization receive? Who would be easiest to convince?

As Your Instructor Directs,

a. Share your answers orally with a small group of students.
b. Present your answers in an oral presentation to the class.
c. Write a paragraph developing the best reader benefit you identified. Remember to use you-attitude.

3–5   Identifying and Developing Reader Benefits for Different Audiences

Assume that you want to encourage people to do one of the activities listed below.

1. Becoming more physically fit.
   Audiences: College students on the job market.
   Workers whose jobs require heavy lifting.
   Sedentary workers.
   People diagnosed as having high blood pressure.
   Managers who travel frequently on business.
   Older workers.

2. Getting advice about interior decorating.
   Audiences: Young people with little money to spend.
   Parents with small children.
   People upgrading or adding to their furnishings.
   Older people moving from single-family homes into smaller apartments or condominiums.
   Builders furnishing model homes.

3. Getting advice on investment strategies.
   Audiences: New college graduates.
                People earning over
                $100,000 annually.
                People responsible for
                investing funds for a
                church or synagogue.
                Parents with small
                children.
                People within 10 years of
                retirement.

4. Gardening.
   Audiences: People with small children.
                People in apartments.
                People concerned about
                reducing pesticides.
                People on tight budgets.
                Retirees.
                Teenagers.

5. Buying a laptop computer.
   Audiences: College students.
                Financial planners who
                visit clients at home.
                Sales representatives who
                travel constantly.
                People who make
                PowerPoint
                presentations.

6. Teaching adults to read.
   Audiences: Retired workers.
                Business people.
                Students who want to
                become teachers.
                High school and college
                students.
                People concerned about
                poverty.

7. Vacationing at a luxury hotel.
   Audiences: Stressed-out people who
                want to relax.
                Tourists who like to
                sightsee and absorb the
                local culture.
                Business people who want
                to stay in touch with the
                office even on vacation.
                Parents with small
                children.
                Weekend athletes who
                want to have fun.

As Your Instructor Directs,

a. Identify needs that you could meet for
   the audiences listed here. In addition to
   needs that several audiences share,
   identify at least one need that would be
   particularly important to each group.

b. Identify a product or service that could
   meet each need.

c. Write a paragraph or two of reader
   benefits for each product or service.
   Remember to use you-attitude.

3–6   Understanding Generations*

1. In which age group are people most
   likely to have moved in the last year?
   a. 20–24
   b. 30–44
   c. 45–64
   d. 65 or older

2. In which age group are people most
   likely to have moved out of state?
   a. 20–24
   b. 30–44
   c. 45–64
   d. 65 or older

3. Who is most likely to own a gun?
   a. 18–20
   b. 21–29
   c. 30–49
   d. 50 or older

4. Who is most likely to believe that unions
   are a good influence on the nation?
   a. 20–24
   b. 30–34
   c. 50–64
   d. 65 or older

5. Households headed by people of which
   age are most likely to include
   preschoolers?
   a. 20–24
   b. 25–34
   c. 35–39
   d. 40–44

6. Households headed by people of which
   age are most likely to include three or
   more children?
   a. 20–24
   b. 25–34
   c. 35–39
   d. 40–44

7. Who is most likely to feel that the
   influence of religion is declining?
   a. 18–29
   b. 30–49
   c. 50–64
   d. 65 or older

8. Who are the best customers for TVs,
   radios, and sound equipment?

a. Under age 25
b. 25–34
c. 35–44
d. 45–54

9. Among full-time, year-round workers, which men (part I) and which women (part II) have the highest median incomes?

a. 25–34
b. 35–44
c. 45–54
d. 55–64

10. In which age group are people most likely to have a bachelor's degree?

a. 25–34
b. 35–44
c. 45–54
d. 55–64

Once you know the answers (ask your professor to check *The Instructor's Manual*) what generalizations would you draw about different generations? How well do you understand generations other than your own? How could you learn more?

*Source: Susan Mitchell, "The Generations Quiz," *American Demographics*, February 1996, 52–53.

3–7   Announcing a Stock Option Program

Assume that your company has decided to give stock options to all workers, not just top executives (see Problem 7–16). As Chief Financial Officer (CFO), you want to write a memo about the program that will answer employees' questions and build support for the program. Pick a specific company that you know something about and answer the following questions about it.

1. Is the company's stock traded on the NYSE or NASDAQ? Or is the stock privately held?
2. What is the value of a share? What has happened to the value in the last three years? the last year? the last month? What changes seem likely in the future?
3. Why has the company made this decision? Are options designed to recruit and retain much-in-demand employees? to offset low salaries? to motivate workers to increase profits? Or something else?
4. What is the company's competitive position? Is the company growing rapidly, going along without much change, or struggling? Are its products in demand? Does it have a reputation for quality and service?
5. How much do employees know about the stock market and about options?
6. Is it likely that most employees have enough extra cash to exercise their options?
7. How old are employees? Are they saving for first homes, for children's college funds, or for their own retirement?

3–8   Announcing a Wellness Program

Assume that your organization has decided to implement a wellness program that will give modest rebates to employees who adopt healthy practices. (See Problem 7–17). As Director of Human Resources, you must explain the program and build support for it. Pick a specific organization that you know something about and answer the following questions about it.

1. What percent of employees currently (a) smoke? (b) drink heavily? (c) are overweight? (d) don't exercise? (e) have high blood pressure or (f) high cholesterol? (g) use seat belts? (h) get annual physicals?
2. Why don't people already follow healthy lifestyles?
3. Do company vending machines, cafeteria, and other facilities make it easy for employees to get low-fat snacks and meals?
4. How much exercise do people get on the job? What work-related injuries are most common?
5. What exactly do people do on the job? Will being healthier help them work more efficiently? Better deal with stress? Have more confidence in interacting with clients and customers?
6. How much do employees know about how much their health insurance costs the organization?
7. What aspects of health and fitness would employees like to know more about? What topics might seem boring or "old hat"?

3–9   Replacing Overtime with Compensatory Time Off

Your organization will no longer pay overtime; instead, workers can receive time off during subsequent pay periods to compensate for the extra hours they've worked. (See Problem 8–17.) You must write a memo explaining the change and minimizing resentment employees may feel. Pick a specific organization that you know something about and answer the following questions about it.

1. Do most employees work overtime, or is overtime concentrated in certain divisions or at certain levels of the organization?

2. Is overtime seasonal or year-round? Does it result from travel? From working extra hours in the office? Is it predictable? How much control do individual employees have over whether they work extra hours?

3. How important was the extra money from overtime to employees? How do you know?

4. Is it likely that employees can take compensatory time off easily, or do pressures of work make it hard to be out of the office?

3–10   Convincing Your Organization to Hire Permanent Workers

Your organization hires many "temporary" workers, some of whom have held temporary jobs for years. You want to persuade the organization to convert at least some of these temporary jobs into full-time permanent positions. (See Problem 10–10.) You plan to write a memo and create a presentation designed to make your case to upper management.

Pick an organization you know something about and answer the following questions.

1. What exactly do "temps" do?
2. Will it cost the organization money to convert the lines to permanent positions?

3. What are the advantages and disadvantages from the organization's position of hiring permanent workers?

4. How are temps treated? Are they well paid? Do they get benefits? Can they grow professionally?

5. Is it likely that the people who hold the temporary positions will be able to compete successfully for the permanent positions? How competitive is the job market?

6. What is the organization's competitive position? Is it growing? Shrinking?

COMMUNICATING AT WORK

3–11   Analyzing Your Boss

What goals matter most to your boss? What pressures is he or she under? Does your boss want details or just the big picture? What are his or her pet peeves? Is punctuality more important than creativity and thoroughness, or vice versa? If you have a question, would your boss rather answer in person, by e-mail, or in a memo? Is he or she more approachable in the morning or the afternoon?

As Your Instructor Directs,

a. Share your answers orally with a small group of students.

b. Present your answers in an oral presentation to the class.

c. Present your answers in a memo to your instructor.

d. Share your answers with a small group of students and write a joint memo reporting the similarities and differences you found.

3–12   Analyzing Your Co-Workers

What do your co-workers do? What hassles and challenges do they face? To what extent do their lives outside work affect their responses to work situations? What do your co-workers value? What are their pet peeves? How committed are they to organizational goals? How satisfying do they find their jobs?

Are the people you work with quite similar to each other, or do they differ from each other? How?

As Your Instructor Directs,

a. Share your answers orally with a small group of students.

b. Present your answers in an oral presentation to the class.

c. Present your answers in a memo to your instructor.

d. Share your answers with a small group of students and write a joint memo reporting the similarities and differences you found.

MEMO ASSIGNMENTS

3–13 Analyzing an Organization's Culture

Interview several people about the culture of their organization. Possible organizations include

- Businesses, government agencies, and nonprofit organizations.
- Sports teams.
- Sororities, fraternities, and other social groups.
- Churches, synagogues, and temples.
- Departments in a community college, college, or university.

Questions to ask include those in this chapter and the following:

- Tell me about someone in this organization you admire. Why is he or she successful?
- Tell me about someone who failed in this organization. What did he or she do wrong?
- What ceremonies and rituals does this organization have? Why are they important?
- Why would someone join this group rather than a competitor?

As Your Instructor Directs,
a. Share your results orally with a small group of students.
b. Present your results in an oral presentation to the class.
c. Present your results in a memo to your instructor.
d. Share your results with a small group of students and write a joint memo reporting the similarities and differences you found.

3–14 Analyzing a Discourse Community

Analyze the way a group you are part of uses language. Possible groups include

- Work teams.
- Sports teams.
- Sororities, fraternities, and other social groups.
- Churches, synagogues, and temples.
- Geographic or ethnic group.
- Groups of friends.

Questions to ask include the following:

- What specialized terms might not be known to outsiders?
- What topics do members talk or write about? What topics are considered unimportant or improper?
- What channels do members use to convey messages?

- What forms of language do members use to build goodwill? to demonstrate competence or superiority?
- What strategies or kinds of proof are convincing to members?
- What formats, conventions, or rules do members expect messages to follow?

As Your Instructor Directs,
a. Share your results orally with a small group of students.
b. Present your results in an oral presentation to the class.
c. Present your results in a memo to your instructor.
d. Share your results with a small group of students and write a joint memo reporting the similarities and differences you found.

CHAPTER 4

Making Your Writing Easy to Read

Chapter Outline

An Inside Perspective:
Making Your Writing Easy to Read

Dee Castner, Senior Auditor, KPMG Peat Marwick LLP

Dee Castner prepares financial statements and audit opinions and documents audit findings for superiors in KPMG. Headquartered in New York City, KPMG Peat Marwick is the global leader of the service organizations that provide audit, tax, and consulting services to the international business community.

Good audit writing is

1. Tight.
2. Complete while remaining positive.
3. Easy to understand for all audiences.

Tight writing is important since working papers and memos go to busy people. Wordy sentences waste time and paper. Parallel structure in bulleted or numbered lists, like the one above, is often used in working papers to show the different events that have affected an account. The items in the list are short and easy to follow. Transition words such as *however* and *but* allow the writer to explain multiple fluctuations during the year in a single sentence or paragraph, keeping related ideas together.

I try to be both complete and sensitive to the image my words convey to the client, especially in explaining transactions in complicated or unusual situations. For example, *minimizing taxes* represents a positive, well-managed image of an entity, while *avoiding taxes* sounds illegal. An auditor must be aware of the connotations of the words chosen to describe an event, as certain words may convey the wrong message to the reader.

An auditor must consider the audience to whom he or she is writing. Our audiences could include other KPMG professionals, employees of the client, or even members of the courts. Since each group has different levels of knowledge about accounting matters, documents should be easy to understand. In external documents, jargon would inhibit the reader's ability to understand. In internal workpapers, however, specialized terms such as PFAW (pass further audit work), P/Minor (pass minor), and PBC (prepared by client) are acceptable since they are commonly understood by auditors. An employee of the client or a member of the court would need to have such terms spelled out.

Writing is the most important communication method within KPMG. We write to clients to communicate the necessities and timeliness of audits. We write to apprise the audit team of internal and external situations. We document in writing the evidence which supports an audit opinion. For each different document, the audience's level of knowledge affects the words we choose.

Dee Castner, April 21, 1997

Visit KPMG's Web site: http://www.kpmg.com

"Tight writing is important since working papers and memos go to busy people."

Dee Castner, KPMG

Good business and administrative writing should sound like a person talking to another person. Unfortunately, much of the writing produced in organizations today seems to have been written by faceless bureaucrats rather than by real people.

Using an easy-to-read style makes the reader respond more positively to your ideas. You can make your writing easier to read in two ways. First, you can make individual sentences and paragraphs easy to read, so that skimming the first paragraph or reading the whole document takes as little work as possible. Second, you can make the document look visually inviting and structure it with signposts to guide readers through the document. This chapter focuses on ways to make words, sentences, and paragraphs easier to read. Chapter 6 will discuss ways to make the document as a whole easier to read.

HALF-TRUTHS ABOUT STYLE

Many generalizations about style are half-truths and must be applied selectively, if at all.

Half-Truth 1: "Write as You Talk."

One of the best tests of style is to read what you've written out loud to someone sitting about three feet away. If a passage sounds stiff and overly formal when you read it out loud, revise it; almost certainly it will sound stiff and perhaps even rude to the reader. If you wouldn't say it, don't write it.

However, unless our speech is exceptionally fluent, "writing as we talk" can create awkward, repetitive, and badly organized prose. It's OK to write as you talk to produce your first draft, but edit to create a good written style.

Half-Truth 2: "Never Use *I*."

Using *I* too often can make your writing sound self-centered; using it unnecessarily will make your ideas seem tentative. However, when you write about things you've done or said or seen, using *I* is both appropriate and smoother than resorting to awkward passives or phrases like *this writer*.

Half-Truth 3: "Never Begin a Sentence with *And* or *But*."

Beginning a sentence with *and* or *also* makes the idea that follows seem like an afterthought. That's OK when you want the effect of spontaneous speech in a written document, as you may in a sales letter. If you want to sound as though you have thought about what you are saying, put the *also* in the middle of the sentence or use another transition: *moreover, furthermore*.

But tells the reader that you are shifting gears and that the point which follows not only contrasts with but also is more important than the preceding

In focus groups, Iomega learned that computer users either hated or were bored by the idea of data storage. But they liked the idea of getting easier access to their "stuff." So Iomega created an ad campaign for the Zip drive using the friendly, colloquial word.

ideas. Presenting such verbal signposts to your reader is important. Beginning a sentence with *but* is fine if doing so makes your paragraph read smoothly.

Half-Truth 4: "Never End a Sentence with a Preposition."

Prepositions are those useful little words that indicate relationships: *with, in, under, at.* The prohibition against ending sentences with them is probably based on two facts: (1) The end of a sentence (like the beginning) is a position of emphasis. A preposition may not be worth emphasizing. (2) When the reader sees a preposition, he or she expects something to follow it. At the end of a sentence, nothing does.

In job application letters, reports, and important presentations, avoid ending sentences with prepositions. Most letters and memos are less formal; it's OK to end an occasional sentence with a preposition. Analyze your audience and the situation, and use the language that you think will get the best results.

Half-Truth 5: "Big Words Impress People."

Learning an academic discipline requires that you master its vocabulary. After you get out of school, however, no one will ask you to write just to prove that you understand something. Instead, you'll be asked to write or speak to people who need the information you have. Sometimes you may want the sense of formality or technical expertise that big words create. But much of the time, big words just distance you from your audience and increase the risk of miscommunication. When people misuse big words, they look foolish. If you're going to use big words, make sure you use them correctly.

EVALUATING "RULES" ABOUT WRITING

Some "rules" are grammatical conventions. For example, standard edited English requires that each sentence have a subject and verb and that they

Figure 4.1   **Different Levels of Style**

Conversational Style	Good Business Style	Traditional Term Paper Style
Highly informal	Conversational: sounds like a real person talking	More formal than conversation would be, but retains a human voice
Many contractions	OK to use occasional contractions	Few contractions, if any
Uses *I*, first- and second-person pronouns	Uses *I*, first- and second-person pronouns	First- and second-person pronouns kept to a minimum
Friendly	Friendly	No effort to make style friendly
Personal; refers to specific circumstances of conversation	Personal; may refer to reader by name; refers to specific circumstances of readers	Impersonal; may generally refer to *readers* but does not name them or refer to their circumstances
Short, simple words; slang	Short, simple words but avoids slang	Many abstract words, scholarly, technical terms
Incomplete sentences; no paragraphs	Short sentences and paragraphs	Sentences and paragraphs usually long
Can be ungrammatical	Uses standard edited English	Uses standard edited English
Not applicable	Attention to visual impact of document	No particular attention to visual impact

agree. Business writing normally demands standard grammar, but exceptions exist. Promotional materials such as brochures, advertisements, and sales and fund-raising letters may use sentence fragments to gain the effect of speech.

Other "rules" may be conventions adopted by an organization so that its documents will be consistent. For example, a company might decide to capitalize job titles (e.g., *Production Manager*) even though grammar doesn't require the capitals, or always to use a comma before *and* in a series, even though a sentence can be grammatical without the comma. A different company might make different choices.

Still other "rules" are attempts to codify "what sounds good." "Never use *I*" and "use big words" are examples of this kind of "rule." To evaluate these "rules," you must consider your audience, the discourse community (➤ p. 61), your purposes, and the situation. If you want the effect produced by an impersonal style and polysyllabic words, use them. But use them only when you want the distancing they produce.

Good Style in Business and Administrative Writing

The style of writing that has traditionally earned high marks in college essays and term papers is more formal than good business and administrative writing. (See Figure 4.1.) However, many business professors also like term papers that are easy to read and use good visual impact.

Most people have several styles of talking, which they vary instinctively depending on the audience. Good writers have several styles, too. A memo to your boss complaining about the delays from a supplier will be informal, perhaps even chatty; a letter to the supplier demanding better service will be more formal.

Keep the following points in mind as you choose a level of formality for a specific document:

- Use a friendly, informal style to someone you've talked with.
- Avoid contractions, slang, and even minor grammatical lapses in paper documents to people you don't know. Abbreviations are OK in e-mail messages if they're part of the group's culture.
- Pay particular attention to your style when you have to write uncomfortable messages: when you write to people you fear or when you

must give bad news. Reliance on nouns rather than on verbs and a general deadening of style increase when people are under stress or feel insecure.[1] Confident people are more direct. Edit your writing so that you sound confident, whether you feel that way or not.

BUILDING A BETTER STYLE

To improve your style,

- Get a clean page or screen, so that you aren't locked into old sentence structures.
- Try WIRMI: *What I Really Mean Is.*[2] Then write the words.
- Try reading your draft out loud to someone sitting about three feet away. If the words sound stiff, they'll seem stiff to a reader, too.
- Ask someone else to read your draft out loud. Readers stumble because the words on the page aren't what they expect to see. The places where that person stumbles are places where your writing can be better.
- Read widely and write a *lot.*
- Use the 10 techniques in the next section to polish your style.

TEN WAYS TO MAKE YOUR WRITING EASIER TO READ

Direct, simple writing is easier to read. James Suchan and Robert Colucci tested two versions of a memo report. The "high impact" version had the "bottom line" (the purpose of the report) in the first paragraph, simple sentences in normal word order, active verbs, concrete language, short paragraphs, headings and lists, and first- and second-person pronouns. The "high impact" version took 22% less time to read. Readers said they understood the report better, and tests showed that they really did understand it better.[3] We'll talk about layout, headings, and lists in Chapter 6.

Ten techniques make words, sentences, and paragraphs easier to read:

As you choose words,
1. Use words that are accurate, appropriate, and familiar.
2. Use technical jargon only when it is essential and known to the reader. Eliminate business jargon.

As you write and revise sentences,
3. Use active verbs most of the time.
4. Use verbs—not nouns—to carry the weight of your sentence.
5. Tighten your writing.
6. Vary sentence length and sentence structure.
7. Use parallel structure. Use the same grammatical form for ideas that have the same logical function.
8. Put your readers in your sentences.

As you write and revise paragraphs,
9. Begin most paragraphs with topic sentences so that readers know what to expect in the paragraph.
10. Use transitions to link ideas.

As You Choose Words

The best word depends on context: the situation, your purposes, your audience, the words you have already used.

E-Mail Acronyms

The following abbreviations often show up in e-mail messages:

BTW	By the way
FAQ	Frequently asked questions
IMHO	In my humble opinion
OTOH	On the other hand
TTYL	Talk to you later

What's in a Name? (1)*

Effective brand names depend on both denotation and connotation.

In 1989, Straight Arrow Products sold $500,000 worth of Mane 'n Tail horse shampoo. But 10 out of 12 bottles were used on people. The company created a new brand, Conceived by Nature: the same product, the same price. Sales in 1995 and 1996 averaged $45 million—a 90-fold increase made possible by a new positioning and a new name.

At Sun Microsystems, Kim Polese called a brainstorming meeting to find a cooler name for Oak software, a product she believed would "wake up the Web." Oak became Java, now the standard for multimedia and animation on Web pages.

*Based on Jennifer DeCoursey, "Straight Arrow," *Advertising Age,* June 24, 1996, s33; Bradley Johnson, "Java: Kim Polese," *Advertising Age,* June 24, 1996, s20.

1. Use Words That Are Accurate, Appropriate, and Familiar.   Accurate words mean what you want to say. Appropriate words convey the attitudes you want and fit well with the other words in your document. Familiar words are easy to read and understand.

Meaning arises in context. Many cities use "911" as an easy-to-dial number to get help in an emergency. Microsoft employees use "911" in subject lines of e-mail messages to signal that the message is urgent.[4]

Some meanings have already evolved before we join the conversation. We may learn the meaning of words, of actions, or of office layouts by being alert and observant. We learn some meanings by formal and informal study: the importance of "generally accepted accounting principles," the best strategies for increasing the size of donations in a fund-raising letter, or what the trashcan on a computer screen symbolizes. Some meanings are constrained by the social or work communities in which we move. Some meanings are negotiated as we interact one-on-one with another person, attempting to communicate.

To be accurate, a word's denotation must match the meaning the writer wishes to convey. **Denotation** is a word's literal or dictionary meaning; **connotation** means the emotional colorings or associations that accompany a word. Most common words in English have more than one denotation. The word *pound,* for example, means, or denotes, a unit of weight, a place where stray animals are kept, a unit of money in the British system, and the verb *to hit.* Coca-Cola spends an estimated $20 million a year to protect its brand names so that *Coke* will denote only that brand and not just any cola drink.

When two people use the same word to mean, or denote, different things, **bypassing** occurs. For example, negotiators for Amoco and for the Environmental Protection Agency (EPA) used *risk* differently. At Amoco, *risk* was an economic term dealing with efficiency; for the EPA, the term "was a four-letter word that meant political peril or health risk."[5] Progress was possible only when they agreed on a meaning.

Problems also arise when writers misuse words.

The western part of Ohio was transferred from Chicago to Cleveland.[6] (Ohio did not move. Instead, a company moved responsibility for sales in western Ohio.)

Three major associations of property-liability companies are poised to strike out in opposite directions.[7] (Three different directions can't be opposite each other.)

Earn a free lunch.[8] (A lunch one earns isn't free.)

Accurate denotations can make it easier to solve problems. In one production line with a high failure rate, the largest category of defects was *missed operations.* At first, the supervisor wondered if the people on the line were lazy or irresponsible. But some checking showed that several different problems were labeled *missed operations:* parts installed backwards, parts that had missing screws or fasteners, parts whose wires weren't connected. Each of these problems had a different solution. Using accurate words redefined the problem and enabled the production line both to improve quality and cut repair costs.[9]

Words are appropriate when their **connotations,** that is, their emotional associations or colorings, convey the attitude you want. A great many words carry connotations of approval or disapproval, disgust or delight. Words in the first column below suggest approval; words in the second column suggest criticism.

Positive word	Negative word
assume	guess
curious	nosy
negotiate	haggle
cautious	fearful
careful	nit-picking
firm	obstinate
flexible	wishy-washy

A supervisor can "tell the truth" about a subordinate's performance and yet write either a positive or a negative performance appraisal, based on the connotations of the words in the appraisal. Consider an employee who pays close attention to details. A positive appraisal might read, "Terry is a meticulous team member who takes care of details that others sometimes ignore." But the same behavior might be described negatively: "Terry is hung up on trivial details."

Advertisers carefully choose words with positive connotations. Expensive cars are never *used*; instead, they're *pre-owned, experienced,* or even *preloved.* An executive for Rolls-Royce once said, "A Rolls never, never breaks down. Of course," he added, with a twinkle in his eye, "there have been occasions when a car has failed to proceed."[10]

Words may also connote status. Both *salesperson* and *sales representative* are nonsexist job titles. But the first sounds like a clerk in a store; the second suggests someone selling important items to corporate customers.

Although connotations rarely appear in a dictionary, they are not individual or idiosyncratic. The associations a word evokes will be consistent in any one culture but may differ among cultures. One scholar reports that while "the term discussion is connotatively neutral for North Americans, it possesses a negative connotation for Latin Americans, who view it as an attempt to change someone else's mind."[11] Even within a culture, connotations may change over time. The word *charity* had acquired such negative connotations by the 19th century that people began to use the term *welfare* instead. Now, *welfare* has acquired negative associations and we may be ready for another term.

How positively can we present something and still be ethical? Certainly the words we use can shape response. A *defense budget* sounds essential; a *military budget* sounds less positive. A *nuclear accident* is scary; a *nuclear event* is neutral. We have the right to package our ideas attractively, but we have the responsibility to give the public or our superiors all the information they need to make decisions.

Use familiar words, words that are in almost everyone's vocabulary. Use the word that most exactly conveys your meaning, but whenever you can choose between two words that mean the same thing, use the shorter, more common one. Try to use specific, concrete words. They're easier to understand and remember.[12]

A series of long, learned, abstract terms makes writing less interesting, less forceful, and less memorable. Will big words make you sound more intelligent? Only if they're needed to communicate. Consider this memo, from the superintendent of schools of the Houston School District to "All Administrative Staff:"

> Subject: Sequential Page Numbering of Documents
>
> Please give immediate attention to insure that the pages of all documents prepared for distribution are numbered sequentially and in a place of optimum visibility. This is needed to facilitate our ability to refer to items during meetings.[13]

What's in a Name? (2)*

Choosing product names is even more complicated when translation is involved.

When Coca-Cola was introduced in China in the 1920s, a group of Chinese characters were chosen that sounded like the English name. Unfortunately, those characters meant "bite the wax tadpole." Today, the characters used on Coke bottles in China denote "happiness in the mouth."

Chevrolet introduced its "Nova" in Latin America, forgetting that "no va" is Spanish for "it doesn't go." The car was renamed "Caribe," and sales increased.

Mazda sells the Xedos 9 in Europe. Americans didn't like the name, so the company launched the car in the United States as the Millenia [sic].

*Based on David A. Ricks, *Blunders in International Business* (Cambridge, MA: Blackwell, 1993), 34–36, and Joel Achenbach, "Dance of Death Easy to Explain," *The Columbus Dispatch,* July 14, 1996, 3B.

The Ethics of Word Choice*

People can use accurate words to lie.

As a prize for visiting a condominium resort, a woman "won" an all-terrain vehicle. She had to pay $29.95 for "handling, processing, and insurance" to get it.

Then she saw her prize: a lawn chair with four wheels that converts into a wheeled cart.

The company claims it told the truth: "It is a vehicle. It's a four-wheel cart you can take anywhere—to the beach, to the pool. It may not be motorized, but [we] didn't say it was motorized."

The company may be guilty of deceptive trade practices: the courts will have to decide that. But whether or not the practice is illegal, it isn't ethical to use words that most people will misinterpret.

*Based on Carmella M. Padilla, "It's a . . . a . . . a . . . All-Terrain Vehicle, Yeah, That's It, That's the Ticket," *The Wall Street Journal,* July 17, 1987, 17.

Impressive? No. Silly? Yes. When you have something simple to say, use simple words.

The following list gives a few examples of short, simple alternatives.

Formal and stuffy	Short and simple
ameliorate	improve
commence	begin
enumerate	list
finalize	finish, complete
prioritize	rank
utilize	use
viable option	choice

There are four exceptions to the general rule that "shorter is better."

1. Use a long word if it is the only word that expresses your meaning exactly.
2. Use a long word if it is more familiar than a short word. *Send out* is better than *emit* and *a word in another language for a geographic place or area* is better than *exonym* because more people know the first item in each pair.
3. Use a long word if its connotations are more appropriate. *Exfoliate* is better than *scrape off dead skin cells.*
4. Use a long word if the discourse community (p. 61) prefers it.

2. Use Technical Jargon Sparingly; Eliminate Business Jargon.   There are two kinds of **jargon.** The first kind of jargon is the specialized terminology of a technical field. *LIFO* and *FIFO* are technical terms in accounting; *byte* and *baud* are computer jargon; *scale-free* and *pickled and oiled* designate specific characteristics of steel. A job application letter is the one occasion when it's desirable to use technical jargon: using the technical terminology of the reader's field helps suggest that you're a peer who also is competent in that field. In other kinds of messages, use technical jargon only when the term is essential and known to the reader.

If a technical term has a "plain English" equivalent, use the simpler term:

Jargon: Foot the average monthly budget column down to Total Variable Costs, Total Management Fixed Costs, Total Sunk Costs, and Grand Total.

Better: Add the figures in the average monthly budget column for each category to determine the Total Variable Costs, the Total Management Fixed Costs, and the Total Sunk Costs. Then add the totals for each category to arrive at the Grand Total.

The revision here is longer but better because it uses simple words. The original will be meaningless to a reader who does not know what *foot* means.

It is especially important to replace jargon with plain English when the specialized meaning of the technical term is not in fact being used. Consider this example:

Jargon: Additional parameters for price exception reporting were established for nonstock labor buy costs.

Better: We decided to include nonstock labor buys of over $_____ in the price exception report.

The word *parameters* means factors that are held constant while other variables change. It is a term that is essential in mathematics and statistics,

Companies with strong corporate cultures develop their own jargon. At IBM, a *hypo* is a high-potential employee—one destined for management.

but it is rarely used properly in general business and administrative writing. As the revision shows, the real meaning here was simple; no technical term was needed.

Terms that have technical meanings but are used in more general senses may be called **business slang.** Business slang includes *bottom line, GIGO, blindsiding,* and *downsize.* Used sparingly, these terms are appropriate in job application letters and in messages for people in your own organization, who are likely to share the vocabulary.

General slang includes words like *awesome, diss,* and *going postal.* Slang is sometimes used in business conversations and presentations, but it is too casual for business and administrative writing.

The second kind of jargon is the **businessese** that some writers still use: *as per your request, enclosed please find, please do not hesitate.* None of the words in this second category of jargon are necessary. Indeed, some writers call these terms *deadwood,* since they are no longer living words. Some of these terms, however, seem to float through the air like germs. If any of the terms in the first column of Figure 4.2 show up in your writing, replace them with more modern language.

As You Write and Revise Sentences

At the sentence level, you can do many things to make your writing easy to read.

3. Use Active Verbs Most of the Time.   "Who does what" sentences with active verbs make your writing more forceful.

A verb is **active** if the grammatical subject of the sentence does the action the verb describes. A verb is **passive** if the subject is acted upon. Passives are usually made up of a form of the verb *to be* plus a past participle. *Passive* has nothing to do with *past.* Passives can be past, present, or future:

were received	(in the past)
is recommended	(in the present)
will be implemented	(in the future)

Figure 4.2   **Getting Rid of Business Jargon**

Instead of	Use	Because
At your earliest convenience	The date you need a response	If you need it by a deadline, say so. It may never be convenient to respond.
As per your request; 55 miles per hour	As you requested; 55 miles an hour	*Per* is a Latin word for *by* or *for each*. Use *per* only when the meaning is correct; avoid mixing English and Latin.
Enclosed please find	Enclosed is; Here is	An enclosure isn't a treasure hunt. If you put something in the envelope, the reader will find it.
Forward same to this office	Return it to this office	Omit legal jargon.
Hereto, herewith	Omit	Omit legal jargon
Please be advised, Please be informed	Omit—simply start your response	You don't need a preface. Go ahead and start.
Please do not hesitate	Omit	Omit negative words.
Pursuant to	According to; or omit	*Pursuant* does not mean *after*. Omit legal jargon in any case.
Said order	Your order	Omit legal jargon.
This will acknowledge receipt of your letter.	Omit—start your response	If you answer a letter, the reader knows you got it.
Trusting this is satisfactory, we remain	Omit	Eliminate *-ing* endings. When you are through, stop.

To spot a passive, find the verb. If the verb describes something that the grammatical subject is doing, the verb is active. If the verb describes something that is being done to the grammatical subject, the verb is passive.

Active	**Passive**
The customer received 500 widgets.	Five hundred widgets were received by the customer.
I recommend this method.	This method is recommended by me.
The state agencies will implement the program.	The program will be implemented by the state agencies.

Verbs can be changed from active to passive by making the direct object the new subject. To change a passive verb to an active one, you must make the agent ("by _____") the new subject. If no agent is specified in the sentence, you must supply one to make the sentence active.

Active	**Passive**
The plant manager approved the request.	The request was approved by the plant manager.
The committee will decide next month.	A decision will be made next month.
Send the customer a letter informing her about the change.	A letter will be sent informing the customer of the change.

If the sentence does not have a direct object in its active form, no passive equivalent exists.

Active	**No passive exists**
I would like to go to the conference. The freight charge will be about $1,400. The phone rang.	

Passive verbs have at least three disadvantages:

1. If all the information in the original sentence is retained, passive verbs make the sentence longer. Passives take more time to understand.[14]
2. If the agent is omitted, it's not clear who is responsible for doing the action.
3. When many passive verbs are used, or when passives are used in material that has a lot of big words, the writing can be boring and pompous.

Passive verbs are desirable in these situations:

1. Use passives to emphasize the object receiving the action, not the agent.

    Your order was shipped November 15.

    The customer's order, not the shipping clerk, is important.
2. Use passives to provide coherence within a paragraph. A sentence is easier to read if "old" information comes at the beginning of a sentence. When you have been discussing a topic, use the word again as your subject even if that requires a passive verb.

    The bank made several risky loans in the 1980s. These loans were written off as "uncollectible" in 1995.

    Using *loans* as the subject of the second sentence provides a link between the two sentences, making the paragraph as a whole easier to read.
3. Use passives to avoid assigning blame.

    The order was damaged during shipment.

    An active verb would require the writer to specify *who* damaged the order. The passive here is more tactful.

4. Use Strong Verbs—Not Nouns—to Carry the Weight of Your Sentence.
Put the weight of your sentence in the verb. Strong verbs make sentences more forceful and up to 25% easier to read.[15] When the verb is a form of the verb *to be*, revise the sentence to use a more forceful verb.

Weak:	The financial advantage of owning this equipment instead of leasing it is 10% after taxes.
Better:	Owning this equipment rather than leasing it will save us 10% after taxes.

Nouns ending in *-ment, -ion,* and *-al* often hide verbs.

make an adjustment	adjust
make a payment	pay
make a decision	decide
reach a conclusion	conclude
take into consideration	consider
make a referral	refer
provide assistance	assist

Use verbs to present the information more forcefully.

Weak:	We will perform an investigation of the problem.
Better:	We will investigate the problem.
Weak:	Selection of a program should be based on the client's needs.
Better:	Select the program that best fits the client's needs.

5. Tighten Your Writing. Writing is **wordy** if the same idea can be expressed in fewer words. Unnecessary words increase typing time, bore your reader, and make your meaning more difficult to follow, since the reader must hold all the extra words in mind while trying to understand your meaning.

What I Really Mean Is . . .*

I wrote asking someone if he could "provide information for" the group he had mentioned on a Web page. He replied that he was too busy to make a submission, and added that he was in full support of the group.

 I got an answer, but a useless one. I had wanted the group's address! I could have avoided confusion (and embarrassment) by simply asking, "Do you have the group's address?"

*Quoted from Margo Metegrano, Letter to the Editor, *Intercom,* May 1996, 2.

Using Your Computer to Improve Style*

Laser copies look so perfect that it can be hard to edit them. But your computer can be an ally, not an enemy, as you revise and edit.

- Use the "search" or "find" command to find potential errors. One student replaces every "is" and "are" with capital letters ("IS" and "ARE") so that he can easily check his draft for weak verbs. Another replaces periods with several asterisks to check sentence integrity.
- Change the font or size. Putting your text in an unusual font or 24-point type can help you really see what you've said. (Just remember to change back to a standard font in a standard size before printing out the final version!)
- Ask a friend to edit, putting changes in all caps, so you can easily find them.

*Based on Todd Taylor, " 'Soft Copy' and the Illusion of Laser-Printed Text," *Technical Communication*, 42.1 (February 1995): 169–70.

Good writing is tight. Tight writing may be long because it is packed with ideas. In Chapter 2, we saw that revisions to create you-attitude and positive emphasis and to develop reader benefits were frequently *longer* than the originals because the revision added information not given in the original.

Sometimes you may be able to look at a draft and see immediately how to tighten it. When the solution isn't obvious, try the following strategies for tightening your writing.

a. Eliminate words that say nothing.
b. Use gerunds (the *-ing* form of verbs) and infinitives to make sentences shorter and smoother.
c. Combine sentences to eliminate unnecessary words.
d. Put the meaning of your sentence into the subject and verb to cut the number of words.

The purpose of eliminating unnecessary words is to save the reader's time, not simply to see how few words you can use. You aren't writing a telegram, so keep the little words that make sentences complete. (Incomplete sentences are fine in lists where all the items are incomplete.)

The following examples show how to use these methods.

a. Eliminate Words That Say Nothing.   Cut words that are already clear from other words in the sentence. Substitute single words for wordy phrases.

Wordy: Keep this information on file for future reference.
Tighter: Keep this information for reference.
or: File this information.

Wordy: Ideally, it would be best to put the billing ticket just below the CRT screen and above the keyboard.
Tighter: If possible, put the billing ticket between the CRT screen and the keyboard.

Phrases beginning with *of, which,* and *that* can often be shortened.

Wordy: the question of most importance
Tighter: the most important question

Wordy: the estimate which is enclosed
Tighter: the enclosed estimate

Sentences beginning with *There are* or *It is* can often be tighter.

Wordy: There are three reasons for the success of the project.
Tighter: Three reasons explain the project's success.

Wordy: It is the case that college graduates advance more quickly in the company.
Tighter: College graduates advance more quickly in the company.

Check your draft. If you find these phrases, or any of the unnecessary words shown in Figure 4.3, eliminate them.

b. Use Gerunds and Infinitives to Make Sentences Shorter and Smoother. A **gerund** is the *-ing* form of a verb; grammatically, it is a verb used as a noun. In the sentence, "Running is my favorite activity," *running* is the subject of the sentence. An **infinitive** is the form of the verb that is preceded by *to: to run* is the infinitive.

In the revision below, a gerund (*purchasing*) and an infinitive (*to transmit*) tighten the revision.

Wordy: A plant suggestion has been made where they would purchase a QWIP machine for the purpose of transmitting test reports between plants.
Tighter: The plant suggests purchasing a QWIP machine to transmit test reports between plants.

Figure 4.3

Words to Cut

The following words can usually be cut:

quite

really

very

Cut redundant words.

~~a period of~~ three months

during ~~the course of~~ the negotiations

during ~~the year of~~ 1996

maximum ~~possible~~

~~past~~ experience

plan ~~in advance~~

refer ~~back~~

~~the color~~ blue

~~true~~ facts

Substitute a single word for a wordy phrase.

~~at the present time~~	now
~~due to the fact that~~	because
~~in the event that~~	if
~~in the near future~~	soon (or give the date)
~~prior to the start of~~	before
~~on a regular basis~~	regularly

Even when gerunds and infinitives do not greatly affect length, they often make sentences smoother and more conversational.

c. Combine Sentences to Eliminate Unnecessary Words.   In addition to saving words, combining sentences focuses the reader's attention on key points, makes your writing sound more sophisticated, and sharpens the relationship between ideas, thus making your writing more coherent.

Wordy: I conducted this survey by telephone on Sunday, April 21. I questioned two groups of upperclassmen—male and female—who, according to the Student Directory, were still living in the dorms. The purpose of this survey was to find out why some upperclassmen continue to live in the dorms even though they are no longer required by the University to do so. I also wanted to find out if there were any differences between male and female upperclassmen in their reasons for choosing to remain in the dorms.

Tighter: On Sunday, April 21, I phoned upperclassmen and women living in the dorms to find out (1) why they continue to live in the dorms even though they are no longer required to do so, and (2) whether men and women had the same reasons for staying in the dorms.

d. Put the Meaning of Your Sentence into the Subject and Verb to Cut the Number of Words.   Put the core of your meaning into the subject and verb of your main clause. Think about what you *mean* and try saying the same thing in several different ways. Some alternatives will be tighter than others. Choose the tightest one.

Wordy: The reason we are recommending the computerization of this process is because it will reduce the time required to obtain data and will give us more accurate data.

Better: We are recommending the computerization of this process because it will save time and give us more accurate data.

Tight: Computerizing the process will give us more accurate data more quickly.

Wordy: The purpose of this letter is to indicate that if we are unable to mutually benefit from our seller/buyer relationship, with satisfactory material and

Legally, GI Joe Is a Doll*

Ask any eight-year-old boy if he wants to play with dolls, and he may paste you one. Better not tell him that a court has ruled that his GI Joe is a doll. Hasbro, which introduced GI Joe in 1964, has always used macho euphemisms like "action figure" to describe the soldier. Since 1982, though, when Hasbro began importing its GI Joe toys from Hong Kong, the U.S. Customs Service has classified it as a doll.

Under Customs rules, imported dolls are subject to a 12% import tariff, while toy soldiers are not. The U.S. Court of Appeals for the District of Columbia has now upheld Customs, reasoning that, like other dolls, GI Joe is "a representation of a human being used as a child's plaything." But for little boys everywhere, says Donald Robbins, the firm's general counsel, "GI Joe is still one of the guys."

*Quoted from "Soldier Boy, You're a Doll," Time, July 31, 1989, 41.

satisfactory payment, then we have no alternative other than to sever the relationship. In other words, unless the account is handled in 45 days, we will have to change our terms to a permanent COD basis.

Better: A good buyer/seller relationship depends upon satisfactory material and satisfactory payment. You can continue to charge your purchases from us only if you clear your present balance in 45 days.

6. Vary Sentence Length and Sentence Structure. Readable prose mixes sentence lengths and varies sentence structure. A really short sentence (under 10 words) can add punch to your prose. Really long sentences (over 30 or 40 words) are danger signs.

You can vary sentence patterns in several ways. First, you can mix simple, compound, and complex sentences. **Simple sentences** have one main clause:

We will open a new store this month.

Compound sentences have two main clauses joined with *and, but, or,* or another conjunction. Compound sentences work best when the ideas in the two clauses are closely related.

We have hired staff, and they will complete their training next week.

We wanted to have a local radio station broadcast from the store during its grand opening, but the DJs were already booked.

Complex sentences have one main and one subordinate clause; they are good for showing logical relationships.

When the stores open, we will have balloons and specials in every department.

Because we already have a strong customer base in the northwest, we expect the new store to be just as successful as the store in the City Center Mall.

You can also vary sentences by changing the order of elements. Normally the subject comes first.

We will survey customers later in the year to see whether demand warrants a third store on campus.

To create variety, occasionally begin the sentence with some other part of the sentence.

Later in the year, we will survey customers to see whether demand warrants a third store on campus.

To see whether demand warrants a third store on campus, we will survey customers later in the year.

Use these guidelines for sentence length and structure:

- Always edit sentences for tightness. Even a 17-word sentence can be wordy.
- When your subject matter is complicated or full of numbers, make a special effort to keep sentences short.
- Use long sentences
  To show how ideas are linked to each other.
  To avoid a series of short, choppy sentences.
  To reduce repetition.
- Group the words in long and medium-length sentences into chunks that the reader can process quickly.[16]
- When you use a long sentence, keep the subject and verb close together.

Let's see how to apply the last three principles.

- **Use long sentences to show how ideas are linked to each other, to avoid a series of short, choppy sentences, and to reduce repetition.** The following sentence is hard to read not simply because it is long but because it is shapeless. Just cutting it into a series of short, choppy sentences doesn't help. The best revision uses medium-length sentences to show the relationship between ideas.

Too long:	It should also be noted in the historical patterns presented in the summary, that though there were delays in January and February which we realized were occurring, we are now back where we were about a year ago, and that we are not off line in our collect receivables as compared to last year at this time, but we do show a considerable over-budget figure because of an ultraconservative goal on the receivable investment.
Choppy:	There were delays in January and February. We knew about them at the time. We are now back where we were about a year ago. The summary shows this. Our present collect receivables are in line with last year's. However, they exceed the budget. The reason they exceed the budget is that our goal for receivable investment was very conservative.
Better:	As the summary shows, although there were delays in January and February (of which we were aware), we have now regained our position of a year ago. Our present collect receivables are in line with last year's, but they exceed the budget because our goal for receivable investment was very conservative.

■ **Group the words in long and medium-length sentences into chunks.** The "better" revision above has seven chunks. In the list below, the chunks starting immediately after the numbers are main clauses. The chunks that are indented are subordinate clauses and parenthetical phrases.

1.   As the summary shows,
2.   although there were delays in January and February
3.   (of which we were aware),
4. we have now regained our position of a year ago.
5. Our present collect receivables are in line with last year's,
6. but they exceed the budget
7.   because our goal for receivable investment was very conservative.

The first sentence has four chunks: an introductory phrase (1), a subordinate clause (2) with a parenthetical phrase (3), followed by the main clause of the first sentence (4). The second sentence begins with a main clause (5). The sentence's second main clause (6) is introduced with *but,* showing that it will reverse the first clause. A subordinate clause explaining the reason for the reversal completes the sentence (7). At 27 and 24 words, respectively, these sentences aren't short, but they're readable because no chunk is longer than 10 words.

Any sentence pattern will get boring if it is repeated sentence after sentence. Use different sentence patterns—different kinds and lengths of chunks—to keep your prose interesting.

■ **Keep the subject and verb close together.** Often you can move the subject and verb closer together if you put the modifying material in a list at the end of the sentence. For maximum readability, present the list vertically.

Hard to read:	Movements resulting from termination, layoffs and leaves, recalls and reinstates, transfers in, transfers out, promotions in, promotions out, and promotions within are presently documented through the Payroll Authorization Form.
Smoother:	The following movements are documented on the Payroll Authorization Form: termination, layoffs and leaves, recalls and reinstates, transfers in and out, and promotions in, out, and within.

Writing to Be Translated*

When you know that something will be translated into another language, avoid figurative language, images, and humor. They don't translate well.

"Consider the American copywriter who prepared a campaign on snowblowers for the European market without giving a thought to translations. . . . 'Super Snow Hound' [was] the most powerful model. . . . The copywriter wrote the headline: 'Super Snow Hound Blows Up a Storm.' You can imagine the difficulty of retaining the idiom and connotations of 'blows' for snowblower and 'up a storm' for heavy duty performance in a snow storm."

*Paragraph 2 quoted from Robert F. Roth, *International Marketing Communications* (Chicago: Crain, 1982), 139.

| Still better: | The following movements are documented on the Payroll Authorization Form:
■ Termination.
■ Layoffs and leaves.
■ Recalls and reinstates.
■ Transfers in and out.
■ Promotions in, out, and within. |

Sometimes you will need to change the verb and revise the word order to put the modifying material at the end of the sentence.

| Hard to read: | The size sequence code that is currently used for sorting the items in the NOSROP lists and the composite stock list is not part of the online file. |
| Smoother: | The online file does not contain the size sequence code that is currently used for sorting the items in the composite stock lists and the NOSROP lists. |

7. Use Parallel Structure.   Words or ideas that share the same logical role in your sentence must also be in the same grammatical form. Parallelism is also a powerful device for making your writing smoother and more forceful. Note the parallel portions in the following examples.

Faulty:	I interviewed juniors and seniors and athletes.
Parallel:	I interviewed juniors and seniors. In each rank, I interviewed athletes and nonathletes.
Faulty:	Errors can be checked by reviewing the daily exception report or note the number of errors you uncover when you match the lading copy with the file copy of the invoice.
Parallel:	Errors can be checked by reviewing the daily exception report or by noting the number of errors you uncover when you match the lading copy with the file copy of the invoice.
Also parallel:	To check errors, note 1. The number of items on the daily exception report. 2. The number of errors discovered when the lading copy and the file copy are matched.

Note that a list in parallel structure must fit grammatically into the umbrella sentence that introduces the list.

8. Put Your Readers in Your Sentences.   Use second-person pronouns (*you*) rather than third-person (*he, she, one*) to give your writing more impact. *You* is both singular and plural; it can refer to a single person or to every member of your organization.

| Third-person: | Funds in a participating employee's account at the end of each six months will automatically be used to buy more stock unless a "Notice of Election Not to Exercise Purchase Rights" form is received from the employee. |
| Second-person: | Once you begin to participate, funds in your account at the end of each six months will automatically be used to buy more stock unless you turn in a "Notice of Election Not to Exercise Purchase Rights" form. |

Be careful to use *you* only when it refers to your reader.

| Incorrect: | My visit with the outside sales rep showed me that your schedule can change quickly. |
| Correct: | My visit with the outside sales rep showed me that schedules can change quickly. |

As You Write and Revise Paragraphs

Paragraphs are visual and logical units. Use them to chunk your sentences.

9. Begin Most Paragraphs with Topic Sentences. A good paragraph has **unity;** that is, it is about only one idea, or topic. The **topic sentence** states the main idea and provides a scaffold to structure your document. Your writing will be easier to read if you make the topic sentence explicit and put it at the beginning of the paragraph.[17]

The Benefits of Plain English*

Allen-Bradley spent two years converting its manuals to plain English. The work is paying off in five ways. (1) Phone calls asking questions about the products have dropped from 50 a day to only 2 a month. (2) The sales force is selling more systems because people can learn about them more quickly. (3) Distributors spend less time on site teaching customers about products. (4) The clearer documents are easier to translate into Japanese, German, and French for international sales. (5) The tighter documents cost less to print, especially when translated into Arabic and German, which require 125% more space than the same content in English.

*Based on Barry Jereb, "Plain English on the Plant Floor," *Plain Language: Principles and Practice,* ed. Edwin R. Steinberg (Detroit: Wayne State University Press, 1991), 213.

Hard to read: (no topic sentence)	In fiscal 1997, the company filed claims for refund of federal income taxes of $3,199,000 and interest of $969,000 paid as a result of an examination of the company's federal income tax returns by the Internal Revenue Service (IRS) for the years 1993 through 1995. It is uncertain what amount, if any, may ultimately be recovered.
Better: (paragraph starts with topic sentence)	The company and the IRS disagree about whether the company is liable for back taxes. In fiscal 1997, the company filed claims for a refund of federal income taxes of $3,199,000 and interest of $969,000 paid as a result of an examination of the company's federal income tax returns by the Internal Revenue Service (IRS) for the years 1993 through 1995. It is uncertain what amount, if any, may ultimately be recovered.

A good topic sentence forecasts the structure and content of the paragraph.

Plan B also has economic advantages.
(Prepares the reader for a discussion of B's economic advantages.)

We had several personnel changes in June.
(Prepares the reader for a list of the month's terminations and hires.)

Employees have complained about one part of our new policy on parental leaves.
(Prepares the reader for a discussion of the problem.)

When the first sentence of a paragraph is not the topic sentence, readers who skim may miss the main point. Move the topic sentence to the beginning of the paragraph. If the paragraph does not have a topic sentence, you will need to write one. If you can't think of a single sentence that serves as an "umbrella" to cover every sentence, the paragraph lacks unity. To solve the problem, either split the paragraph into two or eliminate the sentence that digresses from the main point.

10. Use Transitions to Link Ideas. Transition words and sentences signal the connections between ideas to the reader. Transitions tell whether the next sentence continues the previous thought or starts a new idea; they can tell whether the idea that comes next is more or less important than the previous thought. Figure 4.4 lists some of the most common transition words and phrases.

READABILITY FORMULAS AND GOOD STYLE

Readability formulas attempt to measure objectively how easy something is to read. However, since they don't take many factors into account, the formulas are at best a very limited guide to good style.

Computer packages that analyze style may give you a readability score. Some states' "plain English" laws require consumer contracts to meet a certain readability score. Some companies require that warranties and other consumer documents meet certain scores. Figure 4.5 shows how to calculate the

Figure 4.4   **Transition Words and Phrases**

To show addition or continuation of the same idea
and
also
first, second, third
in addition
likewise
similarly

To introduce the last or most important item
finally
furthermore
moreover
finally

To introduce an example
for example (e.g.)
for instance
indeed
to illustrate
namely
specifically

To contrast
in contrast
on the other hand
or

To show that the contrast is more important than the previous idea
but
however
nevertheless
on the contrary

To show cause and effect
as a result
because
consequently
for this reason
therefore

To show time
after
as
before
in the future
next
then
until
when
while

To summarize or end
in conclusion

Figure 4.5

How to Calculate Readability Formulas

How to Calculate the Gunning Fog Index

1. Calculate the average sentence length. If the document is long, calculate the average using several samples of 100 words spaced through the document.
2. Calculate the percentage of words that have three or more syllables. In a long document, calculate the percentage in several 100-word sections. In the count of words with three or more syllables,
   Omit capitalized words.
   Omit easy words (e.g., *bookkeeper, butterfly*).
   Omit verbs that have three syllables because of *-ed* or *-es*.
3. Multiply the two numbers (average sentence length, percent of words with three or more syllables) by .4. This yields a grade level for the education necessary to understand the passage:
   8 = eighth-grade.
   11 = high school junior.
   13 = first year of college.

How to Calculate the Flesch Reading Ease Scale

1. Calculate the average number of words in a sentence. Multiply that number by 1.015.
2. Calculate the average number of syllables in a word. Multiply that number by .846.
3. Subtract both results from 206.835. This yields a number between 0 (very difficult) and 100 (very easy). The higher the score, the better.

Based on Janice C. Redish, "Readability," *Document Design: A Review of the Relevant Research,* ed. Daniel B. Felker (Washington, DC: American Institutes for Research, 1980), 73–75.

two best known formulas, the Gunning Fog Index and the Flesch Reading Ease Scale.

As you can see, readability formulas depend heavily on word length and sentence length. But as Janice C. Redish and Jack Selzer have shown,[18] using shorter words and sentences will not necessarily make a passage easy to read.

Short words are not always easy to understand, especially if they have technical meanings (e.g., *waive, bear market, liquid*). Short, choppy sentences and sentence fragments are actually harder to understand than well-written medium-length sentences.

No reading formula yet devised takes into account three factors that influence how easy a text is to read: the complexity of the ideas, the organization of the ideas, and the layout and design of the document.

Instead of using readability formulas to measure style, the Document Design Center recommends that you test your draft with the people for whom it is designed. How long does it take them to find the information they need? Do they make mistakes when they try to use the document? Do they think the document is easy to use? Answers to these questions can give us much more accurate information than any readability score.

ORGANIZATIONAL PREFERENCES FOR STYLE

Different organizations and bosses may legitimately have different ideas about what constitutes good writing. If the style the company prefers seems reasonable, use it. If the style doesn't seem reasonable—if you work for someone who likes flowery language or wordy paragraphs, for example—you have several choices.

- Go ahead and use the techniques in this chapter. Sometimes seeing good writing changes people's minds about the style they prefer.
- Help your boss learn about writing. Show him or her this book or the research cited in the notes to demonstrate how a clear, crisp style makes documents easier to read.
- Recognize that a style may serve other purposes than communication. An abstract, hard-to-read style may help a group forge its own identity. James Suchan and Ronald Dulek have shown that Navy officers preferred a passive, impersonal style because they saw themselves as followers. An aircraft company's engineers saw wordiness as the verbal equivalent of backup systems. A backup is redundant but essential to safety, because parts and systems do fail.[19] When big words, jargon, and wordiness are central to a group's self-image, change will be difficult, since changing style will mean changing the corporate culture.
- Ask. Often the documents that end up in files aren't especially good; later, other workers may find these and copy them, thinking they represent a corporate standard. Bosses may in fact prefer better writing.

Building a good style takes energy and effort, but it's well worth the work. Good style can make every document more effective; good style can help make you the good writer so valuable to every organization.

SUMMARY OF KEY POINTS

- Good style in business and administrative writing is less formal, more friendly, and more personal than the style usually used for term papers.
- To improve your style,

  - Get a clean page or screen, so that you aren't locked into old sentence structures.
  - Try WIRMI: *What I Really Mean Is.* Then write the words.
  - Try reading your draft out loud to someone sitting about three feet away. If the words sound stiff, they'll seem stiff to a reader, too.

The Boss Won't Let Me Write That Way

When a writing consultant urged them to use *I*, the engineers in Research and Development (R&D) at one firm claimed they couldn't: "Our boss won't let us." The consultant checked with their boss, the vice president for Research and Development. He said, "I don't care what words they use. I just want to be able to understand what they write."

The vice president had a PhD and had once done experiments in R&D himself, but he'd spent several years in management. He no longer knew as many technical details as did his subordinates. Their efforts to impress him backfired: he was annoyed because he couldn't understand their reports and had to tell subordinates to rewrite them.

Moral 1: If you think your boss doesn't want you to use a word, ask. A few bosses do prize formal or flowery language. Most don't.

Moral 2: Even if your boss has the same background you do, he or she won't necessarily understand what you write. Revise your memos and reports so they're clear and easy to read.

Moral 3: What's in the file cabinet isn't necessarily a guide to good writing for your organization.

- Ask someone else to read your draft out loud. Readers stumble because the words on the page aren't what they expect to see. The places where that person stumbles are places where your writing can be better.
- Write a *lot.*

- Use the following techniques to make your writing easier to read:
  As you choose words,
  1. Use words that are accurate, appropriate, and familiar. **Denotation** is a word's literal meaning; **connotation** is the emotional coloring that a word conveys.
  2. Use technical jargon only when it is essential and known to the reader. Eliminate business jargon.

  As you write and revise sentences,
  3. Use active verbs most of the time. Active verbs are better because they are shorter, clearer, and more interesting.
  4. Use verbs—not nouns—to carry the weight of your sentence.
  5. Tighten your writing. Writing is **wordy** if the same idea can be expressed in fewer words.
     a. Eliminate words that say nothing.
     b. Use gerunds and infinitives to make sentences shorter and smoother.
     c. Combine sentences to eliminate unnecessary words.
     d. Put the meaning of your sentence into the subject and verb to cut the number of words.
  6. Vary sentence length and sentence structure.
  7. Use parallel structure. Use the same grammatical form for ideas that have the same logical function.
  8. Put your readers in your sentences.

  As you write and revise paragraphs,
  9. Begin most paragraphs with topic sentences so that readers know what to expect in the paragraph.
  10. Use transitions to link ideas.

- Readability formulas are not a sufficient guide to style. They imply that all short words and all short sentences are equally easy to read; they ignore other factors that make a document easy or hard to read: the complexity of the ideas, the organization of the ideas, and the layout and design of the document.
- Different organizations and bosses may legitimately have different ideas about what constitutes good writing.

Exercises and Problems
For Chapter 4

4–1 Identifying Words with Multiple Denotations _____

a. Each of the following words has several denotations. How many can you list without going to a dictionary? How many additional meanings does a good dictionary list?

browser	log
court	table

b. List five words that have multiple denotations.

4–2 Explaining Bypassing

Show how different denotations make bypassing possible in the following examples.

a. France and Associates: Protection from Professionals

b. We were not able to account for the outstanding amount of plastic waste generated each year.

c. I scanned the résumés when I received them.

4–3 Evaluating Connotations

a. Identify the connotations of each of the following metaphors for a multicultural nation.

melting pot
mosaic
tapestry
crazy quilt
garden salad
stew
tributaries

b. Which connotations seem most positive? Why?

4–4 Evaluating the Ethical Implications of Connotations

In each of the following pairs, identify the more favorable term. Is its use justified? Why or why not?

1. wastepaper   recovered fiber
2. feedback   criticism
3. deadline   due date
4. scalper   ticket reseller
5. budget   spending plan

4–5 Correcting Errors in Denotation and Connotation

Identify and correct the errors in denotation or connotation in the following sentences.

1. I will take credit for the mistake.
2. The technology for virtual reality looms over the horizon.
3. The three proposals are diametrically opposed to each other.
4. In her search for information, she literally devours *The Wall Street Journal* and several business magazines each week.
5. Approximately 489 customers answered our survey.

4–6 Using Connotations to Shape Response

Write two sentences to describe each of the following situations. In one sentence, use words with positive connotations; in the other, use negative words.

1. Lee talks to co-workers about subjects other than work, such as last weekend's ball game.
2. Lee spends a lot of time sending e-mail messages and monitoring e-mail newsgroups.
3. As a supervisor, Lee rarely gives specific instructions to subordinates.

4–7 Choosing Levels of Formality

Identify the more formal word in each pair. Which term is better for most business documents? Why?

1. adapted to   geared to
2. befuddled   confused
3. assistant   helper
4. pilot project testing the waters
5. cogitate   think

4–8 Eliminating Jargon and Simplifying Language

Revise these sentences to eliminate jargon and to use short, familiar words. In some sentences, you'll need to reword, reorganize, or add information to produce the best revision.

1. Computers can enumerate pages when the appropriate keystroke is implemented.

2. Any alterations must be approved during the 30-day period commencing 60 days prior to the expiration date of the agreement.
3. As per your request, the undersigned has compiled a report on claims paid in 1997. A copy is attached hereto.
4. Please be advised that this writer is unable to attend the meeting on the fifteenth due to an unavoidable conflict.
5. Enclosed please find the schedule for the training session. In the event that you have alterations which you would like to suggest, forward same to my office at your earliest convenience.

4–9 Changing Verbs from Passive to Active

Identify the passive verbs in the following sentences and convert them to active verbs. In some cases, you may need to add information to do so. You may use different words as long as you retain the basic meaning of the sentence. Remember that imperative verbs are active, too.

1. The marketing plan was prepared by Needra Smith.
2. With the assistance of computers, inventory records are updated and invoices are automatically issued when an order is entered by one of our customers.
3. When the Web page is finalized it is recommended that it be routed to all managers for final approval.
4. As stated in my résumé, I speak Spanish fluently.
5. All employees being budgeted should be listed by name and position. Any employee whose name does not appear on the "September Listing of Salaried Employees" must be explained. If this employee is a planned replacement, indicate who will be replaced and when. If it is an addition, the reason must be explained.

4–10 Using Strong Verbs

Revise each of the following sentences to use stronger verbs.

1. The advantage of using color is that the document is more memorable.
2. Customers who make payments by credit card will receive a 1% rebate on all purchases.
3. When you make an evaluation of media buys, take into consideration the demographics of the group seeing the ad.
4. We provide assistance to clients in the process of reaching a decision about the purchase of hardware and software.
5. We maintain the belief that Web ads are a good investment.

4–11 Reducing Wordiness

1. Eliminate words that say nothing. You may use different words.
   a. It is necessary that we reach a decision about whether or not it is desirable to make a request that the office be allowed the opportunity and option of hiring additional workers.
   b. The purchase of a new computer will allow us to produce form letters quickly. In addition, return-on-investment could be calculated for proposed repairs. Another use is that the computer could check databases to make sure that claims are paid only once.
   c. There are many subjects which interest me.
2. Use gerunds and infinitives to make these sentences shorter and smoother.
   a. The completion of the project requires the collection and analysis of additional data.
   b. The purchase of laser printers will make possible the in-house production of the newsletter.
   c. The treasurer has the authority for the investment of assets for the gain of higher returns.
3. Combine sentences to show how ideas are related and to eliminate unnecessary words.
   a. Some buyers want low prices. Other buyers are willing to pay higher prices for convenience or service.

b. We projected sales of $34 million in the third quarter. Our actual sales have fallen short of that figure by $2.5 million.

c. We conducted this survey by handing out questionnaires January 10, 11, and 12. Our office surveyed 100 customers. We wanted to see whether they would like to be able to leave voice-mail messages for their representatives. We also wanted to find out if our hours are convenient for them. Finally, we asked whether adequate parking was available.

4–12   Improving Parallel Structure

Revise each of the following sentences to create parallelism.

1. Training programs
   - Allow employees to build skills needed for current and future positions.
   - Employees enjoy the break from routine work.
   - Training programs are a "fringe benefit" that helps to attract and retain good employees.
2. Newsletters enhance credibility, four times as many people read them as read standard ad formats, and allow soft-sell introduction to prospective customers.
3. When you leave a voice-mail message,
   - Summarize your main point in a sentence or two.
   - The name and phone number should be given slowly and distinctly.
   - The speaker should give enough information so that the recipient can act on the message.
   - Tell when you'll be available to receive the recipient's return call.

4–13   Putting Readers in Your Sentences

Revise each of the following sentences to put readers in them. As you revise, use active verbs and simple words.

1. Mutual funds can be purchased from banks, brokers, financial planners, or from the fund itself.
2. Every employee will receive a copy of the new policy within 60 days after the labor agreement is signed.
3. Another aspect of the university is campus life, with an assortment of activities and student groups to participate in and lectures and sports events to attend.

4–14   Editing Sentences to Improve Style

Revise these sentences to make them smoother, less wordy, and easier to read. Eliminate jargon and repetition. Keep the information; you may reword or reorganize it. If the original is not clear, you may need to add information to write a clear revision.

1. The table provided was unclear due to hard-to-understand headings.
2. By working a co-op or intern position, you may have to be in school an additional year to complete the requirements for graduation, but this extra year is paid for by the income you make in the co-op or intern position.
3. There is a seasonality factor in the workload, with the heaviest being immediately prior to quarterly due dates for estimated tax payments.
4. Informational meetings will be held during next month at different dates and times. These meetings will explain the HMO options. Meeting times are as follows:
   October 17, noon–1 pm.
   October 20, 4–5 pm.
   October 23, 2–3 pm.
5. Listed below are some benefits you get from an HMO:
   1. Routine doctors' visits will charge only a $10 co-payment.
   2. No hassle of prescription reimbursements later. You only pay the co-payment when you fill your prescription.
   3. Hospitalization is covered 100%.

4—15   Using Topic Sentences

Make each of the following paragraphs more readable by opening each paragraph with a topic sentence. You may be able to find a topic sentence in the paragraph and move it to the beginning. In other cases, you'll need to write a new sentence.

1. At Disney World, a lunch put on expense account is "on the mouse." McDonald's employees "have ketchup in their veins." Business slang flourishes at companies with rich corporate cultures. Memos at Procter and Gamble are called "reco's" because the model P&G memo begins with a recommendation.

2. The first item on the agenda is the hiring for the coming year. George has also asked that we review the agency goals for the next fiscal year. We should cover this early in the meeting since it may affect our hiring preferences. Finally, we need to announce the deadlines for grant proposals, decide which grants to apply for, and set up a committee to draft each proposal.

3. Separate materials that can be recycled from your regular trash. Pass along old clothing, toys, or appliances to someone else who can use them. When you purchase products, choose those with minimal packaging. If you have a yard, put your yard waste and kitchen scraps (excluding meat and fat) in a compost pile. You can reduce the amount of solid waste your household produces in four ways.

4—16   Writing Paragraphs

Write a paragraph on each of the following topics.

a. Discuss your ideal job.
b. Summarize a recent article from a business magazine or newspaper.
c. Explain how technology is affecting the field you plan to enter.
d. Explain why you have or have not decided to work while you attend college.
e. Write a profile of someone who is successful in the field you hope to enter.

As Your Instructor Directs,
a. Label topic sentences, active verbs, and parallel structure.
b. Edit a classmate's paragraphs to make the writing even tighter and smoother.

CHAPTER 5

Planning, Composing, and Revising

Chapter Outline

An Inside Perspective:
Planning, Composing, and Revising

Daniel R. Zevchik, Associate Project Leader
Abbott Laboratories Ross Products Division

Daniel Zevchik composes memos and reports for a variety of internal and external audiences. Ross Products, headquartered in Columbus, Ohio, is most noted for its infant and nutritional formulas. Ross Products provides superior nutritional products that advance the quality of life for people of all ages.

In preparing to write, I spend approximately one-third of my time planning. I feel that analyzing the purpose and audience before beginning to write is one of the most important parts of writing.

I begin by analyzing the purpose of the document. Before putting my hands on the keyboard and beginning to type, I must know what message I am trying to get across—persuasion, informative, and so forth.

Secondly, I think about my audiences. It's important to make sure the audience can easily follow a document. The audience may be a group of people. My manager is always an important part of my audience. I write many documents that go to upper management, and I know that being able to write well is crucial so that I can advance to the next level on the corporate ladder.

Recently, I wrote a report to persuade a group of people to implement a new process which was not only new, but new to the company's way of thinking. This required educating my audience with data on why the project was good for the company. The education portion of this report was probably the most difficult. The audience had varied backgrounds and experiences, so I had to make sure the information was general enough for everyone, but specific for those with a need to know.

When beginning a memo or report, I like to outline it. I break the document into the appropriate headings. For example, with long reports I use an abstract or background section to give the reader important information on previous events that led to this one. This is the foundation for the report. A good introduction that is easy to follow creates an overview that helps the reader comprehend the message. Once you have put together your outline or abstract, you should be able to fill in the information under each of the headings you have chosen.

Once the document is complete, I go back to revise and edit—tightening up sentences, substituting words, and spell checking. Some documents need just one pass; some require multiple revisions. After revising, I spell check once again. Then I print a hard copy of the document and read it over for typos and grammatical structure. Once this is finished, I ask a colleague to review the document and make comments. If that person can follow the document easily, my audience also should.

Writing can have a direct impact on your career. Being able to present a well-written document to your manager that he or she can send on without revising will directly affect your upward mobility.

Daniel R. Zevchik, January 28, 1997

Visit Abbott Labs' Web site: http://www.abbott.com/

"In preparing to write, I spend approximately one-third of my time planning. . . . Once the document is complete, I go back to revise and edit."

Daniel R. Zevchik, Abbott Laboratories Ross Products Division

Skilled performances look easy and effortless. In reality, as every dancer, musician, and athlete knows, they're the products of hard work, hours of practice, attention to detail, and intense concentration. Like skilled performances in other arts, writing rests on a base of work.

To get the best results from the time you spend, spend only a third of your time actually "writing." Spend at least one-third of your time analyzing the situation and your audience, gathering information, and organizing what you have to say. Spend another third evaluating what you've said, revising the draft(s) to meet your purposes and the needs of the audience and the organization, editing a late draft to remove any errors in grammar and mechanics, and proofreading the final typed copy.

ACTIVITIES IN THE COMPOSING PROCESS

Most researchers would agree that writing processes can include eight activities: planning, gathering, writing, evaluating, getting feedback, revising, editing, and proofreading. The activities do not have to come in this order. Not every writing task demands all eight.

Planning includes all the thinking you do. It includes such activities as analyzing the problem, defining your purposes, and analyzing the audience; thinking of ideas; choosing a pattern of organization or making an outline; and so on. Planning includes not only devising strategies for the document as a whole but also generating "mini-plans" that govern sentences or paragraphs.

Gathering includes physically getting the data you need. It can mean simply getting a copy of the letter you're responding to; it can also include informal and formal research—everything from getting a computer printout or looking something up in a reference book to administering a questionnaire or conducting a focus group.

Writing is the act of putting words on paper or on a screen, or of dictating words to a machine or a secretary. Writing can be lists, fragmentary notes, stream-of-consciousness writing, or formal drafts.

Evaluating means rereading your work and measuring it against your goals and the requirements of the situation and audience. The best evaluation results from *re-seeing* your draft as if someone else had written it. Will your audience understand it? Is it complete? Convincing? Friendly?

You can evaluate *every* activity in the process, not just your draft. Is your view of purposes adequate? Do you have enough information to write? Are your sources believable? Do your revisions go far enough?

Getting feedback means asking someone else to evaluate your work. Again, you could get feedback on every activity, not just your draft. Is your pattern of organization appropriate? Does a revision solve an earlier problem? Are there any typos in the final copy?

Revising means making changes in the draft suggested by your own evaluation or by feedback from someone else: adding, deleting, substituting,

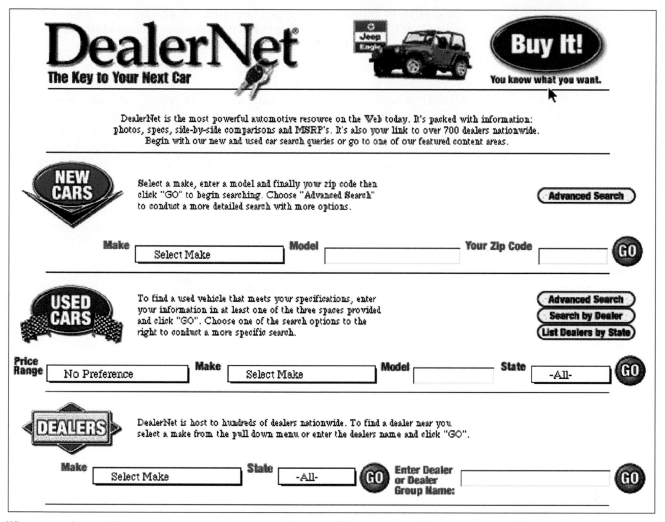

Whatever you're creating—a memo, a brochure, a presentation, or a Web page—you'll be more successful if you plan the message before you compose it and then revise and edit your draft.

or rearranging. Revision can be changes in single words, but more often it means major additions, deletions, or substitutions as the writer measures (evaluates) the draft against purpose and audience and reshapes the document to make it more effective.

Editing means checking the draft to see that it satisfies the requirements of standard English and the principles of business writing. Here you'd correct spelling and mechanical errors and check word choice and format. Unlike revision, which can produce major changes in meaning, editing focuses on the surface of writing.

Proofreading means checking the final copy to see that it's free from typographical errors.

Note the following points about these eight activities:

- **The activities do not have to come in this order.** Some people may gather data *after* writing a draft when they see that they need more specifics to achieve their purposes.
- **You do not have to finish one activity to start another.** Some writers plan a short section and write it, plan the next short section and write it, and so on through the document. Evaluating what is already written may cause a writer to do more planning or to change the original plan.

- **Most writers do not use all eight activities for all the documents they write.** You'll use more activities when you write a certain kind of document, about a subject, or to an audience that's new to you.

Research about what writers really do has destroyed some of the stereotypes we used to have about the writing process. Consider planning. Traditional advice stressed the importance of planning and sometimes advised writers to make formal outlines for everything they wrote. But we know now that not all good documents are based on outlines.[1] George Jensen and John DiTiberio have found that extraverts do little planning and prefer to work out their ideas as they go along, while introverts prefer to work out their ideas fully before they begin writing.[2] Either method can produce good writing. A study on writer's block found that some ineffective writers spent so much time planning that they left too little time to write the assignment.[3] "Plan!" is too simplistic to be helpful. Instead, we need to talk about how much and what kind of planning for what kind of document.

THE WAYS GOOD WRITERS WRITE

No single writing process works for all writers all of the time. However, good writers seem to use different processes than poor writers.[4] Good writers are more likely to

- Realize that the first draft will not be perfect.
- Write regularly.
- Break big jobs into small chunks.
- Have clear goals focusing on purpose and audience.
- Have several different strategies to choose from.
- Use rules flexibly.
- Wait to edit until after the draft is complete.

Research shows that experts differ from novices in identifying and analyzing the initial problem more effectively, understanding the task more broadly and deeply, drawing from a wider repertory of strategies, and seeing patterns more clearly. Experts actually composed more slowly than novices, perhaps because they rarely settled for work that was just "OK." Finally, experts were better at evaluating their own work.[5]

Thinking about the writing process and consciously adopting "expert" processes will help you become a more expert writer.

BRAINSTORMING, PLANNING, AND ORGANIZING BUSINESS DOCUMENTS

Spend at least one-third of your time planning and organizing before you begin to write. The better your ideas are when you start, the fewer drafts you'll need to produce a good document. Start by using the analysis questions from Chapter 1 to identify purpose and audience. Use the strategies described in Chapter 3 to analyze audience (➤ p. 58) and identify reader benefits (➤ p. 69). Gather information you can use for your document.

Sometimes your content will be determined by the situation. Sometimes, even when it's up to you to think of reader benefits or topics to include in a report, you'll find it easy to think of ideas. If ideas won't come, try the following techniques.

- Try **brainstorming.** Think of all the ideas you can, without judging them. Consciously try to get at least a dozen different ideas before you stop.

Writing with Information*

Good writers write with information. Michelle Russo writes reports appraising how much a hotel is worth. Gathering information is a big part of her composing process.

She visits the site. She talks to the general manager. She gets occupancy rates, financial statements, and tax forms. She talks to the tax assessor and all the managers of competing hotels. If it's a convention hotel, she talks to the convention bureau and gets the airlines' passenger traffic counts. Gathering all this information takes about four days. When she gets back to the office, she uses databases for even more information.

*Based on Michelle S. Russo, telephone conversation with the author, December 8, 1993.

Clustering Helps Generate Ideas   **Figure 5.1**

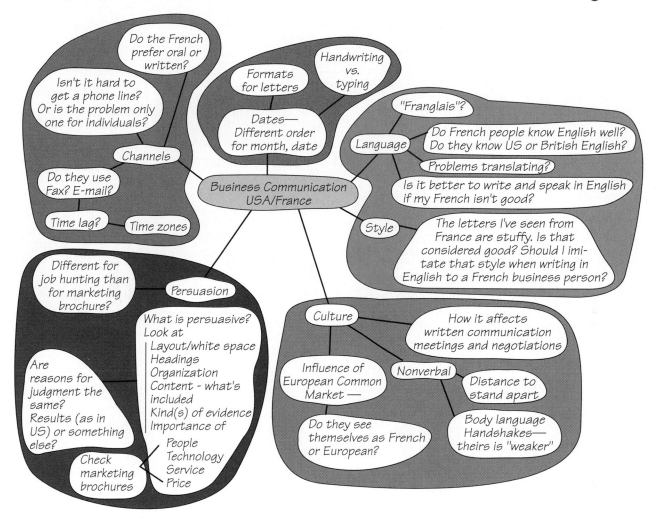

Brainstorming helps writers get over the tendency to be overcritical or to develop a mental block after they've thought of one idea or approach. The first idea you have may not be the best.

- Try **freewriting.**[6] Make yourself write, without stopping, for 10 minutes or so, even if you must write "I will think of something soon." At the end of 10 minutes, read what you've written, identify the best point in the draft, then set it aside, and write for another 10 uninterrupted minutes. Read this draft, marking anything that's good and should be kept, and then write again for another 10 minutes. By the third session, you will probably produce several sections that are worth keeping—maybe even a complete draft that's ready to be revised.

- Try **clustering.**[7] Write your topic in the middle of the page and circle it. Write down the ideas the topic suggests, circling them, too. (The circles are designed to tap into the non-linear half of your brain.) When you've filled the page, look for patterns or repeated ideas. Use different colored pens to group related ideas. Then use these ideas to develop reader benefits in a memo, questions for a survey, or content for the body of a report. Figure 5.1 presents the clusters that one writer created about business communication in the United States and France.

Figure 5.2   **Storyboards Structure Ideas Visually**

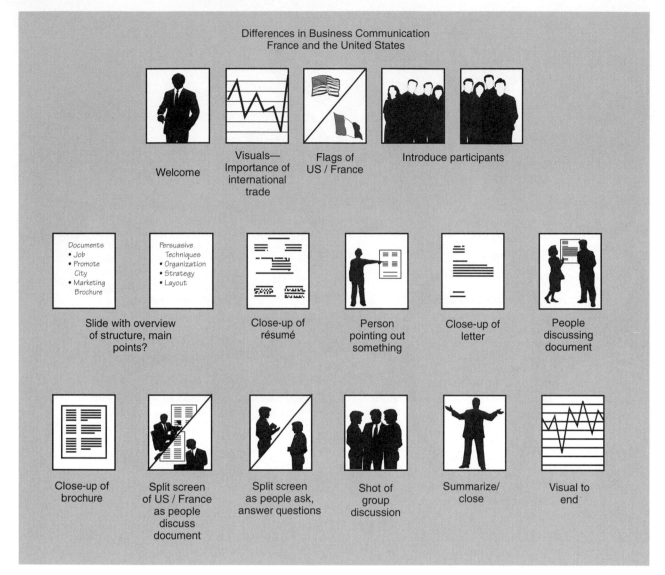

Thinking about the content, layout, or structure of your document can also give you ideas. For long documents, write out the headings you'll use. For anything that's under five pages, less formal notes will probably work. You may want to jot down ideas to use as the basis for a draft. For an oral presentation, a meeting, or a document with lots of visuals, try creating a **storyboard,** with a rectangle representing each page or unit. Draw a box with a visual for each main point. Below the box, write a short caption or label.

Figure 5.2 presents the first draft of a storyboard for a videoconference about business communication between France and the United States. The formless ideas from clustering are starting to take shape. The author still has lots of work to do, but the ideas are now in a form that other people can discuss, criticize, revise, and implement.

Letters and memos will go faster if you choose a basic organizational pattern before you start. Chapters 7, 8, and 9 give detailed patterns of organization for the most common kinds of letters and memos. You may want to customize those patterns with a **planning guide**[8] to help you keep

Figure 5.3

Customized Planning Guides for Specific Documents

Planning Guide for a Trip Report

The Big Picture from the Company's Point of View: We Can Go Forward on the Project.

Criteria/Goals

What We Did

Why We Know Enough to Go Forward

Next Steps

Planning Guide for a Proposal

Customer's Concern #1
    Our Proposal/Answer

Customer's Concern #2
    Our Proposal/Answer

Customer's Concern #3
    Our Proposal/Answer

Customer's Concern #4
    Our Proposal/Answer

Ask for Action

Planning Guide for an E-Mail Message

My Purpose

Points I Want to Make

Document(s) to Attach

Next Steps

Planning Guide for a Credit Rejection

Reason

Refusal

Alternative (Layaway/Co-signer/Provide more information)

Goodwill Ending

Source: E-mail and proposal guides based on Fred Reynolds, "What Adult Work-World Writers Have Taught Me About Adult Work-World Writing," *Professional Writing in Context: Lessons from Teaching and Consulting in Worlds of Work* (Hillsdale, NJ: Lawrence Erlbaum Associates, 1995), 18, 20.

the "big picture" in mind as you write. Figure 5.3 shows planning guides developed for specific kinds of documents.

REVISING, EDITING, AND PROOFREADING

Good writers make their drafts better by judicious revising, editing, and proofreading. **Revising** means making changes that will better satisfy your purposes and your audience. **Editing** means making surface-level changes that make the document grammatically correct. **Proofreading** means checking to be sure the document is free from typographical errors.

What to Look for When You Revise

Every chapter in this book suggests questions you should ask as you revise as well as when you initially plan your document. When you write to an audience you know well, you may be able to check everything at once. When you're writing to a new audience or have to solve a particularly difficult problem, plan to revise the draft at least three times. The first time, look for content and clarity. The second time, check the organization and layout. Finally, check style and tone, using the information in Chapters 2 and 4. Figure 5.4 summarizes the questions you should ask.

Often you'll get the best revision by setting aside your draft, getting a blank page or screen, and redrafting. This strategy takes advantage of the

Good writers revise their drafts to improve content and clarity, organization and layout, and style and tone.

Figure 5.4

Thorough Revision Checklist

Content and Clarity

☐ Is your view of purposes complete? Does your document meet the needs of the organization and of the reader—and make you look good?

☐ Have you given readers all the information they need to understand and act on your message?

☐ Is all the information accurate?

☐ Is each sentence clear? Is the message free from apparently contradictory statements?

☐ Is the logic clear and convincing? Are generalizations and benefits backed up with adequate supporting detail?

Organization and Layout

☐ Is the pattern of organization appropriate for your purposes, audience, and situation?

☐ Are transitions between ideas smooth? Do ideas within paragraphs flow smoothly?

☐ Does the design of the document make it easy for readers to find the information they need? Is the document visually inviting?

☐ Are the points emphasized by layout ones that deserve emphasis?

☐ Are the first and last paragraphs effective?

Style and Tone

☐ Is the message easy to read?

☐ Is the message friendly and free from sexist language?

☐ Does the message build goodwill?

thinking you did on your first draft without locking you into the sentences in it. Use WIRMI (☞ p. 87) to replace awkward phrasing with what you really want to say.

As you revise, be sure to read the document through from start to finish. This is particularly important if you've composed in several sittings or if

Figure 5.5

**Light Revision
Checklist**

☐ Are the first and last paragraphs effective?

☐ Does the design of the document make it easy for readers to find the information they
   need?

☐ Have you told the reader what to do?

you've used text from other documents. Researchers have found that such documents tend to be well organized but don't flow well.[9] You may need to add transitions, cut repetitive parts, or change words to create a uniform level of formality throughout the document.

If you're really in a time bind, do a light revision, as outlined in Figure 5.5. The quality of the final document may not be as high as with a thorough revision, but even a light revision is better than skipping revision altogether.

What to Look for When You Edit

Even good writers need to edit, since no one can pay attention to surface correctness while thinking of ideas. Editing should always *follow* revision. There's no point in taking time to fix a grammatical error in a sentence that may be cut when you clarify your meaning or tighten your style. Some writers edit more accurately when they print out a copy of a document and edit the hard copy. But beware: laser printing makes a page look good but does nothing to correct errors.

Check to be sure that the following are accurate:

- Sentence structure.
- Subject–verb and noun–pronoun agreement.
- Punctuation.
- Word usage.
- Spelling—including spelling of names.
- Numbers.

You need to know the rules of grammar and punctuation to edit. Appendix B reviews grammar and punctuation, numbers, and words that are often confused. Most writers make a small number of errors over and over. If you know that you have trouble with dangling modifiers or subject–verb agreement, for example, specifically look for them in your draft. Also look for any errors that especially bother your boss and correct them.

How to Catch Typos

Proofread every document both with a spell checker and by eye, to catch the errors a spell checker can't find.

To proofread, you must slow your reading speed so you see each individual letter. One way to do that is to read just one line at a time, using a ruler or card to block the text below. Proofreading is hard because writers tend to see what they know should be there rather than what really is there. Since it's always easier to proof something you haven't written, you may want to swap papers with a proofing buddy.

The ideal way to proofread is to have one person read the document aloud, voicing punctuation and spelling out names, while another person follows along the longhand or original typed copy. This way is so slow and so expensive that it is reserved for very important documents or for documents like phone books where it is the only way possible.

**Using Spelling and
Grammar Checkers**

If you use a computer to prepare your documents, use a spell checker to catch typos.

But you still need to proofread by eye.

Spell checkers work by matching words: they will signal any group of letters not listed in their dictionaries. However, they cannot tell that a word is missing or that the meaning demands *of* rather than *or*, or *not* rather than *now*.

Check numbers and the spelling of names. In international business communication, be sure that you have the right currency symbols: £30 million may be over twice as much as $30 million.

Writers with a good command of grammar and mechanics can do a better job than the computer grammar checkers currently available. Grammar checkers can help a writer whose command of grammar and mechanics is weak. However, since grammar checkers do not catch all errors, it's worth taking the time to master grammar and mechanics so you can edit and proofread yourself.

How Feedback Helped Win the Gulf War*

The United States and its allies won the Persian Gulf War quickly in part because they persuaded 87,000 Iraqi soldiers to surrender rather than continuing to fight. US aircraft dropped 29 million surrender leaflets behind enemy lines.

Feedback on draft leaflets was crucial. Cooperative Iraqi prisoners of war told the designers what parts didn't work. As a result, words, colors, and drawings were revised.

Red was removed since it was a signal for danger in Iraq.

In one drawing, the Allied soldier shown receiving some Iraqis' surrender was given a chin beard, since feedback showed that beards rather than clean-shaven faces conveyed trust and brotherhood. In another drawing, a bowl of fruit was changed to include bananas, an Iraqi delicacy. A thought bubble over one soldier's head was removed when feedback showed that the Iraqi culture didn't use bubbles to show cartoon characters' thoughts.

Revising the drafts made the leaflets successful and ended the war more quickly.

*Based on R. John Brockmann and Sal Sinatra, "How the Iterative Process Helped the Allies Win the Persian Gulf War," *STC Intercom*, 42.9 (November 1995): 1, 44.

An acceptable alternative is to read the document twice. Read once quickly for meaning, to see that nothing has been left out. Read a second time, slowly. When you find an error, correct it and then *reread that line.* Readers tend to become less attentive after they find one error and may miss other errors close to the one they've spotted. Always triple-check numbers, headings, the first and last paragraphs, and the reader's name.

Reading out loud and reading lines backward or pages out of order can help you proofread a document you know well.

GETTING AND USING FEEDBACK

Getting feedback almost always improves a document. In many organizations, it's required. All external documents must be read and approved before they go out. The process of drafting, getting feedback, revising, and getting more feedback is called **cycling.** Dianna Booker reports that documents in her clients' firms cycled an average of 4.2 times before reaching the intended audience.[10] Susan Kleimann studied a 10-page document whose 20 drafts made a total of 31 stops on the desks of nine reviewers on four different levels.[11] Being asked to revise a document is a fact of life in businesses, government agencies, and nonprofit organizations.

You can improve the quality of the feedback you get by telling people which aspects you'd especially like comments about. For example, when you give a reader the outline or planning draft,[12] you might want to know whether the general approach is appropriate. After your second draft, you might want to know whether reader benefits are well developed. When you reach the polishing draft, you'll be ready for feedback on style and grammar. Figure 5.6 lists questions to ask.

It's easy to feel defensive when someone criticizes your work. If the feedback stings, put it aside until you can read it without feeling defensive. Even if you think that the reader hasn't understood what you were trying to say, the fact that the reader complained usually means the section could be improved. If the reader says "This isn't true" and you know the statement is true, several kinds of revision might make the truth clear to the reader: rephrasing the statement, giving more information or examples, or documenting the source.

USING BOILERPLATE

Boilerplate is language—sentences, paragraphs, even pages—from a previous document that a writer includes in a new document. In academic papers, material written by others must be quoted and documented. However, because businesses own the documents their employees write, old text may be included without attribution.

In some cases, boilerplate may have been written years ago. For example, many legal documents, including apartment leases and sales contracts, are almost completely boilerplated. In other cases, writers may use boilerplate they wrote for earlier documents. For example, a section from a proposal describing the background of the problem could also be used in the final report after the proposed work was completed. A section from a progress report describing what the writer had done could be used with only a few changes in the methods section of the final report.

Writers use boilerplate both to save time and energy and to use language that has already been approved by the organization's legal staff. However, as Glenn Broadhead and Richard Freed point out, using boilerplate creates two

Outline or Planning Draft
☐ Does the plan seem "on the right track"?
☐ What topics should be added? Should any be cut?
☐ Do you have any other general suggestions?

Revising Draft
☐ Does the message satisfy all its purposes?
☐ Is the message adapted to the audience(s)?
☐ Is the organization effective?
☐ What parts aren't clear?
☐ What ideas need further development?
☐ Do you have any other suggestions?

Polishing Draft
☐ Are there any problems with word choice or sentence structure?
☐ Did you find any inconsistencies?
☐ Did you find any typos?
☐ Is the document's design effective?

Figure 5.6

Questions to Ask Readers

Improving the Corporate Writing Process*

A fertilizer company sued several of its competitors, charging that they mislabeled their bags of composted manure. One of the defendants countersued, charging that the original company also mislabeled its bags. All the company's bags contained the same product (compost made of 7% sheep manure, 33% pig manure, and 60% cow manure), but some were called "sheep manure" while others were called "cow manure."

This inconsistency arose from a compartmentalized, linear composing process. Operations filled the bags; marketing wrote the labels. No one noticed that the labels didn't match the contents.

The case was settled out of court after much time and expense. The companies may have lost goodwill by appearing to mislead consumers. By bringing everyone together during the process of writing the labels, these companies could have saved time and money—and written better labels in the first place.

*Based on James E. Porter, "Ideology and Collaboration in the Classroom and in the Corporation," *The Bulletin of the Association for Business Communication* 53, no. 2 (1990): 21.

problems.[13] First, using unrevised boilerplate can create a document with incompatible styles and tones. Second, boilerplate can encourage writers to see as identical situations and audiences that have subtle differences.

Before you incorporate old language in a new document,

- Check to see that the old section is well written.
- Consciously look for differences between the two situations, audiences, or purposes that may require different content, organization, or wording.
- Read through the whole document at a single sitting to be sure that style, tone, and level of detail are consistent in the old and new sections.

OVERCOMING WRITER'S BLOCK AND PROCRASTINATION

You probably know students who put off assignments until 10 PM the night before they're due. Some managers whose reports are due in two months will spend seven weeks worrying and one week frantically trying to complete the work. These avoiders paint themselves into a corner, sometimes leaving too little time to do a decent job, and never enough time to do their best work. The next time you face writer's block or are tempted to put off writing, use the tricks in the following lists to see what works for you.

Overcoming Writer's Block

If words won't come, you need to get them flowing again. Try everything on this list at least once to see which strategies work best for you.

- Try to redefine the problem, purpose, or audience. If a fact, constraint, or rule is making it hard for you to write, abandon it—at least for this draft.
- Try brainstorming, freewriting, or clustering.

Sooner or Later You'll Hit the Ball*

In baseball, you only get three swings and you're out. In rewriting, you get almost as many swings as you want and you know, sooner or later, you'll hit the ball.

*Quoted from Neil Simon, in Paul D. Zimmerman, "Neil Simon: Up from Success," *Newsweek*, February 2, 1970, 55.

- Write the part that's easiest to write: the headings, the table that will go in the middle of the report, the history of the problem, whatever you *can* write. The parts of a document don't need to be composed in the order in which they'll appear in the final document.
- Do something you can do without thinking: take a walk, wash the car, fold your laundry. As you work, try "saying" ideas to yourself in your head.
- Try explaining what you mean to a friend. It may be easier to talk to a real audience than to try to imagine your audience as you write.
- Draw a picture or diagram of what you mean. Some people think more easily in pictures rather than words.
- Try dictating the document. If you don't have dictating equipment, use a tape recorder.
- Put the document away for a while. Sometimes ideas need time to germinate.

Overcoming the Tendency to Procrastinate

If your problem is sitting down to write at all, some of the techniques for getting past blocks won't help. Putting a document aside, for example, will only make the problem worse. Instead, you need techniques that help create an environment that favors writing. Again, try all of these techniques to see what works for you.

- Set a regular time to write. Sit down and stay there for the time you've planned, even if you write nothing usable.
- Develop a ritual for writing. Choose tools—paper, pen, computer, chair—that you find comfortable. Use the same tools in the same place every time you write.
- Try freewriting—writing for 10 minutes without stopping.
- Write down the thoughts and fears you have as you write. If the ideas are negative, try to substitute more positive statements: "I can do this." "I'll keep going and postpone judging." "If I keep working, I'll produce something that's OK."
- Identify the problem that keeps you from writing. Deal with that problem; then turn back to writing.
- Set modest goals (a paragraph, not the whole document) and reward yourself for reaching them.

Technology and the Writing Process

Technology is changing not only the way we produce and transmit messages but also the way readers respond to documents.

Even if you're using a manual typewriter or paying a typist to type your papers right now, you should be aware of ways in which word processing affects writers and readers.

- You need to master the system to get the most out of your program. Many colleges offer short courses in some of the most popular programs. Time spent now learning the system will pay off later in better documents that you produce more quickly.
- Writers using word processing need to pay special attention to revising and proofreading their documents. Since changes are so easy to make with a word processor, some writers plan, revise, edit, and proofread less

To avoid head and neck aches, position the center of the monitor about 4–8 inches below your eyes and about 26 inches away. Rest your eyes and hands for a few seconds every 10 minutes by looking away from the computer and taking your hands off the keyboard. Every now and then, stand up and stretch.

Ethics and the Writing Process*

As you plan a message,

■ Brainstorm choices and alternatives. In hard situations, seek allies in your organization and discuss your options with them.
■ Check your sources.
■ Assume that no document is confidential. Paper documents can be subpoenaed for court cases; e-mail documents can be forwarded and printed out without your knowledge.

As you compose,

■ Promise only what you can deliver.
■ Warn your readers of dangers or limits in your information.
■ Be accurate and complete.

As you revise,

■ Use feedback to revise words and visuals that your audience may misunderstand.

*Based on J. C. Mathes and Dwight Stevenson, *Designing Technical Reports*, 2nd ed. (New York: Macmillan, 1991), 469, and John M. Lannon, *Technical Writing*, 5th. ed. (New York: HarperCollins, 1991), 74.

efficiently.[14] Instead of reading the whole draft through carefully, some writers skim until they reach one error. They fix it, print out the document again, but then find more errors as they read further. Even worse, because documents produced on a good printer look so neat, some writers don't revise or proofread at all. But keying in a document is no more accurate than typing on a traditional typewriter. Editing and proofreading are still necessary.

■ The widespread use of word processors is raising readers' expectations. Readers are more likely to ask for a revision; they care more about the physical appearance of documents. Because word processing makes it easy to correct typos, change spacing and margins, and insert graphics, readers are less tolerant of badly designed documents and of documents with obvious corrections—even if the document is typed on a manual typewriter.

If you use e-mail, consider these implications for writers and readers:

■ Writers using e-mail feel as if they're speaking, so they may not worry about logic, grammar, or spelling. Receivers know that they're reading the message and judge it as they would any written document. Even worse, the e-mail message may be printed out and shown around, preserving all the flaws of the sender's "quick and dirty" message.

■ Writers using e-mail are much less inhibited than they would be on paper or in person, sending insults, swearing, name-calling, and hostile statements.[15] The time required to produce a typed document on paper may encourage writers to think before they commit their feelings to paper; a typist or boss who sees such a message may counsel moderation. But writers using e-mail can send out messages quickly—and thoughtlessly. **Flaming** is the term used to denote this imprudence.

■ If the subject line of an e-mail message doesn't seem interesting or relevant, the receiver will choose not to call up the message.

■ An e-mail screen holds fewer lines of type than does a single-spaced typed page. The shorter screen length puts a greater premium on highlighting important points and being concise.

COMPOSING COLLABORATIVE DOCUMENTS

Many business documents are planned, composed, evaluated, and revised by groups. Working in a group goes most smoothly when members are aware of their own writing processes and discuss them with other members.

Often different people have different processes: one person always waits till the night before to finish assignments, while someone else wants to finish early. One member wants to work alone; someone else needs the stimulation of conversation to come up with the best ideas. When you know about your own style, you can see how it might fit with other work styles and solve any potential problems in advance.

Chapter 13 discusses the strategies that make collaborative writing easier and more effective.

SUMMARY OF KEY POINTS

- Writing processes can include eight activities: planning, gathering, writing, evaluating, getting feedback, revising, editing, and proofreading. **Revising** means changing the document to make it better satisfy the writer's purposes and the audience. **Editing** means making surface-level changes that make the document grammatically correct. **Proofreading** means checking to be sure the document is free from typographical errors. The activities do not have to come in any set order. It is not necessary to finish one activity to start another. Most writers use all eight activities only when they write a document whose genre, subject matter, or audience is new to them.
- Processes that help writers write well include not expecting the first draft to be perfect, writing regularly, modifying the initial task if it's too hard or too easy, having clear goals, knowing many different strategies, using rules as guidelines rather than as absolutes, and waiting to edit until after the draft is complete.
- To think of ideas, try brainstorming, **freewriting** (writing without stopping for 10 minutes or so), and **clustering** (brainstorming with circled words on a page). **Storyboarding** organizes ideas visually, with a rectangle representing each page or unit of a message.
- You can improve the quality of the feedback you get by telling people which aspects of a draft you'd like comments about. If a reader criticizes something, fix the problem. If you think the reader misunderstood you, try to figure out what caused the misunderstanding and revise the draft so that the reader can see what you meant.
- If the writing situation is new or difficult, plan to revise the draft at least three times. The first time, look for content and clarity. The second time, check the organization and layout. Finally, check style and tone.
- **Boilerplate** is language from a previous document that a writer includes in a new document. Using unrevised boilerplate can create a document with incompatible styles and tones and can encourage writers to see as identical situations and audiences that have subtle differences.
- To overcome writer's block, use strategies that reduce tension, simplify the writing problem, and "lower the stakes." To overcome the tendency to procrastinate, modify your behavior by rewarding yourself for the actions that *lead to* writing, whether or not you produce anything usable at a particular session.

Exercises and Problems

For Chapter 5

5–1   Interviewing Writers about Their Composing Processes

Interview someone about the composing process(es) he or she uses for on-the-job writing. Questions you could ask include the following:

- What kind of planning do you do before you write? Do you make lists? formal or informal outlines?
- When you need more information, where do you get it?
- How do you compose your drafts? Do you dictate? Draft with pen and paper? Compose on screen? How do you find uninterrupted time to compose?
- When you want advice about style, grammar, and spelling, what source(s) do you consult?
- Does your superior ever read your drafts and make suggestions? How do you feel about that?
- Do you ever work with other writers to produce a single document? Describe the process you use.

- Describe the process of creating a document where you felt the final document reflected your best work. Describe the process of creating a document you found difficult or frustrating. What sorts of things make writing easier or harder for you?

As Your Instructor Directs,

  a. Share your results orally with a small group of students.
  b. Present your results in an oral presentation to the class.
  c. Present your results in a memo to your instructor.
  d. Share your results with a small group of students and write a joint memo reporting the similarities and differences you found.

5–2   Analyzing Your Own Writing Processes

Save your notes and drafts from several assignments so that you can answer the following questions.

- Which of the eight activities discussed in Chapter 5 do you use?
- How much time do you spend on each of the eight activities?
- What kinds of revisions do you make most often?
- Do you use different processes for different documents, or do you have one process that you use most of the time?
- Which practices of good writers do you follow?
- What parts of your process seem most successful? Are there any places in the process that could be improved? How?

- What relation do you see between the process(es) you use and the quality of the final document?

As Your Instructor Directs,

  a. Discuss your process with a small group of other students.
  b. Write a memo to your instructor analyzing in detail your process for composing one of the papers for this class.
  c. Write a memo to your instructor analyzing your process during the term. What parts of your process(es) have stayed the same throughout the term? What parts have changed?

5–3   Checking Spelling and Grammar Checkers

Each of the following paragraphs contains errors in grammar, spelling, and punctuation. Which errors does your spelling or grammar checker catch? Which errors does it miss? Does it flag as errors any words that are correct?

  a. Answer to an Inquiry
  Enclosed are the tow copies you requested of our pamphlet, "Using the Internet to market Your products. The pamphelt walks you through the steps

of planning the Home Page (The first page of the web cite, shows examples of other Web pages we have designed, and provide a questionaire that you can use to analyze audience the audience and pruposes.

b. Performance Appraisal

Most staff accountants complete three audits a month. Ellen has completed 21 audits in this past six months she is our most productive staff accountant. Her technical skills our very good however some clients feel that she could be more tactful in suggesting ways that the clients accounting practices courld be improved.

c. Brochure

Are you finding that being your own boss crates it's own problems? Take the hassle out of working at home with a VoiceMail Answering System. Its almost as good as having your own secretary.

d. Presentation Slides

How to Create a Web résumé

- Omit home adress and phone number
- Use other links only if they help an employer evalaute you.
  - ☐ Be Professional.
  - ☐ Carefully craft and proof read the phrase on the index apage.

How to Create a Scannable Résumé

- Create a 'plain vanilla" document.
- Use include a "Keywords" section. Include personality trait sas well as accomplishments.
- Be specific and quantifyable.

CHAPTER 6

Designing Documents, Slides, and Screens

Chapter Outline

An Inside Perspective:
Designing Documents, Slides, and Screens

Kate Molitor, Technical Writer/Senior Research Associate
The Information Design Center

Kate Molitor designs, writes, edits, and tests policy and procedure manuals. The Information Design Center (IDC), in Washington, DC, develops paper and online documents in clear English that are attractive, understandable, and easy for people to use. IDC's parent organization, the American Institutes for Research in the Behavioral Sciences, conducts research, development, and evaluation studies for clients in government and in the private sector.

Creating a good design requires writers to consider three important elements: layout, organization, and content. For example, a good start at creating an effective layout would include using white space to visually chunk information for readers and using different fonts to give readers visual cues for working their way through the document.

Organizing the document with a clear hierarchy of information helps readers work their way through and learn from the document. The document will be easier to understand when the relationship between topics is clearly stated with the help of devices such as headings, rather than leaving readers to make sense of the structure for themselves.

To be right for readers, the content must include what readers came to the document wanting or needing to learn or understand.

One of IDC's current projects involves revising a chapter of a manual that Veterans Benefits Administration employees use to process claims. Revising the chapter has required IDC to address all aspects of design. We introduced white space and chose effective fonts. We had to revise organization and content extensively to help readers

who need to work with it every day to find what they're looking for.

Testing the document showed that the original chapter didn't answer all the questions readers had. Although we do our best to consider readers when creating or revising a document, testing with readers and getting their feedback is the best way to be certain that we've addressed the topics readers need and expect from the document.

Computers are raising readers' expectations of documents. A plain typewritten page with a single font is unappealing to readers who expect a more helpful and visually appealing document. Speakers have no excuse for creating slides in 12-point type that the audience will have trouble reading even from the front of a room.

Computers help writers create quality documents. But whatever the computer can create is not necessarily acceptable. A computer program that lets writers use many typefaces and sizes and a color printer that lets writers create more colorful documents won't automatically result in a quality document. Writers need to think—to determine what's appropriate for their readers.

Kate Molitor, February 14, 1997

**Visit The American Institutes for Research's Web site:
http://www.air-dc.org**

"Creating a good design requires writers to consider three important elements: layout, organization, and content."

Kate Molitor, The Information Design Center

Good document design saves time and money, reduces legal problems, and builds goodwill. A well-designed document looks inviting, friendly, and easy to read. Effective design also groups ideas visually, making the structure of the document more obvious so the document **is** easier to read. Research shows that easy-to-read documents also enhance your credibility and build an image of you as a professional, competent person.[1] Good design is important not only for reports, Web pages, and newsletters but also for announcements and one-page letters and memos.

GUIDELINES FOR PAGE DESIGN

Use the following eight guidelines to create visually attractive documents.

1. Use white space to separate and emphasize points.
2. Use headings to group points and lead the reader through the document.
3. Limit the use of words set in all capital letters.
4. Limit the number of typefaces in a single document.
5. Decide whether to justify margins based on the situation and the audience.
6. Put important elements in the top left and lower right quadrants of the page.
7. Use a grid of imaginary columns to unify the elements in a document.
8. Use highlighting, decorative devices, and color in moderation.

1. Use White Space.

White space—the empty space on the page—makes material easier to read by emphasizing the material that it separates from the rest of the text. Normally, margins should be 1 inch. Use bigger margins to line up text with letterhead or other visual elements (see Appendix A). Smaller margins may be acceptable for elements that are not part of the main text. For example, a page number could be closer to the top of the page than 1 inch as long as the actual text was surrounded by enough white space. In the body of your document, create white space by varying paragraph lengths and using lists.

Try for a good mix of medium-length, shorter, and very short paragraphs. A page looks easier to read when most of the paragraphs are short (six typed lines or less). First and last paragraphs should be quite short—just three to five typed lines. It's even OK to have a paragraph that's just one sentence. Middle paragraphs should be no longer than seven to eight typed lines.

Use lists to emphasize material. You can use lists for phrases, sentences, or even paragraphs. Lists are normally indented on the left. Since different numbers have different widths in proportional type, use tabs or indents—not spacing—to align items vertically.

- Use numbered lists when the number or sequence of items is exact.
- Use **bullets** (large dots or squares like those in this list) when the number and sequence don't matter.

When you use a list, make sure that all of the items in it are parallel (✖ p. 98) and fit into the structure of the sentence that introduces the list.

Faulty: The following suggestions can help employers avoid bias in job interviews:
        1. Base questions on the job description.
        2. Questioning techniques.
        3. Selection and training of interviewers.

Parallel: The following suggestions can help employers avoid bias in job interviews:
        1. Base questions on the job description.
        2. Ask the same questions of all applicants.
        3. Select and train interviewers carefully.

Also parallel: Employers can avoid bias in job interviews by
        1. Basing questions on the job description.
        2. Asking the same questions of all applicants.
        3. Selecting and training interviewers carefully.

Figure 6.1 shows an original typed document. In Figure 6.2, the same document is improved by using shorter paragraphs, lists, and headings. These devices take space. When saving space is essential, it's better to cut the text and keep white space and headings.

2. Use Headings.

As George Miller has shown, our short-term memories can hold only seven plus or minus two bits of information.[2] Only after those bits are processed and put into long-term memory can we assimilate new information. Large amounts of information will be easier to process if they are grouped into three to seven chunks rather than presented as individual items.

Headings are words, short phrases, or short sentences that group points and divide your letter, memo, or report into sections. Headings enable your reader to see at a glance how the document is organized, to turn quickly to sections of special interest, and to compare and contrast points more easily. Headings also break up the page, making it look less formidable and more interesting.

If you use headings at all, you'll normally have several. Headings should be specific. "Part-Time Personnel in the Dallas Office" is better than "Personnel." Headings must also cover all the material until the next heading. Normally, you will spend at most two or three paragraphs on a subject before you switch your focus—and need a new heading.

Headings can also be complete sentences or questions. Figure 6.2 uses questions for headings. The headings at any one level should be parallel: all noun phrases, for example, or all complete sentences.

In a letter or memo, type main headings even with the left-hand margin in bold. Capitalize the first letters of the first word and of other major words; use lowercase for all other letters. (See Figure 6.2 for an example.) In single-spaced text, triple space between the previous text and the heading; double space between the heading and the text that follows.

If you need **subdivisions within a head,** underline the subheading (or use bold type) and put a period after it. Begin the paragraph on the same line. Use subheadings only when you have at least two subdivisions under a given main heading.

In a report, you may need more than two levels of headings. Chapter 15 shows how to set up five levels of headings for reports.

How Big Is Your Short-Term Memory?

One way to test the capacity of your short-term memory is to think about phone numbers. Telephone numbers in the United States are seven digits. If you sometimes forget a phone number while you are dialing it and have to look back at the listing in order to finish dialing, your short-term memory holds only five or six bits of information. If you never have to look back at the book, your memory holds at least seven bits of information.

Figure 6.1   **A Document with Poor Visual Impact**

Full capital letters make title hard to read

MONEY DEDUCTED FROM YOUR WAGES TO PAY CREDITORS

When you buy goods on credit, the store will sometimes ask you to sign a Wage Assignment form allowing it to deduct money from your wages if you do not pay your bill. When you buy on credit, you sign a contract agreeing to pay a certain amount each week or month until you have paid all you owe. The Wage Assignment Form is separate. It must contain the name of your present employer, your social security number, the amount of money loaned, the rate of interest, the date when payments are due, and your signature. The words "Wage Assignment" must be printed at the top of the form and also near the line for your signature. Even if you have signed a Wage Assignment agreement, Roysner will not withhold part of your wages unless all of the following conditions are met: 1. You have to be more than forty days late in payment of what you owe; 2. Roysner has to receive a correct statement of the amount you are in default and a copy of the Wage Assignment form; and 3. You and Roysner must receive a notice from the creditor at least twenty days in advance stating that the creditor plans to make a demand on your wages. This twenty-day notice gives you a chance to correct the problems yourself. If these conditions are all met, Roysner must withhold 15% percent of each paycheck until your bill is paid and give this money to your creditor.

Long para- graph is visually uninviting

If you think you are not late or that you do not owe the amount stated, you can argue against it by filing a legal document called a "defense." Once you file a defense, Roysner will not withhold any money from you. However, be sure you are right before you file a defense. If you are wrong, you have to pay not only what you owe but also all legal costs for both yourself and the creditor. If you are right, the creditor has to pay all these costs.

Important information is hard to find

3. Limit the Use of Words Set in All Capital Letters.

We recognize words by their shapes.[3] (See Figure 6.3.) In capitals, all words are rectangular; letters lose the descenders and ascenders that make reading go 19% more quickly.[4] Use full capitals sparingly.

4. Limit the Number of Typefaces.

Typefaces are unified styles of type. Each typeface comes in several sizes and usually in several fonts (bold, italic, etc.). Typewriter typefaces are **fixed;** that is, every letter takes the same space. An *i* takes the same space as a *w.* Courier and Prestige Elite are fixed typefaces. Computers usually offer **proportional** typefaces as well, where wider letters take more space than narrower letters. Times Roman, Palatino, Zapf Chancery, Helvetica, and Futura are propor-tional typefaces.

   Serif typefaces have little extensions, called serifs, from the main strokes. (In Figure 6.4, look at the feet on the *r*s in Courier and the flick on the top of the *g* in Prestige.) Courier, Elite, Times Roman, Palatino, and Zapf Chancery are serif typefaces. Serif typefaces are easier to read since the serifs help the

A Document Revised to Improve Visual Impact   **Figure 6.2**

**Money Deducted from Your Wages
to Pay Creditors**

*First letter
of each main
word capitalized—
Title split onto
two lines*

When you buy goods on credit, the store will sometimes ask you to sign a Wage Assignment form allowing it to deduct money from your wages if you do not pay your bill.

Have You Signed a Wage Assignment Form?   *Headings divide
document into
chunks*

When you buy on credit, you sign a contract agreeing to pay a certain amount each week or month until you have paid all you owe. The Wage Assignment Form is separate. It must contain

- The name of your present employer,
- Your social security number,
- The amount of money loaned,
- The rate of interest,
- The date when payments are due, and
- Your signature.

*List with
bullets where
order of
items
doesn't
matter*

The words "Wage Assignment" must be printed at the top of the form and also near the line for your signature.

When Would Money Be Deducted from Your Wages to Pay a Creditor?

*Headings
must be
parallel.*   *Here all
are questions*

Even if you have signed a Wage Assignment agreement, Roysner will not withhold part of your wages unless all of the following conditions are met:

*White space
between
items
emphasizes
them*

1. You have to be more than forty days late in payment of what you owe;

2. Roysner has to receive a correct statement of the amount you are in default and a copy of the Wage Assignment form; and

*Numbered
list where
number,
order of
items matter*

3. You and Roysner must receive a notice from the creditor at least twenty days in advance stating that the creditor plans to make a demand on your wages. This twenty-day notice gives you a chance to correct the problem yourself.

If these conditions are all met, Roysner must withhold fifteen percent (15%) of each paycheck until your bill is paid and give this money to your creditor.

What Should You Do If You Think the Wage Assignment Is Incorrect?

If you think you are not late or that you do not owe the amount stated, you can argue against it by filing a legal document called a "defense." Once you file a defense, Roysner will not withhold any money from you. However, be sure you are right before you file a defense. If you are wrong, you have to pay not only what you owe but also all legal costs for both yourself and the creditor. If you are right, the creditor has to pay all these costs.

Figure 6.3

Full Capitals Hide the Shape of a Word

Full capitals hide the shape of a word.

FULL CAPITALS HIDE THE SHAPE OF A WORD.

Figure 6.4

Examples of Different Typefaces

Courier **Bold** Underlined
Prestige Elite Bold Underlined *Italic*
Times Roman **Bold** Underlined *Italic*
Palatino **Bold** Underlined *Italic*
Zapf **Bold** Underlined *Italic*
Helvetica **Bold** Underlined *Italic*
Futura **Bold** Underlined *Italic*

eyes move from letter to letter. Helvetica and Geneva are **sans serif** typefaces since they lack serifs (*sans* is French for *without*). Sans serif typefaces are good for titles and tables.

Use black type on white paper. White letters on dark paper take longer to read. Shadow or outline fonts are also hard to read; save them for big letters on signs or in ads.

Most business documents use just one typeface—usually Times Roman or Helvetica. You can create emphasis and levels of headings by using bold, italics, and different sizes. Bold is easier to read than italics, so use bolding if you only need one method to emphasize text. In a complex document, use bigger type for main headings and slightly smaller type for subheadings and text. Avoid Shadow and Outline fonts, which are hard to read. If you combine two typefaces in one document, choose one serif and one sans serif typeface.

Eleven-point Times Roman is the same size as typewriter type. Twelve-point type will seem a bit big; 10-point type may seem a bit small. Use 9- or 10-point type to get the effect of a printed book or brochure.

If your material will not fit in the available pages, cut one more time. Putting some sections in tiny type will save space but creates a negative response—a negative response that may extend to the organization that produced the document.

5. Decide Whether to Justify Margins Based on the Situation and the Audience.

Computers often allow you to **justify** margins, so that type on the right side of the page is evenly lined up. This paragraph justifies margins. Justified margins let you get up to 20% more text on the page; they create a finished look. However, use them only with a proportional typeface in a fairly long line (45 characters or so). Justification used with narrow columns or fixed type leaves wide spaces between words. These "rivers" that run down the page are distracting to readers.

Unjustified margins are sometimes called **ragged right margins.** Lines end in different places because words are of different lengths. Anyone using a typewriter will produce ragged right margins. The Sidebar columns use ragged right margins. Ragged right margins are better in narrow lines, since justification would produce "rivers." Ragged right margins are usually less expensive to produce, especially if a document is typeset by a professional compositor. If a change is made in a line of justified type, it affects the spacing for that line and perhaps for the whole page or document. Because ragged right margins are uneven, you probably can change a word or two without affecting other pages. Research suggests that poor readers find unjustified type easier to read than justified type.[5]

Use justified margins when you

- Can use proportional typefaces.
- Want the document to look typeset and professional.
- Want to use as few pages as possible.
- Write to skilled readers.

Use ragged right margins when you

- Do not have proportional typefaces.
- Want an informal look.
- Want to be able to revise an individual page without reprinting the whole document.
- Use very short line lengths.
- Write to poor readers.

6. Put Important Elements in the Top Left and Lower Right Quadrants.

Readers of English start in the upper left-hand corner of the page and read to the right and down. The eye moves in a Z pattern.[6] (See Figure 6.5.) Therefore, as Philip M. Rubens notes, the four quadrants of the page carry different visual weights. The top left quadrant where the eye starts is the most important; the bottom right quadrant where the eye ends is next most important.[7] Titles should always start in the top left; reply coupons or another important element should be in the bottom right.

7. Use a Grid to Unify Graphic Elements.

For years, graphic designers have used a **grid system** to design pages. In its simplest form, a grid imposes two or three imaginary columns on the page. In more complex grids, these columns can be further subdivided. Then all the graphic elements—text indentations, headings, visuals, and so on—are lined up within the columns. The resulting symmetry creates a more pleasing page[8] and unifies long documents.

Figure 6.6 uses grids to organize a page with visuals and a résumé.

8. Use Highlighting, Decorative Devices, and Color in Moderation.

Many word-processing programs have arrows, pointing fingers, and a host of other **dingbats** that you can insert. Clip art packages allow you to insert more and larger images into your text. The Document Design Center used icons as well as better page design when it revised Ford's warranty booklet. (See Figure 6.7.) Used in moderation, highlighting and decorative devices make pages more interesting. However, don't overdo them. A page that uses every possible highlighting device just looks busy and hard to read.

Color works well to highlight points. Use color for overviews and main headings, not for small points. Blue, green, or violet type is most legible for younger readers, but perception of blue diminishes for readers over 50.[9] Red is appropriate for warnings in North America. Since the connotations of colors vary among cultures, check Chapter 12 before you use color with international or multicultural audiences. If a document will be copied on a regular photocopier, avoid color: blue may not be picked up at all, and other colors may be hard to identify.

Cultural Differences in Document Design*

Cultural differences in document design are based on reading practices and experiences with other documents. For example, one laundry detergent company printed ads in the Middle East showing soiled clothes on the left, its box of soap in the middle, and clean clothes on the right. But, because people in that part of the world read not from left to right but from right to left, many people thought the ads meant that the soap actually soiled the clothes.

Different cultures also judge and value aesthetics differently. A Japanese executive explained that the company's annual report was designed to create a visually attractive document which would create a good impression of the company. Visuals, which did not need to be related to the company, were the most important part of the document. US readers of the report were frustrated and found the report "flashy" because they expected visuals to have a direct relationship to the words.

*Based on David A. Ricks, *Blunders in International Business* (Cambridge, MA: Blackwell, 1993), 53, and Kaushiki Maitra and Dixie Goswami, "Responses of American Readers to Visual Aspects of a Mid-Sized Japanese Company's Annual Report: A Case Study," *IEEE Transactions on Professional Communication* 38, no. 4 (December 1995): 197–203.

Figure 6.5

Put Important Elements in the Top Left and Bottom Right Quadrants

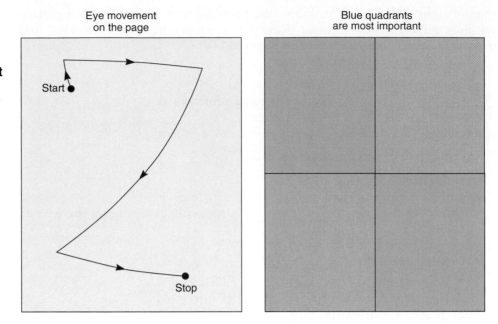

Eye movement on the page

Start

Stop

Blue quadrants are most important

Based on Russel N. Baird, Arthur T. Turnbull, and Duncan McDonald, *The Graphics of Communication: Typography, Layout, Design, Production,* 5th Ed. (New York: Holt, Rinehart, and Winston, 1987), 37.

Figure 6.6   **Examples of Grids to Design Pages**

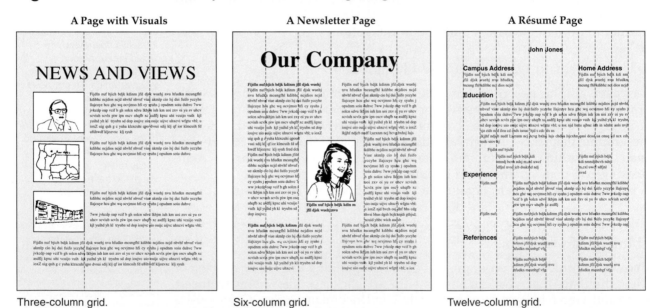

A Page with Visuals

NEWS AND VIEWS

Three-column grid.

A Newsletter Page

Our Company

Six-column grid.

A Résumé Page

John Jones

Twelve-column grid.

When you use color,

- Use glossy paper to make colors more vivid.
- Be aware that colors on a computer screen always look brighter than the same colors on paper because the screen sends out light.

DESIGNING BROCHURES AND NEWSLETTERS

To design brochures and newsletters, first think about audience and purpose. An "image" brochure designed to promote awareness of your company will

"Before" and "After" Pages from Ford's Warranty Booklet   **Figure 6.7**

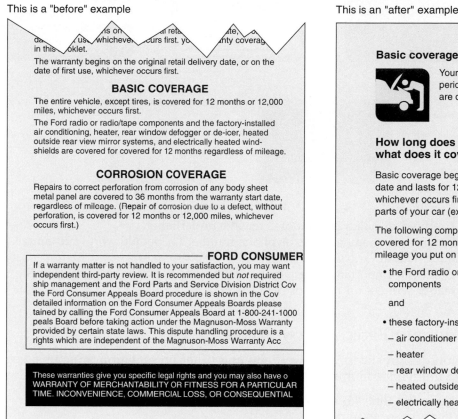

Source: Lee L. Gray, "Ford Offers a Readable Warranty Booklet," *Simply Stated . . . in Business,* no. 18 (March 1987): 2.

have a different look than an "information" brochure telling people how to do something and persuading them to do it.

Start your process by planning content. Create thumbnail sketches (see Figure 5.2) to test various design options. Use a consistent design for a series of brochures or for issues of a newsletter.

When you design a brochure, think how the reader will get the document. Do you need to leave the back third of the page for a mailing label? Must the brochure compete against many others in a display rack?

When you design a newsletter,

- Put your strongest image in the top half of the page.
- Arrange small photos in one column of the grid or in the shape of a *C,* a *U,* or a *T.*
- Pull out interesting quotes or statements that summarize a section of a long story. Put these in larger type in the middle of columns to draw the eye to the story.
- Decide how much space to give a story *before* you write it.

In both kinds of documents,

- Keep pictures near the text they illustrate.
- Use small tab indentations when you have small type and narrow columns.
- Justify type and use rules (thin lines) between columns for a more formal look.

Figure 6.8

Colors for Presentation Slides

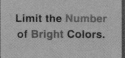

- Use bold or italics instead of extensive underlining.
- Provide an e-mail address or phone number for people who want more information.
- Don't put important information on the back of a page or panel that the reader will cut off to fax or mail to you.

Designing Presentation Slides

As you design slides for PowerPoint and other presentation programs, keep these guidelines in mind.

- Use a big font: 44- or 50-point for titles, 32-point for subheads, and 28-point for examples.
- Use bullet-point phrases rather than complete sentences.
- Use clear, concise language.
- Make only three to five points on each slide. If you have more, consider using two slides.
- Customize your slides with the company logo, charts, downloaded Web pages, and scanned-in photos and drawings.

Use clip art only if the art is really appropriate to your points and only if you are able to find nonsexist and nonracist images. (In 1996, Marilyn Dyrud has shown, the available clip art was biased.[10])

Choose a consistent template, or background design, for the entire presentation. Make sure that the template is appropriate for your subject matter. For example, use a globe only if your topic is international business and palm trees only if you're talking about tropical vacations. One problem with PowerPoint is that the basic templates may seem repetitive to people who see lots of presentations made with the program. For a very important presentation, you may want to consider customizing the basic template.

Choose a light background if the lights will be off during the presentation and a dark background if the lights will be on. Slides will be easier to read if you use high contrast between the words and backgrounds. See Figure 6.8 for examples of effective and ineffective color combinations.

Designing Web Pages

Good Web pages have both good content and an interesting design.

Your opening screen is crucial. Jakob Nielsen claims that only 10% of users scroll beyond the first screen.[11] To make it more likely that visitors to your page will scroll down, on the first screen

Good Document Design Saves Money, I*

Clearer forms and computer screen prompts enable Motorola Corporate Finance department to close its books in 4 days, down from 12. The savings: $20 million a year.

After rewriting its rules for citizen band radios, the Federal Communications Commission was able to transfer to other jobs five employees who spent all day answering telephone questions about the rules.

Revised forms cut training time for Citibank employees in half—while improving the accuracy of the information that employees give to customers.

Simplifying its billing statement reduced customer inquiries at Southern Gas Company and is saving the company an estimated $252,000 a year.

*Based on Karen A. Schriver, "Quality in Document Design: Issues and Controversy," *Technical Communication* 40, no. 2 (1993): 250–51.

- Provide an introductory statement or graphic orienting the surfing reader to the organization sponsoring the page.
- Offer an overview of the content of your page, with links to take readers to the parts that interest them.
- Put information that will be most interesting and useful to most readers on the first screen.

The rest of the page can contain information that only a limited number of readers will want. When a Web document reaches four pages or more, think about dividing it into several documents. Specialized information can go on another page, which readers can click on if they want it.

Make it clear what readers will get if they click on a link.

Ineffective
phrasing: Employment. Openings and skills levels are determined by each office.
Better
phrasing: Employment. Openings listed by skills level and by location.

As you design pages,

- Keep graphics small. Specify the width and height so that the text can load while the graphics are still coming in.
- Provide visual variety. Use indentations, bulleted or numbered lists, and headings.
- Unify multiple pages with a small banner, graphic, or label so surfers know who sponsors each page.
- On each page, provide a link to the home page, the name and e-mail address of the person who maintains the page, and the date when the page was last revised.

TESTING THE DESIGN

A design that looks pretty may or may not work for the audience. To know whether your design is functional, test it with your audience.

The best way to test a document is to watch someone as he or she uses the document to do a task. Where does the reader pause, reread, or seem confused? To find out the reader's thought processes, you can (1) ask the reader to "think aloud" while completing the task, (2) interrupt the reader at key points to ask what he or she is thinking, or (3) ask the reader to describe the thought process after completing the document and the task. Learning the reader's thought processes is important, since a reader may get the right answer for the wrong reasons. In such a case, the design still needs work.

If your document will be used by a wide variety of people, test it with those who are most likely to have trouble with it: very old or young readers, people with little education, people who read English as a second language.

DOCUMENT DESIGN AS PART OF YOUR WRITING PROCESS(ES)

Document design isn't something to "tack on" when you've finished writing. Indeed, the best documents are created when you think about design at each stage of your writing process(es).

- As you plan, think about your audience. Are they skilled readers? Are they busy? Will they read the document straight through or skip around in it?
- As you write, incorporate lists and headings. Use visuals to convey numerical data clearly and forcefully.

**Designing Documents
for Mutual Funds***

Putnam Investments manages over $150 billion in mutual fund and retirement assets. Says its CEO, Lawrence Lasser, "Visually, we started with two objectives: First, we wanted to differentiate ourselves. . . . We wanted to break through the clutter . . . to get both the intermediary's and the investor's attention.

"Our second objective was to simplify. We wanted to simplify the language by getting rid of jargon, and make our literature visually inviting and user-friendly. In this industry, companies typically jam as much as they can into every piece, thinking more is better. We took the opposite approach, saying let's give people something they can comprehend and absorb. We used vivid colors and icons. . . . We added white space, . . . and key messages were highlighted, so that if you just read the headlines and subheads you got a story. . . .

"Design has provided a major way for us to communicate clearly and convincingly what is sometimes pretty archaic stuff."

*Quoted from "Putnam's Lawrence J. Lasser on Design," @Issue 2, no. 2 (Fall 1996): 1–5.

Good design improves image and saves money. Changing "Federal Express" to "FedEx" allows big letters which can be read across an airfield. Limiting the use of purple in the new logo saves thousands of dollars on each plane and vehicle. White pigment weighs less than purple and absorbs 40% less heat, cutting fuel and operating costs.

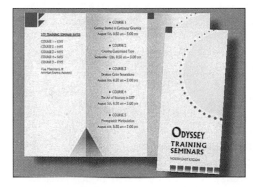
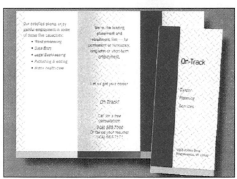

PaperDirect provides special stationery to use with your laser printer or photocopier to produce brochures and newletters.

- Get feedback from people who will be using your document. What parts of the document do they think are hard to understand? Is there additional information they need?
- As you revise, check your draft against the guidelines in this chapter.

THE IMPORTANCE OF EFFECTIVE DESIGN

When document design is poor, both organizations and society suffer.

The defect that caused the nuclear accident at Three Mile Island appeared 17 months earlier in a Toledo power plant.[12] At the Toledo plant, workers were able to control damage before a serious problem arose. However, it was clear that a problem existed that might occur again either at that plant or at other locations. A supervisor recommended new guidelines—and put them on the second page of a two-page memo. None of the 12 people on the distribution list for that memo responded. A not-quite-right subject line, ineffective writing, and poor document design caused the memo to be ignored. On March 28, 1979, the same defect led to America's worst nuclear accident to this date—an accident that might have been avoidable if writers had been able to design documents that readers could understand and act on.

SUMMARY OF KEY POINTS

■ An attractive document looks inviting, friendly, and easy to read. The visual grouping of ideas also makes the structure of the document more obvious so it is easier to read.

■ Good document design can save time, money, and legal problems.

■ Eight guidelines help writers create visually attractive documents.
1. Use white space.
2. Use headings.
3. Limit the use of words set in all capital letters.
4. Limit the number of typefaces in a single document.
5. Decide whether to justify margins based on the situation and the audience.
6. Put important elements in the top left and lower right quadrants of the page.
7. Use a grid of imaginary columns to unify the elements in a document.
8. Use highlighting, decorative devices, and color in moderation.

■ To design brochures and newsletters, first think about audience and purpose. Use a consistent design for a series of brochures or for issues of a newsletter.

■ As you design slides for PowerPoint and other presentation programs,

   ■ Use a big font.
   ■ Use bullet-point phrases.
   ■ Make only three to five points on each slide.
   ■ Customize your slides.

■ Good Web pages have both good content and an interesting design.

   ■ Orient the surfing reader to the organization sponsoring the page.
   ■ Offer an overview of the content of your page, with links to take readers to the parts that interest them.
   ■ Make it clear what readers will get if they click on a link.
   ■ Keep graphics small.
   ■ Provide visual variety.

■ The best documents are created when you think about design at each stage of the writing process.

   ■ As you plan, think about the needs of your audience.
   ■ As you write, incorporate lists, headings, and visuals.
   ■ Get feedback from people who will be using your document.
   ■ As you revise, check your draft against the guidelines in this chapter.

■ To test a document, observe readers, ask them to "think aloud" while completing the task, interrupt them at key points to ask what they are thinking, or ask them to describe the thought process after completing the document and the task.

Good Document Design Saves Money, II*

The British government began reviewing its forms in 1982. Since then, it has eliminated 27,000 forms, redesigned 41,000, and saved over $28 million.

Revising the British lost-baggage form for airline passengers cut a 55% error rate to 3%.

In Australia, rewriting one legal document saved the Victorian government the equivalent of $400,000 a year in staff salaries.

In the Netherlands, revising the form for educational grants reduced by two-thirds the number of forms applicants filled out incompletely or incorrectly. The government saved time and money; the applicants got decisions more quickly.

*Based on Karen A. Schriver, "Quality in Document Design: Issues and Controversy," *Technical Communication* 40, no. 2 (1993): 250–51.

GETTING STARTED

6–1 Evaluating Page Designs

Use the guidelines in Chapter 6 to evaluate each of the following page designs. What are their strong points? What could be improved?

Source: Ad for AD-Ex, *Technical Communication*, 40, no. 4 (November 1993), inside back cover.

Source: Diane Burns and S. Venit, "What's Wrong with This Paper" *PC Magazine* 6, no. 17 (October 13, 1987): 174–75.

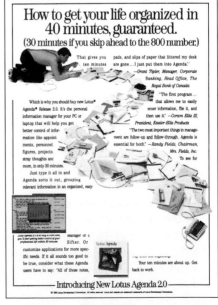

Source: Ad for Lotus Agenda, *PC Magazine,* 10, no. 3 (February 12, 1991): 233.

6–2   Evaluating the Ethics of Design Choices

Indicate whether you consider each of the following actions ethical, unethical, or a gray area. Which of the actions would you do? Which would you feel uncomfortable doing? Which would you refuse to do?

1. Putting the advantages of a proposal in a bulleted list, while discussing the disadvantages in a paragraph.
2. Using a bigger type size so that a résumé visually fills a whole page.
3. Putting reasons to buy a product in the upper-left and lower-right quadrants, and the price in a part of the page that will get less emphasis.
4. Using a line at the bottom of the first page so it appears that the document is finished, and then putting the price and limitations on the back of that page.
5. Putting the services that are not covered by your health plan in full caps to make it less likely that people will read the page.

6–3   Using Headings

Reorganize the items in each of the following lists, using appropriate headings. Use bulleted or numbered lists as appropriate.

a. Rules and Procedures for a Tuition Reimbursement Plan
1. You are eligible to be reimbursed if you have been a full-time employee for at least three months.
2. You must apply before the first class meeting.
3. You must earn a "C" or better in the course.
4. You must submit a copy of the approved application, an official grade report, and a receipt for tuition paid to be reimbursed.
5. You can be reimbursed for courses related to your current position or another position in the company, or for courses which are part of a degree related to a current or possible job.
6. Your supervisor must sign the application form.
7. Courses may be at any appropriate level (high school, college, or graduate school).

b. Activities in Starting a New Business
 - Getting a loan or venture capital
 - Getting any necessary city or state licenses
 - Determining what you will make, do, or sell
 - Identifying the market for your products or services
 - Pricing your products or services
 - Choosing a location
 - Checking zoning laws that may affect the location
 - Identifying government and university programs for small business development
 - Figuring cash flow
 - Ordering equipment and supplies
 - Selling
 - Advertising and marketing

COMMUNICATING AT WORK

6–4   Analyzing Documents at Work

1. Collect several documents: letters and memos, newsletters, ads and flyers, and reports. Use the guidelines in Chapter 6 to evaluate each of them.
2. Compare documents or pages produced by your competitors to those produced by your own organization in a specific category (for example, brochures, instructions, Web pages). Which documents are more effective? Why?

As Your Instructor Directs,

a. Discuss the documents with a small group of classmates.
b. Write a memo to your instructor evaluating three or more of the documents. Include originals or photocopies of the documents you discuss as an appendix to your memo.
c. Write a memo to your supervisor recommending ways the organization can improve its documents.

d. In an oral presentation to the class, explain what makes one document good and another one weak. If possible, use transparencies so that classmates can see the documents as you evaluate them.

DOCUMENT ASSIGNMENTS

6–5   Evaluating Page Designs

Collect several documents that you receive as a consumer: forms, letters, newsletters, ads, and flyers. Use the guidelines in Chapter 6 to evaluate each of them.

As Your Instructor Directs,
   a. Discuss the documents with a small group of classmates.
   b. Write a memo to your instructor evaluating three or more of the documents. Include originals or photocopies of the documents you discuss as an appendix to your memo.
   c. Write a letter to an organization recommending ways it can improve the design of the documents.
   d. In an oral presentation to the class, explain what makes one document good and another one weak. If possible, use transparencies so that classmates can see the documents as you evaluate them.

6–6   Evaluating Web Pages

Compare five Web pages in the same category (for example, nonprofit organizations, car companies, university departments, sports information). Which page(s) are most effective? Why? What weaknesses do the pages have?

As Your Instructor Directs,
   a. Discuss the pages with a small group of classmates.
   b. Write a memo to your instructor evaluating the pages. Include URLs of the pages in your memo.
   c. In an oral presentation to the class, explain what makes one page good and another one weak. If possible, put the pages on screen so that classmates can see the pages as you evaluate them.

6–7   Creating a Brochure

Create a brochure for a campus, nonprofit, government, or business organization. Write a memo to your instructor explaining your choices for content and design.

6–8   Creating a Web Page

Create a Web page for an organization that does not yet have one. Write a memo to your instructor explaining your choices for content and design.

6–9   Testing a Document

Ask someone to follow a set of instructions or to fill out a form. (Consider consumer instructions, forms for financial aid, and so forth.)

   ■ Time the person. How long does it take? Is the person able to complete the task?
   ■ Observe the person. Where does he or she pause, reread, seem confused?
   ■ Interview the person. What parts of the document were confusing?

As Your Instructor Directs,
   a. Discuss the changes needed with a small group of classmates.
   b. Write a memo to your instructor evaluating the document and explaining the changes that are needed. Include the document as an appendix to your memo.
   c. Write to the organization that produced the document recommending necessary improvements.
   d. In an oral presentation to the class, evaluate the document and explain what changes are needed. If possible, use a transparency of the document so that classmates can see it.

Letters and Memos

CHAPTER 7

Informative and Positive Messages

Chapter Outline

An Inside Perspective:
Managing E-Mail

Gloria J. Pfeif, Group Program Manager
Microsoft

Gloria Pfeif is in charge of the quarterly releases for the Microsoft Developer Network (MSDN), the Web sites for MSDN, and the Visual Tools products from Microsoft. She receives 150–200 e-mail messages a day—more, during peak release times. Microsoft, headquartered in Redmond, Washington, is a multimillion-dollar software company that produces systems and application software, including Windows, Microsoft Word, Access, and Visual Tools.

Managing incoming e-mail is a crucial skill, especially when you get a lot of mail. Set priorities, and read the mail from your manager, your team, and other important items first. Learn the advanced features of your e-mail system so that you can filter out messages you don't need to read and file messages you need to save in appropriate folders.

I like to end each day with my mail caught up—which in the ideal world means that I have read and responded to all messages. This doesn't always happen, so when I arrive in the morning I try to wrap up messages from the previous day. (If you get involved in international activities you'll find a full inbox from the night before.) When I read a message, I try to respond immediately. I've found that letting opened mail pile up is very time-consuming because I have to reread the message to regain the context.

Sometimes I can forward requests to other team members for them to answer. When issues require discussion, I send a message that says "I'll schedule a meeting" to resolve the issue. An issue requiring a longer response can be resolved with a high-level summary to "all" with the indication that a more detailed summary will follow. This type of response lets everyone know that you are on top of the issue—and, of course, you must now follow up with the detailed document.

During the day, I check mail between meetings. First, I scan for any items flagged as "high priority"—critical "work stopping" issues that require immediate action. Understand the conventions for your business. Use "high priority" flagging sparingly but use it when it's appropriate. Otherwise, you'll sit idle or be blocked because you didn't show colleagues that they needed to stop work to resolve the issue.

Using descriptive subject lines will improve the effectiveness of your mail. Since many e-mail systems now display the subject line and the first line or two of the message, choose those words carefully and include all the relevant contact information.

No matter who is listed in the "To:" line, assume that your e-mail message is public. Once sent, your message can be easily forwarded to others.

Good e-mail is short and direct. Use two or three paragraphs for basic communications. Some systems permit you to attach a document or insert a pointer in the document when you must send longer messages.

Learn from your colleagues. Note the effective communication styles within your company and build your own style.

Gloria Pfeif, March 11, 1997

Visit Microsoft's Web site: http://microsoft.com/

"[D]escriptive subject lines will improve the effectiveness of your mail."

Gloria Pfeif, Microsoft

Business messages solve communication problems. To do that, they must meet the needs of the writer (and the writer's organization), be sensitive to the audience, and accurately reflect the topic being written about. Informative and positive messages are the bread-and-butter correspondence within an organization; they are also written to people outside the organization.

We categorize messages both by **the author's purposes** and by **the initial response we expect from the reader.** When we need to convey information to which the reader's basic reaction will be neutral, the message is **informative.** If we convey information to which the reader's reaction will be positive, the message is a **positive** or **good news message.** Neither message immediately asks the reader to do anything. However, you may want the reader to save the information and to act on it later. You usually do want to build positive attitudes toward the information you are presenting, so in that sense, even an informative message has a persuasive element. Chapter 8 will discuss messages where the reader will respond negatively; Chapters 9, 10, and 11 discuss messages where you want the reader to act.

Informative and positive messages include acceptances; positive answers to reader requests; information about procedures, products, services, or options; announcements of policy changes that are neutral or positive; and changes that are to the reader's advantage.

Even a simple informative or good news message usually has several purposes:

Primary Purposes:

To give information or good news to the reader or to reassure the reader.
To have the reader read the message, understand it, and view the information positively.
To deemphasize any negative elements.

Secondary Purposes:

To build a good image of the writer.
To build a good image of the writer's organization.
To cement a good relationship between the writer and reader.
To reduce or eliminate future correspondence on the same subject so the message doesn't create more work for the writer.

Informative and positive messages are not necessarily short. Instead, the length of a message depends on your purposes, the audience's needs, and the complexity of the situation. A public health inspector got a lot of teasing from his colleagues because he wrote 10-page inspection reports; the other inspectors rarely wrote more than 4. He got the last laugh, however, when the lawyers in the enforcement division complimented him on his reports. For the first time, they were getting enough information to win cases against companies and individuals charged with violating the public health statutes. The shorter reports didn't give enough information.

How easy a message is to write depends on your familiarity with the situation and your readers as well as on the kind of message. It isn't easy to decide how to present complex information or how to present routine information in an interesting way. Even good news can be hard to convey when you have lots of facts to include or when you need to develop reader benefits.

WRITING LETTERS AND MEMOS

Letters go to someone outside your organization; memos go to someone in your own organization.

In large organizations where each unit is autonomous, the organization's culture determines whether people in different units send letters or memos to each other. In some universities, for example, faculty send letters if they need to write to faculty in other departments.

Letters and memos use different formats. The most common formats are illustrated in Appendix A. The AMS Simplified Letter Format is very similar to memo format: it uses a subject line and omits the salutation and the complimentary close.

The differences in audience and format are the only differences between letters and memos. Both kinds of messages can be long or short, depending on how much you have to say and how complicated the situation is. Both kinds of messages can be informal when you write to someone you know well, or more formal when you write to someone you don't know, to several audiences, or for the record. Both kinds of messages can be simple responses that you can dash off in 15 minutes; both can take hours of analysis and revision when you've never faced that situation before or when the stakes are high.

ORGANIZING INFORMATIVE AND POSITIVE MESSAGES

The patterns of organization in this chapter and the chapters that follow will work for 70 to 90% of the writing situations most people in business and government face. Using the appropriate pattern can help you compose more quickly and create a better final product.

- Be sure you understand the rationale behind each pattern so that you can modify the pattern if necessary. (For example, if you write instructions, any warnings should go up front, not in the middle of the message.)
- Not every message that uses the basic pattern will have all the elements listed. The elements you do have will go in the order presented in the pattern.
- Sometimes you can present several elements in one paragraph. Sometimes you'll need several paragraphs for just one element.

In real life, writing problems don't come with labels that tell you which pattern to use. Chapters 7 through 11 offer advice about when to use each pattern.

Present informative and positive messages in the following order:

1. **Give any good news and summarize the main points.** Include the date policies begin, the percent of a discount, etc. If the reader has already raised the issue, make it clear that you're responding.

   Share good news immediately.
2. **Give details, clarification, background.** Don't repeat information you've already given. Do answer all the questions your reader is likely to have; provide all the information necessary to achieve your purposes. Present details in the order of importance to the reader.

Good News, Good Business*

In 1995, an industrial fire destroyed Malden Mills' factory in Lawrence, Massachusetts. Owner, president, and CEO Aaron Feuerstein pledged to rebuild—and to pay his more than 1,000 employees full salaries until the new factory was ready for them to work in.

Was he foolish to spend $15 million on employees who couldn't work? *Fortune* reporter Thomas Teal doesn't think so. From 1982 to 1995, general US productivity increased just over 1% a year. At Malden Mills in the same period, revenues in constant dollars tripled—while the workforce barely doubled. Feuerstein has always valued having superior employees. And the employees produce superior products. Malden is best known for its lightweight, thermal, wool-like fabrics sold under the brand names Polarfleece and Polartec by Lands' End, L.L. Bean, Patagonia, Eddie Bauer, and a dozen more upscale companies.

The factory is now rebuilt, and the company is back in business and doing well. At a European trade show in Brussels in September 1996, buyers snapped up Malden Mills' broad new line of high-end upholstery fabrics.

*Based on Thomas Teal, "Not a Fool, Not a Saint," *Fortune*, November 11, 1996, 201–204.

3. **Present any negative elements—as positively as possible.** A policy may have limits; information may be incomplete; the reader may have to satisfy requirements to get a discount or benefit. Make these negatives clear, but present them as positively as possible.

4. **Explain any reader benefits.** Most informative memos need reader benefits. Show that the policy or procedure helps readers, not just the company. Give enough detail to make the benefits clear and convincing. In letters, you may want to give benefits of dealing with your company as well as benefits of the product or policy.

   In a good news message, it's often possible to combine a short reader benefit with a goodwill ending in the last paragraph.

5. **Use a goodwill ending: positive, personal, and forward-looking.** Shifting your emphasis away from the message to the specific reader suggests that serving the reader is your real concern.

Figures 7.1 and 7.2 illustrate two ways that the basic pattern can be applied.

The letter in 7.1 authorizes a one-year appointment that the reader and writer have already discussed and describes the organization's priorities. Since the writer knows that the reader wants to accept the job, the letter doesn't need to persuade. The opportunity for the professor to study records that aren't available to the public is an implicit reader benefit; the concern for the reader's needs builds goodwill.

The memo in 7.2 announces a new employee benefit. The first paragraph summarizes the policy. Paragraphs 2–5 give details. Negative elements are in paragraphs 3–5, stated as positively as possible. The last section of the memo gives reader benefits and shows that everyone—even part-timers who are not eligible for reimbursement—will benefit from the new program.

SUBJECT LINES FOR INFORMATIVE AND POSITIVE MESSAGES

A **subject line** is the title of a document. It aids in filing and retrieving the document, tells readers why they need to read the document, and provides a framework in which to set what you're about to say.

Subject lines are standard in memos. Letters are not required to have subject lines (see Appendix A, Formats for Letters and Memos). However, a survey of business people in the southwest found that 68% of them considered a subject line in a letter to be important, very important, or essential; only 32% considered subject lines to be unimportant or only somewhat important.[1]

A good subject line meets three criteria: it is specific, concise, and appropriate to the kind of message (positive, negative, persuasive).

Making Subject Lines Specific

The subject line needs to be specific enough to differentiate that message from others on the same subject, but broad enough to cover everything in the message.

Too General:	Training Sessions
Better:	Dates for 19— Training Sessions
or	Evaluation of Training Sessions on Conducting Interviews
or	Should We Schedule a Short Course on Proposal Writing?

A Positive Letter

Figure 7.1

 INTERSTATE FIDELITY INSURANCE COMPANY

100 Interstate Plaza
Atlanta, GA 30301
404-555-5000
Fax: 404-555-5270

March 8, 1998

Professor Adrienne Prinz
Department of History
Duke University
Durham, North Carolina 27000

Dear Professor Prinz:

Good news — Your appointment as archivist for Interstate Fidelity Insurance has been approved. When you were in Atlanta in December, you said that you could begin work June 1. We'd like you to start then if that date is still good for you. *Tactful*

The Board has outlined the following priorities for your work: *Assumes reader's primary interest is the job*

Negative about lighting and security presented impersonally

Details

1. **Organize and catalogue the archives.** You'll have the basement of the Palmer Building for the archives and can requisition the supplies you need. You'll be able to control heat and humidity; the budget doesn't allow special lighting or security measures.

2. **Prepare materials for a 4-hour training session in October** for senior-level managers. We'd like you to cover how to decide what to send to the archives. If your first four months of research uncover any pragmatic uses for our archives (like Wells Fargo's use of archives to teach managers about past pitfalls), include those in the session.

3. **Write an article each month for the employee newsletter** describing the uses of the archives. When we're cutting costs in other departments, it's important to justify committing funds to start an archive program.

4. **Study the IFI archives to compile** information that (a) can help solve current management problems, (b) could be included in a history of the company, and (c) might be useful to scholars of business history.

These provisions will appeal to the reader

5. **Begin work on a corporate history of IFI.** IFI will help you find a publisher and support the book financially. You'll have full control over the content.

Negative that reader will have to reapply presented as normal procedure

Your salary will be $23,000 for six months; your contract can be renewed twice for a total of 18 months. You're authorized to hire a full-time research assistant for $8,000 for six months; you'll need to go through the normal personnel request process to request that that money be continued next year. A file clerk will be assigned full-time to your project. You'll report to me. At least for the rest of this calendar year, the budget for the Archives Project will come from my department.

Salary is deemphasized to avoid implying that reader is "just taking the job for the money"

Figure 7.1   **A Positive Letter (Concluded)**

Professor Adrienne Prinz
March 8, 1998
Page 2

IFI offices are equipped with Pentium computers with FoxPro, WordPerfect, and Excel. Is there any software that we should buy for cataloguing or research? Are there any office supplies that we need to have on hand June 1 so that you can work efficiently?

In the meantime,

Goodwill ending

1. Please send your written acceptance right away.

2. Let me know if you need any software or supplies.

3. Send me the name, address, and Social Security number of your research assistant by May 1 so that I can process his or her employment papers.

4. If you'd like help finding a house or apartment in Atlanta, let me know. I can give you the name of a real estate agent.

On June 1, you'll spend the morning in Personnel. Stop by my office at noon. We'll go out for lunch and then I'll take you to the office you'll have while you're at IFI.

Welcome to IFI!

Cordially,

Cynthia Yen

Cynthia Yen
Director of Education and Training

Making Subject Lines Concise

Most subject lines are relatively short—usually no more than 10 words, often only 3 to 7 words.[2]

Wordy:	Survey of Student Preferences in Regards to Various Pizza Factors
Better:	Students' Pizza Preferences
or	The Feasibility of a Cassano's Branch on Campus
or	What Students Like and Dislike about Giovanni Pizza

If you can't make the subject both specific and short, be specific.

A Positive Memo   **Figure 7.2**

Memo

January 26, 1998

To: All Crossroads Counselling Center Employees

From: Darlene Bonifas, Director of Human Resources

*Good news in subject
line and first paragraph*

Subject: New Tuition Reimbursement Program

Starting February 1st, full-time employees who have worked at Crossroads three months or more can be reimbursed for up to $3500 a year for tuition and fees when you take courses related to your current position (including courses needed to keep your licenses), courses that would prepare you for another position you might someday hold at Crossroads, or courses required for a job-related degree program.

You can take the courses at any level: high school, college, or graduate school. You can find a selection of catalogs from nearby schools and colleges in the Office of Human Resources.

How to Apply for the Program   *Headings chunk material
and provide good visual impact*

To apply, pick up an application form in the Office of Human Resources, fill it out, and have it signed by your immediate supervisor. Return it to the Office of Human Resources at least two weeks before classes start: your application must be approved before classes start.

How to Get Reimbursed   *Negatives presented as positively
as possible*

You'll be reimbursed when you earn a "C" grade or better in the course. Just bring the follow-ing documents to the Office of Human Resources:

     1. A copy of the approved application.
     2. An official grade report.
     3. A statement of the tuition and fees paid.

If you are eligible for other financial aid (scholarships, grants, or veterans' benefits), you will be reimbursed for the tuition and fees not covered by that aid, up to $3500 during one calendar year. Reimbursements for undergraduate and basic education programs are currently tax-free.

Goals of the Program

This program will help us stay on top of developments in our field. For example, we're

Figure 7.2   **A Positive Memo (concluded)**

All Employees—New Tuition Reimbursement Program   *page 2 of memo*
January 26, 1998   *doesn't use*
Page 2   *letterhead*

working with more and more people who have tested HIV-positive. Some counselors might want to take courses on medical treatments for AIDS. The more we understand about the physical pressures our clients are under, the better we can help them cope with their emotional challenges. Knowing that AIDS leaves patients exhausted may help us understand why someone needs a little extra time or tolerance during an appointment.

Courses about anxiety and stress could help us deal with the increasing number of clients who fear that their jobs will disappear. Perhaps someone would like to take a course in money management or career counseling so that we could offer practical as well as psychological advice. Counselors may want to become registered to administer the MBTI or learn how to use computers to score the MMPI. ———————————————————— *Jargon appropriate for the audience*

Reader Benefits

Counselors can use this program to earn their doctorates so that they can be the primary psychologist seeing a patient. Having more certified counselors would enable us to enlarge our practice.

But courses don't have to relate to psychology and counselling. Maybe someone would like to learn how to use advanced features in WordPerfect, Access, or Excel. (Could someone learn how to improve our database or chart our client profiles?) Management courses might help us run a tighter ship. And interpersonal courses might sharpen our skills so that we do an even better job of working together to solve problems.

Including Benefits for people who are not eligible to partici- pate

In spite of cutbacks by some insurance providers last fall, Crossroads continues to be financially as well as professionally strong. This program gives us the opportunity to build on our strength as we prepare to help people in Columbus face the challenges of the approaching millennium.

Goodwill ending

Making Subject Lines Appropriate for the Pattern of Organization

Since your subject line introduces your reader to your message, it must satisfy the psychological demands of the situation; it must be appropriate to your purposes and to the immediate response you expect from your reader. In general, do the same thing in your subject line that you would do in the first paragraph.

When you have good news for the reader, build goodwill by highlighting it in the subject line. When your information is neutral, summarize it concisely for the subject line.

> Subject: Discount on Rental Cars Effective January 2
>
> Starting January 2, as an employee of Amalgamated Industries you can get a 15% discount on cars you rent for business or personal use from Roadway Rent-a-Car.

> Subject: Update on Arrangements for Videoconference with France
>
> In the last month, we have chosen the participants and developed a tentative agenda for the videoconference with France scheduled for March 21.

USING READER BENEFITS IN INFORMATIVE AND POSITIVE MESSAGES

Not all informative and positive messages need reader benefits (☛ p. 69). You don't need reader benefits when

- You're presenting factual information only.
- The reader's attitude toward the information doesn't matter.
- Stressing benefits may make the reader sound selfish.
- The benefits are so obvious that to restate them insults the reader's intelligence.

You do need reader benefits when

- You are presenting policies.
- You want to shape readers' attitudes toward the information or toward your organization.
- Stressing benefits presents readers' motives positively.
- Some of the benefits may not be obvious to readers.

Messages to customers or potential customers sometimes include a sales paragraph promoting products or services you offer in addition to the product or service that the reader has asked about. Sales promotion in an informative or positive message should be low-key, not "hard sell."

Reader benefits are hardest to develop when you are announcing policies. The organization probably decided to adopt the policy because it appeared to help the organization; the people who made the decision may not have thought at all about whether it would help or hurt employees. Yet reader benefits are most essential in this kind of message so readers see the reason for the change and support it.

Conveying Information to International Audiences*

Traditionally, other countries have organized messages in different ways.

In Muslim countries, a business letter might begin by invoking Allah's blessing on the reader and the reader's family—especially if the business is family-owned.

Traditional Japanese letters began with a reference to the season: "It is autumn and the red leaves cover the ground with color."

But business people who have worked or studied in North America are increasingly adopting North American patterns of communication. When they write in English, they get to the point, using plain, explicit language.

When you write to a stranger, it's safest to use the pattern traditionally preferred in his or her country. But when you write to someone you know, use the pattern he or she uses with you. For good news, it will probably look very much like the "US" pattern described in this chapter.

*Based on Linda Beamer and Iris Varner, *Intercultural Business Communication* (Burr Ridge, IL: Richard D. Irwin, 1995), 129; and Daphne A. Jameson, "New Ways in the New World: Cultural Imperialism and the Empire of American Business Communication," *Proceedings,* 1993 Southeast Regional Conference of the Association for Business Communication, ed. Shirley Kuiper (1993), 5.

When you present reader benefits, be sure to present advantages *to the reader*. Most new policies help the organization in some way, but few workers will see their own interests as identical with the organization's. Even if the organization saves money or increases its profits, workers will benefit directly only if they own stock in the company, if they're high up enough to receive bonuses, if the savings enables a failing company to avoid layoffs, or if all of the savings goes directly to employee benefits. In many companies, any money saved will go to executive bonuses, shareholder profits, or research and development.

To develop reader benefits for informative and positive messages, use the steps suggested in Chapter 2. Be sure to think about **intrinsic benefits** (➤ p. 70) of your policy, that is, benefits that come from the activity or policy itself, apart from any financial benefits. Does a policy improve the eight hours people spend at work?

WRITING THE ONE-PAGE MEMO

Some organizations force writers to be concise by requiring or encouraging one-page memos. In simple situations, a page may be more than you need. Sometimes, careful revising and editing may enable you to cut your memo to a page. When you can't get everything on one page even with careful revision, put the key points on one well-designed page and attach appendixes for readers who need more information.

ENDING INFORMATIVE AND POSITIVE LETTERS AND MEMOS

Ending a letter or memo gracefully can be a problem in short informative and positive messages. In a one-page memo where you have omitted details and proof, you can tell readers where to get more information. In long messages, you can summarize your basic point. In persuasive messages, as you'll learn in Chapter 9, you can tell readers what you want them to do. But none of these strategies works in a short message containing all the information readers need. In those situations, either write a goodwill paragraph that refers directly to the reader or the reader's organization or just stop.

Goodwill endings should focus on the business relationship you share with your reader rather than on the reader's hobbies, family, or personal life. When you write to one person, a good last paragraph fits that person so specifically that it would not work if you sent the same basic message to someone else or to a person with the same title in another organization. When you write to someone who represents an organization, the last paragraph can refer to your company's relationship to the reader's organization. When you write to a group (for example, to "All Employees") your ending should apply to the whole group.

Use a paragraph that shows you see your reader as an individual. Possibilities include complimenting the reader for a job well done, describing a reader benefit, or looking forward to something positive that relates to the subject of the message.

In the following examples, a letter answers the question, "When a patient leaves the hospital and returns, should we count it as a new stay?" For one company the answer was that if a patient was gone from the hospital overnight or longer, the hospital should start a new claim when the patient was readmitted.

Weak closing paragraph:	Should you have any questions regarding this matter, please feel free to call me.
Goodwill paragraph:	Many employee-patients appreciate the freedom to leave the hospital for a few hours. It's nice working with a hospital which is flexible enough to offer that option.
Also acceptable:	Omit the paragraph; stop after the explanation.

Some writers end every message with a standard invitation:

If you have questions, please do not hesitate to ask.

That sentence lacks positive emphasis. But revising it to say "feel free to call" is rarely a good idea. Most of the time, the writer should omit the sentence entirely.

Inviting readers to call suggests that you have not answered the question fully. In very complicated situations, it may be simpler to let people call with individual questions. But in simple situations, you can answer the question clearly.

A state agency sent out a memo explaining when the state would pay for the cost of lunch that was included in a conference registration fee. The state would pay for lunch if the conference was out of town. If the conference was in the same town as the employee's office, the employee had to pay for lunch. Either the conference is in the same town or a different town. The answer is simple; no further explanation is necessary.

One of the reasons you write is to save the time needed to tell everyone individually. People in business aren't shrinking violets; they will call if they need help. Don't make more work for yourself by inviting calls to clarify simple messages.

WRITING E-MAIL MESSAGES

E-mail is an essential tool for millions of workers. Readers read and reply to e-mail quite rapidly. Dealing with 80 to 100 message in 20 or 30 minutes is normal. Write messages so that readers can deal with them quickly.

As you use e-mail, keep these guidelines in mind:

- Although e-mail feels informal, it is not private, as a conversation might be. Your employer may legally check your messages. And a message sent to one person can be printed out or forwarded to others without your knowledge or consent. Don't be indiscreet on e-mail.
- All the principles of good business writing still apply with e-mail. Remember you-attitude and positive emphasis. Use reader benefits when they're appropriate. Use the pattern of organization that fits the purpose of the message.
- Because e-mail feels like talking, some writers give less attention to spelling, grammar, and proofreading. Many e-mail programs have spell checkers; use them. Check your message for grammatical correctness and to be sure that you've included all the necessary information.
- Reread and proofread your message before sending it out.

E-mail allows you to be a bit playful in language, as Figure 7.3 shows.

Voice Mail Information

Before you make a phone call, think of the information you'll need if you must leave a voice mail message.

- Summarize the purpose of your message in a sentence or two.
- Give your name and phone number early in the message. Speak slowly and distinctly.
- Give the recipient enough information to act.
- Tell when you'll be at your desk to receive a return call.

Figure 7.3   **A Positive E-Mail Message**

The system automatically puts in date and time the message was written and sent.

```
>From server@ebbs.english.vt.edu Wed Oct 23 10:50:26
1996
Date: Wed, 23 Oct 1996 10:43:05 -0400 (EDT)
From: EBBS Listproc <server@ebbs.english.vt.edu>
Subject: Re: Problem Posting to BizCom
To: locker.1@osu.edu (Kitty O. Locker)
```

System automatically puts in this "Re:" when you respond to an earlier message.

You don't have to put in the reader's name, but it makes the message more friendly.

```
Kitty:
```

Carats indicate words quoted from original message

```
>I'm getting all the BizCom mailings, but when I try to
>reply, I get a message saying that I'm not a member!
>This has happened twice now.
```

Abbreviations are OK in e-mail if reader will know what they mean.

```
This has happened because the computer mail folk at OSU
have changed your e-mail return address--probably w/o
your realizing it. They also put an alias in place so
that mail sent to the old address(KLOCKER@MAGNUS.ACS.
OHIO-STATE.EDU) would be automatically forwarded to
your new and current address (locker.1@osu.edu).
```

Important information in first screen

```
Naturally, our dim but sincere list robot had no idea
that 'locker.1@osu.edu' was really you, so it refused
to post messages from the interloper.

I've had a chat w/the robot, so now it thinks that you
are you,
and you should be able now both to receive and to send
mail to BIZCOM.

Let me know if there's anything else . . .
```

When you send a message through a listserv, add your name and e-mail address. Your job title is optional.

```
                          Len Hatfield
                          EBBS List Mgr.
```

Subject Lines for E-Mail

Subject lines in e-mail are even more important than those in letters and memos. Subject lines must be specific, concise, and catchy. Some e-mail users get so many messages that they don't bother reading messages if they don't recognize the sender or if the subject doesn't catch their interest. If you have good news to convey, be sure it's in the subject line. Most e-mail systems print only the first three or four words of the subject line. Be as brief as you can. The following subject lines would be acceptable for informative and good news e-mail messages:

> Travel Plans for Sales Meeting
> Your Proposal Accepted
> Reduced Prices During February
> Your Funding Request Approved

When you reply to a message, the e-mail system automatically creates a subject line "Re: [subject line of message to which you are responding]." If the subject line is good, that's fine. If it isn't, you may want to create a new subject line. And if a series of messages arises, create a new subject line. "Re: Re: Re: Re: Question" is not an effective subject line.

Format for E-Mail Messages

Most e-mail systems start by asking you to indicate whom the message is to and what the subject line is. The computer puts in the date, time of day, and your name and address automatically. Send yourself an e-mail message so you can see the relationship between what appears on the screen and what the recipient receives.

Putting the reader's name at the beginning of the message isn't necessary, but some people like to do it to make the message more friendly.

You don't need a close such as "Sincerely." But do put your name after your message, since some e-mail systems strip out the automatic header. If you're sending the message through a listserve, put your e-mail address as well, since the header will print the listserve's address, not the address of the individual sender (see Figure 7.3).

E-mail usually can't do larger font sizes, bullets, underlining, or bold. To indent, you'd have to space over rather than tabbing or indenting. To create good visual impact, use vertical spacing.

E-Mail Etiquette

Follow these guidelines to be a good "netizen":

- Use full caps only to emphasize a single word or two. Putting the whole message in caps is considered as rude as shouting.
- Never send angry messages by e-mail. If you have a conflict with someone, work it out face-to-face, not electronically.
- Send people only messages they need. Send copies to your boss or CEO only if he or she has asked you to.
- Find out how your recipient's system works and adapt your messages to it. Most people would rather get a separate short message on each of several topics, so that the messages can be stored in different mailboxes. But people who pay a fee to download each message may prefer longer messages that deal with several topics.

■ When you respond to a message, include only the part of the original message that is essential so that the reader understands your posting. Delete the rest. If the quoted material is long, put your response first, then the original material.

■ When you compose a message in your word processor and call it up in e-mail, use short line lengths (set the right margin at 2.5 or 3 inches).

Using E-Mail Effectively

To get the most out of e-mail, learn to use your system's advanced features, such as setting up nicknames or aliases for people you write frequently, creating mailboxes to store messages on various topics, and using attachments to send documents with formatting. Most colleges and universities offer workshops on using e-mail programs.

VARIETIES OF INFORMATIVE AND POSITIVE MESSAGES

Many messages can be informative, negative, or persuasive depending on what you have to say. A transmittal, for example, can be positive when you're sending glowing sales figures or persuasive when you want the reader to act on the information. A performance appraisal is positive when you evaluate someone who's doing superbly, negative when you want to compile a record to justify firing someone, and persuasive when you want to motivate a satisfactory worker to continue to improve. A collection letter is persuasive; it becomes negative in the last stage when you threaten legal action. Each of these messages is discussed in the chapter of the pattern it uses most frequently. However, in some cases you will need to use a pattern from a different chapter.

Transmittals

When you send someone something in an organization, attach a memo or letter of transmittal explaining what you're sending. A transmittal can be as simple as a small yellow Post-it™ note with "FYI" written on it ("for your information") or it can be a separate typed document.

Organize a memo or letter of transmittal in this order:

1. Tell the reader what you're sending.
2. Summarize the main point(s) of the document.
3. Indicate any special circumstances or information that would help the reader understand the document. Is it a draft? Is it a partial document that will be completed later?
4. Tell the reader what will happen next. Will you do something? Do you want a response? If you do want the reader to act, specify exactly what you want the reader to do and give a deadline.

Frequently transmittals have important secondary purposes. Consider the writer's purpose in Figure 7.4, a transmittal from a lawyer to her client. The primary purpose of this transmittal is to give the client a chance to affirm that his story and the lawyer's understanding of it are correct. If there's anything wrong, the lawyer wants to know *before* she files the brief. But an important secondary purpose is to build goodwill: "I'm working on your case; I'm earning my fee." The greatest number of complaints officially

A Transmittal

Figure 7.4

100 Barkley Plaza • Denver, CO 80210 • 303.555.4783 • Fax 303.555.4784

October 8, 1997

Mr. Charles Gibney
Personnel Manager
Roydon Interiors
146 East State Street
Denver, CO 80202

Dear Mr. Gibney:

Paragraph one tells reader what is enclosed and summarizes main points

Here is a copy of the brief we intend to file with the Tenth Circuit Court in support of our position that the sex discrimination charge against Roydon Interiors should be dropped.

Will you please examine it carefully to make sure that the facts it contains are correct? If you have changes to suggest, please call my office by October 22nd, so that we can file the brief by October 24th.

Last paragraph asks for action by a specific date.

Sincerely,

Diana Drew

Diana Drew

lodged against lawyers are for the lawyer's neglect—or what the client perceives as neglect—of the client's case.

News Releases

News releases package information about your company that you would like announced in local and national media: promotions, expansions, new programs, new products. They give you a way to tell your side of the story about negative events: the firing of a CEO, a downturn in profits, a plant closing, a strike, or an organizational error.

The mechanics of writing a news release are simple:

- Open the release with a **lead:** an attention-getting statement, quotation, or question.
- Early in the release, answer the 5 Ws and H: who, what, when, where, why, and how.
- Put the most important information early in the release. Editors cut releases, like other news stories, to fit the space or time available.
- Triple-space the release for easy reading and editing. Put "MORE" at the bottom of every page except the last one.
- At the top of the first page, give the name and phone number of someone in the organization who can be contacted for more information.
- At the top of the first page, indicate the release date.

Every week, however, hundreds of news releases that satisfy these rules are thrown away. Your news release has to compete not only against hard news but also against dozens, perhaps hundreds, of other news releases. To increase the chances that your release will be used,

- Get the name of the editor and address the release to him or her specifically. A phone call can give you the name. Or check *Broadcasting Yearbook* for radio and TV editors and *Editor and Publisher International Yearbook* for newspaper and magazine editors.
- Adapt your lead and your details to the audience that reads the paper or watches the newscast. Many small papers will print news releases only if they have a strong local slant. As Iris and Carson Varner point out, in a story on a plant closing, a local paper will be concerned about the effects on jobs and on the economy. What will happen to the people who are losing their jobs? What will happen to the town's tax revenues? A national business paper will be more concerned about the effect of this belt-tightening on the organization's profitability.[3]
- When you have a choice, time your release for the day after Thanksgiving or Christmas. Papers have lots of holiday ads, but few news stories since little hard news occurs on holidays. Therefore, papers are more likely to run news releases.[4]

Adjustments and Responses to Complaints

A study sponsored by Travelers Insurance showed that when people had gripes but didn't complain, only 9% would buy from the company again. But when people did complain—and their problems were resolved quickly—82% would buy again.[5]

When you grant a customer's request for an adjusted price, discount, replacement, or other benefit to resolve a complaint, do so in the very first sentence.

> Your bill for a night's lodging VISA bill has been adjusted to $63. Next month a credit of $37 will appear on your bill to reimburse you for the extra amount you were originally asked to pay.

Don't talk about your own process in making the decision. Don't say anything that sounds grudging. Give the reason for the original mistake only if it reflects credit on the company. (In most cases, it doesn't, so the reason should be omitted.)

Solving a Sample Problem

Real-life problems are richer and less well defined than textbook problems and cases. But even textbook problems require analysis before you begin to write. Before you tackle the assignments for this chapter, examine the following problem. See how the analysis questions probe the basic points required for a solution. Study the two sample solutions to see what makes one unacceptable and the other one good. Note the recommendations for revision that could make the good solution excellent.[6] The checklist at the end of the chapter in Figure 7.7 can help you evaluate a draft.

Problem

Interstate Fidelity Insurance (IFI) uses computers to handle its payments and billings. There is often a time lag between receiving a payment from a customer and recording it on the computer. Sometimes, while the payment is in line to be processed, the computer sends out additional notices: past-due notices, collection letters, even threats to sue. Customers are frightened or angry and write asking for an explanation. In most cases, if they just waited a little while, the situation would be straightened out. But policyholders are afraid that they'll be without insurance because the company thinks the bill has not been paid.

IFI doesn't have the time to check each individual situation to see if the check did arrive and has been processed. It wants you to write a letter that will persuade customers to wait. If something is wrong and the payment never reached IFI, IFI would send a legal notice to that effect saying the policy would be canceled by a certain date (which the notice would specify) at least 30 days after the date on the original premium bill. Continuing customers always get this legal notice as a third chance (after the original bill and the past-due notice).

Prepare a form letter that can go out to every policyholder who claims to have paid a premium for automobile insurance and resents getting a past-due notice. The letter should reassure readers and build goodwill for IFI.

Analysis of the Problem

1. Who is (are) your audience(s)? What characteristics are relevant to this particular message? If you are writing to more than one reader, how do the readers differ?

   Automobile insurance customers who say they've paid but have still received a past-due notice. They're afraid they're no longer insured. Since it's a form letter, different readers will have different situations: in some cases payments did arrive late, in some cases the company made a mistake, in some the reader never paid (check was lost in mail, unsigned, bounced, etc.)

2. What are your purposes in writing?

   To reassure readers: they're covered for 30 days. To inform them they can assume everything is OK *unless* they receive a second notice. To avoid further correspondence on this subject. To build goodwill for IFI: (a) we don't want to suggest IFI is error-prone or too cheap to hire enough people to do the necessary work; (b) we don't want readers to switch companies; (c) we do want readers to buy from IFI when they're ready for more insurance.

The Political Uses of Memos*

How the memo is routed is at least as important as what it says. . . . For example, if I put my immediate supervisor's name AND the vice-president's name on the top, it means that . . . I have direct access to the VP. If I give the VP a copy but don't indicate that on the supervisor's memo, I am withholding information from my supervisor and asserting that my "real" boss is the vice president. If I want to cooperate with my immediate supervisor, I address the memo to him and allow him to route it—he or she, thereby, gets credit for my activities. . . .

If you author a memo, then you are putting yourself up one or one down with respect to the receivers.

For example, I recently won an award. A peer sent me a memo saying, "Congratulations . . . keep up the fine work," to position himself as a superior. Very irritating. Very effective. He has been promoted. . . .

The simplest way to take credit [for an idea] is to attach your memo ("the attached may be of interest to you") to someone else's work. A slightly more sophisticated technique is to write a memo attaching your name to the idea of someone else or, more honestly, write a memo attaching your name to your own idea before somebody else pirates it.

*Quoted from Carla Butenhoff, "Bad Writing Can Be Good Business," *ABCA Bulletin* 40, no. 2 (June 1977): 12–13.

3. What information must your message include?

> Readers are still insured. We cannot say whether their checks have now been processed (company doesn't want to check individual accounts). Their insurance will be canceled if they do not pay after receiving the second past-due notice (the legal notice).

4. How can you build support for your position? What reasons or reader benefits will your reader find convincing?

> Computer helps us provide personal service to policyholders. We offer policies to meet all their needs. Both of these points would need specifics to be interesting and convincing.

5. What objection(s) can you expect your reader(s) to have? What negative elements of your message must you deemphasize or overcome?

> Computers appear to cause errors. We don't know if the checks have been processed. We will cancel policies if their checks don't arrive.

6. What aspects of the total situation may affect reader response? The economy? The time of year? Morale in the organization? The relationship between the reader and writer? Any special circumstances?

> The insurance business is highly competitive—other companies offer similar rates and policies. The customer could get a similar policy for about the same money from someone else. Most people find that money is tight, so they'll want to keep insurance costs low. On the other hand, the fact that prices are steady or rising means that the value of what they own is higher—they need insurance more than ever.

Figure 7.5 **An Unacceptable Solution to the Sample Problem**

Need date

Dear Customer:

Not necessarily true. Reread problem.

Relax. We got your check.

This explanation makes company look bad. There is always a time lag between the time payments come in and the time they are processed. While payments are waiting to be processed, the computer with super-human quickness is sending out past-due notices and threats of cancellation.

Too negative

Need to present this positively Cancellation is not something you should worry about. No policy would be canceled without a legal notice to that effect giving a specific date for cancellation which would be at least 30 days after the date on the original premium notice.

If you want to buy more insurance, just contact your local Interstate Fidelity agent. We will be happy to help you.

This paragraph isn't specific enough to work as a reader benefit. It lacks you-attitude and positive emphasis.

Sincerely,

A Good Solution to the Sample Problem   **Figure 7.6**

Need date

Dear Customer: *Better: use computer to personalize. Put in name and address of a specific reader*

Your auto insurance is still in effect.   *Good ¶ 1. True for all readers*

Good to treat notice as information, tell reader what to do if it arrives   Past-due notices are mailed out if the payment has not been processed within three days after the due date. This may happen if a check is delayed in the mail or arrives without a signature or account number. When your check arrives with all the necessary information, it is promptly credited to your account.   *Good you-attitude*

Even if a check is lost in the mail and never reaches us, you still have a 30-day grace period. If you do get a second notice, you'll know that we still have not received your check. To keep your insurance in force, just stop payment on the first check and send a second one.

Benefits of using computers   Computer processing of your account guarantees that you get any discounts you're eligible for: multicar, accident-free record, good student. If you have a claim, your agent uses computer tracking to find matching parts quickly, whatever car you drive. You get a check quickly—usually within 3 working days—without having to visit dealer after dealer for time-consuming estimates.   *Better to put in agent's name, phone number*

Too negative

Need to add benefits of insuring with IFI   Today, your home and possessions are worth more than ever. You can protect them with Interstate Fidelity's homeowners' and renters' policies. Let your local agent show you how easy it is to give yourself full protection. If you need a special rider to insure a personal computer, a coin or gun collection, or a fine antique, you can get that from IFI, too.   *Good specifics*

Whatever your insurance needs—auto, home, life, or health—one call to IFI can do it all.   *Acceptable ending*

Sincerely,

Many insurance companies are refusing to renew policies (car, liability, malpractice insurance). These refusals to renew have gotten lots of publicity, and many people have heard horror stories about companies and individuals whose insurance has been canceled or not renewed after a small number of claims. Readers don't feel very kindly toward insurance companies.

People need car insurance. If they have an accident and aren't covered, they not only have to bear the costs of that accident alone but also (depending on state law) may need to place as much as $50,000 in a state escrow account to cover future accidents. They have a legitimate worry.

Discussion of the Sample Solutions

The solution in Figure 7.5 is unacceptable. The red marginal comments show problem spots. Since this is a form letter, we cannot tell customers we have their checks; in some cases, we may not. The letter is far too negative. The explanation in paragraph 2 makes IFI look irresponsible and uncaring. Paragraph 3 is far too negative. Paragraph 4 is too vague; there are no reader

Figure 7.7

Checklist for Informative and Positive Messages

☐ In positive messages, does the subject line give the good news? In either message, is the subject line specific enough to differentiate this message from others on the same subject?

☐ Does the first paragraph summarize the information or good news? If the information is too complex to fit into a single paragraph, does the paragraph list the basic parts of the policy or information in the order in which the memo discusses them?

☐ Is all the information given in the message? [What information is needed will vary depending on the message, but information about dates, places, times, and anything related to money usually needs to be included. When in doubt, ask!]

☐ In messages announcing policies, is there at least one reader benefit for each segment of the audience? Are all reader benefits ones that seem likely to occur in this organization?

☐ Is each reader benefit developed, showing that the benefit will come from the policy and why the benefit matters to this organization? Do the benefits build on the job duties of people at this organization and the specific circumstances of the organization?

☐ Does the message end with a positive paragraph—preferably one that is specific to the readers, not a general one that could fit any organization or policy?

And, for all messages, not just informative and positive ones,

☐ Does the message use you-attitude and positive emphasis?

☐ Is the style easy to read and friendly?

☐ Is the visual design of the message inviting?

☐ Is the format correct?

☐ Does the message use standard grammar? Is it free from typos?

Originality in a positive or informative message may come from

- Creating good headings, lists, and visual impact.
- Developing reader benefits.
- Thinking about readers and giving details that answer their questions and make it easier for them to understand and follow the policy.

Good Communication Leads to Corporate Success*

Emerson Electronics is a world-class competitor. One way it achieved that status was using effective communication to outline corporate economic goals for employees and to explain why those goals affect jobs, salaries, and survival. Sharing information and shaping attitudes toward it enabled Emerson to excel.

Martin Marietta Government Electronic Systems, a union shop, speeded up information so that changes were communicated within 48 hours of any decision. Once everyone knew what was going on at all times, grievances dropped from 281 a year to just 12. Information creates openness and a sense of trust.

*Based on James L. Gibson, John M. Ivancevich, and James H. Donnelly, *Organizations: Behavior, Structure, Processes* (Burr Ridge, IL: Richard D. Irwin, 1995), 408.

benefits; the ending sounds selfish. A major weakness with the solution is that it lifts phrases straight out of the problem; the writer does not seem to have thought about the problem or about the words he or she is using. Measuring the draft against the answers to the questions for analysis suggests that this writer should start over.

The solution in Figure 7.6 is much better. The blue marginal comments show the letter's strong points. The message opens with the good news that is true for all readers. (Whenever possible, one should use the good news pattern of organization.) Paragraph 2 explains IFI's policy. It avoids assigning blame and ends on a positive note. The negative information is buried in paragraph 3 and is presented positively: the notice is information, not a threat; the 30-day extension is a "grace period." Telling the reader now what to do if a second notice arrives eliminates the need for a second exchange of letters. Paragraph 4 offers benefits for using computers, since some readers may blame the notice on computers, and offers benefits for being insured by IFI. Paragraph 5 promotes other policies the company sells and prepares for the last paragraph.

As the red comments indicate, this good solution could be improved by personalizing the salutation and by including the name and number of the local agent. Computers could make both of those insertions easily. This good letter could be made excellent by revising paragraph 4 so that it doesn't end on a negative note and by using more reader benefits. For instance, do computers help agents advise clients of the best policies for them? Does IFI offer good service—quick, friendly, nonpressured—that could be stressed? Are agents well trained? All of these might yield ideas for additional reader benefits.

SUMMARY OF KEY POINTS

- Informative and positive messages normally use the following pattern of organization:
  1. Give any good news and summarize the main points.
  2. Give details, clarification, background.
  3. Present any negative elements—as positively as possible.
  4. Explain any reader benefits.
  5. Use a goodwill ending: positive, personal, and forward-looking.
- **Letters** go to people in other organizations. **Memos** go to people within your own organization.
- A **subject line** is the title of a document. A good subject line meets three criteria: it's specific; it's reasonably short; and it's adapted to the kind of message (positive, negative, persuasive). If you can't make the subject both specific and short, be specific.
- The subject line for an informative or positive message should highlight any good news and summarize the information concisely.
- Use reader benefits in informative and positive messages when

  - You are presenting policies.
  - You want to shape readers' attitudes toward the information or toward your organization.
  - Stressing benefits presents readers' motives positively.
  - Some of the benefits may not be obvious to readers.

- **Goodwill endings** should focus on the business relationship you share with your reader or the reader's organization. The last paragraph of a message to a group should apply to the whole group.
- Use the analysis questions listed in Chapter 1 to probe the basic points needed for successful informative and positive messages.

Exercises and Problems
For Chapter 7

GETTING STARTED

7–1 Evaluating Subject Lines

Identify the strengths and weaknesses of each of the following subject lines. Which is the best subject line in each group? Why?

1. a. Subject: New Employee Benefit
   b. Subject: Tuition Reimbursement Will Now Be Offered to Yomans Employees Who Take Work-Related Classes and Earn at Least a "C"
   c. Subject: New Tuition Reimbursement Policy

2. a. Subject: HTML Web Page Memo
   b. Subject: Search Strategies and Design Choices for My Toronto Web Pages
   c. Subject: Surfing the Net and Catching Waves

3. a. Subject: Schedule for 1999 Campus Interviews at California Colleges and Universities
   b. Subject: Times and Places for Campus Interviews with Job Candidates during the 1999 Recruiting Season at California Colleges and Universities

   c. Subject: Interview Schedule

4. a. Subject: Your Memo of August 14
   b. Subject: Progress on Joint Venture Projects in Japan
   c. Subject: Problems with Joint Venture Projects in Japan

7-2 Evaluating First Paragraphs

Identify the strengths and weaknesses of each of the following first paragraphs. Which is the best paragraph in each group? Why?

1. a. Our employees have some concerns about teams.
   b. Thank you for authorizing the questionnaire on what people like and dislike about working in teams. As you know, teams are crucial to our organization, and finding out where people are is the first step to making teams better.
   c. Our employees would like workshops or training sessions on three aspects of working in teams: dealing with difficult team members, resolving conflicts, and rewarding people for their efforts.

2. a. We have evaluated the grade point averages of all students in the School of Business.
   b. It has been a long term, and all of you who have worked so hard are to be commended.
   c. Congratulations on making the Dean's List this past term!

7-3 Revising a Letter

Your assistant gives you the following letter to sign:

Dear Ms. Hebbar:

I received your request to send a speaker to participate in "Career Day" at King Elementary School next month. I am pleased to be able to send Audrey Lindstrom to speak at your school about her job at the child care center.

Audrey has been working in the child care center for over five years. She trains contracted center personnel on policies and procedures of the department.

Another commitment later that day will make it impossible for her to spend the whole day at your school. She will be happy to spend two hours with your class participating in the event.

Call Audrey to coordinate the time of the program, the expected content, and the age group of the audience.

Your students will see the importance of trained day care providers in our neighborhoods.

Thank you for asking our agency to be part of your school's special event. Our future lies in the hands of today's students.

Sincerely,

This draft definitely needs some work. It lacks you-attitude and positive emphasis, it isn't well organized, and it doesn't have enough details. Though employees in your office call each other by their first names, in a letter to another group, "Ms. Lindstrom" would be more professional than "Audrey." And more information is needed. Exactly when should she show up? Will she be giving a speech (how long?), speaking as a member of a panel, or sitting at a table to answer questions? Will all grade levels be together, or will she be speaking to specific grades? Will all students hear each speaker, or will there be several concurrent speakers from which to choose?

As Your Instructor Directs,
   a. Write a memo to your subordinate, explaining what revisions are necessary.
   b. Revise the letter.

E-MAIL MESSAGES

7–4   Telling Workers to Take a Break
To reduce medical expenses, your company has hired a stress consultant. Today, you get this e-mail message from him:

Subject: Low-Cost Way to Relieve Stress

Though my research isn't finished, one thing is already clear. Many workers sit at computers and telephones all day, almost glued to their chairs. They should get up to stretch and move at least twice a day. In other companies I've worked with, people take group breaks; some companies play music or positive affirmations. I recommend that you implement this immediately.

You decide this is worth a try, as long as people are back at work quickly—10 minutes at the most. Group breaks sound like a good idea, so that people on break don't bother people who are still trying to work and so that everyone actually stretches. Music? Maybe, as long as the whole group agrees and it doesn't bother people in other units. If the idea doesn't work, it can be dropped after a trial.

As Your Instructor Directs,
   a. Write to all employees, encouraging them to take breaks to stretch and move twice a day.
   b. Write to all supervisors, telling them to monitor the breaks and end them on time.
   c. Write to the consultant, saying you're implementing the idea on a trial basis.

7–5   Responding to a Supervisor's Request
You've received this e-mail message from your supervisor:

Subject: Need "Best Practices"

Please describe something our unit does well—ideally something which could be copied by or at least applied to other units. Our organization is putting together something on "Best Practices" so that good ideas can be shared as widely as possible.

Be specific. For example, don't just say "serve customers"—explain exactly what you do and how you do it to be effective. Anecdotes and examples would be helpful.

Also indicate whether a document, a videotape, or some other format would be the best way to share your practice. We may use more than one format, depending on the response.

I need your answer asap so that I can send it on to my boss.

Answer the message, describing something that you or others in your unit do well.

7–6   Making Personal Time More Flexible

You're manager of Human Resources at your company. Two weeks ago, you got this e-mail message.

Subject: Flexibility Needed

Higher-up people routinely take time off from work to play golf, coach soccer, or go to school plays. We peons have to fight to stay home with a sick child. It isn't fair. Can you do something about it?

Yesterday, the Executive Committee voted that a change was in order. As long as people tell their supervisors, get their own work done, and aren't out of the office more than a couple of hours a day a couple of times a week, requests for time off will be granted and will be "free"—that is, they won't be deducted from personal or vacation time. But someone who is going to be out all day does have to use sick, personal, or vacation time.

Write an e-mail message to all employees, telling them about the new policy.

7–7   Accepting Suggestions

For years, businesses have asked employees to suggest ways to save money. Your city government has adopted the same program, asking city employees to suggest ways to help balance the city budget. The suggestion committee, which you chair, has voted to adopt five money-saving suggestions.

1. Direct deposit paychecks to save distribution and printing costs. Suggested by Poh-Kim Lee, in Recreation and Parks.
2. Buy supplies in bulk. Suggested by Jolene Zigmund, in Maintenance.
3. Charge nearby towns and suburbs a fee for sending their firefighters through the city fire academy. Suggested by Charles Boxell, in Fire Safety.
4. Set up an honor system for employees to reimburse the city for personal photocopies or phone calls. Suggested by Maria Echeverria, in Police.
5. Install lock boxes so that meter readers don't have to turn off water valves when people move. This causes wear and tear, and broken valves must be dug up and replaced. Suggested by Travis Gratton, in Water Line Maintenance.

Each suggester gets $100. The Accounting Department will cut checks the first Monday of next month; checks should reach people in interoffice mail a few days later.

As Your Instructor Directs,
   a. Write to one of the suggesters, giving the good news.
   b. Write to all employees, announcing the award winners.

WEB PAGES

7–8   Creating a Human Resources Web Page

As firms attempt to help employees balance work and family life (and as employers become aware that personal and family stresses affect performance at work), Human Resource departments sponsor an array of programs and provide information on myriad subjects. However, some people might be uncomfortable asking for help, either because the problem is embarrassing (who wants to admit needing help to deal with drug or spouse abuse or addiction to gambling?) or because focusing on nonwork issues (e.g., child care) might lead others to think they aren't serious about their jobs. The World Wide Web allows organizations to post information that employees can access privately—even from home.

Create a Web page that could be posted by Human Resources to help employees with one of the challenges they face. Possible topics include

- Appreciating an ethnic heritage.
- Buying a house.

- Caring for dependents: child care, helping a child learn to read, living with teenagers, elder care, and so forth.
- Dealing with a health issue: exercising, having a healthy diet, and so forth.
- Dealing with a health problem: alcoholism, cancer, diabetes, heart disease, obesity, and so forth.
- Dressing for success or dressing for casual days.
- Financial management: basic budgeting, deciding how much to save, choosing investments, and so forth.
- Nourishing the spirit: meditation, religion.
- Getting out of debt.
- Planning for retirement.
- Planning vacations.
- Reducing stress.
- Resolving conflicts on the job or in families.

Assume that this page can be accessed from another of the organization's pages. Offer at least seven links. (More is better.) You may offer information as well as links to other pages with information. At the top of the page, offer an overview of what the page covers. At the bottom of the page, put the creation/update date and your name and e-mail address.

As Your Instructor Directs,

a. Turn in two laser copies of your page(s). On another page, give the URLs for each link.
b. Turn in one laser copy of your page(s) and a disk with the HTML code and .gif files.
c. Write a memo to your instructor (1) identifying the audience for which the page is designed, (2) explaining the search strategies you used to find material on this topic, (3) why you chose the pages and information you've included, and (4) why you chose the layout and graphics you've used.
d. Present your page orally to the class.

Hints:

- Pick a topic you know something about.
- Realize that audience members will have different needs. You could explain the basics of choosing day care or stocks, but don't recommend a specific day care center or a specific stock.
- If you have more than nine links, chunk them in small groups under headings.
- Create a good image of the organization.

COMMUNICATING AT WORK

7–9 Praising Work Done Well

Write a memo to a co-worker (with a copy to the person's supervisor) thanking him or her for helping you or complimenting him or her on a job well done.

7–10 Giving Good News

Write to a customer or client, to a vendor or supplier, or to your boss announcing good news. Possibilities include a product improvement, a price cut or special, an addition to your management team, a new contract, and so forth.

7–11 Recording Information for Other Workers

You have a lot of information in your head. Perhaps you've figured out a machine's quirks; you know a customer's idiosyncrasies; you understand the history of a situation. Write a memo that could be used by a vacation replacement or a new hire who might be asked to fill in for you.

7–12 Easing New Hires' Transition into Your Unit

Prepare a document to help new hires adjust quickly to your unit. You may want to focus solely on work procedures; you may also want to discuss aspects of the corporate culture.

LETTER AND MEMO ASSIGNMENTS

7–13 Correcting a Misconception

As the Executive Director for a local charity, you've received an angry letter from a donor:

> According to the *Suburban News,* 89% of the money you raise goes to administrative expenses. Is that true? I always thought you did good work, but now I wonder.
>
> Sincerely,
>
> (Mrs.) Eva Corey

The paper had a major misprint: 89% of the money you raise goes to the work you do; only 11% goes to fund-raising and administrative costs.

As Your Instructor Directs,

a. Write a letter to Mrs. Corey, reassuring her that her donations to your organization indeed go to do good work.

b. Write a letter to the editor of the *Suburban News,* correcting the story.

Hints:

- Pick an organization you know something about.
- Use specifics about what the money supports.

7–14   Reminding Guests about the Time Change

Twice a year in the United States, cities switch to daylight saving time and back again. The time change can be disruptive for hotel guests, who may lose track of the date, forget to change the clocks in their rooms, and miss appointments as a result.

Prepare a form letter to leave in each hotel room reminding guests of the impending time change. What should guests do?

Write the letter.

Hints:

- Use an attention-getting page layout so readers don't ignore the message.

- Pick a specific hotel or motel chain you know something about.
- Use the letter to build goodwill for your hotel or motel chain. Use specific references to services or features the hotel offers, focusing not on what the hotel does for the reader, but on what the reader can do at the hotel.

7–15   Announcing a 360-Degree Feedback System

Following in the footsteps of Chase Manhattan Bank, Pitney Bowes, and Du Pont, your organization has decided to implement a 360-degree feedback system. (See Brian O'Reilly, "360 Feedback Can Change Your Life," *Fortune,* October 17, 1994, 93–100.) Under this system, supervisors and managers will be evaluated not only by their own supervisors (as has always been the case) but also by their peers and subordinates. Everyone will fill out a lengthy, anonymous questionnaire (Are you crisp, clear, and articulate? Abrasive? Spreading yourself too thin? Trustworthy?), including the person being evaluated. A computer will tally and graph the results. Then someone from Human Resources will meet with each supervisor or manager to explain how the person's own opinion of himself or herself is or isn't shared by subordinates, peer group, and boss. The Human Resources officer will help the employee identify ways to work on two or three of the major shortcomings.

The purpose of this system is to enable people to be more effective supervisors and managers. The system will not replace the existing system of performance evaluations; the results will not be placed in official personnel files.

Companies that use the system find that only one-third of managers produce self-assessments that match the judgments of their co-workers. (One-third rank themselves higher than do their subordinates; one-third rank themselves lower.) Many managers are surprised to find out that they're perceived to be cold and uncaring. Sometimes miscommunication has resulted from different conversational styles; sometimes a behavior that may have worked in earlier circumstances no longer works when the person is a supervisor.

The evaluation focuses on the ways people relate to each other. Companies that use the system report that it improves teamwork and management planning; it does not affect creativity or inventing new products.

As Vice President for Human Resources, write a memo to all employees explaining the system and building support for it.

Hints:
- Pick a business, nonprofit, or government organization you know something about. What does the organization do? How big is it? Has it recently gotten larger or smaller?
- Identify the proportion of people who are supervisors and managers.
- Identify the pressures that supervisors and managers are under. Have these changed recently?
- Identify the concerns that each of the following groups might have:
  a. People who will receive feedback from this system.
  b. Subordinates who will evaluate their superiors.
  c. Superiors who will still need to do performance reviews and recommend raises.
- How does this system relate to the organization's values and culture?
- What external pressures must the organization deal with? How will this system help?

7–16   Announcing a Stock Option Program

PepsiCo Inc., Delta Air Lines, and Starbucks are among the estimated 2,000 companies using stock options to motivate employees "to think like owners and build our wealth," in the words of Sanford Weill, CEO of Travelers Group, Inc., a diversified financial services company (*Business Week*, July 22, 1996, 80–84).

Assume that you're Director of Human Resources for a publicly traded company that has decided to offer stock options to all full-time employees, not just the high-level executives who have received them for years.

Effective the first Monday of next month, every full-time employee will be granted a 10-year option to buy 500 shares of company stock at today's stock price. Employees do not actually buy the stock until they exercise their options. That is, if the stock rises 10 points, someone could "cash in" the options, paying the option price rather than the market price and thus making an immediate profit of $5,000. If the stock price falls, the option is worthless. Additional options equal to 5% of each full-time employee's salary will be granted each year when the employee's performance is appraised.

People must be employed by the company to exercise their options. Someone who leaves gives up any unexercised options. When the option is exercised, the employee will pay a commission to a stockbroker. If someone needs to borrow money to cash in options, the broker will lend money on margin; this money plus fees and interest must be repaid. Other ways of financing the purchase will have other costs; people should discuss options with a broker. The difference between the option price and the market value when the option is exercised is taxable as ordinary income. If one holds the stock after exercising the option (rather than selling it for a quick profit), the post-exercise gain or loss is taxed as a capital gain or loss. People should consult a tax professional to learn what strategy is best for them.

Write a memo to all employees, announcing the program.

Hints:
- Pick a company you know something about whose stock is publicly traded. To learn more about a company, check its Web site or talk to someone who works there.
- Use your analyses from problems 3–7 and 3–12.
- Specify the stock price employees would pay to exercise the option. Check *The Wall Street Journal* or the Web for stock prices.
- Think about why the company would offer this program. Is it a motivational device, to get people to work harder? Is it a way to recruit and retain people who have many job options? Does it come out of a sense of fairness in an egalitarian organization?
- Some employees may know a lot about the stock market; some may not know what a "stock option" is. Putting information under a separate heading and using "As you may know" are two ways to provide information to those who may need it without

"talking down" to people who understand.

- Think about benefits for workers of different ages, at different levels of the company, and in different income brackets. Include intrinsic benefits for people who are not eligible to participate in this program.
- Many factors affect stock market prices; you cannot promise that this program will make people rich. But when

employees are productive and creative, the company is more likely to do well and its stock is more likely to rise.

- Think about how the market is doing now. If the market is rising, how can you encourage people not to take further increases for granted? If the market is falling, how can you convince people that this program will benefit them?

7–17   Introducing a Wellness Program

The very best way for a company to save money on health insurance costs is to have healthy employees. Studies show that people who smoke, who are moderate or heavy drinkers, who are overweight, and who do not exercise regularly have significantly higher health care costs: they visit doctors more often, need more prescription drugs, and are hospitalized more often and for longer periods of time. In addition, health costs are also higher for people who do not use seat belts, who indulge in dangerous hobbies like skydiving, and for babies whose mothers do not get adequate prenatal care.

Your company has decided to launch a comprehensive wellness program in an effort to get employees to adopt healthier lifestyles. Employees in your organization pay about 40% of the cost of their health insurance; the organization pays the rest. On January 1 (or July 1) rates are going up, as they have every year for the last nine years. Singles will pay $65 a month; people who also insure a spouse or partner pay $140 a month; the cost for the employee and one child is $130 a month; the family rate is $225 a month.

People who follow good health practices can get several rebates. You'll give a $100 rebate (annually) to each employee who doesn't smoke or use chewing tobacco. An employee who doesn't drink to excess (more than an average of at least 6 ounces of beer or 3 ounces of wine or 1.5 ounces of hard liquor a day) can also get a rebate of $100, as can those who don't use illegal drugs and those whose cholesterol isn't over 150. Employees who exercise at least 30 minutes a day, three times a week will get rebates of $50. Exercise doesn't have to be difficult: walking and gardening count. Other employee rebates are for (1) a

waist-to-hip ratio not over 0.8 for women or 0.95 for men: $50; (2) using a seat belt: $25; (3) getting an annual physical: $25. Rebates will not be available until the end of each year. (Spouses and partners get half the rebate amount in each category. There are no discounts for children.)

As part of the wellness program, the company cafeteria and vending machines will offer healthier foods and the company will offer a monthly informational health fair on some aspect of wellness. These parts of the program will begin next month.

Write a memo to all employees informing them about the wellness program and the rates for insurance.

Hints:
- Pick an organization you know something about to use for this message.
- Use your analyses from problems 3–8 and 3–12.
- Much of the program is described negatively. How can you present it positively?
- Specify the date, time, place, and topic of the first health fair and when the new rates start. If the financial program's start is several months away, suggest that people begin to change habits now.
- Is the organization self-insured, or does it buy insurance?
- If the organization saves money, will employees benefit?
- Why don't people already follow healthy practices? What can you do to overcome these objections?
- Saving money may not motivate everyone. Offer intrinsic benefits as well.

7–18   Lining up a Consultant to Teach Short Courses in Presentations

As Director of Education and Training you oversee all in-house training programs. Five weeks ago, Runata Hartley, Director of Human Resources, asked you to set up a training course on oral presentations. After making some phone calls, you tracked down Brian Barreau, a Communication professor at a nearby college.

"Yes, I do short courses on oral presentations," he told you on the phone. "I would want at least a day and a half with participants—two full days would be better. They need time to practice the skills they'll be learning. I'm free Thursdays and Fridays. I'm willing to work with up to 20 people at a time. Tell me what kind of presentations they make, whether they know how to use PowerPoint, and what kinds of things you want me to emphasize. I'll need a videocamera to record each participant's presentations and a tape for each person. My fee is $2,000 a day."

You told him you thought a two-day session would be feasible, but you'd have to get back to him after you got budget approval. You wrote a quick memo to Runata explaining the situation and asking about what the session should cover.

Two weeks ago, you received this memo.

I've asked the Veep for budget approval for $4000 for a two-day session plus no more than $500 for all expenses. I don't think there will be a problem.

We need some of the basics: how to plan a presentation, how to deal with nervousness. Adapting to the audience is a big issue: our people give presentations to varied audiences with very different levels of technical knowledge and interest. Most of our people have PowerPoint on their computers, but the slide shows I've seen have been pretty amateurish.

I don't want someone to lecture. I don't want some ivory tower theorist. We need practical exercises that can help us practice skills that we can put into effect immediately.

Attached is a list of 18 people who can attend a session Thursday and Friday of the second week of next month. Note that we've got a good mix of people. If the session goes well, I may want you to schedule additional sessions.

Today, you got approval from the Vice President to schedule the session and pay Professor Barreau's fee and reimburse him for expenses to a maximum of $500. He will have to keep all receipts and turn in an itemized list of expenses to be reimbursed; you cannot reimburse him if he does not have receipts.

You also need to explain the mechanics of the session. You'll meet in the Conference Room, which has a screen and flip charts. You have an overhead projector, a slide projector, a videocamera, and a VCR, but you need to reserve these if he wants to use them. Will he bring his own laptop computer, or does he want you to provide the computer?

Write to Professor Barreau. You don't have to persuade him to come since he's already informally agreed, but you do want him to look forward to the job and to do his best work.

Hints:

- Choose an organization you know something about.
- What audiences do people speak to? How formal are these talks? What are their purpose(s)?
- Is this session designed to hone the skills of people who are competent, or is it designed to help people who are very weak, perhaps even paralyzed by fright?
- What role do presentations play in the success of the organization and of individuals in it?
- Check the calendar to get the dates. If there's any ambiguity about what "the second week of next month" is, "call" Runata to check.

7–19   Lining up a Consultant to Help Workers Deal with Diversity _____

As Director of Education and Training you oversee all in-house training programs. Five weeks ago, Cameron Jones, Director of Human Resources, asked you to set up a training course on dealing more effectively with fellow workers of the opposite sex and from different cultural, racial, and ethnic backgrounds. After making some phone calls, you tracked down Roberta Lyons, a professor of Business Communication at a nearby college.

"Yes, I'd be willing to do a session for you," she told you on the phone. "I would want two days with the participants—three would be better. They need time to practice the skills they'll be learning. And they should read the first 60 pages of my book, *Difference as a Source of Strength*. I'm free Mondays and Tuesdays; I might be able to free up a Wednesday if I had enough notice. I'm willing to work with a group of up to 30 people. Tell me what kinds of groups they work in, what they already know, and what kinds of things you want me to emphasize. My fee is $2,400 a day. Of course, you'd reimburse me for expenses."

You told her you thought a two-day session would be feasible, but you'd have to get back to her after you got budget approval. You wrote a quick memo to Cameron explaining the situation and asking about what the session should cover.

Two weeks ago, you received this memo from him.

I've asked the Veep for budget approval for $4,800 for a two-day session plus no more than $750 for all expenses. I don't think there will be a problem.

You know that many of the women and minorities in our office are at lower levels. We're doing a good job of hiring a diverse work force, but we may not do an adequate job mentoring people. Some people claim that we have miscommunication between men and women, between blacks and whites, and between recent immigrants and people whose families have been here for a hundred years. All the predictions call for an even more diverse workforce in the coming years.

We do not need someone to preach at us. We know we need to be egalitarian—people here are not consciously prejudiced. But we need to realize that what we say and do could be misinterpreted by people from different backgrounds.

Don't get some ivory tower theorist. We need practical exercises that can help us practice skills that we can put into effect immediately.

Attached is a list of 28 people who are free Monday and Tuesday of the second week of next month. We've got a good mix of people from different levels and different departments. If the session goes well, I may want you to schedule additional sessions.

Today, you got approval from the Vice President to schedule the session and pay Professor Lyons the fee and reimburse her for expenses to a maximum of $750. She will have to keep all receipts and turn in an itemized list of expenses to be reimbursed; you cannot reimburse her if she does not have receipts.

You also need to explain the mechanics of the session. You always have the sessions at a downtown hotel; you've tentatively reserved the Lakota Room, which can be divided into smaller rooms for small group exercises. It has a screen and overhead projector; if she wants anything else, you can provide it but you'll need to know what she needs. You can't get the book to participants in time unless she gives you a phone number to call to order 28 copies quickly.

Write to Professor Lyons. You don't have to persuade her to come since she's already informally agreed, but you do want her to look forward to the job and to do her best work.

Hints:
- Choose an organization you know something about.
- What different racial, ethnic, and cultural groups do its employees come from?

- Does the organization have a long record of helping employees communicate and cooperate with each other, or will Professor Lyons have to overcome a good deal of resistance?
- Why is it especially important for people in this organization to communicate well with each other? Why is it important that both sexes and all groups be given an equal opportunity to excel?
- Check the calendar to get the dates. If there's any ambiguity about what "the second week of next month" is, "call" Cameron to check.

7–20   Answering an International Inquiry

Your business, government, or nonprofit organization has received the following inquiries from international correspondents. (You choose the country the inquiry is from.)

1. Please tell us about a new product, service, or trend so that we can decide whether we want to buy, license, or imitate it in our country.
2. We have heard about a problem [technical, social, political, or ethical] that occurred in your organization. Could you please tell us what really happened and estimate how it is likely to affect the long-term success of the organization?
3. Please tell us about college programs in this field. We are interested in sending some of our managers to your country to complete a college degree.
4. We are considering setting up a plant in your city. We have already received adequate business information. However, we would also like to know how comfortable our nationals will feel. Do people in your city speak our language? How many? What opportunities exist for our nationals to improve their English? Does your town already have people from a wide mix of nations? Which are the largest groups?
5. Our organization would like to subscribe to an English-language trade journal. Which one would you recommend? Why? How much does it cost? How can we order it?

As Your Instructor Directs,
a. Answer one or more of the inquiries. Assume that your reader either reads English or can have your message translated.
b. Write a memo to your instructor explaining how you've adapted the message for your audience.

Hints:
- Even though you can write in English, English may not be your reader's native language. Write a letter that can be translated easily.
- In some cases, you may need to spell out background information that might not be clear to someone from another country.

7–21   Responding to a Customer Complaint

As a customer service representative for Gerber Products, you've been asked to write a form letter that can be sent to parents who write asking that sugar and starch be taken out of baby foods. You've already removed sugar and starch from 42 kinds of baby foods; when the change is complete, 121 of your 190 products will be free of added starch and sugar.

Gerber is working to make sure that the new formulations still taste good. For example, your researchers learned that hand-peeling bananas and removing the bitter strings on the fruit makes a sweeter mash that babies like even without added sugar.

Write a form letter. Assume that your computer program will put in the reader's name and inside address and print each letter individually.

Source: Based on "Gerber Bows to Moms' Pleas," *Business Week,* July 8, 1996, 42.

7–22   Announcing a Premium Holiday

Rather than paying fees to an insurer, your company is self-insured. That is, you set aside corporate funds to pay for medical bills. If claims are light, the company saves money.

Employees pay a monthly fee for part of the amount of their health insurance. However, with one month to go in the fiscal year, you have more than enough set aside to cover possible costs. You're going to pass along some of the savings to employees (who, by staying healthy, have kept medical costs down). Next month will be a "premium holiday." You will not deduct the monthly premium from employees' checks. As a result, they will have a slightly higher take-home pay next month. The holiday is just for one month; after it, the premium for health insurance will again be deducted each month.

Write a memo to all employees.

7–23   Announcing a Center for Sick Children

Your company has subsidized an on-site day-care center for children from infants to age six for several years. However, until now, this center, like most day care centers, has not accepted sick children. A national survey showed that 82% of working parents said they missed days at work, were late, left early, or used work time to deal with child care problems.

So that parents don't have to stay home when their children are sick, your company-subsidized day care center will open a "Sniffles and Snuggles" room for mildly sick children 12 and under. A student nurse or pediatrician will staff the room. The program will begin on the 15th of next month. Any worker can use the service, even if the child is not enrolled in the day care center. Sick children will stay in bed, watch videos, or play quiet games. No more than six sick children will be accepted on any one day.

Parents whose children already attend the center will pay no additional fee if the child is ill. Parents whose children do not attend the center must preregister to use this service and pay $20 a day (the fee includes meals and snacks).

On days when there are no sick children, the sickroom care givers will work with children in the regular day care program.

Write a memo to all employees, announcing the change.

Hints:
- What proportion of your employees have small children? How can you make people without small children see this as a good use of company funds?
- Why do people need to be at their desks, even if a child is ill?

7–24   Sending Tapes to a Customer

Two months ago, your business school sponsored a colloquium with many local and out-of-town business people. A highlight of the colloquium were small group discussions. The discussions were taped, and people could order tapes and transcripts.

Some of the tapes turned out well: "Ethics in Small Business," "How the Internet Is Changing Business," and "When Your Business Partner Is Your Spouse." But the audio tapes of "Valuing Diversity" and "Small Businesses Can Be Exporters Too" didn't turn out well. You haven't been able to transcribe them, and the quality isn't good enough to distribute.

Write to Paul Cambiaso. You're enclosing the tape on the Internet that he ordered. But he also ordered the tape on diversity. Since it isn't available, you're sending him a check of $12.62 to reimburse him. He's one of several people you have to write. He has a local address, but you don't know him.

7–25   Summarizing *The Wall Street Journal*

Today, your in-basket contains this message from your boss:

As you know, I'm leaving tomorrow for a vacation in Egypt. While I'm gone, will you please scan *The Wall Street Journal* every day and summarize any articles that are relevant to our business? I'd like your summary in hard copy on my desk when I return.

As Your Instructor Directs,

  a. Scan *The Wall Street Journal* for one week, two weeks, or until you find 3–5 relevant articles for the company you have chosen.

  b. Summarize the articles in a memo.

  c. Compare summaries with a small group of students. Do summaries of the same article for different organizations focus on different points?

  d. Present one of your summaries to the class.

Hints:

- Pick an organization you know something about. If the organization is large, focus on one division or department.
- Provide an overview to let your boss know whether the articles you've summarized are on a single topic or on several topics.
- Show how each article relates to the organization.
- Give the full citation (see Chapter 14) so that it's easy to track down articles if the boss wants to see the original.

Negative Messages

Chapter Outline

An Inside Perspective:
Negative Messages

Karl P. Keller, Vice President
First Chicago NBD Investment Services, Inc.

In his 14 years in the investments industry, Karl Keller has written more negative messages than he can count. First Chicago NBD Investment Services is part of the First Chicago NBD bank, which has more than 700 bank branches in Michigan, Illinois, and Indiana.

Negative messages can be tricky. First consider your audience. Are you writing to customers? fellow employees? vendors? You might be more direct to vendors and employees, while you might want to "soften" a negative message to customers. The degree of directness also depends on your purposes. Are you disclosing something negative and that's it? Are you informing people of a goof you made and correcting it or offering some restitution? Categorize your message in this way, and you'll get some ideas on how to handle it.

I only use buffers when they mean something. Let's face it, most people see right through buffers. The real reason to use one is to save face, to be nice, or for other cultural reasons—important, but issues of style, not substance. Of course, you need to be polite and civil in your correspondence and in life in general. But ask whether your buffer or positive idea is real and credible. Is it really connected to what you're talking about? If not, don't bother.

I'm a firm believer in giving the real reason for doing something, unless the reason is too technical or creates liabilities for the business. Sometimes it's enough to give the facts and let the reader draw the conclusions. For example, when we merged the retail investments operations of First Chicago NBD in 1996, our 40,000 investors received only three money market choices from the bank's own family of funds, instead of the dozen choices from other fund providers they had before. We made the change for two reasons: first, we wanted to build assets in our own products, and second, it wasn't cost effective to support all the other alternatives. A sound business decision for us, but the customer gave up choice and, even more important, some yield with our products. We explained the reasons in the letter and talked about some of the positive changes in products and services the new platform would provide. But we chose to simply use a chart to show yield differential and let customers draw the obvious conclusion. A handful were upset and left. Most stayed.

If disclosure creates potential liabilities, or is too complex, or will create a firestorm of negative reaction, you've got to think hard. Fortunately, only the rare negative message falls into those categories. Most negative events are temporary, and very few, if any, mean a meltdown of your business or your career. Most customers and employees know you have a business to run and that you need to make and implement business decisions.

Karl P. Keller, April 8, 1997

Visit First Chicago NBD's Web site: http://www.fcnbd.com

"[G]ive the real reason for doing something, unless the reason is too technical or creates liabilities."

Karl P. Keller, First Chicago NBD Investment Services

In a **negative message,** the basic information we have to convey is negative; we expect the reader to be disappointed or angry.

Negative messages include rejections and refusals, announcements of policy changes that do not benefit customers or consumers, requests the reader will see as insulting or intrusive, negative performance appraisals, disciplinary notices, and product recalls or notices of defects.

A negative message always has several purposes:

Primary Purposes:

To give the reader the bad news.
To have the reader read, understand, and accept the message.
To maintain as much goodwill as possible.

Secondary Purposes:

To build a good image of the writer.
To build a good image of the writer's organization.
To reduce or eliminate future correspondence on the same subject so the message doesn't create more work for the writer.

In many negative situations, the writer and reader will continue to deal with each other. Even when further interaction is unlikely (for example, when a company rejects a job applicant or refuses to renew a customer's insurance), the firm wants anything the reader may say about the company to be positive or neutral rather than negative.

Some messages that at first appear to be negative can be structured to create a positive feeling. Even when it is not possible to make the reader happy with the news we must convey, we still want readers to feel that

- They have been taken seriously.
- Our decision is fair and reasonable.
- If they were in our shoes, they would make the same decision.

ORGANIZING NEGATIVE LETTERS

The following pattern for negative messages helps writers maintain goodwill:

1. **When you have a reason that readers will understand and accept, give the reason before the refusal.** A good reason prepares the reader to expect the refusal. Research shows that readers who described themselves as "totally surprised" had much more negative feelings and described their feelings as being stronger than did those who expected the refusal.[1]
2. **Give the negative information or refusal just once, clearly.** Inconspicuous refusals can be missed, making it necessary to say *no* a second time.
3. **Present an alternative or compromise, if one is available.** An alternative not only gives readers another way to get what they want but also suggests that you care about readers and helping them meet their needs.
4. **End with a positive, forward-looking statement.**

Figures 8.1 illustrates how that the basic pattern for negative messages can be used.

A Negative Letter   **Figure 8.1**

Insurance Company

3373 Forbes Avenue
Rosemont, PA 19010
(215) 572-0100

Negative information highlighted so reader won't ignore message

**Liability Coverage
Is Being Discontinued—
Here's How to Replace It!**

Negative Alternative

Dear Policyholder:

Negative

When your auto insurance is renewed, it will no longer include liability coverage unless you select the new Assurance Plan. Here's why.

Positive information underlined for emphasis

Liability coverage is being discontinued. It, and the part of the premium which paid for it, will be dropped from all policies when they are renewed.

This could leave a gap in your protection. But you can replace the old Liability Coverage with Vickers' new Assurance Plan.

Alternative

With the new Assurance Plan, you receive benefits for litigation or awards arising from an accident--regardless of who's at fault. The cost for the Assurance Plan at any level is based on the ages of drivers, where you live, your driving record, and other factors. If these change before your policy is renewed, the cost of your Assurance Plan may also change. The actual cost will be listed in your renewal statement.

No reason is given. The change probably benefits the company rather than the reader, so it is omitted.

To sign up for the Assurance Plan, just check the level of coverage you want on the enclosed form and return it in the postage-paid envelope within 14 days. You'll be assured of the coverage you select.

Forward-looking ending emphasizes reader's choice

Sincerely,

C. J. Morgan

C. J. Morgan
President

Alternative

P.S. The Assurance Plan protects you against possible legal costs arising from an accident. Sign up for the Plan today and receive full coverage from Vickers.

Organizing Negative Memos

The best way to organize a negative memo depends on whether you're writing to a superior or to a peer or subordinate and on the severity of the negative information.

Giving Bad News to Superiors

Your superior expects you to solve minor problems by yourself. But sometimes, solving a problem requires more authority or resources than you have. When you give bad news to a superior, also recommend a way to deal with the problem. Turn the negative message into a persuasive one.

1. **Describe the problem.** Tell what's wrong, clearly and unemotionally.
2. **Tell how it happened.** Provide the background. What underlying factors led to this specific problem?
3. **Describe the options for fixing it.** If one option is clearly best, you may need to discuss only one. But if the reader will think of other options, or if different people will judge the options differently, describe all the options, giving their advantages and disadvantages.
4. **Recommend a solution and ask for action.** Ask for approval so that you can go ahead to make the necessary changes to fix the problem.

Giving Bad News to Peers and Subordinates

When you must pass along serious bad news to peers and subordinates, use a variation of the pattern to superiors:

1. **Describe the problem.** Tell what's wrong, clearly and unemotionally.
2. **Present an alternative or compromise, if one is available.** An alternative not only gives readers another way to get what they want but also suggests that you care about readers and helping them meet their needs.
3. **If possible, ask for input or action.** People in the audience may be able to suggest solutions. And workers who help make a decision are far more likely to accept the consequences.

No serious negative (such as being downsized or laid off) should come as a complete surprise. Managers can prepare for possible negatives by giving full information as it becomes available. It is also possible to let the people who will be affected by a decision participate in setting the criteria. Someone who has bought into the criteria for awarding cash for suggestions or retaining workers is more likely to accept decisions using such criteria. And in some cases, the synergism of groups may make possible ideas that management didn't think of or rejected as "unacceptable." Some workplaces, for example, might decide to reduce everyone's pay slightly rather than laying off some individuals. To avoid firing workers, Scherer Brothers Lumber in Minneapolis, Minnesota, saved money by temporarily cutting top officers' pay 25%, eliminating fresh flowers on receptionists' desks, and no longer buying professional sports tickets.

When the bad news is less serious, as in Figure 8.2, use the pattern for negative letters unless your knowledge of the reader(s) suggests that another pattern will be more effective. For example, in some organizations each person takes the Myers-Briggs Personality Inventory and puts a sign up indicating his or her "type." In such an organization, someone sending a negative message to a "feeling type" might want to delay the negative by

The Necessary Negative

His five Seattle restaurants were losing money. If he closed his newest restaurant—his biggest money-loser—he'd have to repay immediately the $1 million he'd borrowed to open it. So he decided to eliminate the central office and give individual managers 100% power and responsibility: 100% PAR.

He announced the new program—and the layoffs—on what he called "Just-Do-It-Day." He prepared packets for managers, employees, suppliers, bankers, and the press explaining the restructuring, the new reward structure, and new menus and promotional plans. He drove to every restaurant to explain the plan and left copies for employees. He mailed packets to suppliers, bankers, and the press. And he met with 17 people to tell them that they were losing their jobs.

In each conversation, the owner explained his thinking and offered severance pay. Telling them wasn't easy. But it saved the company. And today, all five restaurants are profitable. The former money-loser—Sharps Fresh Roasting restaurant—is now doing so well that it has been franchised.

Based on Timothy W. Firnstahl, "The Center-Cut Solution," *Harvard Business Review,* May–June 1993, 62–71.

A Negative Memo   **Figure 8.2**

Memo

**Board of County Commissioners
Olentangy County, Nebraska**

Date: January 9, 1997

To: All Employees

From: Floyd E. Loer, Dorothy A. Walters, and Stewart Mattson

Subject: Accounting for Work Missed Due to Bad Weather

Reason

As you know, Olentangy County Services are always open for our customers, whatever the weather. Employees who missed work during the snowstorm last week may count the absence as vacation, sick day(s), or personal day(s).

Refusal, stated as positively as possible

Hourly workers who missed less than a day have the option of taking the missed time as vacation, sick, or personal hours or of being paid only for the hours they worked.

One small positive

Approval of vacation or personal days will be automatic; the normal requirement of giving at least 24 hours' notice is waived.

Goodwill ending

Thanks for all the efforts you have made to continue giving our customers the best possible service during one of the snowiest winters on record.

---

using a buffer (a neutral or positive sentence) even though the organization's discourse community (✖ p. 61) as a whole favored directness.

For memos, the context of communication is crucial. The reader's reaction is influenced by the following factors:

- Do you and the reader have a good relationship?
- Does the organization treat people well?
- Have readers been warned of possible negatives?
- Have readers "bought into" the criteria for the decision?
- Do communications after the negative build goodwill?

THE PARTS OF A NEGATIVE MESSAGE

This section provides more information about wording each part of a negative message.

Subject Lines

When you write to superiors, use a subject line (➤ p. 148) that focuses on solving the problem.

> Subject: Improving Our Subscription Letter

When you write to peers and subordinates, put the topic (but not your action on it) in the subject line.

> Subject: Status of Conversion Table Program
> Due to heavy demands on our time, we have not yet been able to write programs for the conversion tables you asked for.

Use a negative subject line in e-mail messages.

> Subject: Delay in Converting Tables

Use a negative subject line in letters when you think readers may ignore what they think is a routine message.

Buffers

Traditionally, textbooks recommended that negative messages open with buffers. A **buffer** is a neutral or positive statement that allows you to delay the negative. Since recent research suggests that buffers do not make readers respond more positively, and since good buffers are very hard to write, the standard patterns for negative messages no longer include them for every message. However, in special situations, you may want to use a buffer.

To be effective, a buffer must put the reader in a good frame of mind, not give the bad news but not imply a positive answer either, and provide a natural transition to the body of the letter. The kinds of statements most often used as buffers are good news, facts and chronologies of events, references to enclosures, thanks, and statements of principle.

1. **Start with any good news or positive elements the letter contains.**

> Starting Thursday, June 26, you'll have access to your money 24 hours a day at First National Bank.

Letter announcing that the drive-up windows will be closed for two days while automatic teller machines are installed

2. **State a fact or provide a chronology of events.**

> As a result of the new graduated dues schedule—determined by vote of the Delegate Assembly last December and subsequently endorsed by the Executive Council—members are now asked to establish their own dues rate and to calculate the total amount of their remittance.

Announcement of a new dues structure that will raise most members' dues

3. **Refer to enclosures in the letter.**

> Enclosed is a new sticker for your car. You may pick up additional ones in the office if needed. Please *destroy* old stickers bearing the signature of "L.S. LaVoie."

Letter announcing increase in parking rental rates

Never Say *No*

In some cultures, it's rude to say *no.*

Japanese prefer to avoid direct confrontations. Changing the subject—even to something irrelevant—apologies, and silence are ways to avoid saying *no.*

When Japanese businessmen write rejection letters, they begin with buffers and offer reasons, apologies, and appreciation.

To avoid saying *no,* Czechs and Slovaks may say "We will see."

In Hungary, it is considered impolite to say *no* directly to a social equal or superior. Someone who doesn't want to do something may give a series of excuses, until the other person realizes that he or she should stop asking.

Based on Shoji Azuma, "Rejection Strategy in Business Japanese," Association for Business Communication Annual Meeting, Orlando, FL, November 1–4, 1995; Yale Richmond, *From Da to Yes: Understanding the East Europeans* (Yarmouth, ME: Intercultural Press, 1995), 89, 110.

4. **Thank the reader for something he or she has done.**

> Thank you for scheduling appointments for me with so many senior people at First National Bank. My visit there March 14 was very informative.

Letter refusing a job offer

5. **State a general principle.**

> Good drivers should pay substantially less for their auto insurance. The Good Driver Plan was created to reward good drivers (those with 5-year accident-free records) with our lowest available rates. A change in the plan, effective January 1, will help keep those rates low.

Letter announcing that the company will now count traffic tickets, not just accidents, in calculating insurance rates—a change that will raise many people's premiums

Use a buffer only when the reader (individually or culturally) values harmony or when the buffer serves another purpose. For example, when you must thank the reader somewhere in the letter, putting the "thank you" in the first paragraph allows you to start on a positive note.

Buffers are hard to write. Even if you think the reader would prefer to be let down easily, use a buffer only when you can write a good one.

Reasons

Make the reason for the refusal clear and convincing. The following reason is inadequate.

Weak reason: The goal of the Knoxville CHARGE-ALL Center is to provide our customers faster, more personalized service. Since you now live outside the Knoxville CHARGE-ALL service area, we can no longer offer you the advantages of a local CHARGE-ALL Center.

If the reader says, "I don't care if my bills are slow and impersonal," will the company let the reader keep the card? No. The real reason for the negative is that the bank's franchise allows it to have cardholders only in a given geographical region.

Real reason: Each local CHARGE-ALL center is permitted to offer accounts to customers in a several-state area. The Knoxville CHARGE-ALL center serves customers east of the Mississippi. You can continue to use your current card until it expires. When that happens, you'll need to open an account with a CHARGE-ALL center that serves Texas.

Don't hide behind "company policy": readers will assume the policy is designed to benefit you at their expense. If possible, show how readers benefit from the policy. If they do not benefit, don't mention policy at all.

Weak reason: I cannot write an insurance policy for you because company policy does not allow me to do so.

Better reason: Gorham insures cars only when they are normally garaged at night. Standard insurance policies cover a wider variety of risks and charge higher fees. Limiting the policies we write gives Gorham customers the lowest possible rates for auto insurance.

Avoid saying that you *cannot* do something. Most negative messages exist because the writer or company has chosen certain policies or cutoff points. In the example above, the company could choose to insure a wider variety of customers if it wanted to do so.

A Profitable Alternative

Long before Christmas, all of Mattel's holiday-themed Barbie dolls had been sold. But there wasn't time to manufacture more dolls and get them on the shelves.

So Mattel prepared an alternative. It rushed substitute packages to toy stores. Each package contained a framable Barbie poster and an IOU for the holiday doll as soon as it became available.

The alternative meant presents under the tree for Barbie fans—and an additional 300,000 units sold for Mattel.

Based on "Barbie: Diana Troup," *Advertising Age,* June 24, 1996, S32.

Often you as a middle manager will enforce policies that you did not design and announce decisions that you did not make. Don't pass the buck by saying, "This was a terrible decision." In the first place, carelessly criticizing your superiors is never a good idea. In the second place, if you really think a policy is bad, try to persuade your superiors to change it. If you can't think of convincing reasons to change the policy, maybe it isn't so bad after all.

If you have several reasons for saying *no,* use only those that are strong and watertight. If you give five reasons and readers dismiss two of them, readers may feel that they've won and should get the request.

Weak reason:	You cannot store large bulky items in the dormitory over the summer because moving them into and out of storage would tie up the stairs and the elevators just at the busiest times when people are moving in and out.
Way to dismiss the reason:	We'll move large items before or after the two days when most people are moving in or out.

If you do not have a good reason, omit the reason rather than use a weak one. Even if you have a strong reason, omit it if it makes the company look bad.

Reason that hurts company:	Our company is not hiring at the present time because profits are down. In fact, the downturn has prompted top management to reduce the salaried staff by 5% just this month, with perhaps more reductions to come.
Better:	Our company does not have any openings now.

Refusals

Deemphasize the refusal by putting it in the same paragraph as the reason, rather than in a paragraph by itself.

Sometimes you may be able to imply the refusal rather than stating it directly.

Direct refusal:	You cannot get insurance for just one month.
Implied refusal:	The shortest term for an insurance policy is six months.

Be sure the implication is crystal clear. Any message can be misunderstood, but an optimistic or desperate reader is particularly unlikely to understand a negative message. One of your purposes in a negative message is to close the door on the subject. You do not want to have to write a second letter saying that the real answer is *no.*

Alternatives

Giving the reader an alternative or a compromise, if one is available, is a good idea for several reasons:

- It offers the reader another way to get what he or she wants.
- It suggests that you really care about the reader and about helping to meet his or her needs.
- It enables the reader to reestablish the psychological freedom you limited when you said *no.*
- It allows you to end on a positive note and to present yourself and your organization as positive, friendly, and helpful.

When you give an alternative, give readers all the information they need to act on it, but don't take the necessary steps. Let readers decide whether to try the alternative.

Negative messages limit the reader's freedom. People may respond to a limitation of freedom by asserting their freedom in some other arena. Jack W. Brehm calls this phenomenon **psychological reactance.**[4] Psychological reactance is at work when a customer who has been denied credit no longer buys even on a cash basis or a subordinate who has been passed over for a promotion gets back at the company by deliberately doing a poor job.

An alternative allows the reader to react in a way that doesn't hurt you. By letting readers decide for themselves whether they want the alternative, you allow them to reestablish their sense of psychological freedom.

The specific alternative will vary depending on the circumstances. In Figure 8.3, the company is unwilling to quote a price on an item on which it cannot be competitive. In different circumstances, the writer might offer different alternatives.

Endings

If you have a good alternative, refer to it in your ending: "Let me know if you can use A515 grade 70."

The best endings look to the future.

> Wherever you have your account, you'll continue to get all the service you've learned to expect from CHARGE-ALL, and the convenience of charging items at over a million stores, restaurants, and hotels in the U.S. and abroad—and in Knoxville, too, whenever you come back to visit!

Letter refusing to continue charge account for a customer who has moved

Avoid endings that seem insincere.

> We are happy to have been of service, and should we be able to assist you in the future, please contact us.

This ending lacks you-attitude and would not be good even in a positive message. In a situation where the company has just refused to help, it's likely to sound sarcastic or sadistic.

Tone in Negative Messages

Tone—the implied attitude of the author toward the reader and the subject—is particularly important when you want readers to feel that you have taken their requests seriously. Check your draft carefully for positive emphasis (⬌ p. 39) and you-attitude (⬌ p. 34), both at the level of individual words and at the level of ideas.

Figure 8.4 lists some of the phrases to avoid in negative messages.

Even the physical appearance and timing of a letter can convey tone. An obvious form rejection letter suggests that the writer has not given much consideration to the reader's application. An immediate negative suggests that the rejection didn't need any thought. A negative delivered just before a major holiday seems especially unfeeling. AT&T was widely criticized for telling a man that he had been fired when he arrived at work with his daughter on "Take Your Daughter to Work" Day. AT&T later found another job for him, but the cost to the company's image was high.

Workplace Violence

An increasing number of people respond violently to bad news.

The American Management Association found that nearly a quarter of the companies it surveyed reported that an employee had been killed or attacked. A union steward was killed by an employee who was suspended for refusing a drug test. Eight lawyers were killed by former clients who felt they'd been given bad advice. In several incidents, Postal Service employees who were fired killed co-workers. An employee critically wounded a co-worker at a small California market-research company.

Better negative messages and programs in violence prevention can redirect this psychological reactance into less lethal channels.

Based on "Companies See More Workplace Violence," *The Wall Street Journal*, April 12, 1994, B1; "Waging War in the Workplace," *Newsweek*, July 19, 1993, 30; "It's Murder in the Workplace," *Fortune*, August 9, 1993, 12; and "Preventing On-the-Job Violence," *Inc.*, June 1996, 116.

Figure 8.3   **A Refusal with an Alternative**

ROYSNER
Steel Fabrication
"Serving the needs of America since 1890"

April 27, 1998

Mr. H. J. Moody
Canton Corporation
2407 North Avenue
Kearney, NE 68847

Subject: Bid Number 5853, Part Number D-40040

Dear Mr. Moody:

Buffer Thank you for requesting our quotation on your Part No. D-40040.

Your blueprints call for flame-cut rings 1/2" thick A516 grade 70. To use that grade, we'd have to grind down from 1" thick material. However, if you can use A515 grade 70, which we stock in 1/2" thick, you can cut the price by more than half.

Quantity	Description	Gross Weight	Price/Each
75	Rings Drawing D-40040, A516 Grade 70 1" thick x 6" O.D. x 2.8" I.D. ground to .5" thick.	12 lbs.	$15.08
75	Rings Drawing D-40040, A515 Grade 70 1/2" thick x 6" O.D. x 2.8" I.D.	6 lbs.	$6.91

Alternative (Depending on circumstances, different alternatives may exist.)

If you can use A515 grade 70, let me know.

Leaves decision up to reader to re-establish psychological freedom

Sincerely,

Valerie Prynne

Valerie Prynne

VP:wc

1800 Olney Avenue • Philadelphia, PA 19140 • 215•555•7800 • Fax: 215•555•9803

Phrase	Because
I am afraid that we cannot	You aren't fearful. Don't hide behind empty phrases.
I am sorry that we are unable	You probably are *able* to grant the request; you simply choose not to. If you are so sorry about saying *no,* why don't you change your policy and say *yes?*
I am sure you will agree that	Don't assume that you can read the reader's mind.
Unfortunately	*Unfortunately* is negative in itself. It also signals that a refusal is coming.

Figure 8.4

Avoid These Phrases in Negative Messages

ALTERNATE STRATEGIES FOR NEGATIVE SITUATIONS

Whenever you face a negative situation, consider recasting it as a positive or persuasive message.

Recasting the Situation as a Positive Message

If the negative information will directly lead to a benefit that you know readers want, use the pattern of organization for informative and positive messages:

Situation:	You're raising parking rates to pay for lot maintenance, ice and snow removal, and signs so renters can have cars towed away that park in their spots—all services renters have asked for.
Negative:	Effective May 1, parking rentals will go up $5 a month.
Positive emphasis:	Effective May 1, if someone parks in your spot, you can have the car towed away. Signs are being put up announcing that all spaces in the lot are rented. Lot maintenance is also being improved. The lot will be resurfaced this summer, and arrangements have been made for ice and snow removal next winter.

Recasting the Situation as a Persuasive Message

Often a negative situation can be recast as a persuasive message. If your organization has a problem, ask readers to help solve it. A solution that workers have created will be much easier to implement.

When The Association for Business Communication's Board of Directors voted to raise dues, the Executive Director wrote a persuasive letter urging members to send in renewals early so they could beat the increase. The letter shared some of the qualities of any persuasive letter: an attention-getting opener, offsetting the negative by setting it against the benefits of membership, telling the reader what to do, and ending with a picture of the benefit the reader received by acting. (Yes, the letter worked.)

If you are criticizing someone, your real purpose may be to persuade the reader to act differently.[5] Chapter 9 offers patterns for direct requests and problem-solving persuasive messages.

Humor in Negative Messages

Humor can defuse negative messages. In Figure 8.5, a university library uses language to make its rule against food in the library friendly instead of fierce.

Office Politics May Dictate an Alternate Strategy

Several years ago, when I was running a department in a large corporation, I believed I wasn't receiving the cooperation I needed from our company's publicity department. I wrote the company president a memo, complaining about the publicity department's lassitude.

To my astonishment, several days later I received a call from Al, the head of the publicity department, who said that *he* had been given my memo, and that he felt his department *was* doing a competent job, thank you.

. . . Where had I gone wrong? Well, first I didn't calculate that my charming boss might show the memo to Al . . . I was blunt about my feelings toward Al's department . . . The result: I lost a potential ally and made an enemy instead . . .

I would have been a more astute gameplayer, and won a gold star rather than a slap on the wrist, if I had appealed to Al in terms of *his* interests, suggesting how helping me would actually help him.

Quoted from Victoria Pelligrino, "Office Politics: Running a Clean Campaign," *The Working Woman's Success Book* (New York: Ace, 1981), 63–64.

We fell. We got up. End of apology.

Schwinn needed a new product line to attract sophisticated cyclists. This apology for its old, boring line moves quickly to a discussion of its new technology. By evoking an experience every cyclist has had, the headline also suggests that falling is a minor event.

Kathryn McGrath, head of the SEC division of investment management, needed to tell an investment firm that its ad was illegal. The ad showed an index finger pointing up and large bold letters saying that performance was "up," too. Tiny print at the bottom of the page admitted that performance figures hadn't been adjusted to include front-end sales charges. Rather than writing a heavy-handed letter, McGrath sent the firm a photocopy of a thumb pointing down. The ad never ran again.[6]

Humor works best when it's closely related to the specific situation and the message. Humor that seems tacked on is less likely to work. Never use humor that belittles readers.

WRITING NEGATIVE E-MAIL MESSAGES

Major negatives, like firing someone, should be delivered in person, not by e-mail. But e-mail is appropriate for many less serious negatives.

Never write e-mail messages when you're angry. If a message infuriates you, wait until you're calmer before you reply—and even then, reply only if you must. Flaming (p. 121) does not make you look like a mature, level-headed candidate for bigger things. And since employers have the right to read all e-mail, flaming—particularly if directed at co-workers, regulators, suppliers, or customers—may cause an employee to be fired.

Effective Humor in a Negative Message   **Figure 8.5**

PLEASE DO NOT EAT, feed, devour, gulp, dine, gourmandize, nibble, gnaw, drink, imbibe, quaff, sip, sup, tipple, smoke, chew, or spit IN THE LIBRARY!

© copyright Friends of the Libraries of The Ohio State University, 1986.

The best subject line for negative e-mail messages depends on whether you're refusing a request or initiating the negative. When you say "no" to an e-mail request, just hit "reply" and use "Re:" plus whatever the original subject line was for your response. When you write a new message, you will have to decide whether to use the negative in the subject line. The subject line should contain the negative when

- The negative is serious. Many people do not read all their e-mail messages. A neutral subject line may lead the reader to ignore the message.
- The reader needs the information to make a decision or act.
- You report your own errors (as opposed to the reader's).

Thus the following would be acceptable subject lines in e-mail messages:

Subject: We Lost McDonald's Account
Subject: Power to Be Out Sunday, March 8
Subject: Error in Survey Data Summary

When you write to people whom you know well, exaggerated subject lines are acceptable:

Subject: Gloom, Despair, and Agony

In other situations, a neutral subject line is acceptable.

Subject: Results of 360° Performance Appraisals

In the body of the e-mail message, give a reason only if it is watertight and reflects well on the organization. Give an alternative, if one exists. Remember that negative messages do not contain reader benefits.

Use a friendly, conversational tone. Keep the message short. Edit and proofread your message carefully. An easy way for an angry reader to strike back is to attack typos or other errors.

Remember that e-mail messages, like any documents, can become documents in lawsuits. When a negative e-mail is hard to write, you may want to compose it offline so that you can revise and even get feedback before you send the message.

VARIETIES OF NEGATIVE MESSAGES

Three of the most difficult kinds of negative messages to write are rejections and refusals, disciplinary notices and negative performance appraisals, and layoffs and firings.

Rejections and Refusals

When you refuse requests from people outside your organization, try to use a buffer. Give an alternative if one is available. For example, if you are denying credit, it may still be possible for the reader to put an expensive item on layaway.

Politeness and length help. Graduating seniors at a southwestern university preferred rejection letters that addressed them as *Mr./Ms.* rather than calling them by their first names, that said something specific about their good qualities, that phrased the refusal itself indirectly, and that were longer.[7] An experiment using a denial of additional insurance found that subjects preferred a rejection letter that was longer, more tactful, and more personal. The preferred letter started with a buffer, used a good reason for the refusal, and offered sales promotion in the last paragraph. The finding held both for English-speaking US subjects and for Spanish-speaking Mexican subjects.[8]

Double-check the words in the draft to be sure the reason can't backfire if it is applied to other contexts. As Elizabeth McCord has shown, the statement that a plant is "too noisy and dangerous" for a group tour could be used as evidence against the company in a worker's compensation claim.[9]

When you refuse requests within your organization, use your knowledge of the organization's culture and of the specific individual to craft your message. In some organizations, it may be appropriate to use company slogans, offer whatever help already-established departments can give, and refer to the individual's good work (if you indeed know that it is good). In other less personal organizations, a simple negative without embellishment may be more appropriate.

Disciplinary Notices and Negative Performance Appraisals

Performance appraisals are discussed in detail in Chapter 9. Performance appraisals will be positive when they are designed to help a basically good employee improve. But when an employee violates a company rule or fails to improve after repeated negative appraisals, the company may discipline the employee or build a dossier to support firing him or her.

Present disciplinary notices and negative performance appraisals directly, with no buffer. A buffer might encourage the recipient to minimize the message's importance—and might even become evidence in a court case that the employee had not been told to shape up "or else." Cite quantifiable observations of the employee's behavior, rather than generalizations or inferences based on it. If an employee is disciplined by being laid off without pay, specify when the employee is to return.

Layoffs and Firings

If a company is in financial trouble, management needs to communicate the problem clearly. Sharing information and enlisting everyone's help in finding solutions may make it possible to save jobs. Sharing information also means that layoff notices, if they become necessary, will be a formality; they should not be new information to employees.

Before you fire someone, double-check the facts. Give the employee the real reason for the firing. Offering a face-saving reason unrelated to poor performance can create legal liabilities. But avoid broadcasting the reason: to do so can leave the company liable to a defamation suit.[10]

Information about layoffs and firings is normally delivered orally but accompanied by a written statement explaining severance pay or unemployment benefits that may be available.

SOLVING A SAMPLE PROBLEM

Solving negative problems requires careful analysis. The checklist at the end of the chapter in Figure 8.8 can help you evaluate your draft.

Problem

You're Director of Employee Benefits for a Fortune 500 company. Today, you received the following memo:

Legal Layoffs

Federal law requires that companies with 100 or more workers give 60 days' notice before closing a plant or laying off two-thirds of the workers.

Employees cannot be fired on the basis of race, sex, or age. To withstand a lawsuit, a company needs to be able to show that a fired employee failed to meet objective, uniform standards for performance. A record of negative performance appraisals is essential to make the case.

Companies need to follow their own written guidelines. If they don't, employees may sue for wrongful discharge.

Based on Arthur S. Hayes, "Layoffs Take Careful Planning to Avoid Losing the Suits That Are Apt to Follow," *The Wall Street Journal*, November 2, 1990, B1.

From: Michelle Jagtiani   *MJ*
Subject: Getting My Retirement Benefits

Next Friday will be my last day here. I am leaving [name of company] to take a position at another firm.

Please process a check for my retirement benefits, including both the deductions from my salary and the company's contributions for the last six and a half years. I would like to receive the check by next Friday if possible.

You have bad news for Michelle. Although the company does contribute an amount to the retirement fund equal to the amount deducted for retirement from the employee's paycheck, employees who leave with less than 10 years of employment get only their own contributions. Michelle will get back only the money that has been deducted from her own pay, plus 4½% interest compounded quarterly. Her payments and interest come to just over $17,200; the amount could be higher depending on the amount of her last paycheck, which will include compensation for any unused vacation days and sick leave. Furthermore, since the amounts deducted were not considered taxable income, she will have to pay income tax on the money she will receive.

You cannot process the check until after her resignation is effective, so you will mail it to her. You have her home address on file; if she's moving, she needs to let you know where to send the check. Processing the check may take two to three weeks.

Write a memo to Michelle.

Analysis of the Problem

1. Who is (are) your audience(s)? What characteristics are relevant to this particular message? If you are writing to more than one reader, how do the readers differ?

    Michelle Jagtiani. Unless she's a personal friend, I probably wouldn't know why she's leaving and where she's going.

    There's a lot I don't know. She may or may not know much about taxes; she may or may not be able to take advantage of tax-reduction strategies. I can't assume the answers because I wouldn't have them in real life.

2. What are your purposes in writing?

    To tell her that she will get only her own contributions, plus 4½% interest compounded quarterly; that the check will be mailed to her home address two to three weeks after her last day on the job; and that the money will be taxable as income.

    To build goodwill so that she feels that she has been treated fairly and consistently. To minimize negative feelings she may have.

    To close the door on this subject.

3. What information must your message include?

    When the check will come. The facts that her check will be based on her contributions, not employer's, and that the money will be taxable income. How lump-sum retirement benefits are calculated. The fact that we have her current address on file but need a new address if she's moving.

4. How can you build support for your position? What reasons or reader benefits will your reader find convincing?

An Unacceptable Solution to the Sample Problem   **Figure 8.6**

April 20, 1998

To: Michelle Jagtiani

From   Lisa Niaz *LN*

Subject   Receiving Employee Contributions from Retirement Accounts

Give reason before refusal   You cannot receive a check the last day of work and you will get only your own contributions, not a matching sum from the company, because you have not worked for the company for at least ten years.

Better to be specific

This is lifted straight from the problem. The language in problems is often negative and stuffy; information is disorganized.   Your payments and interest come to just over $17,200; the amount could be higher depending on the amount of your last paycheck, which will include compensation for any unused vacation days and sick leave. Furthermore, since the amounts deducted were not considered taxable income, you will have to pay income tax on the money you receive.

The check will be sent to your home address. If the address we have on file is incorrect, please correct it so that your check is not delayed.   *— Negative —*

How will reader know what you have on file? Better to give current address as you have it.

Think about the situation and use your own words to create a satisfactory message.

Giving the amount currently in her account may make her feel that she is getting a significant sum of money. Suggesting someone who can give free tax advice (if the company offers this as a fringe benefit) reminds her of the benefits of working with the company. Wishing her luck with her new job is a nice touch.

5. What objection(s) can you expect your reader(s) to have? What negative elements of your message must you deemphasize or overcome?

She is getting about half the amount she expected, since she gets no matching funds. She might have been able to earn more than $4\frac{1}{2}\%$ interest if she had invested the money herself. Depending on her personal tax situation she may pay more tax on the money as a lump sum than would have been due had she paid it each year as she earned the money.

Discussion of the Sample Solutions

The solution in Figure 8.6 is not acceptable. The subject line gives a bald negative with no reason or alternative. The first sentence has a condescending tone that is particularly offensive in negative messages. The last sentence

Figure 8.7   **A Good Solution to the Sample Problem**

April 20, 1998

To: Michelle Jagtiani

From   Lisa Niaz *LN*

Subject   Receiving Employee Contributions from Retirement Accounts

Good to state reason in third-person to deemphasize negative.   Employees who leave the company with at least ten years of employment are entitled both to company contributions and the retirement benefit paycheck deductions contributed to retirement accounts. Those employees who leave the company with less than ten years of employment will receive the employee paycheck contributions made to their retirement accounts.

Good to be specific   You now have $17,240.62 in your account which includes 4.5% interest compounded quarterly. The amount you receive could be even higher since you will also receive payment for any unused leave and vacation days.

Good to show how company can help   Because you now have access to the account, the amount you receive will be considered income. Beth Jordan in Employee Financial Services can give you information about possible tax deductions and financial investments which can reduce your income taxes.

Good to be specific   The check will be sent to your home address on May 16. The address we have on file is 2724 Merriman Road, Akron, Ohio 44313. If your address changes, please let us know so you can receive your check promptly.

Positive

Good luck with your new job!

Forward-looking

---

focuses on what is being taken away rather than what remains. Paragraph 2 lacks you-attitude and is vague. The memo ends with a negative. There is nothing anywhere in the memo to build goodwill.

The solution in Figure 8.7, in contrast, is very good. The policy serves as a buffer and explanation. The negative is stated clearly but is buried in the paragraph to avoid overemphasizing it. The paragraph ends on a positive note by specifying the amount in the account and the fact that the sum might be even higher.

Paragraph 2 contains the additional negative information that the amount will be taxable but offers the alternative that it may be possible to reduce taxes. The writer builds goodwill by suggesting a specific person the reader could contact.

Paragraph 3 tells the reader what address is in the company files (Michelle may not know whether the files are up to date), asks that she update it if necessary, and ends with the reader's concern: getting her check promptly.

The final paragraph ends on a positive note. This generalized goodwill is appropriate when the writer does not know the reader well.

Figure 8.8

Checklist for Negative Messages

☐ Is the subject line appropriate?

☐ If a buffer is used, does it avoid suggesting either a positive or a negative response?

☐ Is the reason, if it is given, presented before the refusal? Is the reason watertight, with no loopholes?

☐ Is the negative information clear?

☐ Is an alternative given if a good one is available? Does the message provide all the information needed to act on the alternative but leave the choice up to the reader?

☐ Does the last paragraph avoid repeating the negative information?

☐ Is tone acceptable—not defensive, but not cold, preachy, or arrogant either?

And, for all messages, not just negative ones,

☐ Does the message use you-attitude and positive emphasis?

☐ Is the style easy to read and friendly?

☐ Is the visual design of the message inviting?

☐ Is the format correct?

☐ Does the message use standard grammar? Is it free from typos?

Originality in a negative message may come from

- An effective buffer, if one is appropriate.
- A clear, complete statement of the reason for the refusal.
- A good alternative, clearly presented, which shows that you're thinking about what the reader really needs.
- Adding details that show you're thinking about a specific organization and the specific people in that organization.

Summary of Key Points

- In a negative message, the basic information is negative; we expect the reader to be disappointed or angry.
- A good negative message conveys the negative information clearly while maintaining as much goodwill as possible. The goal is to make readers feel that they have been taken seriously, that the decision is fair and reasonable, and that they would have made the same decision. A secondary purpose is to reduce or eliminate future correspondence on the same subject so that the message doesn't create more work for the writer.
- Organize negative letters in this way:
  1. Give the reason for the refusal before the refusal itself when you have a reason that readers will understand and accept.
  2. Give the negative just once, clearly.
  3. Present an alternative or compromise, if one is available.
  4. End with a positive, forward-looking statement.
- Organize negative memos to superiors in this way.
  1. Describe the problem.
  2. Tell how it happened.
  3. Describe the options for fixing it.
  4. Recommend a solution and ask for action.
- When you must pass along serious bad news to peers and subordinates, use a variation of the pattern to superiors:
  1. Describe the problem.
  2. Present an alternative or compromise, if one is available.
  3. If possible, ask for input or action.

- When the bad news is less serious, use the pattern for negative letters unless your knowledge of the reader(s) suggests that another pattern will be more effective.
- A **buffer** is a neutral or positive statement that allows you to bury the negative message. Buffers must put the reader in a good frame of mind, not give the bad news but not imply a positive answer either, and provide a natural transition to the body of the letter. Use a buffer only when the reader values harmony or when the buffer serves a purpose in addition to simply delaying the negative.
- The kinds of statements most often used as buffers are (1) good news, (2) facts and chronologies of events, (3) references to enclosures, (4) thanks, and (5) statements of principle.
- A good reason must be watertight. Give several reasons only if all are watertight and are of comparable importance. Omit the reason for the refusal entirely if it is weak or if it makes your organization look bad.
- Make the refusal crystal clear.
- Giving the reader an alternative or a compromise
  - Offers the reader another way to get what he or she wants.
  - Suggests that you really care about the reader and about helping to meet his or her needs.
  - Enables the reader to reestablish the psychological freedom you limited when you said *no.*
  - Allows you to end on a positive note and to present yourself and your organization as positive, friendly, and helpful.
- People may respond to limits by striking out in some perhaps unacceptable way. This effort to reestablish freedom is called **psychological reactance.**
- When you give an alternative, give the reader all the information he or she needs to act on it, but don't take the necessary steps for the reader. Letting the reader decide whether to try the alternative allows the reader to reestablish a sense of psychological freedom.
- Many negative situations can be redefined to use the patterns of organization for informative and positive or for persuasive messages. Humor sometimes works to defuse negative situations.
- Use the analysis questions in Chapter 1 to solve negative problems.

Exercises and Problems For Chapter 8

GETTING STARTED

8–1 Choosing Organizational Patterns for Negative Messages
Which negative pattern would you use in each situation? Why?

1. Rejecting a worker's suggestion for saving money.
2. Telling a colleague who wanted to attend a workshop that it is full.
3. Telling employees that they cannot post personal Web pages on the company's Web site.
4. Telling your supervisor about a problem in your unit.
5. Informing customers that prices are going up.
6. Giving a subordinate a negative performance appraisal.
7. Turning down an internship that you've been offered.

8−2   Evaluating Buffers

Evaluate the following buffers. Are any good enough to use without change? Might any be acceptable with revision?

a. Refusing to grant credit:

1. Your request to have a Saks Fifth Avenue charge account shows that you are a discriminating shopper. Saks Fifth Avenue sells the finest merchandise available in the United States.

2. We have received your application for a Saks Fifth Avenue charge account.

3. In the current economic climate, all stores have to limit the credit they extend.

b. Refusing to use a software package developed by another state agency:

1. My staff and I have spent many long hours evaluating the software developed by the Department of Transportation to see if the software would be appropriate for our agency to use.

2. The Department of Transportation seems to think that no other state agency has computer personnel capable of developing effective programs. I am delighted to assure you that, whatever the dismal state of some agencies, our agency enjoys the talents of many capable people.

3. Thank you for giving me a chance to evaluate the payroll software developed by DOT.

c. Refusing to admit a rookie golfer to the roster of athletes for whom you negotiate commercials, endorsements, and speaking engagements:

1. It's been a great year for golf, with more people viewing tournaments than ever before.

2. I'm glad to hear that you're on the Pro Golf Tour this year. So many people play golf recreationally, but very few people possess the determination, talent, and love of the sport that you do to make golf a career.

3. Congratulations on winning the Boneyard Creek Country Club Pro-Am Tournament last month!

8−3   Evaluating Reasons for Refusals

Evaluate the following reasons for refusals.

a. Refusing to grant credit:

Your income is not high, and records indicate that you carry large balances on student loans. If you were given a Saks Fifth Avenue charge account, and if you charged a large amount on it, you might have difficulty paying the bill, particularly if you had other unforeseen expenses (car repair, moving, medical emergency) or if your income dropped suddenly. If you were unable to repay, with your other debt you would be in serious difficulty. We would not want you to be in such a situation, nor would you yourself desire it.

b. Refusing to use a software package developed by another state agency:

We already have a package which works well for us. We have already made the necessary changes in it and initialized it to fit our needs. If we used your package, we would have to repeat this initialization. The program we're currently using meets both our current needs and those projected for the next 3−5 years. Furthermore, it allows us to generate reports quickly which would be more difficult with the software developed for the Department of Transportation.

c. Refusing to admit a rookie golfer to the roster of athletes for whom you negotiate commercials, endorsements, and speaking engagements:

We are so busy representing well-known athletes that we are unable to accept any new clients for the next six months.

8−4   Revising a Negative Message

Rewrite and reorganize the following negative message to make it more positive. Eliminate any sentences that are not needed.

Dear Client:

A change is needed so that Travel Globe can continue to make a profit. Effective the first of next month, you'll need to pay the cost of overnight delivery if you want tickets sent to you overnight.

If your business has an account with Airborne, FedEx, or United Parcel Service, you may want to give us your account number so that deliveries can be billed directly to you. You'll write fewer checks and, depending on the volume of overnight mail you send, may even be able to get a discount.

Let us know whether you'd like to pay us for deliveries, be billed directly, come in to pick your tickets up, or just have them sent to you by first-class mail.

As you may know, airlines have reduced the commissions they pay travel agents on tickets. We can no longer afford the cost—over $300 a month—of sending your tickets by overnight delivery. As a result, each service must pay for itself. The alternative would be to charge a fee for each transaction, and that doesn't seem fair to customers who do pick up their tickets or for whom regular mail is fast enough.

Sincerely,

Chris Conrad

Chris Conrad, President
Travel Globe

E-MAIL MESSAGES

8–5   Refusing to Give More Information on Your Web Page

You maintain the Caples Web page, which provides information about award-winning direct mail campaigns. Today, you get this e-mail message:

Subject: Text of Letters

The text of the letters is too small to actually read. Even when I click on the pictures, the next picture isn't much bigger. Please provide pages that we can actually read.

You can't do it. You don't have the copyrights for the letters (most are held by the companies sponsoring the letters, though occasionally the ad agency retains the copyright). Some award-winners aren't willing for the text to be released because they don't want their successful strategies to be imitated by competitors. Asking the company or the advertising agency for a copy might work, depending on who was asking and how the letter would be used.

Write the message.

8–6   Refusing to Provide Graduates' Addresses on Your Web Page

You maintain the Web page for your college or community college department. Today, you get the following e-mail message:

Subject: Add Graduates' Names?

I really like your Web site. Could you please add the names and addresses (snail and e-mail) of recent graduates? That would help us keep in touch and would be really useful for networking.

You don't want to do this. Probably someone in the college or community college has this information, but you don't know who. You've got enough to do without tracking down the information, posting it on the Web, and updating it as people move. But you don't want to offend the person who asked, since recent graduates are asked to help in many ways (sponsor internships, give money, etc.). So you need to say *no* while maintaining goodwill.

Write the message.

8–7 Telling a Co-Worker that a Workshop Is Full

As Director of Human Resources, you sponsor a variety of workshops for employees. You received this e-mail message today:

Subject: Re: Oral Presentation Workshops

Please register me for the Workshop on giving oral presentations next week. My supervisor has told me I should attend this.

Unfortunately, the workshop is full, and you already have three people on a waiting list to fill vacancies if anyone should cancel. You would repeat the workshop only if you have guarantees for at least 15 participants.

Write the message.

8–8 Rejecting Employees' Suggestions

For years, businesses have had suggestion programs, rewarding employees for money-saving ideas. Now your city government has adopted such a program (see Problem 7–7). But not all of the suggestions are adopted. Today, you need to send messages to the following people. Since their suggestions are being rejected, they will not get any cash award.

1. Diane Hilgers, secretary, Mayor's office. Suggestion: Charge for 911 calls. Reason for rejection: "This would be a public relations disaster. People call because they've got emergencies. We already charge for ambulance or paramedic trips; to charge just for the call will offend people. And it might not save money. It's a lot cheaper to prevent a burglary or murder than to track down the person afterwards—to say nothing of the trauma of the loss or death. Bad idea."

2. Steve Rieneke, building and grounds supervisor. Suggestion: Fire the city's public relations specialists. Reason for rejection: "Positive attitudes toward city workers and policies make the public more willing to support public programs and taxes. In the long run, we think this is money well spent."

3. Jose Rivera, Accountant I. Suggestion: Schedule city council meetings during the day to save on light bills and staff overtime. Reason for rejection: "Having the meetings in the evening enables more citizens to attend. People have to be able to comment. Open meetings are essential so that citizens don't feel that policies and taxes are being railroaded through."

Write the messages.

8–9 Limiting the Software on Office Computers

Today, your e-mail includes this message from Ralph Jared, a newly hired employee:

Subject: Need Upgrade

I need an upgrade on WordPerfect. I called Kami Nygen because the keystrokes weren't working—only to discover that the version on my computer isn't the current software on which I've been trained but an earlier version. Kami told me that everybody here has the old version. I want a copy of the new version. According to reviews in *PC Magazine*, it has several useful features.

Company policy is to upgrade software only when the new version offers a major improvement. In the judgment of your company's computer experts, the newest version of WordPerfect doesn't offer enough additional features to warrant upgrading. And you won't upgrade just for one person. People sometimes need to share documents, and that's simpler when everyone uses the same version.

Write the message.

Ralph responds:

> Well, I really want the new version of WordPerfect. I have it on my computer at home, and it's a nuisance not to have it here, too. I'll bring in a copy from home.

Company policy prohibits employees' installing programs other than those officially approved (and purchased by the company). What Ralph is suggesting is almost certainly illegal. And you want to keep all programs the same so that documents can easily be shared.

Respond to Ralph's message.

8–10   Telling Clients That Hackers Have Entered Your System

Your company provides computer-network support to a variety of corporate clients. Yesterday, you realized that hackers had gotten into your computer site. From your system, the hackers got passwords for many of your biggest clients.

As soon as you discovered the damage, you took your system off the Internet to prevent further attacks. Then you contacted a "firewall" vendor, who installed hardware and software that allows you to limit the people who have access to various parts of your system. Now, your system is up again, and you need to tell your clients about the break-in. Each client should reinstall data from the last backup before the break-in. (Fortunately, you've always required your clients to do daily backups.) Your people will help restore damaged data—at no charge to the client. And passwords need to be changed immediately. Finally, clients will need to monitor their systems to see whether additional damage has occurred. Again, your people can provide the technical expertise to do this.

Write an e-mail message to your clients whose sites have been hacked into.

Based on "Case Study: On-Line Crime (Part II)," *Inc.*, June 1996, 123.

8–11   Telling Employees to Remove Personal Web Sites

You're Director of Management and Information Systems (MIS) in your organization. At your monthly briefing for management, a vice president complained that some employees have posted personal Web pages on the company's Web server.

"It looks really unprofessional to have stuff about cats and children and musical instruments. How can people do this?"

You took the question literally. "Well, some people have authorization to post material—price changes, job listings, marketing information. Someone who has authorization could put up anything."

Another manager said, "I don't think it's so terrible—after all, there aren't any links from our official pages to these personal pages."

A third person said, "But we're paying for what's posted—so we pay for server space and connect time. Maybe it's not much right now, but as more and more people become Web-literate, the number of people putting up unauthorized pages could spread. We should put a stop to this now."

The vice president agreed. "The Web site is carefully designed to present an image of our organization. Personal pages are dangerous. Can you imagine the flak we'd get if someone posted links to pornography?"

You said, "I don't think that's very likely. If it did happen, as system administrator, I could remove the page."

The third speaker said, "I think we should remove all the pages. Having any at all suggests that our people have so much extra time that they're playing on the Web. That suggests that our prices are too high and may make some people worry about quality. In fact, I think that we need a new policy prohibiting personal pages on the company's Web server. And any pages that are already up should be removed."

A majority of the managers agreed and told you to write a message to all employees. Create an e-mail message to tell employees that you will remove the personal pages already posted and that no more will be allowed.

Hint:

- Suggest other ways that people can post personal Web pages. Commercial services such as Compuserve and America Online are possibilities. Students at Plugged In (http://www.pluggedin.org) can also provide Web access for a fee. (Check to be sure that the groups you recommend are still offering Web sites. If possible, get current prices.)
- Give only reasons that are watertight and make the company look good.

COMMUNICATING AT WORK

As Your Instructor Directs in 8–12 through 8–16,

a. Prepare notes for a meeting with or phone call to the person to whom you must give the bad news.
b. Write a paper or e-mail document to achieve the goal.
c. Write a memo to your instructor describing the situation and culture at your workplace and explaining your rhetorical choices (medium, strategy, tone, wording, graphics or document design, and so forth).
d. Examine your organization's files for messages responding to similar situations in the past. Are the messages effective? Why or why not? Write a memo to your instructor analyzing the messages, including copies of them, or make a presentation to the class, using the messages as handouts, transparencies, or slides.

8–12   Telling the Boss about a Problem

In any organization, things sometimes go wrong. Tell your supervisor about a problem in your unit and recommend what should be done.

8–13   Telling Customers That Prices Are Going Up

From time to time, organizations raise prices or impose separate fees for services that were previously free. Think of an increase in the prices your customers pay and tell them about it.

8–14   Reprimanding a Subordinate

One of a manager's duties is to reprimand subordinates who fail to meet organizational expectations. Think of a situation when someone's performance was below standard. Prepare notes for a meeting with the subordinate, and write a memo documenting your meeting.

8–15   Refusing a Customer Request

The customer isn't always right. Sometimes customers ask for things you're truly unable to provide. Even more frequently, you say *no* because the refusal serves your organization's needs. Think of a situation where a customer asked for something your organization could not provide or felt was unreasonable. Write a response refusing the request.

8–16   Giving a Supplier Bad News

Sometimes a company must drop a supplier because its prices are too high or its quality is too low. Think of a situation when you've had to give bad news to a supplier, and create the necessary message.

Hint:

Do you want to close the door to future communication? Or would you be willing to do business with this supplier if the company could offer you a lower price or higher quality?

LETTER AND MEMO ASSIGNMENTS

8–17   Replacing Overtime with Compensatory Time Off

As part of a money-saving campaign, the governor has directed that state workers will no longer receive overtime pay. When they work more than 80 hours in a two-week pay period, they may take "compensatory time off." That is, someone who works 85 hours during one pay period may take off five hours in later weeks to "compensate" for the original overtime.

Compensatory time off must be approved by the supervisor. During very busy times, no compensatory time off will be approved. And normally only half a day may be taken off in any one week. That is, someone can't work 120 hours during the first half of the month and then take off the next week.

As director of a state agency, it's your job to pass the word along to your people. Write a memo.

Hints:

- How do people in your state view government workers? How willing are

voters to approve tax increases to fund state programs?
- What kinds of jobs do government workers do?
- In some agencies, overtime will be seasonal (winter snow removal, budget season). In others, it may depend on the workload and be less predictable.
- The change will benefit people who would rather have time than money. But some people may experience this policy as a pay cut.
- What is the job market in your state? How likely is it that disgruntled workers will quit their jobs?

8–18   Refusing Part of a Guest's Request

As Director of Guest Services for a hotel that is part of a national chain, you've received the following letter:

> To Whom It May Concern:
>
> I really don't need to have my room cleaned and made up every day. Every third or fourth day would be fine. That would save you money and reduce the load on the environment (less washing of towels and bedding).
>
> I'll be staying at your hotel when I come to your city next month for a week-long business trip. What arrangements do I need to make so that my room isn't made up? And how much of a discount from the room rate will I get for the days that no one has to clean my room?
>
> Sincerely,
>
> *Rod Bannister*
>
> Rod Bannister

Cleaning a room costs about $18 a day ($6 for supplies, $7 for the worker's salary and benefits, and $5 for utilities and other expenses). But your contract with the workers' union guarantees them a certain number of hours a week—if they didn't work, you'd still have to pay them. And the recordkeeping involved—which guests wanted which days—would be a nightmare.

However, to use less water, last summer your hotel started a policy of asking guests to put in the tub towels that need to be replaced. Towels hanging on the towel rack are not replaced, even if they've been used. Each guest decides when a towel need to be replaced. But you don't keep track of how many towels or washcloths each guest uses, and you don't give a price break to people who use the fewest possible.

Mr. Bannister, you find out, is a member of the "Frequent Guest Club" of the chain, though he hasn't stayed at your hotel for nine months.

Write Mr. Bannister a letter.

8-19   Analyzing Job Rejection Letters

Collect job rejection letters mailed to seniors on your campus. Analyze the letters, answering the following questions:

- What percentage of the letters use a buffer?
- What reasons do the letters give, if any?
- Does the format build goodwill?
- How do the recipients feel about the letters? Which (if any) do they like best?

As Your Instructor Directs,
   a. Discuss your findings in a small group.
   b. Present your findings orally to the class.
   c. Present your findings orally in a memo to your instructor.
   d. Join with other students to write a report based on your findings.

8-20   Refusing a Gift

As the head of a charitable organization, you spend a lot of your time asking for money. But today, you're turning down a gift: a time-share condominium in another state. Time-shares are so difficult to sell that regular real estate agents do not list them. Places that list time-shares frequently charge a nonrefundable up-front fee (not just a commission that is paid if and when the unit sells). If you accepted the gift, your organization would have to pay maintenance fees charged by the homeowners' association and taxes until the unit sold (if it sold). And you'd probably have to hire someone to check on the property occasionally, since the maintenance fee covers general building maintenance, not repairs for a specific unit. You don't want the expense and hassle of something that may or may not ever yield funds for your organization, so you're going to refuse the gift.

Write a letter to the would-be donors, Benjamin and Sarah Mellon, refusing the gift.

As Your Instructor Directs,
Write letters for one or more of the following situations.

   a. Yours is a well-known national charity. You have never met the Mellons, but your records show that they have given small gifts (under $100) in three of the last five years.

   b. Yours is a local religious organization; the Mellons are prominent members. They don't give much money, but they're active and faithful.
   c. Yours is a local charitable organization that struggles to stay open. The Mellons are major contributors. Sarah Mellon served on your Board of Directors, in a term ending three years ago.
   d. Yours is a national charity. No one in the office has ever heard of the Mellons. They haven't contributed in the last three years—your records don't go back further.

Hints:
- Choose a charitable organization you know something about.
- Give the real reason for the refusal. You *would* accept real estate that seemed easy to sell.
- In situations a–c, thank the Mellons for their past support. Be specific about what they've done.
- Use a salutation and complimentary close that are appropriate to the situation.
- In all of the situations, you want to encourage the donor to give other (more liquid) gifts to you in the future. Tell about upcoming opportunities for giving.

8-21   Telling Retirees They Must Switch to HMOs

Your company has traditionally provided health insurance not only to employees but also to retirees who have worked for the company for at least 20 years at the time of retirement. However, the cost of that insurance has been skyrocketing. To cut costs, you have decided to require that retirees switch to health maintenance organizations (HMOs).

Under the current plan, the retiree pays 20% of all costs (up to a yearly ceiling of $10,000 and a lifetime ceiling of $100,000) and you pay 80%. The good news for retirees is that in an HMO, more costs will be covered. Routine doctors' visits, for example, charge only a $10 copayment. Most tests, such as mammograms, X-rays, and blood work, are covered 100%. Hospitalization is covered completely. And there's much less paperwork. By presenting one's card when one fills a prescription, one pays only the copayment, rather than having to pay the entire amount and then filing for partial reimbursement later.

The bad news for retirees is that they have to go to a physician listed with the HMO. If their current physician is not on the list, the retirees will have to switch doctors to retain benefits. Furthermore, the primary care physician must refer the patient to any other health care providers. That is, someone who wants to see a specialist or go to the emergency room must call the primary care physician first. Primary care physicians always approve such referrals whenever they seem medically advisable, but the requirement does limit the patients' freedom. Further, since HMOs are paid a flat fee and therefore have an incentive to give care that costs less than that fee, some people fear that HMOs will be reluctant to prescribe expensive treatments, even when those treatments are essential.

Seven years ago, you cut costs for employee health insurance by switching from open-ended insurance to HMOs. At that time, you kept open-ended insurance for retirees because they wanted to keep their current doctors. But the high cost of that program gives you no choice: to continue to insure retirees, you must hold down costs, and HMOs offer the best way of doing that.

Your company offers a choice of HMOs. Informational meetings will be held next month for retirees (and anyone else who wishes to attend) to explain the various options. Retirees must return a card within two months, indicating which plan they prefer. The card will be enclosed in the mailing. Anyone who does not return a card will be assigned by the company.

As Vice President for Human Resources, write a form letter to all retirees, explaining the change and telling them how to indicate which HMO they prefer.

Hints:

■ Choose a business, government, or nonprofit organization that you know something about.

■ About how many retirees do you have? What percentage are "young old" (under 80, in reasonably good health)? What percentage are "old old" (80 and over, sometimes with more serious health problems)?

■ How well educated are your retirees? How easy will it be for them to understand the HMO options?

■ What times would be convenient for the retirees to come to meetings? Should you have extra times for them, beyond those you've scheduled for employees?

■ Specify the date, time, and place of informational meetings.

■ Specify the date by which retirees must return the cards indicating their choices.

8–22 Refusing Frequent Flyer Credit

As customer service representative of a major airline, you need to answer the following letter:

Please update my Frequent Flyer Account #123-45-6789 to include the three cross-country trips I took on your airline last year. Copies of the flight coupon with the price I paid and itinerary are attached.

Sincerely,

Chris Cattermole

Chris Cattermole

Actually, you require boarding passes to credit someone's account retroactively, not just a coupon showing that a ticket was purchased. But these flights took place 14, 18, and 21 months ago, respectively. You grant retroactive credit only for mileage earned in the last year.

You know that customers have a choice of airlines, and you'd like this customer to continue to choose your airline. But you won't grant credit for these three flights.

Write the letter.

8–23   Refusing to Grant Credit

You are Credit Director at a major furniture store in town. When people apply for credit, you ask for three references. You've found that the best credit risks are people who own their own homes, who've held the same job for a number of years, and who can furnish good credit references. Your store has a more conservative credit policy than some stores, but as a result, you rarely have to repossess furniture from someone who can't pay.

Today, you have an application from R. B. Geddes that lists only one credit reference: a VISA card that has never been used. The applicant is renting an apartment and has lived at the current address for one month. The application form lists two jobs: server at a local restaurant—again, for one month—and "singer." "Previous occupation" was "college student."

Many new graduates who apply for credit have extensive credit histories, paying back college loans, paying off credit cards, paying utility bills. It's a bit surprising to deal with someone who has so little credit history.

Six months from now, if this applicant has either a credit history or six months with the same employer (or both), you might be willing to grant credit. But for now, you're going to say *no*.

Write the letter.

Hints:
- How else can people buy furniture at your store besides cash and credit?
- What benefits do you offer that might persuade this applicant to buy from you—even if it means waiting a bit?
- Six months from now, what information would be necessary to convince you to grant credit?

8–24   Turning Down an Internship

Your hard work has turned up several internship leads and two actual offers. Ten days ago, Beverly Dunn called to offer you an internship at Dunn and Associates in another city in your state. You said you were really interested in the job but wanted two weeks to weigh your options. Three days later, Emergent Enterprises called. You accepted the job provisionally, and now the written offer has arrived. EE is your first choice, since it offers the most interesting work and is in your city. It's a very small organization, so you'll get to do a wide variety of things. The internship at Dunn and Associates offers a higher salary but seems more like "go-fer" work. Moreover, the job would require relocating, and the extra money isn't worth having to move and find another place to live for three months.

Though you're turning down Dunn and Associates, you don't want to burn your bridges. The company is a successful midsize organization with good growth prospects. You might be interested in an internship there next summer or a full-time job after you finish your degree.

Write the letter to Beverly Dunn, President. Refuse the internship, but maintain goodwill.

8–25   Conveying Bad News about a Club Event

In addition to events from September to May, the Business Club at State University also hosts a summer weekend from Friday to Sunday at a local hotel with sports events and a panel of business people. It's a popular event, and you get a good turnout even though many members have summer jobs in other cities and have to come back for this event.

The Social Chair makes the reservations and plans the sports events; the Program Chair lines up the panel members. As President, you asked both of them to get to work early, and the Program Chair had panelists lined up three months before the event. At that time, the Social Chair still hadn't made reservations, but he said he'd get right to it. You were really busy and assumed he'd take care of it. Six weeks later, you realized you hadn't heard anything, so you called him. He said he was working two jobs, hadn't made the reservations, and didn't have time to. Berating him wouldn't do any good, so you called the hotel. It was booked solid for the weekend you'd planned (and announced). Of all the weekends that month, only the weekend before was available. You took it. You've left messages on the Program Chair's answering machine asking her to notify the original panelists, see how many of them are free the week before, and line up some additional speakers if necessary.

Now you must notify club members that the date of the event has been changed. Some of them may be able to make changes easily, but some will have scheduled time off or bought nonrefundable airline tickets. You don't know how many panelists you'll have, or who they'll be. And the letters will arrive at most a month before the event.

Write a form letter to members.

Hints:

- None of this is your fault. How detailed should you be about the reason for the change and the person responsible?
- See Chapters 9 and 11 for information about writing persuasive letters.

8–26   Rejecting a Would-Be Client

You've just joined Sportstars Inc., a company that represents athletes who want to increase their incomes by doing commercials, making speeches and personal appearances, and endorsing products. Sportstars persuades the sponsor to hire the athlete and helps to negotiate the contract. In addition, a considerable amount of hand-holding is necessary to see the client through rough times. For these services, Sportstars receives 20% of the fees paid to the athlete.

As part of your orientation, your boss points out what you know already: a well-known athlete can command much higher fees than someone who's less well known; normally, people who win championships net much higher fees than someone who is consistently good but who has not caught the public eye. "The big problem," your boss says, "is what to do about young athletes. We can't afford to represent the also-rans; we'd go broke spending time on them. But some rookies will eventually make it big, and we want to represent them when they get to the top. We've evolved a foolproof way to do this. When an unknown comes to us and asks to hire us as his or her personal representative, we decline but suggest a competing firm that we know does a terrible job representing its clients. Then, when the winner emerges from the pack, we approach that person and offer to represent him or her. We know we'll do a better job—and we can prove it. We've signed everyone we've approached this way."

Today you have a letter from Lee Ann Bezazian, a figure skater who won a bronze medal in the US championships last year.

She's decided to join a professional skating touring show and wants a representative to negotiate endorsements for her. A bit of research shows that while she's a very good skater, she isn't yet a star—and may never be. Under Sportstars' policy, you can't grant her request.

As Your Instructor Directs,

a. Write a letter to Lee Ann.
b. Write a memo to your boss at Sportstars suggesting that the company's policy be modified.
c. Write a memo to your instructor listing the choices you made and giving the reasons for your choices.

Hints:

- You have no obligation to give a contract to everyone who asks for one, but is it ethical to deliberately recommend the worst of your competitors? At a minimum, you're depriving Lee Ann of income, since you know that the competitor doesn't seek commercials and endorsements aggressively for athletes and doesn't get them nearly as favorable terms as Sportstars has been able to do.
- What will happen to you if you disobey your boss and recommend a competent competitor, several competitors, or no competitor at all?
- How can you build goodwill so that Lee Ann will have a positive image of Sportstars?

Based on Mark H. McCormack, *What They Don't Teach You at Harvard Business School* (New York: Bantam, 1984).

8–27   Refusing to Participate on a Panel

As a prominent executive, you get many requests to appear before various groups. Today, you've received a request to participate in a panel of 3-5 professionals who will talk about "Succeeding in the Real World." The session will run from 2-5 PM of the second Sunday of next month.

You're trying to cut back on outside commitments. Work continues to take much of your time; you have major obligations in a volunteer organization; and you want some

time for yourself and your family. This request does not fit your priorities.

Decline the invitation.

As Your Instructor Directs, assume that the request is from

a. A college business honor society which expects 250 students at the session.
b. The youth group at the church, synagogue, or temple you attend.
c. The Chinese Student Association at the local college or university.

8–28   Announcing Cost-Savings Measures

Your company has to cut costs but would prefer to avoid laying off workers. Therefore, you have adopted the following money-saving ideas. Some can be implemented immediately; some will be implemented at renewal dates. The company will no longer pay for

- Flowers at the receptionist's desk and in executive offices.
- Sky boxes for professional sporting events.
- Employees' dues for professional and trade organizations.
- Liquor at business meals.

Only essential business travel will be approved. The company will pay only for the lowest cost of air travel (coach, reservation made 7 or 14 days in advance, stay over Saturday night).

The company will no longer buy tables or blocks of tickets for charitable events and will not make any cash donations to charity until money is less tight.

Counters will be put on the photocopiers. People must have access numbers to make photocopies; personal photocopies will cost 10 cents a page.

As the Chief Financial Officer, write a memo to all employees, explaining the changes.

8–29   Closing Bill-Payment Offices

For many years, City Gas & Electric had five suburban offices to which people could take their payments. On the first of the month following next month, you're closing these offices. On that date, 100 local merchants, such as grocers, will begin to accept utility payments. Closing the free-standing offices will save your company almost $3 million a year. Customers will still be able to mail in payments or have them deducted automatically from their paychecks.

Write a notice that can be inserted in utility bills this month and next month.

8–30   Rejecting a Member's Request

All nonsupervisory workers employed by your state government are union members. As a paid staff person for the union, you spend about a third of your time writing and editing the monthly magazine, *Public [Your State] Employee*. You receive this letter:

Dear Editor:

Every month, we get two copies of the union magazine—one addressed to me, one to my husband. We have different last names, so your computer may not realize that we're connected, but we are, and we don't need two copies. Sending just one copy will save printing and postage costs and reduce environmental waste. My name is Dorothy Livingston; my husband is Eric Beamer. Please combine our listings to send just one copy.

Sincerely,

Dorothy Livingston

Dorothy Livingston

As it happens, a couple of years ago you investigated possible savings of sending just one mailing to couples who both work for the state. Sophisticated computerized merge/purge programs to eliminate duplicates are far too expensive for the union's tight budget. And going through the mailing list manually to locate and change duplications would cost more than would be saved in postage. Printing costs wouldn't necessarily drop either, since it actually costs less for each copy to print big runs.

But you want to build goodwill—both to this writer, and for the union in general. Extra copies of the magazine (whether a double mailing or simply a copy someone is finished with) could be given to a nonmember or taken to a doctor's or dentist's waiting room or a barber or beauty shop. Such sharing would help spread public support for the union and state workers.

Write a letter to Ms. Livingston, explaining why you can't combine mailings.

Writing Persuasive Messages

Chapter Outline

Persuasive Messages

Ellen Fu, Vice President/Broker Associate
George Realty Group

Ellen Fu, a top producer in real estate for 18 years, speaks three languages. She works with Asian and American clients and recruits and trains new Realtors. George Realty, in Alhambra, California, is a multicultural real estate company with 300-plus associates and over $1 million in sales every day for the last seven years.

George Realty advertises in American, Hispanic, Chinese, Vietnamese, and Korean newspapers. As a result, we get lots of phone calls from speakers of different languages. Our office is just like a small version of the United Nations. We have associates who speak English, Chinese, Taiwanese, Korean, Cantonese, and Japanese. We have people who are Malaysian, Indonesian, Filipino, Hispanic, Caucasian, East Indian, Middle Eastern, Yugoslav, and Vietnamese. We understand clients' concerns and talk to them in their own language.

In our area, the majority of the buyers are Asians, while most of the sellers are Americans. They list with us because they want an agent who understands Asian culture and customs. For example, one owner was insulted when a young Chinese couple offered a price much lower than her asking price. I explained to her that most Chinese like to negotiate or bargain—it's part of the culture. In Taiwan, people even bargain at the supermarket. For example, if oranges are priced at 80 cents a pound, we bargain for 40 cents a pound. The merchant may say "yes" or may settle on a price in between.

In many cases, I feel like I am acting as a diplomat, overcoming cultural gaps and building better relationships and communications for our community.

Chinese people rely on "Feng Shui" very much. Feng Shui (literally "wind and water") means the art of living in harmony with the land, in alignment with the environment and in balance with nature. Before they buy property, some people will bring their Feng Shui master to look at the orientation and location of the house to see whether the house has "good luck" for that person. Most of our American-born sellers don't have a clue on this subject.

More and more builders are incorporating good Feng Shui into the design of their homes. Some Asians will pay top dollar for a property with good Feng Shui.

I try to help the buyer and seller realize they each have an opportunity, no matter what the current market condition may be. To sell, study the client's background. People buy what they are familiar with. What benefits and goals do they wish to achieve? Be very sensitive, very patient. If you are truly watching out for their interests and they are satisfied with your service, you earn their trust and they are your friends for life.

Ellen Fu, January 29, 1997

**Visit George Realty's Web site: http://
www.georgerealty@homeseekers.com**

"We understand clients' concerns and talk to them in their own language."

Ellen Fu, George Realty

How to Ask for a Raise*

Few companies offer automatic raises any more. Getting a raise in the late 90s depends on working in hot product areas, having skills the company wants, and doing your homework before negotiating.

Taking on important projects is a good strategy. You can even ask your boss at your appraisal interview, "What do I need to do to get a big raise next year?" The task you're assigned may be hard, but doing it successfully will bring rewards.

Document your achievements, because your boss won't necessarily notice them. Summarize the most important in a one-page memo that you send to your boss a week before your appraisal. Your boss will have to get approval from his or her boss to give you a raise, so you need to provide the necessary ammunition.

Check salary surveys in trade magazines and ask other people in your field about salaries. Some jobs have pay ceilings; to get a significant increase, you'd have to move into another area of the company.

Finally, be polite. Make your request in person (not in a memo or through e-mail).

*Based on "How Not to Ask the Boss for a Raise," *Fortune*, June 26, 1995; and Hal Lancaster, "They Are Scarce, But You Can Still Get Yourself a Raise," *The Wall Street Journal*, August 27, 1996, B1.

Persuasion depends on talking to people in their own language, literally and figuratively. Whether you're selling houses or ideas, effective persuasion is based on accurate logic, effective emotional appeal, and credibility or trust. Reasons have to be reasons the audience finds important; emotional appeal is based on values the audience cares about; credibility is in the eye of the beholder.

Persuasive messages include orders and requests, proposals and recommendations, sales and fund-raising letters, job application letters, and efforts to change people's behavior, such as collection letters, criticisms or performance appraisals where you want the subordinate to improve behavior, and public-service ads designed to reduce drunk driving, drug use, and so on. Reports are persuasive messages if they recommend action.

This chapter gives general guidelines for persuasive messages. Chapter 10 discusses situations where the audience is quite resistant. Chapter 11 covers sales and fund-raising letters. Chapter 14 discusses grants and proposals; reports are the subject of Chapter 15. Chapter 19 covers job application letters.

All persuasive messages have several purposes:

Primary Purposes:

To have the reader act.
To provide enough information so that the reader knows exactly what to do.
To overcome any objections that might prevent or delay action.

Secondary Purposes:

To build a good image of the writer.
To build a good image of the writer's organization.
To cement a good relationship between the writer and reader.
To reduce or eliminate future correspondence on the same subject so the message doesn't create more work for the writer.

Choosing a Persuasive Strategy

Choose a persuasive strategy based on your answers to four questions:

1. What do you want people to do?
2. What objections, if any, will the audience have?
3. How strong a case can you make?
4. What kind of persuasion is best for the organization and the culture?

1. What Do You Want People to Do?

Identify the specific action you want and the person who has the power to do it. If your goal requires several steps, specify what you want your audience to do *now*. For instance, your immediate goal may be to have people come to a meeting or let you make a presentation, even though your long-term goal is a major sale or a change in policy.

2. What Objections, if Any, Will the Audience Have?

If you're asking for something that requires little time, money, or physical effort and for an action that's part of the person's regular duties, the audience is likely to have few objections. For example, when you order a product, the firm is happy to supply it.

Often, however, you'll encounter some resistance. People may be busy and have what they feel are more important things to do. They may have other uses for their time and money. To be persuasive, you need to show your audience that your proposal meets their needs; you need to overcome any objections.

The easiest way to learn about objections your audience may have is to ask. Particularly when you want to persuade people in your own organization or your own town, talk to knowledgeable people. Phrase your questions nondefensively, in a way that doesn't lock people into taking a stand on an issue: "What concerns would you have about a proposal to do *x?*" "Who makes a decision about *y?*" "What do you like best about [the supplier or practice you want to change]?" Ask follow-up questions to be sure you understand: "Would you be likely to stay with your current supplier if you could get a lower price from someone else? Why?"

People are likely to be most willing to be aware of and to be willing to share objective concerns such as time and money. They will be less willing to tell you that their real objection is emotional. Readers have a **vested interest** in something if they benefit directly from keeping things as they are. People who are in power have a vested interest in retaining the system that gives them their power. Someone who designed a system has a vested interest in protecting that system from criticism. To admit that the system has faults is to admit that the designer made mistakes. In such cases, you'll need to probe to find out what the real reasons are.

Both individuals and organizations have self-images. It's easier for readers to say *yes* when you ask for something that is consistent with that self-image. For example, a marine biologist used a financial argument to persuade Phillips Petroleum to let him harvest the mussels that grow on oil platforms: "I hear you've just written a check for $100,000 to a hydro-blasting company. I could remove those mussels for free." (The biologist sells the mussels to restaurants.)[1] Aramis persuaded men to buy its over-the-counter skin peel, Lift Off, by linking it to shaving: men who exfoliated with the product could reduce their shaving time by one-third.[2]

3. How Strong Is Your Case?

The strength of your case is based on three aspects of persuasion: argument, credibility, and emotional appeal.

Argument refers to the reasons or logic you offer. Sometimes you may be able to prove conclusively that your solution is best. Sometimes your reasons may not be as strong, the benefits may not be as certain, and obstacles may be difficult or impossible to overcome. For example, suppose that you wanted to persuade your organization to offer a tuition reimbursement plan for employees. You'd have a strong argument if you could show that tuition reimbursement would improve the performance of marginal workers or that reimbursement would be an attractive recruiting tool in a tight job market. However, if dozens of fully qualified workers apply for every opening you have, your argument would be weaker. The program might be nice for workers, but you'd have a hard job proving that it would help the company.

Credibility is the audience's response to you as the source of the message. People are more easily persuaded by someone they see as expert, powerful,

What Do Lawyers Want?*

Sales at Tom Carns' PDQ Printing in Las Vegas are 19 times the average for small print shops. He succeeds by analyzing his audience, identifying decision makers, and meeting their needs.

To enter the market for law-firm photocopying, Tom identified the head of the professional association of paralegals in Las Vegas. He met with her for two hours twice a month for three months to learn about the market, paying $500 for each consultation.

The meetings taught him that price didn't really matter when a legal firm needed photocopying. Quality, timeliness, and confidentiality were crucial. So he made some small changes in his procedures to meet those needs and then advertised the changes in a brochure with "Confidential" on the cover in bright red letters. Inside, his employees promised to treat documents confidentially and to shred any flawed copies. PDQ Printing itself would be liable for any breach of confidentiality.

In the first year of the promotion, law-firm copying generated $600,000 in revenues.

*Based on Edward O. Welles, "Quick Study," *Inc.*, April 1992, 67–76.

By offering a big selection of quality shoes at competitive prices, Larry's Shoes in Fort Worth, Texas, gives customers logical reasons to buy. Emotional appeal is created by complimentary cappuccino, foot massages, and displays of celebrities' shoes, like this pair Clark Gable wore.

attractive, or trustworthy. A sexual abstinence program in Atlanta was effective in large part because the lessons on how to say *no* without hurting the other person's feelings were presented by teenagers slightly older than the students in the program. Adults would have been much less credible.[3]

When you don't yet have the credibility that comes from being an expert or being powerful, build credibility by the language and strategy you use:

- **Be factual.** Don't exaggerate.
- **Be specific.** If you say "X is better," show in detail *how* it is better. Show the reader exactly where the savings or other benefits come from so that it's clear that the proposal really is as good as you say it is.
- **Be reliable.** If you suspect that a project will take longer to complete, cost more money, or be less effective than you originally thought, tell your audience *immediately*. Negotiate a new schedule that you can meet.

Emotional appeal means making the reader *want* to do what you ask. People don't make decisions—even business decisions—based on logic alone. J. C. Mathes and Dwight W. Stevenson cite the following example. During his summer job, an engineering student who was asked to evaluate his company's waste treatment system saw a way that the system could be redesigned to save the company over $200,000 a year. He wrote a report recommending the change and gave it to his boss. Nothing happened. Why not? His supervisor wasn't about to send up a report that would require him to explain why *he'd* been wasting over $200,000 a year of the company's money.[4]

4. What Kind of Persuasion Is Best for the Organization and the Culture?

A strategy that works in one organization may not work somewhere else. James Suchan and Ron Dulek point out that DEC's corporate culture values no-holds-barred aggressiveness. "Even if opposition is expected, a subordinate should write a proposal in a forceful, direct manner."[5] In another organization with different cultural values, an employee who used a hard-sell for a request antagonized the boss.[6]

Corporate culture (✖ p. 61) isn't written down; it's learned by imitation and observation. What style do high-level people in your organization use? When you show a draft to your boss, are you told to tone down your statements or to make them stronger? Role models and advice are two ways organizations communicate their culture to newcomers.

Different cultures also have different preferences for gaining compliance. In one study, students who were native speakers of American English judged direct statements ("Do this"; "I want you to do this") clearer and more effective than questions ("Could you do this?") or hints ("This is needed"). Students who were native speakers of Korean, in contrast, judged direct statements to be *least* effective. In the Korean culture, the clearer a request is, the ruder and therefore less effective it is.[7]

Using Your Analysis to Choose a Persuasive Strategy

If your organization prefers a specific approach, use it. If your organization has no preference, or if you do not know your reader's preference, use the following guidelines to choose a strategy.

- Use the **direct request pattern** when the audience will do as you ask without any resistance. Also use the direct request pattern for busy readers in your own organization who do not read all the messages they receive.
- Use the **problem-solving pattern** when the audience may resist doing what you ask and you expect logic to be more important than emotion in the decision.
- Use the **star-chain-knot pattern** in Chapter 11, "Sales and Fund-Raising Letters," when the audience may resist doing what you ask and when you expect emotion to be more important than logic in the decision.

WRITING DIRECT REQUESTS

When you expect quick agreement, save the reader's time by presenting the request directly.

1. **Consider asking immediately for the information or service you want.** Delay the request if it seems too abrupt or if you have several purposes in the message.
2. **Give readers all the information they will need to act on your request.** Number your questions or set them off with bullets so the reader can check to see that all of them have been answered.

   In a claim (where a product is under warranty or a shipment was defective), explain the circumstances so that the reader knows what happened. Be sure to include all the relevant details: date of purchase, model or invoice number, and so on.

   In more complicated direct requests, anticipate possible responses. Suppose you're asking for information about equipment meeting certain specifications. Explain which criteria are most important so that the reader can recommend an alternative if no single product meets all your needs. You may also want to tell the reader what your price constraints are and ask whether the item is in stock or must be special-ordered.
3. **Ask for the action you want.** Do you want a check? A replacement? A catalogue? Answers to your questions? If you need an answer by a certain time, say so. If possible, show the reader why the time limit is necessary.

Figures 9.1 and 9.2 illustrate direct requests. Note that direct requests do not contain reader benefits and do not need to overcome objections: they simply ask for what is needed.

Direct Requests Don't Translate*

Making a direct request may not be the most direct way to get what you want in other cultures.

In Saudi Arabia, it's rude to say to a taxi driver, "Take me to the airport." Instead say that a ride to the airport might be pleasant. Instead of ordering, suggest.

If you have a problem in China, start by thanking your hosts for all the things that make the experience a good one, praising the people, the accommodations and food and even the scenery. Only after that should you mention "one little problem." Express confidence that your hosts will fix it. Instead of asking for immediate action, indicate that you'll check back in a few days. And leave behind a small gift.

*Based on Myron W. Lustig and Jolene Koester, *Intercultural Competence* (New York: HarperCollins, 1993), 228; and Iris Varner and Linda Beamer, *International Business Communication* (Chicago: Richard D. Irwin, 1995), pp. 123–24.

Figure 9.1   **A Direct Request**

BCS Interoffice Memo
Keep each message to one topic.

Date: May 15, 1997

To: Michael Antonucci

From: David Anthony, Chair, BCS Suggestion Committee   *DA*

Subject: Suggestion #97204   *Topic of request in subject line*

Please evaluate the attached suggestion by May 29. *Put request in ¶ 1.*

Spell out subquestions

- Should BCS adopt it? Why or why not?
- Will it save the company money? If so, how much a year?
- If the suggestion is adopted, how large an award should be given?

Make action easy

You may put your answers and brief reasons for them at the bottom of this page or send them to me by e-mail (anthony.37@bcs.com). Please get your response *Ask for the* in by May 29 as the suggestion committee is meeting on May 30.   *action you want.*

Thanks!   *Reason to act promptly*

Direct requests should be direct. Don't make the reader guess what you want.

Indirect request: Is there a newer version of the 1995 *Accounting Reference Manual?*

Direct request: If there is a newer version of the 1995 *Accounting Reference Manual*, please send it to me.

Subject Lines for Direct Requests

In a direct request, put the request, the topic of the request, or a question in the subject line.

Subject: Request for Updated Software
My copy of HomeNet does not accept the aliases for Magnus accounts.

Subject: Status of Account #3548-003
Please get me the following information about account #3548-003.

Subject: Do We Need an Additional Training Session in October?
The two training sessions scheduled for October will accommodate 40 people. Last month, you said that 57 new staff accountants had been hired. Should we schedule an additional training session in October? Or can the new hires wait until the next regularly scheduled session in February?

A Direct Request to a Superior   **Figure 9.2**

Subject   Request for Additional Travel Funds
Request in subject line

Date   February 18, 1997

From   Kitty Locker   KOL

COMMUNICATION

To   Jim Phelan

Background   *Request in ¶ 1*
Last October, I requested travel funds for ABC and MLA. Now, if the department has any travel money left, I would like to request funding for CCCC in Phoenix.

More background justifies request
Since I turned in my request, I've learned that I will be on the program at CCCC, chairing the ABC special interest group meeting. My expenses will be $532.80 ($232.80 for airfare, $60 for registration, and $240 toward hotel expenses). If full funding isn't possible, I would appreciate partial funding.   *Breakdown of cost*

Specific request
Will you please let me know whether I can receive funding for this trip? Thank you.

The Ohio State University
Form 701—Rev. 1/87 Stores 53605

Direct Requests with Multiple Purposes

In some direct requests, your combination of purposes may suggest a different pattern of organization. For example, in a letter asking an employer to reimburse you for expenses after a job interview, you'd want to thank your hosts for their hospitality and cement the good impression you made at the interview. To do that, you'd spend the first several paragraphs talking about the trip and the interview. Only in the last third of the letter (or even in the P.S.) would you put your request for reimbursement.

Similarly, in a letter asking about a graduate program, a major purpose might be to build a good image of yourself so that your application for financial aid would be viewed positively. To achieve that goal, provide information about your qualifications and interest in the field as well as asking questions.

WRITING PROBLEM-SOLVING MESSAGES

Use an indirect approach and the problem-solving pattern of organization when you expect resistance from your reader but can show that doing what you want will solve a problem you and your reader share. This pattern

**A Writer Explains Her
Rhetorical Choices**

In fall 1996, our chair told us
that we could each ask for
funding to two conferences.
This memo got me an extra
$266 to partially fund a third
conference. (See page 217.)

Paragraph 1 of Figure 9.2 is
designed to be low-key since
money is tight. This reader
will know what the
abbreviations stand for. I've
toned down my request by
using the subjunctive "if . . . I
would like." I want to sound
reasonable and to show that
I'm aware of the realities of
departmental budgeting.

In paragraph 2, I list the
change—I'm now on the
program—that justifies my
request. The last sentence of
paragraph 2 again tones
down my request.

Asking the chair to
authorize the expense feels
too pushy given our budget
constraints. The vague,
toned-down request in
paragraph 3 is designed to be
polite and friendly and a little
deferential (I am writing to my
boss, after all). "Thank you!"
seems to end on the right
note, so that I don't sound as
though I'm taking a *yes* for
granted.

allows you to disarm opposition by showing all the reasons in favor of your position before you give your readers a chance to say *no*.

1. **Catch the reader's interest by mentioning a common ground.** Show that your message will be interesting or beneficial. You may want to catch attention with a negative (which you will go on to show can be solved).

2. **Define the problem you both share (which your request will solve).** Present the problem objectively: don't assign blame or mention personalities. Be specific about the cost in money, time, lost goodwill, and so on. You have to convince readers that *something* has to be done before you can convince them that your solution is the best one.

3. **Explain the solution to the problem.** If you know that the reader will favor another solution, start with that solution and show why it won't work before you present your solution.

   Present your solution without using the words *I* or *my*. Don't let personalities enter the picture; don't let the reader think he or she should say *no* just because you've had other requests accepted recently.

4. **Show that any negative elements (cost, time, etc.) are outweighed by the advantages.**

5. **Summarize any additional benefits of the solution.** The main benefit—solving the problem—can be presented briefly since you described the problem in detail. However, if there are any additional benefits, mention them.

6. **Ask for the action you want.** Often your reader will authorize or approve something; other people will implement the action. Give your reader a reason to act promptly, perhaps offering a new reader benefit. ("By buying now, we can avoid the next quarter's price hikes.")

Figure 9.3 uses the problem-solving pattern of organization. Reader benefits can be brief in this kind of message since the biggest benefit comes from solving the problem.

Subject Lines for Problem-Solving Messages

When you have a reluctant reader, putting the request in the subject line just gets a quick *no* before you've had a chance to give all your arguments. One option is to use a **directed subject line** that makes your stance on the issue clear.[8] In the following examples, the first is the most neutral. The remaining two increasingly reveal the writer's preference.

Subject: A Proposal to Change the Formula for Calculating Retirees' Benefits
Subject: Arguments for Expanding the Marysville Plant
Subject: Why Cassano's Should Close Its West Side Store

Another option is to use common ground or a reader benefit—something that shows readers that this message will help them.

Subject: Reducing Energy Costs in the New Orleans Office

Energy costs in our New Orleans office have risen 12% in the last three years, even though the cost of gas has fallen and the cost of electricity has risen only 5%.

Although your first paragraph may be negative in a problem-solving message, your subject line should be neutral or positive.

Both directed subject lines and benefit subject lines can also be used as report titles.

A Problem-Solving Persuasive Message   **Figure 9.3**

Memorandum

February 16, 1998

To: All Staff Members

From: Melissa J. Gutridge *MJG*

Subject: Why We Are Implementing a New Sign-Out System

Directed subject line indicates writer's position

Common ground

Problem

Successfully mainstreaming our clients into the community is very important and daily interaction with the public is necessary. Our clients enjoy the times they get to go to the mall or out to lunch instead of remaining here all day.   Recently, however, clients have been taken out on activities without a staff member's knowing where the client is and whom the client is with.

Specific example of problem

We need to know where all clients are at all times because social workers, psychologists, and relatives constantly stop by unannounced. Last week Janet's father stopped by to pick her up for a doctor's appointment and she was not here. No one knew where she was or whom she was with. Naturally her father was very upset and wanted to know what kind of program we were running. Staff members' not knowing where our clients are and whom they are with is damaging to the good reputation of our staff and program.

Solution presented impersonally

Additional reader benefit

Starting Monday, February 26, a sign-out board will be located by Betty's desk. Please write down where you and the client are going and when you expect to be back. When signing out, help clients sign themselves out. We can turn this into a learning experience for our clients. Then when a social worker stops by to see someone who isn't here, we can simply look at the sign-out board to tell where the client is and when he or she will return.

Tells reader what to do

Please help keep up the superb reputation you have helped Weststar earn as a quality center for adults with handicaps. Sign out yourself and clients at all times.

Developing a Common Ground

A common ground avoids the me-against-you of some persuasive situations and suggests that both you and your audience have a mutual interest in solving the problems you face. To find a common ground, we analyze the audience, understand their biases, objections, and needs, and identify with them so that we can make them identify with us. This analysis can be carried out in a cold, manipulative way. It can also be based on a respect for and sensitivity to the audience's position.

Readers are highly sensitive to manipulation. No matter how much you disagree with your audience, respect their intelligence. Try to understand why they believe or do something and why they may object to your position. If you can understand your readers' initial position, you'll be more effective—and you won't alienate your readers by talking down to them.

In your common ground, emphasize the parts of your proposal that fit with what your audience already does or believes. An employee of 3M wanted to develop laser disks. He realized that 3M's previous products were thin and flat: Scotch tape, Post-it Notes, magnetic tape. When he made his presentation to the group that chose new products for development, he held his prototype disk horizontally, so his audience saw a flat, thin object rather than a large, round, recordlike object. Making his project fit with the audience's previous experience was a subtle and effective emotional tool to make it easier for the audience to say *yes.*[9]

Use audience analysis to evaluate possible common grounds. Suppose you want to install a system to play background music in a factory. To persuade management to pay for the system, a possible common ground would be increasing productivity. However, to persuade the union to pay for the system, you'd need a different common ground. Workers would see productivity as a way to get them to do more work for the same pay. A better common ground would be that the music would make the factory environment more pleasant.

Dealing with Objections

If you know that your readers will hear other points of view, or if your audience's initial position is negative, you have to deal with their objections to persuade them. The stronger the objection is, the earlier in your message you should deal with it.

The best way to deal with an objection is to eliminate it. To sell Jeep Cherokees in Japan, Mitsuru Sato convinced Chrysler to put the driver's seat on the right side, to make an extra pre-shipment quality check, and to rewrite the instruction booklet in Japanese style, with big diagrams and cartoons.[10]

If an objection is false, based on misinformation, give the response to the objection without naming the objection. In a brochure, you can present responses with a "question/answer" format. When objections have already been voiced, you may want to name the objection so that your audience realizes that you are responding to that specific objection. However, to avoid solidifying the opposition, don't attribute the objection to your audience. Instead, use a less personal attribution: "Some people wonder . . . "; "Some citizens are afraid that . . . ."

If real objections remain, try one or more of the following strategies to counter objections:

1. Specify how much time and/or money is required—it may not be as much as the reader fears.

> Distributing flyers to each house or apartment in your neighborhood will probably take two afternoons.

2. Put the time and/or money in the context of the benefits they bring.

> The additional $152,500 will (1) allow The Open Shelter to remain open 24 rather than 16 hours a day, (2) pay for three social workers to help men find work and homes, and (3) keep the Neighborhood Bank open, so that men don't have to cash Social Security checks in bars and so that they can save up the $800 they need to have up front to rent an apartment.

3. Show that money spent now will save money in the long run.

> By replacing the boiler now, we'll no longer have to release steam that the overflow tank can't hold. Depending on how severe the winter is, we could save $100 to $750 a year in energy costs. If energy costs rise, we'll save even more.

4. Show that doing as you ask will benefit some group or cause the reader supports, even though the action may not help the reader directly. This is the strategy used in fund-raising letters, discussed in detail in Chapter 11.

> By being a Big Brother or a Big Sister, you'll give a child the adult attention he or she needs to become a well-adjusted, productive adult.

5. Show the reader that the sacrifice is necessary to achieve a larger, more important goal to which he or she is committed.

> These changes will mean more work for all of us. But we've got to cut our costs 25% to keep the plant open and to keep our jobs.

6. Show that the advantages as a group outnumber or outweigh the disadvantages as a group.

> None of the locations is perfect. But the Backbay location gives us the most advantages and the fewest disadvantages.

7. Turn a disadvantage into an opportunity.

> With the hiring freeze, every department will need more lead time to complete its own work. By hiring another person, the Planning Department could provide that lead time.

Offering a Reason for the Reader to Act Promptly

The longer people delay, the less likely they are to carry through with the action they had decided to take. In addition, you want a fast response so you can go ahead with your own plans.

Just asking for prompt action can help speed a response. Request action by a specific date. Try to give people at least a week or two: they have other things to do besides respond to your requests. Set deadlines in the middle of the month, if possible. If you say, "Please return this by March 1," people will think, "I don't need to do this till March." Ask for the response by February 28 instead. If you can use a response even after the deadline, say so. Otherwise, people who can't make the deadline may not respond at all.

Readers may ignore deadlines that seem arbitrary. Show why you need a quick response:

- **Show that the time limit is real.** Perhaps you need information quickly to use it in a report that has a due date. Perhaps a decision must be made by a certain date to catch the start of the school year, the Christmas selling season, or an election campaign. Perhaps you need to be ready for a visit from out-of-town or international colleagues.
- **Show that acting now will save time or money.** If business is slow and your industry isn't doing well, then your company needs to act now (to economize, to better serve customers) in order to be competitive. If

Are You Doing the Right Thing?*

Pressures of business sometimes create an environment where people think that anything goes. To be sure that you're doing the right thing, ask the following questions:

- Whom will your action hurt?
- Can you discuss the problem with the people who will be affected before you act?
- How would you define the problem if you stood on the other side of the fence?
- How would you feel if your action were known to your boss, your CEO, your family, or society as a whole?
- What symbolic message will people get if they understand your action? If they misunderstand it?

*Based on Laura L. Nash, "Ethics without the Sermon," *Executive Success: Making It in Management*, ed. Eliza G. Collins (New York: John Wiley & Sons, 1983), 497.

Visa capitalized on wide acceptance with its campaign "It's everywhere you want to be." Suddenly exclusivity was bad: "And they don't take American Express." (Reprinted with permission VISA U.S.A.).

Creative Response to an Objection, I*

To cut costs, banks want customers to use ATM machines rather than expensive tellers. But older customers prefer talking to a person. And retirees want their errands to provide social contact.

Canada's second-largest bank, CIBC, hires greeters to train people how to use the ATM machines and to provide human contact at teller-less branches.

And humor helps. Victoria Brink Guillot, manager of a Citibank branch in San Mateo, California, tells her mature customers, "ATMs are just like slot machines, only you never lose."

*Based on Paco Underhill, "Seniors in Stores," *American Demographics,* April 1996, 48.

business is booming and everyone is making a profit, then your company needs to act now to get its fair share of the available profits.

■ **Show the cost of delaying action.** Will labor or material costs be higher in the future? Will delay mean more money spent on repairing something that will still need to be replaced?

Building Emotional Appeal

Stories and psychological description are effective ways of building emotional appeal. Emotional appeal works best when people want to be persuaded.

Even when you need to provide statistics or numbers to convince the careful reader that your anecdote is a representative example, telling a story first makes your message more persuasive. Experiments with both high school teachers and quantitatively trained MBA students show that people are more likely to believe a point and more likely to be committed to it when points were made by examples, stories, and case studies. Stories alone were more effective than a combination of stories and statistics; the combination was more effective than statistics alone. In another experiment, attitude changes lasted longer when the audience had read stories than when they had only read numbers. Recent research suggests that stories are more persuasive because people remember them.[11]

Sense impressions—what the reader sees, hears, smells, tastes, feels—evoke a strong emotional response. **Psychological description** means creating a scenario rich with sense impressions so readers can picture themselves using your product or service and enjoying its benefits. You can also use psychological description to describe the problem your product will solve. Psychological description works best early in the message to catch readers' attention.

Feature:	Snooze alarm
Benefit:	If the snooze button is pressed, the alarm goes off and comes on again nine minutes later.
Psychological description:	Some mornings, you really want to stay in bed just a few more minutes. With the Sleepytime Snooze Alarm, you can snuggle under the covers for a few extra winks, secure in the knowledge that the alarm will come on again to get you up for that breakfast meeting with an important client. If you don't have to be anywhere soon, you can keep hitting the snooze alarm for up to an additional 63 minutes of sleep. With Sleepytime, you're in control of your mornings.
Feature:	Tilt windows
Benefit:	Easier to clean
Psychological description	It's no wonder so many cleaners "don't do windows." Balancing precariously on a rickety ladder to clean upper-story windows . . . shivering outside in the winter winds and broiling in the summer sun as you scrub away . . . running inside, then outside, then inside again to try to get the spot that always seems to be on the other side. Cleaning traditional windows really is awful.
	In contrast, cleaning is a breeze with Tilt-in Windows. Just pull the inner window down and pull the bottom toward you. The whole window lifts out! Repeat for the outer window. Clean them inside in comfort (sitting down or even watching TV if you choose). Then replace the top of the outer window in its track, slide up, and repeat with the inner window. Presto! Clean windows!

Someone who's already looking for a product may need only the feature or the benefit. Good psychological description uses vivid details and sensory imagery to motivate uncommitted readers. The flyer for a university's food services in Figure 9.4 gets your gastric juices flowing.

In psychological description, you're putting your reader in a picture. If the reader doesn't feel that the picture fits him or her, the technique backfires. To prevent this, psychological description often uses subjunctive verbs ("if you like . . ." "if you were . . .") or the words *maybe* and *perhaps*.

> You're hungry but you don't want to bother with cooking. Perhaps you have guests to take to dinner. Or it's 12 noon and you only have an hour for lunch. Whatever the situation, the Illini Union has a food service to fit your needs. If you want convenience, we have it. If it's atmosphere you're seeking, it's here too. And if you're concerned about the price, don't be. When you're looking for a great meal, the Illini Union is the place to find it.

Illini Union brochure

Creative Response to an Objection, II*

Jim Young sold apples by direct mail order. One year, a hailstorm just before the harvest bruised the apples.

At first, the obstacle appeared insurmountable. For years, his selling point had been that these apples looked as good as they tasted.

But Jim was able to turn the disadvantage into an advantage.

He knew that cold weather (partially responsible for the hailstorm) improves the flavor of ripening apples. So he filled the orders, inserting a note in each box:

Note the hail marks which have caused minor skin blemishes in some of these apples. They are proof of their growth at a high mountain altitude where the sudden chills from hailstorms help firm the flesh, develop the natural sugars, and give these apples their incomparable flavor.

Not one customer asked for a refund. In fact, the next year, some people wrote on their orders, "Send the hail-marked apples if possible."

*Based on Ray Considine and Murray Raphael, *The Great Brain Robbery* (Pasadena, CA: The Great Brain Robbery, 1981), 95–96.

Figure 9.4   **Using Psychological Description to Develop Reader Benefits**

You–attitude psychological description

The Colonial

When you dine in the Illini Union Colonial Room, it's easy to imagine yourself a guest in a fine Virginian mansion. Light from the gleaming chandeliers reflects from a hand-carved mirror hanging over the dark, polished buffet. Here you can dine in quiet elegance amid furnishings adapted from 18th century Williamsburg and the Georgian homes of the James River Valley in Virginia.

Perhaps you'd like a dinner of stuffed rainbow trout. Or the pork fricassee. The menu features a variety of complete meals which are changed daily, as well as the regular a la carte service. Whatever your choice, you'll enjoy an evening of fine dining at very reasonable prices.

The Illini Union Colonial Room is located on the northeast corner of the first floor. Dinners are served Monday through Friday from 5:30 to 7:30 p.m. Please call 333-0690 for reservations, and enjoy the flavor of the Colonies tonight.

Visual details

Details appeal to sight, taste, smell

Emphasis on reader's choice— Not every reader will want the same thing

The Cafeteria

In the Illini Union Cafeteria, you start out with an empty tray and silverware. Then comes the food, several yards of it, all yours for the choosing. By the time you've finished, your empty tray has become a delicious meal.

In the morning, the warm aroma of breakfast fills the air. Feast your eyes and then your appetite on the array of eggs, bacon, pancakes, toast, sausage, rolls, juices, and coffee . . . They're all waiting to wake you up with good taste. Have a hearty breakfast or make it quick and tasty. The warm, freshly baked sweet rolls and coffeecakes practically beg to be smothered in butter and savored with a cup of hot coffee.

By 11 a.m. the breakfast menu has made way for lunch. Here come the plump Reuben sandwiches and the toasty grilled cheese. Soups and salads make their appearance. A variety of vegetables are dressed up to entice you and several main dishes lead the luncheon parade. Any number of complete meals can take shape as you move along.

What? Back for dinner? Well, no wonder! The Cafeteria sets out a wide selection of entrees and side dishes. Veal parmigiana steams for your attention but the roast beef right next to it is rough competition. Tomorrow the fried chicken might be up for selection. Choose the dinner combination that best fits your appetite and your pocket.

The newly remodeled Cafeteria is on the ground floor and is open for breakfast from 7 to 11 a.m. Monday through Saturday and 8 to 11 a.m. on Sunday. Lunch is from 11 a.m. to 1:15 p.m. Monday through Saturday and 11 a.m. to 2 p.m. on Sunday. Dinner is served from 4:45 to 7 p.m. Monday through Fridy.

A meal in a restaurant is expensive. A meal at home is a chore. But a meal at the Cafeteria combines good food and reasonable prices to make dining a pleasure.

TONE IN PERSUASIVE MESSAGES

The best phrasing depends on your relationship to the reader. When you ask for action from people who report directly to you, you have several choices. Even orders ("Get me the Ervin file") and questions ("Do we have the third-quarter numbers yet?") will work. When you need action from co-workers, superiors, or people outside the organization, you need to be more forceful but also more polite.

How you ask for action affects whether you build or destroy positive relationships with other employees, customers, and suppliers. Professor and consultant Dan Dieterich notes that the calls to action in many messages are

- Buried somewhere deep in the middle of the correspondence.
- Disguised as either statements or questions.
- Insulting because they use "parental language."

Such messages, Dieterich points out, "lower productivity within the organization and reduce or eliminate the goodwill customers have toward the organization. . . . [T]hose two things . . . can put the organization out of business."[12]

Avoiding messages that sound parental or preachy is often a matter of tone. Saying "Please" is a nice touch, especially to people on your level or outside the organization. Tone will also be better when you give reasons for your request or reasons to act promptly.

| Parental: | Everyone is expected to comply with these regulations. I'm sure you can see that they are commonsense rules needed for our business. |
| Better: | Even on casual days, visitors expect us to be professional. So leave the gym clothes at home! |

When you write to people you know well, humor can work. Just make sure that the message isn't insulting to anyone who doesn't find the humor funny.

Writing to superiors is trickier. You may want to tone down your request by using subjunctive verbs and explicit disclaimers that show you aren't taking a *yes* for granted.

| Arrogant: | Based on this evidence, I expect you to give me a new computer. |
| Better: | If department funds permit, I would like a new computer. |

Passive verbs and jargon sound stuffy. Use active imperatives—perhaps with "Please" to create a friendlier tone.

| Stuffy: | It is requested that you approve the above-mentioned action. |
| Better: | Please authorize us to create a new subscription letter. |

WRITING PERSUASIVE E-MAIL MESSAGES

It can be particularly tricky to control tone in e-mail messages, which always tend to sound less friendly than paper documents or conversations. For important requests, it's worth taking the time to compose your message offline and revise it carefully before you send it.

Paper messages can work up to the request since readers will normally skim the first page. But e-mail messages have to catch the reader's eye in the subject line. If the message is longer than one screen, the first screen must interest the reader enough to make him or her continue. E-mail messages to people who report directly to you are easy, since people will read anything from their supervisors. But writing to people who are not in a direct reporting relationship or to people outside your unit or organization takes more care.

The subject line of a persuasive e-mail message should make it clear that you're asking for something. If you're sure that the reader will read the message, something as vague as "Request" may work. Most of the time, it's better to be more specific.

Subject:	Move Meeting to Tuesday?
Subject:	Need Your Advice
Subject:	Provide Story for Newsletter?
Subject:	Want You for United Way Campaign

Creative Response to an Objection, III*

WearGuard Corporation in Norwell, Massachusetts, makes uniforms and rugged work clothes. Orders are heaviest in the fall, when the company needs 400 more workers than it needs the rest of the year. Training costs soar; quality falls.

Managers didn't like any of the conventional solutions. Lisa Zankman, Vice President for Human Resources, said, "Wouldn't it be great if we could find a company with a different peak season?" They did. Cross Country Motor Club takes distress calls from car owners who need towing. Its workload is busiest summer and winter. Employees at each company learn to take calls for the other; telephone switches carry the calls.

Each company gets trained workers in its busy season, with no need to lay off people when calls are lighter.

*Based on "Lisa Zankman Solved Her Staffing Woes with a Wacky Plan," *The Wall Street Journal,* June 21, 1996, B1.

Try to keep the subject line short. If that's difficult, put the most important part into the first few words since many e-mail programs only show the first 28 characters of the subject line.

When you ask for something small or for something that it is part of the reader's job duties to provide, your request can be straightforward. In the body of the message, give people all the information they need to act. At the end of the message, ask for the action you want. Make the action as easy as possible, and specify when you need a response. You may want an immediate response now ("Let me know asap whether you can write a story for the newsletter so that I can save the space") and a fuller one later ("we'll need the text by March 4").

When you ask for something big or something which is not a regular part of that person's duties, the first paragraph must not only specify the request but also make the reader view it positively. Use the second paragraph to provide an overview of the evidence that the rest of the message will provide: "Here's why we should do this." "Let me describe the project. Then, if you're willing to be part of it, I'll send you a copy of the proposal." Use audience analysis to find a reason to do as you ask that the reader will find convincing. Everyone is busy, so you need to make the reader *want* to do as you ask. Be sure to provide complete information that the reader will need to act on your request. Ask for the action you want.

Major requests that require changes in values, culture, or lifestyles should not be made in e-mail messages.

VARIETIES OF PERSUASIVE MESSAGES

Collection letters, performance appraisals, and letters of recommendation are among the most common varieties of persuasive messages.

Collection Letters

Most businesses find that phoning rather than writing results in faster payment. But as more and more companies install voice mail systems, you may sometimes need to write letters when leaving messages doesn't work.

Collection letters ask customers to pay (as they have already agreed to do) for the goods and services they have already received. Instead of sending one letter, or repeated copies of the same letter, good credit departments send a **series** of letters. Letters in the series should be only a week or two apart. Waiting a month between letters implies that you're prepared to wait a long time—and the reader will be happy to oblige you!

Early letters are gentle, assuming that the reader intends to pay but has forgotten or has met with temporary reverses. Early letters can be obvious form letters or even just a second copy of the bill with the words "Second Notice" or "Past Due" stamped on it.

A student who had not yet been reimbursed by a company for a visit to the company's office put the second request in the P.S. of a letter refusing a job offer:

> P.S.   The check to cover my expenses when I visited your office in March hasn't come yet. Could you check to see whether you can find a record of it? The amount was $490 (airfare $290, hotel room $185; taxi $15).

Early collection letters sometimes use humor to defuse negative feelings and to set themselves apart from other mail. Since readers' senses of humor differ, the real test of a collection letter using humor should be: Does it enrage readers who think they have already paid? Does it make the request seem trivial, as though the bill is a joke? If the answer to either of these questions is *yes*, don't use the humor.

If one or two early letters don't result in payment, it's worth calling the customer to ask if your company has created a problem. It's possible that you shipped something the customer didn't want or sent the wrong quantity. It's possible that the invoice arrived before the product and was filed and forgotten. It's possible that the invoice document is poorly designed, so customers set it aside until they could figure it out. If any of these situations apply, you'll build goodwill by solving the problem rather than arrogantly asking for payment.[13]

Middle letters are more assertive in asking for payment. Figure 9.5 gives an example of a middle letter. This form letter is merged with database information about the customer's name, the amount due, and the magazine the customer is receiving. Other middle letters offer to negotiate a schedule for repayment if the reader is not able to pay the whole bill immediately, may remind the reader of the importance of a good credit rating (which will be endangered if the bill remains unpaid), educate the reader about credit, and explain why the creditor must have prompt payment.

Unless you have firm evidence to the contrary, middle letters should assume that readers have some legitimate reason for not yet paying. Perhaps they've been out of town. Perhaps their checks were lost in the mail. Perhaps they're waiting to receive payments due them so that they can pay their own creditors. Even people who are "juggling" payments because they do not have enough money to pay all their bills or people who will put payment off as long as possible will respond more quickly if you do not accuse them. If a reader is offended by your assumption that he or she is dishonest, that anger can become an excuse to continue delaying payment.

Late letters threaten legal action if the bill is not paid. Under federal law, the writer cannot threaten legal action unless he or she actually intends to sue. Other regulations also spell out what a writer may and may not do in a late letter.

Many small businesses find that establishing personal relationships with customers is the best way to speed payment.

Performance Appraisals

At regular intervals, supervisors evaluate, or appraise, the performance of their subordinates. In most organizations, employees have access to their files; sometimes they must sign the appraisal to show that they've read it. The superior normally meets with the subordinate to discuss the appraisal.

As a subordinate, you should prepare for the appraisal interview by listing your achievements and goals. Where do you want to be in a year or five years? What training and experience do you need to reach your goals? Also think about any weaknesses. If you need training, advice, or support from the organization to improve, the appraisal interview is a good time to ask for this help.

Appraisals need to both protect the organization and motivate the employee. These two purposes conflict. Most of us will see a candid appraisal as negative; we need praise and reassurance to believe that we're valued and can do better. But the praise that motivates someone to improve can come back to haunt the company if the person does not eventually do acceptable work. An organization is in trouble if it tries to fire someone whose evaluations never mention mistakes.

Getting Action with Voice Mail

If your action is small and easy, you can ask for it in a voice mail message: "Please fax me a copy of your price list."

When you want something more complicated or that the other person may be less willing to give, prepare a 30-second summary of your request, including the benefit to the person whose action you want. Put energy into your voice, so that you sound interesting to talk to.

As in any voice mail message, state your name and phone number slowly and clearly. If you want something sent by e-mail, fax, or mail, give the appropriate number or address clearly. Specify when you'll be available to take return calls. If possible, give the person several options.

Figure 9.5   **A Middle Collection Letter**

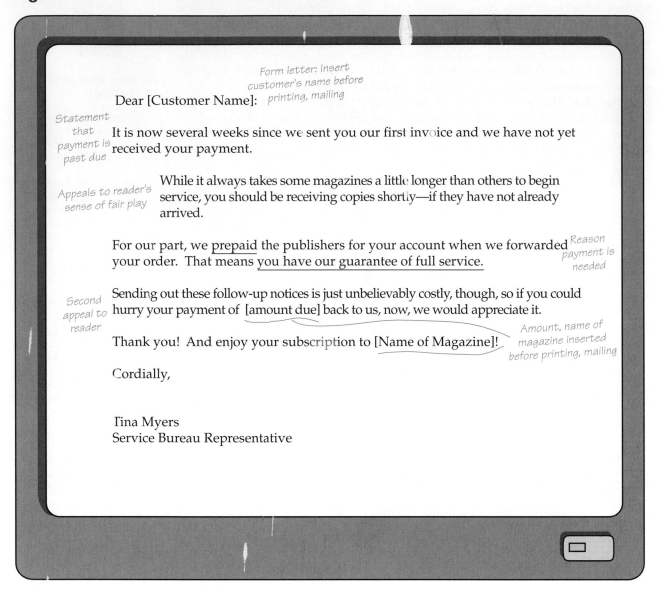

Form letter: Insert customer's name before printing, mailing

Dear [Customer Name]:

Statement that payment is past due

It is now several weeks since we sent you our first invoice and we have not yet received your payment.

Appeals to reader's sense of fair play

While it always takes some magazines a little longer than others to begin service, you should be receiving copies shortly—if they have not already arrived.

For our part, we <u>prepaid</u> the publishers for your account when we forwarded your order. That means <u>you have our guarantee of full service.</u>

Reason payment is needed

Second appeal to reader

Sending out these follow-up notices is just unbelievably costly, though, so if you could hurry your payment of [amount due] back to us, now, we would appreciate it.

Thank you! And enjoy your subscription to [Name of Magazine]!

Amount, name of magazine inserted before printing, mailing

Cordially,

Tina Myers
Service Bureau Representative

Avoid labels (*wrong, bad*) and inferences. Instead, cite specific observations that describe behavior.

Inference:	Sam is an alcoholic.
Vague observation:	Sam calls in sick a lot. Subordinates complain about his behavior.
Specific observation:	Sam called in sick a total of 12 days in the last two months. After a business lunch with a customer last week, Sam was walking unsteadily. Two of his subordinates have said that they would prefer not to make sales trips with him because they find his behavior embarrassing.

Sam might be an alcoholic. He might also be having a reaction to a physician-prescribed drug; he might have a mental illness; he might be showing symptoms of a physical illness other than alcoholism. A supervisor who jumps to conclusions creates ill will, closes the door to solving the problem, and may provide grounds for legal action against the organization.

Be specific in an appraisal.

Too vague: Sue does not manage her time as well as she could.
Specific: Sue's first three weekly sales reports have been three, two, and four
              days late, respectively; the last weekly sales report for the month is
              not yet in.

Without specifics, Sue won't know that her boss objects to late reports. She may think that she is being criticized for spending too much time on sales calls or for not working 80 hours a week. Without specifics, she might change the wrong things in a futile effort to please her boss.

Good supervisors try not only to identify the specific problems in subordinates' behavior but also in conversation to discover the causes of the problem. Does the employee need more training? Perhaps a training course or a mentor will help. Does he or she need to work harder? Then the supervisor needs to motivate the worker and help him or her manage distractions. Is a difficult situation causing the problem? Perhaps the situation can be changed. If it can't be changed, the supervisor and the company should realize that the worker is not at fault.

Sometimes performance appraisals reflect mostly the month or week right before the appraisal, even though it is supposed to cover six months or a year. Many managers record specific observations of subordinates' behavior two or three times a month. These notes jog the memory so that the appraisal doesn't focus unduly on recent behavior.

Appraisals are more useful to subordinates if they make clear which areas are most important and contain specific recommendations for improvement. No one can improve 17 weaknesses at once. Which two should the employee work on this month? Is getting in reports on time more important than increasing sales? The supervisor should explicitly answer these questions during the appraisal interview.

Phrase goals in specific, concrete terms. The subordinate may think that "considerable progress toward completing" a report may mean that the project should be 15% finished. The boss may think that "considerable progress" means 50% or 85% of the total work.

Figure 9.6 shows a performance appraisal for a member of a collaborative business communication group.

Letters of Recommendation

In an effort to protect themselves against lawsuits, some companies state only how long they employed someone and the position that person held. Such bare-bones letters have themselves been the target of lawsuits when employers did not reveal relevant negatives. Whatever the legal climate, there may be times when you want to recommend someone for an award or for a job.

Letters of recommendation must be specific. General positives that are not backed up with specific examples and evidence are seen as weak recommendations. Letters of recommendation that focus on minor points also suggest that the person is weak.

Either in the first or the last paragraph, summarize your overall evaluation of the person. Early in the letter, perhaps in the first paragraph, show how well and how long you've known the person. In the middle of the letter, offer specific details about the person's performance. At the end of the letter, indicate whether you would be willing to rehire the person and repeat your overall evaluation.

Speedier Collections*

Art Allen, the CEO of Allen Systems Groups, a software manufacturer in Naples, Florida, cut his average collection time from 61 days to 45 days with a combination of computerized "tickler" files and low-tech phone calls.

Before invoices go out, accounts receivable staffers call clients to ask how long payment typically takes and to make certain that the computer information (address, etc.) is correct.

A few days after invoices are mailed, a staffer calls to make sure the bill arrived. If it didn't, a copy of the invoice is faxed.

If the payment doesn't arrive on the expected payment date (based on information about typical payment times), staffers call to find out what went wrong.

Because he's now paid more quickly, Allen has been able to pay off his corporate debt.

*Based on "Speedier Collection," *Inc.*, June 1995, 93.

Figure 9.6   **A Performance Appraisal**

February 13, 1998

To: Barbara Buchanan

From: Brittany Papper   *BAP*

Subject line indicates that memo is a performance appraisal

Subject: Your Performance Thus Far in Our Collaborative Group

Overall evaluation

You have been a big asset to our group. Overall, our business communication group has been one of the best groups I have ever worked with, and I think that only minor improvements are needed to make our group even better.

What You're Doing Well

You demonstrated flexibility and compatibility at our last meeting before we turned in our proposal on February 12 by offering to type the proposal since I had to study for an exam in one of my other classes. I really appreciated this because I really did not have the time to do it. I will definitely remember this if you are ever too busy with your other classes and cannot type the final report.

Specific observations provide dates, details of performance

Another positive critical incident occurred February 5. We had discussed researching the topic of sexual discrimination in hiring and promotion at Midstate Insurance. As we read more about what we had to do, we became uneasy about reporting the information from our source who works at Midstate. I called you later that evening to talk about changing our topic to a less personal one. You were very understanding and said that you agreed that the original topic was a touchy one. You offered suggestions for other topics and had a positive attitude about the adjustment. Your suggestions ended my worries and made me realize that you are a positive and supportive person.

Other strengths

Your ideas are a strength that you definitely contribute to our group. You're good at brainstorming ideas, yet you're willing to go with whatever the group decides. That's a nice combination of creativity and flexibility.

Areas for Improvement

Two minor improvements could make you an even better member.

The first improvement is to be more punctual to meetings. On February 5 and February 8 you were about 10 minutes late. This makes the meetings last longer. Your ideas are valuable to the group, and the sooner you arrive the sooner we can share in your suggestions.

Specific recommendations for improvement

The second suggestion is one we all need to work on. We need to keep our meetings

A Performance Appraisal   **Figure 9.6**

Barbara Buchanan   2   February 13, 1998

Specific behavior to be changed

positive and productive. I think that our negative attitudes were worst at our first group meeting February 5. We spent about half an hour complaining about all the work we had to do and about our busy schedules in other classes. In the future if this happens, maybe you could offer some positive things about the assignment to get the group motivated again.

Overall Compatibility

Positive, forward-looking ending

I feel that this group has gotten along very well together. You have been very flexible in finding times to meet and have always been willing to do your share of the work. I have never had this kind of luck with a group in the past and you have been a welcome breath of fresh air. I don't hate doing group projects any more!

Experts are divided on whether you should include negatives. Some people feel that any negative weakens the letter. Other people feel that presenting but not emphasizing honest negatives makes the letter more convincing.

In many discourse communities, the words "Call me if you need more information" in a letter of recommendation mean "I have negative information that I am unwilling to put on paper. Call me and I'll tell you what I really think."

SOLVING A SAMPLE PROBLEM[14]

Problem

In one room in the production department of Nakamura Electronics Company, employees work on TV picture tubes under conditions that are scarcely bearable due to the heat. Even when the temperature outside is only 75°, it is over 100° in the "tube room." In June, July, and August, 24 out of 36 workers quit because they couldn't stand the heat. This turnover happens every summer.

In a far corner of the room sits a quality control inspector in front of a small fan (the only one in the room). The production workers, in contrast, are carrying 20-pound TV tubes. As Production Supervisor, you tried to get air-conditioning two years ago, before Nakamura acquired the company, but management was horrified at the idea of spending $300,000 to insulate and air-condition the warehouse (it is impractical to air-condition the tube room alone).

What Evaluations Mean in the US Air Force*

In the Air Force, reports a former officer, inflation has hit the labels used in evaluations:

"Good"—This person is terrible.

"Excellent"—This person can barely get through the day without written instructions.

"Outstanding"—This person does good work but not the best.

"Absolutely superior"—This person should be the first to be promoted.

*Based on Captain Phoebe S. Spinrad, conversation with the author, August 20, 1987.

Credit Collection and the Law*

The Fair Debt Collection Practices Act (15 U.S.C. § 1601 and following) limits the actions of attorneys and debt collectors.

Collectors are **not** allowed to

■ Harass debtors on the phone or in person, threaten violence, use obscenities or profanity, or publish a list of debtors.
■ Call debtors at work or late at night.
■ Misrepresent the legal status of the debt, the creditor's actual intent to take legal action, or the consequences of not paying.

Collectors are **required** to

■ Specify the amount of the debt and the name of the creditor.
■ Specify that the debtor has 30 days to dispute the validity of the debt.
■ Offer to provide the name and address of the original creditor, if the debtor asks for it, and if the collector is not the original creditor.

*Based on Fredric A. Kannensohn, "Attorney Beware: Fair Debt Collection Practices Act," Gregory L. Karam, "Drafting a Demand Letter in Compliance with the Fair Debt Collection Practices Act," both in *Ohio State Bar Association Report* 60, no. 30 (July 20, 1987): 1236–44.

Inflation has pushed the price of insulation and air-conditioning up to $500,000, but with such high turnover, you're losing money every summer. Write a memo to Jennifer M. Kirkland, Operations Vice President, renewing your request.

Analysis of the Problem

1. Who is (are) your audience(s)? What characteristics are relevant to this particular message? If you are writing to more than one reader, how do the readers differ?

   The Operations Vice President will be concerned about keeping costs low and keeping production running smoothly. Kirkland may know that the request was denied two years ago, but another person was Vice President then; Kirkland wasn't the one who said *no*.

2. What are your purposes in writing?

   To persuade Kirkland to authorize insulation and air-conditioning. To build a good image of myself.

3. What information must your message include?

   The cost of the proposal. The effects of the present situation.

4. How can you build support for your position? What reasons or reader benefits will your reader find convincing?

   Cutting turnover may save money and keep the assembly line running smoothly. Experienced employees may produce higher-quality parts. Putting in air-conditioning would relieve one of the workers' main complaints; it might make the union happier.

5. What objection(s) can you expect your reader(s) to have? What negative elements of your message must you deemphasize or overcome?

   The cost. The time operations will be shut down while installation is taking place.

6. What aspects of the total situation may affect reader response? The economy? The time of year? Morale in the organization? The relationship between the reader and writer? Any special circumstances?

   The electronics industry is having a shakeout; money is tight; the company will be reluctant to make a major expenditure. Despite moderate unemployment, filling vacancies in the tube room is hard—we are getting a reputation as a bad place to work. Summer is over, and the problem is over until next year.

Discussion of the Sample Solutions

Solution 1, shown in Figure 9.7, is unacceptable. By making the request in the subject line and the first paragraph, the writer invites a *no* before giving all the arguments. The writer does nothing to counter the objections that any manager will have to spending a great deal of money. By presenting the issue in terms of fairness, the writer produces defensiveness rather than creating a common ground. The writer doesn't use details or emotional appeal to show that the problem is indeed serious. The writer asks for fast action but doesn't show why the reader should act now to solve a problem that won't occur again for eight months.

Solution 2, shown in Figure 9.8, is an effective persuasive message. The writer chooses a positive subject line. The opening sentence is negative, catching the reader's attention. However, the paragraph makes it clear that the memo offers a solution to the problem. The problem is spelled out in detail. Emotional impact

An Unacceptable Solution to the Sample Problem   **Figure 9.7**

Date: October 12, 19--

To: Jennifer M. Kirkland, Operations Vice President

From: Arnold M. Morgan, Production Supervisor **AMM**

Subject: Request for Air-Conditioning the Tube Room   *Request in subject line stiffens resistance when reader is reluctant*

Please put air-conditioning in the tube room. This past summer, 2/3 of our employees quit because it was so hot. It's (not fair) that they should work in unbearable temperatures when management sits in air-conditioned comfort.   *attacks reader*

Inappropriate emphasis on writer (I) propose that we solve this problem by air-conditioning the tube room to bring down the temperature to 78°.

Insulating and air-conditioning the tube room would cost $500,000.

Please approve this request promptly.   *Cost sounds enormous without a context*

Memo sounds arrogant.
Logic isn't developed.
This attacks reader instead of enlisting reader's support.

is created by taking the reader through the day as the temperature rises. The solution is presented impersonally. There are no *I*'s in the memo.

The memo stresses reader benefits: the savings that will result once the investment is recovered. The last paragraph tells the reader exactly what to do and links prompt action to a reader benefit. The memo ends with a positive picture of the problem solved.

Figures 9.9 and 9.10 provide checklists for direct requests and problem-solving persuasive messages.

Figure 9.8   **A Good Solution to the Sample Problem**

Date: October 12, 19--

To: Jennifer M. Kirkland, Operations Vice President

From: Arnold M. Morgan, Production Supervisor   *AMM*

Subject: Improving Summer Productivity

Reader benefit in subject line

Problem creates a common ground

Nakamura forfeited a possible $186,000 in profits last summer due to a 17% drop in productivity. That's not unusual: Nakamura has a history of low summer productivity. But we can reverse the trend and bring summer productivity in line with the rest of the year's.

Good to show problem can be resolved

Cause of problem

The problem starts in the tube room. Due to high turnover and reduced efficiency from workers who are on the job, we just don't make as many TV tubes as we do during the rest of the year. And when we don't have tubes, we can't make TV sets.

Both the high turnover and reduced efficiency are due to the unbearable heat in the tube room. Temperatures in the tube room average 25° over the outside temperature. During the summer, when work starts at 8, it's already 85° in the tube room. By 11:30, it's at least 105°. On six days last summer, it hit 120°. When the temperatures are that high, we may be violating OSHA regulations.

Additional reason to solve problem

Production workers are always standing, moving, or carrying 20-lb. TV tubes. When temperatures hit 90°, they slow down. When no relief is in sight, many of them quit.

We replaced 24 of the 36 employees in the tube room this summer. When someone quits, it takes an average of five days to find and train a replacement; during that time, the trainee produces nothing. For another five days, the new person can work at only half speed. And even "full speed" in the summer is only 90% of what we expect the rest of the year.

More details about problem

Here's where our losses come from:

Normal production = 50 units a person each day (upd)

Loss due to turnover:
    loss of 24 workers for 5 days =   6,000 units
    24 at $^1/_2$ pace for 5 days =   3,000 units
        Total loss due to turnover =   9,000 units

Shows detail— Set up like an arithmetic problem

Loss due to reduced efficiency:
    loss of 5 upd x 12 workers x 10 days =   600 units
    loss of 5 upd x 36 x 50 days =   9,000 units
        Total loss due to reduced efficiency = 9,600 units

Total Loss =   18,600 units

Concluded   **Figure 9.8**

Jennifer M. Kirkland   2   October 12, 19--

According to the accounting department, Nakamura makes a net profit of $10 on every TV set we sell. And, as you know, with the boom in TV sales, we sell every set we make. Those 18,600 units we don't produce are costing us $186,000 a year.

Shows where numbers in paragraph 1 come from

Additional benefit

Bringing down the temperature to 78° (the minimum allowed under federal guidelines) from the present summer average of 112° will require an investment of $500,000 to insulate and air-condition the tube room. Extra energy costs for the air-conditioning will run about $30,000 a year. We'll get our investment back in less than three years. Once the investment is recouped, we'll be making an additional $150,000 a year—all without buying additional equipment or hiring additional workers.

Reason to act promptly

Tells reader what to do

By installing the insulation and air-conditioning this fall, we can take advantage of lower off-season rates. Please authorize the Purchasing Department to request bids for the system. Then, next summer, our productivity can be at an all-time high.

Ends on positive note of problem solved, reader enjoying benefit

---

Figure 9.9

Checklist for Direct Requests

☐ If the message is a memo, does the subject line indicate the request? Is the subject line specific enough to differentiate this message from others on the same subject?

☐ Does the first paragraph summarize the request or the specific topic of the message?

☐ Does the message give all of the relevant information? Is there enough detail?

☐ Does the message answer questions or overcome objections that readers may have without introducing unnecessary negatives?

☐ Does the last paragraph tell the reader exactly what to do? Does it give a deadline if one exists and a reason for acting promptly?

And, for all messages, not just direct requests,

☐ Does the message use you-attitude and positive emphasis?

☐ Is the style easy to read and friendly?

☐ Is the visual design of the message inviting?

☐ Is the format correct?

☐ Does the message use standard grammar? Is it free from typos?

Originality in a direct request may come from

- Good lists and visual impact.
- Thinking about readers and giving details that answer their questions, overcome any objections, and make it easier for them to do as you ask.
- Adding details that show you're thinking about a specific organization and the specific people in that organization.

Figure 9.10

Checklist for Problem-Solving Persuasive Messages

☐ If the message is a memo, does the subject line indicate the writer's purpose or offer a reader benefit? Does the subject line avoid making the request?

☐ Does the first paragraph create a common ground?

☐ Is the problem presented as a joint problem both writer and reader have an interest in solving, rather than as something the reader is being asked to do for the writer?

☐ Does the message give all of the relevant information? Is there enough detail?

☐ Does the message overcome objections that readers may have?

☐ Does the message avoid phrases that sound dictatorial, condescending, or arrogant?

☐ Does the last paragraph tell the reader exactly what to do? Does it give a deadline if one exists and a reason for acting promptly?

And, for all messages, not just persuasive ones,

☐ Does the message use you-attitude and positive emphasis?

☐ Is the style easy to read and friendly?

☐ Is the visual design of the message inviting?

☐ Is the format correct?

☐ Does the message use standard grammar? Is it free from typos?

Originality in a problem-solving persuasive message may come from

- A good subject line and common ground.
- A clear and convincing description of the problem.
- Thinking about readers and giving details that answer their questions, overcome objections, and make it easier for them to do as you ask.
- Adding details that show you're thinking about a specific organization and the specific people in that organization.

SUMMARY OF KEY POINTS

- The primary purposes in a persuasive message are to have the reader act, to provide enough information so that the reader knows exactly what to do, and to overcome any objections that might prevent or delay action. Secondary purposes are to build a good image of the writer and the writer's organization, to cement a good relationship between the writer and reader, and to reduce or eliminate future correspondence on the same subject.
- Readers have a vested interest in something if they benefit directly from keeping things as they are.
- **Credibility** is the audience's response to you as the source of the message. You can build credibility by being factual, specific, and reliable.
- Use the persuasive strategy your organization prefers.
- Use the **direct request pattern** when the audience will do as you ask without any resistance. Also use the direct request pattern for busy readers in your own organization who do not read all the messages they receive.
- Use the **problem-solving pattern** when the audience may resist doing what you ask and you expect logic to be more important than emotion in the decision.
- Use the **star-chain-knot pattern** in Chapter 11, "Sales and Fund-Raising Letters," when the audience may resist doing what you ask and when you expect emotion to be more important than logic in the decision.
- In a direct request, consider asking in the first paragraph for the information or service you want. Give readers all the information they will need to act on your request. In the last paragraph, ask for the action you want.

- Organize a problem-solving persuasive message in this way:
  1. Catch the reader's interest by mentioning a common ground.
  2. Define the problem you both share (which your request will solve).
  3. Explain the solution to the problem.
  4. Show that any negative elements (cost, time, etc.) are outweighed by the advantages.
  5. Summarize any additional benefits of the solution.
  6. Ask for the action you want.
- In a direct request, put the request, the topic of the request, or a question in the subject line. Do not put the request in the subject line of a problem-solving persuasive message. Instead, use a **directed subject line** that reveals your position on the issue or a reader benefit. Use a positive or neutral subject line even when the first paragraph will be negative.
- Use one or more of the following strategies to counter objections:
  - Specify how much time and/or money is required.
  - Put the time and/or money in the context of the benefits they bring.
  - Show that money spent now will save money in the long run.
  - Show that doing as you ask will benefit some group the reader identifies with or some cause the reader supports.
  - Show the reader that the sacrifice is necessary to achieve a larger, more important goal to which he or she is committed.
  - Show that the advantages as a group outnumber or outweigh the disadvantages as a group.
  - Turn the disadvantage into an opportunity.
- To encourage readers to act promptly, set a deadline. Show that the time limit is real, that acting now will save time or money, or that delaying action will cost more.
- Build emotional appeal with stories and psychological description.
- Performance appraisals should cite specific observations, not inferences. They should contain specific suggestions for improvement and identify the two or three areas that the worker should emphasize in the next month or quarter.
- Letters of recommendation must be specific and tell how well and how long you've known the person.
- Early in the collection series, remind the reader about the debt matter-of-factly. In middle letters, be more assertive. Try to negotiate for partial payment if the reader is not able to pay the full amount.
- Use the analysis questions from Chapter 1 to analyze persuasive situations.

Exercises and Problems For Chapter 9

GETTING STARTED

9–1   Writing Psychological Description

For one or more of the following groups, write two or three paragraphs of psychological description that could be used in a brochure, news release, or direct mail letter directed to members of that group.

1. Having a personal trainer.
   Audiences: Professional athletes.
   Busy managers.
   Someone trying to lose weight.

Someone making a major lifestyle change after a heart attack.
2. Buying a cellular phone.
Audiences: People who do a lot of big-city driving.
People who do a lot of driving in rural areas.
People who do a lot of flying.
3. Buying a laptop computer.
Audiences: College students.
Financial planners who visit clients at home.
Sales representatives who travel constantly.
People who make PowerPoint presentations.
4. Vacationing at a luxury hotel.
Audiences: Stressed-out people who want to relax.
Tourists who like to sightsee and absorb the local culture.
Business people who want

to stay in touch with the office even on vacation.
Parents with small children.
Weekend athletes who want to have fun.
5. Attending a fantasy sports camp (you pick the sport), playing with and against retired players who provide coaching and advice.
6. Attending a health spa where clients get low-fat and low-calorie meals, massages, beauty treatments, and guidance in nutrition and exercise.

Hints:
- For this assignment, you can combine benefits or programs as if a single source offered them all.
- Add specific details about particular sports, cities, tourist attractions, activities, etc., as material for your description.
- Be sure to move beyond reader benefits to vivid details and sense impressions.
- Put your benefits in you-attitude.

9–2 Evaluating Subject Lines

Evaluate the following subject lines. Is one subject line in each group clearly best? Or does the "best" line depend on company culture, whether the message is a paper memo or an e-mail message, or on some other factor?

a. Subject: Request
Subject: Why I Need a New Computer
Subject: Increasing My Productivity
b. Subject: Who Wants Extra Hours?
Subject: Holiday Work Schedule
Subject: Working Extra Hours During the Holiday Season

c. Subject: Student Interviews
Subject: Request for Volunteers to Conduct Information and Mock Job Interviews
Subject: Volunteers Needed for Student Interviews
d. Subject: More Wine and Cheese
Subject: Today's Reception for Japanese Visitors
Subject: Reminder
e. Subject: Reducing Absenteeism
Subject: Opening a Day Care Center for Sick Children of Employees
Subject: Why We Need Expanded Day Care Facilities

9–3 Brainstorming Reasons to Act Promptly

Brainstorm one or more reasons that readers should act promptly in each of the following situations:

1. Persuading CPAs to take a continuing education course about changes in the tax law
a. In May.
b. In October.
c. In December.
2. Persuading customers to install storm windows and insulation

a. In March.
b. In June.
c. In October.

3. Persuading your office to make a major change in its computer hardware and software
a. Just before the end of the fiscal year.
b. Right before the busiest season of the year.
c. During the least busy time of the year.

9—4   Identifying Observations

Susan has taken the following notes about her group's meetings. Which of the following are specific observations that she could use in a performance appraisal of group members? If she had it to do over again, what kinds of details would turn the inferences into observations?

1. Feb. 22: Today was very frustrating. Sam was totally out of it—I wonder if he's on something. Jim was dictatorial. I argued, but nobody backed me up. Masayo might just as well have stayed home. We didn't get anything done. Two hours, totally wasted.

2. February 24: Jim seems to be making a real effort to be less domineering. Today he asked Sam and me for our opinions before proposing his own. And he noticed that Masayo wasn't talking much and brought her into the conversation. She suggested some good ideas.

3. February 28: Today's meeting was OK. I thought Masayo wasn't really focusing on the work at hand. She needs to work on communicating her ideas to others. Sam was doing some active listening, but he needs to work at being on time. Jim was involved in the project. He has strong leadership skills. There were some tense moments, but we got a lot done, and we all contributed. I got to say what I wanted to say, and the group decided to use my idea for the report.

4. March 5: This week most of us had midterms, and Masayo had an out-of-town gymnastics trip. We couldn't find a time to meet. So we did stuff by e-mail. Sam and Jim found some great stuff at the library and on the Web. Jim created a tentative schedule which he sent to all of us and then revised. I wrote up a draft of the description of the problem. Then Masayo and I put everything together. I sent my draft to her; she suggested revisions (in full caps so I could find them in the e-mail message). Then I sent the message to everyone. Masayo and Jim both suggested changes, which I made before we handed the draft in.

5. March 15: We were revising the proposal, using Prof. Jones' comments. When we thought we were basically done, Masayo noticed that we had not responded to all of the specific comments about our introductory paragraph. We then went back and thought of some examples to use. This made our proposal better and more complete.

9—5   Revising a Form Memo

You've been hired as a staff accountant; one of your major duties will be processing expense reimbursements. Going through the files, you find this form memo:

Subject: Reimbursements

Enclosed are either receipts that we could not match with the items in your request for reimbursement or a list of items for which we found no receipts or both. Please be advised that the Accounting Department issues reimbursement checks only with full documentation. You cannot be reimbursed until you give us a receipt for each item for which you desire reimbursement. We must ask that you provide this information. This process may be easier if you use the Expense Report Form which is available in your department.

Thank you for your attention to this matter. Please do not hesitate to contact us with questions.

You know this memo is horrible. In addition to wordiness, a total lack of positive emphasis and you-attitude, and a vague subject line, the document design and organization of information bury the request.

Create a new memo that could be sent to people who do not provide all the documentation they need in order to be reimbursed.

E-MAIL MESSAGES

9–6   Asking a Question

You're Director of Management Information Systems for your organization. This morning at the Budget Committee meeting, you presented a proposal to buy new laptop computers. One person asked whether it would be cheaper to stop buying desktop computers and buy only laptops. "Today's laptops are really powerful," one person said. "This way no one would need two computers," someone else added. The committee tabled your proposal, asking you to investigate the idea and report back at the next meeting in two weeks.

There's some merit in the idea, though desktop computers, which can be big, are much less expensive than laptops with the same features. And laptops are much more likely to be dropped, have coffee spilled on them, or be stolen.

As you think about the report you'll need to make in two weeks, you realize it isn't just a matter of comparing dollars and cents. You really need information about how people *use* their computers. Maybe some people need both. Maybe others could use just one or the other—especially if there were a few "loaner" laptops for people who don't travel much and a few "community" desktop machines for people in the office. Do the laptops need to be full-featured? Are people using multimedia and CD-ROMs on the road? Do they need big hard drives and good screens to show graphics? Or would a stripped down (and cheaper) machine do the job?

Write an e-mail message to all employees, asking them about their computer use and preferences. You need responses early enough to put together your own recommendation and support for the Budget Committee.

9–7   Asking for Something for Your Unit

You've received this e-mail message from the Chief Financial Officer (CFO) of your organization:

> Subject: RFP for New Money
>
> Nearly $100,000 in new capital has become available. Argue for an item you need, up to $15,000. E-mail your request, a ballpark price, and the justification by Friday. We'll notify winners within two weeks.

Write the message.

Hints:

- Pick an organization you know well (for example, a college computer lab, your workplace, an organization where you volunteer). Ask for something that's really needed.
- Show how the item will enable your unit to contribute to the organization's mission.

9–8   Finding Out Whether a Client Can Receive Attachments

You've finished preparing a draft of brochure text for a client. Before you do the artwork, you want to get approval on the text and page layout. You've been sending messages back and forth through e-mail, but you want your client to see the layout, font sizes, and so forth. Your document is in Microsoft Word for Office 97. If your client also has that program (or a newer version), you could send the document as an attachment, preserving the layout codes. If she doesn't, you'll need to send the document by overnight delivery. Send an e-mail message to your client, Carole Romano, to find out whether you can send the document as an attachment.

9–9   Persuading People to Come to a Session

Several months ago, your organization brought in a consultant to recommend ways your organization could improve and become a "learning organization." One of the recommendations was that regular seminar sessions be held to acquaint people with the "best practices" in each unit, so that they could spread more quickly. You were put in charge of scheduling these sessions. The first few went well, but attendance has fallen. As a result, it's harder to persuade people to present: with a small audience, they don't feel like taking the time to create a polished presentation.

Perhaps the usefulness of the sessions has run its course. But when you tried tactfully to suggest that maybe it was time to end the sessions, your manager, Earl Stanwyk, vetoed the idea.

From: Earl Stanwyk

Subject: Re: Continue Best Practices Sessions?

Of course we should continue them. So far, we've heard from fewer than half the areas in the organization.

You may need to tinker with the time or format to get people to come to them. I'll authorize payment for modest refreshments. And if you're having a hard time getting speakers, ask Alodie. She developed our Web pages, which have been getting a very good response. Tell her I told you to ask her.

The Director likes this program. It's your job to make it succeed.

Write an e-mail message to Alodie Sun, asking her to give a presentation six weeks from now. Assume that she says *yes*, and send an e-mail message to everyone in the organization, persuading them to attend the talk.

Hints:

- Pick an organization you know something about and pick a time and format that will attract people. What kind of refreshments should you have? What time of day is best? Would people prefer a session with more discussion? Would a plain presentation or one with slick graphics be more successful?

- Pick a subject line that will attract people without misleading them. "Free donuts" will backfire when people find out they have to come to a session to get them.

- How busy are people going to be when this presentation is scheduled? If it's crunch time, how can you make them want to come? What kind of presentation (in terms of content or involvement) could Alodie give that will be easy for you to sell?

9–10   Persuading the CEO to Attend Orientation

As the Director of Education and Training of your organization, you run orientation sessions for new hires. You're planning next quarter's session (new quarters start in January, April, July, and October) for a big group of new college graduates. You'd really like the organization's president and CEO to come in and talk to the group for at least 15 minutes. Probably most of the employees have seen the CEO, but they haven't had any direct contact. The CEO could come any time during the three-day session. Speaking just before or after lunch would be ideal, because then the CEO could also come to lunch and talk informally with at least a few people. Next best would be speaking just before or after the midmorning or midafternoon breaks. But the CEO is busy, and you'll take what you can get.

As Your Instructor Directs,

a. Assume that your instructor is your CEO, and send an e-mail message persuading him or her to come to orientation.

b. Send an e-mail message to your instructor, asking him or her to address new members of a campus organization.

c. Address the CEO of your college or your workplace, asking him or her to speak to new employees.

COMMUNICATING AT WORK

As Your Instructor Directs in 9–11 through 9–17,
   a. Create a document or presentation to achieve the goal.
   b. Write a memo to your instructor describing the situation at your workplace and explaining your rhetorical choices (medium, strategy, tone, wording, graphics or document design, and so forth).

9–11   Writing a Performance Appraisal

Write an appraisal of someone with whom you work. You may appraise a subordinate, or you may assume that your organization uses 360° appraisals (see problem 7–15) and appraise a peer or a superior.

9–12   Recommending a Co-Worker for a Bonus or an Award

Recommend someone at your workplace for a bonus or an award. The award can be something bestowed by the organization itself ("Employee of the Month," "Dealership of the Year," and so forth), or it can be a community or campus award ("Business Person of the Year," "Volunteer of the Year," an honorary degree, and so forth).

9–13   Justifying Your Position

Organizations facing downsizing have to decide which positions to keep and which to cut. Imagine that your organization is facing financial problems and that your supervisor, who wants to keep you, has asked you to draft something explaining why your position should be retained and why you are the best person to keep in the position. Create a memo or presentation to do the job.

Hints:
   ■ Show how you contribute to the unit's and the organization's goals.
   ■ Write your memo in the third person, so that your supervisor can send it upward without having to revise it.

9–14   Asking for a Raise or Reclassification

Do you deserve a raise? Should your job be reclassified to reflect your increased responsibilities (with more pay, of course!)? If so, write a memo to the person with the authority to determine pay and job titles, arguing for what you want.

9–15   Writing a Collection Letter

Identify a customer or client whose payment is late, and write a collection letter or prepare notes for a phone call.

9–16   Requesting Information from a Co-worker

Often, you need information from other people to do your own work. Write to a co-worker, asking for the information you need.

9–17   Asking to Take a Course or Attend a Conference

Write to your supervisor, asking to take a course or attend a conference (at the organization's expense) that will help you do your job better.

Hints:
   ■ How much does your supervisor know about this course or conference? Have others in your unit taken or attended it, or are you the first?
   ■ How will your work be covered while you're away?
   ■ Include the cost of registration, materials, travel, and lodging so that your supervisor knows what you're asking for.

MEMO AND LETTER ASSIGNMENTS

9-18 Persuading a Magazine to Change Its Subscription Letter _____

You're Director of Customer Service for a new magazine named *Parenting 2000*. (Actually, you're the whole customer service department, but you negotiated the higher title when you took the job six weeks ago.) Much of your work is routine, but you also respond to customer complaints. In the last three weeks, you've received 36 letters complaining about a direct mail letter soliciting new subscriptions. The complaints fall into three categories:

1. The largest category, with 19 complaints. Here's a sample:

> You claim your magazine will "help you persuade your husband to do his share of the parenting, whether it's changing diapers or helping enforce curfews." This implies that most men have to be "persuaded" to "help"—as if raising kids were really the wife's job. We, like many couples we know, are both actively involved in our children's care and have been from the very beginning. Your letter insults men and parents.

2. The next biggest category, with 14 complaints. Here's a sample:

> Your letter assumes that every mother has a husband who can share the work of raising a child. It's really odd that a magazine that claims to be about parenting at the turn of the century doesn't seem to realize that there are a lot of single parents out there, doing the best we can. Why exclude us? And why should I subscribe to a magazine that isn't for me?

3. A category with three complaints. Here's one of them:

> Many of the examples in your letter (how to choose a nanny, should your child be in a private school) suggest that your magazine is really for rich, conservative, white families. You don't mention any concerns of parents of color or of people who are trying to prepare their children to be good citizens in a multiracial world. Shame on you!

From your training and experience in customer service, you know that few people take the time to write letters of complaint, even when they are disappointed or angered by a product, service, or ad. So these three dozen letters likely represent a much larger sample of recipients who didn't like the subscription letter. Even worse, judging from these complaints, the subscription letter misrepresented the magazine: the issues you've seen (in print and in preparation) have useful information for all parents, whatever their politics, marital status, ethnicity, or income level.

You told the editor, Lance Dittrich, about the problem and that the letter needed to be changed. He said that he didn't have anything to do with the letter. "That's all done by the parent company. Actually, they probably hired some freelancer to write the letter, and the person just wasn't very sensitive. But if the results are poor, they'll change the letter. Companies keep using the same letter only if it works."

You think this letter needs to be changed immediately, whether it "works" or not. And people at the magazine should get a chance to comment on drafts before a final letter is mailed out. If you or other staffers had seen the letter, you could have recommended changes in wording and examples to create a more balanced picture of the magazine.

Write to the CEO of the publishing group, Lana Salazar, urging that this subscription letter be replaced and that future letters come to your office for comments before they go out.

9–19   Solving the Coffee Break Problem

Once upon a time, the generic office pot of coffee was good enough. But now employees have to get just the right blend at their favorite java haunt. The only problem is that by the time they walk there, wait, order, and walk back, they may have been gone 20 minutes or more. And the elevators are tied up with all this going down and up.

Create a message to solve the problem.

Hints:

- Use a business, government office, or nonprofit organization you know well.

- Be sure to answer possible objections:
  a. "It's healthy to get up, stretch, and walk for a few minutes."
  b. "Smokers go outside for cigarettes. I've got the right to go out for coffee."
  c. "Coffee helps me be creative and more productive."
- Why is it important that people be in the office rather than at a coffee shop?

9–20   Persuading Guests to Allow Extra Time for Checkout

Your hotel has been the headquarters for a convention, and on Sunday morning you're expecting 5,000 people to check out before noon. You're staffing the checkout desk to capacity, but if everyone waits till 11:30 to check out, things will be a disaster.

So you want to encourage people to allow extra time. And they don't have to stand in line at all: by 4 AM, you'll put a statement of current charges under each guest's door. If that statement is correct and the guest is leaving the bill on the credit card used at check-in, the guest can just leave the key in the room and leave. You'll mail a copy of the final bill together with any morning charges by the end of the week.

Write a one-page message that can be put on pillows when the rooms are made up Friday and Saturday night.

9–21   Asking for Sick-Child Care

Day care is a fact of life for working parents in the United States. But day care centers won't accept sick children. So when their kids are sick, parents may have to call in sick themselves. The problem wreaks havoc on schedules for production, travel, meetings, and presentations.

Write a memo to the upper management of your organization, urging that it provide sick care service. One model is to create a site in a central area. An organization big enough to need a site just for its employees' children may be able to create one on-site. Small companies will want to team up with several other small businesses and split the cost. Another option is to have a visiting caregiver stay with the child in the employee's home.

Hints:

- Pick a business, government office, nonprofit agency, or educational institution that you know something about.
- Use your analysis from problems 3–11 and 3–12. How will this program help individuals? And how will that help the organization?
- Will your organization be more persuaded by a dollars-and-cents comparison showing how much this benefit could save the company? Or would stories be more persuasive?

9–22   Persuading Disability Services to Increase the Handivan's Hours

State University has a "Handivan" that takes students in wheelchairs from their residences or apartments to campus locations and back again. But the van stops at 6 PM (even though there are evening classes, lectures, and events). And it doesn't take people to off-campus restaurants, movies, grocery stores, or shopping centers. Write to the Director of Disability Services, urging that the Handivan's services be increased.

9–23   Persuading Your Campus to Keep Computer Labs Open Longer Hours

Only a few of State University's computer labs are open 24 hours a day. From midterms on, there always seems to be a waiting line for the computers in those labs.

Identify the person(s) with the authority and power to determine lab hours, and write a message that will persuade him, her, or them to keep more labs open longer.

Hints:

- Use your college, community college, or university.
- Do all the labs need to be kept open 24 hours a day all term? If not, what hours in which labs at what points in the term would be most helpful?
- How much would it cost (in terms of hiring people to staff the labs, paying for electricity and building safety) to keep the labs open longer? Where could this money come from?
- Administrators may not know a lot about students' lives and schedules. How can you persuade readers that students will indeed come in to use the labs?
- Revise, edit, and proofread carefully. Mistakes weaken your credibility.

9–24   Recommending a "Telecard"

Everyone from the Salvation Army to Burger King is experimenting with telecards. These credit-card-size cards give the holder prepaid long-distance time—usually 5 or 10 minutes, though the amount is up to the organization paying for the cards ("Playing the 'Telecard' Hand," *Inc.*, January 1996, 84). The cards can be given away as a premium or sold to people who will use them or distribute them as gifts. Users of the cards hear a short promotional message before getting the access number to make calls.

Write a memo to the person in charge of marketing for your organization, recommending that it adopt telecards.

Hints:

- Pick a business, government office, nonprofit agency, or educational institution that you know something about.
- Should the cards be given away? To whom? Should they be sold?
- Can the cards enhance the organization's image and build goodwill?
- What kind of promotional message would be most appropriate for your organization?

9–25   Handling a Sticky Recommendation

As a supervisor in a state agency, you have a dilemma. You received this e-mail message today:

From: John Inoye, Director of Personnel, Department of Taxation

Subject: Need Recommendation for Peggy Chafez

Peggy Chafez has applied for a position in the Department of Taxation. On the basis of her application and interview, she is the leading candidate. However, before I offer the job to her, I need a letter of recommendation from her current supervisor.

Could you please let me have your evaluation within a week? We want to fill the position as quickly as possible.

Peggy has worked in your office for 10 years. She designed, writes, and edits a monthly statewide newsletter that your office puts out; she designed and maintains the department Web site. Her designs are creative; she's a very hard worker; she seems to know a lot about computers.

However, Peggy is in many ways an unsatisfactory staff member. Her standards are so high that most people find her intimidating.

Some find her abrasive. People have complained to you that she's only interested in her own work; she seems to resent requests to help other people with projects. And yet both the newsletter and the Web page are projects that need frequent interaction. She's out of the office a lot. Some of that is required by her job (she takes the newsletters to the post office, for example), but some people don't like the fact that she's out of the office so much. They also complain that she doesn't return voice mail and e-mail messages.

You think managing your office would be a lot smoother if Peggy weren't there. You can't fire her: state employees' jobs are secure once they get past the initial six-month probationary period. Because of budget constraints, you can hire new employees only if vacancies are created by resignations. You feel that it would be pretty easy to find someone better.

If you recommend that John Inoye hire Peggy, you will be able to hire someone you want. If you recommend that John hire some-

one else, you may be stuck with Peggy for a long time.

As Your Instructor Directs,

    a. Write an e-mail message to John Inoye.

    b. Write a memo to your instructor listing the choices you've made and justifying your approach.

Hints:

- Polarization may make this dilemma more difficult than it needs to be. What are your options? Consciously look for more than two.
- Is it possible to select facts or to use connotations so that you are truthful but still encourage John to hire Peggy? Is it ethical? Is it certain that John would find Peggy's work as unsatisfactory as you do? If you write a strong recommendation and Peggy doesn't do well at the new job, will your credibility suffer? Why is your credibility important?

9–26 Persuading Employees to Join the Company Volleyball Team

Your company has decided to start a company volleyball team to play in the city recreation league. Now, you need to get people to sign up for the team. Ideally, you'd like to have several teams to involve as many people as possible and build company loyalty. If you have enough teams, they can play each other once a week in a round-robin company tournament.

Write a memo to all employees persuading them to sign up.

Hints:

- How young and how athletic are your employees? How busy are they? Will

this be an easy or a difficult thing to persuade them to do?

- Some people may be reluctant to join because their skills are rusty. How can you persuade people that you want everyone to participate even if they're not athletic?
- Will the people who sign up have to pay anything or buy uniforms?
- How do people sign up? Is there a deadline?

9–27 Writing Collection Letters

You have a small desktop publishing firm. Today, you've set aside some time to work on overdue bills.

As Your Instructor Directs, write letters for one or more of the following situations.

    a. A $750 bill for producing three monthly newsletters for a veterinarian to mail to her clients. The agreement was that you'd bill her $250 each month. But somehow you haven't sent out bills for the last two months, so they'll go on this month's bill. You'd like payment for the whole bill, and you want to

continue this predictable income of $250 a month.

    b. A $200 bill for creating flyers for a rock band to post. You've called twice and left messages on an answering machine, but nothing has happened. The bill is only three weeks overdue, but the band doesn't seem very stable, and you want to be paid now.

    c. A $3,750 bill for designing and printing a series of brochures for Creative Interiors, a local interior decorating shop, is three weeks past due. When you billed Creative Interiors, you got a note saying that the design was not acceptable and that you would not be paid until you redesigned it (at no extra charge) to the owner's satisfaction. The owner had approved the preliminary design on which the brochures were based; he did not explain in the note what was wrong with the final product. He's never free when you are; indeed, when you call to try to schedule an appointment, you're told the owner will call you back—but he never does. At this point, the delay is not your fault; you want to be paid.

9-28 Getting Permission from Parents for a School Project

As part of a community cleanup program, all public-school students will spend the afternoon of the second Friday of April picking up trash. Younger students will pick up trash on school grounds, in parks, and in parking lots; older students will pick up trash downtown. Schoolteachers will supervise the students; where necessary, school buses will transport them. After students are finished, they'll return to their school's playground, where they'll be supervised until the end of the school day. Each school will maintain a study hall for any students whose parents do not give them permission to participate. Trash bags and snacks have been donated by local merchants.

Write a one-page cover letter that students can take home to their parents telling them about the project and persuading them to sign the necessary permission form. You do NOT need to create the permission form, but do refer to it in your letter.

Hints:
- What objections may parents have? How can you overcome these?
- Where should parents who drive their kids to school pick them up?
- Should students wear their normal school clothing?
- When must the form be returned? Who gets it? Whom can parents call if they have questions before they sign the form?

9-29 Asking an Instructor for a Letter of Recommendation

You're ready for the job market or graduate school, and you need letters of recommendation.

As Your Instructor Directs,
- a. Assume that you've orally asked an instructor for a recommendation, and he or she has agreed to write one. "Why don't you write up something to remind me of what you've done in the class? Tell me what else you've done, too. And tell me what they're looking for. Be sure to tell me when the letter needs to be in and whom it goes to."
- b. Assume that you've been unable to talk with the instructor whose recommendation you want. When you call, no one answers the phone; you stopped by once and no one was in. Write asking for a letter of recommendation.
- c. Assume that the instructor is no longer on campus. Write him or her a letter asking for a recommendation.

Hints:
- Be detailed about the points you'd like the instructor to mention.
- How well will this instructor remember you? How much detail about your performance in his or her class do you need to provide?
- Specify the name and address of the person to whom the letter should be written; specify when the letter is due. If there's an intermediate due date (for example, if you must sign the outside of the envelope to submit the recommendation to law school), say so.

9-30 Writing a Performance Appraisal for a Member of a Collaborative Group

During your collaborative writing group meetings, keep a log of events. Record specific observations of both effective and ineffective things that group members do. Then evaluate the performance of the other members in your group. (If there are two or more other people, write a separate appraisal for each of them.)

In your first paragraph, summarize your evaluation. Then in the body of your memo, give the specific details that led to your evaluation by answering the following questions:

- What specifically did the person do in terms of the task? Brainstorm ideas? Analyze the information? Draft the text? Suggest revisions in parts drafted by others? Format the document or create visuals? Revise? Edit? Proofread? (In most cases, several people will have done each of these activities together. Don't overstate what any one person did.) What was the quality of the person's work?

- What did the person contribute to the group process? Did he or she help schedule the work? Raise or resolve conflicts? Make other group members feel valued and included? Promote group cohesion? What roles did the person play in the group?

Support your generalizations with specific observations. The more observations you have and the more detailed they are, the better your appraisal will be.

As Your Instructor Directs,
  a. Write a midterm performance appraisal for one or more members of your collaborative group. In each appraisal, identify the two or three things the person should try to improve during the second half of the term.
  b. Write a performance appraisal for one or more members of your collaborative group at the end of the term. Identify and justify the grade you think each person should receive for the portion of the grade based on group process.
  c. Give a copy of your appraisal to the person about whom it is written.

CHAPTER 10

Handling Difficult Persuasive Situations

Chapter Outline

An Inside Perspective:
Handling Difficult Persuasive Situations

Ray Hood-Phillips, Chief Diversity Officer
Flagstar Companies

Ray Hood-Phillips helps companies see diversity as a strength and create more inclusive workplaces. Headquarted in Spartanburg, South Carolina, Flagstar is the parent company of Denny's and five other restaurant chains. Flagstar is the second largest restaurant chain company in the United States, with over 3,200 restaurants.

In today's downsized or "right-sized" world, face-to-face contact with your direct reports may be limited to monthly or quarterly meetings. Broadened wingspans (more direct reports) and management's expectation of doing more with less make communicating persuasively a critical skill.

Our Diversity Affairs unit is responsible for formulating strategies and supporting tactics to increase the representation of women and minorities throughout all business operations at Flagstar. Our aim is to build an inclusive organization in all six restaurant chains. We manage all diversity issues and intervene in crises. We must be persuasive to present, sell, or negotiate our point of view to satisfy all parties.

I remember an incident in which a local civil rights group felt one of our chains was discriminating against a specific minority group in its hiring practices. The civil rights leaders were angry and confrontational. Management felt the accusations were wrong and were somewhat defensive. Handling this conflict required face-to-face meetings with restaurant management and the civil rights leaders.

It was important to first meet with each side privately to give people a chance to openly air all their issues, concerns, and wounds. I took notes and asked a lot of questions to clarify the main issues. Both sides had powerful arguments. I then called a joint meeting to let each party hear the other's side. Before the meeting, I pulled the workforce availability statistics for the market. (It's important to work with facts and not opinions, anecdotes, or hearsay.) The research supported the civil rights group's claims.

I mediated the meeting, with a goal of satisfying each party's bottom-line issues. We found a common meeting ground. In the end, management learned new tactics for attracting nontraditional workers. The civil rights group learned the difficulties the restaurants were having in recruiting minorities and offered to help. As a result, six months later the demographic composition of the local restaurants changed significantly to be more reflective of the surrounding market. Restaurant management was recently featured on a local radio show to discuss the radical transformation and to show other companies how to do it. Everybody won.

Ray Hood-Phillips, February 18, 1997

251

"[G]ive people a chance to openly air all their issues, concerns, and wounds[,] . . . work with facts . . . [and find] a common meeting ground."

Ray Hood-Phillips, Flagstar Companies

Some persuasive situations are very difficult. Perhaps your audience's initial position is negative; they may be highly committed to their position; doing as you ask raises fears about their comfort, security, and self-images. However, if you understand the situation and your audience, and if you use tight logic and control your tone, you can sometimes find a common meeting ground.

Three sample situations show how difficult persuasion can be:

- People tune out messages they don't want to hear.

    An apartment manager urges residents to pay their rent on time, to take their trash out to the dumpster, and to obey the "no pets" rules. The manager tries everything from pleading to insults, but nothing works.

    Because the apartment manager's messages are unpleasant and limit their freedom, most residents ignore them. That way, they can do what they want without disturbing their images of themselves as reasonable people.

- People are reluctant to say *yes* if doing so requires them to admit they've been wrong all along.

    A Traffic Manager finds that buying trucks rather than continuing to lease them would save his company $10 million over the first three years and an additional $1 million a year after that.

    This isn't an open-and-shut case because the Traffic Manager must convince a reader who has decided every year to lease. Yet the reader will simply become defensive if the Traffic Manager says, "You should have made this change years ago."

- People deny realities that are too much for them to cope with.

    A lab worker becomes infected with the AIDS virus. A government report shows that if lab workers follow safety procedures—if they wear gowns and gloves, and perhaps masks and goggles—they'll be safe. But workers don't follow the procedures.

    When the risk is so great, why don't workers protect themselves? Perhaps because the thought of contracting AIDS is too scary. Many people who deal every day with something life-threatening practice **denial:** they persuade themselves that "nothing will happen" to them. Taking precautions seems to make the risk too real.

Fortunately, even a brief view of history shows that societies, organizations, and people can change. Societies can reject racism and sexism. Companies can abandon unprofitable products and follow the market into new ventures. People can change their minds even about such deeply held beliefs as sexual behavior and how to raise their children. Conversions—both religious and secular—do happen.

When you want readers to do something specific,

1. Limit your audience. Go with the people you can persuade and forget about the rest.
2. Try to bring everyone on board.

Major changes may take months or years and a series of formal and informal messages. These changes will be most successful if you use a third strategy:

3. Involve the audience. Let them find the solution.

This chapter discusses these three strategies and the logical arguments needed to support them.

LIMITING YOUR AUDIENCE

Sometimes you don't need everyone. A political candidate, for example, needs to persuade only enough people to win the election. A shelter for runaway teens doesn't need money from everyone—just enough money to meet the budget.

Figure 10.1 shows a letter that resulted when a company couldn't persuade everyone to respond to a request. Combustion Engineering had decided, as a matter of policy, to favor minority suppliers. Most suppliers ignored its request to let it know their demographic makeup. Suppliers that qualified were happy to respond, but there just weren't reader benefits for those who didn't qualify. But it didn't matter if many—perhaps most—companies didn't respond. Combustion Engineering just needed to hear from the companies it wanted to buy from.

BRINGING EVERYBODY ON BOARD

Some changes, such as motivating people in your organization to save money or to adopt diversity goals, will succeed only if most people cooperate. To change people's minds, you need to offer reasons.

Sometimes people think they will be able to mandate change by ordering or threatening subordinates. Real managers disagree. Research shows that managers use threats only for obligatory duties such as coming to work on time. For more creative duties—like being part of a team or thinking of ways to save the company money—managers give reasons.[1] A survey showed that sales representatives were motivated by selling a good product; getting backup, support, training, and commissions; and being affiliated with a good company. Threats ("perform or else") were rated dead last, with 86% saying threats offered little or no motivation.[2] And threats are even less effective in trying to persuade people whose salaries you don't pay.

Why Threats Are Less Effective than Persuasion

A **threat** is a statement—explicit or implied—that someone will be punished if he or she does (or doesn't do) something. Six reasons explain why punishment and threats don't work.[3]

1. **Threats don't produce permanent change.** Many people obey the speed limit only when a marked police car is in sight.
2. **Threats won't necessarily produce the action you want.** If you embarrass or punish people who take too many felt-tip pens or too much paper, they might write fewer reports—hardly the response you'd want!
3. **Threats may make people abandon an action—even in situations where it would be appropriate.** Criticizing workers for talking about nonbusiness topics such as sports may reduce communication about business topics as well.
4. **Threats produce tension.** People who feel threatened put their energies into ego defense rather than into productive work.
5. **People dislike and avoid anyone who threatens them.** A supervisor who is disliked will find it harder to enlist cooperation and support on the next issue that arises.
6. **Threats can provoke counteraggression.** Getting back at a boss can run the gamut from complaints to work slowdowns to sabotage.

Olympic Persuasion*

How did Salt Lake City get the Winter Olympics in 2002, just six years after the Summer Games had been held in Atlanta? Credit the quiet persuasion of Anita DeFrantz, lawyer, former US medalist in rowing, and the only woman on the 11-member Executive Board of the International Olympic Committee (IOC). She told Salt Lake City boosters about the interests of each IOC member, so that they could adapt messages and gifts.

DeFrantz's behind-the-scenes work is also credited with persuading the IOC to accept softball as a women's sport. She worked comments about softball into conversations with swing voters on bus rides and at breakfasts. "You can't hit these people over the head with a two-by-four," she says. Frequently she didn't see much response. But she reassured herself, "if I wasn't persuasive today, I might be tomorrow." She was. Now softball is also an Olympic sport.

*Based on "Inside Moves: Former U.S. Medalist Emerges as Quiet Force in the Olympic Arena," *The Wall Street Journal,* June 28, 1996, A1, A6.

Figure 10.1   **A Request to Persuade Only Those Who Will Directly Benefit**

COMBUSTION ❯ENGINEERING

Is at Least 50%
of Your Business
Owned by Women
or Minorities?

Question catches attention, takes visual place of inside address, salutation

If it is, we want to try to use you as a supplier.

Question, paragraph 1 limit audience

You qualify for this favorable treatment if one of the following situations applies:

List creates visual interest

   a.   50% of the business or 51% of the stock is owned by women.

   b.   50% of the business or 51% of the stock is owned by minority group members: Blacks, Asian Americans, Native Americans, or Hispanic Americans.

Combustion Engineering is committed to affirmative action programs to prevent discrimination based on race, color, creed, sex, age, or national origin. We believe that the pursuit of profit and the pursuit of social goals are compatible. We try to act affirmatively in hiring and promoting employees. We also try to act affirmatively in choosing suppliers.

If at least 50% of your company is owned by women or minorities, please send us written evidence by May 15.

If we don't hear from you, we'll assume that you're not a minority business.

Asks for action by a specific date

Sincerely,

J.R. Tran

Reminds readers that they must reply to get favorable treatment

J. R. Tran
Director, Purchasing

Process Automation Business
Combustion Engineering, Inc.

650 Ackerman Road
Post Office Box 02650
Columbus, Ohio 43202-1502

Tel: (614) 261-2000
Fax: (614) 261-2172
Telex: 246675

How to Develop a Persuasive Strategy

Use the following five analysis steps in difficult persuasive situations:

1. **Find out why your audience members resist what you want them to do.** Ray Hood-Phillips suggests sitting down one-on-one with people and listening: "You don't even try to persuade. You just try to understand."
2. **Try to find a win-win solution.** People will be much more readily persuaded if they see benefits for themselves. Sometimes your original proposal may have benefits that the audience had not thought of, and explaining the benefits will help. Sometimes you'll need to modify your original proposal to find a solution that solves the real problem and meets everyone's needs. Chapter 13 has more information about solving the real problem.
3. **Let your audience save face.** Don't ask people to admit that they have been wrong all along. If possible, admit that the behavior may have been appropriate in the past. Whether you can do that or not, always show how changed circumstances or new information call for new action.
4. **Ask for something small.** When you face great resistance, you won't get everything at once. Ask for one step that will move toward your larger goal. For example, if your ultimate goal is to eliminate prejudice in your organization, a step toward that goal might be to convince managers to make a special effort for one month to recognize the contributions of women or members of minorities in group meetings.
5. **Present your arguments from your audience's point of view.** Offer benefits that help the reader, not just you. Take special care to avoid words that attack or belittle readers. Present yourself as someone helping readers achieve their goals, not someone criticizing or giving orders from above.

The draft in Figure 10.2 makes the mistake of attacking readers in a negative message. Making the memo less accusatory would help, but the message doesn't need to be a negative message at all. Instead, the writer can take the information in paragraph 3 and use it as the attention-getter and common ground for a problem-solving persuasive message. Figure 10.3 shows a possible revision.

INVOLVING YOUR AUDIENCE

Organizational changes work best when the audience buys into the solution. And that happens most easily when they themselves find it. Management can

1. Help people see and own the problem.
2. Identify values and cultures that need to change.
3. Let people discover solutions.
4. Support change tangibly and symbolically.

Simply admitting that a serious problem exists is difficult. Videotapes of customer complaints, a visit to a Japanese factory with a more efficient production process, or evidence that the current source of revenue is drying up may help people see the problem. But the tendency is just to keep doing the same thing (perhaps a bit more efficiently). People need to realize that the system is at fault.

For KPMG Netherlands, moving from auditing and tax preparation into new growth areas required recognizing that the company's culture inhibited change. KPMG named 100 of its professionals to work on 14 task forces.

Vision Engineering*

Bridgestone/Firestone faced a major decision: should it spend $100 million on a new information system? Gemini Consulting used a process it calls "vision engineering" to help the company decide.

Top executives came into a room to find stacks of cards, each with a single fact. Some facts are general (Americans save less than 5% of their personal income; work schedules are more flexible). Other facts are industry-specific.

Everyone studied the cards, then combined sets of them under a headline representing a change or trend. After small groups debated, edited, and perhaps combined the headlines, the group agreed on 6 to 10 of them. Because leaders had come up with the ideas themselves, they were less likely to say "yes, but."

Bridgestone/Firestone used this process to get past the split between Japanese and Americans, manufacturing and marketing. While the list of 10 business influences is confidential, in general people decided that technology will change how companies market tires, share information with buyers, and forecast and schedule production. Technology—even with a big price tag—was thus even more important than the company had realized. With that understanding, deciding to spend $100 million was an easier call.

*Based on Thomas A. Stewart, "A Refreshing Change: Vision Statements that Make Sense," *Fortune*, September 30, 1996, 195.

Figure 10.2   **Original Memo Attacking Readers**

BIERNAT
LABORATORIES

Inter-office Memorandum

October 25, 1997

To: Todd Neumann

From: Heather Johnson

Subject: Problems with Instrument Lab Results

Negative *Makes reader feel incompetent*

Accusatory tone The Instrument Technicians Lab again(seems to believe)that if a result is printed out, it is the correct answer.(It doesn't seem to matter)that the chromatogram is terribly noisy. the calibration standards are over a month old, or the area of the internal standards is about half what it should be. What does it matter if the correction factor is 1286 and at the very minimum it should be 1300? That's an average of two results—so what if the calibration standard is six weeks old? I'm *Lacks YA* aware that the conditions in the lab have contributed to the discouraged atmosphere, but I don't *Attacks reader* feel it's an excuse for the shape of the lab and the equipment. The G.C. columns are in bad shape just from abuse. I've lost count of the number of 10 ml. syringes the lab has buried (at least $20 each) mainly because they were not properly rinsed and the plungers were lost trying to push through dried protein material. When was the last time the glass insert in the B column was changed or even looked at? Has anyone checked the filter on the Autolab I?

Lacks YA

Insults and attacks reader During the last six months, I have either reminded the technician of such things or written reminders in the log book. Isn't it time for our responsible lab technicians to take on this responsibility? Shouldn't they have fresh standards made up, especially when they know a run is coming? Granted, we've had many false starts, but I am still uncomfortable that the technicians will be ready when the time comes.

Lacks YA

Problem presented as reader's fault, not a common problem that both share I don't feel that I should have to go over the chromatograms, printouts and G.C. book every time we submit samples for analysis. However, just two weeks ago I sent out results without doing this and immediately received a call that the results were impossible—and they were because unacceptable KF was used, the result of an old calibration standard.

Lacks YA

One other item bothers me. I don't know how to get the technicians interested in the way the Autolab integrates each peak when they don't seem to look at anything other than the answer. I feel it's very important they learn this so they will know when a peak has been incorrectly integrated.

Attacks and insults reader I think it's time they either take hold and run the lab themselves or they be treated as if they were children and told what to do which means they'll need a baby-sitter. I also would like to see them read the Autolab I Instruction Manual and take the tape courses on the gas chromatograph and the Autolab I. I really think the above should be a mandatory part of their training. *Whole ¶ lacks YA*

The overall attitude and morale of the lab must be raised and a step in that direction is to give them the responsibility which they were supposed to have in the first place and expect them to accept it. These people are being called technicians but they are actually classed as chemists and should be assuming more initative and responsibility.

Attacks reader

Revised Memo Creating a Common Ground   **Figure 10.3**

Inter-office Memorandum

October 25, 1997

To: Todd Neumann

From: Heather Johnson

Subject: Cutting Requests for Re-Work   *Positive Subject Line*

Problem writer and reader share

Two weeks ago a customer called to tell me that the results we'd sent out were impossible. I checked, and the results were wrong because we'd used an old calibration standard.

Redoing work for outside customers and for in-house projects doubles our workload. Yet because people don't trust our results, we're getting an increasing number of requests for re-work.

Writer shows understanding of reader's problems

Part of the problem is that we've had so many false starts. Customers and especially in-house engineers say they'll need a run but then don't have the materials for another day or even a week. Paul Liu has told me that these schedule glitches are inevitable. We'll just have to prepare fresh calibration standards every time a run is scheduled—and prepare them again when the run actually is ready.

You've told me that the equipment in the lab is unreliable. The Capital Expenditures Request includes a line item for G.C. columns and a new gas chromatograph. We'll be able to be more persuasive at the Board meeting if we can show that we're taking good care of the equipment we have. Please remind your staff to

- Rinse the 10-ml. syringes every day.

List emphasizes what reader needs to do

- Check the glass insert in the B column every week.

Treats reader as an equal who can help solve the problem

- Check the filter on the Autolab I every week.

Do workers find the Autolab I instruction manual and the tape courses on the gas chromatograph and the Autolab I helpful? If the manual is hard to use or the tape course is boring, perhaps we should ask the manufacturer to redo them and, in the meantime, to send a service worker to offer a short course for our workers. What do you think would be the best way to increase the technical expertise of our staff?

By getting our results right the first time, we can eliminate the re-work and give both customers and in-house clients better service.

Links desired action to benefit and picture of the problem being solved

People in every culture make decisions "logically"—but what counts as evidence and convincing support varies from culture to culture. To be convincing, use the kind of evidence your audience prefers.

Working Together*

Procter & Gamble and Wal-Mart turned a win–lose way of doing business into a win–win relationship. At one time, P&G tried to sell its products to Wal-Mart for as much money as possible, while Wal-Mart tried to pay as little as possible.

Today, P&G and Wal-Mart work together instead of at cross-purposes. Wal-Mart sends continuous sales data to P&G by satellite. P&G figures out what products and sizes are needed and ships directly from the factory to Wal-Mart. Wal-Mart has a smaller inventory but also fewer stockouts. P&G gets paid more quickly. As a result, sales and profits are higher for both companies.

*Based on "Two Tough Companies Learn to Dance Together," *Harvard Business Review*, November-December 1996, 102.

Choosing people from different levels in the organization and asking them to work with people from different areas was itself an important symbolic change in a company that was based on hierarchy and fiefdoms. The project manager helped task force members compare the culture they wanted to the culture they actually had and eventually to see how they would have to change to create the new culture. The process wasn't easy. It required formal meetings and one-on-one dialogs. People had to learn to confront conflict openly and resolve it. One strategy that the company developed was to distribute yellow cards like those used by soccer referees to call "foul" when someone refused to listen to co-workers. Over time, the company changed its culture. The task forces identified $50 to $60 million worth of new business opportunities in helping firms create and shape corporate visions and develop learning organizations.[4]

Symbolism makes it easier for people to change, but symbols alone aren't enough. Tangible rewards in performance appraisals, raises, and promotions must support organizational change if it is to succeed.[5]

CONVINCING THE READER

Any argument has a better chance if it is logically sound and well presented. Tight logic is crucial when you face a hostile audience hoping to defeat you by picking holes in your logic. While any system of logic will help you craft solid arguments, **Toulmin logic,** developed by Stephen Toulmin,[6] is particularly useful for business communication since it can help you both to see whether an argument is valid and to decide how much—or what kind of—evidence you need to provide.

The Toulmin Model

In everyday life, the first part of the argument to emerge is frequently the **claim** we wish to make. When the reader is already on our side, all we have to do is state the claim. But when the reader resists the claim, we must support it with **data** or **evidence.**

Just providing evidence may not be enough in difficult situations. The reader has to see the relationship between the evidence and the claim. If the reader doesn't see the relationship (doesn't know it, agree with it, or happen to think of it at the moment), he or she won't be convinced. Adding more evidence won't help. Instead, we need to spell out the assumption or **bridge** that links the evidence to the claim. (In the old movie, *If Today is Tuesday, This Must Be Belgium*, the bridge is that we're on a whirlwind package trip through Europe that sticks to the itinerary. Without that assumption, there would be no bridge between the evidence that today is Tuesday and a claim about where we are.)

If the audience may disagree with the bridge, we need to prove it. When the proof is made explicit, the statement supporting the bridge is called the **foundation.** Sometimes the reader may accept the bridge but think of a **counterclaim** that negates the claim. If a counterargument exists, we must provide a **rebuttal** to it to be convincing.

Here's an example, labeling the parts of an argument that a college sports team needs to communicate more often with high school athletes it wants to recruit.

Claim:	Better communication will improve our recruiting record.
Evidence:	We are losing recruits to other schools.
Bridge:	Recruits don't necessarily go to the most prestigious school they can. Instead, recruits are more likely to choose schools that communicate with them often during the recruiting process.
Foundation:	Research shows that frequency and quality of communication were key factors in influencing recruits to attend a specific school. Communication strengthened recruits' initial interest and helped overcome objections. Our informal surveys of recruits show that they receive more mail and phone calls from other schools than from us.
Counterclaim:	Our communication might be poor. Frequent communication might hurt rather than help.
Rebuttal:	We will hire a consultant to help our coaches write effective letters.

Many claims cannot be made with 100% certainty. If the claim is only *probably* and not *necessarily* true, we need to **limit** it. You can limit a claim with the words *probably, help,* and *may be* and with explicit disclaimers: "These results are accurate within ± 5.6%." "This projection is based on surveys taken October 28th." Qualifying your claims will build your credibility as a person who promises only what you can deliver.

In a paragraph, the parts of the Toulmin model can come in almost any order; choose the one that makes ideas flow most smoothly. In a longer document—a letter, memo, or report—claims, once you prove them, become data or evidence (now that the reader accepts them) that can be used to support bigger claims. Thus logic becomes a pyramid: small claims support medium-sized claims, which, when proven, in turn support major claims.

In a job application letter, the major claim is "I can do the job." That major claim rests on several smaller claims: "I have the necessary technical skills," "I work well with people," and "I have relevant experience." But each of these smaller claims needs support before it is convincing in supporting the major claim. For example, to prove that she had relevant experience, a student might describe the cost accounting system she developed for a small business, enabling it to save money. She could support that claim by giving details (evidence) about her contribution (to rebut the counterargument that she only used an already-written software package) and by being specific about how the system saved money and how much money it saved. The amount of money limits the claim and makes it more convincing. How specific the applicant needs to be—whether a statement can stand on its own as evidence or whether it first needs to be treated as a claim and proved—depends on how critically the reader will scrutinize the logic. If people who

Limiting Statements in Accounting Reports*

Accountants carefully limit the claims they make in their reports. The following paragraph from a review contains four limiting phrases:

Based on our review we are not aware of any material modifications that should be made to the accompanying financial statements in order for them to be in conformity with generally accepted accounting principles.

"Based on our review" and "we are not aware" acknowledge that evidence may exist which the auditors have not seen. To say that "material modifications" are not needed leaves the door open for possible minor improvements. Finally, "generally accepted accounting principles" is itself limited. CPAs are not claiming that these principles are unchanging or that everyone in the world accepts them.

*Based on Aletha S. Hendrickson, "How to Appear Reliable without Being Liable: C.P.A. Writing in its Rhetorical Context," *Worlds of Writing: Teaching and Learning in Different Discourse Communities*, ed. Carolyn Matalene (New York: Random House, 1989), 308–13.

can do cost accounting are in short supply, the simple claim "I can do it" may net an interview. But if the job market is tight, proof will be necessary.

Using Toulmin Logic in a Memo to Subordinates

Figure 10.4 illustrates the use of the Toulmin model in a problem-solving persuasive message (✖ p. 218). The memo is written to persuade employees not to make personal calls on office phones. The numbers in the margins identify the words, phrases, sentences, or paragraphs that

1. Build a common ground.
2. Offer evidence of the problem.
3. Prove that the problem hurts the organization.
4. Rebut the counterclaim that phones are tied up on business, not personal, calls.
5. Present the solution to the problem in general terms.
6. Present the complete solution in specific terms.
7. Picture the problem being solved.
8. Limit the claims about additional reader benefits that may arise from the solution but are not certain to occur.
9. Ask for action.
10. Create a win-win solution and build an image of the writer as someone who's on the same side as readers, helping them to solve their problems and achieve their goals.

How Much of the Full Toulmin Model To Use

It is possible to outline the full Toulmin model for any claim, even simple ones such as "Your order will arrive Thursday." However, it is not always necessary to do so. Decide how much of the model to use by analyzing the reader and the situation.

The following guidelines can help.

1. **Make both the claim and the evidence explicit** unless you are *sure* the reader will accept what you say totally without questions. Present obvious evidence in a subordinate clause beginning with "since" or "because" to avoid giving the impression that this information is new and surprising.

Since employers prefer job candidates with work experience, we should set up an internship program for our students.

Here the claim "we need an internship program" is supported by evidence in the introductory subordinate clause: "employers prefer candidates with experience."

2. **Include the bridge**
   a. **If it is new information to the reader.**
   b. **If the reader may have heard the bridge but forgotten it.**
   c. **If the reader may disagree with the bridge.**
   d. **If invalid as well as valid bridges exist.**

All of the money saved in the cost-reduction program will go into salaries and benefits, not into research and development, executive bonuses, or stockholder dividends. Therefore employees will benefit if the company saves money.

A Problem-Solving Memo   **Figure 10.4**

Inter-office Memorandum

Date: February 19, 1998

From: James Christopher Smith *JCS*

Subject: ① Improving Service of Customers' Phone Orders *Common ground as subject line*

To: All Sales Representatives
             ⑩ *Writer as problem solver*

Common ground ①
All of you have told me that your customers are experiencing difficulties in placing orders because all the phone lines are tied up, and that some customers are ordering from other wholesalers as a result. This is causing you a loss in sales commissions.

Evidence ② ③
The recent opening of the Johnson Wholesale House in Decatur has made competition in our field of wholesale drugs even keener. With the addition of this new warehouse, Johnson can service customers in all our sales areas almost as quickly as we can, and for approximately the same price. This new availability makes it even easier for our customers to call Johnson's instead of us. In fact, Glenn and Jack report that Walgreen's has increased its business with Johnson's from a sixth to a third of its total drug business. Sue and Jerry also say that several of the small independent drug stores in central Illinois, such as the ones in Effingham and Tuscola, have switched to Johnson's from us. With competition as fierce as this, we must make ordering from us a quick and easy operation.

Rebuttal of counter-claim ④ ⑤
Most orders are phoned in between 9:30 and 11:30 in the morning and 1:00 and 2:00 in the afternoon, according to the times indicated on the order forms from last month. Computer records of our phone use, however, show that the lines are tied up throughout the day, usually by calls from the sales department. In order to relieve congestion, then, it is necessary to reduce phone activity in the sales department.

Solution presented impersonally ⑥ ⑦
This reduction can be made by using the pay phones for personal calls during the peak ordering hours. Calls on company business should be made during non-peak hours too, if possible. This will enable us to keep more lines open during the peak ordering hours without spending money on costly new lines.

Additional reader benefits ⑧
With the lines open to incoming calls, customers will find that they can place their orders quickly and easily. This will encourage them to keep calling us instead of our competitors, which can mean greater sales for you. In addition, good service helps build goodwill which may enable you to get a bigger share of your customers' business. The easy phone ordering service will also serve you as an additional selling point for new customers.

Links action to solution of problem ⑩ ⑨
In order to improve customer relations and realize greater sales, then, use the pay phones for personal calls between the peak hours of 9:30-11:30 and 1:00-2:00, and make outgoing business calls during non-peak hours.

Asks for action; tells readers exactly what to do

The best ads persuading kids not to smoke are often created by kids. In the 1990s, macabre humor has been effective. This poster, one of the winners in a contest sponsored by the nonprofit organization SmokeFree, was created by a fifth grader.

The first sentence is a bridge connecting saving money to the claim, "employees will benefit." The bridge is necessary because invalid bridges exist: any money saved might be spent on several things other than salaries and benefits.

3. **Make the foundation explicit**
   a. **If it is new information to the reader.**
   b. **If the reader will disagree with the bridge.**
   c. **If invalid as well as valid foundations exist.**
   d. **If there are arbitrary demands for documentation (e.g., in a term paper or a paper you are submitting for publication, where you must indicate your sources for each fact).**

XYZ university will have trouble developing a top-20 football team because its academic standards are high. After practicing four hours a day, football players don't have the time or energy to complete complex, lengthy assignments. Long practices are necessary both to reduce the risk of injury and to make the moves automatic.

The implicit bridge here is "good football players can't meet high academic standards." Readers who think of the possible but invalid foundation "Good football players are dumb" will reject the argument. Giving the valid foundation (the last two sentences) makes the argument more persuasive.

4. **Always offer rebuttals to counterclaims.** Failure to dispose of loopholes is, after failure to provide a valid bridge, probably the most common cause of unconvincing—and unaccepted—recommendations.

> Three of our best customers got busy signals for two straight hours Monday. Business was slow Monday: quotes were down 11%, and the logs compiled by the inside sales reps don't show many outgoing business calls. But the phones were busy, and it seems likely that they were tied up with personal calls.

A reader who accepts the evidence "our phones were tied up" may offer the counterclaim "all the calls were to business customers." If that claim were true, customers would get busy signals even though no one was making personal calls. The middle sentence rebuts that counterclaim by showing that business activity was down. That rebuttal is crucial to making convincing the claim in the last clause: the phones were tied up with personal calls.

5. **Limit any claim whose truth is uncertain or relative.**

> This procedure should produce more accurate results.

The word *should* limits the claim. Without it, we would be promising that the procedure would definitely bring an improvement. But many things could go wrong. Limiting the claim makes it more persuasive because it is now more realistic.

Evaluating Arguments

By comparing an argument to the Toulmin model, you can see what kind of statements you need to make an argument convincing. Each of the examples is unconvincing, but the solutions differ.

Argument 1	By using XTROCUT tubing, you can cut production time and reduce scrap loss.
Problem with Argument	This argument needs evidence to support each of its claims.
Revised Argument	Because XTROCUT comes in the lengths and shapes you use most often, you spend less time cutting down longer tubes. Since you can order just the length you want, you don't waste 2 feet every time you need a 10-foot tube.
Argument 2	The workers I talked to were split 50/50. The workers at our plant don't agree whether the benefits package is adequate.
Problem with Argument	No bridge shows that the "workers I talked to" were a representative or sufficiently large sample. The audience may also wonder whether things have changed since the date of the poll.
Revised Argument	I talked to a random sample of 60 workers. They were split 50/50. Last week, the workers didn't agree whether the benefits package is adequate.
Argument 3	Our national advertising campaign will run during the most popular TV shows this month. This ad campaign will increase our sales dramatically.
Problem with Argument	Such a claim cannot be made with certainty: too many variables affect sales.

Why Students Sign Organ Donor Cards*

What makes healthy young adults sign organ donor cards? Research shows that college students who have signed cards are knowledgeable, altruistic, and unafraid.

Students who said they intended to sign donor cards but had not done so had less knowledge and more fears. Some mistakenly believed that a card had to be filed with the federal government. Many didn't know that most religious groups support the concept of organ donation and that it is considered unethical for the same doctor to care for both the organ donor and the organ recipient.

Students who said they were unlikely to sign donor cards had even less knowledge and more fears. Some didn't know about the need for organ donors. People in this group weren't altruistic but did care about the opinions of others. Encouraging them to talk about organ donation with family and friends may make them more likely to consider donation.

Different messages are needed for people who view organ donation positively and negatively. For the latter group, a series of messages will be necessary.

*Based on Jenifer E. Kopfman and Sandi W. Smith, "Understanding the Audiences of a Health Communication Campaign: A Discriminant Analysis of Potential Organ Donors Based on Intent to Donate," *Journal of Applied Communication Research,* 24 (1996): 33–49.

One Step at a Time*

If your readers have a stake in what you are arguing against, you . . . must resist your impulse to change their beliefs. You have to set your sights much lower. The best you can hope for—and it is hoping for a great deal—is to get your readers just to *understand* your point of view even while not changing theirs in the slightest. . . .

In short, stop trying to persuade the enemy and settle for planting a seed. . . .

What does this mean in practice? . . . [I]f I were writing a short article or leaflet to readers with a stake in what I'm trying to refute, I wouldn't say, "Here's why *you* should believe nuclear power is bad." How can I get them to invest themselves in words which translate "Here's why you've been bad or stupid"? I would take an approach which said, "Here are the reasons and experiences that have made *me* believe nuclear power is bad. Please try to understand them for a moment."

*Quoted from Peter Elbow, *Writing with Power: Techniques for Mastering the Writing Process* (New York: Oxford University Press, 1981), 203–04.

Revised Argument	Our national advertising campaign will run during the most popular TV shows this month. This ad campaign will support our sales reps' efforts to increase sales 5% over last month's.

SUMMARY OF KEY POINTS

- Persuasion is often difficult because
  - People tune out messages they don't want to hear.
  - People are reluctant to say *yes* if doing so requires them to admit that they've been on the wrong side all along.
  - People deny realities that are too much for them to cope with.
- When you need action quickly, you have two choices:
  1. Limit your audience to the people you can persuade.
  2. Try to bring everyone on board.
  For a major change,
  3. Involve the audience. Let them find the solution.
- If you don't need everyone's cooperation, use a direct request to get action from the people who already agree with you.
- Threats don't produce permanent change; they won't necessarily produce the action you want; they may make people abandon an action entirely—even in situations where it would be appropriate; they produce tension. People dislike and avoid anyone who threatens them. Threats can provoke counteraggression.
- Base persuasion in difficult persuasive situations on the following five analysis steps:
  1. Find out why your audience members resist what you want them to do.
  2. Try to find a win-win solution.
  3. Find a way to let your audience save face.
  4. Ask for something small.
  5. Present your arguments from your audience's point of view.
- When you want people to change their behavior, don't criticize them. Instead, show that you're on their side, that you and they have a mutual interest in solving a problem.
- Toulmin logic is useful in labeling the parts of an argument and showing you how much information you need to include.
- In Toulmin logic, the **claim** is the point we want the audience to accept. **Evidence** is material the audience already accepts. The **bridge** is the assumption that allows us to infer the claim from the evidence. The **foundation** supports (proves) the bridge. **Counterclaims** are statements that invalidate the claim even when the evidence and bridge are sound. The **rebuttal** answers the counterclaim. The **limiter** shows under what circumstances, or with what limitations, the claim is true.
- Use these guidelines to determine how much of the full Toulmin model to use.
  1. Make both the claim and the evidence explicit.
  2. Include the bridge
     a. If it is new information to the reader.
     b. If the reader may have heard the bridge but forgotten it.
     c. If the reader may disagree with the bridge.
     d. If invalid as well as valid bridges exist.
  3. Make the foundation explicit
     a. If the reader will disagree with the bridge.
     b. If invalid as well as valid foundations exist.
     c. If there are arbitrary demands for documentation.
  4. Always offer rebuttals to loopholes the reader may find in the main claim.
  5. Limit any claim whose truth is uncertain or relative.

Exercises and Problems
For Chapter 10

GETTING STARTED

10–1   Evaluating Logic

Miswording creates logical errors in the following sentences. Explain what's wrong in each sentence and revise so that it makes logical sense. (If the sentence is ambiguous, pick one logical meaning.)

1. My parents believe students should speak a foreign language. Therefore I spent a summer in France and another summer in Mexico.
2. We do not issue building keys to employees because we want to keep security to a minimum.
3. If you need to reach me, I'll be at 555-1234 all day Thursday.
4. At an annual subscription price of only US$799 the *Asian Markets Monitor* is no doubt the least costly investment you will make this year. It will also certainly prove to be the most vital and useful.
5. As a result of the questionnaire, many students felt that more computers were needed on campus.

10–2   Using Toulmin Logic

In each of the following arguments, identify the claim and the evidence (if any). What bridge could link the evidence to the claim? Is it valid? Why or why not?

1. When you work harder, our customers are more satisfied. And that in turn raises the price of the company's stock.
2. Tom majored in accounting and he got five job offers. I should major in accounting, too.
3. I've worked for two large companies and hated both of them. I'd be happier starting my own business.
4. Of all the applicants, Bob got the highest score on the test. He's the person who should get the job.
5. Last month we spent 34% more on paper than we did six months ago. People are either wasting it or stealing it.
6. The vote on whether to move to a four-day work week was 50/50. Our employees can never agree on whether or not a shorter work week would be beneficial.
7. The vote on whether to move to a four-day work week was split 50/50. Our employees don't care whether or not we change the work week.
8. Since profits are falling, we need to downsize.
9. Customers already believe that our microwave meals taste better than other brands. So we should use our new advertising campaign to stress other advantages, such as their convenience or nutrition.
10. This company is a team. And just as every player does what the coach says, so each of you needs to run the game plan that your manager creates.

10–3   Rebutting Counterclaims

Brainstorm a way to respond to each of the counterclaims to the following goal that a writer might have.

1. Using less paper
   a. If paper costs more, we'll just pass the cost on to customers or deduct it as a business cost on our taxes.
   b. Sure, paper is expensive. But good documents are crucial to our business.
   Using less paper will cut the quality of our work. We'll lose goodwill, reputation, and, ultimately, income.
   c. Reformatting documents to get them on one page and waiting till the printer cools to print on both sides takes time. We just can't afford the time it will take to comply with these "cost-saving" measures.

    d. Reusing scraps of paper is incompatible with our image as a successful organization.

  2. Increasing flextime
    a. It will be too hard to hold staff meetings if everyone works different hours.
    b. Managers won't be able to supervise people they can't see.
    c. Representatives will be out of the office when their clients call.

    d. If people get the hours they want, at some times there will be no one in the office at all.

  3. Reducing use of the minibar
    a. The company can afford the cost.
    b. When I have to be away from home on business, I deserve the luxury of a snack or drink in my room.

E-MAIL MESSAGES

10–4 Persuading People to Use Better Passwords

Your computer system requires each employee to change his or her password every three months. But many people choose passwords that are easy to guess. According to Deloitte & Touche's fraud unit, the 10 most commonly used passwords are (1) the employee's name or child's name, (2) "secret," (3) stress-related words ("deadline," "work"), (4) sports teams or terms, (5) "payday," (6) "bonkers," (7) the current season ("autumn," "spring"), (8) the employee's ethnic group, (9) repeated characters ("AAAAA"), (10) obscenities and sexual terms ("Hackers' Delight," *Business Week*, February 10, 1997, 4).

As Director of Management Information Systems (MIS), you want employees to choose passwords that hackers can't guess based on knowing an employee's background. The best passwords contain numbers as well as letters, use more characters (at least five; eight possible), and aren't real words.

Write an e-mail message to all employees, urging them to choose better passwords.

10–5 Asking for Something Different for Secretary's Day

Your clerical job gives you the flexibility you need while you're in school. Secretary's Day is approaching, and you really don't want flowers or a free lunch. You'd much rather have a bonus or at least time off to attend an educational seminar (whose cost the company should bear). You'd be willing to go to a seminar that would make you even more useful to the company—perhaps learning advanced features of a computer program, for example.

Write an e-mail to the person who supervises clerical workers in your unit, asking that Secretary's Day give you something useful.

Hints:
- Assume that you work in an organization you know something about.

- Specify one or more seminars you'd like to attend.
- Some seminars may cost a lot more than flowers or lunch; some may cost less. How much financial flexibility does the organization have?
- Are there other clerical workers? Would they also like bonuses or seminars, or do some prefer flowers or lunch?
- How well does the person who will make the decision know you? How positively does he or she view you and any other clerical workers?

10–6 Not Doing What the Boss Asked

Today, you get this e-mail message:

To: All Unit Managers

Subject: Cutting Costs

Please submit five ideas for cutting costs in your unit. I will choose the best ideas and implement them immediately.

You think your boss's strategy is wrong. Cutting costs will be easier if people "buy into" the decision rather than being handed orders. Instead of gathering ideas by e-mail, the boss should call a meeting so that people can brainstorm, teaching each other why specific strategies will or won't be easy for their units to implement.

Reply to your boss's e-mail request. Instead of suggesting specific ways to cut costs, persuade the boss to have a meeting where everyone can have input and be part of the decision.

COMMUNICATING AT WORK

As Your Instructor Directs in 10–7 through 10–9,

a. Create a document or presentation to achieve the goal.
b. Write a memo to your instructor describing the situation at your workplace and explaining your rhetorical choices (medium, strategy, tone, wording, graphics, or document design, and so forth).

10–7   Motivating Workers
Motivate workers in your unit to do their best work.

10–8   Changing What's Wrong
No workplace is perfect. Pick one of the things you'd like to change about your workplace, identify the decision maker(s), and create a memo or presentation to start the persuasion process.

10–9   Asking for More Resources for Your Unit
Write a memo or prepare a presentation to persuade your organization to give more resources to your unit.

Hints:
- Who in the organization decides the level of resources your unit receives? What are the values of that person or group?
- How much do the decision makers know about your unit? How much evidence do you need to provide about your contribution to organization goals?
- What kind of evidence is most persuasive in your organization. Should you talk about customers or clients? About internal clients? Give numbers?
- Will you be more persuasive if you ask for funds to take on new tasks, or argue that additional resources will help you do current tasks better?

MEMO AND LETTER ASSIGNMENTS

10–10   Replacing Temporary Workers with Permanent Employees
Your organization hires many "temporary" workers, some of whom have held temporary jobs for years. You want to persuade the organization to convert at least some of these temporary jobs into full-time permanent positions. (Note: If you work for an organization that hires lots of part-timers, you may modify this assignment to replace at least some of the part-time positions with full-time positions.)

Write a memo to upper management, persuading the appropriate people to hire permanent workers.

Hint:
- Use your analysis from exercise 3–10.

10–11   Persuading Employees to Use Less Paper
Your office uses lots of paper. Environmentalists have always felt that the office should reduce its paper use, but now that the cost of paper is skyrocketing, fiscal policy also mandates restraint.

Write a memo to all employees urging them to use less paper, while still producing high-quality work.

Hints:
- Pick an organization you know well. Think about the documents—internal and external—it creates.
- Brainstorm ways that people could use less paper without changing their documents, such as single-spacing all

documents and printing on both sides of the page. People who are now double-spacing may not know how to create good visual impact with a single-spaced document, so explain the basics. Also tell people how to print double-sided on laser printers designed for single-side printing.

■ Brainstorm ways that people could use less paper: using discards and the backs of documents for notes and drafts, cutting documents so they fit on fewer pages, using proportional type with justified margins, using a smaller font (11 point rather than 12), making fewer copies of documents, making more revisions on screen before printing out a new draft, and so forth.

■ Remind people to use paper only for work—not to print out flyers for kids or clubs. (Or, if you allow personal use, raise the cost per page you charge.)

■ Show people how to recycle the paper they discard.

■ Allow readers to save face. What changes in the external environment make it necessary to change behavior?

■ Rebut the counterarguments from 10–3 (1).

■ Present yourself as a problem solver who's on the reader's side, not an authoritarian figure who's on the other side.

10–12   Persuading an Organization to Expand Flextime

County government offices are open 9 to 5. Employees have limited flextime: they can come in and leave half an hour early or half an hour late. But employees want much more flexible hours. Some people want to start at 6 AM so they can leave at 2 PM; others want to work 11 AM to 7 PM.

When the idea has been proposed, supervisors have been very negative. "How will we hold staff meetings? How can we supervise people if everyone works different hours? We have to be here for the public, and we won't be if people work whatever hours they please."

But conversations with co-workers and a bit of research show that there are solutions. Many firms that use flextime require everyone to be at work (or at lunch) between 10 and 2 or 11 and 2, so that staff meetings can be scheduled. Right now, when clients call, a representative is frequently on the phone and has to call back. Voice mail and better message forms

could solve the problem. And flextime might actually let offices stay open longer hours—say 8 to 6, which would be helpful for taxpayers who themselves work 9 to 5 and now can come in only on their own lunch hours.

Write a memo to the County Commissioners, persuading them to approve a change in work hours.

Hints:

■ Assume that this situation is happening in your own county government. What services does the county offer?

■ Use any facts about your county that are helpful (for example, being especially busy right now, having high turnover, whether tax issues have been voted up or down).

■ Use what you know about managing to allay managers' fears.

■ Rebut the counterarguments from 10–3 (2).

10–13   Persuading Employees to Save Money on Trips

Rising travel costs are eating into your company's budget. Keeping salespeople on the road is important, but they could travel more cheaply. For example, sometimes it's possible to get a cheaper room rate by talking to the hotel directly rather than to the 800-number; people should call both numbers to find out. And most hotels give discounts for "corporate" rates or AAA membership. Sometimes one hotel will lower its rates to meet another hotel's rates. People who want a snack in their rooms should

stop by a nearby deli or grocery rather than eating the $18 jar of cashews in the minibar.

Write a memo to employees, persuading them to use company travel funds more frugally.

Hints:

■ Pick an organization you know something about.

■ Rebut the counterarguments from 10–3 (3).

10–14   Persuading Tenants to Follow the Rules

As resident manager of a large apartment complex, you receive free rent in return for collecting rents, doing simple maintenance, and enforcing the complex's rules. You find the following notice in the files:

To: All Residents

Subject: Cleaning, Garbage, and Extermination

Some of you are failing to keep any kind of standard sanitation code resulting in the unnecessary cost on our part to hire exterminators to rid the building of roaches.

Our leases state breach of contract in the event that you are not observing your responsibility to keep your apartment clean.

We are in the process of making arrangements for an extermination company to rid those apartments that are experiencing problems. Get in touch with the manager no later than 10 PM Monday to make arrangements for your apartment to be sprayed. It is a fast, odorless operation. You are also required to put your garbage in plastic bags. Do not put loose garbage or garbage in paper bags in the dumpster, as this leads to rodent or roach problems.

Should we in the course of providing extermination service to the building find that your apartment is a source of roaches, then you will be held liable for the cost incurred to rid your apartment of them.

The message is horrible. The notice lacks you-attitude; it seems to threaten anyone who asks to have his or her apartment sprayed.

The annual spraying scheduled for your complex is coming up. Under the lease, you have the right to enter apartments once a year to spray. However, for spraying to be fully effective, residents must empty the cabinets, remove kitchen drawers, and put all food in the refrigerator. People and pets need to leave the apartment for about 15 minutes while the exterminator sprays.

Tell residents about the spraying. Persuade them to prepare their apartments to get the most benefit from it, and persuade them to dispose of food waste quickly and properly so that the bugs don't come back.

Hints:

- What objections may people have to having their apartments sprayed for bugs?
- Why don't people already take garbage out promptly and wrap it in plastic? How can you persuade them to change their behavior?
- Analyze your audience. Are most tenants students, working people, or retirees? What tone would be most effective for this group?

10–15   Persuading Your Campus to Make a Change

Persuade your campus to make some change.

As Your Instructor Directs,

- a. Write a memo to the person or office with the authority to make the change.
- b. Join with a small group of students to write a memo about a change all of you want.
- c. Make an oral presentation to the class urging this change.

Hints:

- Find out who would have the authority to make the decision. How difficult would it be to make the change, assuming that you convinced your audience?
- What is your campus's mission? Can you show that the change you want will make it easier to meet those goals?
- Will your change create extra work for already-burdened administrators, instructors, or workers? Could you minimize this work?
- How much emotional investment does the audience have in this issue? How can you phrase your request so that you don't sound as though you're criticizing the people you're trying to persuade?
- Is the audience more likely to be persuaded by a short, snappy message or a longer persuasive memo packed with details?

CHAPTER 11

Sales and Fund-Raising Letters

Chapter Outline

Sales and Fund-Raising Letters

David Rose, Direct Response Account Supervisor
Sive/Young & Rubicam

David Rose supervises the development and execution of direct mail/direct response advertising programs for Sive/Young & Rubicam in Cincinnati, Ohio. Sive/Young & Rubicam is a full-service advertising agency with clients in various consumer, business-to-business, and fund-raising categories.

To create a good direct mail package, you need to make an offer to the right target market, provide enough information to make a decision, and provide a call to action with a means to respond. The more you know about your market—who they are, what they buy, where they shop—the more relevant and effective you can make your package. People with aging eyes who order fine arts books by mail, for example, may respond well to large type and long copy for fine arts, travel, and related mail order offers.

The right amount of information in your package depends on the complexity of your message and the commitment you are asking one to make. New, complex products call for thorough descriptions, in text and in pictures. Direct sales call for more information than inquiries. People do read long copy—if it interests them. But nobody was ever bored into buying anything.

The more time people spend with your package, the more likely they'll respond to it—and to your future offers. Get attention with bold graphics and clear, straightforward headlines. Stimulate interest by raising a question, concern, doubt, or by making news. Exploit the "nod" factor by relating to your reader's lifestyle, values, previous purchases, etc. Use inserts and action devices to increase involvement. Make reading the package a fun and memorable experience with the brand.

In writing fund-raising copy, explain that things are great for your organization, but that there's a problem and that the donor is the solution. People like to associate with successful organizations. Be sincere (think about the way you write to your mother), ask early and often, show how contributions will lead to success, talk about the need rather than the organization, and thank donors.

Make it easy for people to respond to your offer or appeal. Give them choices: call, write, fax, e-mail, visit a store, or pay by check or credit card. Some people will want to talk with a representative; others will want to "kick the tires."

Above all, be mindful of trends and responsive to them.

David Rose, April 28, 1997

**Visit Sive/Young & Rubicam's Web site for its kids marketing division:
http://www.Small-Talk.com**

"[M]ake an offer to the right target market, provide enough information to make a decision and [ask for] action."

David Rose, Sive/Young & Rubicam

Time-Life Books, Buick, FedEx—these are only a few of the companies that use letters to persuade customers to buy their products, visit their showrooms, and use their services. The American Cancer Society, the Republican National Committee, Gallaudet University—these are only a few of the organizations that use letters to persuade people to donate time or money to their causes.

Sales and fund-raising letters may be even more useful for local charities or small businesses with small advertising budgets. The Country Charm store in a Detroit suburb sent letters to its customers: letters announcing special promotions, "thank you" letters with gift certificates based on the customer's past purchases. As a result, within five years the store's sales multiplied eight times and it had hired 14 employees. The store grew so big that it had to move. Another established business gladly moved into Country Charm's old location, thinking the location was great. But that store didn't send letters, and it didn't get much traffic. It closed in a year.[1]

Sales and fund-raising letters are a special category of persuasive messages. They are known as **direct mail** because they ask for an order, inquiry, or contribution directly from the reader. Direct mail is one form of direct marketing. **Direct marketing** also includes catalog sales, space ads in magazines and newspapers that have reply cards so that the reader can buy or contribute directly, telemarketing (telephone sales), and TV direct response ads, where the viewer calls an 800 number to place an order. In 1995, direct mail sold almost $220 billion worth of products in the United States and raised over $57 billion for charities.[2]

Fortune 500 companies and well-endowed charitable or political organizations hire professionals to write their direct mail. Professionals charge $3,000 to $25,000 to create a package. And that's just the creative cost: you still have to pay for printing and postage. If you own your own business, you can save money by doing your firm's own direct mail. If you are active in a local group that needs to raise money, writing the letter yourself is likely to be the only way your group can afford to use direct mail. The principles in this chapter will help you write solid, serviceable letters that will build your business and help fund your group.

Sales and fund-raising letters have several purposes.

Primary Purposes:

To motivate the reader to read the message.
To have the reader act (order the product, schedule a demonstration, send a donation).
To provide enough information so that the reader knows exactly what to do (even if he or she keeps only the reply coupon).
To overcome any objections that might prevent or delay action.

Secondary Purpose:

To build a good image of the writer's organization (to strengthen the commitment of readers who act, and make readers who do not act more likely to respond positively next time).

COMPONENTS OF GOOD DIRECT MAIL

Good direct mail has three components: a good product, service, or cause; a good mailing list; and a good appeal. A **good product** appeals to a specific segment of people, is not readily available in stores, can be mailed, and provides an adequate profit margin. A **good service or cause** fills an identifiable need. A **good mailing list** has accurate addresses and is a good match to the product. Most professional direct mailers rent their lists from companies that specialize in compiling and maintaining lists. Small businesses and charities can use in-house lists of their customers or members and can compile lists of prospects from city directories or other local sources. A **good appeal** offers a believable description of benefits, links the benefits of the product or service to a need or desire that motivates the reader, makes the reader want to read the letter, and motivates the reader to act. The appeal is made up of the words in the letter, the pictures in the brochure, and all the parts of the package, from outer envelope to reply card.

All three elements are crucial: the best letter in the world won't persuade someone who doesn't have a garden to buy a Rototiller. However, this chapter will examine only the elements of a good appeal: how to create a message that will motivate a reader to act, assuming that you already have a good product to sell or a worthy cause to raise funds for, and that you already have a good list of people who might be interested in that product or organization.

Industry wisdom is that a **cold list**—a list of people with no prior connection to your group—will have a 2% response rate. Good timing, a good list, and a good appeal can double or even triple that percentage.

You can raise the response rate 1% or 2% by including an 800 number as another way for people to respond. Following up the mailing with a phone call 24 to 72 hours after the reader receives the mailing can bring in another 2% to 14%. If people on your list have some connection with your organization (e.g., have been patients at the hospital or have visited the museum you're raising money for), you can expect a higher response rate. From a list of people who have bought from or given *to your organization* before, the response rate can be well over 50% and for some groups can approach 90%.[3]

IS IT "JUNK" MAIL?

Almost everyone claims to dislike "junk" mail. However, people do like to get mail that interests them: ads for products they want to buy, information about groups they like, letters about subjects they care about. One study found that 75% of the people who got political direct mail read the letters.[4]

To reduce the amount of direct mail you get, write to the Mail Preference Service, Direct Marketing Association, PO Box 9008, Farmingdale, NY 11735-9008. If you want mail only from certain organizations, ask them not to rent your name to other organizations. Many companies have a box on the reply card that you can check to indicate this. American Express reports that only 7% of its cardholders say they don't want "bonus" mail.

Much direct mail is bundled by the mailer for each carrier route in the nation, so that the Post Office does not have to sort it. (If your mailing label carries the letters CAR-RT SORT, it has been "carrier route sort"ed.)

The quality of the direct mail written today varies widely. A great deal of research has been done about what works in direct mail, but unlike academic research, this research is not generally available. To learn about direct mail, talk to someone who is experienced in the field, join the Direct Marketing Association and read its publications, or read a book like this one.

Lists, Lists, and More Lists*

Nearly 40,000 mailing lists are available commercially. Among the lists available from one company are

130,310	Women accountants
3,953	Owners of balloon aircraft
171,983	High school athletic directors
6,195,311	Dog owners
263,877	Republican contributors
59,641	Highest salaried executives (home addresses)
2,450	Rabbis
4,600,000	Hispanic Families
204,443	Heads of households ages 18–34 in Utah
2,046	Yacht owners in Illinois
62,301	Californians with annual income over $100,000

*Based on Best Mailing Lists, Inc., *1996 Catalog.*

The Web site for Hot Hot Hot gets 1,000 hits a day and generates 20% of total sales for Perry Lopez and Monica Bosserman Lopez' specialty hot sauce company.

BASIC DIRECT MAIL STRATEGY

Direct mail strategies start with three basic steps: (1) learn about the product, service, or organization, (2) choose and analyze the target audience, and (3) choose a central selling point. These steps interact. An understanding of your target audience may suggest questions to ask about your product. Information you find in researching the product may suggest an idea for a possible central selling point.

1. Understand Your Product, Service, or Organization.

Try to use the product or service. Talk to volunteers who work for your charitable organization; if possible, visit the site where the good work is done.

For a sales letter, ask

- What needs does the product meet? What benefits does it provide? What problems does it remove?
- What are the product's objective features? Size? Color? Materials? How does it work? What options are available?
- How much does it cost? What does the buyer get for the money?
- How is it different from or better than competing products? (If the *details* of differences or superiority are interesting, jot them down. They may work well in a letter.)
- How easy is it to install? To use? To maintain?

For a fund-raising letter, ask

- What is the problem your group is helping to solve? (If possible, collect examples to illustrate the need.)
- How, specifically, is your group helping? (Collect stories about specific people who have been helped, specific gains that have been achieved. Also get overall figures.)
- What support does your group already get from tax dollars, user fees, ticket sales, and so on? Why are private funds necessary?
- What are the group's immediate goals? How much will it cost to achieve them? (Try to get costs for some of the specific subgoals as well as the total budget needed.)

If you're writing a letter for a local organization, visit its office or center and talk to the people who work there. If you're writing a letter for a national group, check the phone book to see if there's a local chapter where you can get brochures, flyers, and information. The library may also have information. For fund-raising letters, you can learn about the problem the group is working to solve by checking *The Reader's Guide to Periodical Literature* or the *Business Periodicals Index*. Magazine articles about the problem may have anecdotes and specifics you can use. Also check the Web.

2. Identify and Analyze Your Target Audience.

The **target audience** is all of the people who are likely to be interested in buying the product, using the service, or contributing to the cause. In direct mail, you do not try to sell a subscription to *Sports Illustrated* to someone who loathes sports; you do not ask Republicans to contribute to a Democratic candidate's campaign. In the latter case you might, however, include Independents or people who had never indicated a party preference. In addition

Databases and Direct Mail*

For almost 20 years, computers have allowed direct mailers to "personalize" letters by inserting the reader's name, city, amount of last year's gift, or other information in a basic form letter. Today, sophisticated databases can help organizations match the appeal to the reader.

Memorial Sloan Kettering Cancer Center sent solicitations for a new nursing fund to former patients who might be expected to appreciate the nurses' care.

Several organizations match the size of the request to the prospective donor's wealth. The World Jewish Congress matched its donor list against a list of wealthy people to identify multimillionaires who could be approached for major gifts. Juniata College ran its alumni list against one of the wealth lists and found a dozen potential donors who might be able to give $100,000 or more each "who were a total surprise."

*Based on Michael Shorland and Michael Zodrow, "Bear Creek Builds In-House Gold Mine," *Direct Marketing,* January 1993, 38, and William M. Bulkeley, "Nonprofits Dig into Databases for Big Donors," *The Wall Street Journal,* September 8, 1992, B1, B6.

to the small number of people who are already interested in your product or committed to your cause, the audience always includes people who could be persuaded if you gave them enough evidence.

As Chapter 3 explains, you can analyze your audience in terms of **demographics** (⊷ p. 62)—objective, measurable features: "This letter is going to homeowners who have children between the ages of 4 and 10." You can also use **psychographic characteristics** (⊷ p. 62)—values, beliefs, goals, and lifestyles: "I'm writing to people who care about protecting the environment." Often a combination of demographic and psychographic characteristics works best: college students may have different reasons for using a health club than do 45-year-old executives, even though both groups want to look good and deal with stress. Commercial lists for direct mail can be based on demographics, psychographics, or both.

Whenever possible, think of specific people you know while you write the letter. What do they care about? What would motivate *them*?

3. Choose a Central Selling Point.

Since even a well-defined audience will have people with different motivations and different objections to buying or giving, a direct mail letter needs several selling points. To unify the letter, use a central selling point. A **central selling point** is a reader benefit which by itself could motivate your readers to act and which can serve as an umbrella under which all the other benefits can fit.

Suppose you want to sell copies of a book that explains how to grow vegetables in home gardens. Whenever you try to sell a book or magazine by mail, you are really selling the activity; the book helps readers do the activity successfully. Any of the following statements could be used as central selling points:

- Fresh vegetables from your own garden taste better than store-bought vegetables that are ripened with chemicals.
- Vegetables from your own garden are healthier. You control the chemicals you put on them; you can avoid insecticides and wax you don't want.
- It's cheaper to grow your own vegetables than to buy them in a grocery store.
- Growing vegetables is fun for the whole family. Children will be fascinated by growing plants.
- Growing your own vegetables is a way to get back to nature, to have a simpler, more natural lifestyle.

A professional direct mailer might test two or more different approaches with samples of the target market, then send the best letter to the whole list. When you can't run a test, how do you choose? First, eliminate any central selling points that don't fit your target audience. Next, use your own understanding of people to decide whether to stress taste or health or economy or fun or working with nature. If two or more appeals seem equally effective, try writing each of them. In your assignment, use the one that you can develop most effectively.

In a fund-raising letter, you must also choose the appeal that will be most powerful for the target audience. A fund-raising letter to college alumni could use nostalgia, the obligation to repay the college, the feeling of making an investment in young people, or a sense of social responsibility. To create a sense of nostalgia, refer to events that happened when readers were in school. (Check back issues of the college newspaper or yearbook for ideas.) If you're writing to members of a sorority or fraternity, refer to events the house is proud of, and use a salutation and complimentary close that will remind readers of their membership. If you are writing to a group that sees the Bible as an authority, use appropriate Biblical quotes and allusions.

When you hope to raise funds from two different target audiences, you may need two separate mailing pieces with different central selling points. Ducks Unlimited can appeal to both hunters and nonhunting environmentalists. Its letters remind hunters that preserving wetlands is essential to maintain the duck populations that hunters need. Environmentalists will be interested in saving the wetlands for their own sake.

How to Organize a Sales or Fund-Raising Letter

Use the Star-Chain-Knot pattern[5] to organize your letter:

1. Open your letter with a *star* designed to catch the reader's attention.
2. In the body, provide a *chain* of reasons and logic.
3. End by telling the reader what to do and providing a reason to act promptly. Tie up the motivation you have created and turn it into action.

Opener (Star)

The opener of your letter gives you 30 to 60 seconds to motivate readers to read the rest of the letter. If the opener fails to do that, your letter will be thrown away.

A good star opener will make readers want to read the letter and provide a reasonable transition to the body of the letter. A very successful subscription letter for *Psychology Today* started out,

> Do you still close the bathroom door when there's no one in the house?

The question is both intriguing in itself and a good transition into the content of *Psychology Today:* practical psychology applied to the quirks and questions we come across in everyday life.

It's essential that the opener not only get the reader's attention but also be something that can be linked logically to the body of the letter. A sales letter started,

> Can You Use $20 This Week?

Certainly that gets attention. But the letter only offered the reader the chance to save $20 on a product. Readers may feel disappointed or even cheated when they learn that instead of getting $20, they have to spend money to save $20.

It's hard to write a brilliant opener the minute you sit down. Two reliable strategies are (1) write four or five openers, and pick the best; (2) just start writing. A good opener may in fact appear on your second or third page; sometimes you can throw away much of the prose that preceded it.

To brainstorm possible openers, use the four basic modes: **questions, narration, startling statements,** and **quotations.**

1. Question

> Dear Writer:
>
> What is the best way to start writing?

Ethics and Direct Mail, I

Deception in direct mail is all too easy to find.

Some mailers have sent "checks" to readers. But the "check" can only be applied toward the purchase of the item the letter is selling.

Some mailings now have yellow Post-it notes with "handwritten" notes signed with initials or a first name only—to suggest that the mailing is from a personal friend.

One letter offers a "free" membership "valued at $675" (note the passive—who's doing the valuing?) but charges—up front—$157 for "maintenance fees."

Such deception has no place in well-written direct mail.

This letter selling subscriptions to *Writer's Digest* goes on to discuss Hemingway's strategy for getting started on his novels and short stories. *Writer's Digest* offers practical advice to writers who want to be published. The information in the letter is useful to any writer so the recipient keeps reading; the information also helps to prove the claim that the magazine will be useful.

Good questions challenge but don't threaten the reader. They're interesting enough that readers want the answers, so they read the letter.

Poor
question: Do you want information about investments?
Better
question: Can you still make money investing in land?

A series of questions (as in Figure 11.1 later in the chapter) can be an effective opener.

2. Narration, Stories, Anecdotes

Dear Reader:

She hoisted herself up noiselessly so as not to disturb the rattlesnakes snoozing there in the sun.

To her left, the high desert of New Mexico. Indian country. To her right, the rock carvings she had photographed the day before. Stick people. Primitive animals.

Up ahead, three sandstone slabs stood stacked against the face of the cliff. In their shadow, another carving. A spiral consisting of rings. Curious, the young woman drew closer. Instinctively, she glanced at her watch. It was almost noon. Then just at that moment, a most unusual thing happened.

Suddenly, as if out of nowhere, an eerie dagger of light appeared to stab at the topmost ring of the spiral. It next began to plunge downwards—shimmering, laser-like.

It pierced the eighth ring. The seventh. The sixth. It punctured the innermost and last. Then just as suddenly as it had appeared, the dagger of light was gone. The young woman glanced at her watch again. Exactly twelve minutes had elapsed.

Coincidence? Accident? Fluke? No. What she may have stumbled across that midsummer morning three years ago is an ancient solar calendar. . . .

This subscription letter for *Science84* argues that it reports interesting and significant discoveries in all fields of science—all in far more detail than do other media. The opener both builds suspense so that the reader reads the subscription letter and suggests that the magazine will be as interesting as the letter and as easy to read.

3. Startling Statements

Dear Membership Candidate:

I'm writing to offer you a job.

It's not a permanent job, understand. You'll be working for only as much time as you find it rewarding and fun.

It's not even a paying job. On the contrary, it will cost *you* money.

This fund-raising letter from Earthwatch invites readers to participate in its expeditions, subscribe to its journal, and donate to its programs. Earthwatch's volunteers help scientists and scholars dig for ruins, count bighorns, and monitor changes in water; they can work as long as they like; they pay their own (tax-deductible) expenses.

4. Quotation

> "I never tell my partner that my ankle is sore or my back hurts. You can't give in to pain and still perform."
>
> —Jill Murphy
> Soloist

The series of which this letter is a part sells season tickets to the Atlanta Ballet by focusing on the people who work to create the season. Each letter quotes a different member of the company. The opening quote is used on the envelope over a picture of the ballerina and as an opener for the letter. The letters encourage readers to see the artists as individuals, to appreciate their hard work, and to share their excitement about each performance.

Body (Chain)

The *chain* is the **body** of the letter. It provides the logical and emotional links that move readers from their first flicker of interest to the action that is wanted. A good chain answers readers' questions, overcomes their objections, and involves them emotionally.

All this takes space. One of the industry truisms is "The more you tell, the more you sell." Tests show that longer letters bring in more new customers or new donors than do shorter letters. A four-page letter is considered ideal for mailings to new customers or donors. Why? As direct mail expert Bill Jayme says,

> A single mailing package must . . . do the work . . . of many hundreds of people.
>
> It must create a need for your product, like the print ad, radio commercial, or billboard. . . .
>
> It must show how your product looks, like the TV commercial. . . .
>
> It must explain how your product works, like the in-store demonstrator. . . .
>
> Finally, it must ring up the sale, like the person at the checkout counter. Do you take credit cards? Can I give you a postdated check? If he hates it, can I bring it back?[6]

To get that length, some letters use large type and margins. Expensive mailings sometimes use one uncut, folded 17-inch-by-11-inch sheet, printed on the first and third sides, to give a two-page letter the psychological weight of four pages. And many letters now use bullet points or graphics to make the page easy to read.

Can short letters work? Yes, when you're writing to old customers or when the mailing is supported by other media. One study showed that a one-page letter was just as effective as a two-page letter in persuading recent purchasers of a product to buy a service contract.[7] The shortest letter on record may be the two-word postcard that a fishing lake resort sent its customers: "They're biting!"

Content for the body of the letter can include

- Information readers will find useful even if they do not buy or give.
- Stories about how the product was developed or what the organization has done.
- Stories about people who have used the product or who need the organization's help.
- Word pictures of readers using the product and enjoying its benefits.

Long, Longer, Longest

Some tests show that six- or even eight-page letters outpull shorter letters. Many political fund-raising letters are six pages (particularly during the primary seasons when candidates are not yet well known).

Long letters are especially good for expensive items, publications, or high-involvement categories like health and investing. Liberty Mint used an eight-page letter to sell 100 castings of Remington's "The Bronco Buster" made of pure silver for $25,000 each. In 1993, *American Speaker* used a 12-page letter to sell a $400 book on giving speeches; "Richard Band's Profitable Investing" used a 24-page self-mailer to sell subscriptions to a financial newsletter.

Even long letters should look easy to read. Many long letters use Courier-10 type and short paragraphs (just a sentence or two).

So that they look inviting and easy to read, many direct mail letters now use color and graphics. This fund-raising letter from UNICEF breaks up the text with photos and drawings.

How You Can Help Save Children's Lives...

As a supporter of the U.S. Committee for UNICEF, you know we are working to help save children in more than 140 countries around the world. But I want to tell you specifically what is being done to increase crop production in drought-affected areas and how you can help...

In Africa, UNICEF distributes improved seed strains especially suited to the climate and areas where most of the world's hungry children live. Special packages of seeds and farm implements designed to help a family become self-sufficient within 18 months have been developed.

Each package contains seeds such as drought-resistant sorghum, African maize used to bake bread, beans, and ground nuts -- which are excellent sources of protein -- and upland rice to provide an important source of carbohydrates.

All of these specially selected plants grow well in sub-Saharan Africa, which suffers from numerous droughts...

...all grow hearty, disease-resistant plants...

...and all have been proven to increase yields tremendously in every part of the world where they've been distributed.

As little as 40 pounds of these specially selected seeds can produce more than 1,600 pounds of nutritious food! How much does it cost for a package of these special seeds? Only $30...to put an entire family on the road to recovery and help them become self-sufficient

Action Close (Knot)

The action close in the letter must do four things:

1. **Tell the reader what to do:** respond. Avoid *if* ("if you'd like to try . . .") and *why not* ("why not send in a check?"). They lack positive emphasis and encourage your reader to say *no*.
2. **Make the action sound easy:** fill in the information on the reply card, sign the card (for credit sales), put the card and check (if payment is to accompany the order) in the envelope, and mail the envelope. If you provide an envelope and pay postage, stress those facts.
3. **Offer a reason for acting promptly.** Readers who think they are convinced but wait to act are less likely to buy or contribute. Reasons for acting promptly are easy to identify when a product is seasonal or there is a genuine limit on the offer—time limit, price rise scheduled, limited supply, and so on. Sometimes you can offer a premium or a discount if the reader acts quickly. When these conditions do not exist, remind

How Does UNICEF Work To Save Even MORE Children?

Besides distributing special seed grains to increase food production, UNICEF has developed other simple, low-cost methods that can work IMMEDIATELY to reduce the child mortality rate by a third!

Clean Water

In developing countries, diarrheal disease -- usually caused by drinking unclean water -- is the second leading cause of child mortality. In fact, diarrheal disease causes the death of approximately 3 million children every year!

Water supplies in developing countries often become contaminated with parasites and bacteria -- especially in times of low rainfall. When children drink the water, they are struck by dysentery and the subsequent massive loss of fluids. This rapid loss of body fluids and salts quickly leads to dehydration... and often death.

To replace body fluids and prevent deaths due to dehydration, UNICEF distributes packets of oral rehydration salts. These packets contain a mixture of sugar and essential salts that are mixed with clean water to replace the lost fluids. One treatment -- at a cost of only 15 cents per dose -- will often be enough to save a child suffering from dysentery. In fact, oral rehydration therapy programs saved over 1 million lives last year alone!

UNICEF also works to provide clean water supplies to prevent waterborne diseases from affecting children. Last year, UNICEF helped improve the water supply and sanitation systems in almost 100 developing countries by drilling wells, constructing water systems, and by providing sanitation systems and education in hygiene.

Immunization

Six "childhood" diseases kill millions of children every year: measles, polio, TB, tetanus, whooping cough, and diptheria. In the United States, these diseases are easily prevented through vaccination programs... but in developing countries, access to medical care is extremely limited.

readers that the sooner they get the product, the sooner they can benefit from it; the sooner they contribute funds, the sooner their dollars can go to work to solve the problem.

4. **End with a positive picture** of the reader enjoying the product (in a sales letter) or of the reader's money working to solve the problem (in a fund-raising letter). The last sentence should never be a selfish request for money.

The action close can also remind readers of the central selling point, stress the guarantee, and mention when the customer will get the product.

Using a P.S.

Studies of eye movement show that people often look to see who a letter is from before they read the letter. Therefore, direct mail often uses a deliberate P.S. after the signature block. The P.S. may offer a reader benefit or a make a point not made in the letter. If it restates the central selling point, or some other point the letter makes, it should do so in different words so that it won't sound repetitive when the reader reads the letter through from start to finish.

Here are four of the many kinds of effective P.S.'s.

- Reason to act promptly:

> P.S. Once I finish the limited harvest, that's it! I do not store any SpringSweet Onions for late orders. I will ship all orders on a first-come, first-served basis and when they are gone they are gone. Drop your order in the mail today . . . or give me a call toll free at 800-531-7470! (In Texas: 800-292-5437)

Sales letter for Frank Lewis Alamo Fruit

- Description of a premium the reader receives for giving:

> P.S. And . . . we'll be pleased to send you—as a *new* member—the exquisite, full-color 1998 Sierra Club Wilderness Calendar. It's our gift . . . absolutely FREE to you . . . to show our thanks for your membership at this critical time.

Fund-raising letter for Sierra Club

- Reference to another part of the package:

> P.S. Photographs may be better than words, but they still don't do justice to this model. Please keep in mind as you review the enclosed brochure that your SSJ will look even better when you can see it firsthand in your own home.

Sales letter for the Danbury Mint's model of the Duesenberg SSJ

- Restatement of central selling point:

> P.S. It is not easy to be a hungry child in the Third World. If your parents' crops fail or if your parents cannot find work, there are no food stamps . . . no free government-provided cafeteria lunches.
> Millions of hungry schoolchildren will be depending on CARE this fall. Your gift today will ensure that we will be there—that CARE won't let them down.

Fund-raising letter for CARE

STRATEGY IN SALES LETTERS

The basic strategy in sales letters is satisfying a need. People buy to get something or to get rid of something. Your letter must remind people of the need your product meets, prove that the product will satisfy that need, show why your product is better than similar products, and make readers *want* to have the product. Use psychological description (➤ p. 223) to show readers how the product will help them. Testimonials from other buyers can help persuade them that the product works; details about how the product is made can carry the message of quality.

Dealing with Price

Many sales letters make the offer early in the letter—even on the envelope. The exact price, however, is not mentioned until the last fourth of the letter,

Gimmicks and Gadgets in Business-to-Business Sales*

Direct mail letters to business customers often use enclosures to get the attention of busy executives.

To catch attention for its business loans, CIT Group sent baseballs autographed by Willie Mays, Stan Musial, and Mickey Mantle. Of the 98 executives who received the first package, 89 responded. The campaign cost $17,664; it brought in sales of over $120 million.

Airborne Express sent a plastic pouch of shredded US currency to persuade executives that "air express shipping with someone else is like tearing up money."

Taking the term *cold call* literally, James Productions, a corporate events producer, sent Coleman coolers to 75 local human resource directors. On the ice inside was a sealed bag with the letter: "I'll bring some soft drinks for you and your staff to enjoy during our presentation meeting. . . . Let's get together before the ice melts." The campaign netted 15 new accounts.

*Based on "CIT Group Scores Big Points," *Direct Marketing*, November 1992, 38; *Direct Marketing*, February 1988, 80; and Wingfield Hughes, "Promotional Products Can *Boost* Direct Mail Responses," *Direct Marketing*, July 1996, 30–31.

after the copy makes the reader *want* the product. The only exception is when you're selling something that has a reputation for being expensive (a luxury car, *Encyclopaedia Britannica*). Then you may want to deal with the price issue early in the letter, especially if your readers want the product but think they can't afford it.

You can make the price more palatable with the following techniques:

1. **Link the price to the benefit the product provides.** "Your piece of history is just $39.95."
2. **Show how much the product costs each day, each week, or each month.** "You can have all this for less than the cost of a cup of coffee a day." Make sure that the amount seems small and that you've convinced people that they'll use this product all year long.
3. **Allow customers to charge sales or pay in installments.** Your bookkeeping costs will rise, and some sales may be uncollectible, but the total number of sales will increase.

Always offer a guarantee, usually right after the price. The best guarantees are short, convincing, and positive.

Negative:	If the magazine fails to meet your expectations, you can cancel at any time and receive a refund on any unmailed copies.
Better:	You'll be satisfied or we'll refund your money. I guarantee that.

You can increase the number of orders simply by repeating your message. A repeat copy of the original sales letter, mailed about three weeks later, will bring in about 70% of the original response rate.[8]

Sample Sales Letter

The sample letter in Figure 11.1 is a subscription letter for *3-2-1 Contact*, a magazine for children ages 8–14. The letter uses an elite typeface on white paper with blue ink for the logo, the "ABSOLUTELY FREE!" and the signature. The folded, uncut 17-inch-by-11-inch paper is printed on four sides.

The letter opens with its central selling point: *3-2-1 Contact* educates kids in a fun way. Since the letter is addressed to parents, the opening questions are designed to be ones that will interest adults so that they'll read to find the answers. The body of the letter builds credibility by pointing out that the magazine is published by a nonprofit group. Material from the magazine itself helps to prove the claim that it teaches in an interesting way. The action close asks the reader to send in the reply card to subscribe.

STRATEGY IN FUND-RAISING APPEALS

In a fund-raising letter, the basic emotional strategy is **vicarious participation.** By donating money, readers participate vicariously in work they are not able to do personally. This strategy affects the pronouns you use. Throughout the letter, use *we* to talk about your group. However, at the end, talk about what *you* the reader will be doing. End positively, with a picture of the reader's dollars helping to solve the problem.

To achieve both your primary and secondary purposes in fund-raising letters, you must give a great deal of information. This information (1) helps to persuade readers; (2) gives supporters evidence to use in conversations with others; and (3) gives readers who are not yet supporters evidence that may make them see the group as worthwhile, even if they do not give money now.

Talking about Taxes*

Even if your group is not required to pay taxes, contributions may not be tax-deductible. Such groups with incomes over $100,000 a year must "state conspicuously" in all fund-raising solicitations, including phone calls, that the gift is not tax-deductible.

Stressing what the group will achieve with the money can make donors feel that the gift is still worth giving:

Your dues and gifts to the Sierra Club support our effective citizen-based advocacy and lobbying programs, and therefore are not tax-deductible.

Sometimes, particularly in December, people will give because a gift is tax-deductible. However, you should never suggest that that is the *reason* people would give. In your letter, mention that gifts are tax-deductible (if they are), but subordinate that fact to the work of the organization that the reader's gift makes possible.

*Based on "Tax Report," *The Wall Street Journal,* February 3, 1988, 1; Sierra Club reply card.

Figure 11.1   **A Magazine Subscription Letter**

PL-CN1

Children's Television Workshop ▪ One Lincoln Plaza, New York, NY 10023

* * * * * * * * * * *

This letter is not for everyone. But if you're
the parent of a youngster between the ages of 8
and 14 . . .   *Identifies*
                                                    target
                                                    audience
. . . then I invite you to send for a free copy
of 3-2-1 CONTACT, the <u>award-winning</u> magazine of   *Statement of*
science, nature and math for the middle grades.   *central selling*
                                                    point
Like the other Children's Television Workshop
publications -- <u>Sesame Street</u> and <u>Kid City</u> --
3-2-1 CONTACT is so spirited, so entertaining, so
amusing that its readers seldom notice the fact
that it's "educational."

Yet every issue is chock-full of mind-stretching
puzzles, mazes, games and mysteries . . . amazing
facts . . . and articles and features that promote
analytical thinking, encourage patience and
concentration, and generally help prepare your
child for the world of tomorrow.

Keeps door   Don't worry -- I'm not asking you to <u>subscribe</u> to
open for   this magazine, at least not yet. All I'm asking
reluctant   is your permission to send an issue of 3-2-1
reader   CONTACT to your home,

                                                    Repeats powerful
                                                    word "Free"
ABSOLUTELY FREE!

* * * * * * * * * * *

Dear Fellow Parent,
                                                    Attention-getting
"Why is the ocean salty?"   *questions*

   "When you take an aspirin, how does it know where you hurt?"

      "What are eyelashes for?"

         "How does a magnifying glass work?"

                                        (over, please . . .)

Continued   **Figure 11.1**

"Why is my image upside down when I see myself in a spoon?"

"How do fireworks work?"

"Why do some objects glow in the dark?"

"Why is the sky blue?"

                    *   *   *   *   *   *

Good you-attitude— avoids making reader feel inferior

I don't know about you, but I'm often stumped by the science questions my kids throw at me. I have no trouble helping them with spelling, or simple arithmetic, or even state capitals . . . but when it comes to explaining why teeth chatter, or how roosters know what time it is -- I guess I'm not as well-educated as I should be!

And yet our children are growing up into a world that is more technological than ever . . .

. . . a world where familiarity with computers is becoming essential, not just for scientists but for office workers, farmers, teachers, doctors, librari-ans, almost everyone . . .

Paragraphs indented for emphasis, visual appeal

. . . a world in which many of the most interesting, most challenging career opportunities call for a background in science and technology.

That's why I'm pleased that my children read 3-2-1 CONTACT, a magazine for 3rd through 8th graders that does for them what <u>Sesame Street</u> does for younger children: It educates without tears, using cartoons, games, jokes, and the attention-getting tricks of television to stimulate, enrich, and enlighten.

3-2-1 CONTACT is published by the non-profit Children's Television Workshop. It is a glossy, colorful magazine, loosely based on the television show of the same name. Like the show, the magazine has high production values: lively graphics, good writing, clear, full-color photographs and amusing illustrations throughout. Issue after issue, your youngsters will be entertained and challenged by such features as . . .

Builds credibility

<u>EXTRA!</u> The puzzles-and-games pages of the magazine, and the section most readers turn to first. Perhaps there'll be a "what's wrong with this picture" game, designed to promote logic and attention to detail. Sometimes there's a maze to get through, or a simple hands-on experiment, or a word-search puzzle.

There's often something to write away for -- for example, a free booklet from Kodak on how to make a pin-hole camera. Sometimes there's a riddle your child can solve by doing a series of math problems. (Can you imagine? Fun math!)

<u>TNT: Tomorrow's News Today</u> -- is a popular monthly column that brings our readers interesting news, often before their parents know of it. Have you heard about pop rice? (It tastes like pop corn, but is made from rice.) Did you know that the planet Pluto is a lot smaller than previously thought, and may be downgraded to a "minor planet"? Have

Figure 11.1   **Continued**

you heard about the plans for a two-mile-long elevated freeway in Los
Angeles -- for bicycles only? Do you know about the new aerosol spray
that protects against poison ivy? 3-2-1 CONTACT readers know about
all these, and more!

The famous magician Blackstone is a contributor to 3-2-1 CONTACT, usually with
a remarkable math trick, such as this one:

> Using a calculator, punch in any three-digit
> number. (Example: 627.) Then punch it in again,
> so you have a six-digit number. (Example: 627,627.)
> Then divide the six-digit number by seven, divide
> the answer by 11, and divide that answer by 13.
> Amazingly, you'll always end up with the original
> three-digit number! Try it!

*Example of material
in magazine —
helps to prove
claims*

THE TIME TEAM is another popular feature of 3-2-1 CONTACT. In each
month's story, two teenagers -- with the help of a science fair
project gone awry -- travel into the past or the future. Transported
to different eras and cultures, the heroes become caught up in
exciting historical moments, and have adventures with people both
famous and ordinary. In one episode, set in the 1920s, they use their
mental agility to help Walt Disney solve a mystery involving the
original Mickey Mouse cartoon. In another, they find themselves in
the middle of the Civil War. An entertaining blend of fact and
fiction, the stories make history and science come alive!

FACTOIDS, too, is a popular monthly column, one that provides our
readers with curious little facts which they can share with their
friends. For example, did you know that . . .

*   In one day, Americans eat enough pizza to cover 75 football
    fields.

*Facts to
interest
parents as
well as kids*

*   A codfish lays up to four million eggs at one time, but on
    average only two will become fish.

*   Lions sleep about 18 hours a day.

*   One hundred years ago, the average 9-year-old was about six
    inches shorter than a 9-year-old today.

*   In one year, your heart beats about 36,000,000 times.

And of course, every issue of 3-2-1 CONTACT contains several major articles
spanning the depth and breadth of science today. For example, recently we had
a special issue on Water, with articles on Rescuing a Coral Reef . . . River
Rafting Catches On . . . and Are We Running Out of Water?

We've also had cover stories on Why Baby Animals Are Cute (in some species,
it's what makes adults take care of their young!) . . . on Finding Homes for
Wild Horses . . . and on Memory, including an article on how memory works,
with tricks and techniques for greatly improving your own memory!

*   *   *   *   *   *

Concluded   **Figure 11.1**

Need to improve positive emphasis here

(If) these examples of what you'll find in 3-2-1 CONTACT have convinced you to subscribe for your family, then indicate "I ACCEPT" on the enclosed Free Issue Request Card. Send no money now -- (we'll send) you your first issue, enter your subscription, and bill you later.

Lacks you–attitude

(If) you'd like to see the magazine before making up your mind, indicate "I'M NOT SURE" on the Free Issue Request Card. (We'll send) you an issue at no cost and with no obligation to subscribe.

When you receive your first issue, show it to your children. Look through it together, and decide if becoming a subscriber is a good idea for you.

Action close

(If) not, write "cancel" on our invoice, return it, and owe nothing. The first issue will be yours to keep, free. But if you like 3-2-1 CONTACT -- the <u>only</u> children's magazine ever to receive the National Magazine Award for General Excellence -- and wish to continue receiving it, (we'll send) you 9 more issues (10 issues in all) for the low price of $1.59 per issue.

Should use you–attitude

There's really nothing to lose -- and the exciting world of science and technology to gain. Say "I ACCEPT" or "I'M NOT SURE," but please -- return your Free Issue Card today!

                          Sincerely,

                          Nina B. Link

                          Nina B. Link
                          Publisher
                          3-2-1 CONTACT

Lacks you–attitude

    P.S.   If yours is one of the first fifty request cards to be processed,
           (we'll send) you -- absolutely FREE -- a NINTENDO Entertainment
           System Control Deck. The system includes the Control Deck and
           two precision-engineered controls designed for instant reflex
           action! You can play the complete library of NINTENDO games on
           this system. And its exclusive microchips give you brilliant
           color, 3-D images and actual shadows -- the most advanced
           graphics ever! To be considered for this state-of-the-art home
           entertainment system, remove the "FREE NINTENDO" sticker from the
           outer envelope and affix it to the postpaid reply envelope
           provided. Then enclose your request card and mail it
           immediately!

Split long P.S. into two paragraphs for better visual impact

Even though The Salvation Army raises most of its funds by direct mail, it still has holiday collection buckets in malls. The traditional collection gets mostly single dollar bills, but it builds visibility and goodwill.

In your close, in addition to asking for money, suggest other ways the reader can help: doing volunteer work, scheduling a meeting on the subject, writing letters to Congress or the leaders of other countries, and so on. By suggesting other ways to participate, you not only involve readers but also avoid one of the traps of fund-raising letters: sounding as though you are selfish, only interested in readers for the money they can give.

Deciding How Much to Ask For

Most letters suggest a range of amounts, from $15 or $25 (for employed people) up to perhaps double what you *really* expect to get from a single donor. A second strategy is to ask for a small, set amount that nearly everyone can afford ($5 or $10).

You can increase the size of gifts by using the following techniques:

1. **Suggest amounts in descending order.** Both in your close and on the reply card, say "$100, $50, $25, or whatever amount you prefer" rather than starting with the smallest and going up.
2. **Ask for gifts slightly higher than the normal cut-off points.** Most people think in terms of a gift of $5, $25, $50, and so on, even though they could afford to give slightly more. You can increase the average gift by asking for $6, $30, $60, and so on.
3. **Link the gift to what it will buy.** Tell how much money it costs to buy a brick, a hymnal, or a stained glass window for a church; a book or journal subscription for a college library; a meal for a hungry child. Linking amounts to specific gifts helps readers feel involved and often motivates them to give more: instead of saying, "I'll write a check for $25," the reader may say, "I'd like to give a _____" and write a check to cover it.
4. **Offer a premium for giving.** Public TV and radio stations have used this ploy with great success, offering books, umbrellas, and carryall bags for gifts at a certain level. The best premiums are things that people both

want and will use or display, so that the organization will get further publicity when other people see the premium.

5. **Ask for a monthly pledge.** People on tight budgets could give $5 or $10 a month; more prosperous people could give $50 a month or more. These repeat gifts not only bring in more money than the donors could give in a single check but also become part of the base of loyal supporters which is essential to the continued success of any organization that raises funds.

Always send a thank-you letter to people who respond to your letter, whatever the size of their gifts. By telling about the group's recent work, a thank-you letter can help reinforce donors' commitment to your cause.

Logical Proof in Fund-Raising Letters

The body of a fund-raising letter must prove that (1) the problem deserves the reader's attention, (2) the problem can be solved or at least alleviated, (3) your organization is helping to solve it, (4) private funds are needed, and (5) your organization will use the funds wisely.

1. The problem deserves the reader's attention. No reader can support every cause. Show why the reader should care about solving this problem.

If your problem is life-threatening, give some statistics: you cannot count on everyone's knowing how many people are killed in the United States every year by drunk drivers, or how many children in the world go to bed hungry every night. Also tell about one individual who is affected.

If your problem is not life-threatening, show that the problem threatens some goal or principle your readers find important. For example, a fund-raising letter to boosters of a high school swim team showed that team members' chances of setting records were reduced because timers relied on stopwatches. The letter showed that automatic timing equipment was accurate and produced faster times, since the timer's reaction time was no longer included in the time recorded.

2. The problem can be solved or alleviated. People will not give money if they see the problem as hopeless: why throw money away? Sometimes you can reason by analogy. Cures have been found for other deadly diseases, so it's reasonable to hope that research can find a cure for cancer and AIDS. Sometimes you can show that short-term or partial solutions exist. For example, a UNICEF letter showed that four simple changes could save the lives of millions of children: oral rehydration, immunization, promoting breast feeding, and giving mothers cardboard growth charts so they'll know if their children are malnourished. Those solutions don't affect the underlying causes of poverty, but they do keep children alive while we work on long-term solutions.

3. Your organization is helping to solve or alleviate the problem. Prove that your organization is effective. Be specific. Talk about your successes in the past. Your past success helps readers believe that you can accomplish your goals.

4. Private funds are needed to accomplish your group's goals. We all have the tendency to think that taxes, or foundations, or church collections yield enough to pay for medical research or basic human aid. If your group does get some tax or foundation money, show why more money is needed. If the organization helps people who might be expected to pay for the service, show why they cannot pay, or why they cannot pay enough to cover the full cost. If some of the funds have been raised by the people who will benefit, make that clear.

5. Your organization will use the funds wisely. Prove that the money goes to the cause, not just to the cost of fund-raising.

Enclosures in Fund-Raising Letters

Fund-raising letters sometimes use inexpensive enclosures to add interest and help carry the message.

Brochures are inexpensive, particularly if you photocopy them. Mailings to alumni have included "Why I Teach at Earlham" (featuring three professors) and letters from students who have received scholarships.

Seeds don't cost much. Mailings from both Care and the New Forests Fund include four or five seeds of the leucaena, a subtropical tree that can grow 20 feet in a year. Its leaves feed cattle; its wood provides firewood or building materials; its roots reduce soil erosion. (Indeed, the enclosure easily becomes the theme for the letter.)

Reprints of newspaper or magazine articles about the organization or the problem it is working to solve add interest and credibility. Pictures of people the organization is helping build emotional appeal.

School songs and sports broadcasts on thin vinyl records or audiocassettes motivate people to give to a university and its athletic program.

Major campaigns may budget for enclosures: pictures of buildings, tapes of oral history interviews, even sea shells and Mason jars.

Canadian Culture and Direct Mail*

In the United States, direct mail letters to total strangers often begin "Dear Friend." Canadian letters, in contrast, are more formal and less likely to imply any relationship other than business to be transacted.

US letters often offer some extrinsic reward (✖ p. 70) for responding: a cash rebate, a credit on a bank card, a tote bag. Canadian letters avoid such rewards, perhaps because they suggest that if the product itself is not worth purchasing, the cause is not worth supporting.

*Based on Roger Graves, " 'Dear Friend' (?): Culture and Genre in American and Canadian Direct Marketing Letters," forthcoming, *The Journal of Business Communication.*

Emotional Appeal in Fund-Raising Letters

Emotional appeal is needed to make people pull out their checkbooks. How strong should emotional appeal be? A mild appeal is unlikely to sway any reader who is not already committed, but readers will feel manipulated by appeals they find too strong and reject them. Audience analysis may help you decide how much emotional appeal to use. If you don't know your audience well, use the strongest emotional appeal *you* feel comfortable with.

Emotional appeal is created by specifics. It is hard to care about, or even to imagine, a million people; it is easier to care about one specific person. Details and quotes help us see that person as real. A letter for a New York hospital talked about four people who owed their lives to the hospital: a baby, a young girl, a businessman, and an elderly woman. The letter brought in a greater response than previous mailings that simply used statistics.[9]

Sample Fund-Raising Letter

The Nature Conservancy's "baby heron" letter uses both logic and emotional appeal effectively. (See Figure 11.2.) The mailing list includes people who have given to other causes but not necessarily to wildlife or environmental causes specifically.

The letter is printed in a serif font on two pages front and back. Bolding, indenting, and short paragraphs provide visual variety.

The letter opens with a startling statement that builds emotional appeal. The second paragraph acknowledges the reader's other commitments. The first bold indented paragraph asks for a small amount to make the action seem easy. And since many people distrust requests for funds, the bold indented statement at the bottom of the page stresses the fact that this organization uses funds effectively. The letter cites the Conservancy's past successes to suggest that it will be successful here, shows why money is still needed, and explains what the money will be used for. The action close ends with a picture of the reader's dollars protecting the earth for the next generation.

WRITING STYLE

Direct mail is the one kind of business writing where elegance and beauty of language matter; in every other kind, elegance is welcome but efficiency is all that finally counts. Direct mail imitates the word choice and rhythm of conversation. The best sales and fund-raising writing is closer to the language of poetry than to that of academia: it shimmers with images, it echoes with sound, it vibrates with energy.

Many of the things that make writing vivid and entertaining *add* words because they add specifics or evoke an emotional response. Individual sentences should be tight. The passage as a whole may be fun to read precisely because of the details and images that "could have been left out."

1. Make Your Writing Tight.

If the style is long-winded and boring, the reader will stop reading. Eliminating wordiness (✖ p. 93) is crucial. You've already seen ways to tighten your writing in Chapter 4. Direct mail goes further, breaking some of

A Fund-Raising Letter   **Figure 11.2**

Donna Cherel
Director of Membership

The **Nature Conservancy**®   1815 North Lynn Street

Dear Friend of the Family,   *Opener: Starting Statement . . .*

Builds emotional appeal.

It goes (almost) without saying that the (baby) black-crowned night heron on our envelope depends on you for her survival.

. . . that moves to a question—one that reflects the cynicism some people feel toward fund-raising

But you have dependents, concerns of your own. So why should you help this short-legged, short-necked bird who's usually awake only at night?

Answer to the question.

Because her future is your future. The wetlands our baby calls home are vanishing -- under the plow, bulldozer, cement truck. And the streams, bogs, ponds and marshes that are <u>basic</u> to both your lives are being destroyed as never before.

This letter uses the strategy of asking for a small amount from everyone.

Saving them is imperative . . . and worth the cost.
Just $10 from you and we can do it.
The Nature Conservancy can <u>buy</u> the land this heron
-- all of us -- need to breed, roost, survive.

Central selling point.

Home for our heron chick is the Virginia Coast Reserve, the last intact fully functioning, barrier island ecosystem on the Atlantic coast of the United States. We are rescuing this, one of America's Last Great Places, through a coordinated plan of purchases and agreements.

And we'd like to let <u>you</u> in on the deal.

Since 1951, The Nature Conservancy has been protecting wetlands, rain forests, prairies and beaches. To date, we've helped protect more than 8.1 million acres in the U.S. and millions more through our Latin American, Caribbean and Pacific programs. Our work has already rescued numerous species from extinction.

Not a bad record. And it explains why in a recent poll by <u>The Chronicle of Philanthropy</u>,

The Nature Conservancy was rated
America's #1 environmental organization,
with regard to accountability
and expenditure of funds.

Fund-raising letters need to prove that the group uses funds wisely. A testimonial from a third party builds credibility.

Our night heron chick and I are inviting you to join this most influential, effective and prestigious environmental organization at <u>a price that's less than half what others might</u>

Recycled Paper   *(over, please)*

Figure 11.2 **Continued**

-2-

White space gives this powerful word extra emphases.

pay.* More on this (bargain) in a moment.

Only a few lucky souls ever hear the nocturnal heron's flat and eerie "quawk." And only a few informed and intelligent folks -- like you -- ever get a chance to join such an auspicious real estate deal. One that's advantageous to us all.

The Nature Conservancy works with special partners throughout America to safeguard the shrinking natural areas of our country. We're not out to save the world, just the most important parts of it.

Our strategy is simple. And amazingly effective. We find natural habitats that are in danger and we buy them. It's the best of America, combining good ethics, sound business and visionary outlook.

The large number of members explains how only $10 can help.

Right now, we have more than 825,000 members who each contribute $10 (or often more!) a year. With their support, we're able to exercise some muscle on behalf of those animals, plants and natural places that need it.

Prepares way for bigger gifts, too.

So in addition to black-crowned night herons in Virginia, we help provide homes for free-ranging bison in Tallgrass Prairie. Black spectacled bear in Ecuador. Chinook salmon in California. Uakari monkeys in the Amazon basin. Sandhill cranes in Florida. Margays in Central America. And many, many more than I can list here.

Past successes.

Some of our protected wildlife are noble. Some are cute. Many, like the night heron chick, have faces only a mother could love.

But we don't save species because they're cute or appealing. We save them because, given the interdependence of life on this planet, a threat to any of them is a threat to us all.

Each year, the U.S. loses 290,000 acres of wetlands -- an area larger than half of our national parks. Over a quarter million acres, gone forever. Those wetlands absorb contaminants and sediments from the water we drink, make a buffer against coastal flooding, and give safe haven to 600 wildlife species and 5,000 plant species.

Why more help is needed.

**So just as our baby heron needs her mother to bring her fish
parts to eat, she needs <u>you</u> to invest
just $10 to protect what's left of her -- <u>our</u> -- home.**

Last year, with contributions of $10 or more from people just like you, we completed

Continued   **Figure 11.2**

-3-

744 projects and brought under our protection a total land area over one-third the size of Connecticut.

Past successes.

In that state alone, we oversee 55 preserves. And with 62 Nature Conservancy chapters in all 50 states, we currently own and manage more than 1,500 preserves throughout the U.S., the largest private system of nature sanctuaries in the world.

If we're doing so well, why do I ask you to join?

Because you're exactly the kind of person we need right now.

Why more help is needed.

And while we've been extremely successful, the problem we face is extremely large. Also, we've discovered it's not enough just to protect acreage.

We must protect ecosystems. Set up buffers between protected habitats and "civilization." Engineer cooperation among government, business and people. And discover ways that allow human beings to live more wisely on the land.

Now, in this new era of new environmentalism, a top priority is saving America's Last Great Places: like Adirondak Park in northern New York state; Nipomo Dunes, California; the embattled Florida Keys; and the Virginia Coast Reserve, where our heron chick lives.

How money will be spent.

In many parts of the world, we're saving land. Using creative techniques like debt-for-nature swaps and Adopt-an-Acre programs. Trading know-how with partners in the tropics through staff exchange projects. And investing, each and every day, in an additional 600 acres of critical habitat for the survival of rare and endangered species.

By saving just a fraction of our country's undeveloped land, we can save our natural heritage.

Deals with an objection some people have to environmental groups.

I know it's fashionable these days to talk about making a choice between environmental protection and prosperity. Between birds and jobs.

But you can't ask people to choose between protecting the environment and feeding their families. And you don't have to. Instead, join The Nature Conservancy.

When you do, you'll save thousands of broken homes and keep your own planetary habitat from shattering as well. You'll join a savvy partnership of real estate and business experts, lawyers, ecologists, biologists, foresters and more.

Emotional appeal.

(over, please)

Figure 11.2   **Concluded**

- 4 -

And you'll receive:

White space, bolding emphasize premiums for giving.

A full year's subscription to the full-color magazine, <u>Nature Conservancy</u>, filled with engrossing articles and gorgeous photographs of the animals and places you're helping to save.

A 10% discount on most purchases from The Nature Company catalog and stores.

A newsletter from your state chapter regularly detailing how your support is protecting natural habitats right where you live.

Exclusive invitations to special social events and field trips at Nature Conservancy preserves near you.

An official membership card.

Of course, the most important benefit is a little harder to quantify -- the advantage of *Central selling point.* living on a planet that still provides a home for black-crowned night herons. The intangible, immeasurable value of keeping our earthly family intact.

Think how much we stand to gain. Then remember how little this costs.

Just $10 for 12 months. Less than 20 cents a week. *Breaks down cost.*

That's an amount you can't afford <u>not</u> to spend. *Better omitted. Reader is likely to disagree.*

<u>So join us, America's leading conservation group, today</u>. Send your check now for just $10 in the return envelope. Or send more if your bank account and commitment allow. *Reference to bigger gifts allows someone who wants to give more to do so.*

But do it <u>now</u>. If you don't do it for yourself, do it for the younger generation. On whose behalf your membership will protect our Earth.

Ends with picture of reader helping to protect next generation & the earth.

Sincerely,

Donna Cherel

Donna Cherel
Director of Membership

P.S.   Although the black-crowned night heron on our envelope is not yet a threatened *Effective* species, the wetlands she calls home are still in danger. With your help, we can save *P.S.s* America's wetlands and their species before it is too late.

P.P.S.   During breeding season, the night heron proudly grows long white plumes on the back of its head. You'll have a good self-image, too, when you join us. Just check the appropriate box on the enclosed form and I'll send your FREE 1996 CALENDAR and other valuable membership gifts as soon as I hear from you.

NH • LT • ABCAL • 12 • 1 * Dues are normally $25. You can join for $10 through this special invitation only.

the rules of grammar. In the following examples, note how sentence fragments and ellipses (spaced dots) are used in parallel structure to move the reader along:

> So tiny, it fits virtually unnoticed in your pocket. So meticulously hand-assembled by unhurried craftsmen in Switzerland, that production may never exceed demand. So everyday useful, that you'll wonder how you ever got along without it.

Letter asking for inquiries about Dictaphone

> Dear Member-elect:
>
> If you still believe that there are only nine planets in our solar system . . . . . . that wine doesn't breathe . . . and that you'd recognize a Neanderthal man on sight if one sat next to you on the bus . . .
> . . . check your score. There aren't. It does. You wouldn't.

Subscription letter for *Natural History*

2. Use Sound Patterns to Emphasize Words.

When you repeat sounds, you create patterns that catch the reader's attention, please the ear, and emphasize the words they occur in. **Alliteration** occurs when several syllables begin with the same sound. **Rhyme** is the repetition of the final vowel sounds and, if the words end with consonants, the final consonant sounds. **Rhythm** is the repetition of a pattern of accented and unaccented syllables. The **rule of three** explains that when you have a series of three items that are logically parallel, the last receives the most emphasis.

Alliteration marks the opener-anecdote quoted earlier. The *s* and *z* sounds in the first sentence focus our attention on the snakes. The repetition of *st* in the second indented paragraph emphasizes those words. (Note that these paragraphs also use sentence fragments.)

> She hoisted herself up noiselessly so as not to disturb the rattlesnakes snoozing there in the sun.
> To her left, the high desert of New Mexico. Indian country. To her right, the rock carvings she had photographed the day before. Stick people. Primitive animals.
> Up ahead, three sandstone slabs stood stacked against the face of the cliff.

Subscription letter for *Science84*

Rhythm, rhyme, and the rule of three emphasize words in the following example:

> Nightcalls, pratfalls, and jungle shrieks . . . a scattering of wings, a chattering of monkeys and big, yellow eyes in my headlights!

Headline, sales letter for Tom Timmins cigars

This letter goes on to tell the story of a search for tobacco in a tropical jungle—in a style that evokes the feeling of the Bogart-Hepburn movie *The African Queen*.

3. Use Psychological Description.

Psychological description (✂ p. 223) means describing your product or service in terms of reader benefits. In a sales letter, you can use psychological description to create a scenario so the reader can picture himself or herself using your product or service and enjoying its benefits. You can also use psychological description to describe the problem your product will solve.

A *Bon Appétit* subscription letter uses psychological description in its opener and in the P.S., creating a frame for the sales letter:

> Dear Reader:
>
> First, fill a pitcher with ice.
> Now pour in a bottle of ordinary red wine, a quarter cup of brandy, and a small bottle of Club soda.
> Sweeten to taste with a quarter to half cup of sugar, garnish with slices of apple, lemon, and orange. . . .
> . . . then *move your chair to a warm, sunny spot.* You've just made yourself Sangria—one of the great glories of Spain, and the perfect thing to sit back with and sip while you consider this invitation. . . .
> . . .
> P.S. One more thing before you finish your Sangria. . . .

It's hard to imagine any reader really stopping to follow the recipe before finishing the letter, but the scenario is so vivid that one can imagine the sunshine even on a cold, gray day.

4. Make Your Letter Sound Like a Letter, Not an Ad.

Maintain the image of one person writing to one other person that is the foundation of all letters. Use an informal style with short words and sentences, and even slang.

You can also create a **persona**—the character who allegedly writes the letter—to make the letter interesting and keep us reading. Use the rhythms of speech, vivid images, and conversational words to create the effect that the author is a "character."

The following opening creates a persona who fits the product:

> Dear Friend:
>
> There's no use trying. I've tried and tried to tell people about my fish. But I wasn't rigged out to be a letter writer, and I can't do it. I can close-haul a sail with the best of them. I know how to pick out the best fish of the catch, I know just which fish will make the tastiest mouthfuls, but I'll never learn the knack of writing a letter that will tell people why my kind of fish—fresh-caught prime-grades, right off the fishing boats with the deep-sea tang still in it—is lots better than the ordinary store kind.

Sales letter, Frank Davis Fish Company

This letter, with its "Aw, shucks, I can't sell" persona, with language designed to make you see an unassuming fisherman ("rigged out," "close-haul"), was written by a professional advertiser.[10]

PARTS OF A DIRECT MAIL PACKAGE

The letter is the most important part of a direct mail package, but several other parts help accomplish your purpose. The **package** includes the outer

Ethics and Direct Mail, II*

Direct mail letters are rarely written by the people who sign the letter. (President Clinton probably didn't actually draft the fund-raising letter you received. And his signature was printed, not personally signed.)

Sometimes, to create the effect of personal letters, direct mail includes a typo or two.

And one company specializes in producing handwritten letters: letters written by real people (but people whose only connection with the product or cause is that they're being paid as scribes).

Each of these practices is, strictly speaking, misleading. I would argue, however, that these tactics are acceptable. Savvy consumers know that actors and actresses in TV ads are being paid to enthuse about the product. Similarly, ghostwriters (and signers) in direct mail seem acceptable.

*Paragraph 3 based on Bethany McLean, "The Lost Art of Writing Meets the Black Art of Direct Mail," *Fortune*, February 5, 1996, 36.

envelope and everything that goes in it: the main letter, brochures, samples, secondary letters, reply card, and the reply envelope.

The **envelope** can do more than simply protect the contents during mailing. One test found that an envelope marked "OPEN NOW" produced an 18% higher response rate than a plain envelope (the rest of the package parts were identical). Words on the envelope are called **teaser copy.** Like openers, teasers must get the reader's attention and have some logical link to the body of the letter.

Brochures give more information about the product or organization and, especially if they have color pictures, can involve the sense of sight and contribute to the package's emotional appeal. Magazines and products relating to food, decorating, scenery, gardening, sports, and history seem especially to lend themselves to good brochures, but you can use a brochure in almost any package.

Samples give the reader something to touch and may help sell your product. Swatches of cloth enable readers to check color and quality of the clothing you're selling; a small packet of seeds may motivate readers to order your book on gardening; a scratch-and-sniff card can help sell perfume or scented soap.

Many packages contain **secondary letters:** letters on small paper to readers who have decided not to accept the offer, letters from people who have benefited from the charity in the past, letters from recognized people corroborating the claims made in the main letter.

The **reply card** can be a separate card, a tear-off stub of the letter or brochure, or even the (large) inside flap of the reply envelope. Make the card easy to fill out. A good reply card not only has space for the reader to fill in mailing and ordering information but also repeats information from the letter such as the central selling point, basic product information, and price. Information from the letter is repeated because readers who plan to order or donate may throw away the letter and just keep the reply card.

If readers will be sending in checks, a separate **reply envelope** is necessary. In sales packages, the postage is normally paid. In fund-raising appeals, even if the postage is paid, the letter often invites the reader to affix a stamp, so that more of the organization's money can go to the cause. A postage-paid **reply card,** with no envelope, is possible if you are just asking for inquiries or if only credit sales are possible, but be careful—some readers prefer not to make their requests or their credit card numbers public.

The Power of Touch*

A classic direct mail package has eight critical surfaces: the front and back of the outer envelope; above the salutation of the letter; the salutation, first line, and first paragraph of the letter; the P.S.; the response device; and the front and back of the brochure. You try to put the right icons on the right surfaces. And you try to build in tactile involvement: the more people handle direct mail, the better the response. Why? Handling the pieces prolongs the time people spend with the package, and subliminally suggests the direct mail transaction, which always involves the hand filling out a form or dialing a phone. Touch, by the way, is processed by the right hemisphere, so it adds a whole brain dimension.

*Quoted from James R. Rosenfield, interview with the author, November 24, 1993.

Summary of Key Points

- Calling direct mail "junk mail" may cause us to respond to the symbol rather than to the reality.
- The first three steps in writing a sales or fund-raising letter are to (1) learn about the product or service, (2) choose and analyze the target audience, and (3) choose a central selling point. The **target audience** is the group of people one expects to be interested in the product, service, or cause. A **central selling point** is a reader benefit that by itself motivates your readers to act and covers all the other benefits.
- A good **star** (opener) makes readers want to read the letter and provides a reasonable transition to the body of the letter. Four modes for openers are **questions, narration, startling statements,** and **quotations.** A good **chain** (body) answers readers' questions, overcomes their objections, and involves them emotionally. A good **knot** (action close) tells readers what to do, makes the action sound easy, gives them a reason for acting promptly, and ends with a reader benefit or a picture of the reader's money helping to solve the problem.

■ Specify price in the last fourth of a sales letter, after you've given your evidence and made the reader *want* the product.

■ In a fund-raising letter, the basic strategy is vicarious participation. By donating money, readers participate vicariously in work they are not able to do personally.

■ The primary purpose in a fund-raising letter is to get money. An important secondary purpose is to build support for the cause, so that readers who are not persuaded to give will still have favorable attitudes toward the group and will be sympathetic when they hear about it again.

■ The body of a fund-raising letter must prove that (1) the problem deserves the reader's attention, (2) the problem can be solved or at least alleviated, (3) your organization is helping to solve it, (4) private funds are needed, and (5) your organization will use the funds wisely.

■ To increase the size of gifts, suggest amounts in descending order; ask for gifts slightly higher than the normal cut-off points; link the gift to what it will buy; offer a premium for giving; and ask for a monthly pledge.

■ Good writing in direct mail is tight. It uses sound patterns to emphasize words, uses psychological description, and is specific and conversational.

■ A **direct mail package** includes the outer envelope and everything that goes in it: the main letter, brochures, samples, secondary letters, reply card, and the reply envelope.

Exercises and Problems
For Chapter 11

GETTING STARTED

11–1   Evaluating Envelope Teasers

In the following examples, the words in square brackets describe the appearance of the envelope or lettering. The name in parentheses is from the return address. If no name is listed, either the return address is a street address only or there is no return address. Unless otherwise noted, the teaser copy appeared on the front (address side) of the envelope.

Would you open the envelope? Why or why not? Do others in the class agree?

1. [Large 6-inch-by-11½-inch envelope. Through the address window, below your name, a red "Fast Company" shows. On the envelope, in big black letters]
   THROW AWAY
   this envelope, and you'll be canning your job, career, business, and future. [In smaller type:] (*Open it, and you'll learn the one best survival secret for you . . .*)

   [in lower left-hand corner, in black type on gray background:]
   CHARTER INVITATION—
   FREE ISSUE—RSVP
   [Through a round window, a red sticker with the word "FREE" in white shows.]

2. (United Farm Workers)
   Question: What's at the top of a 40-foot palm tree? [Drawing of palm tree]
   Answer:
   A farm worker!

3. (World Vision.) [Green 7¼-inch-by-5¼-inch envelope. Black box in upper left-hand corner.]
   Shake this envelope
      and
         hear
            the
               sound
                  of
                     hope
   [When shaken, envelope makes a soft rattling noise.]

4. (ACLU)
   Personalized Address Labels Enclosed
   For:
   [Address box with your name]

5. (Heart and Stroke Foundation of
   Ontario)

43% of the people reading this letter will die from heart disease or stroke.

The improved *"Ticker Test"* inside will tell what you can do to reduce *your* risk!

11–2   Evaluating P.S.'s

Evaluate the following P.S.'s. Will they motivate readers to read the whole letter if readers do turn to them first? Do they create a strong ending for those who have already read the letter?

1. P.S.   Because many of our friends have enjoyed the soup recipes we've offered in the past, I've included another one at the bottom of this letter. I hope it brings back to you and your loved ones the warmth you've shared generously with others. [Recipe for "Ground Beef & Vegetable Soup" below, in outline shaped like a recipe card.]

2. P.S.   I am enclosing three color postcards of your scenic public lands as a beautiful reminder of just how much you have at stake in this fight for our natural heritage. We really need your support. Please join NRDC today and help us send Congress a message loud and clear that: *"Our Natural Heritage Is Not For Sale!"*

3. P.S.   Send no money now. Just send your reply. There's no risk. No commitment. No obligation at all.

P.P.S.   You'll get answers to *101 Health Questions* just for sending your reply. It's yours to keep no matter what.

4. P.S.   I almost forgot! To thank you for taking the time to preview GOOD HEALTH FOR AFRICAN AMERICANS, we'd like to send you another book *absolutely free.* It's called *Heart & Soul's Guide to Looking Good Naturally,* and it contains a treasure trove of natural beauty secrets for African American men and women. In this 48-page manual (not sold in stores), you'll learn how to bring out the natural good looks you were born to enjoy. This book is *yours free* just for giving GOOD HEALTH FOR AFRICAN AMERICANS a try. And it's *yours to keep,* regardless of whether or not you choose to buy my book.

5. P.S.   I hope to hear from you right away so we can make 1998 Habitat's most exciting year of building ever!

11–3   Evaluating Sales and Fund-Raising Letters

Collect the sales and fund-raising letters that come to you, your co-workers, landlord, neighbors, or family. Use the following questions to evaluate each package:

- What mode does the opener use? Is it related to the teaser, if any? Is it related to the rest of the letter? How good is the opener?
- What central selling point or common ground does the letter use?
- What kinds of proof does the letter use? Is the logic valid? What questions or objections are not answered?
- How does the letter create emotional appeal?

- Is the style effective? Where does the letter use sound to emphasize points?
- Does the close tell readers what to do, make action easy, give a reason for acting promptly, and end with a positive picture?
- Does the letter use a P.S.? How good is it?
- Is the letter visually attractive? Why or why not?
- What other items besides the letter are in the package?

As Your Instructor Directs,
a. Share your analysis of one or more letters with a small group of your classmates.

b. Analyze one letter in a presentation to the class. Make overhead transparencies or photocopies of the letter to use as a visual aid in your presentation.

c. Analyze one letter in a memo to your instructor. Provide a copy or photocopy of the letter along with your memo.

d. With several other students, write a group memo or report analyzing one

part of the letter (e.g., openers) or one kind of letter (e.g., political letters, organizations fighting hunger, etc.). Use at least 10 letters for your analysis if you look at only one part; use at least six letters if you analyze one kind of letter. Provide copies or photocopies as an appendix to your report.

11–4 Brainstorming Openers for a Magazine Subscription Letter

a. Using at least **two** of the four different modes—question, narration, startling statement, and quotation—write **three** possible openers for a letter urging readers to subscribe to a magazine (you pick the magazine).

b. For each opener indicate (1) what mode it uses and (2) how you would make a

transition to the body of the letter. (You may write out the transition or just describe it, whichever is easier.)

c. Rate the three openers in terms of their effectiveness, and briefly explain the reason for your ratings.

E-MAIL MESSAGES

11–5 Raising Money at the Office

A charity you support needs funds.

As Your Instructor Directs,

a. Write an e-mail message to your boss, to find out if it's OK to post fund-raising messages to the entire workforce.

b. Write a fund-raising e-mail message to everyone at your workplace. Be sure to tell where to send cash or checks.

11–6 Answering an Ethics Question

You're a senior staffer in a charitable organization. Today, you get this message from your boss.

Subject: Using "Handwritten" Messages

I'd like your feedback on the suggestion from our direct mail consultant to use a mailing with handwritten notes. I understand the argument that this will increase response. But the idea of hiring people who don't have any relation to us to write notes—and implying that the notes are by loyal donors—seems unethical. And frankly, I worry about the image we'd create if our real donors learned that we'd done this.

What do you think?

As Your Instructor Directs,

a. Answer the question, using a charitable organization that you know something about.

b. Answer the question, assuming that it comes from a congressional candidate.

c. Answer the question, assuming that the strategy has been recommended for a sales rather than for a fund-raising letter.

d. Write an e-mail message to your instructor, justifying your answer.

WEB PAGES

11–7 Creating a Web Page

The World Wide Web enables individuals and companies to sell products and services and organizations, causes, and candidates to raise funds. The cost can be much lower than other forms of marketing, and, because the consumer chooses to go to the page, Web pages may create a more positive response than other forms of marketing.

Create a Web page to sell a product or service or to raise funds for an organization or candidate. At the top of the page, catch the reader's attention, so that he or she is motivated to scroll down. Provide both a "snail mail" address to which funds can be sent and a form on which people can buy or contribute online by entering their credit card numbers. At the bottom of the page, put the creation/update date and your name and e-mail address.

As Your Instructor Directs,
a. Turn in two laser copies of your page(s). On another page, give the URLs for any links.
b. Turn in one laser copy of your page(s) and a disk with the HTML code and .gif files.
c. Write a memo to your instructor (1) identifying the audience for which the page is designed and explaining (2) the search strategies you used to find material on this topic, (3) why you chose the information you've included, and (4) why you chose the layout and graphics you've used.
d. Present your page orally to the class.

Hints:
- Pick a product, service, candidate, or organization you know something about.
- If you have a lot of information, divide it into several pages.
- Interest readers so that they stay with your page(s) as long as possible.
- Use links to pages sponsored by other organizations only if they support your purposes.
- Offer a reason for people to return to the page after their initial visit.

LETTER ASSIGNMENTS

11–8 Writing a Magazine Subscription Letter

Write a 2½- to 4-page letter persuading **new subscribers** to subscribe to a magazine of your choice. Assume that your letter would have a reply card and postage-paid envelope. You do NOT have to write these, but DO refer to them in your letter.

Choose a magazine you read or one that deals with a subject or sport you know something about. You may choose a narrower target audience for this letter than the magazine uses. For example, if the magazine is designed to appeal to women ages 18–35, for this assignment you could write to college women, ages 18–25. If you narrow the target audience, be sure to tell your instructor.

Hints:
- Read several issues of the magazine, looking both at editorial content and at ads, to identify the magazine's target audience. Choose a central selling point that will appeal to that audience.
- Pay special attention to language. To keep your letter moving quickly, consider occasionally using sentence fragments or ellipses. Try to choose vivid, evocative language; try your hand at alliteration or other repetitive patterns.
- Everyone has had the experience of seeing interesting headlines on a magazine cover but then being disappointed by the stories inside. Be sure to prove your claims by giving examples and specifics. You may use material from previous issues of the magazine; you may need to edit or rewrite it for maximum effect. Choose details that will interest your reader.
- Get current figures about subscription rates from the magazine itself. It's OK to offer a free issue, a premium, or a discount, but do not depend on the offer alone to motivate people. Your letter must be fully persuasive even without the special premium.

11–9   Persuading Students to Join a Campus Organization

Write a letter persuading eligible students to join a campus organization.

As Your Instructor Directs,

a. Assume that your organization can afford only a one-page mailing, with address and postage on the back of the page. Write a one-page letter.

b. Assume that postage is not an issue. Write a 2- to 3-page letter.

c. Create a brochure to publicize the organization.

d. Make a 3- to 5-minute presentation persuading students to join.

e. Write a memo to your instructor describing your target audience and your strategy.

Hints:

- How much do students know about the organization? What information must you give about programs, cost, time commitment, benefits, etc.?
- What percentage of eligible students have joined in the past? What would motivate students to join? What obstacles must you overcome?
- Will students at your school respond best to a low-key appeal, to humor, to a hard sell, or to some other approach?

11–10   Selling a Campus Product or Service

In a marketing class, you and a group of other students have come up with a product or service that you could sell on campus and in your community. It's such a good idea that you decide to get the necessary permissions. Now, you're ready to market it. (Use your own idea for a product or service or pick one of the following: a "smart" [debit] card, creating Web pages, temporary tattoos with the school logo or mascot, reusable bins to collect materials for recycling, an income-tax service, a shopping service.)

As Your Instructor Directs,

a. Write a memo to your instructor describing your target audience and the best central selling point and media for reaching them.

b. Design a one-page flyer that you can post on campus advertising your product or service.

c. Write a letter to students and faculty marketing your product or service.

d. Write a letter to businesses urging them to buy your product or service for employees or clients.

e. Create a brochure for your product or service.

f. Make a 3- to 5-minute presentation persuading people to buy your product or service.

11–11   Selling a Book on Bird Watching

Assume that your state's land-grant college has prepared a paperback book, *Bird Watching in [Your State]*. The book has pictures, descriptions, and a brief statement about the behaviors of 25 birds. It also explains how to attract birds to feeders and plants that birds like. The book is written by a professor of Biology of the land-grant university; the price is $9.95, which includes postage and handling.

Pick a target audience and write a 2½- to 4-page letter persuading them to buy the book.

If your instructor directs, also prepare a reply card.

Hints:

- Give as much information as possible that could be found in the book.
- Use psychological description and sensory details.
- Include benefits for people with kids and for childless people, for people with big yards as well as those in apartments, for those who have already put up feeders and birdbaths as well as for those who may be considering doing so for the first time.

11–12   Writing a Fund-Raising Letter

Write a 2½- to 4-page letter to raise money from **new donors** for an organization you support. You must use a real organization, but it does not actually have to be conducting a fund-raising drive now. Assume that your letter would have a reply card and postage-paid envelope. You do NOT have to write these, but DO refer to them in your letter. Options for organizations include

- Tax-deductible charitable organizations—churches, synagogues, hospitals, groups working to feed, clothe, and house poor people.
- Lobbying groups—Mothers Against Drunk Driving, the National Abortion Rights Action League, the National Rifle Association, groups working against nuclear weapons, etc.
- Groups raising money to fight a disease or fund research.

- Colleges trying to raise money for endowments, buildings, scholarships, faculty salaries.
- Athletic associations raising money for scholarships, equipment, buildings, facilities.

For this assignment, you may also use groups which do not regularly have fund-raising drives but which may have special needs. Perhaps a school needs new uniforms for its band or an automatic timing device for its swimming pool. Perhaps a sorority or fraternity house needs repairs, remodeling, or expansion.

11–13 Writing a Fund-Raising Letter for a Political Candidate

One of the problems in running for office is financing the campaign. Direct mail is a primary means of raising money. A letter can give far more information about a candidate's views than a TV or radio spot; unlike those media, it can target a specific group of voters. For presidential elections, direct mail is essential: candidates must demonstrate national support to qualify for federal matching funds.

Choose a real candidate and write a letter to raise funds for him or her. Use real information about the candidate's positions and the issues in the race. Let readers know ways to help the campaign instead of or in addition to giving money. Assume that your letter would have a reply card and postage-paid envelope. You do NOT have to write these, but DO refer to them in your letter.

Choose a target audience that would be likely to support this candidate. In a memo to your instructor, describe the audience and explain your decision to personalize or not to personalize the letter with the name and address of a specific voter.

Hints:
- Read newspapers and pick up the candidate's literature to find out where the candidate stands on the issues. The League of Women Voters can help you find each candidate's headquarters.
- Talk to some of the people who live in the district to see what their concerns are. Read material from other candidates so you'll know what you have to combat.

11–14 Attracting People to Your State or Province

Create a brochure or letter to attract people to your state or province. Possible audiences and purposes include the following:

a. Persuade people with high-tech skills to work in your state or province.
b. Persuade growing businesses to move to your state or province.

c. Persuade movie and TV producers to film in your state or province.
d. Persuade retirees to move to your state or province.

Interpersonal Communication

CHAPTER 12

International Communication

Chapter Outline

An Inside Perspective:
International Communication

Brenda Arbeláez, President, PALS International

Brenda Arbeláez designs the cross-cultural and language programs needed for successful international business ventures. PALS International in Troy, Michigan, provides customized training in languages and cultures for US business people who are going to other countries and to business people from other countries who are coming to the United States.

Many US employees have learned, often through costly mistakes, that the key to successful international business relationships lies in a real understanding of the values, priorities, and practices of the counterparts in the host nation.

For example, to do business in Mexico, you need to develop a personal relationship. Tell me about you as a person. That's very important. Then I tell you about me, and we do this sometimes not just one time but several times. Then I will trust you and I will value your qualities. Then I will like to work with you. So that's the first step. In Mexican values, work is number 2, family is number 1. So if something happens, they take off to be there for their families.

The best people for international assignments are

- Flexible, with a flexible family.
- Sincerely interested in the target country and its culture.
- Ready to study the target language.
- Modest about the home country and culture.
- Open to growing personally and developing friendships.

These traits are the key to adaptation; they enable executives to overcome most of the hurdles caused by differences in culture.

Thorough preparation is essential before starting the new assignment, not only for the employee, but also for the family. An American couple from an international supplier took our Mexican Cross-Cultural Program and 120 hours of Spanish classes before going to Mexico. The employee invited me to the grand opening of the company's plant in Chihuahua. Knowing the culture and language has made him a manager who is loved and respected by his employees and his Mexican counterparts. He even developed a great relationship with the governor. His wife is an incredible asset to him and his company. She not only knows how to entertain and network with the Mexican spouses, but she also became the lead interpreter and liaison of the American spouses, some of whom did not speak the language. It was extremely satisfying to see how well our students had adapted to a new culture.

Even within the United States, you can learn about other cultures. You can watch Spanish TV channels and listen to Spanish radio. You can buy tapes and cassettes, you have concerts, you have the Hispanic community growing in every single city. The language is incredible, and the culture is here for you to pick up.

Brenda Arbeláez, December 12, 1996

Call PALS International at 1-810-362-2060

"The key to successful international business relationships lies in a real understanding of the values, priorities, and practices of the counterparts in the host nation."

Brenda Arbeláez, PALS International

Mission Statement*

For more than a century, the Mormons have been sending their young overseas. . . . Some stay on as long-term expatriates, many hail from Utah and return there eventually, and a lot . . . go into business, capitalizing on language skills and contacts developed over the years. . . .

On a hill near the University of Utah, Evans & Sutherland Computer Corp. designs display systems for flight simulators. A cadre of former missionaries can speak Mandarin with the Taiwanese air force, German with German customers, and Hebrew with the Israelis. Nearly 50% of the firm's revenue of $113 million a year is from international sales. . . .

[L]iving abroad in such large numbers has created a better grasp of something important: that large parts of the business world puts [sic] much store in personal relationships. "A lot of US business is blind to relationships," says David Janke, a vice president at Evans & Sutherland, the maker of flight simulator displays. "Everything is very by-the-book. The rest of the world lives on relationships and trust."

*Quoted from "Utah's Economy Goes Global, Thanks in Part to Role of Missionaries," The Wall Street Journal, March 28, 1996, A1, A8.

Our values, priorities, and practices are shaped by the culture in which we grow up. Understanding other cultures is crucial if you want to sell your products in other countries, manage an international plant or office, or work in this country for a multinational company headquartered in another country.

This chapter focuses on cultural differences that are linked to national origin. Other kinds of diversity are discussed in Chapter 13.

As Brenda Arbeláez suggests, the successful international communicator is

- Aware that his or her preferred values and behaviors are influenced by culture and are not necessarily "right."
- Flexible and open to change.
- Sensitive to verbal and nonverbal behavior.
- Aware of the values, beliefs, and practices in other cultures.
- Sensitive to differences among individuals within a culture.

THE IMPORTANCE OF INTERNATIONAL BUSINESS

As we saw in Chapter 1, exports are essential to the success both of individual businesses and to a country's economy as a whole. Less technologically advanced countries may offer special opportunities for businesses in mature markets in the United States. For example, the market for buses in Mexico City is greater than the entire bus market in the whole United States.[1]

The web of international business is not confined to exports and imports. Many companies—even service businesses—depend on vendors or operations in other countries. The Bombay Furniture Company orders products from more than 30 countries. If you call an 800 number to reserve a hotel room, your call may be taken by a clerk working in a large room equipped with telephones and computers in Montego Bay, Jamaica. Calls to Quarterdeck's customer service line are answered by highly trained, multilingual computer experts in Ireland—who also field questions from Europe.[2]

For executives in global companies, international experience is often essential for career advancement. At Tupperware, each of the nine members of the executive committee speaks two to four languages and has worked outside his or her home country.[3] Robert Staley, Vice Chairman of Emerson Electric, says,

> If you want to be a senior manager in this company 20 years from now, you'd better get some experience in Asia.[4]

DIVERSITY IN THE UNITED STATES AND CANADA

Even if you never go outside mainland United States or Canada, you'll deal with people whose background is international.

Figure 12.1

Views of Communication in High- and Low-Context Cultures

	High Context (Examples: Japan, United Arab Emirates)	Low Context (Examples: Germany, North America)
Preferred communication strategy	Indirectness, politeness, ambiguity	Directness, confrontation, clarity
Reliance on words to communicate	Low	High
Reliance on nonverbal signs to communicate	High	Low
Importance of written word	Low	High
Agreements made in writing	Not binding	Binding
Agreements made orally	Binding	Not binding
Attention to detail	Low	High

Source: Adapted from David A. Victor, *International Business Communication* (New York: HarperCollins, 1992), 148, 153, 160.

Bilingual Canada has long compared the diversity of its people to a "mosaic." But now immigrants from Italy, Greece, and Hong Kong add their voices to the medley of French, English, and Inuit. Radio station CHIN in Toronto broadcasts in 32 languages.[5] People in the United States increasingly use the metaphor of "a crazy quilt" to describe the country's growing diversity. In the 1990 census, 25% of the people in the United States chose to identify themselves as members of minorities.[6] Forty percent of Californians are African American, Latino, or Asian.[7] The United States now has 1,100 mosques and Islamic centers, 1,500 Buddhist centers, and 800 Hindu centers.[8] According to one estimate, there may be twice as many Muslims as Episcopalians.[9] People work in Japanese plants in Peterborough, New Hampshire; Marysville, Ohio; and Smyrna, Tennessee. Employees at the Digital Equipment plant in Boston come from 44 countries and speak 19 languages; the plant's announcements are printed in English, Chinese, French, Spanish, Portuguese, Haitian Creole, and Vietnamese.[10]

Ways to Look at Culture

Each of us grows up in a **culture** that provides patterns of acceptable behavior and belief. We may not be aware of the most basic features of our own culture until we come into contact with people who do things differently. If we come from a culture where dogs are pets, that interpretation may seem "natural" until we learn that in other cultures, dogs, like chickens, are raised for food.

We can categorize cultures as high-context or low-context. In **high-context cultures,** most of the information is inferred from the context of a message; little is explicitly conveyed. Japanese, Arabic, and Latin American cultures are high-context. In **low-context cultures,** context is less important; most information is explicitly spelled out. German, Scandinavian, and North American cultures are low-context.

As David Victor points out, high- and low-context cultures value different kinds of communication and have different attitudes toward oral and written channels (✖ p. 64).[11] As Figure 12.1 shows, low-context cultures like those of the United States favor direct approaches and may see indirectness as dishonest or manipulative. The written word is seen as more important than oral statements, so contracts are binding but promises may be broken. Details matter. Business communication practices in the United States reflect these low-context preferences.

Living and doing business in another country require being sensitive to religious beliefs and practices. Here, thousands of Muslims in India gather to attend a prayer service marking the last day of Islam's holy month of Ramadan.

VALUES, BELIEFS, AND PRACTICES

Values and beliefs, often unconscious, affect our response to people and situations. Most North Americans, for example, value "fairness." "You're not playing fair" is a sharp criticism calling for changed behavior. In some countries, however, people expect certain groups to receive preferential treatment. Most North Americans accept competition and believe that it produces better performance. The Japanese, however, believe that competition leads to disharmony. US business people believe that success is based on individual achievement and is open to anyone who excels. In England and in France, success is more obviously linked to social class. And in some countries, people of some castes or races are prohibited by law from full participation in society.

Many people in the United States value individualism. Other countries may value the group. In traditional classrooms, US students are expected to complete assignments alone; if they get much help from anyone else, they're "cheating." In Japan, in contrast, groups routinely work together to solve problems. In US white culture, quiet is a sign that people are working. In Japan people talk to get the work done.[12]

Values and beliefs are influenced by religion. Christianity coexists with a view of the individual as proactive. In some Muslim and Asian countries, however, it is seen as presumptuous to predict the future by promising action by a certain date. The Puritan work ethic legitimizes wealth by seeing it as a sign of divine favor. In other Christian cultures, a simpler lifestyle is considered to be closer to God.

A Sampling of International Holidays   **Figure 12.2**

Holiday	Date	Celebrated in	Commemorates
Chinese New Year (Spring Festival)	January or February (date varies)	Countries with Chinese residents	Beginning of lunar new year
Independence Day	March 6	Ghana	1957 independence from Great Britain
St. Patrick's Day	March 17	Ireland	Ireland's patron saint
Cinco de Mayo	May 5	Mexico	1867 victory over the French
St. Jean-Baptiste Day	June 24	Québec province of Canada	Québec's national holiday
Canada Day	July 1	Canada	1867 proclamation of Canada's status as dominion
Bastille Day	July 14	France	1789 fall of the Bastille prison during the French Revolution
Ramadan	Ninth month of lunar year	Countries with Muslim residents	Atonement; fasting from sunup to sundown
Respect for the Aged Day	September 15	Japan	Respect for elderly relatives and friends
Chun Ben	Last week of September	Cambodia, other Buddhist countries	The dead and actions for one's salvation
Mahatma Ghandi's birthday	October 2	India	Birth of father of Indian independence
Guy Fawkes Day	November 5	England	Capture of Guy Fawkes, who plotted to blow up Parliament
Hanukkah	December (dates vary)	Countries with Jewish residents	Rededication of the temple in Jerusalem
Christmas	December 25	Countries with Christian residents	Birth of Jesus
Boxing Day	December 26	British Commonwealth	Tradition of presenting small boxed gifts to service workers

Religion affects what foods may be eaten and on what days businesses are open. For example, Hindus do not eat beef; Muslims consider pork unclean; orthodox Jews eat only kosher meats. In many Muslim countries, Friday, a day of prayer, is an official holiday. During the twelfth month of the Muslim lunar calendar, a devout Muslim may be on a pilgrimage to Mecca.[13] An ordinary business day may be a holiday in the country you're visiting. A sampling of international holidays appears in Figure 12.2.

Even everyday practices differ from culture to culture. North Americans and Europeans put the family name last; Asians put it first. North American and European printing moves from top to bottom and from left to right. Arabic reads from right to left, but still from top to bottom. Japanese reads from right to left and from bottom to top, so Japanese and English books start at opposite ends. An American carpenter pushes a saw; a Japanese pulls it. Light switches and door knobs turn the opposite way in Japan and in the United States.[14]

Values are more pervasive than we sometimes realize. A US manager whose company was owned by the Japanese was asked to estimate the US sales potential for a piece of construction equipment that is widely used in Japan. The manager believed that the equipment was too small for US construction sites and knew that US builders were happy with the equipment they were using. But smallness is a virtue in crowded Japan, and

International sales require adapting to local tastes. Coca-Cola dominates Japanese vending machines by offering drinks based on tea, coffee, and fermented milk.

technological innovation is more important. The manager felt that he had to defer to the values of the parent company in his report. He presented the potential problems of the equipment as mildly as possible and ended his report with a statement that if management decided to sell the equipment in the United States, he would do everything possible to market it. The statement was necessary, the man believed, so that his superiors in Japan would not see him as disloyal and attacking the company.[15]

NONVERBAL COMMUNICATION

Nonverbal communication—communication that doesn't use words—takes place all the time. Smiles, frowns, who sits where at a meeting, the size of an office, how long someone keeps a visitor waiting—all these communicate pleasure or anger, friendliness or distance, power and status. Most of the time we are no more conscious of interpreting nonverbal signals than we are conscious of breathing.

Yet nonverbal signals can be misinterpreted just as easily as can verbal symbols (words). And the misunderstandings can be harder to clear up because people may not be aware of the nonverbal cues that led them to assume that they aren't liked, or respected, or approved. An Arab student assumed that his US roommate disliked him intensely because the US student sat around the room with his feet up on the furniture, soles toward the Arab roommate. Arab culture sees the foot in general and the sole in particular as unclean; showing the sole of the foot is an insult.[16]

Learning about nonverbal language can help us project the image we want to present and make us more aware of the signals we are interpreting. However, even within a single culture a nonverbal symbol may have more than one meaning.

Body Language

The Japanese value the ability to sit quietly. They may see the US tendency to fidget and shift as an indication of lack of mental or spiritual balance. Even in North America, interviewers and audiences usually respond negatively to nervous gestures such as fidgeting with a tie or hair or jewelry, tapping a pencil, or swinging a foot.

People from different cultures learn to walk differently. Carmen Judith Nine-Curt observes that Caribbean people move the torso as though it was made up of separable parts, while North American Anglos and Northern Spaniards carry the torso as if it were one piece.[17] People from one culture often react negatively to another culture's walk. The French see the American walk as "uncivilized."[18] Anglo Americans sometimes see the way African-American men walk as threatening and the way Latinos walk as sexual, although there is no evidence that these walks carry such meanings in the cultures where people have learned them.

Eye Contact

North American whites see **eye contact** as a sign of honesty. But in many cultures, dropped eyes are a sign of appropriate deference to a superior. Puerto Rican children are taught not to meet the eyes of adults.[19] The Japanese are taught to look at the neck.[20] In Korea, prolonged eye contact is considered rude. The lower-ranking person is expected to look down first.[21]

Arab men in laboratory experiments looked at each other more than did two American men or two Englishmen.[22] Eye contact is so important that Arabs dislike talking to someone wearing dark glasses or while walking side by side. It is considered impolite not to face someone directly. In Muslim countries, women and men are not supposed to have eye contact.

These differences can lead to miscommunication in the multicultural workplace. Superiors may feel that subordinates are being disrespectful when the subordinate is being fully respectful—according to the norms of his or her culture.

Smiling

In the United States, smiling varies from region to region. Twenty years ago, Ray Birdwhistell found that "middle-class individuals" from Ohio, Indiana, and Illinois smiled more than did people from Massachusetts, New Hampshire, and Maine, who in turn smiled more than did western New Yorkers. People from cities in southern and border states—Atlanta, Louisville, Memphis, and Nashville—smiled most of all.[23] Some scholars speculate that northeasterners may distrust the sincerity of southerners who smile a lot (like former President Jimmy Carter). Students from other countries who come to US universities may be disconcerted by the American tendency to smile at strangers—until they realize that the smiles don't "mean" anything. In Germany, smiles are reserved for friends.[24] The Japanese smile not only when they are pleased or amused, but also to say "That's none of your business" and to cover embarrassment, sadness, and even anger.[25]

The Japanese learn to control their emotions. In situations of strong emotion, it is considered acceptable to smile or laugh, but not to frown or cry. In some US businesses, it is considered acceptable to frown, swear, and yell, but not to cry. Yet both "anger" and "crying" may be expressions of the same emotion: frustration at not getting what we want.

Gestures

Americans sometimes assume that they can depend on gestures to communicate if language fails. But Birdwhistell reported that "although we have been searching for 15 years [1950–65], we have found no gesture or body

Ethics Away from Home*

What should you do in a country that seems to demand bribes, approve of racial or sex discrimination, and allow dangerous practices, like dumping unprocessed toxic wastes?

Thomas Donaldson urges businesses to turn down projects that violate the core human values of dignity, basic rights, and good citizenship. If a practice does not violate those values and is necessary to doing business, he sees it as acceptable.

Donaldson also urges moral creativity. Rather than simply "going along with the crowd" or leaving the playing field altogether, it may be possible for a firm to act in a way that is genuinely helpful. Coca-Cola has turned down requests for bribes from Egyptian officials but has gained public trust by planting fruit trees. When Levi Strauss found that two of its Bangladesh suppliers were employing children, just firing the children wouldn't have guaranteed that they went to school. Instead, Levi Strauss forged an agreement that the suppliers would pay the children while they attended school, and that Levi Strauss would pay for tuition, books, and uniforms.

*Based on Thomas Donaldson, "Values in Tension: Ethics Away from Home," *Harvard Business Review*, September–October 1996, 48–62.

motion which has the same meaning in all societies."[26] In Bulgaria, for example, people may nod their heads to signify *no* and shake their heads to signify *yes*.[27]

Gestures that mean approval in the United States may have very different meanings in other countries. The "thumbs up" sign, which means "good work" or "go ahead" in the United States and most of Western Europe, is a vulgar insult in Greece. The circle formed with the thumb and first finger that means *OK* in the United States is obscene in Southern Italy and can mean "you're worth nothing" in France and Belgium.[28]

In the question period after a lecture, a man asked the speaker, a Puerto Rican professor, if shaking the hands up and down in front of the chest, as though shaking off water, was "a sign of mental retardation." The professor was horrified: in her culture, the gesture meant "excitement, intense thrill."[29] Studies have found that Spanish-speaking doctors rate the mental abilities of Latino patients much higher than do English-speaking doctors. The language barrier is surely part of the misevaluation of English-speaking doctors. Cultural differences in gestures may contribute to the misevaluation. Similarly, Anglo supervisors in the workplace may underestimate the abilities of Hispanics because gestures differ in the two cultures.

Space

Personal space is the distance someone wants between himself or herself and other people in ordinary, nonintimate interchanges. Observation and limited experimentation show that most North Americans, North Europeans, and Asians want a bigger personal space than do Latin Americans, French, Italians, and Arabs. People who prefer lots of personal space are often forced to accept close contact on a crowded elevator or subway.

Even within a culture, some people like more personal space than do others. One US study found that men took more personal space than women did.[30] In many cultures, people who are of the same age and sex take less personal space than do mixed-age or mixed-sex groups. Latin Americans will stand closer to people of the same sex than North Americans would, but North Americans stand closer to people of the opposite sex.[31] Similarly, Laotians of the same sex sit very close together, almost "on top of each other" according to the space norms of the United States. But people of the opposite sex sit at a distance from each other.[32]

Touch

Repeated studies have shown that babies need to be touched to grow and thrive and that older people are healthier both mentally and physically if they are touched. But some people are more comfortable with touch than others. Each kind of person may misinterpret the other. A person who dislikes touch may seem unfriendly to someone who's used to touching. A toucher may seem overly familiar to someone who dislikes touch. Studies in the United States have shown that touch is interpreted as power: more powerful people touch less powerful people. When the toucher had higher status than the recipient, both men and women liked being touched.[33]

Most parts of North America allow opposite-sex couples to hold hands or walk arm-in-arm in public but frown on the same behavior in same-sex couples. People in Asia, the Middle East, and South America have the opposite expectation: male friends or female friends can hold hands or walk arm-in-arm, but it is slightly shocking for an opposite-sex couple to touch in public. In Iran, even handshakes between men and women are seen as improper.[34]

People who don't know each other well may feel more comfortable with each other if a piece of furniture separates them. For example, a group may work better sitting around a table than just sitting in a circle. In North America, a person sitting at the head of a table is generally assumed to be the group's leader. However, one experiment showed that when a woman sat at the head of a mixed-sex group, observers assumed that one of the men in the group was the leader.[35]

Podiums and desks can be used as barricades to protect oneself from other people. One professor normally walked among his students as he lectured. But if anyone asked a question he was uncomfortable with, he retreated behind the podium before answering it.

Spatial Arrangements

In the United States, the size, placement, and privacy of one's office connotes status. Large corner offices have the highest status. An individual office with a door that closes connotes more status than a desk in a common area. Japanese firms, however, see private offices as "inappropriate and inefficient," reports Robert Christopher. Only the very highest executives and directors have private offices in the traditional Japanese company, and even they will also have desks in the common areas.[36]

Time

Differences in time zones complicate international phone calls. But even more important are different views of time and attitudes toward time.

Organizations in the United States—businesses, government, and schools—keep time by the calendar and the clock. Being "on time" is seen as a sign of dependability. Other cultures may keep time by the seasons and the moon, the sun, internal "body clocks," or a personal feeling that "the time is right."

North Americans who believe that "time is money" are often frustrated in negotiations with people who take a much more leisurely approach. Part of the problem is that people in many other cultures want to establish a personal relationship before they decide whether to do business with each other.

The problem is made worse because various cultures mentally measure time differently. Many North Americans measure time in five-minute blocks. Someone who's five minutes late to an appointment or a job interview feels compelled to apologize. If the executive or interviewer is running half an hour late, the caller expects to be told about the likely delay upon arriving. Some people won't be able to wait that long and will need to reschedule their appointments. But in other cultures, 15 minutes or half an hour may be the smallest block of time. To someone who mentally measures time in 15-minute blocks, being 45 minutes late is no worse than being 15 minutes late is to someone who is conscious of smaller units.

Edward T. Hall points out that different cultures have different lead times. In some countries, you need to schedule important meetings at least two weeks in advance. In other countries, not only are people not booked up so far in advance, but a date two weeks into the future may be forgotten. He advises scheduling appointments only three or four days in advance in Arab countries.[37]

Hall also distinguishes between **monochronic** cultures, where one does only one important activity at a time, and **polychronic** cultures, where people do several things at once. The United States has traditionally been considered monochronic, though that may be changing as people close business deals with their cellular car phones. But we are expected to focus on other people when we are with them. It is impolite to read a book during a meeting, even if much of the meeting does not directly concern the person reading. When US managers feel offended because a Latin American manager also sees other people during "their" appointments, the two kinds of time are in conflict.

According to some scholars, Europeans schedule fewer events in a comparable period of time than do North Americans. Perhaps as a result, Germans and German Swiss see North Americans as too time-conscious.[38]

Other Nonverbal Symbols

Many other symbols can carry nonverbal meanings: clothing, colors, age, and height, to name a few.

In North America, certain styles and colors of clothing are considered more "professional" and more "credible." In Japan, clothing denotes not only status but also occupational group. Students wear uniforms. Company badges indicate rank within the organization. Workers wear different clothes when they are on strike than they do when they are working.[39]

Colors can also carry meanings in a culture. In the United States, mourners wear black to funerals, while brides wear white. In Japan, white is the color of death. Purple flowers are given to the dead in Mexico. In Korea, red ink is used to record deaths but never to write about living people.[40] In the United States, the first-place winner gets a blue ribbon. In the United Kingdom, the first-place ribbon is usually red.

In the United States, youth is valued. Some men as well as some women color their hair and even have face-lifts to look as youthful as possible. In Japan, younger people defer to older people. Americans attempting to negotiate in Japan are usually taken more seriously if at least one member of the team is noticeably gray-haired.

Height connotes status in many parts of the world. Executive offices are usually on the top floors; the underlings work below. Even being tall can help a person succeed. Studies have shown that employers are more willing to hire men over 6 feet tall than shorter men with the same credentials. Studies of real-world executives and graduates have shown that taller men make more money. In one study, every extra inch of height brought in an extra $1,300 a year.[41] But being too big can be a disadvantage. A tall, brawny football player complained that people found him intimidating off the field and assumed that he "had the brains of a Twinkie."

ORAL COMMUNICATION

Learning at least a little of the language of the country where you hope to do business will help you in several ways. First, learning the language will give you at least a glimpse into the culture. In English, for example, we say that a clock "runs." The French say, "Il marche,"—or, literally, "it is walking." Second, learning some of the language will help you manage the daily necessities of finding food and getting where you need to go while you're there. If you know enough, you'll even be able to sightsee and take advantage of the unique opportunities business travel can provide. Finally, in

The Bad Guys Wore Black*

Black uniforms make football and hockey players appear—and act—meaner, according to a study by two Cornell University psychologists.

Penalty records of 28 National Football League teams from 1970 to 1986 showed that all five teams that wore predominately black uniforms were among the 12 most penalized teams. Similarly, the three most penalized teams in the National Hockey League in those 17 years wore black. . . .

This prompted the psychologists to launch a series of experiments on the effects of black uniforms. Groups of football fans and referees were shown either of two videotapes of a staged football play. In one tape the defensive team wore black while in the other tape the defenders wore white. Those who saw the black-uniform team rated the defenders as far more aggressive and "dirty" than those who watched the white-clothed defenders making the same moves. . . .

A black uniform may make others think a person is more aggressive or "mean" and, as a result, the person becomes more aggressive, the psychologists speculate.

*Quoted from Jerry E. Bishop, "Athletes Wearing Black Play More Aggressively," *The Wall Street Journal,* February 29, 1988, 21.

business negotiations, knowing a little of the language gives you more time to think. You'll catch part of the meaning when you hear your counterpart speak; you can begin thinking even before the translation begins.

If at all possible, take your own translator when you travel abroad on business. Brief him or her with the technical terms you'll be using; explain as much of the context of your negotiations as possible. A good translator can also help you interpret nonverbal behavior and negotiating strategies.

Understatement and Exaggeration

To understand someone from another culture, you must understand the speaker's conversational style. The British have a reputation for understatement. Someone good enough to play at Wimbledon may say he or she "plays a little tennis." Many people in the United States exaggerate. An American businessman negotiating with a German said, "I know it's impossible, but can we do it?" The German saw the statement as nonsensical: by definition, something that is impossible cannot be done. The American saw "impossible" as merely a strong way of saying "difficult" and assumed that with enough resources and commitment, the job could in fact be done.[42]

Compliments

The kinds of statements that people interpret as compliments and the socially correct way to respond to compliments also vary among cultures. The statement "You must be really tired" is a compliment in Japan since it recognizes the other person has worked hard. The correct response is "Thank you, but I'm OK." An American who is complimented on giving a good oral presentation will probably say "Thank you." A Japanese, in contrast, will apologize: "No, it wasn't very good."[43]

Statements that seem complimentary in one context may be inappropriate in another. For example, women in business are usually uncomfortable if male colleagues or superiors compliment them on their appearance: the comments suggest that the women are being treated as visual decoration rather than as contributing workers.

Silence

Silence also has different meanings in different cultures and subcultures. Muriel Saville-Troike reports that during a period of military tension, Greek traffic controllers responded with silence when Egyptian planes requested permission to land. The Greeks intended silence as a refusal; the Egyptians interpreted silence as consent. Several people were killed when the Greeks fired on the planes as they approached the runway.[44]

Voice Qualities

Tone of voice refers to the rising or falling inflection that tells you whether a group of words is a question or a statement, whether the speaker is uncertain or confident, whether a statement is sincere or sarcastic. Anyone who has written dialog with adverbs ("he said thoughtfully") has tried to indicate tone of voice.

When tone of voice and the meaning of words conflict, people "believe" the tone of voice. Jann Davis reports that one person responded to friends'

Silence, Please!*

In Japan, silence can mean "I don't like your idea," but it can also mean, "I'm thinking." Knowing this is essential for international negotiators. One American businessman offered an apparatus to a Japanese customer for $100,000. The customer sat quietly. After 10 minutes, the American, who couldn't stand the silence any more, lowered his price $10,000.

Reading this through a US lens, you might think that the Japanese customer was happy and perhaps even used silence deliberately. Not so. In fact, he was deeply disappointed by the poor negotiation. Relationships are far more important than price in Japan. How could someone be so impatient?

*Based on J. M. Ulijn, "How Can a Multicultural Workforce of a Company Successfully Communicate in International Trade?" *Acta Universitatis Wratislaviensis*, No. 1774, 264–65.

"How are you?" with the words, "Dying, and you?" Most of the friends responded "Fine." Because the tone of voice was cheerful, they didn't hear the content of the words.[45]

Pitch measures whether a voice uses sounds that are low (like the bass notes on a piano) or high. Low-pitched voices are usually perceived as being more authoritative, sexier, and more pleasant to listen to than are high-pitched voices. Most voices go up in pitch when the speaker is angry or excited; some people raise pitch when they increase volume. Women whose normal speaking voices are high may need to practice projecting their voices to avoid becoming shrill when they speak to large groups.

Stress is the emphasis given to one or more words in a sentence. As the following example shows, emphasizing different words can change the meaning.

> **I'll** give you a raise.
> [Implication, depending on pitch and speed: "Another supervisor wouldn't" or "I have the power to determine your salary."]
> I'll **give** you a raise.
> [Implication, depending on pitch and speed: "You haven't **earned** it" or "OK, all right, you win. I'm saying 'yes' to get rid of you, but I don't really agree," or "I've just this instant decided that you deserve a raise."]
> I'll give **you** a raise.
> [Implication: "But nobody else in this department is getting one."]
> I'll give you **a** raise.
> [Implication: "But just one."]
> I'll give you a **raise.**
> [Implication: "But you won't get the promotion or anything else you want."]
> I'll give **you** a **raise.**
> [Implication: "You deserve it."]
> **I'll** give you a **raise!**
> [Implication: "I've just this minute decided to act, and I'm excited about this idea. The raise will please both of us."]

Speakers who use many changes in tone, pitch, and stress as they speak usually seem more enthusiastic; often they also seem more energetic and more intelligent. Someone who speaks in a monotone may seem apathetic or unintelligent. Nonnative speakers whose first language does not use tone, pitch, and stress to convey meaning and attitude may need to practice varying these voice qualities when they give presentations in the United States.

Volume is a measure of loudness or softness. Very soft voices, especially if they are also breathy and high-pitched, give the impression of youth and inexperience. People who do a lot of speaking to large groups need to practice projecting their voices so they can increase their volume without shouting.

In some cultures, it is considered rude to shout; loud voices connote anger and imminent violence. In others, everyday conversations are loud. Edward Hall and William Whyte report that some Arabs discounted "Voice of America" broadcasts because the signal was so "weak."[46] Arab men who are equals speak loudly by North American standards.

WRITING TO INTERNATIONAL AUDIENCES

Most cultures are more formal than the United States. When you write to international audiences, use titles, not first names; avoid contractions, slang, and sports metaphors. Do write in English unless you're extremely fluent in your reader's language.

Translators Needed*

As the number of people speaking languages other than English has grown in Los Angeles, so has the need for translators.

Los Angeles businesses put up signs and flyers in Mandarin, Farsi, and Hebrew. Students and their parents in Cupertino elementary schools speak 52 different languages and 12 dialects. Hebrew, Russian, and Farsi are among the 10 most common. Cornish and Carey Real Estate handles about 40 tongues.

Translators have been called upon to translate courtroom testimony, Japanese operating manuals, and Arabic business contracts.

Translation, as always, works best when the translator knows connotations and context as well as the dictionary meaning of words. George Rimalower, president of Interpreting Services International in Van Nuys, California, reports that one church newsletter turned "our Lord in heaven" into "our guy in the sky."

*Based on Jan Lonsdale, "The Real L.A. Speak," *Los Angeles Times Magazine,* June 13, 1993, 8; and "New Companies Fuel Silicon Valley Boom," *The Wall Street Journal,* October 8, 1996, A12.

Marcia Sweezey, a manager at Digital Equipment Corporation, offers the following advice for sending e-mail to Japanese recipients.

1. Be clear, but be adult. Don't write in second-grade English.
2. Use complete sentences.
3. Write "Dear Lastname-san" to begin your e-mail: Dear Abo-san. Use this form of address for both men and women. Also use this form to refer to your peers in a formal memo, such as a memo to that person's manager.
4. Tell your peers how to address you. Peers in Japan may write to you "Dear Smith-san" or "Dear Ellen-san." You may wish to invite them to call you by your first name. (The first time you correspond, let them know if you are a man or a woman so they know whether to use "Mr." or "Ms." when they address you formally.)
5. Be honest, friendly, and relaxed.[47]

The patterns of organization that work for North American audiences may need to be modified in international correspondence. For most cultures, buffer negative messages and make requests more indirect. Be aware that the reader benefits and appeals that would motivate a US audience may need to be changed for international readers. Make a special effort to avoid phrases that could seem cold and uncaring. Cultural mistakes made orally float away on the air; those made in writing are permanently recorded.

Business people from Europe and Japan who correspond frequently with North America are beginning to adopt US directness and patterns of organization. If you know that your reader understands North American behavior, you can write just as you would to someone in the United States or Canada. If you don't know your reader well, it may be safer to modify your message slightly.

If you're faxing the message, use at least 12-point type. If the transmission has static or if your message is re-faxed to another reader, the larger type will make it easier to read.[48]

In international business correspondence, list the day before the month:

Not: April 8, 1998
But: 8 April 1998

Spell out the month to avoid confusion. A US professor wrote to the British library to reserve the books he would need for his visit on April 10th. However, he wrote "4/10" and the British assumed he wanted them on October 4th.

LEARNING MORE ABOUT INTERNATIONAL BUSINESS COMMUNICATION

Learning to communicate with people from different backgrounds shouldn't be a matter of learning rules. Instead, use the examples in this chapter to get a sense for the kinds of factors that differ from one culture to another. Test these generalizations against your experience. And when in doubt, ask.

You can deepen your knowledge by reading. Figure 12.3 lists useful sources to check.

You can also learn by seeking out people from other backgrounds and talking with them. Many campuses have centers for international students. Some communities have groups of international business people who meet regularly to discuss their countries. By asking all these people what aspects of the dominant US culture seem strange to them, you'll learn much about what is "right" in their cultures.

Figure 12.3

Sources for More Information about International Business

Culturgrams, updated annually, offer 4-page overviews of every country in the world. Write or call:

Brigham Young University
The David M. Kennedy Center for International Studies
P.O. Box 24538
Provo, UT 84602-4538
1-800-528-6279.

To learn more about a specific country or region, write the embassy for information or consult business magazines and reference books.

Price Waterhouse publishes an excellent series of paperbacks titled *Doing Business in [Country].* Each book covers financial, tax, accounting, and regulatory matters.

American Society for Quality Control. Assistance in meeting manufacturing standards set by the International Organization for Standardization. 1-800-248-1946.

Export Legal Assistance Network. Referrals to local attorneys with experience in international trade. 1-202-778-3000.

Export Opportunity Hot Line. Free information provided by trade experts. Sponsored by the Small Business Foundation of America. 1-800-243-7332. In Washington, DC, call 1-202-223-1104.

Service Corps of Retired Executives (SCORE). Matches small businesses with one of roughly 500 seasoned exporting counselors. 1-800-634-0245.

US Commerce Department Hot Line. How to qualify for low tariffs under NAFTA. Free information. 1-800-USA-TRADE.

US & Foreign Commercial Service. Offices in 68 US cities and in 129 cities in 67 other countries. Offers advice about exports, market research, and sales leads.

Women in International Business*

Since there aren't many women in overseas executive assignments, those women who *are* there stand out and are remembered by their associates and partners. Women also have an advantage when it comes to interpersonal skills. Compared to foreign, male managers, local male employees find women easier to talk to on a wide range of topics. . . . [S]ince so few women are sent abroad the local business community assumes the woman is undoubtedly the foreign company's very best manager. . . .

[M]ost U.S. professional women state than when they work overseas they are seen first as American and second as female, regardless of how the country treats their local women.

*Quoted from Tracey Wilen and Patricia Wilen, *Asia for Women on Business* (Berkeley, CA: Stone Bridge Press, 1995), 222.

SUMMARY OF KEY POINTS

- **Culture** provides patterns of acceptable behavior and beliefs.
- The successful intercultural communicator is
  - Aware that his or her preferred values and behaviors are influenced by culture and are not necessarily "right."
  - Flexible and open to change.
  - Sensitive to verbal and nonverbal behavior.
  - Aware of the values, beliefs, and practices in other cultures.
  - Sensitive to differences among individuals within a culture.
- In **high-context cultures,** most of the information is inferred from the context of a message; little is explicitly conveyed. In **low-context cultures,** context is less important; most information is explicitly spelled out.
- **Nonverbal communication** is communication that doesn't use words. Nonverbal communication can include voice qualities, body language, space, time, and other miscellaneous matters such as clothing, colors, and age.
- Nonverbal signals can be misinterpreted just as easily as can verbal symbols (words).
- No gesture has a universal meaning across all cultures. Gestures that signify approval in North America may be insults in other countries, and vice versa.
- **Personal space** is the distance someone wants between him or herself and other people in ordinary, nonintimate interchanges.
- North Americans who believe that "time is money" are often frustrated in negotiations with people who want to establish a personal relationship before they decide whether to do business with each other or who measure time in 15- or 30-minute increments rather than the 5-minute intervals North Americans are used to.

- In **monochronic** cultures, people do only one important activity at a time. The United States is monochronic. In **polychronic** cultures, people do several things at once.
- The patterns of organization that work for North American audiences may need to be modified in international correspondence.
- In international correspondence, spell out the month.

Exercises and Problems For Chapter 12

GETTING STARTED

12−1 Identifying Sources of Miscommunication

In each of the following situations, identify one or more ways that cultural differences may be leading to miscommunication.

1. Alan is a US sales representative in Mexico. He makes appointments and is careful to be on time. But the person he's calling on is frequently late. To save time, Alan tries to get right to business. But his hosts want to talk about sightseeing and his family. Even worse, his appointments are interrupted constantly, not only by business phone calls, but also by long conversations with other people and even the customers' children who come into the office. Alan's first progress report is very negative. He hasn't yet made a sale. Perhaps Mexico just isn't the right place to sell his company's products.

2. To help her company establish a presence in Japan, Susan wants to hire a local interpreter who can advise her on business customs. Kana Tomari has superb qualifications on paper. But when Susan tries to probe about her experience, Kana just says, "I will do my best. I will try very hard." She never gives details about any of the previous positions she's held. Susan begins to wonder if the résumé is inflated.

3. Stan wants to negotiate a joint venture with a Chinese company. He asks Tung-Sen Lee if the Chinese people have enough discretionary income to afford his product. Mr. Lee is silent for a time, and then says, "Your product is good. People in the West must like it." Stan smiles, pleased that Mr. Lee recognizes the quality of his product, and he gives Mr. Lee a contract to sign. Weeks later, Stan still hasn't heard anything. If China is going to be so inefficient, he wonders if he really should try to do business there.

4. Elspeth is very proud of her participatory management style. On assignment in India, she is careful not to give orders but to ask for suggestions. But people rarely suggest anything. Even a formal suggestion system doesn't work. And to make matters worse, she doesn't sense the respect and camaraderie of the plant she managed in the United States. Perhaps, she decides gloomily, people in India just aren't ready for a woman boss.

E-MAIL MESSAGES

12−2 Sending a Draft to Japan

You've drafted instructions for a consumer product that will be sold in Japan. Before the text is translated, you want to find out if the pictures will be clear. So you send an e-mail to your Japanese counterpart, Takashi Haneda, asking for a response within a week.

Write an e-mail message; assume that you will send the pictures as an attachment.

12−3 Asking about Travel Arrangements

The CEO is planning a trip to visit colleagues in another country (you pick the country). As Executive Assistant to the CEO of your organization, it's your job to make travel plans. At this stage, you don't know anything except dates and flights. (The CEO will arrive in the country at 7 AM local time on the 28th of next month and stay for three days.) It's your job to find out what the plans are and communicate any of the CEO's requirements.

Write an e-mail message to your contact.

Hints:

- Pick a business, nonprofit organization, or government agency you know something about, making assumptions about the kinds of things its executive would want to do during an international visit.
- How much international traveling does your CEO do? Has he or she ever been to this country before? What questions will he or she want answered?

COMMUNICATING AT WORK

12−4 Studying International Communication at Your Workplace

Does your employer buy from suppliers or sell to customers outside the country? Get a sampling of international messages, or interview managers about the problems they've encountered.

As Your Instructor Directs,

 a. Share your results orally with a small group of students.

 b. Present your findings orally to the class.

 c. Summarize your findings in a memo to your instructor.

 d. Join with other students in your class to write a group report.

WEB PAGES

12−5 Creating a Web Page

Create a Web page for international managers who are planning assignments in other countries or who work in this country for a multinational company headquartered in another country.

Assume that this page can be accessed from another of the organization's pages. Offer at least seven links. (More is better.) You may offer information as well as links to other pages with information. At the top of the page, offer an overview of what the page covers. At the bottom of the page, put the creation/update date and your name and e-mail address.

As Your Instructor Directs,

 a. Turn in two laser copies of your page(s). On another page, give the URLs for each link.

 b. Turn in one laser copy of your page(s) and a disk with the HTML code and .gif files.

 c. Write a memo to your instructor (1) identifying the audience for which the page is designed and explaining (2) the search strategies you used to find material on this topic, (3) why you chose the pages and information you've included, and (4) why you chose the layout and graphics you've used.

 d. Present your page orally to the class.

Hints:

- Limit your page to just one country or one part of the world.
- You can include some general information about working abroad and culture, but most of your links should be specific to the country or part of the world you focus on.
- Try to cover as many topics as possible: history, politics, geography, culture, money, living accommodations, transport, weather, business practices, and so forth.
- Chunk your links into small groups under headings.

MEMO AND REPORT ASSIGNMENTS

12–6   Requesting Information about a Country

Use one or more of the following ways to get information about a country. Information you might focus on could include

- Business opportunities.
- History and geography.
- Principal exports and imports.
- Dominant religions.
- Holidays.
- School system.
- Political system.

1. Write to the US & Foreign Commercial Service Office in your district. (Your instructor has the addresses in the *Instructor's Manual*.)

2. Check the country's trade office, if there is one in your city.
3. Interview someone from that country or someone who has lived there.
4. Read published materials about the country.

As Your Instructor Directs,
   a. Share your findings orally with a small group of students.
   b. Summarize your findings in a memo to your instructor.
   c. Present your findings to the class.
   d. Join with a group of classmates to write a group report on the country.

12–7   Recommending a Candidate for an Overseas Position

Your company sells customized computer systems to businesses large and small around the world. The Executive Committee needs to recommend someone to begin a three-year term as Manager of Eastern European Marketing.

As Your Instructor Directs,
   a. Write a memo to each of the candidates, specifying the questions you would like each to answer in a final interview.
   b. Assume that it is not possible to interview the candidates. Use the information here to write a memo to the CEO recommending a candidate.
   c. Write a memo to the CEO recommending the best way to prepare the person chosen for his or her assignment.
   d. Write a memo to the CEO recommending a better way to choose candidates for international assignments.
   e. Write a memo to your instructor explaining the assumptions you made about the company and the candidates that influenced your recommendation(s).

Information about the Candidates:
All the candidates have applied for the position and say they are highly interested in it.

1. **Deborah Gere,** 39, white, single. Employed by the company for eight years in the Indianapolis and New York offices. Currently in the New York office as Assistant Marketing Manager, Eastern United States; successful. University of Indiana MBA. Speaks Russian fluently; has translated for business negotiations that led to the setting up of the Moscow office. Good technical knowledge, acceptable managerial skills, excellent communication skills, good interpersonal skills. Excellent health; excellent emotional stability. Swims. One child, age 12. Lived in the then-Soviet Union for one year as an exchange student in college; business and personal travel in Europe.

2. **Claude Chabot,** 36, French, single. Employed by the company for 11 years in the Paris and London offices. Currently in the Paris office as Assistant Sales Manager for the European Economic Community; successful. No MBA, but degrees from MIT in the United States and l'Ecole Supérieure de Commerce de Paris. Speaks native French; speaks English and Italian fluently; speaks some German. Good technical knowledge, excellent managerial skills, acceptable communication skills, excellent interpersonal skills. Excellent health, good emotional stability. Plays tennis. No children. French citizen; lived in the United States for two years, in London for five years (one year in college, four years in the London office). Extensive business and personal travel in Europe.

3. **Linda Moss,** 35, African American, married. Employed by the company for 10 years in the Atlanta and Toronto offices. Currently Assistant Manager of Canadian Marketing; very successful. Howard University MBA. Speaks some French. Good technical knowledge, excellent managerial skills, excellent communication skills, excellent interpersonal skills. Excellent health; excellent emotional stability. Does Jazzercize classes. Husband is an executive at a US company in Detroit; he plans to stay in the States with their children, ages 11 and 9. The couple plans to commute every two to six weeks. Has lived in Toronto for five years; business travel in North America; personal travel in Europe and Latin America.

4. **Steven Hsu,** 42, of Asian-American descent, married. Employed by the company for 18 years in the Los Angeles office. Currently Marketing Manager, Western United States; very successful. UCLA MBA. Speaks some Korean. Excellent technical knowledge, excellent managerial skills, good communication skills, excellent interpersonal skills. Good health, excellent emotional stability. Plays golf. Wife is an engineer who plans to do consulting work in eastern Europe. Children ages 8, 5, and 2. Has not lived outside the United States; personal travel in Europe and Asia.

Your committee has received this memo from the CEO.

To: Executive Committee

From: Ed Conzachi   *ERC*

Subject: Choosing a Manager for the New Eastern European Office

Please write me a memo recommending the best candidate for Manager of East European Marketing. In your memo, tell me whom you're choosing and why; also explain why you have rejected the unsuccessful candidates.

This person will be assuming a three-year appointment, with the possibility of reappointment. The company will pay moving and relocation expenses for the manager and his or her family.

The Eastern European division currently is the smallest of the company's international divisions. However, this area is poised for growth. The new manager will supervise the Moscow office and establish branch offices as needed.

The committee has invited comments from everyone in the company. You've received these memos.

To: Executive Committee

From: Robert Osborne, US Marketing Manager   *RO*

Subject: Recommendation for Steve Hsu

Steve Hsu would be a great choice to head up the new Moscow office. In the past seven years, Steve has increased sales in the Western Region by 15%—in spite of recessions, earthquakes, and fires. He has a low-key, participative style that brings out the best in subordinates. Moreover, Steve is a brilliant computer programmer. He probably understands our products better than any other marketing or salesperson in the company.

Steve is clearly destined for success in headquarters. This assignment will give him the international experience he needs to move up to the next level of executive success.

To: Executive Committee

From: Becky Exter, Affirmative Action Officer   RRE

Subject: Hiring the New Manager for East European Marketing

Please be sensitive to affirmative action concerns. The company has a very good record of appointing women and minorities to key positions in the United States and Canada; so far our record in our overseas divisions has been less effective.

In part, perhaps, that may stem from a perception that women and minorities will not be accepted in countries less open than our own. But the experience of several multinational firms has been that even exclusionary countries will accept people who have the full backing of their countries. Another concern may be that it will be harder for women to establish a social support system abroad. However, different individuals have different ways of establishing support. To assume that the best candidate for an international assignment is a male with a stay-at-home wife is discriminatory and may deprive our company of the skills of some of its best people.

We have several qualified women and minority candidates. I urge you to consider their credentials carefully.

To: Executive Committee

From: William E. Dortch, Marketing Manager, European Economic Community   WED

Subject: Recommendation for Debbie Gere

Debbie Gere would be my choice to head the new Moscow office. As you know, I recommended in 1996 that Europe be divided and that we establish an Eastern European division. Of all the people from the States who have worked on the creation of the new division, Debbie is the best. The negotiations were often complex. Debbie's knowledge of the language and culture were invaluable. She's done a good job in the New York office and is ready for wider responsibilities. Eastern Europe is a challenging place, but Debbie can handle the pressure and help us gain the foothold we need.

To: Ed Conzachi, President

From: Pierre Garamond, Sales Representative, European Economic Community   PG

Subject: Recommendation for Claude Chabot

Claude Chabot would be the best choice for Manager of Eastern European Marketing. He is a superb supervisor, motivating us to the highest level of achievement. He understands the complex legal and cultural nuances of selling our products in Europe as only a native can. He also has the budgeting and managerial skills to oversee the entire marketing effort.

You are aware that the company's record of sending US citizens to head international divisions is not particularly good. European Marketing is an exception, but our records in the Middle East and Japan have been poor. The company would gain stability by appointing Europeans to head European offices, Asians to head Asian offices, and so forth. Such people would do a better job of managing and motivating staffs which will be comprised primarily of nationals in the country where the office is located. Ending the practice of reserving the top jobs for US citizens would also send a message to international employees that we are valued and that we have a future with this company.

To: Executive Committee   *EC*

From: Elaine Crispell, Manager, Canadian Marketing

Subject: Recommendation for Linda Moss

Linda Moss has done well as Assistant Manager for the last two and a half years. She is a creative, flexible problem solver. Her productivity is the highest in the office. Yet though she could be called a "workaholic," she is a warm, caring human being.

As you know, the Canadian division includes French-speaking Montreal and a large Native Canadian population; furthermore, Toronto is an international and intercultural city. Linda has gained intercultural competence both on a personal and professional level.

Linda has the potential to be our first woman CEO fifteen years down the road. She needs more international experience to be competitive at that level. This would be a good opportunity for her, and she would do well for the company.

Working and Writing in Groups

Chapter Outline

An Inside Perspective:
Working and Writing in Groups

George Fogel, Manager—Engineering
Ameritech

George Fogel regularly writes documents and presentations collaboratively both as a manager at Ameritech and in his MBA program at the University of Chicago. Ameritech serves customers in 50 states and 40 countries, providing a full range of communications services, including local and long distance telephone, cellular, paging, security monitoring, cable TV, electronic commerce, and on-line services, and more.

Working collaboratively is becoming easier with computer networks and software. However, the actual task of collaborative work still can be difficult and time-consuming. Sharing information and data will help a group only if everyone is focused on a common goal.

Technology makes it easier to have people in multiple locations working on the same project. One of the challenges I faced was how to get customer information to numerous different and dispersed work groups quickly so that they could develop customer-specific solutions. My group then needed the information back so that we could build our proposal for the customer. We built a Web-based intranet that combined the power of the Web with e-mail so effectively that we were able to cut our cycle time by days.

Teams must quickly build trust in each other's abilities to effectively produce clear documents and presentations. In most group presentations I have worked on, each individual brings a different skill to help the team. With diverse talents such as a model builder, data analyst, writer, presentation builder, and public speaker, the group can collectively create a presentation that is succinct and meaningful.

An additional benefit to working and writing in groups is the knowledge others bring to the process. Many times I must write not only for my own group but also to share information with other departments and work groups. Including members from other departments upfront enables us to streamline the entire process, requiring fewer follow-up messages.

I have had the opportunity to write in groups not only at work but also in my MBA program at the University of Chicago. The most effective writing process was a truly integrative approach. Our group wrote a paper on leadership that combined six hour-long interviews. The final paper was clear and well organized and read like a single document. One of the worst ways I have approached group writing is the divide-and-conquer model. Of course, it seems easy. On the day before the paper is due, everyone slams the parts together. When you read a paper like this, you realize the problems cut-and-paste writing causes.

Mark Twain wrote that "it is differences of opinion that makes horse races." It is also differences in opinion that can make writing in groups painfully difficult. Everyone's writing style is based on what they have read, where they grew up, where they went to school, etc. Simply pasting sections together makes it painfully obvious that there is no continuous style in the document, and that detracts from the content. Had we done this with our leadership paper, it would have been simply six summations of interviews without any comparison of our leaders' styles and experiences.

As we worked, we shared drafts among the six group members by e-mail. This allowed us to revise and edit the document quickly and efficiently. You simply cannot do this with a faxed copy. One person, usually the strongest writer in the group, should complete the final edit of the document to standardize its look and feel.

Working and writing in groups is essential if I am to reach all of my goals during a year. As the demands of our work life continue to grow, groups can help share the burden of a task and make it easier and more efficient for all.

George Fogel, February 18, 1997

Visit Ameritech's Web site: http://www.ameritech.com

"Teams must quickly build trust in each other's abilities to effectively produce clear documents and presentations."

George Fogel, Ameritech

Teamwork is crucial to success in an organization. Some teams produce products, provide services, or recommend solutions to problems. Other teams—perhaps in addition to providing a service or recommending a solution—also produce documents. **Interpersonal communication** is communication between people. Interpersonal skills such as listening and dealing with conflict are used in one-to-one interchanges, in problem-solving groups, and in writing groups. These skills will make you more successful on the job, in social groups, and in community service and volunteer work. In writing groups, careful attention to both group process and writing process (✖ p. 110) improves both the final product and members' satisfaction with the group.

LISTENING

Listening is crucial to building trust. However, listening on the job may be more difficult than listening in classes. In class you're encouraged to take notes. But you can't whip out a notepad every time your boss speaks. Many classroom lectures are well organized, with signposts and repetition of key points to help hearers follow. But conversations usually wander. A key point about when a report is due may be sandwiched in among statements about other due dates for other projects. Finally, in a classroom you're listening primarily for information. In interchanges with friends and co-workers, you need to listen for feelings, too. Feelings of being rejected or overworked need to be dealt with as they arise. But you can't deal with a feeling unless you are aware of it.

As Appendix C explains, to receive a message, the receiver must first perceive the message, then decode it (that is, translate the symbols into meaning), and then interpret it. In interpersonal communication, **hearing** denotes perceiving sounds. **Listening** means decoding and interpreting them correctly.

Some listening errors happen because the hearer wasn't paying enough attention to a key point. After a meeting with a client, a consultant waited for the client to send her more information, which she would use to draft a formal proposal to do a job for the client. It turned out the client thought the next move was up to the consultant. The consultant and the client had met together, but they hadn't remembered the same facts. To avoid error caused by inattention,

- As early as possible, make a mental or paper list of the questions you have. When is the project due? What resources do you have? What is the most important aspect of this project, from the other person's point of view? During a conversation, listen for answers to your questions.
- At the end of the conversation, check your understanding with the other person. Especially check who does what next.
- After the conversation, write down key points that affect deadlines or how work will be evaluated.

Many listening errors are errors in interpretation. In 1977 when two Boeing 747 jumbo jets ran into each other on the ground in Tenerife, the pilots seemed to have heard the control tower's instructions. The KLM pilot was told to taxi to the end of the runway, turn around, and wait for clearance. But the KLM pilot didn't interpret the order to wait as an order he needed to follow. The Pan Am pilot interpreted *his* order to turn off at the "third intersection" to mean the third *unblocked* intersection. He didn't count the first blocked ramp, so he was still on the main runway when the KLM pilot ran into his plane at 186 miles an hour. The planes exploded in flames; 576 people died.[1]

To reduce listening errors caused by misinterpretation,

- Don't ignore instructions you think are unnecessary. Before you do something else, check with the order giver to see if there is a reason for the instruction.
- Consider the other person's background and experiences. Why is this point important to the speaker? What might he or she mean by it?
- Paraphrase what the speaker has said, giving him or her a chance to correct your understanding.

Listening to people is an indication that you're taking them seriously. **Acknowledgment responses**—nods, *uh huh*s, smiles, frowns—help carry the message that you're listening. However, listening responses vary in different cultures. Research has found that US whites almost always respond nonverbally when they listen closely, but that African Americans respond with words rather than nonverbal cues (⟶ p. 4). This difference in response patterns may explain the fact that some whites think that African Americans do not understand what they are saying. Studies in the mid-1970s showed that white counselors repeated themselves more often to black clients than to white clients.[2] Similarly, black supervisors may miss verbal feedback when they talk to white subordinates who only nod.

In **active listening,** receivers actively demonstrate that they've heard and understood a speaker by feeding back either the literal meaning or the emotional content or both. Other techniques in active listening are asking for more information and stating one's own feelings.

Instead of simply mirroring what the other person says, many of us immediately respond in a way that analyzes or attempts to solve or dismiss the problem. People with problems need first of all to know that we hear that they're having a rough time. Figure 13.1 lists some of the responses that block communication. Ordering and interrogating all tell the other person that the speaker doesn't want to hear what he or she has to say. Preaching attacks the other person. Minimizing the problem suggests the other person's concern is misplaced. Even advising shuts off discussion. Giving a

Do You Hear What I Hear?*

In Center Harbor, Maine, local legend recalls the day some 10 years ago when Walter Cronkite steered his boat into port. The avid sailor, as it's told, was amused to see in the distance a small crowd of people on shore waving their arms to greet him. He could barely make out their excited shouts of "Hello Walter, Hello Walter."

As his boat sailed closer, the crowd grew larger, still yelling, "Hello Walter, Hello Walter." Pleased at the reception, Cronkite tipped his white captain's hat, waved back, even took a bow.

But before reaching dockside, Cronkite's boat abruptly jammed aground. The crowd stood silent. The veteran news anchor suddenly realized what they'd been shouting: "Low water, low water."

*Quoted from Don Oldenburg, "What You Hear Isn't Always What You Get," *The Columbus Dispatch*, April 12, 1987, 1C.

Figure 13.1

Blocking Responses versus Active Listening

1. **Ordering, threatening**
   "I don't care how you do it. Just get that report on my desk by Friday."
   Possible active response: Paraphrasing content
   "You're saying that you don't have time to finish the report by Friday."

2. **Preaching, criticizing**
   "You should know better than to air the department's problems in a general meeting."
   Possible active response: Mirroring feelings
   "It sounds like the department's problems really bother you."

3. **Interrogating**
   "Why didn't you *tell* me that you didn't understand the instructions?"
   Possible active response: Stating one's own feelings
   "I'm frustrated that the job isn't completed yet, and I'm worried about getting it done on time."

4. **Minimizing the problem**
   "You think *that's* bad. You should see what *I* have to do this week."
   Possible active response: Asking for information or clarification
   "What parts of the problem seem most difficult to solve?"

5. **Advising**
   "Well, why don't you try listing everything you have to do and seeing which items are most important?"
   Possible active response: Offering to help solve the problem together
   "Is there anything I could do that would help?"

Source: The 5 responses that block communication are based on a list of 12 in Thomas Gordon and Judith Gordon Sands, *P.E.T. in Action* (New York: Wyden, 1976), 117–18.

quick answer minimizes the pain the person feels and puts him or her down for not seeing (what is to us) the obvious answer. Even if it is a good answer from an objective point of view, the other person may not be ready to hear it. And sometimes, the off-the-top-of-the-head solution doesn't address the real problem.

Active listening takes time and energy. Even people who are skilled active listeners can't do it all the time. Furthermore, as Thomas Gordon and Judith Gordon Sands point out, active listening works only if you genuinely accept the other person's ideas and feelings. Active listening can reduce the conflict that results from miscommunication, but it alone cannot reduce the conflict that comes when two people want apparently inconsistent things or when one person wants to change someone else.[3]

GROUP INTERACTIONS

Groups can focus on three different dimensions. **Informational** messages focus on content: the problem, data, and possible solutions. **Procedural** messages focus on method and process. How will the group make decisions? Who will do what? When will assignments be due? **Interpersonal** messages focus on people, promoting friendliness, cooperation, and group loyalty. As Figure 13.2 shows, different kinds of communication dominate during the four stages of the life of a task group: orientation, formation, coordination, and formalization.[4]

During **orientation,** when members meet and begin to define their task, groups need to develop some sort of social cohesiveness and to develop procedures for meeting and acting. Interpersonal and procedural comments reduce the tension that always exists in a new group. Insistence on information in this first stage can hurt the group's long-term productivity.

During **formation,** conflicts almost always arise when the group chooses a leader and defines the problem. Successful leaders make the procedure clear so that each member knows what he or she is supposed to do. Interpersonal communication is needed to resolve the conflict that surfaces during this

Communication Activities and Phases of Group Development   **Figure 13.2**

Phase	Events during Phase	Communication Activities during Phase	Focus
Orientation	Group meets. Members decide how to relate to each other. Group tries to define task.	Members make tentative comments, seek information. Statements skip from one topic to another. Members agree more with each other than in any other phase.	Interpersonal and procedural.
Formation	Members begin to specialize. Leader emerges. Group develops strategy, objectives, and procedures to meet goals.	Conflict emerges as leader and strategy are chosen. Positions are stated clearly; ambiguity decreases. Members argue with each other.	Procedural, some interpersonal and informational.
Coordination	Group finds, organizes, and interprets information; examines its assumptions. Group considers alternatives but no one advocates a specific conclusion.	Information flows freely but prompts questions, trial interpretations and solutions. Comments include diagnosis, explanation, and substantiation. Conflict is accepted as part of the effort to find the best solution.	Informational, some procedural and interpersonal.
Formalization	Group makes and formalizes decision.	Members compliment and congratulate each other.	Procedural and interpersonal.

Source: Based on Thomas J. Knutson, "Communication in Small Decision-Making Groups: In Search of Excellence," *Journal for Specialists in Group Work* 10, no. 1 (March 1985): 31–33.

phase. Successful groups analyze the problem carefully before they begin to search for solutions.

Coordination is the longest phase and the phase during which most of the group's work is done. While procedural and interpersonal comments help maintain direction and friendliness, most of the comments need to deal with information. Good information is essential to a good decision. Conflict occurs as the group debates alternate solutions.

In **formalization,** the group seeks consensus. The success of this phase determines how well the group's decision will be implemented. In this stage, the group seeks to forget earlier conflicts.

Roles in Groups

Individual members can play several roles in groups. These roles can be positive or negative.

Positive roles and actions that help the group achieve its task goals include the following:[5]

- **Seeking information and opinions**—asking questions, identifying gaps in the group's knowledge.
- **Giving information and opinions**—answering questions, providing relevant information.
- **Summarizing**—restating major points, pulling ideas together, summarizing decisions.
- **Evaluating**—comparing group process and products to standards and goals.
- **Coordinating**—planning work, giving directions, and fitting together contributions of group members.

Positive roles and actions that help the group build loyalty, resolve conflicts, and function smoothly include the following:

- **Encouraging participation**—demonstrating openness and acceptance, recognizing the contributions of members, calling on quieter group members.

The Power and Peril of Teams*

- **Relieving tensions**—joking and suggesting breaks and fun activities.
- **Checking feelings**—asking members how they feel about group activities and sharing one's own feelings with others.
- **Solving interpersonal problems**—opening discussion of interpersonal problems in the group and suggesting ways to solve them.
- **Listening actively**—showing group members that they have been heard and that their ideas are being taken seriously.

Negative roles and actions that hurt the group's product and process include the following:

- **Blocking**—disagreeing with everything that is proposed.
- **Dominating**—trying to run the group by ordering, shutting out others, and insisting on one's own way.
- **Clowning**—making unproductive jokes and diverting the group from the task.
- **Withdrawing**—being silent in meetings, not contributing, not helping with the work, not attending meetings.

Some actions can be positive or negative depending on how they are used. Criticizing ideas is necessary if the group is to produce the best solution, but criticizing every idea raised without ever suggesting possible solutions blocks a group. Jokes in moderation can defuse tension and make the group more fun. Too many jokes or inappropriate jokes can make the group's work more difficult.

Leadership in Groups

You may have noted that "leader" was not one of the roles listed above. Being a leader does *not* mean doing all the work yourself. Indeed, someone who implies that he or she has the best ideas and can do the best work is likely playing the negative roles of blocking and dominating.

Effective groups balance three kinds of leadership, which parallel the three group dimensions. Providing information leadership (by generating ideas and text) is joined by providing interpersonal leadership (monitoring the group's process, checking people's feelings, and resolving conflicts) and procedural group management (setting an agenda, making sure everyone knows what's due for the next meeting, communicating with absent group members, checking to be sure assignments are carried out). While it's possible for one person to do all of these responsibilities, in many groups, the three kinds of leadership are taken on by three (or more) different people. Some groups formally or informally rotate or share these responsibilities, so that everyone—and no one—is a leader.

Several studies have shown people who talk a lot, listen effectively, and respond nonverbally to other members in the group are considered to be leaders.[6]

Decision-Making Strategies

Probably the least effective decision-making strategy is to let the person who talks first, last, loudest, or most determine the decision.

Voting is quick but may leave people in the minority unhappy with and uncommitted to the majority's plan.

Coming to consensus takes time but results in speedier implementation of ideas.

Two strategies that are often useful in organizational groups are the standard agenda and dot planning.

The **standard agenda** is a seven-step process for solving problems.

1. Understand what the group has to deliver, in what form, by what due date. Identify available resources.
2. Identify the problem. What exactly is wrong? What question(s) is the group trying to answer?
3. Gather information, share it with all group members, and examine it critically.
4. Establish criteria. What would the ideal solution include? Which elements of that solution would be part of a less-than-ideal but still acceptable solution? What legal, financial, moral, or other limitations might keep a solution from being implemented?
5. Generate alternate solutions. Brainstorm and record ideas for the next step.
6. Measure the alternatives against the criteria.
7. Choose the best solution.[7]

Dot planning offers a way for large groups to choose priorities quickly. First, the group brainstorms ideas, recording each on pages that are put on the wall. Then each individual gets two strips of three to five adhesive dots in different colors. One color represents high priority, the other lower priority. People then walk up to the pages and affix dots by the points they care most about. Some groups allow only one dot from one person on any one item; others allow someone who is really passionate about an idea to put all of his or her dots on it. As Figure 13.3 shows, the dots make it easy to see which items the group believes are most important.

Characteristics of Successful Student Groups

A case study of six student groups completing class projects found that students in successful groups were not necessarily more skilled or more experienced than students in less successful groups. Instead, successful and less successful groups communicated differently in three ways.[8]

First, in the successful groups, the leader set clear deadlines, scheduled frequent meetings, and dealt directly with conflict that emerged in the group. In less successful groups, members had to ask the leader what they were supposed to be doing. The less successful groups met less often, and they tried to pretend that conflicts didn't exist.

Second, the successful groups listened to criticism and made important decisions together. Perhaps as a result, everyone in the group could articulate the group's goals. In the less successful groups, a subgroup made decisions and told other members what had been decided.

Third, the successful groups had a higher proportion of members who worked actively on the project. The successful groups even found ways to use members who didn't like working in groups. For example, one student who didn't want to be a "team player" functioned as a "free-lancer" for her group, completing assignments by herself and giving them to the leader. The less successful groups had a much smaller percentage of active members and each had some members who did very little on the final project.

Rebecca Burnett has shown that student groups produce better documents when they disagree over substantive issues of content and document design. The disagreement does not need to be angry: a group member can simply say, "Yes, and here's another way we could do it." Deciding among two (or more) alternatives forces the proposer to explain the rationale for an idea. Even when the group adopts the original idea, considering alternatives rather than quickly accepting the first idea produces better writing.[9]

Figure 13.3   **Dot Planning Allows Groups to Set Priorities Quickly**

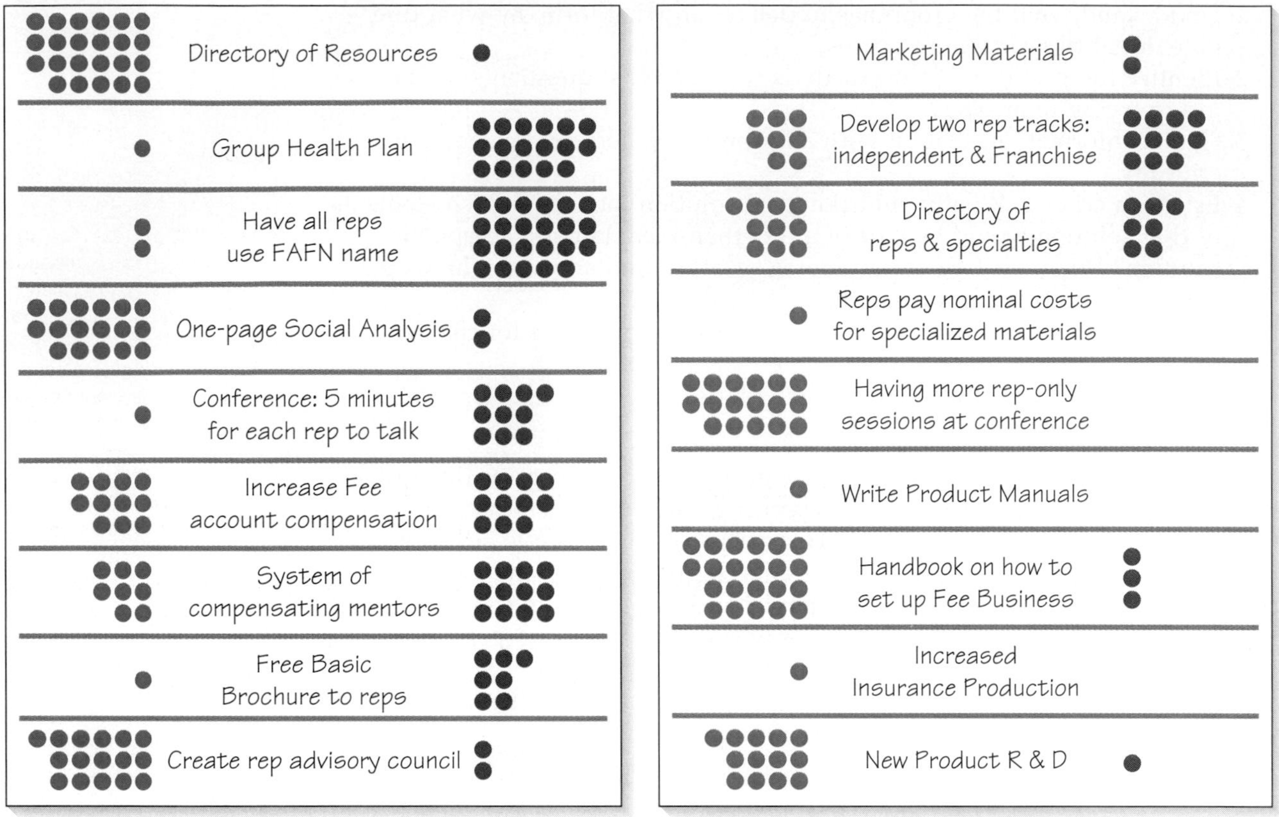

Here, green dots mean "high priority;" blue dots mean "low priority." One can see at a glance which items have widespread support, which are controversial, and which are low priority.

Source: "The Color-Coded Priority Setter," *Inc.,* June 1995, pp. 70–71.

Kimberly Freeman found that the students who spent the most time meeting with their groups had the highest grades—on their individual as well as on group assignments.[10]

Peer Pressure and Groupthink

Groups that never express conflict may be experiencing groupthink. **Groupthink** is the tendency for groups to put such a high premium on agreement that they directly or indirectly punish dissent.

Many people feel so much reluctance to express open disagreement that they will say they agree even when objective circumstances would suggest the first speaker cannot be right. In a series of experiments in the 1950s, Solomon Asch showed the influence of peer pressure. People sitting around a table were shown a large card with a line and asked to match it to the line of the same length on another card. It's a simple test: people normally match the lines correctly almost 100% of the time. However, in the experiment, all but one of the people in the group have been instructed to give false answers for several of the trials. When the group gave an incorrect answer, the focal person accepted the group's judgment 36.8% of the time. When someone else also gave a different answer—even if it was another wrong answer—the focal person accepted the group's judgment only 9% of the time.[11]

The experimenters varied the differences in line lengths, hoping to create a situation in which even the most conforming subjects would trust their own senses. But some people continued to accept the group's judgment, even when one line was seven inches longer than the other.

Groups that "go along with the crowd" and suppress conflict ignore the full range of alternatives, seek only information that supports the positions they already favor, and fail to prepare contingency plans to cope with foreseeable setbacks. A business suffering from groupthink may launch a new product that senior executives support but for which there is no demand. Student groups suffering from groupthink turn in inferior documents.

The best correctives to groupthink are to consciously search for additional alternatives, to test one's assumptions against those of a range of other people, and to protect the right of people in a group to disagree.

WORKING IN DIVERSE GROUPS

In any organization, you'll work with people whose backgrounds differ from yours. Residents of small towns and rural areas have different notions of friendliness than do people from big cities. Californians look, talk, and dress differently from people in the Midwest. Advertising executives and truck drivers have different lifestyles.

Even people who come from the same part of the country and who have the same jobs may differ in personality type. Savvy group members play to each other's strengths and devise strategies for dealing with differences. Figure 13.4 shows what people with various Myers-Briggs profiles (⬥ p. 59) can bring to groups.

In addition, differences arise from gender, class, race and ethnicity, religion, age, sexual orientation, and physical ability. A growing body of literature shows that ethnically diverse teams produce more and higher-quality ideas.[12] One problem with our awareness of difference, however, is that when someone feels shut out, he or she can attribute the negative interaction to prejudice, when other factors may be responsible. Conversational style and nonverbal communication are two of the areas that may cause miscommunication.

Conversational Style

Deborah Tannen uses the term **conversational style** to denote our conversational patterns and the meaning we give to them: the way we show interest, politeness, appropriateness.[13] Your answers to the following questions reveal your own conversational style:

- How long a pause tells you that it's your turn to speak?
- Do you see interruption as rude? or do you say things while other people are still talking to show that you're interested and to encourage them to say more?
- Do you show interest by asking lots of questions? or do you see questions as intrusive and wait for people to volunteer whatever they have to say?

Tannen concludes that the following features characterize her own conversational style:

Fast rate of speech.
Fast rate of turn-taking.
Persistence—if a turn is not acknowledged, try again.
Preference for personal stories.
Tolerance of, preference for simultaneous speech.
Abrupt topic shifting.

"Assertiveness" May Be a Matter of Conversational Style*

Rachel regularly led training groups with a male colleague. He always did all the talking, and she was always angry at him for dominating and not giving her a chance to say anything. . . . He would begin to answer questions from the group while she was still waiting for a slight pause to begin answering. And when she was in the middle of talking, he would jump in—but always when she had paused. So she tried pushing herself to begin answering questions a little sooner than felt polite, and not to leave long pauses when she was talking. The result was that she talked a lot more, and the man was as pleased as she was. Her supervisor complimented her on having become more assertive.

Whether or not Rachel actually became more assertive is debatable. . . . [S]he solved her problem with a simple and slight adjustment of her way of speaking, without soul-searching, self-analysis, external intervention, and—most important— without defining herself as having an emotional problem or a personality defect: unassertiveness.

*Quoted from Deborah Tannen, *That's Not What I Meant!* (New York: William Morrow, 1986), 177–78.

Figure 13.4

The Strengths Myers-Briggs Types Bring to Groups

Sensing Type	Intuitive Type
Notices what needs to be done.	Deals with ill-structured problems well.
Keeps track of details and essentials.	Generates ideas.
Seeks data.	Finds patterns and relationships.
Thinking Type	**Feeling Type**
Analyzes and organizes information.	Helps group members communicate with one another.
Critically evaluates alternatives.	Arouses enthusiasm for recommendation and sells action plan.
Stands firm in the face of opposition.	Finds common ground between different viewpoints.

Sources: Based on Harvey J. Brightman, *Group Problem-Solving: An Improved Managerial Approach* (Atlanta: Georgia State University 1988), 105, and Isabel Briggs Myers, *Introduction to Type* (Palo Alto, CA: Consulting Psychologists Press, 1962, 1980), 29–30.

Are Interruptions Impolite?*

In the dominant US culture, interrupting can seem impolite, especially if a lower-status person interrupts a superior.

Simulated negotiations have measured the interruptions by business people in 10 countries. The following list is ordered by decreasing numbers of interruptions:

    Korea
    Germany
    France
    China
    Brazil
    Russia
    Taiwan
    Japan
    United Kingdom
    United States.

This list does not mean that US business people are more polite, but rather that how people show politeness differs from culture to culture. Chinese and Italians (who also interrupt frequently) use interruptions to offer help, jointly construct a conversation, and show eagerness to do business—all of which are polite.

*Based on Jan M. Ulijn and Xiangling Li, "Is Interrupting Impolite? Some Temporal Aspects of Turn-Taking in Chinese-Western and Other Intercultural Encounters," *Text* 15, no 4. (1995): 600, 621.

Different conversational styles are not better or worse than each other, but people with different conversational styles may feel uncomfortable without knowing why. A subordinate who talks quickly may be frustrated by a boss who speaks slowly. People who talk more slowly may feel shut out of a conversation with people who talk more quickly. Someone who has learned to make requests directly ("Please pass the salt") may be annoyed by someone who uses indirect requests ("This casserole needs some salt").

In the workplace, conflicts may arise because of differences in conversational style. Generation Xers often use a rising inflection on statements as well as questions. Xers see this style as gentler and more polite. But baby boomer bosses may see this speech pattern as hesitant, as if the speaker wants advice—which they then proceed to deliver.[14] Thomas Kochman claims that blacks often use direct questions to criticize or accuse.[15] If Kochman is right, a black employee might see a question ("Will that report be ready Friday?") as a criticism of his or her progress. One supervisor might mean the question simply as a request for information. Another supervisor might use the question to mean "I want that report Friday."

Daniel N. Maltz and Ruth A. Borker believe that differences in conversational style (Figure 13.5) may be responsible for the miscommunication that often occurs in male–female conversations. Certainly conversational style is not the same for all men and for all women, but research has found several common patterns in the US cultures studied so far. For example, researchers have found that women are much more likely to nod and to say *yes* or *mm hmm* than men are. Maltz and Borker hypothesize that to women, these symbols mean simply, "I'm listening; go on." Men, on the other hand, may decode these symbols as, "I agree" or at least "I follow what you're saying so far." A man who receives nods and *mms* from a woman may feel that she is inconsistent and unpredictable if she then disagrees with him. A woman may feel that a man who doesn't provide any feedback isn't listening to her.[16]

Nonverbal Communication

Posture and body movements connote energy and openness. North American **open body positions** include leaning forward with uncrossed arms and legs, with the arms away from the body. **Closed** or **defensive body positions** include leaning back, sometimes with both hands behind the head, arms and legs crossed or close together, or hands in pockets. As the labels imply, open positions suggest that people are accepting and open to new ideas. Closed positions suggest that people are physically or psychologically uncomfortable, that they are defending themselves and shutting other people out.

Different Conversational Styles   **Figure 13.5**

	Debating	Relating
Interpretation of Questions	See questions as requests for information.	See questions as way to keep a conversation flowing.
Relation of New Comment to What Last Speaker Said	Do not require new comment to relate explicitly to last speaker's comment. Ignoring previous comment is one strategy for taking control.	Expect new comments to acknowledge the last speaker's comment and relate directly to it.
View of Aggressiveness	See aggressiveness as one way to organize the flow of conversation.	See aggressiveness as directed at audience personally, as negative, and as disruptive to a conversation.
How Topics Are Defined and Changed	Tend to define topics narrowly and shift topics abruptly. Interpret statements about side issues as effort to change the topic.	Tend to define topics gradually, progressively. Interpret statements about side issues as effort to shape, expand, or limit the topic.
Response to Someone Who Shares a Problem	Offer advice, solutions.	Offer solidarity, reassurance. Share troubles to establish sense of community.

Based on Daniel N. Maltz and Ruth A. Borker, "A Cultural Approach to Male-Female Miscommunication," *Language and Social Identity,* ed. John J. Gumperz (Cambridge: Cambridge University Press, 1982), 213, and Deborah Tannen, *Talking from 9 to 5: Women and Men in the Workplace: Language, Sex and Power* (New York: William Morrow, 1995).

People who cross their arms or legs often claim that they do so only because the position is more comfortable. But notice your own body the next time you're in a perfectly comfortable discussion with a good friend. You'll probably find that you naturally assume open body positions. The fact that so many people in organizational settings adopt closed positions may indicate that many people feel at least slightly uncomfortable in school and on the job.

As Chapter 12 explains, even within a culture, a nonverbal sign may have more than one meaning. A young woman took a new idea into her boss, who sat there and glared at her, brows together in a frown, as she explained her proposal. The stare and lowered brows symbolized anger to her, and she assumed that he was rejecting her idea. Several months later, she learned that her boss always "frowned" when he was concentrating. The facial expression she had interpreted as anger had not been intended to convey anger at all.

Misunderstandings are even more common when people communicate with people from other cultures or other countries. A white teacher sends two African-American students to the principal's office because they're "fighting." US whites consider fighting to have started when loud voices, insults, and posture indicate that violence is likely. But the US African-American culture does not assume that those signs will lead to violence: they can be part of nonviolent disagreements.[17]

Knowing something about other cultures may help you realize that a subordinate who doesn't meet your eye may be showing respect rather than dishonesty. But it's impossible to memorize every meaning that every nonverbal sign has in every culture. And in a multicultural workforce, you can't know whether someone retains the meanings of his or her ancestors or has adopted the dominant US meanings. The best solution is to state an observation: "I see you're wearing black." The other person's response will let you know whether the color is a fashion statement or a sign of mourning.

CONFLICT RESOLUTION

Conflicts are going to arise in any group of intelligent people who care about the task. Yet many of us feel so uncomfortable with conflict that we pretend it doesn't exist. However, unacknowledged conflicts rarely go away: they fester, making the next interchange more difficult.

We Are Family*

Who is in your family? Middle-class baby boomers limit "family" to people joined by blood or marriage. Younger whites and people of color have a much more extended sense of family.

Generation Xers include step-parents, adopted and half-siblings, close friends, and live-in lovers.

For US African Americans, "family" may embrace "play kin," the children one played with regularly as a child, and their families. "Family" includes the people who raised one, who may be no blood relationship at all but simply friends who helped out when times were tough.

Similarly, in Hispanic cultures, "family" includes not only people related by blood or marriage but also godparents and the especially close relationship known as the *compadre.*

US businesses normally grant leaves for family emergencies. But the size and extent of the "family" will differ among different subcultures.

*Based on Karen Ritchie, "Marketing to Generation X," *American Demographics,* April 1995, 36; Deneen Shepherd, conversation with the author, July 29, 1993; and H. Ned Seelye and Alan Seelye-James, *Culture Clash* (Lincolnwood, IL: NTC Business Books, 1995), 108–09.

Groups can reduce the number of conflicts by making responsibilities and ground rules clear at the beginning, discussing (rather than just accepting) problems as they arise, and realizing that members are not responsible for each other's happiness. Once a conflict arises, groups may need to reopen discussions about responsibilities and confront a troublesome group member.[18]

Steps in Conflict Resolution

Dealing successfully with conflict requires both attention to the issues and to people's feelings. This four-step procedure will help you resolve conflicts constructively.

1. Make sure the people involved really disagree.   Sometimes someone who's under a lot of pressure may explode. But the speaker may just be **venting** anger and frustration; he or she may not in fact be angry at the person who receives the explosion. One way to find out if a person is just venting is to ask, "Is there something you'd like me to do?"

2. Check to see that everyone's information is correct.   Sometimes different conversational styles, differing interpretations of symbols, or faulty inferences create apparent conflicts when no real disagreement exists. (See Appendix C for a discussion of symbols and inferences.) During a negotiation between a US businessman and a Balinese businessman, the Balinese man dropped his voice and lowered his eyes when he discussed price. The US man saw the low voice and breaking of eye contact as an indication of dishonesty. But the Balinese believe that it is rude to mention price specifically. He was embarrassed, but he wasn't lying.[19]

Similarly, misunderstanding can arise from faulty assumptions. A US student studying in Colombia quickly learned that only cold water was available for his evening shower. Since his host family washed dinner dishes in cold water, he assumed the family didn't have hot water. They did. Colombians turn off the water heater in the morning after everyone has bathed; washing later in the day is done with cold water. He could have hot water for his showers if he took them in the morning.[20]

3. Discover the needs each person is trying to meet.   Sometimes determining the real needs makes it possible to see a new solution. The **presenting problem** that surfaces as the subject of dissention may or may not be the real problem. For example, a worker who complains about the hours he's putting in may in fact be complaining not about the hours themselves but about not feeling appreciated. A supervisor who complains that the other supervisors don't invite her to meetings may really feel that the other managers don't accept her as a peer. Sometimes people have trouble seeing beyond the presenting problem because they've been taught to suppress their anger, especially toward powerful people. One way to tell whether the presenting problem is the real problem is to ask, "If this were solved, would I be satisfied?" If the answer is *no,* then the problem that presents itself is not the real problem. Solving the presenting problem won't solve the conflict. Keep probing until you get to the real conflict.

4. Search for alternatives.   Sometimes people are locked into conflict because they see too few alternatives. Indeed, they may see only two polarized choices. Robert Moran tells the story of a large US high-technology company that was having trouble in the Japanese market. At a meeting called to discuss the problem, the president wrote two alternatives on the board:

"GET OUT" and "MAKE THEM DO WHAT WE WANT." Moran suggested a third alternative: "LEARN TO WORK WITH THE JAPANESE."[21]

Responding to Criticism

Conflict is particularly difficult to resolve when someone else criticizes or attacks us directly. When we are criticized, our natural reaction is to defend ourselves—perhaps by counterattacking. The counterattack prompts the critic to defend him- or herself. The conflict escalates; feelings are hurt; issues become muddied and more difficult to resolve.

Just as resolving conflict depends upon identifying the needs each person is trying to meet, so dealing with criticism depends upon understanding the real concern of the critic. Constructive ways to respond to criticism and get closer to the real concern include paraphrasing, checking for feelings, checking inferences, and buying time with limited agreement.

Paraphrasing

To **paraphrase,** repeat in your own words the verbal content of the critic's message. The purposes of paraphrasing are (1) to be sure that you have heard the critic accurately, (2) to let the critic know what his or her statement means to you, and (3) to communicate the feeling that you are taking the critic and his or her feelings seriously.

Criticism:	You guys are stonewalling my requests for information.
Paraphrase:	You think that we don't give you the information you need quickly enough.

Checking for Feelings

When you check the critic's feelings, you identify the emotions that the critic seems to be expressing verbally or nonverbally. The purposes of checking feelings are to try to understand (1) the critic's emotions, (2) the importance of the criticism for the critic, and (3) the unspoken ideas and feelings that may actually be more important than the voiced criticism.

Criticism:	You guys are stonewalling my requests for information.
Feeling Check:	You sound pretty angry.

Always *ask* the other person if you are right in your perception. Even the best reader of nonverbal cues is sometimes wrong.

Checking for Inferences

When you check the inferences you draw from criticism, you identify the implied meaning of the verbal and nonverbal content of the criticism, taking the statement a step further than the words of the critic to try to understand *why* the critic is bothered by the action or attitude under discussion. The purposes of checking inferences are (1) to identify the real (as opposed to the presenting) problem and (2) to communicate the feeling that you care about resolving the conflict.

Criticism:	You guys are stonewalling my requests for information.
Inference:	Are you saying that you need more information from our group?

Inferences can be faulty. In the above interchange, the critic might respond, "I don't need *more* information. I just think you should give it to me without my having to file three forms in triplicate every time I want some data."

Solve the Real Problem*

Consider the story of two men quarreling in a library. One wants the window open and the other wants it closed. They bicker back and forth about how much to leave it open: a crack, halfway, three quarters of the way. No solution satisfies them both.

Enter the librarian. She asks one why he wants the window open: "To get some fresh air." She asks the other why he wants it closed: "To avoid the draft." After thinking a minute, she opens wide a window in the next room, bringing in fresh air without a draft.

*Quoted from Roger Fisher and William Ury, *Getting to YES: Negotiating Agreement Without Giving In* (Boston: Houghton Mifflin, 1981), 41.

Being Taken Seriously*

It's frustrating to speak in a meeting and have people ignore what you say. Here are some tips for being taken seriously.

■ Link your comment to the comment of a powerful person. Even if logic suffers a bit, present your comment as an addition, not a challenge. For example, say, "John is saying that we should focus on excellence, AND I think we can become stronger by encouraging diversity."

■ Show that you've done your homework. Laura Sloate, who is blind, establishes authority by making sure her first question is highly technical: "In footnote three of the 10K, you indicate. . . ."

■ Find an ally in the organization and agree ahead of time to acknowledge each other's contributions to the meeting, whether you agree or disagree with the point being made. Explicit disagreement signals that the comment is worth taking seriously: "Duane has pointed out . . . , but I think that . . . ."

*Based on Joan E. Rigdon, "Managing Your Career," *The Wall Street Journal*, December 1, 1993, B1, and Cynthia Crossen, "Spotting Value Takes Smarts, Not Sight, Laura Sloate Shows," *The Wall Street Journal*, December 10, 1987, A1, A14.

Buying Time with Limited Agreement

Buying time is a useful strategy for dealing with criticisms that really sting. When you buy time with limited agreement, you avoid escalating the conflict (as an angry statement might do) but also avoid yielding to the critic's point of view. To buy time, restate the part of the criticism you agree to be true. (This is often a fact, rather than the interpretation or evaluation the critic has made of that fact.) *Then let the critic respond, before you say anything else.* The purposes of buying time are (1) to allow you time to think when a criticism really hits home and threatens you, so that you can respond to the criticism rather than simply reacting defensively, and (2) to suggest to the critic that you are trying to hear what he or she is saying.

| Criticism: | You guys are stonewalling my requests for information. |
| Limited agreement: | It's true that the cost projections you asked for last week still aren't ready. |

DO NOT go on to justify or explain. A "Yes, but . . ." statement is not a time-buyer.

You-Attitude in Conflict Resolution

You-attitude means looking at things from the audience's point of view, respecting the audience, and protecting the audience's ego. The *you* statements that many people use when they're angry attack the audience; they do not illustrate you-attitude. Instead, substitute statements about your own feelings. In conflict, *I* statements show good you-attitude!

Lacks you-attitude:	You never do your share of the work.
You-attitude:	I feel that I'm doing more than my share of the work on this project.
Lacks you-attitude:	Even you should be able to run the report through a spelling checker.
You-attitude:	I'm not willing to have my name on a report with so many spelling errors. I did lots of the writing, and I don't think I should have to do the proofreading and spell-checking, too.

EFFECTIVE MEETINGS

Meetings have always taken a large part of the average manager's week. The increased number of teams means that meetings are even more frequent. Unfortunately, several surveys have found that of the meetings middle and senior managers attend, only slightly more than half are productive.[22]

Formal meetings are run under strict rules, like the rules of parliamentary procedure summarized in *Robert's Rules of Order*. Motions must be made formally before a topic can be debated. Each point is settled by a vote. **Minutes** record each motion and the vote on it. Formal rules help the meeting run smoothly if the group is very large or if the agenda is very long. **Informal meetings** are run more loosely. Votes may not be taken if most people seem to agree. Minutes may not be kept. Informal meetings are better for team-building and problem solving.

Planning the agenda is the foundation of a good meeting. A good agenda indicates

■ Whether each item is presented for information, for discussion, or for a decision.

■ Who is sponsoring or introducing each item.

■ How much time is allotted for each item.

The decor of a meeting room can send a powerful message. GSD&M, an advertising agency in Austin, Texas, devotes a "war room" to each major client outfitted with the client's products, marketing statistics, and colors.

Many groups put first routine items on which agreement will be easy. If there's a long list of routine items, save them till the end or dispense with them in an omnibus motion. An **omnibus motion** allows a group to approve many items together rather than voting on each separately. A single omnibus motion might cover multiple changes to operational guidelines, or a whole slate of candidates for various offices, or various budget recommendations. It's important to schedule controversial items early in the meeting, when people's energy level is high, and to allow enough time for full discussion. Giving a controversial item only half an hour at the end of the day or evening makes people suspect that the leaders are trying to manipulate them.

Pay attention to people and process as well as to the task at hand. At informal meetings, a good leader observes nonverbal feedback and invites everyone to participate. If conflict seems to be getting out of hand, a leader may want to focus attention on the group process and ways that it could deal with conflict, before getting back to the substantive issues.

If the group doesn't formally vote, the leader should summarize the group's consensus after each point. At the end of the meeting, the leader must summarize all decisions and remind the group who is responsible for implementing or following up on each item. If no other notes are taken, someone should record the decisions and assignments. Long minutes will be most helpful if assignments are set off visually from the narrative.

If you're planning a long meeting, for example, a training session or a conference, recognize that networking is part of the value of the meeting. Allow

Let's See What We Said*

[O]rganizations from Allstate to McKinsey & Co. have begun to use computers as a medium to manage their meetings. A personal computer is hooked up to an overhead projector and as the participants talk their comments are typed by a designated scribe for all to see. People literally see themselves being heard. Related comments are identified, linked and edited on screen. The digressions and tangents quickly become apparent. Instead of simply swapping ideas, participants are actively collaborating to produce a document— whether it be a spreadsheet, a production manual or a strategic plan. The results are often posted on internal corporate networks for comments and suggestions. These technologies effectively encourage new forms of interaction.

*Quoted from Michael Schrage, "Meetings Don't Have to Be Dull," *The Wall Street Journal*, April 29, 1996, A12.

short breaks at least every two hours and generous breaks twice a day so participants can talk informally to each other. If participants will be strangers, include some social functions so they can get to know each other. If they will have different interests or different levels of knowledge, plan concurrent sessions on different topics or for people with different levels of expertise.

COLLABORATIVE WRITING

Whatever your career, it is likely that some of the documents you produce will be written with a group. Lisa Ede and Andrea Lunsford found that 87% of the 700 professionals in seven fields who responded to their survey sometimes wrote as members of a team or a group.[23] Collaboration is often prompted by one of the following situations:

1. The task is too big or the time is too short for one person to do all the work.
2. No one person has all the knowledge required to do the task.
3. A group representing different perspectives must reach a consensus.
4. The stakes for the task are so high that the organization wants the best efforts of as many people as possible; no one person wants the sole responsibility for the success or failure of the document.

Collaborative writing can be done by two people or by a much larger group. The group can be democratic or run by a leader who makes decisions alone. The group may share or divide responsibility for each of the eight stages in the writing process. The following patterns illustrate three of the many possibilities:

- A group plans the document and divides the work. Individuals gather the necessary material for their parts and each writes a section. The entire group evaluates and revises the document. (Democratic teams in business and students assigned group projects in business classes often organize their work this way.)
- One person plans the work and divides it. Each member of the group carries out his or her assignments. The parts are put together, and the whole group or one person revises it. (Team projects in business may be run this way when the group leader is also the supervisor of the group members.)
- A group gathers information and discusses the topic. A single writer plans and writes a document to reflect the group's position. The group evaluates the document and may suggest possible revisions. The writer revises the document until the group feels it is acceptable. (Many committee reports are written this way.)

Research in collaborative writing is beginning to tell us about the strategies that produce the best writing. Rebecca Burnett found that student groups that voiced disagreements as they analyzed, planned, and wrote a document produced significantly better documents than those that suppressed disagreement, going along with whatever was first proposed.[24] A case study of two collaborative writing teams in a state agency found that the successful group distributed power in an egalitarian way, worked to soothe hurt feelings, and was careful to involve all group members. In terms of writing process, the successful group understood the task as a response to a rhetorical situation, planned revisions as a group, saw supervisors' comments as legitimate, and had a positive attitude toward revision.[25] Ede and Lunsford's detailed case studies of collaborative teams in business, government, and science create an "emerging profile of effective collaborative writers": "They are flexible; respectful of others; attentive and analytical

Who Does What

Working successfully in a group depends on being open about preferences, constraints, and skills and then using creative problem-solving techniques.

A person who prefers to outline the whole project in advance may be in a group with someone who expects to do the project at the last minute. Someone who likes to talk out ideas before writing may be in a group with someone who wants to work on a draft in silence and revise it before showing it to anyone. By being honest about your preferences, you make it possible for the group to find a creative solution that builds on what each person can offer.

In one group, Rob wanted to wait to start the project because he was busy with other class work. David and Susan, however, wanted to go ahead now because their schedules would get busier later in the term. A creative solution would be for David and Susan to do most of the work on parts of the project that had to be completed first (such as collecting data and writing the proposal) and for Rob to do work that had to be done later (such as revising, editing, and proofreading).

listeners; able to speak and write clearly and articulately; dependable and able to meet deadlines; able to designate and share responsibility, to lead and to follow; open to criticism but confident in their own abilities; ready to engage in creative conflict."[26]

Planning the Work and the Document

Collaborative writing is most successful when the group articulates its understanding of the document's purposes and audiences and explicitly discusses the best way to achieve these rhetorical goals. Businesses schedule formal planning sessions for large projects to set up a time line specifying intermediate and final due dates, meeting dates, who will attend each meeting, and who will do what. Putting the plan in writing reduces misunderstandings during the project.

When you plan a collaborative writing project,

- Make your analysis of the problem, the audience, and your purposes explicit so you know where you agree and where you disagree.
- Plan the organization, format, and style of the document before anyone begins to write to make it easier to blend sections written by different authors.
- Build some leeway into your deadlines. It's harder for a group to finish a document when one person's part is missing than it is for a single writer to finish the last section of a document on which he or she has done all the work.

Composing the Drafts

Most writers find that composing alone is faster than composing in a group. However, composing together may reduce revision time later, since the group examines every choice as it is made.

When you draft a collaborative writing project,

- Use word processing to make it easier to produce the many drafts necessary in a collaborative document.
- If the quality of writing is crucial, have the best writer(s) draft the document after everyone has gathered the necessary information.

Revising the Document

Revising a collaborative document requires attention to content, organization, and style. The following guidelines can make the revision process more effective:

- Evaluate the content and discuss possible revisions as a group. Brainstorm ways to improve each section so the person doing the revisions has some guidance.
- Recognize that different people favor different writing styles. If the style satisfies the demands of standard English and the conventions of business writing, accept it even if you wouldn't say it that way.
- When the group is satisfied with the content of the document, one person—probably the best writer—should make any changes necessary to make the writing style consistent throughout.

Editing and Proofreading the Document

Since writers' mastery of standard English varies, a group report needs careful editing and proofreading.

Voices from a Hewlett-Packard Team*

[T]he Hewlett-Packard team that developed an advanced system for speeding delivery of billions of dollars of printers . . . was made up of 35 earnest people, all under 50, . . . a gender-balanced, multi-ethnic group. . . .

On how this team's ethos compares with the corporate mainstream:
- Normal meetings are about assault and battery. You go in to stake out a position, defend it, and make sure you don't give up any ground. Here, we're just accountable for business results . . .

On group intelligence: . . .
- You're used to the expectation that it's your job to have the best idea. But no individual is going to have the best idea, that's not how it works—the best ideas come from the collective intelligence of the team. If you accept that, you're in for a big change in how you think about yourself. . . .

On stress: . . .
- I used to work like a slave, and when I dragged myself home, all I wanted to do was drink. Now I don't feel that distinction between work and personal life. I couldn't tell you whether I work hard. What I know is that I don't suffer any more.

*Quoted from "How Team Members Saw It," *Fortune*, March 18, 1996, 120.

- Have at least one person check the whole document for correctness in grammar, mechanics, and spelling and for consistency in the way that format elements, names, and numbers are handled.
- Run the document through a spell checker if possible.
- Even if you use a computerized spell checker, at least one human being should proofread the document too.

Making the Group Process Work

All of the information in this chapter can help your collaborative writing group listen effectively, run meetings efficiently, and deal with conflict constructively. The following suggestions apply specifically to writing groups:

- Give yourselves plenty of time to discuss problems and find solutions. Purdue students who are writing group reports spend six to seven hours a week outside class in group meetings—not counting the time they spend gathering information and writing their drafts.[27]
- Take the time to get to know group members and to build group loyalty. Group members will work harder and the final document will be better if the group is important to members.
- Be a responsible group member. Attend all the meetings; carry out your responsibilities.
- Be aware that people have different ways of experiencing reality and of expressing themselves. Use the principles of semantics discussed in Appendix C to reduce miscommunication.
- Because talking is "looser" than writing, people in a group can think they agree when they don't. Don't assume that because the discussion went smoothly, a draft written by one person will necessarily be acceptable.

SUMMARY OF KEY POINTS

- **Interpersonal communication** is communication between people.
- In interpersonal communication, **hearing** denotes perceiving sounds. **Listening** means decoding and interpreting them correctly.
- To avoid listening errors caused by inattention,
  - Be conscious of the points you need to know and listen for them.
  - At the end of the conversation, check your understanding with the other person.
  - After the conversation, write down key points that affect deadlines or how work will be evaluated.
- To reduce listening errors caused by misinterpretation,
  - Don't ignore instructions you think are unnecessary.
  - Consider the other person's background and experiences. Why is this point important to the speaker?
  - Paraphrase what the speaker has said, giving him or her a chance to correct your understanding.
- In **active listening,** receivers actively demonstrate that they've heard and understood a speaker by feeding back either the literal meaning or the emotional content or both.
- Effective groups balance information leadership, interpersonal leadership, and procedural group management.
- The **standard agenda** is a seven-step process for solving problems. In **dot planning** the group brainstorms ideas. Then each individual affixes adhesive dots by the points or proposals he or she cares most about.

- A case study of six student groups completing class projects found that students in successful groups had leaders who set clear deadlines, scheduled frequent meetings, and dealt directly with conflict that emerged in the group; an inclusive decision-making style; and a higher proportion of members who worked actively on the project.
- Students who spent the most time meeting with their groups got the highest grades.
- **Groupthink** is the tendency for groups to put such a high premium on agreement that they directly or indirectly punish dissent. The best correctives to groupthink are to consciously search for additional alternatives, to test one's assumptions against those of a range of other people, and to protect the rights of people in a group to disagree.
- **Conversational style** denotes our conversational patterns and the meaning we give to them: the way we show interest, politeness, and appropriateness.
- To resolve conflicts, first make sure that the people involved really disagree. Next, check to see that everyone's information is correct. Discover the needs each person is trying to meet. The **presenting problem** that surfaces as the subject of dissention may or may not be the real problem. Search for alternatives.
- Constructive ways to respond to criticism include paraphrasing, checking for feelings, checking inferences, and buying time with limited agreement.
- Use statements about the speaker's feelings to own the problem and avoid attacking the audience. In conflict, *I* statements are good you-attitude!
- To make meetings more effective,
  - State the purpose of the meeting at the beginning.
  - Distribute an agenda that indicates whether each item is for information, for discussion, for action, and how long each is expected to take.
  - Allow enough time to discuss controversial issues.
  - Pay attention to people and process as well as to the task at hand.
  - If you don't take formal votes, summarize the group's consensus after each point. At the end of the meeting, summarize all decisions and remind the group who is responsible for implementing or following up on each item.
- **Collaborative writing** means working with other writers to produce a single document. Writers producing a joint document need to pay attention not only to the basic steps in the writing process but also to the processes of group formation and conflict resolution.

Exercises and Problems **For Chapter 13**

GETTING STARTED

13–1   Making Ethical Choices

Indicate whether you consider each of the following actions ethical, unethical, or a gray area. Which of the actions would you do? Which would you feel uncomfortable doing? Which would you refuse to do?

1. Taking home office supplies (e.g., pens, markers, calculators, etc.) for personal use.

2. Inflating your evaluation of a subordinate because you know that only people ranked *excellent* will get pay raises.

3. Making personal long-distance calls on the company phone.

4. Writing a feasibility report about a new product and deemphasizing test

results that show it could cause cancer.

5. Coming in to the office in the evening to use the company's word processor and computer for personal projects.

6. Designing an ad campaign for a cigarette brand.

7. Working as an accountant for a company that makes or advertises cigarettes.

8. Working as a manager in a company that exploits its nonunionized hourly workers.

9. Writing copy for a company's annual report hiding or minimizing the fact that it pollutes the environment.

10. "Padding" your expense account by putting on it charges you did not pay for.

11. Writing a subscription letter for a sex magazine that glamorizes rape, violence, and sadism.

12. Doing the taxes of a client who publishes a sex magazine that glamorizes rape, violence, and sadism.

13. Telling a job candidate that the company "usually" grants cost-of-living raises every six months, even though you know that the company is losing money and plans to cancel cost-of-living raises for the next year.

14. Laughing at the racist or sexist jokes a client makes, even though you find them offensive.

15. Reading *The Wall Street Journal* on company time.

13–2   Identifying Responses That Show Active Listening

Which of the following responses show active listening? Which responses block communication?

1. Comment: Whenever I say something, the group just ignores me.
   Responses:
   a. That's because your ideas aren't very good. Do more planning before group meetings.
   b. Nobody listens to me, either.
   c. You're saying that noboby builds on your ideas.

2. Comment: I've done more than my share of work on this project. But the people who have been freeloading are going to get the same grade I've worked so hard to earn.
   Responses:
   a. Yes, we're all going to get the same grade.

   b. Are you afraid we won't do well on the assignment?
   c. It sounds like you feel resentful.

3. Comment: My parents are going to kill me if I don't have a job lined up when I graduate.
   Responses:
   a. You know they're exaggerating. They won't *really* kill you.
   b. Can you blame them? I mean, it's taken you six years to get a degree. Surely you've learned something to make you employable!
   c. If you act the way in interviews that you do in our class, I'm not surprised. Companies want people with good attitudes and good work ethics.

13–3   Practicing Active Listening

Go around the room for this exercise. In turn, let each student complain about something (large or small) that really bothers them. Then the next student(s) will

a. Offer a statement of limited agreement that would buy time.

b. Paraphrase the statement.
c. Check for feelings that might lie behind the statement.
d. Offer inferences that might motivate the statement.

13–4   Experiencing Closed and Open Groups

Let three people stand up and talk together in front of the class. A fourth person will come up to the group and try to join it. If your social security number ends in an even number, observe what the newcomer does and says. If your social security number ends in an odd number, observe what the group does and says.

> **Situation a.** The group makes it easy for the newcomer to join.
> **Situation b.** The group rejects the newcomer and tries to keep the original group unchanged.

After each situation, discuss the following questions:

- What did the newcomer do to try to join the group? How did the newcomer adjust his or her strategy when the group was closed? Did the newcomer succeed in joining the group?
- What did the group do to welcome the newcomer? What did it do to reject the newcomer?

Ask the following questions of the newcomer and the group members:

- How did it feel to be accepted? How did it feel to be rejected?
- How did it feel to welcome the newcomer? How did it feel to shut the newcomer out?

13–5   Brainstorming Ways to Resolve Conflicts

Suggest one or more ways that each of the following groups could deal with the conflict(s) it faces.

1. Mike and Takashi both find writing hard. Elise has been getting better grades than either of them, so they offer to do all the research if she'll organize the document and write, revise, edit, and proofread it. Elise thinks that this method would leave her doing a disproportionate share of the work. Moreover, scheduling the work would be difficult, since she wouldn't know how good their research was until the last minute.

2. Because of their class and work schedules, Lars and Andrea want to hold group meetings from 8–10 PM, working later if need be. But Juan's wife works the evening shift, and he needs to be home with his children, two of whom have to be in bed before 8. He wants to meet from 8–10 AM, but the others don't want to meet that early.

3. Lynn wants to divide up the work exactly equally, with firm due dates. Marcia is trying to get into medical school. She says she'd rather do the lion's share of the work so that she knows it's good. Jessie's father is terminally ill. This group isn't very important in terms of what's going on in her life, and she knows she may have to miss some group meetings.

4. Sherry is aware that she is the person in her group who always points out the logical flaws in arguments: she's the one who reminds the group that they haven't done all the parts of the assignment. She doesn't want her group to turn in a flawed product, but she wonders whether the other group members see her as too critical.

5. Jim's group missed several questions on their group quiz. Talking to Tae-Suk after class, Jim learns that Tae-Suk knew all the answers. "Why didn't you say anything?" Jim asks angrily. Tae-Suk responds quietly, "Todd said that he knew the answers. I did not want to argue with him. We have to work together, and I do not want anyone to lose face."

13–6   Taking Minutes

As your instructor directs, have two or more people take minutes of each class or collaborative group meeting for a week. Compare the accounts of the same meeting.

- To what extent do they agree on what happened?
- Does one contain information missing in other accounts?
- Do any accounts disagree on a specific fact?
- How do you account for the differences you find?

13-7 Keeping a Journal about a Group

As you work in a collaborative writing group, keep a journal after each group meeting.

- What happened?
- What roles did you play in the meeting?
- What conflicts arose? How were they handled?
- What strategies could you use to make the next meeting go smoothly?
- Record one observation about each group member.

E-MAIL MESSAGES

In Problems 13-8 through 13-11, assume that your group has been asked to recommend a solution.

As Your Instructor Directs,

- Send e-mail messages to group members laying out your initial point of view on the issue and discussing the various options.
- As a group, answer the message.
- Write a memo to your instructor telling how satisfied you are with
  a. The decision your group reached.
  b. The process you used to reach it.

13-8 Recommending a Fair Way to Assign Work around the Holidays

You are on the Labor-Management Committee. This e-mail arrives from the general manager:

> Subject: Allocating Holiday Hours
>
> As you know, lots of people want to take extra time off around holidays to turn three-day weekends into longer trips. But we do need to stay open. Right now, there are allegations that some supervisors give the time off to their friends. But even "fair" systems, such as giving more senior workers first choice at time off, or requiring that workers with crucial skills work, also create problems. And possibly we need a different system around Christmas, when many people want to take off a week or more, than around lesser holidays, when most people take only an extra day or two.
>
> Please recommend an equitable way to decide how to assign hours.

Write a group response recommending the best way to assign hours.

Hint:
Agree on an office, factory, store, hospital, or other workplace to use for this problem.

13-9 Recommending Whether the Travel Policy Should Be Changed

You are on the Executive Committee. This e-mail arrives from the Sales Manager.

> Subject: Complaints about Travel Policy
>
> My people really don't like the current travel regulations. As you know, people are reimbursed only for the least expensive airfare, which means they have to stay over Saturday night. People want to leave right after the close of business Friday to get home to spend time with their families.
>
> This company depends on sales people. Let's keep them happy. Please change the travel policy to reimburse people for airfare even if it is not the lowest rate.

Write a group response recommending whether the policy should be changed.

13–10   Recommending Whether a Mall Should Hire Ethnic Santas _____

You're on a committee of store managers elected from all of the managers in a large mall. You get this e-mail from the committee chair.

> Subject: Ethnic Santas?
>
> We've received several complaints that the men we hire to be Santas are always white. Should we change that policy? If so, what to?

Write a group response recommending what the ethnic makeup of people hired to be Santas at the mall should be.

13–11   Recommending an Internet Use Policy _____

You're on the Computers Committee. You get this message from your manager.

> Subject: Need Internet Use Policy
>
> We have no policy on Internet use. Is it OK for people to play games or surf the Web during work hours? Should we block access to certain Web sites?
>
> The biggest problem may be responses to listservs and comments on electronic bulletin boards. There's no problem when people log on from home. But if they post responses from their workstations here, people might think the comment represents the official organizational stance on the issue—and it doesn't.

Write a group response recommending a policy.

Hint:
Agree on an office, factory, store, hospital, or other workplace to use for this problem.

WEB PAGES

As Your Instructor Directs, in Problems 13–12 through 13–14,

a. Turn in two laser copies of your page(s). On another page, give the URL for each link.
b. Turn in one laser copy of your page(s) and a disk with the HTML code and .gif files.
c. Write a group memo to your instructor (1) identifying the audience for which the page is designed and explaining (2) the search strategies you used to find material on this topic, (3) why you chose the pages and information you've included, (4) why you chose the layout and graphics you've used, and (5) who did what on the project.
d. Present your page orally to the class.

13–12   Creating a Web Page for a Campus Group _____

Create a Web page for a campus group that does not yet have one.

13–13   Creating a Web Page for Multicultural Managers and Workers

1. Create a Web page for multicultural managers. What links would help managers better understand the multicultural Workforce 2000?

2. Create a Web page for members of a group that has not traditionally been part of the power structure of US business. (The group could be defined by class, gender, race and ethnicity, religion, physical ability, age, sexual orientation, or education.) What links would provide support to members of this group and help them attain their full potential in their work lives?

3. Create a Web page for a nonprofit, business, or government organization devoted to the advancement of a group that has not traditionally been part of the power structure of US business. (The group could be defined by class, gender, race and ethnicity, religion, physical ability, age, sexual orientation, or education.) You must choose an organization that does not already have a Web page.

13–14   Creating a Web Page on a Topic of Your Choice

Create a Web page on a topic of your choice. Possibilities include

- Information for students new to your campus.
- Study tips for students in your major.
- Links about speakers, bands, or events coming to your town.
- Links to advice about on-line résumés and to good (and poor) résumés on the Web.
- Information about how to construct a Web page.

MEMO AND BROCHURE ASSIGNMENTS

13–15   Recommending a Writing Prompt

You're on the Executive Committee of your union. Today you get a letter from a college professor in your city:

> Dear Union Executive Committee:
>
> As you may know, I was on the team of reviewers reading the applications for the Les Best Scholarship Award, given to children of union members.
>
> The current prompt asks students to write a 1,000 word essay on "What the Union Has Meant to Our Family." The trouble with the topic is that students with poignant stories have a real advantage over those whose parents have had more mundane experiences in the union. So I think you need a new topic for next year. It's OK to have something related to unions, if you choose, but succeeding on the prompt shouldn't depend on how horrific the parents' work experience has been.
>
> Sincerely,
>
> Patricia McKaslin, PhD

Determine what the prompt for next year's competition will be, and notify Professor McKaslin.

13–16   Answering an Ethics Question

You are on your organization's Ethics Committee. You receive the following anonymous note:

> People are routinely using the company letterhead to write letters to members of Congress, Senators, and even the President stating their positions on various issues. Making their opinions known is of course their right, but doing so on letterhead stationery implies that they are speaking for the company, which they are not.
>
> I think that the use of letterhead for anything other than official company business should be prohibited.

Determine the best solution to the problem. Then write a message to all employees stating your decision and building support for it.

13–17   Creating a Form to Approve Internships and Appraise Interns' Work

You are members of the School of Business' Student Advisory Board. The school's Placement Director, Wade Wandowski, tells you:

> As some of you may know, our internship program isn't working as well as we'd like it to. We try to screen employers, but some of them use an intern for go-fer work, so the person doesn't get any real experience. And many of them don't write the detailed evaluations we ask for, so assigning grades is a real problem. We need two things: a form that can be filled out by organizations that want interns, so that we can approve only those projects that will be good learning experiences, and a performance appraisal form that's easy for busy supervisors to fill out but informative enough for us to assign grades.

As Your Instructor Directs,
  a. Create one or both forms.
  b. Write a memo to the Placement Director explaining the choices your group has made.

13–18   Creating Brochures

In a collaborative group, create a series of brochures for an organization and present your design and copy to the class in a group oral presentation. Your brochures should work well as a series but also be capable of standing alone if a reader picks up just one. They should share a common visual design and be appropriate for your purposes and audience. You may use sketches rather than photos or finished drawings. Text, however, should be as it will appear in the final copy.

As you prepare your series, talk to a knowledgeable person in the organization. For this assignment, as long as the person is knowledgeable, he or she does not have to have the power to approve the brochures.

In a manila folder, turn in

1. Two copies of each brochure.
2. A copy of your approved proposal (see Chapter 14).
3. A narrative explaining (a) how you responded to the wishes of the person in the organization who was your contact and (b) five of the choices you made in terms of content, visuals, and design and why you made these choices.

13–19   Interviewing Workers about Listening

Interview someone who works in an organization about his or her on-the-job listening. Possible questions to ask include the following:

- Whom do you listen to as part of your job? Your superior? Subordinates? (How many levels down?) Customers or clients? Who else?
- How much time a day do you spend listening?
- What people do you talk to as part of your job? Do you feel they hear what you say? How do you tell whether or not they're listening?
- Do you know of any problems that came up because someone didn't listen? What happened?
- What do you think prevents people from listening effectively? What advice would you have for someone on how to listen more accurately?

As Your Instructor Directs,
   a. Share your information with a small group of students in your class.
   b. Present your findings orally to the class.
   c. Present your findings in a memo to your instructor.
   d. Join with other students to present your findings in a group report.

13–20 Analyzing the Dynamics of a Group

Analyze the dynamics of a task group of which you are a member. Answer the following questions:

1. Who was the group's leader? How did the leader emerge? Were there any changes in or challenges to the original leader?
2. Describe the contribution each member made to the group and the roles each person played.
3. Did any members of the group officially or unofficially drop out? Did anyone join after the group had begun working? How did you deal with the loss or addition of a group member, both in terms of getting the work done and in terms of helping people work together?
4. What planning did your group do at the start of the project? Did you stick to the plan or revise it? How did the group decide that revision was necessary?
5. How did your group make decisions? Did you vote? reach decisions by consensus?
6. What problems or conflicts arose? Did the group deal with them openly? To what extent did they interfere with the group's task?
7. Evaluate your group both in terms of its task and in terms of the satisfaction members felt. How did this group compare with other task groups you've been part of? What made it better or worse?

As you answer the questions,
   ▪ Be honest. You won't lose points for reporting that your group had problems or did something "wrong."
   ▪ Show your knowledge of good group dynamics. That is, if your group did something wrong, show that you know what *should* have been done. Similarly, if your group worked well, show that you know *why* it worked well.
   ▪ Be specific. Give examples or anecdotes to support your claims.

As Your Instructor Directs,
   a. Discuss these questions with the other group members.
   b. Present your findings orally to the class.
   c. Present your findings in an individual memo to your instructor.
   d. Join with the other group members to write a collaborative memo to your instructor.

Hint:
Use your journal from Problem 13-9.

Reports

CHAPTER 14

Planning, Proposing, and Researching Reports

Chapter Outline

Planning, Proposing, and Researching Reports

Kendra Hatcher, Associate Planner
Leo Burnett Company

Kendra Hatcher is one of Leo Burnett's experts in issues and trends relating to teens, young adults, and African Americans. The Leo Burnett Company, headquartered in Chicago, Illinois, is the sixth largest advertising agency network in the world.

Had I been asked to discuss research and planning a year ago, my response would have been quite different. Within the last year, Burnett has smoothly transitioned from a "research" to a "planning" orientation. As a planner, I don't just "do" research. I "use" insights to answer key marketing and communication questions to support strategic planning for our clients.

For example, traditional practices like focus groups and telephone surveys may not provide the type of human insight needed to make good advertising great. So the account planner may conduct an ethnography, that is, going to consumers in their own environments to observe their behavior as they interact with the product. Checking out the target consumers' favorite movies and reading their favorite magazines are also ways for me to understand what makes people tick. In short, we strive to look at our "target" as people, not just as consumers.

While our crafts are different, good planners are as creative as the best copywriter or the most clever art director. We can invent new ways to find needed information, adapt grassroots marketing tactics to suit our needs, or use out-of-the-box qualitative explorations to reach consumers.

Whatever the approach, there is a blueprint to follow when either the client or someone at the agency asks "Why?" Why do children flip over hamburgers at their favorite restaurant? Why have teens embraced the fashions of the 70s? The questions never end.

Once we identify what we need to know, we usually set up a brainstorming meeting among key agency team members—the planner, the client service and media representatives, and the creative team. Here we develop an action plan, which is presented to the client in a written proposal. The proposal outlines the project background (what led to the initiative), the objectives of the project (what we hope to learn), the recommended methods (how and by whom the study will be conducted), the timeline and cost, and any next steps that need to be taken.

Once the study is complete, the results are analyzed and written in a comprehensive or topline report. A summary of the findings is presented to the client and agency team members. The next place our insights are seen is in our advertising. Whether it is for one of our multinational clients like McDonald's or Coca-Cola, or for a blue-chip national client like Amoco, we know that we have succeeded when our advertising is relevant to our target consumers, delivers the intended message, and moves our clients' business forward.

Kendra Hatcher, March 26, 1997

Visit Leo Burnett's Web site: http://www.leoburnett.com

"Good planners . . . can invent new ways to find needed information."

Kendra Hatcher, Leo Burnett

Proposals and reports depend on research. The research may be as simple as pulling up data with a computer program or as complicated as calling many different people, conducting focus groups and surveys, or even planning and conducting experiments. Care in planning, proposing, and researching reports is needed to produce reliable data.

In writing any report, there are five basic steps:

1. Define the problem.
2. Gather the necessary data and information.
3. Interpret the data.
4. Organize the information.
5. Write the report.

After reviewing the varieties of reports, this chapter focuses on the first two steps. Chapter 15 discusses the last three steps.

VARIETIES OF REPORTS

Many kinds of documents are called *reports*. In some organizations, a report is a long document or a document that contains numerical data. In others, one- and two-page memos are called *reports*. A short report to a client may use letter format. **Formal reports** contain formal elements such as a title page, a transmittal, a table of contents, and a list of illustrations. **Informal reports** may be letters and memos or even computer printouts of production or sales figures. But all reports, whatever their length or degree of formality, provide the information that people in organizations need to make plans and solve problems.

Reports can be called **information reports** if they collect data for the reader, **analytical reports** if they interpret data but do not recommend action, and **recommendation reports** if they recommend action or a solution. It's worth knowing the names of common reports so that you'll understand what your supervisor is asking you to do.

The following reports are usually information reports:

- **Sales reports** (sales figures for the week or month).
- **Quarterly reports** (figures showing a plant's productivity and profits for the quarter).

The following reports are usually analytical reports.

- **Annual reports** (financial data and an organization's accomplishments during the past year).
- **Audit reports** (interpretations of the facts revealed during an audit).
- **Make-good** or **payback reports** (calculations of the point at which a new capital investment will pay for itself).

The following reports are recommendation reports.

- **Feasibility reports** evaluate two or more alternatives and recommend which the organization should choose.

- **Justification reports** justify the need for a purchase, an investment, a new personnel line, or a change in procedure.
- **Problem-solving reports** identify the causes of an organizational problem and recommend a solution.

Often, the name of a report isn't enough to identify its purpose. The following reports can be information, analytical, or recommendation reports:

- **Accident reports** can simply list the nature and causes of accidents in a factory or office. These reports can also recommend changes to make conditions safer.
- **Credit reports** can simply summarize an applicant's income and other credit obligations. These reports can also evaluate the applicant's collateral and creditworthiness.
- **Progress** and **interim reports** can simply record the work done so far and the work remaining on a project. These reports can also recommend that a project be stopped, continued, or restructured.
- **Trip reports** can simply share what the author learned at a conference or during a visit to a customer or supplier. These reports can also recommend action based on that information.
- **Closure reports** can simply document the causes of a failure or of research that is not economically or technically feasible for new products under current conditions. They can also recommend action to prevent such failures in the future.

DEFINING REPORT PROBLEMS

Good report problems grow out of real problems: disjunctions between reality and the ideal, choices that must be made. When you write a report as part of your job, the organization may define the topic. To think of problems for class reports, think about problems that face your college or university; housing units on campus; social, religious, and professional groups on campus and in your city; local businesses; and city, county, state, and federal governments and their agencies. Read your campus and local papers and newsmagazines; watch the news on TV or listen to it on National Public Radio.

A good report problem in business or administration meets the following criteria:

1. The problem is
   - Real.
   - Important enough to be worth solving.
   - Narrow but challenging.
   - Possible to solve with the time and resources available.
   - Something you're interested in.
2. The audience for the report is
   - Real.
   - Able to implement the recommended action.
   - One you can get information about.
3. The data, evidence, and facts are
   - Sufficient to document the severity of the problem.
   - Sufficient to prove that the recommendation will solve the problem.
   - Available to *you*.
   - Comprehensible to *you*.

Often problems need to be narrowed. For example, "improving the college experiences of international students studying in the United States" is far too

Find the Real Problem*

One student group decided that students were not informed about campus events and that the problem could be solved with a campus radio station. In fact, their university already had a radio station that broadcast, among other things, university announcements. But even with this information, the group was unable to change its problem formulation.

Possible real problems could include what the university radio station could do to make its announcements more interesting or why students did not want to participate in a particular campus event.

To be sure that the problem is real, check your perceptions against those of others, especially people in the organization whose problem you hope to solve.

*Based on Meg Morgan, "Case Study Methods and Collaborative Writing," Conference on College Composition and Communication, St. Louis, MO, March 17–19, 1988.

broad. First, choose one college or university. Second, identify the specific problem. Do you want to increase the social interaction between US and international students? Help international students find housing? Increase the number of ethnic grocery stores and restaurants? Third, identify the specific audience that would have the power to implement your recommendations. Depending on the specific topic, the audience might be the Office of International Studies, the residence hall counselors, a service organization on campus or in town, a store, or a group of investors.

Pick a problem you can solve in the time available. Six months of full-time (and overtime) work and a team of colleagues might allow you to look at all the ways to make a store more profitable. If you're doing a report in 6 to 12 weeks for a class that is only one of your responsibilities, limit the topic. Depending on your interests and knowledge, you could choose to examine the prices and styles of clothes a store carried, its inventory procedures, its overhead costs, its layout and decor, or its advertising budget.

How you define the problem shapes the solutions you find. For example, suppose that a manufacturer of frozen foods isn't making money. If the problem is defined as a marketing problem, the researcher may analyze the product's price, image, advertising, and position in the market. But perhaps the problem is really that overhead costs are too high due to poor inventory management, or that an inadequate distribution system doesn't get the product to its target market. Defining the problem accurately is essential to finding an effective solution.

Once you've defined your problem, you're ready to write a purpose statement. The purpose statement goes both in your proposal and in your final report. A good **purpose statement** makes three things clear:

- The organizational problem or conflict.
- The specific technical questions that must be answered to solve the problem.
- The rhetorical purpose (to explain, to recommend, to request, to propose) the report is designed to achieve.

The following purpose statement has all three elements. The report's audience is the Superintendent of Yellowstone National Park.

> Current management methods keep the elk population within the carrying capacity of the habitat but require frequent human intervention. Both wildlife conservation specialists and the public would prefer methods that controlled the elk population naturally. This report will compare the current short-term management techniques (hunting, trapping and transporting, and winter feeding) with two long-term management techniques, habitat modification and the reintroduction of predators. The purpose of this report is to recommend which techniques or combination of techniques would best satisfy the needs of conservationists, hunters, and the public.

To write a good purpose statement, you must understand the basic problem and have some idea of the questions that your report will answer. Note, however, that you can (and should) write the purpose statement before researching the specific alternatives the report will discuss.

WRITING PROPOSALS AND PROGRESS REPORTS

Proposals suggest a method for finding information or solving a problem.[1] Proposals may be competitive or noncompetitive. **Competitive proposals** compete against each other for limited resources. When you collaborate on a group report, each student may propose a topic; only one can be accepted.

Similarly, applications for research funding are often very competitive. The National Science Foundation, for example, funds only 12% of the proposals submitted.[2] Many companies will bid for corporate or government contracts, but only one will be accepted. **Noncompetitive proposals** have no real competition. For example, a company could accept all of the internal proposals it thought would save money or improve quality. Similarly, when students write proposals for reports or theses, the proposals compete not against each other but against standards for doing good research. And often a company that is satisfied with a vendor asks for a noncompetitive proposal to renew the contract.

To write a good proposal, you need to have a clear view of the problem you hope to solve and the kind of research or other action needed to solve it. A proposal must answer the following questions convincingly:

- **What problem are you going to solve?** Show that you understand the problem and the organization's needs. Define the problem as the audience sees it, even if you believe that the presenting problem is part of a larger problem that must first be solved.
- **How are you going to solve it?** Prove that your methods are feasible. Show that a solution can be found in the time available. Specify the topics you'll investigate. Explain how you'll gather data.
- **What exactly will you provide for us?** Specify the tangible products you'll produce; explain how you'll evaluate them.
- **Can you deliver what you promise?** Show that you have the knowledge, the staff, and the facilities to do what you say you will. Describe your previous work in this area, your other qualifications, and the qualifications of any people who will be helping you.
- **What benefits can you offer?** In a sales proposal, several vendors may be able to supply the equipment needed. Show why the company should hire you. Discuss the benefits—direct and indirect—that your firm can provide.
- **When will you complete the work?** Provide a detailed schedule showing when each phase of the work will be completed.
- **How much will you charge?** Provide a detailed budget that includes costs for materials, salaries, and overhead.

Government agencies and companies often issue Requests for Proposals, known as **RFPs**. Follow the RFP exactly when you respond to a proposal. Competitive proposals are often scored by giving points in each category. Evaluators look only under the heads specified in the RFP. If information isn't there, the proposal gets no points in that category.

Proposals for Class Research Projects

You may be asked to submit a proposal for a report that you write for a class. Even when the report and the assignment are addressed to a real person in a real organization, your instructor is the audience for the proposal. Your instructor wants evidence that your problem is not too big and not too small, that you understand it, that your method will give you the information you need, and that you have the knowledge and resources to collect and analyze the data.

A proposal for a student report usually has the following sections:

1. In your first paragraph (no heading), summarize in a sentence or two the topic and purposes of your report.
2. **Problem.** What organizational problem exists? What is wrong? Why does it need to be solved? Is there a history or background that is relevant?
3. **Feasibility.** Are you sure that a solution can be found in the time available? How do you know?

In-House Proposals*

There is no better way to kick-start a career than acting like an entrepreneur. . . .

That's exactly what P. J. Smoot, head of training and development at International Paper in Chicago, did. When she joined International Paper in 1980, she was in the finance department. "I noticed that there wasn't a lot of career development or training going on, except at the college recruitment level, and I saw a real need for it."

So she wrote a proposal to the HR department, where they liked it so much, they hired her to put her ideas into practice. What started as an 18-month assignment has evolved into a full-fledged companywide training program. Smoot, who oversees the program, has since won six promotions—all because she saw a way to help her company and then acted on it.

*Quoted from Anne Fisher, "Six Ways to Supercharge Your Career," *Fortune*, January 13, 1997, 48.

Research for a Proposal*

Patti Douglas, Customer Service Representative for Phelps County Bank in Rolla, Missouri, proposed that her bank implement a marketing program for mature adults. To get the information she needed for her proposal, she

- Read articles in trade journals about mature-adult programs.
- Visited local competitors to find out what (if any) programs they offered for mature adults.
- Called the National Center of Health Statistics to find out how long people lived.
- Asked the switchboard operator to track inquiries about a program for mature adults.
- Found out how much free customer checks and other services for mature adults would cost.
- Assembled a group of current customers to find out what benefits would attract mature adults.

*Based on phone interview with the author, January 26, 1994.

4. **Audience.** Who in the organization would have the power to implement your recommendation? What secondary audiences might be asked to evaluate your report? What audiences would be affected by your recommendation? Will anyone in the organization serve as a gatekeeper, determining whether your report is sent to decision makers? What watchdog audiences might read the report?

For each of these audiences and for your initial audience (your instructor), give the person's name, job title, and business address and answer the following questions:
- What is the audience's major concern or priority?
- What will the audience see as advantages of your proposal? What objections, if any, is the reader likely to have?
- How interested is the audience in the topic of your report?
- How much does the audience know about the topic of your report?

List any terms, concepts, equations, or assumptions that one or more of your audiences may need to have explained. Briefly identify ways in which your audiences may affect the content, organization, or style of the report.

5. **Topics to investigate.** List the questions and subquestions you will answer in your report, the topics or concepts you will explain, the aspects of the problem you will discuss. Indicate how deeply you will examine each of the aspects you plan to treat. Explain your rationale for choosing to discuss some aspects of the problem and not others.

6. **Methods/procedure.** How will you get answers to your questions? Whom will you interview or survey? What published sources will you use? Give the full bibliographic references.

Your METHODS section should clearly indicate how you will get the information needed to answer the questions in the TOPICS TO INVESTIGATE section.

7. **Qualifications/facilities/resources.** Do you have the knowledge and skills needed to conduct this study? Do you have adequate access to the organization? Do you have access to any equipment you will need to conduct your research (computer, books, etc.)? Where will you turn for help if you hit an unexpected snag?

You'll be more convincing if you have already scheduled an interview, checked out books, or printed out online sources.

8. **Work schedule.** List both the total time you plan to spend on and the date when you expect to finish each of the following activities:
- Gathering information.
- Analyzing information.
- Preparing the progress report.
- Organizing information.
- Writing the draft.
- Revising the draft.
- Preparing the visuals.
- Editing the draft.
- Proofreading the report.

Answer this question either in a chart or in a calendar. A good schedule provides realistic estimates for each activity, allows time for unexpected snags, and shows that you can complete the work on time.

9. **Call to action.** In your final section, indicate that you'd welcome any suggestions your instructor may have for improving the research plan. Ask your instructor to approve your proposal so that you can begin work on your report.

Figure 14.1 shows a student proposal for a long report using library research.

Figure 14.1   **Proposal for a Student Report Using Library Research**

February 14, 1997

To: Laura J. Peterson   *In subject line*   ①*indicate that this is a proposal*
                                                          ②*specify the kind of report*
From: Christy West *CW*   ③*specify the topic.*

Subject: Proposal to Write a Report Evaluating the Feasibility of Persuading the NFL to
           Allow Buffalo Bills Fans to Buy the Team

*Summarize
topic and
purposes
of report.*

With the aging of the Buffalo Bills' owner, football fans and community leaders in western New York have begun to look for ways to keep the Bills football franchise in Erie County. For my report, I will assume that my consulting firm has been hired by the City of Buffalo and Erie County to recommend whether it is feasible to persuade the National Football League (NFL) to allow Buffalo Bills fans to buy the team. I will use library and online sources and possibly telephone interviews.

Problem   *If "Problem" section is detailed and well-written,
                  you may be able to use it unchanged in your report.*

In 1959, Ralph Wilson put up the $25,000 necessary to establish an American Football League (AFL) franchise. Mr. Wilson is now 78 years old, and the franchise is worth approximately $200 million. Inheritance taxes for the franchise would run approximately $110 million, and Mr. Wilson's daughters have indicated that they would sell the team to pay the taxes. Given current NFL ownership rules, any new owner would be likely to move the team to another city to maximize revenue.

The richest franchises also have stadiums with luxury boxes for which corporations pay premium prices. The Bills play in Rich Stadium, a 24-year-old dinosaur without adequate luxury boxes. And even if a new stadium were built, Buffalo probably does not have enough wealthy corporations to purchase the requisite number of luxury boxes.

To move the team, the new owner would need the approval of the National Football League. But it seems certain that the owners would approve a move. Since 1994, four NFL franchises have relocated or have made plans to do so. The team that received the most public scrutiny by moving is the franchise owned by Art Modell, the team formerly known as the Cleveland Browns and now known as the Baltimore Ravens. The team Modell moved had been in Cleveland for 50 years and had very loyal fans. If the owner of an NFL franchise could break a lease and move a team without penalty (and with little warning), what are the implications for other loyal football cities, like Buffalo?

The alternative that holds the most promise is to allow Buffalo to buy the Bills. Such a decision would create a situation like that of the Green Bay Packers, a franchise owned by its fans. However, since the Packer fans bought their team, the NFL has enacted rules to prevent another citizen purchase.

Feasibility   *In a feasibility report, you evaluate two or more options
                  for action. Specify what they are. If one option looks
                  more promising, say so.*

Because this is a feasibility study, I will be able to recommend some action whatever my

Figure 14.1   **Continued**

research reveals. If I can make a strong case for allowing the fans to purchase the team, I will recommend that the county and city work to persuade the NFL owners to allow this ownership structure. If I cannot show that public ownership will benefit other NFL teams (thus making it unlikely that they would vote to support a change), I will recommend that this alternative be dropped and that fans investigate other strategies for keeping the Bills in Buffalo.

Audience   *Identify the kinds of audiences and the major concerns or priority of each.*

The City of Buffalo Common Council and the Erie County Legislature will be my primary audience, as they would need to approve my recommendations. They want to keep the Bills in Buffalo and will be eager to get my report. They will want a report that lays out all the arguments so that they can make the strongest possible case to the NFL owners.

Anthony M. Masiello, Mayor of Buffalo, and Dennis T. Gorski, Erie County Executive, serve as gatekeepers. They will schedule my report for discussion and vote only if they think that my evidence is convincing. Because Dennis Gorski has been negotiating the terms of the lease of Rich Stadium with Ralph Wilson, Mr. Gorski is very knowledgeable about the Bills, Ralph Wilson, the state of the franchise, and the possibility of relocation upon Mr. Wilson's death.

The most important secondary audiences are the voters, Ralph Wilson, his daughters, and the Buffalo Bills players and staff.   All of these audiences would favor an alternative that keeps the Bills in Buffalo, while allowing the Wilson daughters to receive their inheritance in cash. These audiences know a lot about what the team means to Buffalo, but they may not be aware of the details of other kinds of ownership and the arguments that may be persuasive to NFL team owners.

Other secondary audiences include the owners of other NFL teams and the Commissioner of the NFL, Paul Tagliabue, who would have to approve a change in ownership rules. Owners of other small-market NFL franchises may face similar dilemmas in the future; the media has been intensely interested in the relocation of NFL franchises since the Browns moved from Cleveland.

You are my initial audience. You are most interested in my report's content, thesis and logic, use of sources, writing style, and adaptation to its audiences. You know something about sports and business, but not about this specific situation, so you may need explanations.

Topics to Investigate   *Indicate what you'll discuss briefly and what you'll discuss in more detail. This list should match your audience's concerns.*

In this report, I will briefly discuss the history of the Buffalo Bills, the current structure of ownership of the Buffalo Bills, the economic hardships Ralph Wilson's daughters stand to face when they inherit the Buffalo Bills, and why moving the team is a real threat.

I will investigate the following topics in detail:
1. Why are the Buffalo Bills important to Buffalo?   *If it is well-written,*
    - What is the economic contribution?   *"Topics to Investigate"*
    - How are the Bills important to Buffalo's culture and sense of identity?   *section will*
2. What are the sources of NFL team owners' revenue?   *become the "Scope"*
    - How is TV revenue distributed among teams?   *section of the report*
                                                            —with minor revisions.

Continued   **Figure 14.1**

Laura J. Peterson   3   February 14, 1997

All items in
list must be   • What other sources of shared revenue exist?
grammatically   • What sources of revenue remain the sole property of the owner?
parallel.   3. What rules govern NFL franchise ownership?
Here, all   4. What kind of ownership does Green Bay have of the Packers?
are questions.   • Is the same model appropriate for Buffalo? If not, what changes are needed?
                      • If cities in smaller markets were allowed to purchase their local franchises (or if pri-
                        vate corporations in smaller markets were allowed to purchase local franchises), how
                        would other NFL owners be affected?
               5. Is it in the other owners' interest for some teams to remain in small markets?
                      • Can all of the small-market teams be moved to larger cities without diluting major
                        markets?
                      • Do small-market teams contribute directly to the overall financial health of the NFL?
                      • Do small-market teams contribute indirectly to goodwill toward the NFL and to
                        enthusiasm for football?

I will not discuss possible owners for the team or the financial feasibility of building a new
stadium.   *Indicate any topics that are relevant to your subject*
            that you choose not to discuss.

If you'll   **Methods**
administer
a survey   I will use library and online research to answer my research questions. The following materials
or conduct in the Ohio State University libraries and the Internet appear to be useful:
interviews,
tell how   Atre, T., Auns, K., Badenhausen, K., McAuliffe, K., Nikolov, C. & Oznian, M. K. (1996, May
many   20). Sports stocks and bonds. *Financial World*, pp. 53-63.
subjects
you'll have,   Deckard, L. (1993, March 22). Expansion, corporate ownership on agenda at NFL owners
how you'll meeting. *Amusement Business*, pp. 14-15.
choose
them,   Green Bay fans aren't just fans, they are the owners. (1995, January 10; visited site February
and what   12, 1997).   http://www.nando.net/newsroom/sports/fbo/1995/nfl/gbp/feat/archive/011096/gbp
you'll   28958.html
ask them.
                  Gridiron groupies. (1994, June; visited site February 12, 1997). *American Demographics*.
              http://www.marketingtools.com/search/nn/NN151.htm

                  Kapner, S. (1995, December 11). Operators, residents seeing red over Browns' departure.
              Nation's Restaurant News, pp. 3-4.

                  King, P. (1996, February 19). Without grace or glory. *Sports Illustrated*, p. 62.

              Save our Bills. (1996, September 29). Buffalo: *The Magazine of the Buffalo News*, pp. 4-8.

              The commish stands up. (1996, April 1). *Sports Illustrated*, pp. 15-16.

                  Was NFL meeting a (yawn) waste? (1996, March 15; visited site February 12, 1997). *San Fran-*
              cisco Examiner. http://www.nando.net/newsroom/sports/fbo/1996/nfl/nfl/feat/archive/
              031596/nfl58946.html
                  Give full bibliographic citations. Here, APA format is used.

Figure 14.1   **Continued**

Laura J. Peterson   4   February 14, 1997

Weintraub, L. C. (1996, April 27). Panel approves preference in granting sports teams. *Congressional Quarterly Weekly Report*, p. 1169.

Wulf, S. (1995, December 11). Bad bounces for the N.F.L. *Time*, pp. 64-65.

Qualifications and Resources

Cite knowledge and skills from other classes, jobs, and activities that will will enable you to conduct the research under "Methods" and interpret your data.

As a student of marketing in the Max M. Fisher College of Business, I have done library research for other classes and am familiar with some of the reference materials available on marketing, demographics, and sports. As a native of Lackawanna, New York, I am familiar with the City of Buffalo and the Buffalo Bills franchise. I interned on *The Buffalo News* last summer and know the sports editor, so that I could phone if I need information not available in print or online. *Show you have access to the materials you'll need.*

Work Schedule

The following schedule will enable me to complete the report by the due date:

Activity	Total Time	Completion Date	
Gathering information	25 hours	February 21	*Time needed*
Analyzing information	16 hours	February 28	*will depend on*
Preparing the progress report	6 hours	March 15	*the length and*
Organizing information	9 hours	March 22	*topic of the*
Writing the draft	12 hours	March 29	*report, your*
Revising the draft	15 hours	April 5	*knowledge of*
Editing the draft	10 hours	April 10	*the topic, and*
Proofreading the report	4 hours	April 11	*your writing skills.*

Allow plenty of time!

Good reports need good revision, editing, and proofreading as well as good research.

Call to Action

Could we set up a conference to discuss my proposal? I would welcome any suggestions you may have for improving the research plan or making the report better. Please approve this proposal so that I can begin work on my report.

It's tactful to indicate you'll accept suggestions. End on a positive note.

Sales Proposals

To sell expensive goods or services, you may be asked to submit a proposal.

Be sure that you understand the buyer's priorities. A phone company lost a $36 million sale to a university because it assumed the university's priority would be cost. Instead, the university wanted a state-of-the-art system. The university accepted a higher bid.

Don't assume that the buyer will understand why your product or system is good. For everything you offer, show the reader benefits (⚹ p. 69) of each feature. Be sure to present the benefits using you-attitude (⚹ p. 34). Consider using psychological description (⚹ p. 223) to make the benefits vivid.

Use language appropriate for your audience. Even if the buyers want a state-of-the-art system, they may not want the level of detail that your staff could provide; they may not understand or appreciate technical jargon (⚹ p. 90).

Sales proposals, particularly for complicated systems costing millions of dollars, are often long. Provide a one-page cover letter to present your proposal succinctly. The best organization for this letter is a modified version of the sales pattern in Chapter 11:

1. Catch the reader's attention and summarize up to three major benefits you offer.
2. Discuss each of the major benefits in the order in which you mentioned them in the first paragraph.
3. Deal with any objections or concerns the reader may have.
4. Mention other benefits briefly.
5. Ask the reader to approve your proposal and provide a reason for acting promptly.

Proposals for Funding

If you need money for a new or continuing public service project, you may want to submit a proposal for funding to a foundation, a corporation, a government agency, or a religious agency. In a proposal for funding, stress the needs your project will meet and show how your project helps fulfill the goals of the organization you are asking for funds.

Every funding source has certain priorities; some have detailed lists of the kind of projects they fund. *The Foundation Directory* indexes foundations by state and city and by field of interest. *The Foundation Grants Index Annual* lists grants of $5,000 or more made by the 425 biggest foundations. Check recent awards to discover foundations that may be interested in your project. *Source Book Profiles* describes 1,000 national and regional foundations.

Progress Reports

When you're assigned to a single project that will take a month or more, you'll probably be asked to file one or more progress reports. A progress report reassures the funding agency or employer that you're making progress and allows you and the agency or employer to resolve problems as they arise. Different readers may have different concerns. An instructor may want to know whether you'll have your report in by the due date. A client may be more interested in what you're learning about the problem. Adapt your progress report to the needs of the audience.

Christine Barabas's study of the progress reports in a large research and development organization found that poor writers tended to focus on what

The Political Uses of Progress Reports

Progress reports can do more than just report progress. You can use progress reports to

■ Enhance your image. Details about the number of documents you've read, people you've surveyed, or experiments you've conducted create a picture of a hardworking person doing a thorough job.

■ Float trial balloons. Explain, "I could continue to do X [what you approved]; I could do Y instead [what I'd like to do now]." The detail in the progress report can help back up your claim. Even if the idea is rejected, you don't lose face because you haven't made a separate issue of the alternative.

■ Minimize potential problems. As you do the work, it may become clear that implementing your recommendations will be difficult. In your regular progress reports, you can alert your boss or the funding agency to the challenges that lie ahead, enabling them to prepare psychologically and physically to act on your recommendations.

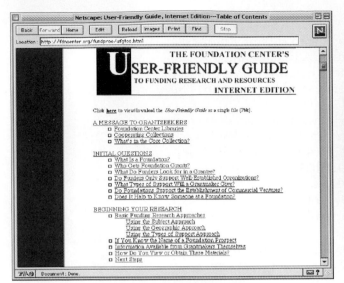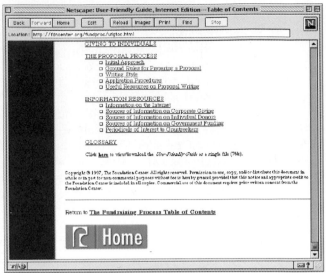

One of the most useful Web sites on writing proposals is The Foundation Center's *User-Friendly Guide to Funding Research and Resources* (http://fdncenter.org/fundproc/ufgtoc.html).

they had done and said very little about the value of their work. Good writers, in contrast, spent less space writing about the details of what they'd done but much more space explaining the value of their work for the organization.[3]

The following pattern of organization focuses on what you have done and what work remains.

1. **Summarize your progress in terms of your goals and your original schedule.** Use measurable statements.

   Poor: My progress has been slow.
   Better: The research for my report is about one-third complete.

2. **Under the heading "Work Completed," describe what you have already done.** Be specific, both to support your claims in the first paragraph and to allow the reader to appreciate your hard work. Acknowledge the people who have helped you. Describe any serious obstacles you've encountered and tell how you've dealt with them.

   Poor: I have found many articles about Procter & Gamble on the Web. I have had a few problems finding how the company keeps employees safe from chemical fumes.
   Better: On the Web, I found Procter & Gamble's home page, its annual report, and mission statement. No one whom I interviewed could tell me about safety programs specifically at P&G. I have found seven articles about ways to protect workers against pollution in factories, but none mentions P&G.

3. **Under the heading "Work to Be Completed," describe the work that remains.** If you're more than three days late (for school projects) or two weeks late (for business projects) submit a new schedule, showing how you will be able to meet the original deadline. You may want to discuss "Observations" or "Preliminary Conclusions" if you want feedback before writing the final report or if your reader has asked for substantive interim reports.

4. **Either express your confidence in having the report ready by the due date or request a conference to discuss extending the due date or limiting the project.** If you are behind your original schedule, show why you think you can still finish the project on time.

The student progress report in Figure 14.2 uses this pattern of organization. Subject lines for progress reports are straightforward. Specify the project on which you are reporting your progress.

> Subject: Progress on Developing a Marketing Plan for TCBY
> Subject: Progress on Group Survey on Campus Parking

If you are submitting weekly or monthly progress reports on a long project, number your progress reports or include the time period in your subject line. Include dates for the work completed since the last report and that to be completed before the next report.

Make your progress report as positive as you honestly can. You'll build a better image of yourself if you show that you can take minor problems in stride and that you're confident of your own abilities.

Negative: I have not deviated markedly from my schedule, and I feel that I will have very little trouble completing this report by the due date.

Positive: I am back on schedule and expect to complete my report by the due date.

RESEARCH STRATEGIES FOR REPORTS

Research for a report may be as simple as getting a computer printout of sales for the last month; it may involve finding published material or surveying or interviewing people. **Secondary research** retrieves information that someone else gathered. Library research and online searches are the best known kinds of secondary research. **Primary research** gathers new information. Observations, surveys, and interviews are common methods for gathering new information for business reports.

Finding Information Online and in Print

You can save time and money by checking online published sources of data before you gather new information. Many college and university libraries provide

- Workshops on research techniques.
- Handouts explaining how to use printed and computer-based sources.
- Free or inexpensive access to computer databases.
- Research librarians who can help you find and use sources.

Categories of sources that may be useful include

- Specialized encyclopedias for introductions to a topic (for example, *Kodansha Encyclopedia of Japan*).
- Indexes to find articles. Most permit searches by keyword, by author, and often by company name.
- Abstracts for brief descriptions or summaries of articles. Sometimes the abstract will be all you'll need; almost always, you can tell from the abstract whether an article is useful for your needs.
- Citation indexes to find materials that cite previous research. Citation indexes thus enable you to use an older reference to find newer articles on the topic. The *Social Sciences Citation Index* is the most useful for researching business topics.
- Newspapers for information about recent events.
- US Census reports, for a variety of business and demographic information.

Bermuda *Not* Onion

Searches on the Web can yield thousands, sometimes hundreds of thousands, matches. The computer just matches words. If you enter "Bermuda" as your search term, you'll get articles and pages about Bermuda onions as well as about the cruise market in Bermuda. "Bermuda *and* Travel" limits the search to articles with both the words *Bermuda* and *travel*. But maybe that's too narrow. What if the article uses the word *cruise* or *vacation* instead of *travel*? To capture those variations, use "Bermuda *and* (Cruise* *or* Vacation* *or* Travel)." The parentheses group the "or" items together to flag any one of them with *Bermuda*. The asterisks are wild card endings allowing for plurals and other forms. Some databases use different symbols for wild cards. Specify articles printed in the last two to three years (maybe even more recently, if your topic has been changing quickly). Then read the articles and pages the search finds. When one is relevant, copy or download it so that you can use it in your research.

Figure 14.2   **A Student Progress Report**

November 10, 1997

To: Kitty O. Locker

From: David G. Bunnel   *DGB*

Subject: Progress on CAD/CAM Software Feasibility Study for the Architecture Firm, Patrick
           and Associates, Inc.

*¶ 1:
Summarize
results in
terms of
purpose,
schedule.*

I have obtained most of the information necessary to recommend whether CADAM or CATIA is
better for Patrick and Associates, Inc. (P&A). I am currently analyzing and organizing this information and am on schedule.

*Underline Headings
or Bold.*

Work Completed

*Be very
specific
about
what
you've
done.*

To learn how computer literate P&A employees are, I interviewed a judgment sample of five
employees. My interview with Bruce Ratekin, the director of P&A's Computer-Aided Design
(CAD) Department on November 3 enabled me to determine the architectural drafting needs of
the firm. Mr. Ratekin also gave me a basic drawing of a building showing both two- and three-
dimensional views so that I could replicate the drawing with both software packages.

*Show how
you've
overcome
minor
problems.*

I obtained tutorials for both packages to use as a reference while making the drawings. First I
drew the building using CADAM, the package designed primarily for two-dimensional architectural drawings. I encountered problems with the isometric drawing because there was a mistake in the manual I was using; I fixed the problem by trying alternatives and finally getting help
from another CADAM user. Next, I used CATIA, the package whose strength is three-dimensional drawings, to construct the drawing. I am in the process of comparing the two packages
based on these criteria: quality of drawing, ease of data entry (lines, points, surfaces, etc.) for
computer experts and novices, and ease of making changes in the completed drawings. Based
on my experience with the packages, I have analyzed the training people with and without
experience in CAD would need to learn to use each of these packages.

Indicate changes in purpose, scope, or recommendations.

Work to Be Completed   *Progress report is a low-risk way to bring the readers on board.*

Making the drawings has shown that neither of the packages can do everything that P&A
needs. Therefore, I want to investigate the feasibility of P&A's buying both packages.

*Specify
the work
that
remains.*

As soon as he comes back from an unexpected illness that has kept him out of the office, I will
meet with Tom Merrick, the CAD systems programmer for The Ohio State University, to learn
about software expansion flexibility for both packages as well as the costs for initial purchase,
installation, maintenance, and software updates. After this meeting, I will be ready to begin the
first draft of my report.

Whether I am able to meet my deadline will depend on when I am able to meet with Mr. Merrick. Right now, I am on schedule and plan to submit my report by the December 1 deadline.

End on a positive note.

Figures 14.3 and 14.4 list a few of the hundreds of online and print sources. More and more resources are going online every month; by the time you read this book, additional online sources will exist. Do a Net search for items in print to see whether they're available.

To use a computer database efficiently, identify the concepts you're interested in and choose keywords that will help you find relevant sources. **Keywords** or **descriptors** are the terms that the computer searches for. If you're not sure what terms to use, check the *ABI/Inform Thesaurus* for synonyms and the hierarchies in which information is arranged in various databases.

Specific commands allow you to narrow your search. For example, to study the effect of the minimum wage on employment in the restaurant industry, you might specify the following:

(minimum wage) *and* (restaurant *or* fast food) *and*
(employment rate *or* unemployment).

This descriptor would give you the titles of articles that treat all three of the topics in parentheses. Without *and,* you'd get articles that discuss the minimum wage in general, articles about every aspect of *restaurants,* and every article that refers to *unemployment,* even though many of these would not be relevant to your topic. The *or* descriptor calls up articles that use the term *fast food* but not the term *restaurant.* An article that used the phrase *food service industry* would be eliminated unless it also used the term *restaurant.* Alta Vista and some other Web search engines allow you to specify words that cannot appear in a source.

Many words can appear in related forms. To catch all of them, use the database's **wild card** or **truncated code** for shortened terms and root words.

Observing Customers and Users

Watching people actually use your product can tell you whether a product, computer program, or documentation is well designed. Observation enables you to spot problems that people might forget by the time they were interviewed or suppress out of a desire to please the interviewer. Honda videotapes drivers as they test new cars. Advertising agency Foote, Cone & Belding sends researchers to bars, car dealers, and even funerals in a small town near Chicago to learn what makes small towns click.[4]

Observation can also be used for in-house research. A custom-machine-parts manufacturer in Danvers, Massachusetts, videotaped tool-setup processes at one milling work center. Management and work teams watched the tape, suggested changes in the processes, and were able to cut set-up time 14 to 20% throughout the work center.[5]

Observation is often combined with other techniques to get the most information. **Think-aloud protocols** ask users to voice their thoughts as they use a document or product: "First I'll try. . . ." These protocols are tape-recorded and later analyzed to understand how users approach a document or product. **Interruption interviews** interrupt users to ask them what's happening. For example, a company testing a draft of computer instructions might interrupt a user to ask, "What are you trying to do now? Tell me why you did that." **Discourse-based interviews** ask questions based on documents that the interviewee has written: "You said that the process is too complicated. Tell me what you mean by that."

Follow Me Home*

"Follow Me Home" is the official name of Intuit's program to observe new customers as they install and use its software. Sometimes the users get tape cassettes on which to record the problems they have.

Looking at how people actually use its products has sparked new product development. For instance, it became clear that small-business owners used Quicken—designed for personal use—for their small businesses. So Quick-books was developed.

*Based on Ronald B. Lieber, "Storytelling: A New Way to Get Closer to Your Customer," *Fortune,* February 3, 1997, 106.

Figure 14.3

Sources for Electronic Research

ABI/Inform (indexes and abstracts 800 journals in management and business)
AGRICOLA (CD-ROM version of *Agricultural Index*)
AIDSLINE
BioethicsLine
Biological and Agricultural Index
Black Studies on Disc
CINAHL (Nursing and Allied Health)
ComIndex (indexes and abstracts journals in communication, including *The Journal of Business Communication*)
Congressional Masterfile
Dun's Million Dollar Disc
EconLit
ERIC (research on education and teaching practices in the US and other countries)
Ethnic Newswatch
Foreign Trade and Economic Abstracts
GPO on SilverPlatter (Government Publications)
Handbook of Latin American Studies
Health Planning
HealthSTAR
Index to Legal Periodicals
Legis-Slate
LEXIS/NEXIS Services
A Matter of Fact
MEDLINE
Newspaper Abstracts
PAIS International—Public Affairs Information Service
Peterson's College Database
Peterson's Gradline
PsychINFO
PsychLIT
Social Sciences Index
Social Work Abstracts
Sociofile
SPORT Discus
Statistical Masterfile (statistics collected by the US government)
Telephone Directory (Business White Pages)
Telephone Directory (Residential White Pages)
Wilson Business Abstracts
Women's Resources International
World Wide Web Search Engines:
    Alta Vista: http://altavista.digital.com
    Open Text: http://index.opentext.net
    NLightN: http://www.nlightn.com   Free searches of the Web and 500 proprietary databases. (Most searchers that check databases charge a fee.)

Designing Questions for Surveys and Interviews

A **survey** questions a large group of people, called **respondents** or **subjects.** The easiest way to ask many questions is to create a **questionnaire,** a written list of questions that people fill out. An **interview** is a structured conversation with someone who will be able to give you useful information. Surveys and interviews can be useful only if the questions are well designed.

Good questions are phrased neutrally, avoid making assumptions about the respondent, and mean the same thing to different people.

Phrase questions in a way that won't bias the response. A state representative mailed out a survey to constituents with the question, "Do you think the Legislature should enact a cost-of-living raise for teachers?" He might have gotten a much less positive response if he had asked, "Would you be willing to pay higher taxes to fund a cost-of-living raise for teachers?" A *New York Times*/CBS News Poll used two different questions about abortion. A

Indexes:
  Accountants' Index
  Ageline (physical, psychological, economic, and political aspects of aging)
  Business Periodicals Index
  Canadian Business Index
  Family Resources
  Forestry Abstracts
  Hospital Literature Index
  Personnel Management Abstracts
  World Textile Abstracts
Facts, Figures, and Forecasts (also check the Web):
  Almanac of Business and Industrial Financial Ratios
  Cost-of-Living Indicators
  Moody's Manuals
  Predicasts
  The Statistical Abstract of the US
  Trades and Securities Statistics
  The Value Line Investment Survey
US Census Reports (also available on the Web):
  Census of Population
  Census of Manufacturers
  Census of Wholesale Trade
  Census of Retail Trade
  Census of Service Industries
Directories (facts about organizations, including the names of officers and directors; more
  up-to-date information may be available on the Web):
  Directory of American Firms Operating in Foreign Countries
  Dun & Bradstreet's *Reference Book of Corporate Managements*
  Dun's Employment Opportunities Directory
  National Directory of Minority-Owned Business Firms
  Poor's Register of Corporations, Directors, and Executives
  Thomas' Register of American Manufacturers
International Business and Government
  Canada Year Book
  Dun and Bradstreet's *Principal International Businesses*
  European Marketing Data and Statistics
  Price, Waterhouse's *Guide to Doing Business in [Name of Country]*
  Statistical Yearbook of the United Nations
  Who Owns Whom: Continental Europe

Figure 14.4

Print Sources for Research

majority opposed "a constitutional amendment prohibiting abortions." But about 20% of the sample changed their answer when presented with a more emotionally charged question: "Should there be a constitutional amendment protecting the life of the unborn child?"[6]

Avoid questions that make assumptions about your subjects. The question "Does your wife have a job outside the home?" assumes that your respondent is a married man.

Use words that mean the same thing to you and to the respondents. If a question can be interpreted in more than one way, it will be. Words like *often* and *important* mean different things to different people. Whenever possible, use more objective measures:

Vague: Do you study in the library frequently?
Better: How many hours a week do you study in the library?

Even questions that call for objective information can be confusing. For example, consider the owner of a small business confronted with the question: "How many employees do you have?" Does the number include the owner as well as subordinates? Does it include both full- and part-time employees? Does it include people who have been hired but who haven't yet started work, or someone who is leaving at the end of the month? A better wording would be

> How many full-time employees were on your payroll the week of May 16?

Bypassing occurs when two people use the same symbol but interpret it differently. To reduce bypassing,

1. Train your observers. Decide on definitions in advance; do some practice coding to allow observers to apply the definitions.
2. Avoid terms that are likely to mean different things to different people.
3. Pretest your questions with several people who are like those who will fill out the survey to catch questions that can be misunderstood. Even a small pretest with 10 people can help you refine your questions.

Questions can be categorized in several ways.

Closed questions have a limited number of possible responses. **Open questions** do not lock the subject into any sort of response. Figure 14.5 gives examples of closed and open questions. Closed questions are faster for subjects to answer and easier for researchers to score. However, since all answers must fit into prechosen categories, they cannot probe the complexities of a subject. You can improve the quality of closed questions by conducting a pretest with open questions to find categories that matter to respondents.

Use an "Other, Please Specify" category when you want the convenience of a closed question but cannot foresee all the possible responses:

> What is the single most important reason that you ride the bus?
> _____ I don't have a car.
> _____ I don't want to fight rush-hour traffic.
> _____ Riding the bus is cheaper than driving my car.
> _____ Riding the bus conserves fuel and reduces pollution.
> _____ Other (Please specify) _____

When you use multiple-choice questions, make sure that any one answer fits only in one category. In the following example of overlapping categories, a person who worked for a company with exactly 25 employees could check either *a* or *b*. The resulting data would be unreliable.

Overlapping
categories:

> Indicate the number of full-time employees in your company on May 16:
> ___ a. 0–25
> ___ b. 25–100
> ___ c. 100–500
> ___ d. over 500

Discrete
categories:

> Indicate the number of full-time employees on your payroll on May 16:
> ___ a. 0–25
> ___ b. 26–100
> ___ c. 101–500
> ___ d. over 500

Branching questions direct different respondents to different parts of the questionnaire based on their answers to earlier questions.

> 10. Have you talked to an academic advisor this year?   yes   no
>   (If "no," skip to question 14.)

Closed Questions

Are you satisfied with the city bus service? (yes/no)

How good is the city bus service?
   Excellent 5 4 3 2 1 Terrible

Indicate whether you agree or disagree with each of the following statements about city bus service:
   A   D   The schedule is convenient for me.
   A   D   The routes are convenient for me.
   A   D   The drivers are courteous.
   A   D   The buses are clean.

Rate each of the following improvements in the order of their importance to you (1 = most important, 6 = least important)
_____Buy new buses.
_____Increase non-rush-hour service on weekdays.
_____Increase service on weekdays.
_____Provide earlier and later service on weekdays.
_____Buy more buses with wheelchair access.
_____Provide unlimited free transfers.

Open Questions

How do you feel about the city bus service?

Tell me about the city bus service.

Why do you ride the bus? (or, Why don't you ride the bus?)

What do you like and dislike about the city bus service?

How could the city bus service be improved?

Figure 14.5

Closed and Open Questions

Use closed multiple-choice questions for potentially embarrassing topics. Seeing their own situation listed as one response can help respondents feel that it is acceptable. However, very sensitive issues are perhaps better asked in an interview, where the interviewer can build trust and reveal information about himself or herself to encourage the interviewee to answer.

Generally, put early in the questionnaire questions that will be easy to answer. Put questions that are harder to answer or that people may be less willing to answer (e.g., age and income) near the end of the questionnaire. Even if people choose not to answer such questions, you'll still have the rest of the survey filled out.

If subjects will fill out the questionnaire themselves, pay careful attention to the physical design of the document. Use indentations and white space effectively; make it easy to mark and score the answers. Include a brief statement of purpose if you (or someone else) will not be available to explain the questionnaire or answer questions. Pretest the questionnaire to make sure the directions are clear. One researcher mailed a two-page questionnaire without pretesting it. Twenty-five respondents didn't answer the questions on the back of the first page.[7]

C. Britt Beamer's research showed that people bought upscale furniture not because they made a lot of money but because they entertained guests in their homes. Beamer's research suggests that *Gourmet* or *Bon Appétit* would be better places to advertise than *Architectural Digest*. (Courtesy Plunkett's Furniture).

Conducting Surveys and Interviews

Face-to-face surveys are convenient when you are surveying a fairly small number of people in a specific location. In a face-to-face survey, the interviewer's sex, race, and nonverbal cues can bias results. Most people prefer not to say things they think their audience will find unacceptable. For that reason, women will be more likely to agree that sexual harassment is a problem if the interviewer is also a woman. Members of a minority group are more likely to admit that they suffer discrimination if the interviewer is a member of the same minority.

Telephone surveys are popular because they can be closely supervised. Interviewers can read the questions from a computer screen and key in answers as the respondent gives them. The results can then be available just a few minutes after the last call is completed.

The major limitation of phone surveys is that they reach only people who have phones and thus underrepresent poor people. Other limitations can be avoided with good designs. Since a survey based on a phone book would exclude people with unlisted numbers, professional survey-takers use automatic random-digit dialing. Since women are more likely to answer the phone than men are,[8] decide in advance to whom you want to speak, and ask for that person rather than surveying whoever answers the phone.

To increase the response rate for a phone survey, call at a time respondents will find convenient. Avoid calling between 5 and 7 PM, a time when many families have dinner.

Mail surveys can reach anyone who has an address. Some people may be more willing to fill out an anonymous questionnaire than to give sensitive information to a stranger over the phone. However, mail surveys are not effective for respondents who don't read and write well. Further, it may be more difficult to get a response from someone who is reluctant to participate. Over the phone, the interviewer can try to persuade the subject and overcome his or her objections.

A major concern with any kind of survey is the **response rate,** the percentage of people who respond. A total response rate of 80% or higher is desirable,[9] since people who refuse to answer may differ from those who respond quickly, and you need information from both groups to be able to generalize to the whole population. However, given the current cynicism about surveys, an 80% response rate is almost impossible to get. In 1992, 31% of people surveyed in the United States refused to participate at least once.[10] Professional pollsters report that 25 to 30% of the people they call refuse to participate in political polls.[11] Even the Census Bureau gets a 5% refusal rate when it conducts its monthly Current Population survey.[12] To get as high a response rate as possible, good researchers follow up, contacting nonrespondents at least once and preferably twice to try to persuade them to participate in the survey.

Selecting a Sample for Surveys and Interviews

To keep research costs reasonable, only a sample of the total population is polled. How that sample is chosen and the attempts made to get responses from nonrespondents will determine whether you can infer that what is true of your sample is also true of the population as a whole. The **population** is the group you want to make statements about. Depending on the purpose of your research, your population might be all Fortune 1000 companies, all business students at your college, or all consumers.

A **convenience sample** is a group of subjects who are easy to get: students who walk through the union, people at a shopping mall, workers in your own unit. Convenience samples are useful for a rough pretest of a questionnaire. However, you cannot generalize from a convenience sample to a larger group.

A **judgment sample** is a group of people whose views seem useful. Someone interested in surveying the kinds of writing done on campus might ask each department for the name of a faculty member who cared about writing, and then send surveys to those people.

In a **random sample,** each person in the population theoretically has an equal chance of being chosen. When people say they did something *randomly* they often mean *without conscious bias*. However, unconscious bias exists. Someone passing out surveys in front of the library will be more likely to

Who Tallies That Survey?*

When we think about information and privacy, we usually think about how a company will use the information we've provided. But sometimes the person who tallies the survey puts the respondent at risk.

One woman filled out a questionnaire that promised she'd receive free product samples for her time and answers about products she used. What the instructions didn't say was that prison inmates were hired to enter the data.

The woman got a 12-page letter from a man imprisoned for rape; the letter referred to the magazines she liked, the fact that she was divorced, and her birthday. The letter spun sexual fantasies involving the products she used.

That company says it no longer uses inmates to tally surveys. But inmates in more than a dozen states routinely process data, answer 800 numbers, and even work as telemarketers.

*Based on James P. Miller, "Privacy Issue Raised in Direct-Mail Case," *The Wall Street Journal*, May 6, 1996, B8.

Affordable Research on Foreign Markets*

A small company interested in exporting products needs inexpensive research. Akihisa Kumayama and Steuart Henderson Britt suggest the following ways to get information cheaply:

■ Use foreign nationals in your city. Take a focus group to a good restaurant and let them discuss your proposal there.

■ Talk to people in government and journalism in another country about laws, competition, the general readiness for a certain product.

■ If you plan to introduce an industrial product in foreign countries, get small samples of knowledgeable people in each country rather than a large sample from only two or three countries.

*Based on Akihisa Kumayama, "Creating a Course Combining Marketing, Language, and Cross-Cultural Communication with Japanese and American Cultures as a Model," Languages and Communication for World Business and the Professions, Sixth Annual Conference, Ann Arbor, MI, May 8–9, 1987, and Steuart Henderson Britt, quoted in Robert A. Roth, *International Marketing Communications* (Chicago: Crain, 1982), 26–27.

approach people who seem friendly and less likely to ask people who seem intimidating, in a hurry, much older or younger, or of a different race, class, or sex. True random samples rely on random digit tables, published in statistics texts and books such as *A Million Random Digits.* Computers can also be programmed to generate random numbers. If you take a true random sample, you can generalize your findings to the whole population from which your sample comes. For example, a random phone survey that shows that 65% of the respondents approve of a presidential policy may be accurate ± 7%. That is, in the population as a whole, between 58% and 72% approve the policy. The accuracy range is based on the size of the sample and the expected variation within the population. Statistics texts tell you how to calculate these figures.

A **simple random sample** requires that you have a list of all the members in your population. To take a simple random sample,

1. Number the list of all the members of a population.
2. Use a random digit table to select the members for the sample. Continue until you have the size sample you need.
3. Ignore numbers in the random digit table that have already been chosen or that are higher than the total number in the population.

A **systematic random sample** requires only that you have a list, such as a phone book or a student directory, even if the list is incomplete. A systematic random sample is much faster because it allows you to create a **template,** or pattern, which you apply to a systematic sample of pages. Figure 14.6 shows one template. To take a systematic random sample,

1. Take a systematic sample of the pages in the book.
   a. Count or estimate the number of lines on each page that will not contain eligible names. (For example, the staff directory may have a new name every third line. In addition, some of the listings will be out of date.) Add that number to the sample size you want. You now have the total number of lines you need.
   b. Divide this total into the number of pages. You now have an interval. If for example, your interval is 5, you will take every fifth page.
   c. Use a random digit table to choose the starting page between one and the interval. Use the starting page and every interval page after that. For example, if your starting page is 2 and the interval is 5, you would use pages 2, 7, 12, 17, etc.
2. Take a systematic sample of items on a page. Use a random digit table to choose a number for the column and a number for the line in that column.
3. Make a template of the location of the random column and line, and use it on every page identified in (1c).
4. If the template hits an ineligible line, go on to the next page interval—not the next item on that page.

A **random cluster sample** allows you to take a random sample of locations and a random sample within each location. This method reduces the time and money needed to survey. To take a random cluster sample,

1. Identify the geographic locations where subjects may be found.
2. If the locations differ in important ways, group them and determine approximately what proportion of subjects may be found in each group. Plan to take 1/5 to 1/20 of your sample at each location. Use more locations when you expect differences among the locations.
3. Take a simple random sample *of the locations.* If the locations are very different, take a simple random sample of *each* group.
4. Sample the number of people you need at each location.

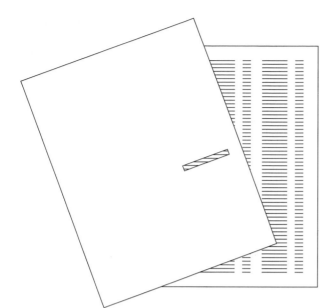

Figure 14.6

A Template for a Systematic Random Sample

A **stratified random sample** builds on your knowledge of the makeup of your overall population. For example, if you know that 17% of the students at your college are older than 28, then 17% of your sample would be students older than 28. Choose the categories, or **strata,** based on the characteristics that are important for your survey. Depending on the survey's purposes, strata might be year in school, occupation, number of employees, or number of years in business. To take a stratified random sample,

1. Calculate the percentage of the population that is in each strata, or division, within the population.
2. Divide the sample size into the same percentages.
3. Within each strata, sample the appropriate number of people.

Conducting Research Interviews

Schedule interviews in advance; tell the interviewee about how long you expect the interview to take. A survey of technical writers (who get much of their information from interviews) found that the best times to interview subject-matter experts are Tuesday, Wednesday, and Thursday mornings.[13]

Interviews can be structured or unstructured. In a **structured interview,** the interviewer uses a detailed list of questions to guide the interview. Indeed, a structured interview may use a questionnaire just as a survey does. In an **unstructured interview,** the interviewer has three or four main questions. Other questions build on what the interviewee says. To prepare for an unstructured interview, learn as much as possible about the interviewee and the topic. Go into the interview with three or four main topics you want to cover.

Interviewers sometimes use closed questions to start the interview and set the interviewee at ease. The strength of an interview, however, is getting at a person's attitudes, feelings, and experiences. Situational questions let you probe what someone would do in a specific circumstance. Hypothetical questions that ask people to imagine what they would do generally yield less reliable answers than questions about **critical incidents** or key past events.

Hypothetical question: What would you say if you had to tell an employee that his or her performance was unsatisfactory?

Ethical Issues in Interviewing

If you're trying to get sensitive information, interviewees may give useful information when the interview is "over" and the tape recorder has been turned off. Is it ethical to use that information?

If you're interviewing a hostile or very reluctant interviewee, you may get more information if you agree with everything you can legitimately agree to, and keep silent on the rest. Is it ethical to imply acceptance even when you know you'll criticize the interviewee's ideas in your report?

Most people would say that whatever public figures say is fair game: they're supposed to know enough to defend themselves. Many people would say that different rules apply when you'll cite someone by name than when you'll use the information as background or use a pseudonym so that the interviewee cannot be identified.

As a practical matter, if someone feels you've misrepresented him or her, that person will be less willing to talk to you in the future. But quite apart from practical considerations, interview strategies raise ethical issues as well.

Critical incident question:	You've probably been in a situation where someone who was working with you wasn't carrying his or her share of the work. What did you do the last time that happened?

A **mirror question** paraphrases the content of the last answer: "So you confronted him directly." "You think that this product costs too much." Mirror questions are used both to check that the interviewer understands what the interviewee has said and to prompt the interviewee to continue talking. **Probes** follow up an original question to get at specific aspects of a topic:

Question:	What do you think about the fees for campus parking?
Probes:	Would you be willing to pay more for a reserved space? How much more?
	Should the fines for vehicles parked illegally be increased?
	Do you think fees should be based on income?

Probes are not used in any definite order. Instead, they are used to keep the interviewee talking, to get at aspects of a subject that the interviewee has not yet mentioned, and to probe more deeply into points that the interviewee brings up.

If you read questions to subjects in a structured interview, use fewer options than you might in a written questionnaire.

> I'm going to read a list of factors that someone might look for in choosing a restaurant. After I read each factor, please tell me whether that factor is Very Important to you, Somewhat Important to you, or Not Important to you.

If the interviewee hesitates, reread the scale.

Always tape the interview. Test your equipment ahead of time to make sure it works. If you think your interviewee may be reluctant to speak on tape, take along two tapes and two recorders; offer to give one tape to the interviewee.[14]

Pulitzer Prize-winner Nan Robertson offers the following advice to interviewers:[15]

- Do your homework. Learn about the subject and the person before the interview.
- To set a nervous interviewee at ease, start with nuts-and-bolts questions, even if you already know the answers.
- Save controversial questions for the end. You'll have everything else you need, and the trust built up in the interview makes an answer more likely.
- Go into an interview with three or four major questions. Listen to what the interviewee says and let the conversation flow naturally.
- At the end of the interview, ask for office and home telephone numbers in case you need to ask an additional question when you write up the interview.

USING AND DOCUMENTING SOURCES

In a good report, sources are cited and documented smoothly and unobtrusively. **Citation** means attributing an idea or fact to its source **in the body of the report.** "According to the 1990 Census...." "Jane Bryant Quinn argues that...." Citing sources demonstrates your honesty and enhances your credibility. **Documentation** means providing the bibliographic information readers would need to go back to the original source. The two usual means of documentation are notes and lists of References.

Note that citation and documentation are used in addition to quotation marks. If you use the source's exact words, you'll use the name of the person you're citing and quotation marks in the body of the report; you'll indicate the source in parentheses and a list of References or in a footnote or endnote. If you put the source's idea into your own words, or if you condense or synthesize information, you don't need quotation marks, but you still need to tell whose idea it is and where you found it.

Long quotations (four typed lines or more) are used sparingly in business reports. Since many readers skip quotes, always summarize the main point of the quotation in a single sentence before the quotation itself. End the sentence with a colon, not a period, since it introduces the quote. Indent long quotations on the left and right to set them off from your text. Indented quotations do not need quotation marks; the indentation shows the reader that the passage is a quote.

You may want to interrupt a quotation to analyze, clarify, or question it.

To make a quotation fit the grammar of your report, you may need to change one or two words. Sometimes you may want to add a few words to explain something in the longer original. In both cases, use square brackets to indicate words that are your replacements or additions. Omit any words in the original source that are not essential for your purposes. Use ellipses (spaced dots) to indicate where your omissions are.

Document every fact and idea that you take from a source except facts that are common knowledge. Historical dates and facts are considered common knowledge. Generalizations are considered common knowledge ("More and more women are entering the work force") even though specific statements about the same topic (such as the percentage of women in the work force in 1965 and in 1995) would require documentation.

The three most widely used formats for footnotes, endnotes, and bibliographies in reports are those of the American Psychological Association (APA), the Modern Language Association (MLA), and the University of Chicago *Manual of Style* format, which this book uses. The APA format uses internal documentation with a list of references; it does not use footnotes or endnotes. **Internal documentation** provides the work and the page number where the reference was found in parentheses in the text. The work may be indicated by the author's last name (if that isn't already in the sentence), by the last name plus the date of the work (if you're using two or more works by the same author, or if the dates of the works are important). The full bibliographical citation appears in a List of References or Works Cited at the end of the report. Figure 14.7 shows two paragraphs from a report using APA format and the matching part of the Works Cited. Figure 14.8 shows the APA and MLA formats for books, government documents, journal and newspaper articles, online sources, and interviews.

If you have used many sources that you have not cited, you may want to list both *Works Cited* and *Works Consulted*. Or you can use the term *Bibliography*, which covers all sources on a topic.

If you use a printed source that is not readily available, consider including it as an appendix in your report. For example, you could copy an ad or include an organization's promotional brochure.

SUMMARY OF KEY POINTS

- **Information reports** collect data for the reader; **analytical reports** present and interpret data; **recommendation reports** recommend action or a solution.
- A good purpose statement must make three things clear:

Market Research Creates an Ad Campaign*

[The tiny company that made Boker knives was considering dropping the brand. But before making the decision, executives and ad agency personnel talked to current and potential customers: people who hunt and fish.]

They knew they were onto something when they ran into a longtime Boker customer who told them what he liked about the knife. He said that whenever he wants to make French fries, he just opens his Boker, puts it in the glove box of his four-by-four pickup with a bunch of potatoes, and drives over a rocky road in second gear. He added, "Of course, for hash browns I use third gear."

As they began to collect stories like this, others poured in. The agency ran a print campaign featuring fanciful pictures of old-time Boker users. The title of the ad ran: IN EVERY LIE ABOUT THE BOKER THERE'S A LITTLE BIT OF TRUTH. The ads recounted the tall tales, which guaranteed high readership. Then the ads told the serious part of the Boker message. Within a year, both market share and profits had doubled.

*Quoted from Robert H. Waterman, *The Renewal Factor* (Toronto: Bantam, 1987), 163.

Figure 14.7   **Report Paragraphs with APA Documentation**

Author and date in parenthesis.

    The main cause of indoor air pollution is inadequate ventilation. The U.S. National Institute of Occupational Safety and Health found that poor ventilation caused problems in 52% of the 450 buildings studied (Moretz, 1988). Health Welfare Canada found that 68% of the 94 buildings it studied had problems with ventilation (Sterling, 1987). Inadequate ventilation can be caused by too little fresh air or by the way the ventilation system recycles air.

All material from citation to parenthesis is from a single source.

    During the 1970s, Robert B. Holtom notes, many buildings were built "with sealed windows, over-insulated roofs and closed air-intake ducts" to save energy. "As a result, in many office buildings, air is recirculated without adequate dilution by fresh air" (1990, p. 66). The American Society of Heating, Refrigeration, and Air-Conditioning Engineers recommends that a building's heating, ventilation, and cooling system deliver 20 cubic feet per minute of outside air for each occupant (White, 1990).

Use page number for quotation.

    Even if a building gets enough outside air, problems may arise from the way the system is used. Systems shut down for the weekend allow microorganisms to grow in the dust and organic matter in filters and ducts. When the system is turned on Monday morning, the microorganisms are, in Sandy Moretz's words, "blown all over the building" (1988, p. 62).

Square brackets indicate a change from the original.

    Stuart E. Salot, a certified industrial hygienist, advises companies not only to improve ventilation, ban smoking, and add plants but also to "[e]mpower complainants" by taking their complaints seriously (Wojcik, 1993, p. 29).

Here, sense of the paragraph requires a lower-case "e" since a capital letter was used in the original, brackets as needed.

Includes all works quoted and paraphrased.

References

Holtom, R. B. (1990, Jan.). Underwriting update--Seeking the SBS cure. Best's
    Review, 64-66, 83.

List source only once, even when used more than once.

Moretz, S. (1988, Feb.). Are your workers safe from sick building syndrome?
    Occupational Hazards, 58-62.

Sterling, T. D., Collett, C. W., and Sterling, E. M. , (1987). Environmental
    tobacco smoke and indoor air quality in modern office work environments.
    Journal of Occupational Medicine, 29(1), 57-62.

White, F. A. (1990, Summer). Indoor air quality: What managers can do.
    Employee Relations Today, 93-101.

Wojcik, J. (1993, Sept.) Indoor air quality causing headaches. Business
    Insurance, 13, 28-29.

List sources alphabetically.

APA and MLA Formats for Documenting Sources   **Figure 14.8**

APA

APA internal documentation gives the author's last name and the date of the work in parentheses in the text. A comma separates the author's name from the date (Cross, 1994). The page number is given only for direct quotations (Thomas, 1997, p. 62). If the author's name is used in the sentence, only the date is given in parentheses. (See Figure 14.7.) A list of REFERENCES gives the full bibliographic citation, arranging the entries alphabetically by the author's last name.

Initials only.

In titles of books and articles, capitalize only
(1) first word
(2) first word of subtitle
(3) proper nouns.

Book

Year. Period outside parenthesis.

    Cross, G. A. (1994). Collaboration and conflict: A contextual
exploration of group writing and positive emphasis. Cresskill, NJ:
Hampton Press.

Book or Pamphlet with a Corporate Author

When information is known to you but not printed in document, put in square brackets.

    Citibank. (1994). Indonesia: An investment guide. [Jakarta]:Author.

Indicates organization authoring document also publishes it.

Indent entries 5 spaces or .4".

Government Document

    House Committee on Interior and Insular Affairs. (1979). Accident
at Three Mile Island nuclear powerplant (H441-18 and H441-26).
Washington, DC: US Government Printing Office.

Article in an Edited Book   *No quotes around title of article.*

Editors before book title.

    Burnett, R. E. (1993). Conflict in collaborative decision-making.
In Nancy Roundy Blyler and Charlotte Thralls (Eds). Professional com-
munication: The social perspective (pp. 144-62). Newbury Park, CA:
Sage.

Underline or italicize book and journal titles.

Italicize or underline volume also!

Article in a Periodical

In titles of journals, magazines, and newspapers, capitalize all main words.

    Thomas, J. (1997). Discourse in the marketplace: The making of
meaning in annual reports. The Journal of Business Communication, 33
(1), 47-66.   *No "pp." when journal has volume number.*

    Kaufman, J. & Markels, A. (1996, November 18). Blacks, whites
differ on lesson of Texaco tape. The Wall Street Journal, pp. B1, B3.

"p." or "pp." for newspapers and magazines without volume number.

Article from an Electronic Database

    Atre, T., Auns, K., Badenhausen, K., McAuliffe, K., Nikolov, C., &
Ozanian, M. K. (1996, May 20). Sports stocks and bonds. Financial
World, p. 53 (11). General Reference Center Gold (GPIP). *Name of database.*

Page article begins on.   Number of pages in article.

Interview Conducted by the Researcher

    Lamela, L. E. (1994, March 8). [Interview conducted by the writer.]

Year comma date.

Figure 14.8   **Continued**

Give author and author's
e-mail address, if known. Can
put addressess in angle brackets <>.   *Subject line*
of posting.

E-Mail Message
    Locker, K. O. locker.1@osu.edu. (1997, April 3). Reschedule call for next week.
    [Personal e-mail.] ⟵ *Use for a private message to one person.*

    Locker, K. O. locker.1@osu.edu. (1997, April 2). Proposed JBC procedures. [E-mail to
ABC Publication Board and JBC Associate Editors].
                Indicate distribution list for organizational messages.

Last name
first for
all authors.   Listserv Message
    Lessig, L., Post, D., Volokh, E., & the Cyberspace Law Institute and Counsel Connect.
(1996, May 3). Cyberspace law for nonlawyers (fwd). H-Net History of Rhetoric <u>Discussion</u>
Date of   Group. <u>h-rhetor@mus.edu</u> (1996, May 6).   *Name of*
original   *E-mail address*   *Date of forwarded posting.*   *listserv.*
posting.   *of listserv.*

World Wide Web Site *Creation/update; date of visit to site.*
    Will, G. (<u>n.d.</u>; visited site October 14, 1996). Archeus: Resume writing resources.
http://www.golden.net/~archeus.reswri.htm
           URL. Can put in angle brackets <>.

MLA

  MLA internal documentation gives the author's last name and page number in parentheses in
the text. Unlike APA, the year is not given, and no comma separates the name and page
number (Thomas 62). If the author's name is used in the sentence, only the page number is
given in parentheses. A list of WORKS CITED gives the full bibliographic citation, arranging
the entries alphabetically by the author's last name.

      Comma.   *Period.*
Book
In titles   Cross, Geoffrey A. <u>Collaboration and Conflict: A Contextual</u> *Include state*
of books,   *when city is not*
journals,   <u>Exploration of Group Writing and Positive Emphasis</u>. Cresskill, *well known.*
articles, &   NJ: Hampton, 1994.
periodicals,   *City colon publisher comma date.*
capitalize
first word Book or Pamphlet with a Corporate Author
and all   Citibank. <u>Indonesia: An Investment Guide</u>. [Jakarta:] Citibank, 1994.
major words.
                 Square brackets for
                 information you supply.

Government Document
    United States. House Committee on Interior and Insular Affairs.
        Accident at Three Mile Island Nuclear Powerplant. 2 vols.
        Washington: GPO, 1979.

Use Article from an Edited Book *Title of article in quotation marks.*
hanging   Burnett, Rebecca E. "Conflict in Collaborative Decision-Making."
indents: <u>Professional Communication: The Social Perspective</u>. Ed.
indent carry-over   Nancy Roundy Blyler and Charlotte Thralls. Newbury Park, CA:
lines 5 spaces   Sage, 1993. 144-62.
or .4".

Concluded   **Figure 14.8**

Title of article in quotation marks.

Article in a Periodical
  Thomas, Jane. "Discourse in the Marketplace: The Making of Meaning
      in Annual Reports." The Journal of Business Communication 34.1
      (1997): 47-66. *Colon space page numbers.*

  Kaufman, Jonathan and Alex Markels. "Blacks, Whites Differ on
      Lesson of Texaco Tape." The Wall Street Journal, November 18,
      1996, B1, B3. *"pp." not used.*

*Italicize
or underline
title of
journal,*   Article from an Electronic Database
newspaper,   Atre, Tushar, Kristine Auns, Kurt Badenhausen, Kevin McAuliffe,
or magazine.   Christopher Nikolov, and Michael K. Ozanian. "Sports Stocks
      and Bonds." Financial World, 53 (11). General Reference Center
      Gold (GPIP).
                Starting page.   *Number of pages in text.*

Interview Conducted by the Researcher
  Lamela, Luis E. Personal interview. 8 Mar. 1994.

            Can put e-mail address
            in angle brackets <>.   *Subject line in quotations.*
E-Mail Message
  Locker, Kitty O. locker.1@osu.edu. "Reschedule Call for Next Week."
      Personal e-mail. (April 3, 1997).

  Locker, Kitty O. locker.1@osu.edu. "Proposed JBC Procedures." E-mail
      to ABC Publication Board and JBC Associate Editors. (April 2,
      1997).

            Use first name first for second and
            subsequent authors.
Listserv Message
  Lessig, Larry, David Post, Eugene Volokh, and the Cyberspace Law
      Institute and Counsel Connect. "Cyberspace Law for Nonlawyers (fwd)."
      H-Net History of Rhetoric Discussion Group. h-rhetor@mus.edu (May 6,
      1996).   *Name of listserv.*   *E-mail address of listserve.*

World Wide Web Site   *Title of site in quotation marks.*
  Will, Gary. "Archeus: Resume Writing Resources." http://www.golden.
      net/~archeus.reswri.htm (n.d.; visited site October 14, 1996).
    Can put URL   *Date you visited*
in angle brackets <>.   *Date site*   *the site.*
                        created or
                        revised or revised
                        [n.d. = no date given].

- The organizational problem or conflict.
- The specific technical questions that must be answered to solve the problem.
- The rhetorical purpose (to explain, to recommend, to request, to propose) that the report is designed to achieve.
- A proposal must answer the following questions:
  - What problem are you going to solve?
  - How are you going to solve it?
  - What exactly will you provide for us?
  - Can you deliver what you promise?
  - When will you complete the work?
  - How much will you charge?
- In a proposal for a class research project, prove that your problem is the right size, that you understand it, that your method will give you the information you need to solve the problem, and that you have the knowledge and resources.
- Use the following pattern of organization for the cover letter for a sales proposal.
  1. Catch the reader's attention and summarize up to three major benefits you offer.
  2. Discuss each of the major benefits in the order in which you mentioned them in the first paragraph.
  3. Deal with any objections or concerns the reader may have.
  4. Mention other benefits briefly.
  5. Ask the reader to approve your proposal and provide a reason for acting promptly.
- In a proposal for funding, stress the needs your project will meet. Show how your project will help fulfill the goals of the organization you are asking for funds.
- To focus on what you have done and what work remains, organize a progress report in this way:
  1. Summarize your progress in terms of your goals and your original schedule.
  2. Under the heading "Work Completed," describe what you have already done.
  3. Under the heading "Work to Be Completed," describe the work that remains.
  4. Either express your confidence in having the report ready by the due date or request a conference to discuss extending the due date or limiting the project.
- Use positive emphasis in progress reports to create an image of yourself as a capable, confident worker.
- Use indexes and directories to find information about a specific company or topic.
- A **survey** questions a large group of people, called **respondents** or **subjects.** A **questionnaire** is a written list of questions that people fill out. An **interview** is a structured conversation with someone who will be able to give you useful information.
- Good questions are phrased neutrally, avoid making assumptions about the respondent, and mean the same thing to different people.
- **Closed questions** have a limited number of possible responses. **Open questions** do not lock the subject into any sort of response. **Branching questions** direct different respondents to different parts of the questionnaire based on their answers to earlier questions. A **mirror question** paraphrases the content of the last answer. **Probes** follow up an original question to get at specific aspects of a topic.

- Good researchers attempt to reach nonrespondents at least once and preferably twice.
- A **convenience sample** is a group of subjects who are easy to get. A **judgment sample** is a group of people whose views seem useful. In a **random sample,** each person in the population theoretically has an equal chance of being chosen. Varieties of random samples include **simple, systematic, cluster,** and **stratified random samples.** Only in a random sample is the researcher justified in inferring that the results from the sample are also true of the population from which the sample comes.
- **Citation** means attributing an idea or fact to its source in the body of the report. **Documentation** means providing the bibliographic information readers would need to go back to the original source.

Exercises and Problems
For Chapter 14

GETTING STARTED

14−1   Identifying the Weaknesses in Problem Statements _____

Identify the weaknesses in the following problem statements.

- Is the problem narrow enough?
- Can a solution be found in a semester or quarter?
- What organization could implement any recommendations to solve the problem?
- Could the topic be limited or refocused to yield an acceptable problem statement?

1. One possible report topic I would like to investigate would be the differences in women's intercollegiate sports in our athletic conference.
2. How to market products effectively to college students.
3. Should Web banners be part of a company's advertising?
4. How can United States and Canadian students get jobs in Europe?
5. We want to explore ways our company can help raise funds for the Open Shelter. We will investigate whether collecting and recycling glass, aluminum, and paper products will raise enough money to help.
6. How can XYZ university better serve students from traditionally underrepresented groups?
7. What are the best investments for the next year?

14−2   Writing a Preliminary Purpose Statement _____

Answer the following questions about a topic on which you could write a formal report. (See Problems 15−4, 15−5, 15−7, 15−8, 15−10, and 15−11.)

As Your Instructor Directs,
   a. Be prepared to answer the questions orally in a conference.
   b. Bring written answers to a conference.
   c. Submit written answers in class.
   d. Give your instructor a photocopy of your statement after it is approved.

1. What problem will you investigate or solve?
   a. What is the name of the organization facing the problem?
   b. What is the technical problem or difficulty?
   c. Why is it important to the organization that this problem be solved?
   d. What solution or action might you recommend to solve the problem?

e. List the name and title of the person in the organization who would have the power to accept or reject your recommendation.

2. Will this report use information from other classes or from work experiences? If so, give the name and topic of the class and/or briefly describe the job. If you will need additional information (that you have not already gotten from other classes or from a job), how do you expect to find it?

3. List the name, title, and business phone number of a professor who can testify to your ability to handle the expertise needed for this report.

4. List the name, title, and business phone number of someone in the organization who can testify that you have access to enough information about that organization to write this report.

14–3   Choosing Research Strategies

For each of the following reports, indicate the kinds of research that might be useful. If a survey is called for, indicate the most efficient kind of sample to use.

   a. How can XYZ store increase sales?
   b. What is it like to live and work in [name of country]?
   c. Are the signs in our airport adequate for foreign visitors?
   d. Is it feasible to start a monthly newsletter for students in your major?
   e. How can we best market to mature adults?
   f. Can compensation programs increase productivity?
   g. What skills are in demand in our area? Of these, which could the local community college offer courses in?

14–4   Comparing Web Search Engines

Using at least three different search engines, search for sources on a topic on which you could write a formal report. (See Problems 15–5, 15–7, 15–8, 15–10, and 15–11.) Compare the top 30 sources. Which sites turn up on all three search engines? Which search engine appears to be most useful for your project?

As Your Instructor Directs,
   a. Share your results orally with a small group of students.
   b. Present your results to the class.
   c. Write a memo to your instructor summarizing your results.
   d. With a small group of students, write a report recommending guidelines for using search engines.

14–5   Choosing Samples for Surveys and Interviews

Indicate the best sample(s) to use in surveys and interviews for reports on the following topics.

   a. Would XYZ organization raise more money if it sold items besides donuts every morning in [classroom building]?
   b. Improving access to computers for students at XYZ College.
   c. How can XYZ organization attract more student members?
   d. How XYZ restaurant can reduce turnover.
   e. Improving communication with international students at XYZ University.
   f. Dealing with hate speech at XYZ College.
   g. How teaching can be improved in [Department].

14–6   Identifying Keywords for Computer Searches

As Your Instructor Directs, identify the keyword combinations that you could use in researching one or more of the following topics:
   a. Ways to evaluate whether recycling is working.
   b. Safety of pension funds.
   c. Ethical issues in accounting.
   d. Effects of advertising on sales of automobiles.
   e. What can be done to increase the privacy of personal data.
   f. Retaining royalties on recordings.
   g. Advantages and problems of Web advertising.

14-7   Compiling a Bibliography

Answer the following questions about a topic of your choice. Ask a reference librarian or another expert for help.

Specific topic: _____

General field: _____

1. List the sources that index or abstract books, journal articles, and dissertations in this field.
2. List any electronic indexes, bibliographies, or databases in this field.
3. How can you locate newspaper articles on this topic?
4. What congressional committees or federal agencies would be most likely to have published documents that might be useful in your research?
5. You don't know whether or not any congressional committees have issued reports that might help. What index can you check to find out?
6. You know that Edward Expert has done important work in your field. How can you find out whether he has testified before a congressional committee?
7. What book is most likely to have statistics or facts that might be relevant to your topic? Give the title of the book and its call number.
8. You know that Susan Scholar has done important work on your subject. How can you find the names and references for other researchers who have extended or challenged her findings? (Hint: researchers who build on someone's work almost always cite that person.) Give the title of the book and its call number.
9. List the name(s), department(s), and phone number(s) of faculty who might know something about this topic.
10. List the name(s), position(s), and phone number(s) of anyone in the community who might know something about this topic.
11. List the name of the reference librarian who could help you find sources on this topic and the hours when he or she is on duty.
12. Give full bibliographic information for 5 to 10 newspaper, journal, or online articles, books, dissertations, or government reports that seem relevant to your topic.

14-8   Evaluating Survey Questions

Evaluate each of the following questions. Are they acceptable as they stand? If not, how can they be improved?

a. Survey of clerical workers:
   Do you work for the government? ☐ or the private sector? ☐

b. Questionnaire on grocery purchases:
   1. Do you *usually* shop at the same grocery store?
      a. Yes
      b. No
   2. Do you use credit cards to purchase items at your grocery store?
      a. Yes
      b. No
   3. How much is your average grocery bill?
      a. Under $25
      b. $25–50
      c. $50–100
      d. $100–150
      e. Over $150

c. Survey on technology:
   1. Would you generally welcome any technological advancement that allowed information to be sent and received more quickly and in greater quantities than ever before?
   2. Do you think that all people should have free access to all information, or do you think that information should somehow be regulated and monitored?

d. Survey on job skills:
   How important are the following skills for getting and keeping a professional-level job in US business and industry today?

	Low				High
Ability to communicate	1	2	3	4	5
Leadership ability	1	2	3	4	5
Public presentation skills	1	2	3	4	5
Selling ability	1	2	3	4	5
Teamwork capability	1	2	3	4	5
Writing ability	1	2	3	4	5

e. Survey of working women:

Are any of the following issues a problem for you at work? (If so, check off how serious a problem it is. If not, check "Doesn't Apply"):

	One of the Most Serious	Very Serious	Somewhat Serious	Not Very Serious	Not at All Serious	Doesn't Apply
I don't get paid what I think my job is worth	_____	_____	_____	_____	_____	_____
I need better benefits	_____	_____	_____	_____	_____	_____
I work too many hours	_____	_____	_____	_____	_____	_____
I worry about losing my job	_____	_____	_____	_____	_____	_____
I don't have the flexibility to meet family responsibilities	_____	_____	_____	_____	_____	_____
I am under too much stress	_____	_____	_____	_____	_____	_____
I do not have the skills to get a better job	_____	_____	_____	_____	_____	_____
It's hard to find quality child or elder care that I can afford	_____	_____	_____	_____	_____	_____
I have lost a job or a promotion because of my race or sex	_____	_____	_____	_____	_____	_____
I know someone who lost a job or promotion because of race or sex	_____	_____	_____	_____	_____	_____
I suffer other problems at my job (please explain below):	_____	_____	_____	_____	_____	_____

14–9   Designing Questions for an Interview or Survey

Submit either a one- to three-page questionnaire or questions for a 20- to 30-minute interview AND the information listed below for the method you choose.

Questionnaire

1. Purpose(s), goal(s).
2. Subjects (who, why, how many).
3. How and where to be distributed.
4. Any changes in type size, paper color, etc., from submitted copy.
5. Rationale for order of questions, kinds of questions, wording of questions.
6. References, if building on questionnaires by other authors.

Interview

1. Purpose(s), goal(s).
2. Subjects (who, and why).
3. Proposed site, length of interview.
4. Rationale for order of questions, kinds of questions, wording of questions, choice of branching or follow-up questions.
5. References, if building on questions devised by others.

As Your Instructor Directs,

a. Create questions for a survey on one of the following topics:
 - Survey students on your campus about their knowledge of and interest in the programs and activities sponsored by a student organization.
 - Survey workers at a company about what they like and dislike about their jobs.
 - Survey people in your community about their willingness to pay more to buy products using recycled materials and to buy products that are packaged with a minimum of waste.
 - Survey students and faculty on your campus about whether adequate parking exists.
 - Survey two groups on a topic that interests you.

b. Create questions for an interview on one of the following topics:
 - Interview an international student about the forms of greetings and farewells, topics of small talk, forms of politeness, festivals and holidays,

meals at home, size of families, and roles of family members in his or her country.

■ Interview a TV producer about what styles and colors work best for people appearing on TV.

■ Interview a worker about an ethical dilemma he or she faced on the job, what the worker did and why, and how the company responded.

■ Interview the owner of a small business about the problems the

business has, what strategies the owner has already used to increase sales and profits and how successful these strategies were, and the owner's attitudes toward possible changes in product line, decor, marketing, hiring, advertising, and money management.

■ Interview someone who has information you need for a report you're writing.

14–10   Choosing Subject Lines for Memo Reports

Identify the strengths and weaknesses of each subject line, and choose the best subject line(s) from each group.

1. A proposal to conduct research.
   a. Membership Survey
   b. Proposal to Survey Former Members to Learn Their Reasons for Not Rejoining
   c. Proposal to Investigate Former Members' Reasons for Not Rejoining

2. A survey to find out why former members did not renew their memberships.
   a. 1998 Delinquency Survey
   b. Results of 1998 Former Member Survey
   c. Why Members Did Not Renew Their Memberships in 1998

3. A progress report.
   a. Progress Report
   b. Work Completed, October 15–November 5
   c. Status of the Survey of Former Members

E-MAIL MESSAGES

14–11   Writing a Progress Report

As Your Instructor Directs, send an e-mail message

a. To the other members of your group, describing your progress since the last group meeting.

b. To your instructor, describing your progress.

c. To your instructor, asking for help solving a problem you have encountered.

COMMUNICATING AT WORK

As Your Instructor Directs in Problems 14–12 through 14–14,

a. Create a document or presentation to achieve the goal.

b. Write a memo to your instructor describing the situation at your workplace and explaining your rhetorical choices (medium, strategy, tone, wording, graphics or document design, and so forth).

14–12   Proposing a Change

No organization is perfect. Propose a change that would improve your organization. The change can affect only your unit or the whole organization; it can relate to productivity and

profits, to quality of life, or to any other aspect your organization can control. Direct your proposal to the person or committee with the power to authorize the change.

14–13 Proposing to Undertake a Research Project

Pick a project you would like to study whose results could be used by your organization. (See Problem 15–5). Write a proposal to your supervisor requesting time away from other duties to do the research. Show how your research (whatever its outcome) will be useful to the organization.

14–14 Writing a Progress Report to Your Superior

Describe the progress you have made this week or this month on projects you have been assigned. You may describe progress you have made individually, or progress your unit has made as a team.

MEMO AND LETTER ASSIGNMENTS

14–15 Writing up a Survey

As Your Instructor Directs,

a. Survey 40 to 50 people on some subject of your choice.

b. Team up with your classmates to conduct a survey and write it up as a group. Survey 50 to 80 people if your group has two members, 75 to 120 people if it has three members, 100 to 150 people if it has four members, and 125 to 200 people if it has five members.

c. Keep a journal during your group meetings and submit it to your instructor.

d. Write a memo to your instructor describing and evaluating your group's process for designing, conducting, and writing up the survey. (See Chapter 13 on working and writing in groups.)

For this assignment, you do **not** have to take a random sample. Do, however, survey at least two different groups so that you can see if they differ in some way. Possible groups are men and women, business majors and English majors, Greeks and independents, first-year students and seniors, students and townspeople.

As you conduct your survey, make careful notes about what you do so that you can use this information when you write up your survey. If you work with a group, record who does what. Use complete memo format. Your subject line should be clear and reasonably complete. Omit unnecessary words such as "Survey of." Your first paragraph serves as an introduction, but it needs no heading. The rest of the body of your memo will be divided into four sections with the following headings: Purpose, Procedure, Results, and Discussion.

In your first paragraph, briefly summarize (not necessarily in this order) who conducted the experiment or survey, when it was conducted, where it was conducted, who the subjects were, what your purpose was, and what you found out. You will discuss all of these topics in more detail in the body of your memo.

In your **Purpose** section, explain why you conducted the survey. What were you trying to learn? What hypothesis were you testing? Why did this subject seem interesting or important?

In your **Procedure** section, describe in detail *exactly* what you did. "The first 50 people who came through the Union on Wed., Feb. 2" is not the same as "The first 50 people who came through the south entrance of the Union on Wed., Feb. 2, and agreed to answer my questions." Explain any steps you took to overcome possible sources of bias.

In your **Results** section, first tell whether your results supported your hypothesis. Use both visuals and words to explain what your numbers show. (See Chapter 16 on how to design visuals.) Process your raw data in a way that will be useful to your reader.

In your **Discussion** section, evaluate your survey and discuss the implications of your results. Consider these questions:

1. What are the limitations of your survey and your results?

2. Do you think a scientifically valid survey would have produced the same results? Why or why not?

3. Were there any sources of bias either in the way the questions were phrased or in the way the subjects were chosen? If you were running the survey again,

what changes would you make to eliminate or reduce these sources of bias?

4. Do you think your subjects answered honestly and completely? What factors may have intruded? Is the fact that you did or didn't know them, were or weren't of the same sex relevant? If your results seem to contradict other evidence, how do you account for the discrepancy? Were your subjects shading the truth? Was your sample's unrepresentativeness the culprit? Or have things changed since earlier data were collected?

5. What causes the phenomenon your results reveal? If several causes together account for the phenomenon, or if it is

impossible be sure of the cause, admit this. Identify possible causes and assess the likelihood of each.

6. What action should be taken?

The discussion section gives you the opportunity to analyze the significance of your survey. Its insight and originality lift the otherwise well-written memo from the ranks of the merely satisfactory to the ranks of the above-average and the excellent.

The whole assignment will be more interesting if you choose a question that interests you. It does not need to be "significant" in terms of major political or philosophic problems; a quirk of human behavior that fascinates you will do nicely.

14–16 Writing a Proposal for a Student Report

Write a proposal to your instructor to do the research for a formal or informal report. (See Problems 15–4, 15–5, 15–7, 15–8, 15–10, and 15–11.)

The headings and the questions in the section titled "Proposals for Class Research Projects" are your RFP; be sure to answer

every question and to use the headings exactly as stated in the RFP. Exception: where alternate heads are listed, you may choose one, combine the two ("Qualifications and Facilities"), or treat them as separate headings in separate categories.

14–17 Writing a Proposal for Funding for a Nonprofit Group

Pick a nonprofit group you care about. Examples include professional organizations, a school sports team, a charitable group, a community organization, a religious group, or your own college or university.

As Your Instructor Directs,
   a. Check a directory of foundations to find one that makes grants to groups like yours. Brainstorm a list of businesses that might be willing to give money for specific projects. Check to

see whether state or national levels of your organization make grants to local chapters.
   b. Write a proposal to obtain funds for a special project your group could undertake if it had the money. Address your proposal to a specific organization.
   c. Write a proposal to obtain operating funds or money to buy something your group would like to have. Address your proposal to a specific organization.

14–18 Writing a Sales Proposal

Pick a project that you could do for a local company or government office. Examples include

- Creating a brochure or Web page.
- Revising form letters.
- Conducting a training program.
- Writing a newsletter or an annual report.
- Developing a marketing plan.
- Providing plant care, catering, or janitorial services.

Write a proposal specifying what you could do and providing a detailed budget and work schedule.

As Your Instructor Directs,
   a. Phone someone in the organization to talk about its needs and what you could offer.
   b. Write an individual proposal.
   c. Join with other students in the class to create a group proposal.
   d. Present your proposal orally.

14–19 Writing a Progress Report

Write a memo to your instructor summarizing your progress on your report.

In the introductory paragraph, summarize your progress in terms of your schedule and your goals. Under a heading titled *Work Completed,* list what you have already done. (This is a chance to toot your own horn: if you have solved problems creatively, say so! You can also describe obstacles you've encountered that you have not yet solved.) Under *Work to Be Completed,* list what you still have to do. If you are more than two days behind the schedule you submitted with your proposal, include a revised schedule, listing the completion dates for the activities that remain.

In your last paragraph, either indicate your confidence in completing the report by the due date or ask for a conference to resolve the problems you are encountering.

14–20 Writing a Progress Report for a Group Report

Write a memo to your instructor summarizing your group's progress.

In the introductory paragraph, summarize the group's progress in terms of its goals and its schedule, your own progress on the tasks for which you are responsible, and your feelings about the group's work thus far.

Under a heading titled *Work Completed,* list what has already been done. Be most specific about what you yourself have done. Describe briefly the chronology of group activities: number, time, and length of meetings; topics discussed and decisions made at meetings.

If you have solved problems creatively, say so! You can also describe obstacles you've encountered that you have not yet solved. In this section, you can also comment on problems that the group has faced and whether or not they've been solved. You can comment on things that have gone well and have contributed to the smooth functioning of the group.

Under *Work to Be Completed,* list what you personally and other group members still have to do. Indicate the schedule for completing the work.

In your last paragraph, either indicate your confidence in completing the report by the due date or ask for a conference to resolve the problems you are encountering.

CHAPTER 15

Analyzing Data and Writing Reports

Chapter Outline

An Inside Perspective: Analyzing Data and Writing Reports

Dayton J. D. Semerjian, Product Marketing Manager
Shiva Corporation

Dayton Semerjian writes reports to develop and implement global product growth strategies. Shiva Corporation, headquartered in Bedford, Massachusetts, is the international market leader for remote access network servers.

Reports are comprised of analysis, conclusions, and recommendations. The quality of the final report is a function of the quality of the content and the quality of the packaging. A beautifully packaged report that has meaningless analysis is as worthless as a powerful analysis that is packaged so poorly that it never gets read. To create an effective report, you must have both.

The single most important recommendation I can give is to know the goal of your report and create a structure or map to help guide you through the analysis and writing. I regularly write reports to senior management summarizing recent actions of our competitors and recommending what we should do to stay competitive. To make my recommendations meaningful, I cover all of the areas of competitive activity in my report, including pricing, advertising, new product development, financial strength, and strategic alliances. So identifying the pieces I must include and understanding how they fit together is the first step. A map of the entire writing process is also important. You should plan how much time you will use to define the problem, research, write, revise and edit, and produce the final copies.

Quality analysis is based on taking a problem and breaking it down into the questions that must be answered to solve it. (This is "critical thinking.") For instance, you may be asked to write a report explaining why your product sales have stopped growing. To answer this question, you must first answer several other questions:

Am I losing market share and if so to whom, and why? Is my product the only one whose growth has slowed or has the entire industry slowed down? Why? Could my product line grow again? What must I do to make that happen? How much investment will it take and what return on investment should I expect?

Quality packaging means that the final report is clear, concise, and well organized. A common format is Executive Summary, body, and Conclusions and Recommendations. Divide the main body into subsections that answer the questions you have already laid out.

The most critical piece of the final report is the Executive Summary. Why? Because most time-pressed executives never read beyond this section. Therefore, the writer should make certain that the key findings, conclusions, and recommendation(s) are laid out clearly here. The rest of the report, in all its detail, is attached so the reader may decide whether he or she would like more information on a particular topic.

How much detail should you include? As much as you believe the audience reading the report will want. A general rule would be the shorter the better. Put yourself in the reader's shoes. Would you rather read about the problem and solution in 5 pages or in 50 pages? In each of the supporting sections, state the question you answer, your analytic method, findings, and conclusions. Put the raw data in appendices.

The final piece of the process is editing and revising. Most people don't leave enough time at the end of a research-intensive project to edit and revise. This step is necessary to "polish" your report and refine your thinking. How well you perform this step is often the difference between a good report and a great report.

Dayton J. D. Semerjian, February 3, 1997

Visit Shiva's Web site: http://www.shiva.com

"A beautifully packaged report that has meaningless analysis is as worthless as a powerful analysis that is packaged so poorly that it never gets read. To create an effective report, you must have both."

Dayton J. D. Semerjian, Shiva Corporation

Careful analysis, smooth writing, and effective document design work together to make effective reports, whether you're writing a 2½-page memo report or a 250-page formal report complete with all the report components.

Chapter 14 covered the first two steps in writing a report:

1. Define the problem.
2. Gather the necessary data and information.

This chapter covers the last three steps:

3. Interpret the data.
4. Organize the information.
5. Write the report.

Other chapters that are especially useful for reports are Chapters 10, 13, 16, and 17 and Appendix C.

A TIMETABLE FOR WRITING REPORTS

To use your time efficiently, think about the parts of the report before you begin writing. Much of the Introduction comes from your proposal with only minor revisions. You can write six sections even before you've finished your research: Purpose, Scope, Assumptions, Methods, Criteria, and Definitions.

The background reading for your proposal can form the first draft of your list of References.

Save a copy of your questionnaire or interview questions to use as an appendix. As you tally and analyze the data, prepare an appendix summarizing all the responses to your questionnaire, your figures and tables, and a complete list of References. You can print appendices before the final report is ready if you number their pages separately. Appendix A pages would be A-1, A-2, and so forth; Appendix B pages would be B-1, B-2, and so forth.

You can write the title page and the transmittal as soon as you know what your recommendation will be.

After you've analyzed your data, write the Executive Summary, the body, and the Conclusions and Recommendations. Prepare a draft of the table of contents and the list of illustrations.

When you write a long report, list all the sections (headings) that your report will have. Mark those that are most important to your reader and your proof, and spend most of your time on them. Write the important sections early. That way, you won't spend all your time on Background or History of the Problem. Instead, you'll get to the meat of your report.

Analyzing Data for Reports

Analyzing the data you have gathered is essential to produce the tight logic needed for a good report. Reports form an interlocking pyramid of evidence (➤ p. 258) and claims (➤ p. 258). You start with small claims; once you've proven them, they become evidence for bigger claims. These bigger claims in turn become the evidence for your thesis or recommendation. (Review Toulmin logic in Chapter 10.)

As you analyze your data, look for answers to your research questions and for interesting nuggets that may not have been part of your original questions but that emerge from the data. For example, Intuit was trying to decide whether to keep a personal inventory feature in Quicken Deluxe. A man in California wrote the company that a few days after he purchased Quicken, brush fires broke out near his house. He ran from room to room with his laptop, recording furniture and valuables. Then he left the house with his floppy disk. Fortunately, the fires spared his house, but had he lost everything, he would have been able to document his possessions to the insurance company.[1] Such stories can be more convincing in reports and oral presentations than pages of computer printouts.

If your report is based upon secondary data from library and online research, look at the sample, the sample size, and the exact wording of questions to see what the data actually measure. Some studies bias results by limiting the alternatives. Ninety percent of students surveyed by Levi Strauss & Co. said Levi's 501 jeans would be the most popular clothes that year. But the Levi's were the only brand of jeans on the list of choices. Some studies ask biased questions. A poll sponsored by the disposable-diaper industry asked, "It is estimated that disposable diapers account for less than 2% of the trash in today's landfills. In contrast, beverage containers, third-class mail, and yard waste are estimated to account for about 21% of the trash in landfills. Given this, in your opinion, would it be fair to ban disposable diapers?" Not surprisingly, 84% of respondents said *no*.[2]

Evaluating online sources, especially Web pages, can be difficult, since anyone can post pages on the Web or contribute comments to chat groups. Check the identity of the writer: is he or she considered an expert? Can you find at least one source printed in a respectable newspaper or journal that agrees with the Web page? If a comment appeared in chat groups, did others in the group support the claim? Does the chat group include people who could be expected to be unbiased and knowledgeable? Especially when the issue is controversial, seek out opposing views.

If your data include words, try to find out what the words mean to the people who said them. Respondents to Whirlpool's survey of 180,000 households said they wanted "clean refrigerators." After asking more questions, Whirlpool found that what people really wanted were refrigerators

Tell Them a Story*

To persuade people, tell them a story or anecdote that proves your point.

Experiments with both high school teachers and quantitatively trained MBA students show that people are more likely to believe a point and more likely to be committed to it when points were made by examples, stories, and case studies. Stories alone were more effective than a combination of stories and statistics; the combinations was more effective than statistics alone. In another experiment, attitude changes lasted longer when the audience had read stories than when they had only read numbers. Recent research suggests that stories are more persuasive because people remember them.

In many cases, you'll need to provide statistics or numbers to convince the careful reader that your anecdote is a representative example. But give the story first. It's more persuasive.

*Based on Daniel J. O'Keefe, *Persuasion* (Newbury Park, CA: Sage Publications, 1990), 168; Joanne Martin and Melanie E. Powers, "Truth or Corporate Propaganda," *Organizational Symbolism*, eds. Louis R. Pondy, Thomas C. Dandridge, Gareth Morgan, and Peter J. Frost (Greenwich, CT: JAI Press 1983), 97–107; and Dean C. Kazoleas, "A Comparison of the Persuasive Effectiveness of Qualitative versus Quantitative Evidence: A Test of Explanatory Hypotheses," *Communication Quarterly* 41, no. 1 (Winter 1993): 40–50.

Truck drivers need parts in two situations: routine maintenance and emergency repairs. Volvo GM set up a warehouse in Memphis, Tennessee, where FedEx is headquartered. Anxious customers eager to get back on the road are happy to pay for same-day service, and the percentage of "out-of-stock" parts has dropped dramatically, even with a smaller inventory. (Courtesy Volvo Trucks of North America).

that *looked* clean, so the company developed models with textured fronts and sides to hide fingerprints.[3] Also try to measure words against numbers. When he researched possible investments, Peter Lynch found that people in mature industries were pessimistic, seeing clouds. People in immature industries saw pie in the sky, even when the numbers weren't great.[4]

Look for patterns. If you have library sources, on which points do experts agree? Which disagreements can be explained by early theories or numbers that have now changed? Which disagreements are the result of different interpretations of the same data? Which are the result of having different values and criteria? In your interviews and surveys, what patterns do you see?

- Have things changed over time?
- Does geography account for differences?
- What similarities do you see?
- What differences do you see?
- What confirms your hunches?
- What surprises you?

If you have numerical data, you'll want to sum it, calculate the average, and perhaps run statistical tests. Often it's useful to simplify the data: rounding it off, combining similar elements. Then you can see that one number is about 2½ times another. Charting it can also help you see patterns in your data. (See Chapter 16 for a full discussion of charts as a way of analyzing and presenting numerical data.) Look at the raw data as well as at percentages. For example, a 50% increase in shoplifting incidents sounds alarming—but an increase from two to three shoplifting incidents sounds well within normal variation.

State accurately what your data show. For example, suppose that you've asked people who use computers if they could be as productive without them and the overwhelming majority say *no*. This finding shows that people *believe* that computers make them more productive, but it does not prove that they in fact *are* more productive.

Don't confuse causation with correlation. **Causation** means that one thing causes or produces another. **Correlation** means that two things happen at the same time. One might cause the other, but both might be caused by a third. For example, suppose you're considering whether to buy PCs for everyone in your company, and suppose your surveys show that the people who currently have computers are, in general, more productive than people who don't use computers. Does having a computer lead to higher productivity? Perhaps. But perhaps productive people are more likely to push to get computers from company funds, while less productive people are more passive. Perhaps productive people earn more and are more likely to be able to buy their own computers if the organization doesn't provide them. Perhaps some third factor—experience in the company, education, or social background—leads both to increased productivity and to acquiring computers.

Consciously search for at least three possible causes for each phenomenon you've observed and at least three possible solutions for each problem. The more possibilities you brainstorm, the more likely you are to find good options. In your report, mention all of the possibilities; discuss in detail only those that will occur to readers and that you think are the real reasons and the best solutions.

When you have identified patterns that seem to represent the causes of the problem or the best solutions, check these ideas against reality. Can you find support in the quotes or in the numbers? Can you answer counterclaims? If you can, you will be able to present evidence for your argument in a convincing way.

Make both the claim and the evidence explicit in reports. Show the bridge (✖ p. 259) that justifies moving from the evidence to the claim. Documenting sources provides the foundation (✖ p. 259) for each bridge. Always offer rebuttals (✖ p. 259) to loopholes the reader may find in the main claim. Limit any claim whose truth is uncertain or relative.

Make the nature of your evidence clear to your reader. Do you have observations that you yourself have made? Or do you have inferences based on observations or data collected by others? Check the principles of semantics in Appendix C. Old data and *either-or* classifications are not good guides to future action. A statement—even one from a computer printout—is never the whole story.

If you can't prove the claim you originally hoped to make, modify your conclusions to fit your data. Even when your market test is a failure or your experiment disproves your hypothesis, you can still write a useful report.

- Identify changes that might yield a different result (for example, selling the product at a lower price might enable the company to sell enough units).
- Divide the discussion to show what part of the test succeeded.
- Discuss circumstances that may have affected the results.
- Summarize your negative findings in progress reports to let readers down gradually and to give them a chance to modify the research design.
- Remember that negative results aren't always disappointing to the audience. For example, the people who commissioned a feasibility report may be relieved to have an impartial outsider confirm their suspicions that a project isn't feasible.[5]

CHOOSING INFORMATION FOR REPORTS

Don't put information in reports just because you have it or just because it took you a long time to find it. Instead, choose the information that your reader needs to make a decision.

What Does the Reader Want? (1)*

What criteria do experienced investors use to read strategic business plans? Researchers Evelyn Pierce, Richard Young, and Thomas Hajduk found that the return on investment and the management team were the most important criteria. Investors didn't really care what product or service the business would provide, and they skipped most of the material in business plans that didn't relate to their criteria.

*Based on Evelyn Pierce, Richard Young, and Thomas Hajduk, "Using Experienced Audience Insights That Reveal How Readers Respond to Business Documents," Southeast Association for Business Communication, Kiawah Island, South Carolina, March 7–9, 1996.

If you know your readers well, you may know what criteria interest them. If you don't know your readers, you may be able to get a sense for what is important by showing them a tentative table of contents (a list of your headings) and asking, "Have I included everything?" When you cannot contact an external audience, show your draft to superiors in your organization.

One report writer was asked to examine a building that had problems with heating, cooling, and air circulation. The client who owned the building wanted quick answers to three questions: Can we do it? What will it cost? When will it pay for itself? The report could have been three pages with a seven-page appendix showing the payback figures.[6]

How much information you need to include depends on whether your audience is likely to be supportive, neutral, or skeptical. As Jeanne Halpern of McKinsey says,

> If the audience is very likely to go along with you, then you can give the message directly and explain how to do it. If you have a message that the people have no conviction about or don't feel happy about, then you have to show the reasons why and explain your thinking in a persuasive way.[7]

You must also decide whether to put information in the body of the report or in appendices. Put material in the body of the report if it is crucial to your proof or if it is short. (Something less than half a page won't interrupt the reader.)

Anything that a careful reader will want but that is not crucial to your proof can go in an appendix. Appendices can include

- A copy of a survey questionnaire or interview questions.
- A tally of responses to each question in a survey.
- A copy of responses to open-ended questions in a survey.
- A transcript of an interview.
- Computer printouts.
- Previous reports on the same subject.

ORGANIZING INFORMATION IN REPORTS

Most sets of data can be organized in several logical ways. Choose the way that makes your information easiest for the reader to understand and use. If you were compiling a directory of all the employees at your plant, for example, alphabetizing by last name would be far more useful than listing people by height, social security number, or length of service with the company, although those organizing principles might make sense in other lists for other purposes.

In one company, a young employee comparing the economics of two proposed manufacturing processes gave his logic and his calculations in full before getting to his conclusion. But his superiors didn't want to wade through eight single-spaced pages; they wanted his recommendation up front.[8]

The following three guidelines will help you choose the arrangement that will be the most useful for your reader:

1. **Process your information before you present it to your reader.** The order in which you became aware of information usually is not the best order to present it to your reader.
2. **When you have lots of information, group it into three to seven categories.** The average person's short-term memory can hold only seven chunks, though the chunks can be of any size.[9] By grouping your

information into seven categories (or fewer), you make your report easier to read.

3. **Work with the reader's expectations, not against them.** Introduce ideas in the overview in the order in which you will discuss them.

Basic Patterns for Organizing Information

Seven basic patterns for organizing information are useful in reports:

1. Comparison/contrast.
2. Problem-solution.
3. Elimination of alternatives.
4. General to particular or particular to general.
5. Geographic or spatial.
6. Functional.
7. Chronological.

Any of these patterns can be used for a whole report or for only part of it.

1. Comparison/Contrast

Many reports use comparison/contrast sections within a larger report pattern. Comparison/contrast can also be the purpose of the whole report. Feasibility studies usually use this pattern.

There are two ways to organize your discussion. The **divided pattern** takes up each alternative in turn: AAA, BBB, CCC. The **alternating pattern** takes up each criteria in turn: ABC, ABC, ABC. See Figure 15.1 for examples of these two patterns in a report.

Divided Pattern	
Alternative A	Opening a New Store on Campus
Criterion 1	Cost of Renting Space
Criterion 2	Proximity to Target Market
Criterion 3	Competition from Similar Stores
Alternative B	Opening a New Store Downtown
Criterion 1	Cost of Renting Space
Criterion 2	Proximity to Target Market
Criterion 3	Competition from Similar Stores
Alternative C	Opening a New Store in the Suburban Mall
Criterion 1	Cost of Renting Space
Criterion 2	Proximity to Target Market
Criterion 3	Competition from Similar Stores
Alternating Pattern	
Criterion 1	Cost of Renting Space for the New Store
Alternative A	Cost of Campus Locations
Alternative B	Cost of Downtown Locations
Alternative C	Cost of Locations in the Suburban Mall
Criterion 2	Proximity to Target Market
Alternative A	Proximity on Campus
Alternative B	Proximity Downtown
Alternative C	Proximity in the Suburban Mall
Criterion 3	Competition from Similar Stores
Alternative A	Competing Stores on Campus
Alternative B	Competing Stores Downtown
Alternative C	Competing Stores in the Suburban Mall

Figure 15.1

Two Ways to Organize a Comparison/ Contrast Report

Use the divided pattern (AAA, BBB, CCC) when

- One alternative is clearly superior.
- The criteria are hard to separate.
- The reader will intuitively grasp the alternative as a whole rather than as the sum of its parts.

Use the alternating pattern (ABC, ABC, ABC) when

- The superiority of one alternative to another depends on the relative weight assigned to various criteria. Perhaps Alternative A is best if we are most concerned about Criterion 1, cost, but worst if we are most concerned about Criterion 2, proximity to target market.
- The criteria are easy to separate.
- The reader wants to compare and contrast the options independently of your recommendation.

A variation of the divided pattern is the **pro and con pattern.** In this pattern, under each specific heading, give the arguments for and against that alternative. A report recommending new plantings for a university quadrangle uses the pro and con pattern:

> Advantages of Monocropping
>   High Productivity
>   Visual Symmetry
> Disadvantages of Monocropping
>   Danger of Pest Exploitation
>   Visual Monotony

Whatever information comes second will carry more psychological weight. This pattern is least effective when you want to deemphasize the disadvantages of a proposed solution, for it does not permit you to bury the disadvantages between neutral or positive material.

2. Problem-Solution

Identify the problem; explain its background or history; discuss its extent and seriousness; identify its causes. Discuss the factors (criteria) that affect the decision. Analyze the advantages and disadvantages of possible solutions. Conclusions and recommendation can go either first or last, depending on the preferences of your reader. This pattern works well when the reader is neutral.

A report recommending ways to eliminate solidification of a granular bleach during production uses the problem-solution pattern:

> Recommended Reformulation for Vibe Bleach
> Problems in Maintaining Vibe's Granular Structure
>   Solidifying during Storage and Transportation
>   Customer Complaints about "Blocks" of Vibe in Boxes
> Why Vibe Bleach "Cakes"
>   Vibe's Formula
>   The Manufacturing Process
>   The Chemical Process of Solidification
> Modifications Needed to Keep Vibe Flowing Freely

3. Elimination of Alternatives

After discussing the problem and its causes, discuss the *impractical* solutions first, showing why they will not work. End with the most practical solution. This pattern works well when the solutions the reader is likely to favor will not work, while the solution you recommend is likely to be perceived as expensive, intrusive, or radical.

A report on toy commercials eliminates alternatives:

> The Effect of TV Ads on Children
> Camera Techniques Used in TV Advertisements
> Alternative Solutions to Problems in TV Toy Ads
>   Leave Ads Unchanged
>   Mandate School Units on Advertising
>   Ask the Industry to Regulate Itself
>   Mandate FTC Authority to Regulate TV Ads Directed at Children

4. General to Particular and Particular to General

General to particular starts with the problem as it affects the organization or as it manifests itself in general and then moves to a discussion of the parts of the problem and solutions to each of these parts. Particular to general starts with the problem as the audience defines it and moves to larger issues of which the problem is a part. Both are good patterns when you need to redefine the reader's perception of the problem in order to solve it effectively.

The directors of a student volunteer organization, VIP, have defined their problem as "not enough volunteers." After studying the subject, the writer is convinced that problems in training, supervision, and campus awareness are responsible both for a high dropout rate and a low recruitment rate. The general to particular pattern helps the audience see the problem in a new way:

> Why VIP Needs More Volunteers
> Why Some VIP Volunteers Drop Out
>   Inadequate Training
>   Inadequate Supervision
>   Feeling That VIP Requires Too Much Time
>   Feeling That the Work Is Too Emotionally Demanding
> Why Some Students Do Not Volunteer
>   Feeling That VIP Requires Too Much Time
>   Feeling That the Work Is Too Emotionally Demanding
>   Preference for Volunteering with Another Organization
>   Lack of Knowledge about VIP Opportunities
> How VIP Volunteers Are Currently Trained and Supervised
> Time Demands on VIP Volunteers
> Emotional Demands on VIP Volunteers
> Ways to Increase Volunteer Commitment and Motivation
>   Improving Training and Supervision
>   Improving the Flexibility of Volunteers' Hours
>   Providing Emotional Support to Volunteers
>   Providing More Information about Community Needs and VIP Services

5. Geographic or Spatial

In a geographic or spatial pattern, you discuss problems and solutions by units by their physical arrangement. Move from office to office, building to building, factory to factory, state to state, region to region, etc.

A sales report uses a geographic pattern of organization:

Sales Have Risen in the European Economic Community
Sales Are Flat in Eastern Europe
Sales Have Fallen Sharply in the Middle East
Sales Are Off to a Strong Start in Africa
Sales Have Risen Slightly in Asia
Sales Have Fallen Slightly in South America
Sales Are Steady in North America

6. Functional

In functional patterns, discuss the problems and solutions of each functional unit. For example, a report on a new plant might divide data into sections on the costs of land and building, on the availability of personnel, on the convenience of raw materials, etc. A government report might divide data into the different functions an office performed, taking each in turn.

A strategy report for a political party uses a functional pattern of organization:

Current Makeup of the House and Senate
Congressional Seats Open in 2002
   Seats Held by a Democratic Incumbent
     Races in Which the Incumbent Has a Commanding Lead
     Races in Which the Incumbent Is Vulnerable
   Seats Held by a Republican Incumbent
     Races in Which the Incumbent Has a Commanding Lead
     Races in Which the Incumbent Is Vulnerable
   Seats Where No Incumbent is Running
Senate Seats Open in 2002
   Seats Held by a Democratic Incumbent
     Races in Which the Incumbent Has a Commanding Lead
     Races in Which the Incumbent Is Vulnerable
   Seats Held by a Republican Incumbent
     Races in Which the Incumbent Has a Commanding Lead
     Races in Which the Incumbent Is Vulnerable
   Seats Where No Incumbent is Running

7. Chronological

A chronological report records events in the order in which they happened or are planned to happen. Many progress reports are organized chronologically:

Work Completed in October
Work Planned for November

How to Organize Specific Varieties of Reports

Informative, feasibility, justification, and annual reports will be more success-ful when you work with the readers' expectations for that kind of report.

Informative and Closure Reports

An **informative** or **closure report** summarizes completed work or research that does not result in action or recommendation.

Informative reports often include the following elements:

- Introductory paragraph summarizing the problems or successes of the project.
- Purpose and Scope section(s) giving the purpose of the report and indicating what aspects of the topic it covers.
- Chronological account of how the problem was discovered, what was done, and what the results were.
- Concluding paragraph with suggestions for later action. In a recommendation report, the recommendations would be based on proof. In contrast, the suggestions in a closure or recommendation report are not proved in detail.

Figure 15.2 presents this kind of informative closure report.

Closure reports also allow a firm to document the alternatives it has considered before choosing a final design and to prove its right to copyrights and patents. Dwight W. Stevenson has shown that firms challenged in product liability suits need to be able to document in detail the evaluation process that led to the product design.[10] In another kind of case, the Wells Fargo bank was sued for $480 million in a suit charging that it had misappropriated someone else's idea for a credit card operation. The bank used materials from its archives going back 20 years to prove that it had developed the idea itself.[11]

Feasibility Reports

Feasibility reports evaluate several alternatives and recommend one of them. (Doing nothing or delaying action can be one of the alternatives.)

Feasibility reports normally open by explaining the decision to be made, listing the alternatives, and explaining the criteria. In the body of the report, each alternative will be evaluated according to the criteria using one of the two comparison/contrast patterns. Discussing each alternative separately is better when one alternative is clearly superior, when the criteria interact, and when each alternative is indivisible. If the choice depends on the weight given to each criterion, you may want to discuss each alternative under each criterion.

Whether your recommendation should come at the beginning or the end of the report depends on your reader. Most readers want the "bottom line" up front. However, if the reader will find your recommendation hard to accept, you may want to delay your recommendation till the end of the report when you have given all your evidence.

Justification Reports

Justification reports recommend or justify a purchase, investment, hiring, or change in policy. If your organization has a standard format for justification reports, follow that format. If you can choose your headings and organization,

Figure 15.2

March 14, 1997

To: Kitty O. Locker

From: Sara A. Ratterman *SAR*   *Informal short reports use letter or memo format.*

First paragraph summarizes main points.   Subject: Recycling at Bike Nashbar

Two months ago, Bike Nashbar began recycling its corrugated cardboard boxes. The program was easy to implement and actually saves the company a little money compared to our previous garbage pickup.

Purpose and scope of report.   In this report, I will explain how, why, and by whom Bike Nashbar's program was initiated; how the program works and what it costs; and why other businesses should consider similar programs.

Bold or underline headings.

The Problem of Too Many Boxes and Not Enough Space in Bike Nashbar

Cause of problem.   Every week, Bike Nashbar receives about 40 large cardboard boxes containing bicycles and other merchandise. As many boxes as possible would be stuffed into the trash bin behind the building, which also had to accommodate all the other solid waste the shop produces. Boxes that didn't fit in the trash bin ended up lying around the shop, blocking doorways, and taking up space needed for customers' bikes. The trash bin was only emptied once a week, and by that time, even more boxes would have arrived.

Triple space before heading.

The Importance of Recycling Cardboard Rather than Throwing It Away

Further seriousness of problem.   Arranging for more trash bins or more frequent pickups would have solved the immediate problem at Bike Nashbar but would have done nothing to solve the problem created by throwing away so much trash in the first place.

Double space between paragraphs within heading.

According to David Crogen, sales representative for Waste Management, Inc., 75% of all solid waste in Columbus goes to landfills. The amount of trash the city collects has increased 150% in the last five years. Columbus's landfill is almost full. In an effort to encourage people and businesses to recycle, the cost of dumping trash in the landfill is doubling from $4.90 a cubic yard to $9.90 a cubic yard next week. Next January, the price will increase again to $12.95 a cubic yard. Crogen believes that the amount of trash can be reduced by cooperation between the landfill and the power plant and by recycling.

Capitalize first letter of major words in heading.

How Bike Nashbar Started Recycling Cardboard

Solution.   Waste Management, Inc., is the country's largest waste processor. After reading an article about how committed Waste Management, Inc., is to waste reduction and recycling, I decided to see whether Waste Management could recycle our boxes. Corrugated cardboard (which is what Bike Nashbar's boxes are made of) is almost 100% recyclable, so we seemed to be a good candidate for recycling.

Continued   **Figure 15.2**

Kitty O. Locker   *Reader's name*
March 14, 1997   *date*
Page 2   *page number.*

To get the service started,

1. I looked up Waste Management's phone number and called the company.

2. I met with a friendly sales rep, David Crogen, that same afternoon to discuss the service.

Waste Management, Inc., took care of all the details. Two days later, Bike Nashbar was recycling its cardboard.

How the Service Works and What It Costs   *Talking heads tell reader what to expect in each section.*

Details of solution. Waste Management took away our existing 8-cubic-yard garbage bin and replaced it with two 4-yard bins. One of these bins is white and has "cardboard only" printed on the outside; the other is brown and is for all other solid waste. The bins are emptied once a week, with the cardboard being taken to the recycling plant and the solid waste going to the landfill or power plant.

Double space between paragraphs. Since Bike Nashbar was already paying more than $60 a week for garbage pickup, our basic cost stayed the same. (Waste Management can absorb the extra overhead only if the current charge is at least $60 a week.) The cost is divided 80/20 between the two bins: 80% of the cost pays for the bin that goes to the landfill and power plant; 20% covers the cardboard pickup. Bike Nashbar actually receives $5.00 for each ton of cardboard it recycles.

Each employee at Bike Nashbar is responsible for putting all the boxes he or she opens in the recycling bin. Employees must follow these rules:

Indented lists provide visual variety.

- The cardboard must have the word "corrugated" printed on it, along with the universal recycling symbol.

- The boxes must be broken down to their flattest form. If they aren't, they won't all fit in the bin and Waste Management would be picking up air when it could pick up solid cardboard. The more boxes that are picked up, the more money and space that will be made.

- No other waste except corrugated cardboard can be put in the recycling bin. Other materials could break the recycling machinery or contaminate the new cardboard.

- The recycling bin is to be kept locked with a padlock provided by Waste Management so that vagrants don't steal the cardboard and lose money for Waste Management and Bike Nashbar.

Figure 15.2   Continued

Kitty O. Locker
March 14, 1997
Page 3

Minor Problems with Running the Recycling Program

Dis-
advantages
of
solution.

The only problems we've encountered have been minor ones of violating the rules. Sometimes employees at the shop forget to flatten boxes, and air instead of cardboard gets picked up. Sometimes people forget to lock the recycling bin. When the bin is left unlocked, people do steal the cardboard, and plastic cups and other solid waste get dumped in the cardboard bin. I've posted signs where the key to the bin hangs, reminding employees to empty and fold boxes and relock the bin after putting cardboard in it. I hope this will turn things around and these problems will be solved.

Advantages of the Recycling Program

Advantages
of
solution.

The program is a great success. Now when boxes arrive, they are unloaded, broken down, and disposed of quickly. It is a great relief to get the boxes out of our way, and knowing that we are making a contribution to saving our environment builds pride in ourselves and Bike Nashbar.

Our company depends on a clean, safe environment for people to ride their bikes in. Now we have become part of the solution. By choosing to recycle and reduce the amount of solid waste our company generates, we can save money while gaining a reputation as a socially responsible business.

Why Other Companies Should Adopt Similar Programs

Argues
that her
company's
experience
is relevant
to other
companies.

Businesses and institutions in Franklin County currently recycle less than 4% of the solid waste they produce. David Crogen tells me he has over 8,000 clients in Columbus alone, and he acquires new ones every day. Many of these businesses can recycle a large portion of their solid waste at no additional cost. Depending on what they recycle, they may even get a little money back.

The environmental and economic benefits of recycling as part of a comprehensive waste reduction program are numerous. Recycling helps preserve our environment. We can use the same materials over and over again, saving natural resources such as trees, fuel, and metals and decreasing the amount of solid waste in landfills. By conserving natural resources, recycling helps the U.S. become less dependent on imported raw materials. Crogen predicts that Columbus will be on a 100% recycling system by the year 2020. I strongly hope that his prediction will come true and the future may start to look a little brighter.

use this pattern when your recommendation will be easy for your reader to suggest:

1. **Indicate what you're asking for and why it's needed.** Since the reader has not asked for the report, you must link your request to the organization's goals.
2. **Briefly give the background of the problem or need.**
3. **Explain each of the possible solutions.** For each, give the cost and the advantages and disadvantages.
4. **Summarize the action needed to implement your recommendation.** If several people will be involved, indicate who will do what and how long each step will take.
5. **Ask for the action you want.**

If the reader will be reluctant to grant your request, use this variation of the problem-solving pattern described in Chapter 9:

1. **Describe the organizational problem (which your request will solve).** Use specific examples to prove the seriousness of the problem.
2. **Show why easier or less expensive solutions will not solve the problem.**
3. **Present your solution impersonally.**
4. **Show that the disadvantages of your solution are outweighed by the advantages.**
5. **Summarize the action needed to implement your recommendation.** If several people will be involved, indicate who will do what and how long each step will take.
6. **Ask for the action you want.**

How much detail you need to give in a justification report depends on your reader's knowledge of and attitude toward your recommendation and on the corporate culture. Many organizations expect justification reports to be short—only one or two pages. Other organizations may expect longer reports with much more detailed budgets and a full discussion of the problem and each possible solution.

Annual Reports

Every firm that sells stock to the public is required by the Securities and Exchange Commission (SEC) to issue an **annual report** every year summarizing the company's financial position. In the last 30 years, annual reports have increasingly become persuasive and image-building documents. In addition to presenting the required financial data, most companies use lavish color photos and graphics to keep readers interested, portray themselves as good corporate citizens, and defend management's record. Annual reports have become so popular that many privately held and nonprofit organizations also issue annual reports as a way to build loyalty among employees, clients or customers, and the various publics to which the organization is accountable.

US companies spend an estimated $5 billion a year on annual reports. In 1996, investors still want paper annual reports, though many firms are also distributing information on the Web and on CD-ROM. The CEO's letter is very important to most portfolio managers and to some individual investors.[12] Writing this short document (sometimes only a page, rarely more than two or three) can be difficult. Geoffrey Cross has shown that poor planning and inadequate analysis sometimes extend unnecessarily the time needed to

How to Make Annual Reports Fit Investors' Needs*

Face up to disappointing results and shortcomings at the outset. Don't try to sugarcoat or play down a bad year. If there are problems, have management take responsibility for solving them. Say what you are doing to solve them—in specifics. . . .

Use clear, appealing graphics and typography to present the mass of financial data required in the back of the report. Select key facts from the required data and highlight them prominently in the early pages of the report. . . .

Assume your reader is intelligent, but knows nothing about your business or its jargon. Where only technical terms are accurate, define them the first time you use them.

Avoid using long words and convoluted sentences. Paraphrase aloud what you're trying to say, and use those words. Employ the active voice, so that management is portrayed as making things happen, rather than having things happen to it.

*Quoted from Ned Raynolds, "What Investors Want From the Annual Report," *The Wall Street Journal,* January 18, 1988, 10.

Since 1993, Harley-Davidson
has included a poster in its
annual report.

prepare a report. In one organization, eight people spent 77 days writing the
two-page executive letter.[13]

If you're involved in the preparation of an annual report,

- Agree on the report's purposes and audiences (primary, secondary,
  immediate, gatekeepers, and watchdogs (✖ p. 58)) early in the planning
  process.
- Allow writers drafting parts of the report that will be signed by someone
  else (e.g., the Executive Letter) to talk directly with the signer to get a
  sense of his or her priorities and style.

■ Make sure that visuals are accurate as well as attractive. Deliberately misleading visuals are one of the factors that have made so many readers skeptical of annual reports.

■ Make the best case possible for management and for the company, but be honest about problems and weaknesses. In the current climate of distrust of annual reports, honesty is the only way to build credibility.

PRESENTING INFORMATION EFFECTIVELY IN REPORTS

The advice about style in Chapter 4 also applies to reports, with three exceptions:

1. **Use a fairly formal style, without contractions or slang.**
2. **Avoid the word *you*.** In a document with multiple audiences, it will not be clear who *you* is. Instead, use the company name.
3. **Include in the report all the definitions and documents needed to understand the recommendations.** The multiple audiences for reports include readers who may consult the document months or years from now; they will not share your special knowledge. Explain acronyms and abbreviations the first time they appear. Explain the history or background of the problem. Add as appendixes previous documents on which you are building.

The following points apply to any kind of writing, but they are particularly important in reports.

1. Say what you mean.
2. Tighten your writing.
3. Introduce sources and visuals gracefully.
4. Use blueprints, transitions, topic sentences, and headings to make your organization clear to your reader.

Let's look at each of these principles as they apply to reports.

1. Say What You Mean.

Not-quite-right word choices are particularly damaging in reports, which may be skimmed by readers who know very little about the subject. Occasionally you can simply substitute a word.

Incorrect:	With these recommendations, we can overcome the solutions to our problem.
Correct:	With these recommendations, we can overcome our problem.
Also correct:	With these recommendations, we can solve our problem.

Putting the meaning of your sentence in the verbs will help you say what you mean.

Vague:	My report revolves around the checkout lines and the methods used to get price checks when they arise.
Better:	My report shows how price checks slow checkout lines and recommends ways to reduce the number of price checks needed.

Sometimes you'll need to completely recast the sentence.

Incorrect:	The first problem with the incentive program is that middle managers do not use good interpersonal skills in implementing it. For example, the hotel chef openly ridicules the program. As a result, the kitchen staff fear being mocked if they participate in the program.

> Better: The first problem with the incentive program is that some middle managers undercut it. For example, the hotel chef openly ridicules the program. As a result, the kitchen staff fear being mocked if they participate in the program.

2. Tighten Your Writing.

Eliminate unnecessary words, use gerunds and infinitives, combine sentences, and reword sentences to cut the number of words.

> Wordy: Campus Jewelers' main objective is to increase sales. Specifically, the objective is to double sales in the next five years by becoming a more successful business.
>
> Better: Campus Jewelers' objective is to double sales in the next five years.

Wordiness in reports may arise from two sources that are less likely to affect shorter messages: writers may deliberately put in extra words to create a longer document, and repetition may occur in different sections that are written at different times.

No reader wants length for the sake of length. Even in a class report, the page requirement is an indication of the complexity of analysis that the instructor expects. If you've chosen an appropriate topic, collected enough data, and analyzed the data thoroughly, you should reach any minimum page requirement easily. (If you suspect that there isn't enough data to yield an adequate report, talk to your instructor well before the due date to revise your topic.)

Some repetition in reports is legitimate. The Conclusion section restates points made in the body of the report; the recommendations appear in the Transmittal, the Abstract or Executive Summary, and in the Recommendations sections of the report. However, repetitive references to earlier material ("As we have already seen") may indicate that the document needs to be reorganized. Read the document through at a single sitting to make sure that any repetition serves a useful purpose. If the repetition is boring, eliminate it.

3. Introduce Sources and Visuals Gracefully.

The first time you cite an author's work, use his or her full name: "Rosabeth Moss Kanter points out. . . ." In subsequent citations, use only the last name: "Kanter shows. . . ." Use active rather than passive verbs.

The verb you use indicates your attitude toward the source. *Says* and *writes* are neutral. *Points out, shows, suggests, discovered,* and *notes* suggest that you agree with the source. Words such as *claims, argues, contends that, believes,* and *alleges* distance you from the source. At a minimum, they suggest that you know that not everyone agrees with the source; they are also appropriate to report the views of someone with whom you disagree.

Use active verbs to refer to visuals, too.

> As Table 1 shows, . . .
> See Figure 4.

4. Use Blueprints, Transitions, Topic Sentences, and Headings.

Blueprints are overviews or forecasts that tell the reader what you will discuss in a section or in the entire report. Make your blueprint easy to read by telling the reader how many points there are and numbering them (either

Who Did What?*

The passive verbs and impersonal constructions in US reports of coal mine disasters ("coal dust was permitted to accumulate" and "an accident occurred") suggest that accidents are inevitable. Who permitted the coal dust to accumulate? What could have been done to prevent the accumulation? Mine disaster reports contain sentences like the following: "The . . . fatality occurred when the victim proceeded into an area . . . before the roof was supported." *Why* did the man who was killed go into the area? Had a supervisor checked to see that the room was supported? Who ordered what?

British reports of mine disasters, in contrast, focus on people and what they did to limit the damage from the disaster. Perhaps as a result, British mines have a much lower incidence of disasters than do US coal mines.

*Based on Beverly A. Sauer, "Sense and Sensibility in Technical Documentation: How Feminist Interpretation Strategies Can Save Lives in the Nation's Mines," *Journal of Business and Technical Communication* 7 (January 1993): 63–83.

with words or figures). In the following example, the first sentence in the revised paragraph tells the reader to look for four points; the numbers separate the four points clearly. This overview paragraph also makes a contract with readers, who now expect to read about tax benefits first and employee benefits last.

Paragraph without numbers:	Employee Stock Ownership Programs (ESOPs) have several advantages. They provide tax benefits for the company. ESOPs also create tax benefits for employees and for lenders. They provide a defense against takeovers. In some organizations, productivity increases because workers now have a financial stake in the company's profits. ESOPs are an attractive employee benefit and help the company hire and retain good employees.
Revised paragraph with numbers:	Employee Stock Ownership Programs (ESOPs) provide four benefits. First, ESOPs provide tax benefits for the company, its employees, and lenders to the plan. Second, ESOPs help create a defense against takeovers. Third, ESOPs may increase productivity by giving workers a financial stake in the company's profits. Fourth, as an attractive employee benefit, ESOPs help the company hire and retain good employees.

Transitions are words, phrases, or sentences that tell the reader whether the discussion is continuing on the same point or shifting points.

There are economic advantages, too.
(Tells the reader that we are still discussing advantages but that we have
     now moved to economic advantages.)

An alternative to this plan is . . . .
(Tells reader that a second option follows.)

The second factor. . . .
(Tells reader that the discussion of the first factor is finished.)

These advantages, however, are found only in A, not in B or C.
(Prepares reader for a shift from A to B and C.)

A **topic sentence** introduces or summarizes the main idea of a sentence. Readers who skim reports can follow your ideas more easily if each paragraph begins with a topic sentence.

Hard to read (no topic sentence):	Another main use of ice is to keep the fish fresh. Each of the seven kinds of fish served at the restaurant requires one gallon twice a day, for a total of 14 gallons. An additional 6 gallons a day are required for the salad bar.
Better (begins with topic sentence):	Twenty gallons of ice a day are needed to keep food fresh. Of this, the biggest portion (14 gallons) is used to keep the fish fresh. Each of the seven kinds of fish served at the restaurant requires one gallon twice a day (7 × 2 = 14). An additional 6 gallons a day are required for the salad bar.

Headings are single words, short phrases, or complete sentences that indicate the topic in each section. A heading must cover all of the material under it until the next heading. For example, *Cost of Tuition* cannot include the cost of books or of room and board. You can have just one paragraph under a heading or several pages. If you do have several pages between headings you may want to consider using subheadings. Use subheadings only when you have two or more divisions within a main heading.

Topic headings focus on the structure of the report. As you can see from the following example, topic headings give very little information.

Recommendation
Problem
    Situation 1
    Situation 2
Causes of the Problem
    Background
    Cause 1
    Cause 2
Recommended Solution

Informative or **talking heads,** in contrast, tell the reader what to expect. Informative heads, like those in the examples in this chapter, provide an overview of each section and of the entire report:

Recommended Reformulation for Vibe Bleach
Problems in Maintaining Vibe's Granular Structure
    Solidifying during Storage and Transportation
    Customer Complaints about "Blocks" of Vibe in Boxes
Why Vibe Bleach "Cakes"
    Vibe's Formula
    The Manufacturing Process
    The Chemical Process of Solidification
Modifications Needed to Keep Vibe Flowing Freely

Headings must be **parallel** (➤ p. 98), that is, they must use the same grammatical structure. Subheads must be parallel to each other but do not necessarily have to be parallel to subheads under other headings.

Not
parallel:
    Are Students Aware of VIP?
        Current Awareness among Undergraduate Students
        Graduate Students
    Ways to Increase Volunteer Commitment and Motivation
        We Must Improve Training and Supervision
        Can We Make Volunteers' Hours More Flexible?
        Providing Emotional Support to Volunteers
        Provide More Information about Community Needs and VIP Services

Parallel:
    Campus Awareness of VIP
        Current Awareness among Undergraduate Students
        Current Awareness among Graduate Students
    Ways to Increase Volunteer Commitment and Motivation
        Improving Training and Supervision
        Improving the Flexibility of Volunteers' Hours
        Providing Emotional Support to Volunteers
        Providing More Information about Community Needs and VIP Services

In a very complicated report, you may need up to five levels of headings. Figure 15.3 illustrates one way to set up headings. When you don't need this many levels, pick the headings you find most attractive. Use a lower level for subheadings.

The example in Figure 15.3 shows only one example of each level of heading. In an actual report, however, you would not use a subheading unless you had at least two subsections under the next higher heading.

Whatever the format for headings, avoid having a subhead come immediately after a heading. Instead, some text should follow the main heading before the subheading. (If you have nothing else to say, give an overview of

Legal Liability and Report Drafts*

During civil litigation (such as a tort case charging that a product has injured a user), rough drafts may be important to establish the state of mind and intent of a document's drafters.

To protect the company, one lawyer recommends labeling all but the final draft "Preliminary Draft: Subject to Change." That way, if there's ever a lawsuit, the company will be able to argue that only the final report, not the drafts, should be used as evidence.

*Based on Elizabeth McCord, " 'But What You Really Meant Was . . .': Multiple Drafts and Legal Liability," paper presented at the Association for Business Communication Midwest Regional Conference, Akron, OH, April 3–5, 1991.

Five Levels of Headings in a Single-Spaced Document   **Figure 15.3**

Center
Bold or underline   *For titles of short reports,*
Full capital letters   **FIRST-LEVEL HEADINGS**   *chapter titles in very long*
                                                                documents

First-level headings are used for the titles of short documents and for chapter titles within long documents. Center them, using full capital letters. You may use bold type or a larger type size if you choose.

This example uses just one heading at each level. However, in a business document use at least two headings at each level.

Center
Bold or underline   *Main divisions in a*
Regular capital letters   **Second-Level Headings**   *medium-length report*

Second-level headings introduce divisions within major points. The first letter of each major word in the heading is capitalized; the heading is either underlined or put in bold type; it is centered on the page. In a single-spaced document, triple space between the previous text and the heading; double space between the heading and the text which follows. In a double-spaced document, double space twice between the previous text and the heading; double space either once or twice between the heading and the following text.

When you do not need five levels of division, you may use "second-level headings" for the major divisions (Roman numerals in an outline) of the report.

                                          Left margin   *Used for subheadings in a medium-*
Third-Level Headings   *Bold or underline*   *length report*
                                          Regular capitals   *Used for main headings in memos*

Third-level headings are flush with the left-hand margin and are either set in bold or underlined. The first letters of the first word and of other major words are capitalized; all other letters are lowercase. In a single-spaced document, triple space between the previous text and the heading; in a double-spaced document, double space twice before the heading. In both, double space between the heading and the text which follows.

In a report using second-level headings for the Roman numerals, third-level headings would indicate capital letter points. Third-level headings are usually used for the main headings in memos.

Bold or underline
Followed   **Fourth-level headings.** Fourth- and fifth-level headings will appear only in a very long or
by a   complicated report. Fourth-level headings use the normal paragraph indentation, if any, are
period   underlined or set in bold, and are followed by a period. Double space between previous text
            and the heading. The paragraph begins on the same line on which the heading is placed.
Bold or underline   *Used only in very long, complex documents*
Part of   **Fifth-level headings** are integral parts of the first sentence of the first paragraph about a
sentence   topic. They are underlined or set in bold. Since they are part of the paragraph, only the first
            letter of the first word is capitalized and only the normal spacing between paragraphs is
            used between previous text and the heading.

the division.) Avoid having a heading or subheading all by itself at the bottom of the page. Instead, have at least one line (preferably two) of type. If there isn't room for a line of type under it, put the heading on the next page. Don't use a heading as the antecedent for a pronoun. Instead, repeat the noun.

WRITING FORMAL REPORTS

Formal reports are distinguished from informal letter and memo reports by their length and by their components. A full formal report may contain the following components:

Cover
Title Page
Letter of Transmittal
Table of Contents
List of Illustrations
Executive Summary
Report Body
  Introduction (Orients the reader to the report. Usually has subheadings for Purpose and Scope; depending on the situation, may also have Limitations, Assumptions, Methods, Criteria, and Definitions.)
  Background/History of the Problem (Orients the reader to the topic of the report. Serves as a record for later readers of the report.)
  Body (Presents and interprets data in words and visuals. Analyzes causes of the problem and evaluates possible solutions. Specific headings will depend on the topic of the report.)
  Conclusions (Summarizes main points of report.)
  Recommendations (Recommends actions to solve the problem. May be combined with Conclusions; may be put at beginning of body rather than at the end.)
  Notes, References, or Works Cited (Documents sources cited in the report.)
Appendixes (Provide additional materials that the careful reader may want: transcript of an interview, copies of questionnaires, tallies of all the questions, computer printouts, previous reports.)

As Figure 15.4 shows, not every formal report necessarily has all these components. In addition, some organizations call for additional components or arrange these components in a different order. As you read each section below, you may want to turn to the corresponding pages of the long report in Figure 15.5 to see how the component is set up and how it relates to the total report.

Title Page

The Title Page of a report usually contains four items: the title of the report, whom the report is prepared for, whom it is prepared by, and the release date. Sometimes reports also contain a brief summary or abstract of the contents of the report; some title pages contain decorative artwork.

The title of the report should be as informative as possible. Like subject lines, report titles are straightforward.

Poor title:	New Plant Site
Better title:	Why Eugene, Oregon, Is the Best Site for the New Kemco Plant
Poor title:	Planting for the Quadrangle
Better title:	Why Honey Locusts Are the Best Trees for the New Quadrangle

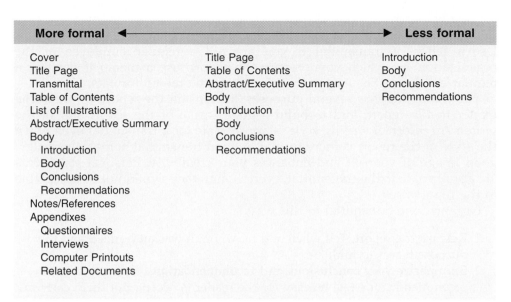

Figure 15.4

The Components in a Report Can Vary

In many cases, the title will state the recommendation in the report: "Why the United Nations Should Establish a Seed Bank." However, the title should omit recommendations when

- The reader will find the recommendations hard to accept.
- Putting all the recommendations in the title would make it too long.
- The report does not offer recommendations.

If the title does not contain the recommendation, it normally indicates what problem the report tries to solve.

Eliminate any unnecessary words:

Wordy: Report of a Study on Ways to Market Life Insurance to Urban Professional People Who Are in Their Mid-Forties

Better: Ways to Market Life Insurance to the Mid-Forties Urban Professional

The statement of whom the report is prepared for normally includes the name of the person who will make a decision based on the report, his or her job title, the organization's name, and its location (city, state, and ZIP code). Government reports often omit the person's name and simply give the organization that authorized the report.

If the report is prepared primarily by one person, the *Prepared by* section will have that person's name, his or her title, the organization, and its location (city, state, and ZIP code). In internal reports, the organization and location are usually omitted if the report writer works at the headquarters office.

If several people write the report, government reports normally list all their names, using a separate sheet of paper if the group working on the report is large. Practices in business differ. In some organizations, all the names are listed; in others, the division to which they belong is listed; in still others, the name of the chair of the group appears.

The **release date,** the date the report will be released to the public, is usually the date the report is scheduled for discussion by the decision makers. The report is due four to six weeks before the release date so that the decision makers can review the report before the meeting.

If you have the facilities and the time, try using different sizes and styles of type, color, and artwork to create a visually attractive and impressive title page. However, a plain typed page is acceptable. The format in Figure 15.5 will enable you to create an acceptable title page by typing it only once.

Letter or Memo of Transmittal

Use a letter of transmittal if you are not a regular employee of the organization for which you prepare the report; use a memo if you are a regular employee. See Appendix A for letter and memo formats.

The transmittal has several purposes: to transmit the report, to orient the reader to the report, and to build a good image of the report and of the writer. An informal writing style is appropriate for a transmittal even when the style in the report is more formal. A good transmittal helps you create a good image of yourself and enhances your credibility. Personal statements are appropriate in the transmittal, even though they would not be acceptable in the report itself.

Organize the transmittal in this way:

1. **Release the report.** Tell when and by whom it was authorized and the purpose it was to fulfill.
2. **Summarize your conclusions and recommendations.** If the recommendations will be easy for the reader to accept, put them early in the transmittal. If they will be difficult, summarize the findings and conclusions before the recommendations.
3. **Mention any points of special interest in the report. Indicate minor problems you encountered in your investigation and show how you surmounted them. Thank people who helped you.** These items are all optional, but they can build goodwill and enhance your credibility.
4. **Point out additional research that is necessary, if any.** Sometimes your recommendation cannot be implemented until further work is done. If you'd be interested in doing that research, or if you'd like to implement the recommendations, say so.
5. **Thank the reader for the opportunity to do the work and offer to answer questions.** Even if the report has not been fun to do, expressing satisfaction in doing the project is expected. Saying that you'll answer questions about the report is a way of saying that you won't charge the reader your normal hourly fee to answer questions (one more reason to make the report clear!).

The Letter of Transmittal on page i of Figure 15.5 uses this pattern of organization.

Table of Contents

In the Table of Contents, list the headings exactly as they appear in the body of the report. If the report is less than 25 pages, you'll probably list all the levels of headings. In a very long report, pick a level and put all the headings at that level and above in the Table of Contents.

Page ii of Figure 15.5 shows the Table of Contents.

List of Illustrations

A List of Illustrations enables readers to refer to your visuals.

Report visuals comprise both Tables and Figures. **Tables** are words or numbers arranged in rows and columns. **Figures** are everything else: bar graphs, pie charts, flow charts, maps, drawings, photographs, computer printouts, etc. Tables and figures are numbered independently, so you may have both a Table 1 and a Figure 1. In a report with maps and graphs but no other visuals, the visuals are sometimes called Map 1 and Graph 1. Whatever you call the illustrations, list them in the order in which they appear in the report; give the name of each visual as well as its number.

See Chapter 16 for information about how to design and label visuals.

Executive Summary

An **Executive Summary** or **abstract** tells the reader what the document is about. It summarizes the recommendation of the report and the reasons for the recommendation or describes the topics the report discusses and indicates the depth of the discussion.

A good abstract is easy to read, concise, and clear. Edit your abstract carefully to tighten your writing and eliminate any unnecessary words.

Wordy: The author describes two types of business jargon, *businessese* and *reverse gobbledygook.* He gives many examples of each of these and points out how their use can be harmful.

Tight: The author describes and gives examples of two harmful types of business jargon, *businessese* and *reverse gobbledygook.*

It's OK to use exactly the same words in the abstract and the report. Abstracts generally use a more formal style than other forms of business writing. Avoid contractions. Use second-person *you* only if the article uses second-person; even then, use *you* sparingly.

It is not necessary to follow the organization, wording, or proportions of the original report or article. The abstract usually uses a logical pattern of organization, putting the thesis first, even though the report may use another pattern (a psychological problem-solving pattern, for instance).

Summary abstracts present the logical skeleton of the article: the thesis or recommendation and its proof. Use a summary abstract to give the most useful information in the shortest space.

> To market life insurance to mid-forties urban professionals, Interstate Fidelity Insurance should advertise in upscale publications and use direct mail.
>
> Network TV and radio are not cost-efficient for reaching this market. This group comprises a small percentage of the prime-time network TV audience and a minority of most radio station listeners. They tend to discard newspapers and general-interest magazines quickly, but many of them keep upscale periodicals for months or years. Magazines with high percentages of readers in this group include *Architectural Digest, Bon Appetit, Business Week, Forbes, Golf Digest, Metropolitan Home, Southern Living,* and *Smithsonian.* Most urban professionals in their mid-forties are already used to shopping by mail and respond positively to well-conceived and well-executed direct mail appeals.
>
> Any advertising campaign needs to overcome this group's feeling that they already have the insurance they need. One way to do this would be to encourage them to check the coverage their employers provide and to calculate the cost of their children's expenses through college graduation. Insurance plans that provide savings and tax benefits as well as death benefits might also be appealing.

Reports of experimental research in the sciences use a formal structure that you can use for scientific abstracts: the purpose of the research; its hypothesis; the experimental method; the significant results; the implications for treatment, action, or further research.

To write abstracts of business and government reports, conference papers, and published articles, write a sentence outline. A **sentence outline** not only uses complete sentences rather than words or phrases but also contains the thesis sentence or recommendation and the points that prove that point.

What Does the Reader Want? (2)*

As Director of the Information Design Center in Washington, DC, Susan Kleimann researched reply forms for a hotel. The managers said they didn't want to read a report. So Kleimann limited the "report" to an executive summary with conclusions and recommendations. Everything else went into "appendices."

*Based on Susan D. Kleimann, "The Need to Test Forms in the Real World," Association for Business Communication Annual Convention, Orlando, FL, November 1–4, 1995.

Combine the sentences into paragraphs, adding transitions if necessary, and you'll have your abstract.

Descriptive abstracts indicate what topics the article covers and how deeply it goes into each topic, but do not summarize what the article says about each topic. Phrases that describe the paper ("this paper reports," "it includes," "it summarizes," "it concludes") are marks of a descriptive abstract. An additional mark of a descriptive abstract is that the reader can't tell what the article says about the topics it covers.

> This report recommends ways Interstate Fidelity Insurance could market insurance to mid-forties urban professionals. It examines demographic and psychographic profiles of the target market. Survey results are used to show attitudes toward insurance. The report suggests some appeals that might be successful with this market.

A **mixed abstract** is a hybrid: part summary, part description. Mixed abstracts enable you both to comment about the kind of information and present the thesis and its proof. Mixed abstracts often are used as headnotes over journal articles. Since the article is right there, the abstract essentially serves as an advertisement for the article. Rather than using a pure summary abstract and starting with the thesis, you may build readership if you start with the purpose or an attention-getter. Mixed abstracts are often the easiest to write, since you do not have to worry about the form of the abstract.

Introduction

The **Introduction** of the report always contains a statement of purpose and scope and may include all the parts in the following list.

- **Purpose.** The Purpose statement identifies the organizational problem the report addresses, the technical investigations it summarizes, and the rhetorical purpose (to explain, to recommend).
- **Scope.** The Scope statement identifies how broad an area the report surveys. For example, Company XYZ is losing money on its line of radios. Does the report investigate the quality of the radios? The advertising campaign? The cost of manufacturing? The demand for radios? A Scope statement allows the reader to evaluate the report on appropriate grounds. If the person who approved the proposal accepted a focus on advertising, then one cannot fault a report that considers only that factor.
- **Limitations.** Limitations make your recommendations less valid or valid only under certain conditions. Limitations usually arise because time or money constraints haven't permitted full research. For example, a campus pizza restaurant considering expanding its menu may ask for a report but not have enough money to take a random sample of students and townspeople. Without a random sample, the writer cannot generalize from the sample to the larger population.

  Many recommendations are valid only for a limited time. For instance, a campus store wants to know what kinds of clothing will appeal to college men. The recommendations will remain in force only for a short time: three years from now, styles and tastes may have changed, and the clothes that would sell best now may no longer be in demand.
- **Assumptions.** Assumptions in a report are like assumptions in geometry: statements whose truth you assume, and which you use to prove your final point. If they are wrong, the conclusion will be wrong too.

  For example, to plan cars that will be built five years from now, an automobile manufacturer commissions a report on young adults' attitudes toward cars. The recommendations would be based on assumptions both about gas prices and about the economy. If gas prices radically rose or fell, the kinds of cars young adults wanted would change. If there were a major recession, people wouldn't be able to buy new cars.

Almost all reports require assumptions. A good report spells out its assumptions so that readers can make decisions more confidently.

- **Methods.** If you conducted a survey, focus groups, or interviews, you need to tell how you chose your subjects, and how, when, and where they were interviewed. Reports based on scientific experiments usually put the Methods section in the body of the report, not in the Introduction.

  If your report is based solely on library or online research, omit Methods; simply cite your sources in the text and document them in Notes or References. See Chapter 14 on how to cite and document sources.

- **Criteria** or **Standards.** The Criteria section outlines the factors that you are considering and the relative importance of each. If a company is choosing a city for a new office, is the cost of office space more or less important than the availability of skilled workers? Check with your audience before you write the draft to make sure that your criteria match those of your readers.

- **Definitions.** When you know that some members of your primary, secondary, or immediate audience will not understand technical terms, define them. If you have only a few definitions, you can put them in the Introduction. If you have many terms to define, use a **Glossary** either early in the report or at the end. If the glossary is at the end, refer to it in the Introduction so that readers know that you've provided it.

Background or History

Formal reports usually have a section that gives the background of the situation or the history of the problem. Even though the current audience for the report probably knows the situation, reports are filed and consulted years later. These later audiences will probably not know the background, although it may be crucial for understanding the options that are possible.

In some cases, the History may cover many years. For example, a report recommending that a US hotel chain open hotels in Romania will probably give the history of that country for at least the last hundred years. In other cases, the History is much briefer, covering only a few years or even just the immediate situation.

Conclusions and Recommendations

Conclusions summarize points you have made in the body of the report; **Recommendations** are action items that would solve or ameliorate the problem. These sections are often combined if they are short: *Conclusions and Recommendations.*

The Conclusions section is the most widely read part of the report.[14] No new information should be included in the Conclusions. Conclusions are usually presented in paragraphs, but you could also use a numbered or bulleted list.

Many readers turn to the Recommendations section first; some organizations ask that recommendations be presented early in the report. Number the recommendations to make it easy for people to discuss them. If the recommendations will seem difficult or controversial, give a brief paragraph of rationale after each recommendation. If they'll be easy for the audience to accept, you can simply list them without comments or reasons. The recommendations will also be in the Executive Summary and perhaps in the title and the transmittal.

Figure 15.5

C. W. Consulting

2424 Circle Road • Columbus, OH 43212 • Voice 614-555-5202 • Fax 614-555-5232

April 11, 1997

Mr. Dennis Gorski, Erie County Executive
95 Franklin Street
Buffalo, NY 14202

Mr. Anthony M. Masiello, Mayor
City Hall
65 Niagara Square
Buffalo, NY 14202

Dear Mr. Gorski and Mr. Masiello:

As you requested on February 10, I have investigated ways to keep the Buffalo Bills in Buffalo.

Early in the project, it appeared that, following the Green Bay Packers' model, the best alternative might be to try to persuade the National Football League (NFL) to allow Buffalo fans to buy the team. However, my research shows that the high value of the team ($200 million) makes a fan purchase impractical.

The only options that seem workable are to try to persuade the NFL to allow corporations or municipalities to buy teams. The experiences of professional baseball and hockey, which allow such ownership, suggest that teams owned by entities who have other interests will continue to be competitive. Municipal ownership would guarantee that the team stays in western New York; however, more money may be available for corporate ownership.

With the recent departure of the Browns from Cleveland, NFL Commissioner Paul Tagliabue and NFL team owners are sensitive to the issue of team relocation. Therefore, if you accept my recommendation to lobby the NFL for a change in team ownership, do so sooner rather than later. The current climate against team relocation may change.

Most of the information for this report came from the libraries of The Ohio State University and Franklin County, from online sources, and from interviews. I appreciate the generosity of Jeff Haza of the NFL, Don Purdy of the Buffalo Bills, Phil Pionek of the Green Bay Packers, Scott Brown of Erie County, and Richard Geiger of the Greater Buffalo Convention and Visitors' Bureau, all of whom answered questions for this report.

Thank you for the opportunity to conduct this research. Like you, I want the Buffalo Bills to remain in western New York, and I enjoyed this opportunity to learn more about the Bills' organization and the NFL. If you have any questions about the report, just call me.

Sincerely,

Christy West

Christy West
General Partner

i

Design a letterhead for yourself if you choose.

In paragraph 1, release the report. Note when and by whom the report was authorized. Note report's purpose.

Give recommendations or thesis.

Thank people who helped you.

Thank the reader for the opportunity to do the research.

If you're doing the report as a consultant, offer to answer questions about the report. Answers would be included in your fee—no extra charge!

Center page number at the bottom of the page. Use a lower-case Roman numeral.

Continued   **Figure 15.5**

Most word processors create leader dots automatically. If yours doesn't, type "space dot space dot" and align dots vertically.

Table of Contents does not list itself.

Use lower-case Roman numerals for front matter.

Table of Contents

Intro begins on page "1".

Indent subheads.

Capitalize first letter of each major word in headings.

These sections may be combined.

Line up right margin (justify).

Headings or subheadings must be parallel within a section. Here, headings are phrases. Subheadings in the body of the report are complete sentences.

Add a "List of Illustrations" at the bottom of the next page if the report has graphs or other visuals.

Figure 15.5   **Continued**

Report title.   **Why Erie County and the City of Buffalo**   *This summary, like the*
          Should Lobby the National Football League to Allow   *report, is organized*
          Corporate and Municipal Ownership of Teams   *by eliminating alternatives.*

Executive Summary

Start with recommendations or thesis.

In order to keep the Bills in Buffalo, Erie County and the City of Buffalo should try to persuade the National Football League (NFL) to allow corporate and municipal ownership of league teams. If the NFL makes this change, additional research will be needed to identify corporate buyers and to determine how to finance a municipal purchase of the Buffalo Bills.

Evidence that action is needed. (In a feasibility study, one option is to do nothing.)

The owner of the Buffalo Bills, Ralph Wilson, is 78 years old. His franchise is worth approximately $200 million. Inheritance taxes for the franchise would run approximately $110 million, and Mr. Wilson's daughters have indicated that they would sell the team to pay the taxes. Current NFL ownership rules require teams to be owned by one or more individuals who do not own other businesses. Any investor interested in buying the team would be likely to move it to another city to maximize revenue. While precise dollar figures on the economic value of the Bills to Buffalo are not yet available, area officials believe the amount to be substantial. And the intangible value of having a professional football team is enormous.

Evidence showing why some actions won't work.

Three of the ways suggested for keeping the Bills in Buffalo are not feasible. It is not feasible to try to persuade the NFL to allow fans to buy the team, following the ownership model of the Green Bay Packers. The NFL leadership is opposed to such purchases, and the high value of the team prohibits such a purchase. Asking Congress to exempt the NFL from antitrust laws so that the NFL can refuse to let a team move might take too long and would in any case be useless if no owner could be found who was willing to keep the team in Buffalo. Sharing all revenues--including rentals of luxury boxes--would remove the incentive for a new owner to relocate the team. However, it seems very unlikely that owners with lucrative luxury boxes and seat licensing programs would want to share these revenues. Indeed, existing revenue sharing practices are under attack with the Cowboys' decision to sign separate contracts with sponsors.

Evidence for recommendations.

Two remaining options are for the NFL to allow corporations or municipalities to buy teams. Current rules prohibit ownership by anyone who runs another business. But the success of nonsport acquisitions suggests that ownership by another company is not a death knell for a team that is purchased. The experiences of professional baseball and hockey, which allow such ownership, suggest that teams owned by entities who have other interests will continue to be competitive. Municipal ownership would guarantee that the team never leaves western New York; however, there may be more money available for corporate ownership. If corporate ownership is allowed, the team may be moved. Corporate owners with strong ties to Buffalo and western New York will be most likely to keep the Bills in Buffalo.

Benefits to the NFL of accepting the proposed lobbying.

Corporate and municipal ownership would allow orderly successions for and sales of other NFL teams as well. NFL Commissioner Paul Tagliabue has indicated that he would like to slow or stop the current trend to relocate NFL teams. Some team owners who voted to approve the move of Mr. Modell's team from Cleveland to Baltimore have expressed publicly their concerns about a potential erosion of the NFL fan base if relocation is allowed to continue. If the fan base erodes, shared revenues from TV rights and the on-site sale of NFL merchandise may drop, affecting not just teams that relocate, but all teams in the NFL.

iii   *The abstract or executive summary contains the logical skeleton of the report: the recommendation(s) and evidence supporting them.*

Continued   **Figure 15.5**

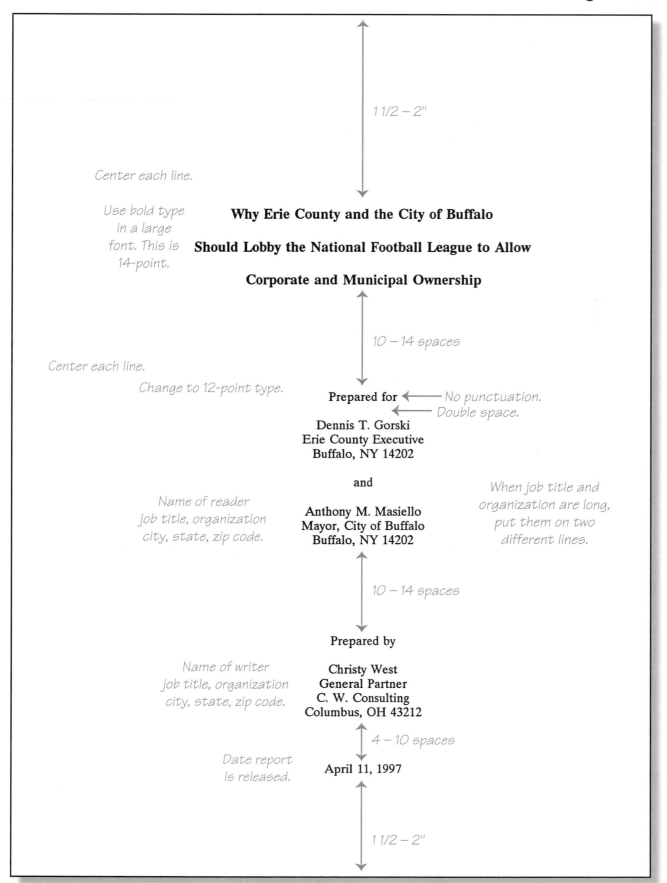

1 1/2 – 2"

Center each line.

Use bold type in a large font. This is 14-point.

Why Erie County and the City of Buffalo

Should Lobby the National Football League to Allow

Corporate and Municipal Ownership

10 – 14 spaces

Center each line.

Change to 12-point type.

Prepared for ← *No punctuation.*
← *Double space.*

Dennis T. Gorski
Erie County Executive
Buffalo, NY 14202

and

Name of reader job title, organization city, state, zip code.

Anthony M. Masiello
Mayor, City of Buffalo
Buffalo, NY 14202

When job title and organization are long, put them on two different lines.

10 – 14 spaces

Prepared by

Name of writer job title, organization city, state, zip code.

Christy West
General Partner
C. W. Consulting
Columbus, OH 43212

4 – 10 spaces

Date report is released.

April 11, 1997

1 1/2 – 2"

Figure 15.5   **Continued**

Lobbying the NFL to Allow Corporate or Municipal Ownership   Page ①

The City of Buffalo and Erie County want to ensure that the Buffalo Bills of the National Football League (NFL) will remain in western New York.

Purpose

With the aging of the Buffalo Bills' owner, Ralph Wilson, football fans and community leaders in western New York have begun to look for ways to keep the Bills football franchise in Erie County. C. W. Consulting has been asked to study the feasibility of various proposals for keeping the Bills in Buffalo.

Information for this report comes from the various libraries at The Ohio State University and the Columbus Metropolitan Libraries, online sources, and from telephone interviews with Jeff Haza of the NFL, Don Purdy of the Buffalo Bills, Phil Pionek of the Green Bay Packers, Scott Brown of Erie County, and Richard Geiger of the Greater Buffalo Convention and Visitors' Bureau. The purpose of this report is to recommend whether, based on this information, Buffalo Bills fans in western New York have a strong case to persuade the NFL to change its rules on franchise ownership.

Scope

In this report, I will briefly review the history of the Buffalo Bills' ownership and the economic hardships Ralph Wilson's daughters stand to face when they inherit the Buffalo Bills. I will discuss the importance of the Bills to Buffalo and the financial and legal factors which make moving the team a real threat. I will examine five proposals for keeing the Bills in Buffalo:

1. Allow Buffalo fans to form a nonprofit corporation to buy the team.
2. Exempt the NFL from antitrust laws.
3. Change the NFL's allocation of revenues to teams.
4. Allow corporations to buy teams.
5. Allow cities and counties to buy teams.

Finally, I will discuss the benefits to the NFL of allowing additional ownership structures.

I will not discuss the following topics: how possible changes in inheritance tax laws might affect the ownership of the Bills, possible corporate owners for the team, the financial feasibility of building a new stadium, or how a municipal purchase should be financed.

Limitations

This report has two limitations. First, although Buffalo has commissioned a report on the economic impact of the Buffalo Bills, the report has not been completed and I was unable to obtain reliable data on the eocnomic impact of the Bills to Buffalo. Second, my report depends primarily on published sources. Before approaching the NFL, the City of Buffalo and Erie County should supplement this research with more in-depth interviews with NFL personnel and with discussions with voters in Buffalo and Erie County.

Continued **Figure 15.5**

Assumptions cannot be proven. But if they are wrong, the report's recommendation may no longer be valid.

Lobbying the NFL to Allow Corporate or Municipal Ownership Page 2

Assumption

My recommendations are based on the assumption that Ralph Wilson will continue to own the Buffalo Bills until he dies. If Ralph Wilson sells the Buffalo Bills in the near future, Buffalo and Erie County may not have time to present their argument for alternate ownership models to the NFL.

Criteria

Each of the proposed ways to keep the Bills in Buffalo is evaluated on how easily approval can be obtained, how quickly the proposal could be implemented, and how successful the proposal seems likely to be.

Give name of source and identifying information to build source's credibility.

The Importance of the Buffalo Bills to Buffalo

Scott Brown, Spokesman for Erie County Executive Dennis Gorski, notes that the Greater Buffalo Parnership is doing a study right now on the economic and social impact of the Buffalo Bills. Although that study is not complete, Brown believes that the Bills create "millions of dollars a year in direct impact, through hotels, concessions, people buying things for tailgate parties, everything associated with football." In addition to income to hotels, restaurants, and stores which generates money for jobs and taxes, the county's income from rent on Rich Stadium, in which the Bills play, a 25-cent surcharge per ticket, and a share of concessions and parking fees comes to between $1.2 and $1.4 million a year (personal communication, March 31, 1997).

Begin most paragraphs with topic sentences.

APA format for phone calls and other sources of data which the reader cannot check.

Richard Geiger, President of the Greater Buffalo Convention and Visitors Bureau, says the benefits are intangible. "The media exposure, the name Buffalo on national television every weekend--those are the subjective attributes that you can't get out of dollars and cents. There's a sense of prestige associated with having an NFL franchise. There's definitely a quality of life issue. . . . The impression is that it makes us bigger than we are. Everyone knows Buffalo" (personal communication, March 31, 1997).

A feature story in *Buffalo: The Magazine of the Buffalo News* agrees: "decades of economic erosion and ill-informed negative press" mean that "to much of America, the Bills are the only thing that sets Buffalo apart from Utica, Columbus, Ohio, or any of a thousand decent but anonymous, decaying and forgettable towns." The team "provides a priceless rallying point for our civic identity." Being in the Super Bowl means being "treated as equals by the big boys" (1996, p. 6). In spite of the implications that Buffalo does not otherwise feel itself to be equal and that this is only a children's game of one-upsmanship, the quote makes clear the importance of the Bills to the city's self-image.

If author or title is in the text, do not repeat it in parenthesis. Give both the year and the page number for a direct quotation from your source.

Why the Bills May Leave Buffalo

In 1959, Ralph Wilson put up the $25,000 necessary to establish an American Football League franchise. Mr. Wilson is now 78 years old, and the franchise is worth approximately $200 million. Inheritance taxes for the franchise would run approximately $110 million, and Mr. Wilson's

Figure 15.5   **Continued**

daughters have indicated that they would sell the team to pay the taxes ("Save Our Bills," 1996).

Use a period after a first- or second-level heading only if it is a complete sentence.

Current NFL Rules Limit Who Can Own Teams.

Current NFL ownership rules limit owners to individuals or small groups (15 people or fewer). If a limited partnership of up to 15 people owns the team, one "general partner must own at least a 30% beneficial interest in the partnership and have complete management control of the club." With the "grandfathered exception" of the Green Bay Packers, "each member club must be operated on a for-profit basis." In 1993, rules were liberalized to permit privately-held entities to operate other businesses in addition to the football team. However, publicly-held entities (such as corporations) and nonprofit organizations are still prohibited from owning teams (National Football League, 1993, p. C84). These ownership policies mean that the buyers for teams will be individuals who buy teams as a way of making money.

This report uses headings—flush with the left margin—for second-level heads. Provide an overview after a heading before you give subheadings.

Owners Can Make More Money Elsewhere.

The combination of Buffalo's small size and the lack of luxury seats in Rich Stadium limits how much money an owner can make as long as the team is in Buffalo. Team revenue can be divided into two categories: revenue that is shared by all owners, and revenue retained by the team generating it.

Third-level headings have periods even when they are not complete sentences.

    TV and Some Sales Revenue Is Shared by All Owners. All teams divide equally revenues from the sale of TV and radio rights and from the licensing of NFL products sold through NFL Properties.

Give author, year, page number the first time you cite a source.

The current TV rights package, which expires after the 1997-98 season, "has brought in $4.3 billion over the last four years from telecasters ABC, ESPN, Fox, NBC and TNT" (Jensen, 1997, p. 3). Under the revenue-sharing system, each team received nearly $40 million in TV revenue last year (J. Haza, personal communication, April 8, 1997). League Commissioner Paul Tagliabue expects "very substantial increases in revenues" when the NFL negotiates its next TV rights package. Tagliabue wouldn't quote a dollar figure, but Oakland Raiders' owner Al Davis predicts the amount of revenue could double (Jensen, p. 3).

The second time you cite a source, omit the year if you have only one source by the author.

When vendors want to sell merchandise with the logo of the NFL or any of its teams, the vendor pays a division of the League offices called NFL Properties a licensing fee of $10,000, plus 9% royalties. The money collected from licensing fees and royalties is distributed equally among all teams (D. Purdy, personal communication, April 8, 1997). Sales of merchandise with the logos of NFL teams bring in more than $3 billion a year (FEATDALRecent, 1995).

Some on line sources have strange titles. Nevertheless, cite them exactly as they appear in the original.

    Owners Retain Stadium and Other Local Revenues. Except for ticket sales, portions of which go to the visiting team and to an NFL fund for stadium renovation, teams are permitted to keep income generated on site. These revenues include income from renting luxury boxes and seat licences. The most lucrative stadium is Texas Stadium, where the Dallas Cowboys play. Its 368 luxury suites yielded almost $40 million in 1995 for Cowboys' owner Jerry Jones (Atre, Auns, Badenhausen, McAuliffe, Nikolov, & Ozanian, 1996). Each team also sells its own logo merchandise at its own stadium, making each team a retailer. Each team gets to keep its own retail profits from sales of licensed logo merchandise (D. Purdy, personal communication, April 8, 1997).

Give all authors' last names the first time you cite an article.

Continued   **Figure 15.5**

Lobbying the NFL to Allow Corporate or Municipal Ownership   Page 4

How much money the team makes from on-site sales depends, perhaps, on the loyalty of fans who attend its games; how much licensed logo merchandise brings in depends on the team's popularity nationwide. Owners have no direct control over these factors. But they can increase their income by selling seat licenses or by moving from a stadium with few luxury boxes to one which will support more of them. Older stadiums may not have the structural integrity to support such renovation. Building a new stadium is easier. And if the new stadium is offered by a city eager to attract an NFL team, the team's owner may get a package for rent, concessions, and parking that is very attractive indeed.

Heading must cover everything under that heading until the next head or subhead at that level.

Legal Fears Limit the NFL's Power to Prevent a Team's Moving.

According to NFL bylaws, a team can move to another city only with the approval of 75% of the other owners. But in fact, the NFL's power to prevent a team's moving has been limited by legal fears.

Vary paragraph length for good visual impact.

As NFL Commissioner Paul Tagliabue explained to the Senate Judiciary's Subcommittee on Antitrust, Business Rights, and Competition (Heartland Institute, 1995), the current legal climate dates from the 1980s litigation with the Oakland Raiders. When the NFL refused to allow the team to leave Oakland, the owner sued for and won the right to move the team to Los Angeles. The NFL paid almost $50 million in legal fees and judgments. By 1995, the NFL was again being sued-- this time for "hundreds of millions of dollars"--as the team decided to leave Los Angeles and return to Oakland. This latter suit, Tagliabue claims, "involves a situation where the club never sought--and the League therefore never held--a vote on the proposed 1994 move."

The threat of lawsuits has forced the NFL to change at least one vote. In 1995, the NFL owners voted not to allow the Rams to move from Los Angeles to St. Louis. As a result, Tagliabue reported to the Judiciary Subcommittee,

Indented quotes don't use quotation marks.

The League's intial decision was immediately met with public and private threats--by the Rams and by the State's Attorney General--to seek "billions" of dollars in antitrust damages from the NFL in suits to be filed in St. Louis.

As a result, the membership eventually reversed its initial decision and reluctantly voted to permit the Rams to move. Even though we believed that we should have prevailed in any lawsuit, the NFL members were unwilling to endure years of antitrust litigation in a St. Louis court (Heartland Institute, testimony, 1995). *If you don't print out an online document, omit the page number—even for a direct quotation.*

After a quote, you may continue the paragraph.

The legal threat is exacerbated by the fact that the antitrust statute mandates that anyone found guilty of violating the statute be assessed punitive damages three times the amount of actual damages. Awards in these cases, therefore, can be very high.

Fear of expensive lawsuits and judgments was surely a factor in the NFL's vote to allow Art Modell to move his team from Cleveland to Baltimore at the end of the 1995 season. Even though the NFL recognizes the value of keeping teams in the cities that support them, the NFL is likely to approve a new owner's request to move the Bills to a more lucrative city.

Rather than have a heading all by itself at the bottom of a page, use a larger-than-usual bottom margin.

Figure 15.5   **Continued**

10 pt.

12 pt.   **Options for Keeping the Bills in Buffalo**

11 pt.   If nothing is done, whoever buys the Bills from Ralph Wilson's heirs will almost certainly move the team out of state. Five options have been proposed which might keep the Bills in Buffalo:

1. Allow Buffalo fans to form a nonprofit corporation to buy the team.
2. Exempt the NFL from antitrust laws.
3. Change the NFL's allocation of revenues to teams.
4. Allow corporations to buy teams.
5. Allow cities and counties to buy teams.

List in the order in which you'll discuss them.

Allow Buffalo Fans to Form a Nonprofit Corporation to Buy the Team.

A notable exception to the NFL's bylaws which prohibit nonprofit operation of a team is the Green Bay Packers. In 1950, in an effort to guarantee that the Packers wouldn't relocate to a larger market, shares of the team were sold to the public for $25 a share. In all, 4,600 shares of stock were sold to 1,800 stockholders. The nonprofit organization channels money left over from paying expenses back into the team. This unique ownership form has ensured that the city of 96,000 will keep its football team.

Vary sentence length and sentence structure.

Although the NFL grandfathered in Green Bay's ownership when the current policies were approved, the NFL leadership is opposed to allowing more fan-owned nonprofit teams (J. Haza, personal communication, April 8, 1997). And even if the NFL could be persuaded to accept fan ownership, such a solution is impractical for Buffalo. The estimated population for the Buffalo/Niagara Falls Metropolitan Statistical Area is only 1.2 million people (Hunt [p. 4]). Since the Buffalo Bills are now worth about $200 million, every man and woman and most of the children in western New York would each have to buy two $100 shares to pay for the team. That's just not going to happen.

Give initial as well as last name of source of personal communication to make it easier for reader to evaluate source.

Web page is a continuous document. When printing clearly divides it into pages, put page number you're using in square brackets.

Exempt the NFL from Antitrust Laws.

If the NFL were exempted from antitrust laws, it would be able to block the movement of teams without fear of legal retribution. Major League Baseball already enjoys an antitrust exemption: it is deemed a "pastime" by Congress, not a business. This definition makes Major League Baseball a single entity, not a collection of individual teams (businesses) competing against each other for profits. Treating the sport in this way has, in part, prevented mass relocation of major league baseball franchises.

NFL Commissioner Paul Tagliabue argues that the same exemption should be applied to the NFL. Several members of Congress sympathize with the desires of fans to keep their professional sports teams. In April 1996, the House Judiciary Committee approved HR 2740, which, according to Lisa Weintraub, would "alter antitrust law to give the leagues expanded powers to approve or disapprove a team move" (1996, p. 1169). Even this limited antitrust exemption has not become law.

Don't need author's name in parenthesis when name is in the sentence.

However, HR 2740 would merely make it more difficult to move teams, not prohibit such moves altogether. Even if the NFL is eventually exempted from antitrust laws, it, like other leagues, will allow teams to move if no local buyer comes forward. In his testimony before the Senate

Continued   **Figure 15.5**

Lobbying the NFL to Allow Corporate or Municipal Ownership   Page 6

Quote when the source is especially credible or the source's words are memorable.

Judiciary Subcommittee on Antitrust, Business Rights, and Competition, Gary B. Bettman, Commissioner of the National Hockey League (NHL), claimed, "I personally spent a tremendous amount of effort trying to preserve the Winnipeg Jets in Winnipeg. But even with the promise of a new arena, nobody was able or willing to buy the team and operated it in Winnipeg" (Heartland Institute, testimony, 1995). Rather than let the team die or require that it be sold for a price lower than market value, the NHL permitted the Jets' sale to an owner who would move the team. Since Buffalo has no individual or small group who is able and willing to buy the Bills and keep them in Buffalo, there is every reason to believe that the NFL would similarly permit the team to be sold to an owner who would move the Bills.

Change the NFL's Allocation of Revenues to Teams.

Identify source. The name alone won't tell reader whether the person is credible.

In his testimony before the Senate Judiciary Subcommittee on Antitrust, Business Rights, and Competition, Professor Stephen F. Ross of the University of Illinois proposed that the NFL require income from the rental of luxury boxes and seat licenses to be shared among all teams. Ross is correct in his claim that such a change would "take away a significant incentive for owners to relocate" (Heartland Institute, executive summary, 1995 [p. 4]). However, it seems highly unlikely that the other owners--particularly the owners who have or hope to soon have such income--would be willing to share it.

Indeed, the current NFL policies on revenue-sharing are under attack (FEATDALRecent, 1995). In 1995, Dallas Cowboys' owner Jerry Jones signed deals with PepsiCo and Nike, competitors of two of the NFL's official sponsors Coca-Cola and Reebok. The deals were possible because Jones owns Texas Stadium, where the Cowboys play; technically, the contracts are with the stadium, not the team. Each multi-year contract is estimated to be worth $2.5 million a year.

Jones has proposed that each NFL team do its own marketing when the NFL's contract with NFL Properties (the entity which markets all 30 NFL teams as a unit) expires in 2003. The NFL argues that dividing TV and licensing revenues is in the best interest of the league, half of whose teams will have a losing season in any given year. If this argument is persuasive to enough owners, Jones' proposal will not prevail. But in the current climate, it does not seem likely that owners who enjoy substantial individual income would want to share it. *Not every idea has to come from a source. You can give your own inferences based on the data and your knowledge of business and people.*

Allow Corporations to Buy Teams.

The NFL has considered the issue of corporte ownership annually since the 1980s (Deckard, 1993) but never accepted the idea. In contrast, the National Hockey League has granted franchises to Blockbuster, the Walt Disney Company, and Paramount. Paramount also owns a National Basketball Association team, as does the Tribune Co. (Deckard, 1993).

Quote when you can't think of any better words than those in the source.

Although the value of NFL teams is skyrocketing, costs are also high. While some cities have voted to increase taxes to pay for new facilities, the most common method of financing new arenas in baseball and basketball is corporate sponsorship. Indeed, *Financial World* predicts that by the end of this decade, every pro team's stadium will be named after a corporation in an industry where brand identity is crucial" (Atre et al., 1996, [p. 2]). *Use "et al." in subsequent citations of a work with many authors.*

The NFL contends that corporate ownership could be bad for the league because corporate

Figure 15.5   **Continued**

owners may have possible conflicts and other priorities. But in this day of mergers and acquisitions, it seems clear that being owned by a parent company does not, in itself, lead to poor management decisions. Corporate ownership may be essential to keep teams competitive. Currently, the gap between the teams worth most and those worth least is widening in football (as it is also in baseball and hockey; Atre et al.) This influx of corporate money could be the difference between a professional franchise's remaining in its current city or moving out of town.

Use square brackets for words you add to quote to make it fit structure of your sentence.

As Linda Deckard notes, corporate ownership may bring other benefits, "such as Disney's fabled marketing expertise. Financial restraints, such as being accountable to stockholders, might [also] be a positive" (1993, p. 2).

Corporate owners, of course, could still move teams from one city to another. However, corporations buying NFL teams would be likely to be more interested in gaining prestige and burnishing their images rather than simply increasing their income. Therefore, a corporation that purchased a football franchise would have less motivation to move it than might an individual owner or a limited partnership, for whom team income might be more important. Corporate owners with strong ties to Buffalo and western New York will be most likely to keep the Bills in Buffalo.

Triple space (2 empty spaces) before new head. Double space after head before paragraph.

Allow Cities and Counties to Buy Teams.

Municipal ownership of teams would guarantee that the team would stay. Local politicians are aware of the aura that professional sports teams give cities. Governments that have announced plans to build new venues for their teams include Hamilton County, Ohio; King County (Seattle); Maryland; Florida; and Atlanta (Atre et al.). Right now, these governments and others which, like New York City, are considering such investments, are committing funds without any guarantee that the teams will remain even for the life of the lease. Art Modell broke his Cleveland Stadium lease when he moved his team to Baltimore. He had to pay the city $9.3 million in damages in addition to $2.25 million in lease fees (King, 1996), but the city got only the money, not the team it worked so hard to keep. Buying a team would be a major financial investment for a municipality, but it would ensure that the team would remain.

Use talking heads. Note how much more informative this is than "Advantages".

Benefits to the NFL of Allowing Additional Ownership Structures

The NFL will not change its rules on ownership solely to benefit Buffalo. Instead, to gain the necessary three-fourths majority, Erie County and Buffalo must convince other team owners that they too will benefit. Fortunately, a strong case can be made that such a change is in the League's best interest. Permitting corporate and municipal ownership of teams would allow orderly successions for and sales of other teams and maintain fan loyalty and goodwill.

Allow Orderly Successions for and Sales of Other Teams.

Given the current value of NFL teams and the current inheritance tax laws in the United States, anyone who inherits an NFL team is likely to be faced with selling the franchise just to pay inheritance taxes. Since teams are owned by single individuals or small partnerships, each team is likely to face this dilemma--some not for many years, some in the next decade. If the NFL were to change its ownership rules to allow corporate or municipal ownership, heirs to NFL teams--such

Continued   **Figure 15.5**

Lobbying the NFL to Allow Corporate or Municipal Ownership   Page 8

as the daughters of Ralph Wilson--would have the option of finding a buyer who could keep a team in its current geographic location. (Granted, corporate buyers might move teams,) but if the rules were changed, owners at least would have more of a chance to sell a team to local interests.

When you cannot rebut a counter argument completely, admit its force. It's ok to use connotations to support your point of view.

Maintain Fan Loyalty and Goodwill.

Many NFL teams have moved or threaten to move in recent years. The Cardinals moved to Phoenix from St. Louis several seasons ago. The Rams just completed their first season in St. Louis after moving from Los Angeles. Cleveland's team has moved to Baltimore. The Houston Oilers will play in Nashville beginning with the 1998 season. The Bears threaten to move from Chicago to Gary, Indiana, unless the city of Chicago builds a new downtown football arena. The Seattle Seahawks want to move to Southern California, possibly Anaheim.

Begin most paragraphs with topic sentences.

These moves are not popular with fans. In a scathing *Time* magazine article in December 1995, author (Steve Wulf) vented the growing frustration of many football fans when he speculated that the NFL could stand for "No Fixed Location," or "No Fan Loyalty," or even "National Flux League":

Always cite the source of a quote in the text.

What does the N.F.L. stand for? Could it be . . . greed? How else do you explain the Arizona Cardinals making eyes at Los Angeles just seven years after they moved from St. Louis to Phoenix? How else do you explain Al Davis moving his Raiders back to Oakland after he cost the N.F.L. $50 million in legal fees and damages by moving them back to Los Angeles? How else do you explain Art Modell betraying the most loyal fans in pro football by taking his Browns from Cleveland to Baltimore? How else do you explain the blood on the hands of the Baltimoreans who are giving Modell a $200 million stadium in order to replace the Colts, who were spirited away 11 years ago in moving vans bound for Indianapolis? (1995, pp. 64-65).

Analyze passages you quote.

The terms used in this article are harsh and indicate a sense of distrust. The language Wulf uses to talk about the Browns' relocation conjures images of betrayal and murder, especially when he talks about "blood on the hands." Out of context, this language seems extreme; if one remembers the nightly reports on national television sports shows about the threats on Art Modell's life, and the attention paid to members of the anguished "Dawg Pound," the loyal end-zone Browns' fans, and the legal battle the city of Cleveland and its mayor, Michael White, raged with the NFL, then one understands how visible this loss of goodwill can be.

Quote to give exact wording of survey question, so reader can interpret data accurately.

Maintaining fan goodwill is important to the enormous revenues the NFL derives from TV, marketing, and sales contracts. A poll conducted by ESPN and Chilton Research Services found that 61% of adults aged 18 to 24 are ("at least somewhat") interested in watching football, while 30% of those are (very interested.") "Watching professional football on television is a part of American life," claims *American Demographics* ("Gridiron Groupies," 1994 [p. 1]).

This large audience is attractive to advertisers. The television market for professional football is relatively young and financially affluent. The poll found that adults with higher incomes are more likely to watch football than their lower-income counterparts. "More than half of adults with household incomes of $35,000 to $49,000 and $75,000 or more are interested in the NFL. Twenty-nine percent and 28 percent, respectively, are very interested in professional football" ("Gridiron Groupies").

Figure 15.5   **Continued**

Only two owners voted against the relocation of Modell's team: Ralph Wilson, and Dan Rooney, owner of the Pittsburgh Steelers. Even so, other team owners are beginning to see the potential erosion of the fan base that could occur if teams continue to bounce around the country. Given the popularity of football on television and the demographics of football fans, the potential loss of revenue that could accompany the loss of goodwill when franchises leave cities is substantial and could affect the finances of every NFL team.

Some companies ask for Conclusions and Recommendations at the beginning of reports.

Conclusions

Conclusions repeat points made in the report. No documentation is needed here, since it has been given earlier.

When Ralph Wilson's daughters inherit the Buffalo Bills, they will sell the team to pay the estimated $110 million in inheritance taxes they will owe. The current NFL ownership rules make it likely that the team willl be bought by someone who will move it to a more lucrative location, where luxury boxes and seat licenses can provide substantial income.

While precise dollar figures on the economic value of the Bills to Buffalo are not yet available, area officials believe the amount to be substantial. And the intangible value of having a professional football team is enormous.

Three of the ways suggested for keeping the Bills in Buffalo are not feasible.

These ideas could be presented in a paragraph. But the list provides visual variety and makes it easier for the reader to skim the page.

- It is not feasible to try to persuade the NFL to allow fans to buy the team, following the ownership model of the Green Bay Packers. The NFL leadership is opposed to such purchases, and the high value of the team prohibits such a purchase.

- Asking Congress to exempt the NFL from antitrust laws so that the NFL can refuse to let a team move might take too long and would in any case be useless if no owner could be found who was willing to keep the team in Buffalo.

- Sharing all revenues--including rentals of luxury boxes--would remove the incentive for a new owner to relocate the team. However, it seems very unlikely that owners with lucrative luxury boxes and seat licensing programs would want to share these revenues. Indeed, existing revenue sharing practices are under attack with the Cowboys' decision to sign separate contracts with sponsors.

Two remaining options are for the NFL to allow corporations or municipalities to buy teams. Current rules prohibit ownership by anyone who runs another business. But the success of nonsport acquisitions suggests that ownership by another company is not a death knell for a team that is purchased. The experiences of professional baseball and hockey, which allow such ownership, do not suggest that teams owned by entities who have other interests will be more poorly managed or less competitive. Municipal ownership would guarantee that the team never leaves western New York; however, there may be more money available for corporate ownership.

Allowing corporate and municipal ownership would make it more likely that teams would stay in their original cities. Allowing these alternate forms of ownership would allow orderly successions for and sales of other teams as well and maintain fan loyalty and goodwill. The NFL depends on income from TV rights, licensed merchandise, and sponsorship. If the fan base erodes, the value of these rights may drop, affecting not just teams that relocate, but all teams in the NFL.

Continued   **Figure 15.5**

Lobbying the NFL to Allow Corporate or Municipal Ownership   Page 10

Recommendations *Recommendations are*
                     actions the reader should take.

I recommend that Erie County and the City of Buffalo lobby the NFL to allow corporate and municipal ownership. While this lobbying is in progress, I recommend that the County and City conduct further research to identify possible corporate buyers for the Bills and to assess taxpayers' willingness to buy the team, so that, when the NFL makes its decision, the County and City will be ready to act.

Numbering the recommendations
makes it easy for the reader
to discuss them.

1.   **Lobby the NFL to Allow Corporate and Municipal Ownership.**

Corporate and municipal ownership offer the best hope for keeping the Bills in Buffalo. Indeed, without such ownership, it is likely that a new owner will move the team to a more lucrative location.

Informal discussions with each NFL owner should precede the formal presention of this proposal to the NFL. In conversations with owners, stress that permitting corporate and municipal ownership of teams would allow orderly successions for and sales of other teams and maintain fan loyalty and goodwill. The NFL depends on income from TV rights, licensed merchandise, and sponsorship. If the fan base erodes, the value of these rights may drop, affecting not just teams that relocate, but all teams in the NFL.

Move quickly on this recommendation both to take advantage of the current climate against relocation and so that the necessary action is taken in time to ensure that the Bills stay in Buffalo.

2.   **Do Further Research to Identify Possible Corporate Buyers.**

While pursuing discussions with the NFL, Erie County and the City of Buffalo should begin to identify possible corporate buyers. When the Wilson daughters inherit, they will need to sell the team quickly. The ideal buyer would have strong ties to western New York and would be committed to keeping the Bills in Buffalo.

3.   **Do Further Research to Assess Taxpayers' Willingness to Buy the Team.**

Surveys of support for the Bills suggest that a municipal purchase may be a popular move. However, it is wise to prepare carefully for a campaign. Voters would want to know about financing structures and the effect of buying the team on taxes and city and county services. Considerable advance work is necessary to determine the most fiscally sound plan so that it can be presented to the voters for approval.

Because many readers turn to the "Recommendations"
first, provide a brief reationale for each,. The ideas in
this section must be logical extensions of the points
made and supported in the body of the report.

Figure 15.5   **Continued**

APT Format

References

Atre, T., Auns, K., Badenhausen, K., McAuliffe, K., Nikolov, C. & Oznian, M. K. (1996, May 20). Sports stocks and bonds. *Financial World,* pp. 53-63.

Deckard, L. (1993, March 22). Expansion, corporate ownership on agenda at NFL owners meet. *Amusement Business,* pp. 14-15. General Reference Center Gold (GPIP), 3 pp.

FEATDALRecent Dallas deal may alter NFL handing of $3 billion a year in marketing. (1995, September 14). Associated press. http://www.nando.net.newsroom/ap/fbo/1995/nfl/dal/feat/archive/091495/dal70497.html

Gridiron groupies. (1994, June; visited site February 12, 1997). *American Demographics.* http://www.marketingtools.com/search/nn/NN151.htm

The Heartland Institute. (1995, November 29; Web pages posted August, 1996; visited sites April 3, 1997). Should Congress stop the bidding war for sports franchises? Hearing before the Subcomittee on Antitrust, Business Rights, and Competition of the Senate Committee on the Judiciary. Executive summary: http://204.120.202.3/stadsumm.htm; full testimony: http://204.120.3/stadps2.htm

Hunt Commercial Real Estate Corporation. Selected area demographics. (N.d.; visited site April 8, 1997). http://www.huntcommercial.com/locdemo.htm#Counties

Jensen, J. (1997, January 20). Tagliabue sees big score ahead for NFL TV rights. *Advertising Age,* pp. 3 and 47.

King, P. (1996, February 19). Without grace or glory. *Sports Illustrated,* p. 62.

National Football League. *NFL Policy Manual. Vol. 1, Administrative/Business Operations--General Ownership Policies.* (1993). New York: Author.

Save our Bills. (1996, September 29). *Buffalo: The Magazine of the Buffalo News,* pp. 4-8.

Weintraub, L. C. (1996, April 27). Panel approves preference in granting sports teams. *Congressional Quarterly Weekly Report,* p. 1169.

Wulf, S. (1995, December 11). Bad bounces for the N.F.L. *Time,* pp. 64-65.

Number of pages in database printout.

To avoid confusion, just divide Web addresses that don't fit on one line. A hyphen might be misread as being part of the address.

When you use two sets of pages that are part of one Web site, combine them in a single entry.

Underline titles of magazines, journals, and books if you don't have italics.

List all the printed and online sources cited in your report. Do not list sources you used for background but did not cite. Do not list interviews, phone calls, or other information to which the reader has no access.

Summary of Key Points

- **Causation** means that one thing causes or produces another. **Correlation** means that two things happen at the same time. One might cause the other, but both might be caused by a third.
- In **comparison/contrast,** the **divided pattern** takes up each alternative in turn: AAA, BBB, CCC. The **alternating pattern** takes up each criterion in turn: ABC, ABC, ABC. The **pro and con pattern** divides the alternatives and discusses the arguments for and against that alternative. A **problem-solving report** identifies the problem, explains its causes, and analyzes the advantages and disadvantages of possible solutions. **Elimination** identifies the problem, explains its causes, and discusses the least practical solutions first, ending with the one the writer favors. **General to particular** begins with the problem as it affects the organization or as it manifests itself in general, then moves to a discussion of the parts of the problem and solutions to each of these parts. **Particular to general** starts with specific aspects of the problem, then moves to a discussion of the larger implications of the problem for the organization. **Geographical or spatial** patterns discuss the problems and solutions by units. **Functional** patterns discuss the problems and solutions of each functional unit.
- Reports use the same style as other business documents, with three exceptions:

  1. Reports use a more formal style than do many letters and memos.
  2. Reports rarely use the word *you.*
  3. Reports should be self-explanatory.

- To create good report style,

  1. Say what you mean.
  2. Tighten your writing.
  3. Introduce sources and visuals gracefully.
  4. Use blueprints, transitions, topic sentences, and headings.

- **Headings** are single words, short phrases, or complete sentences that cover all of the material under it until the next heading. **Informative** or **talking heads** tell the reader what to expect in each section.
- Headings must use the same grammatical structure. Subheads under a heading must be parallel to each other but do not necessarily have to be parallel to subheads under other headings.
- The Title Page of a report usually contains four items: the title of the report, whom the report is prepared for, whom it is prepared by, and the release date.
- The title of a report should contain the recommendations unless

  - The reader will find the recommendations hard to accept.
  - Putting all the recommendations in the title would make it too long.
  - The report does not offer recommendations.

- If the title does not contain the recommendations, it normally indicates what problem the report tries to solve.
- If the report is 25 pages or less, list all the headings in the Table of Contents. In a long report, pick a level and put all the headings at that level and above in the contents.
- Organize the transmittal in this way:

  1. Release the report.
  2. Summarize your conclusions and recommendations.
  3. Mention any points of special interest in the report. Indicate minor problems you encountered in your investigation and show how you surmounted them. Thank people who helped you.

Report Your Way to a Better Job*

Joan was hired by a computer company to find references to the computer industry in current publications. To expand her job description, Joan wrote reports summarizing the data instead of just sending files of clippings. The receivers were delighted because she was saving them time.

Her second step was to meet with the people who got her reports to ask them what sorts of information they needed. Now she was able to target her reports to her readers' needs. People in each unit began to invite her to meetings discussing the projects she was researching.

As a member of the various groups within the company, Joan now had the information she needed to take a third step: drafting the report for decision makers. For example, if the sales department wanted information for a proposal to a client, she presented her information in a sales proposal. If the president wanted material for a speech, she arranged her information in a speech outline.

When the director of business communications resigned, Joan was the obvious choice for the job.

*Based on Janice LaRouche, "I'm Stuck in a Dead-End Job," *Family Circle*, March 24, 1987, 121.

4. Point out additional research that is necessary, if any.
5. Thank the reader for the opportunity to do the work and offer to answer questions.

■ **Summary abstracts** present the logical skeleton of the article: the thesis or recommendation and its proof. **Descriptive abstracts** indicate what topics the article covers and how deeply it goes into each topic, but do not summarize what the article says about each topic. **Mixed abstracts** have some characteristics of both summary and descriptive abstracts. They may list all of the topics covered in an article and summarize some of the points about some of the topics.

■ A summary abstract is based on a sentence outline. A descriptive abstract is based on a topic outline.

■ A good abstract or executive summary is easy to read, concise, and clear. A good abstract can be understood by itself, without the original article or reference books.

■ The **Introduction** of the report always contains a statement of Purpose and Scope. The **Purpose** statement identifies the organizational problem the report addresses, the technical investigations it summarizes, and the rhetorical purpose (to explain, to recommend). The **Scope** statement identifies how broad an area the report surveys. The Introduction may also include **Limitations,** problems or factors that limit the validity of your recommendations; **Assumptions,** statements whose truth you assume, and which you use to prove your final point; **Methods,** an explanation of how you gathered your data; **Criteria** or **Standards** used to weigh the factors in the decision; and **Definitions** of terms readers may not know.

■ A **Background** or **History** section is included because reports are filed and may be consulted years later.

■ **Conclusions** summarize points made in the body of the report; **Recommendations** are action items that would solve or ameliorate the problem. These sections are often combined if they are short.

Exercises and Problems For Chapter 15

GETTING STARTED

15–1   Identifying Assumptions and Limitations

Indicate whether each of the following would be an Assumption or a Limitation in a formal report.

a. Report on Ways to Encourage More Students to Join XYZ Organization
  1. I surveyed a judgment sample rather than a random sample.
  2. These recommendations are based on the attitudes of current students. Presumably, students in the next several years will have the same attitudes and interests.

b. Report on the Feasibility of Building Hilton Hotels in Vietnam
  1. This report is based on the expectation that the country will be politically stable.
  2. All of my information is based on library research. The most recent articles were published two months ago; much of the information was published a year ago or more. Therefore some of my information may be out of date.

c. Report on Car Buying Preferences of Young Adults
   1. These recommendations may change if the cost of gasoline increases dramatically or if there is another deep recession.
   2. This report is based on a survey of adults ages 20 to 24 in California, Texas, Illinois, Ontario, and Massachusetts.
   3. These preferences are based on the cars now available. If a major technical or styling innovation occurs, preferences may change.

15–2   Writing Summary and Descriptive Abstracts

Write both a summary and a descriptive abstract of an article. Turn in a copy of the article along with your abstracts.

COMMUNICATING AT WORK

As Your Instructor Directs, in Problems 15–3 and 15–4,
   a. Create a document or presentation to achieve the goal.
   b. Write a memo to your instructor describing the situation at your workplace and explaining your rhetorical choices (medium, strategy, tone, wording, graphics or document design, and so forth).

15–3   Explaining "Best Practices"

Write a report explaining the "best practices" of your unit that could also be adopted by other units in your organization.

15–4   Recommending Action

Write a report recommending an action that your unit or organization should take. Possibilities include

- Buying more equipment for your department.
- Hiring an additional worker for your department.
- Making your organization more family-friendly.
- Making a change that will make the organization more efficient.
- Making changes to improve accessibility for customers or employees with disabilities.

Address your report to the person who would have the power to approve your recommendation.

REPORT ASSIGNMENTS

15–5   Evaluating Annual Reports

Evaluate one or more annual reports. Is the report interesting and easy to read? Does it create a favorable impression of the company? Does it deal effectively with any problems the company faced that year? Consider the following aspects of the report:

- Financial data. What is included? How is it presented? Can a nonaccountant understand it?
- Visuals and layout. Are visuals used effectively? Are they accurate and free from chartjunk? What image do the pictures and visuals create? Are color and white space used effectively? (See Chapter 16 on visuals.)
- Emphasis. What points are emphasized? What points are deemphasized? What verbal and visual techniques are used to highlight or minimize information?

As Your Instructor Directs,
   a. Write a memo to your instructor analyzing the annual report of a company that interests you.

b. Write a memo to your instructor comparing and contrasting the annual reports of two companies in the same industry.

c. Join with a small group of students to analyze three or more annual reports.

Present your evaluation in an informal group report.

d. Present your evaluation orally to the class.

15–6   Writing a Feasibility Study

Write a report evaluating the feasibility of two or more alternatives. Possible topics include the following:

1. Is it feasible for a local restaurant to open another branch? Where should it be?

2. Is it feasible to create a program to mentor women and minorities in your organization?

3. Is it feasible to produce a video yearbook in addition to or instead of a paper yearbook at your college, community college, or university?

4. Is it feasible to create or enlarge a day care center for the children of students?

5. Could your college host a regional meeting of the Association for Business Communication on campus or in town?

6. Is it feasible to start a monthly newsletter for students in your major?

7. Is it feasible for local grocery stores to stock (or increase their stock of) carambolas, mamey, longans, lychees, atemoyas, sugar apples, jackfruit, and other exotic Asian and Latin American fruits and vegetables? If so, where should the additional space come from: Less space for traditional fruits and vegetables? Less space for another department (which one?)? Store expansion?

Pick a limited number of alternatives, explain your criteria clearly, evaluate each alternative, and recommend the best course of action.

15–7   Writing an Informative or Closure Report

Write an informative report on one of the following topics.

1. What should a US or Canadian manager know about dealing with workers from_____[you fill in the country or culture]? What factors do and do not motivate people in this group? How do they show respect and deference? Are they used to a strong hierarchy or to an egalitarian setting? Do they normally do one thing at once or many things? How important is clock time and being on time? What factors lead them to respect someone? Age? Experience? Education? Technical knowledge? Wealth? Or what? What conflicts or miscommunications may arise between workers from this culture and other workers due to cultural differences? Are people from this culture similar in these beliefs and behaviors, or is there lots of variation?

2. Describe an ethical dilemma encountered by workers in a specific organization. What is the background of the situation? What competing loyalties exist? In the past, how have workers

responded? How has the organization responded? Have "whistle-blowers" been rewarded or punished? What could the organization do to foster ethical behavior?

3. Describe a problem or challenge encountered by an organization where you've worked. Describe the problem, show why it needed to be solved, tell who did what to try to solve it, and tell how successful the efforts were. Possibilities include

   ▪ How the organization is implementing work teams, downsizing, or a change in organizational culture.

   ▪ How the organization uses e-mail or voice mail, statistical process control, or telecommuting.

   ▪ How managers deal with stress, make ethical choices, or evaluate subordinates.

   ▪ How the organization is responding to changing US demographics, the Americans with Disabilities Act, or international competition and opportunities.

15–8 Writing a Consultant's Report—Restaurants

Although the Western Buffet has been packed nearly every night since it opened a year ago, it's been losing thousands of dollars each month. Owners Larry Anton and Boyd Call have never run a restaurant before. They don't want to be among the 60% of restaurants that fail in the first five years, so they've called in your hospitality consulting firm.

After a month of research, you reach these conclusions:

1. Some food disappears because employees are stealing. Locks are needed on the freezers and storage areas.
2. The Buffet must end its practice of providing free drinks and meals for employees. So far this year, the Buffet has given away $36,000 of free liquor. Employees should purchase their own liquor and meals (though the latter could be made available at cost).
3. The Buffet should use less expensive cuts of meat. Switching to cheaper ribs from perfectly square, 4-inch slabs of barbecue ribs would save $2,500 a week.
4. Currently, the Buffet buys its desserts from an upscale bakery. Baking them in-house would save $500 a week—even after the cost of ingredients and hiring a baker is included.
5. Instead of throwing out uneaten kale lettuce each night, the Buffet should refrigerate it and use it to decorate the buffet tables the next day. Eliminating the need to buy decorative lettuce will save $2,000 a year.
6. The Buffet should try to increase liquor sales, which have a higher profit than food sales. Asking customers if they want drinks and offering drink specials are two ways to increase the percentage of customers who order alcohol.

Write a short report to the owners, recommending what they should do.

Hint:
Start the report with the recommendations the owners will find easiest to accept.

15–9 Writing a Library Research Report

Write a library research report.

As Your Instructor Directs,
Turn in the following documents:

a. The approved proposal.
b. Two copies of the report, including
   Cover.
   Title Page.
   Letter or Memo of Transmittal.
   Table of Contents.
   List of Illustrations.
   Executive Summary or Abstract.
   Body (Introduction, all information, recommendations). Your instructor may specify a minimum length, a minimum number or kind of sources, and a minimum number of visuals.
   References or Works Cited.
c. Your notes and rough drafts.

Choose one of the following topics.

1. **Managing Workforce 2000.** Your boss is concerned that traditional management techniques may not work for all the cultures now in the workforce. She hands you an article from her files: "Check this out and update it. What are experts saying now about the best techniques for managing multicultural workers in our industry? Does "what's best" depend on what people are doing or on other factors? Come up with some concrete recommendations that will apply to our organization." Start your research with Catherine Yang, Ann Therese Palmer, Seanna Browder, and Alice Cuneo, "Low-Wage Lessons," *Business Week*, November 11, 1996, 108–16. (Address the report to an organization you know well.)

2. **Retaining Record Royalties.** Your boss is Director of Marketing for a major music label. "We've got a real problem. Labels that let people download music files get a lot more hits on their Web pages than we do. But if we distribute music on the Web, why should anyone buy a CD? As it is, we've got a problem with bootleg recordings that fans post. What can we do?" Start your research with Don Steinberg, "Digital Underground," *Wired*, January 1997, 104–10.

3. **Marketing to the Mature Market.** Your boss is an account executive at an ad agency. "You know, we've always focused on younger buyers because they seemed more profitable. But some of the people who are retired have a lot of discretionary income. Pick one of our clients, and write a report about what kinds of ads, packaging, and promotional events are most promising to increase sales by mature customers." Start your research with George P. Moschis, "Life Stages of the Mature Market," *American Demographics*, September 1996, 44–50. (Address your report to an ad agency; write it about a specific consumer product.)

4. **Reevaluating Recycling.** You work for the Mayor, who hands you a copy of Jeff Bailey, "Waste of a Sort: Curbside Recycling Comforts the Soul, but Benefits Are Scant," *The Wall Street Journal*, January 19, 1995, A1, A6. "I want you to recommend whether we should continue curbside recycling. This article suggests it costs more than it saves. Is that right? And even if it is, should we continue curbside pickup for nonfinancial reasons?" (Pick a city you know well.)

5. **Keeping Workers Safe.** Restaurants, especially fast-food outlets, are increasingly targets of robberies. Your boss says, "I think we need to do more to protect our workers. Lots of them are teenagers, and they don't have lots of experience. What can we do to make them safer? And how can we persuade them to follow security policies *before* there's a robbery?" Start your research with Laurie M. Grossman, "Easy Marks: Fast-Food Industry Is Slow to Take Action against Growing Crime, *The Wall Street Journal*, September 22, 1994, A1, A4. (Address your report to the manager of a specific fast-food store.)

6. **Deciding Whether to Be an Olympic Sponsor.** Your boss is the new marketing director of a major company. "Does it make sense financially to be an Olympic sponsor? If so, what kind of sponsorship should we have? What kind of events or advertising is needed to support sponsorship? Do the answers change depending on whether we're talking about summer or winter games or on where the Olympics are held?" Start your research with Nicole Harris, "The Game's Afoot—and It's Marketing," *Business Week*, January 22, 1996, 95, and Emory Thomas Jr., "The Bottom Line," *The Wall Street Journal*, July 19, 1996, R14. (Address your report to a specific company and recommend whether it should pay to sponsor the Olympics.)

7. **Bringing Hope to the 'Hood.** You're on the Mayor's staff in a major metropolitan city. "We've got some neighborhoods that really need work," he says. "The ideas in this article look promising. Find out what happened—whether these plans worked—and recommend which if any of them we should implement." Start your research with Ron Stodghill, "Bringing Hope Back to the 'Hood," *Business Week*, August 19, 1996, 70–73. (Pick a city you know well. You may need to focus on one part of the problem: public housing, tax policies for individuals or businesses, involving churches or other groups in improving the neighborhood.)

8. **Handling Personal Information.** Your boss is a Congresswoman who's concerned about privacy. "As things get more electronic, more information about people is recorded. It's possible to find out who buys cigarettes, what books and videos someone buys or checks out, and all kinds of medical and financial data. Write a report on what the experts are saying about current problems and solutions in personal data. You don't need to look at legislative issues: I'll use your report to decide whether I want to make this an issue." Start your research with Jim Castelli, "How to Handle Personal Information," *American Demographics*, March 1996, 50–57.

9. **Using Pay to Increase Productivity.** Your boss hands you a copy of Howard Gleckman, Sandra Atchison, Tim Smart, and John A. Byrne, "Bonus Pay: Buzzword or Bonanza?" *Business Week*, November 14, 1994, 62–64. "This

article's kind of old, and I wonder whether it's still true. Would changing our compensation package increase productivity here?" (Address your

report to an organization you know well.)

10. With your instructor's permission, choose your own topic.

15–10   Writing a Recommendation Report

Write an individual or a group report.

As Your Instructor Directs,

Turn in the following documents:

1. The approved proposal.
2. Two copies of the report, including
   Cover.
   Title Page.
   Letter or Memo of Transmittal.
   Table of Contents.
   List of Illustrations.
   Executive Summary or Abstract.
   Body (Introduction, all information, recommendations). Your instructor may specify a minimum length, a minimum number or kind of sources, and a minimum number of visuals.
   Appendixes if useful or relevant.
3. Your notes and rough drafts.

Pick one of the following topics.

1. **Evaluating Airport Signs.** When international students or business people arrive in town, can they easily get information in their own languages? What information needs to be on airport signs? In which languages? What information could be on an interactive kiosk? What languages should it include? Address your report to the manager of the airport.
2. **Recommending Courses for the Local Community College.** Businesses want to be able to send workers to local community colleges to upgrade their skills; community colleges want to prepare students to enter the local workforce. What skills are in demand in your community? What courses at what levels should the local community college offer?

3. **Improving Sales and Profits.** Recommend ways a small business in your community can increase sales and profits. Focus on one or more of the following: the products or services it offers, its advertising, its decor, its location, its accounting methods, its cash management, or any other aspect that may be keeping the company from achieving its potential. Address your report to the owner of the business.

4. **Increasing Student Involvement.** How could an organization on campus persuade more of the students who are eligible to join or to become active in its programs? Do students know that it exists? Is it offering programs that interest students? Is it retaining current members? What changes should the organization make? Address your report to the officers of the organization.

5. **Evaluating a Potential Employer.** What training is available to new employees? How soon is the average entry-level person promoted? How much travel and weekend work are expected? Is there a "busy season," or is the workload consistent year-round? What fringe benefits are offered? What is the corporate culture? Is the climate nonracist and nonsexist? How strong is the company economically? How is it likely to be affected by current economic, demographic, and political trends? Address your report to the Placement Office on campus; recommend whether it should encourage students to work at this company.

6. With your instructor's permission, choose your own topic.

CHAPTER 16

Using Graphs and Other Visuals

Chapter Outline

An Inside Perspective: Using Graphs and Other Visuals

Jeff Evers, Associate Producer
ESPN, Inc.

Jeff Evers conceptualizes and creates graphics for ESPN's college basketball and major league baseball games. He also produces graphics and edits video teasers to get fans "pumped up." With three networks that cover sports 24 hours a day, ESPN is the largest sports cable network in the world. Headquartered in Bristol, Connecticut, ESPN covers every sport, from the NFL to the Extreme Games, from European Soccer to Deep Sea Fishing.

In sports, we give viewers information so that they can feel smart when they talk to their friends the next day: "Hey, did you know that Albert Belle has *averaged* 43 home runs and 120 RBIs a year over the past five years?" My goal as a graphics producer is to choose statistics that will tell fans interesting stories.

Last season, the Red Sox and Yankees were playing the last game of an important series. The Yankees had just taken the lead in the 8th inning, 4–3. From my research, I knew that the Yankees were an incredible 78–0 when leading a game into the 9th inning. As our director showed a shot of John Wetteland, the Yankees' ace reliever, warming up to start the 9th inning, I flashed that graphic. The announcers referred to it, saying it was a "staggering number." Well, the unbelievable happened. The Boston Red Sox scored two runs and won the game 5–4. Our announcers referred again to the 78–0 statistic, saying that our crew might have jinxed the Yankees.

Graphics have to support what the announcers are saying. We discuss possible topics in pregame meetings. Then I input data supporting those topics into a computer for 10 to 12 hours before the game starts. If I am thinking along with the announcers and even trying to anticipate where they are going with a story, I can make the telecast that much better by enhancing it with a pertinent graphic.

Over the last couple of years, ESPN has moved away from "stills" to present graphical information. Information hasn't changed, but the way we present it has. A good example of this was a baseball game I did last year at Coors Field in Denver, CO, which is 5280 feet—one mile—above sea level. I wanted to show that balls travel farther in thin air than they do at sea level. A ball that would travel 400 feet at sea level will travel 430 feet one mile above sea level. I had a graphic designer make models of both Shea Stadium—which is at sea level—and Coors Field. We then showed an animated batter hitting a ball in both stadiums, using animated arrows to show the flights of the balls. With a visual, the story is as clear as day. The graphic not only explained an interesting story but also jazzed up the whole concept and really helped the telecast.

My advice for design would be to keep the information simple. Use animation only when it is necessary to prove a point—and do have a point behind why you are using animation. My job is to think of a concept, bring a storyboard layout of how I want to convey my idea, and then discuss ways to reach this goal with the artist.

Jeff Evers, March 11, 1997

Visit ESPN's Web site: http://espnet.sportszone.com/

"My goal is to choose statistics that will tell fans interesting stories."

Jeff Evers, ESPN

Visuals help make numbers meaningful and thus help communicate your points in telecasts, oral presentations, memos, letters, reports, and meetings. This chapter shows you how to turn data into graphs and other visuals. See Chapter 6 for a discussion of designing slides for oral presentations and Chapter 17 for a discussion of other aspects of good oral presentations.

Visuals can present numbers dramatically. The Consumer Federation of America crystallized discontent with high interest rates on consumer loans by issuing a simple three-page study with a graph showing that while the prime rate was going down, interest on consumer loans was going up. Dan Rather showed the graph and discussed the report on the evening news; the publicity helped persuade Congress to pass laws requiring fuller disclosure and some caps on interest rates.[1]

Numbers are no more "objective" than words are: both require interpretation and context to have meaning. On November 1, 1990, both *The Wall Street Journal* and *The Columbus Dispatch* carried stories about General Motors' third-quarter loss, which had been announced the day before. *The Dispatch*'s headline was negative: "GM's $2 billion quarterly loss biggest ever." *The Wall Street Journal*, in contrast, saw the loss as a positive strategic move: "Smaller Giant: Huge GM Write-Off Positions Automaker to Show New Growth."[2] The two headlines come from and suggest very different ways to view the loss and GM's potential.

The same numbers can be presented in different ways to create very different impressions. During the 1996 presidential campaign, Bob Dole charged that Clinton's 1993 tax increase was the largest in history. In unadjusted dollars, that statement was true. But if one adjusts for inflation or measures taxes as a percent of the gross domestic product, Reagan's 1982 tax increase was bigger. Tax surcharges during World War II were likely even bigger than Reagan's tax increase, but we can't compare because the data isn't available.[3]

WHEN TO USE VISUALS

The ease of creating visuals by computer may make people use them uncritically. When every bit of numerical data is put in a visual, or if the writer chooses the wrong visual, the visual does little more than take up space. Never put in numbers or visuals just because you have them; instead, use them to convey information the audience needs or wants.

In your rough draft, use visuals

- **To see that ideas are presented completely.** A table, for example, can show you whether you've included all the items in a comparison.
- **To find relationships.** For example, charting sales on a map may show that the sales representatives who made quota all have territories on the east or the west coast. Is the central United States suffering a recession? Is the product one that appeals to coastal lifestyles? Is advertising reaching the coasts but not the central states? Even if you don't use the visual in your final document, creating the map may lead you to questions you wouldn't otherwise ask.

Showing Trends and Changes*

Jerry Atkinson gives his clients not only financial statements but also graphs of key trends. Atkinson is managing director of Atkinson and Company, a 62-employee CPA firm in Albuquerque, New Mexico.

Current-month or year information isn't enough, he says. Clients need to see trends and changes. And graphs offer an easy way to show that.

Atkinson personalizes the graphs by using the colors of the company being profiled.

*Based on John von Brachel, "Interpreting Financial Statements: How One Firm Uses the Language of Graphics," *Journal of Accountancy* 180, no. 2 (August 1995): 42–43.

In the final presentation or document, use visuals

- **To make points vivid.** Readers skim memos and reports; a visual catches the eye. The brain processes visuals immediately. Understanding words—written or oral—takes more time.
- **To emphasize material** that might be skipped if it were buried in a paragraph. The beginning and end are places of emphasis. However, especially in a long document, something has to go in the middle. Visuals allow you to emphasize important material, wherever it logically falls.
- **To present material more compactly and with less repetition** than words alone would require. Words can call attention to the main points of the visual, without repeating all of the visual's information.

The number of visuals you will need depends on your purposes, the kind of information, and the audience. You'll use more visuals when you want to show relationships and to persuade, when the information is complex or contains extensive numerical data, and when the audience values visuals. Some audiences and discourse communities (⊷ p. 61) expect oral presentations and reports to use lots of visuals. Other audiences and discourse communities may see visuals as frivolous and time spent making visuals as time wasted. For these audiences, you'd sharply limit the number of visuals you use—but you'd still use them when your own purposes and the information called for them.

DESIGNING VISUALS

Use these six steps to create good visuals:

1. Check the source of the data.
2. Determine the story you want to tell.
3. Choose the right visual for the story.
4. Follow the conventions for designing typical visuals.
5. Use color and decoration with restraint.
6. Be sure the visual is accurate and ethical.

Let's discuss each of these briefly.

1. Check the Source of the Data.

Your chart is only as good as the underlying data. Check to be sure that your data come from a reliable source. When the source has a vested interest (⊷ p. 213) in the results, scrutinize them with special care. In 1995, America Online claimed that its subscribers stayed an average of 41 months. But 60% of its customers had joined in the previous nine months.[4] The news release was image advertising, not reliable data.

Identify the assumptions used in analyzing the data. When studies contradict each other, the explanation sometimes lies in the assumptions. For example, a study that found disposable diapers were better for the environment than cloth diapers assumed that each diaper change used 1.9 or 1.79 diapers and that a cloth diaper lasted for 92.5 uses. A study that found that cloth diapers were better assumed that each diaper change used 1.72 diapers and that each cloth diaper lasted for 167 uses.[5]

Identify exactly what the data measure. For example, using a Dun & Bradstreet database, many people claim that only 28% of small businesses survive for eight years. But that database counts a small business as "surviving" only if it remains under the same ownership. Researcher Bruce

Statistics and Staying Alive*

In 1982, Stephen Jay Gould, author of *The Panda's Thumb* and other essays on evolution, learned that he had a rare, incurable form of cancer. Patients lived a median of eight months after the disease was discovered.

Gould knew that "lived a median of eight months" meant half the people lived longer. Some of them lived a lot longer.

Furthermore, he knew, the statistics referred to cases treated by conventional means. Gould entered an experimental protocol. He thus had the opportunity to be in a new group with a new median and a new distribution curve.

Gould was young; his disease had been caught early; he had excellent medical care; he wanted to live; and he knew enough about statistics to read the data correctly and avoid despair.

As this book goes to press 15 years after the initial diagnosis, Gould is alive and doing well. And he's still writing essays helping us understand science and statistics.

*Based on Stephen Jay Gould, "The Median Isn't the Message," *Discover*, June 1985, 40–42.

Kirchoff found that another 26% survive with ownership changes, for a total survival rate of 54%.[6]

You may be able to use data based on assumptions and definitions in careful titles or notes: "Under the Fast-Growth Scenario, Sales Will Triple." "Over One-Fourth of Small Businesses Last Eight Years under Original Owners." If the data themselves are unreliable, you're better off not using visuals. The visual picture will be more powerful than verbal disclaimers, and the audience will be misled.

2. Determine the Story You Want to Tell.

Every visual should tell a story. Stories can be expressed in complete sentences that describe something that happens or changes. The sentence also serves as the title of the visual.

Not a story:	US Sales, 1992–97
Possible stories:	Forty Percent of Our Sales Were to New Customers.
	Growth Was Highest in the South.
	Sales Increased from 1992 to 1997.
	Most Sales Representatives Have 2–5 Years' Experience.
	Sales Were Highest in the Areas with More Sales Representatives.

Stories that tell us what we already know are rarely interesting. Instead, good stories may

- Support a hunch you have.
- Surprise you or challenge so-called "common knowledge."
- Show trends or changes you didn't know existed.
- Have commercial or social significance.
- Provide information needed for action.
- Be personally relevant to you and the audience.

To find stories,

1. Focus on a topic (starting salaries, who likes rock music, and so forth).
2. Simplify the data on that topic and convert the numbers to simple, easy-to-understand units.
3. Look for relationships and changes. For example, compare two or more groups: do men and women have the same attitudes? Look for changes over time. Look for items that can be seen as part of the same group. For example, to find stories about TV ads, you might group ads in the same product category—ads for cars, for food, for beverages.

When you think you have a story, test it against all the data to be sure it's accurate.

Some stories are simple straight lines: "Sales Increased." But other stories are more complex, with exceptions or outlying cases. Such stories will need more nuanced titles to do justice to the story. And sometimes the best story arises from the juxtaposition of two stories. In Figure 16.1, *Business Week* uses **paired graphs** to tell a surprising story. Normally, when interest rates rise, the stock market falls. But in the six weeks graphed here, despite rising interest rates (story 1), stocks have soared (story 2). The combination is a powerful, interesting story.

Gene Zelazny points out that the audience should be able to *see* what the message *says:*

> [D]oes the chart support the title; and does the title reinforce the chart? So if I *say* in my title that "sales have increased significantly" I want to *see* a trend moving up at a

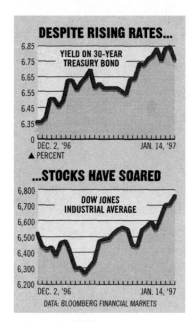

Source: Eric Hoffmann, *Business Week,*
January 27, 1997.

Figure 16.1

**A Complex Story
Using Paired Graphs**

sharp angle. If not, if the trend parallels the baseline, it's an instant clue that the chart needs more thinking.[7]

Almost every data set allows you to tell several stories. You must choose the story you want to tell. Dumps of uninterpreted data confuse and frustrate your audience; they undercut the credibility and goodwill you want to create.

Sometimes several stories will be important. When that's the case, you'll need a separate visual for each.

3. Choose the Right Visual for the Story.

Visuals are not interchangeable. Good writers choose the visual that best matches the purpose of presenting the data.

- Use **tables** when the reader needs to be able to identify exact values. (See Figure 16.2a.)
- Use a chart or graph when you want the reader to focus on relationships.[8]
  - To compare a part to the whole, use a **pie chart.** (See Figure 16.2b.)
  - To compare one item to another item, use a **bar chart** or a **map.** (See Figure 16.2c.)
  - To compare items over time, use a **bar chart** or a **line graph.** (See Figure 16.2d.)
  - To show frequency or distribution, use a **bar chart** or **line graph.** (See Figure 16.2e.)
  - To show correlations, use a **bar chart,** a **line graph,** or a **dot chart.** (See Figure 16.2f.)
- Use **photographs** to create a sense of authenticity or show the item in use. If the item is especially big or small, include something in the photograph that can serve as a reference point: a dime, a person.
- Use **drawings** to show dimensions or emphasize detail.
- Use **maps** to emphasize location.
- Use **Gannt charts** to show timelines for proposals or projects.

Figure 16.2   **Choose the Visual to Fit the Story**

US Sales Reach $44.5 Million			
Millions of Dollars			
	1996	1997	1998
Northeast	10.2	10.8	11.3
South	7.6	8.5	10.4
Midwest	8.3	6.8	9.3
West	11.3	12.1	13.5
Totals	37.4	38.2	44.5

a. Tables show exact values.

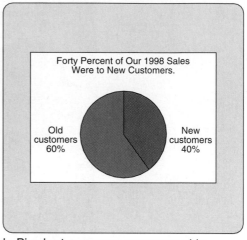

b. Pie charts compare a component to the whole.

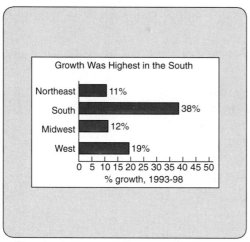

c. Bar charts compare items or show distribution or correlation.

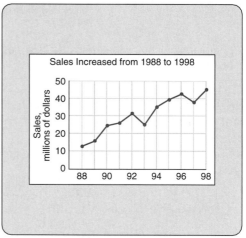

d. Line charts compare items over time or show distribution or correlation.

e. Bar charts can show frequency.

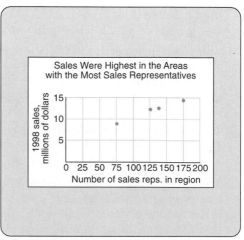

f. Dot charts show correlation.

4. Follow the Conventions for Designing Typical Visuals.

Every visual should contain six components:

1. A title that tells the story that the visual shows.
2. A clear indication of what the data are. For example, what people *say* they did is not necessarily what they really did. An estimate of what a number will be in the future differs from numbers in the past that have already been measured.
3. Clearly labeled units.
4. Labels or legends identifying axes, colors, symbols, and so forth.
5. The source of the data, if you created the visual from data someone else gathered and compiled.
6. The source of the visual, if you reproduce a visual someone else created.

Formal visuals are divided into tables and figures. **Tables** are numbers or words arrayed in rows and columns; **figures** are everything else. In a document, formal visuals have both numbers and titles, e.g., "Figure 1. The Falling Cost of Computer Memory, 1990–97." In an oral presentation, the title is usually used without the number: "The Falling Cost of Computer Memory, 1990–97." The title should tell the story so that the audience knows what to look for in the visual and why it is important. Informal or **spot** visuals are inserted directly into the text; they do not have numbers or titles.

Tables

Use tables only when you want the audience to focus on specific numbers. Graphs convey less specific information but are always more memorable. Figure 16.3 illustrates the basic structure of tables. The **boxhead** is the variable whose label is at the top; the **stub** is the variable listed on the side.

- Use common, understandable units. Round off to simplify the data (e.g., 35% rather than 35.27%; 34,000 rather than 33,942).
- Provide column and row totals or averages when they're relevant.
- Put the items you want readers to compare in columns rather than in rows to facilitate mental subtraction and division.
- When you have many rows, screen alternate entries or double space after every five entries to help readers line up items accurately.

Pie Charts

Pie charts force the audience to measure area. Research shows that people can judge position or length (which a bar chart uses) much more accurately than they judge area. The data in any pie chart can be put in a bar chart.[9] Therefore, use a pie chart only when you are comparing one segment to the whole. When you are comparing one segment to another segment, use a bar chart, a line graph, or a map—even though the data may be expressed in percentages.

- Start at 12 o'clock with the largest percentage or the percentage you want to focus on. Go clockwise to each smaller percentage or to each percentage in some other logical order.
- Make the chart a perfect circle. Perspective circles distort the data.
- Limit the number of segments to five or seven. If your data has more divisions, combine the smallest or the least important into a single "miscellaneous" or "other" category.
- Label the segments outside the circle. Internal labels are hard to read.

Figure 16.3   **Tables Show Exact Values**

Table Number -Title

Source line

**Table 4. US Firms Dominate
the Top Ten**

1996 Rank	Company (Country)	Market Value, Millions of US Dollars
1	General Electric (US)	$136,515
2	Royal Dutch/Shell (Netherlands/UK)	128,206
3	Coca-Cola (US)	117,258
4	NTT (Japan)	113,609
5	Exxon (US)	102,161
6	Bank of Tokyo–Mitsubishi (Japan)	98,191
7	Toyota Motor (Japan)	91,519
8	Philip Morris (US)	86,424
9	AT&T (US)	83,960
10	Merck (US)	78,163

Source: Adapted from "The World's 100 Largest Public Companies," *The Wall Street Journal,* September 26, 1996, R27.

Bar Charts

Bar charts are easy to interpret because they ask people to compare distance along a common scale, which most people judge accurately. Bar charts are useful in a variety of situations: to compare one item to another, to compare items over time, and to show correlations. Use horizontal bars when your labels are long; when the labels are short, either horizontal or vertical bars will work.

- Order the bars in a logical or chronological order.
- Put the bars close enough together to make comparison easy.
- Label both horizontal and vertical axes.
- Put all labels inside the bars or outside them. When some labels are inside and some are outside, the labels carry the visual weight of longer bars, distorting the data.
- Make all the bars the same width.
- Use different colors for different bars only when their meanings are different: estimates as opposed to known numbers, negative as opposed to positive numbers.
- Avoid using perspective. Perspective makes the values harder to read and can make comparison difficult.

Several varieties of bar charts exist. See Figure 16.4 for examples.

- **Grouped bar charts** allow you to compare several aspects of each item, or several items over time.
- **Segmented, subdivided** or **stacked bars** sum the components of an item. It's hard to identify the values in specific segments; grouped bar charts are almost always easier to use.
- **Deviation bar charts** identify positive and negative values, or winners and losers.
- **Paired bar charts** show the correlation between two items.
- **Histograms** or **pictograms** use images to create the bars.

Varieties of Bar Charts

Figure 16.4

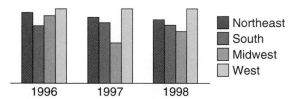

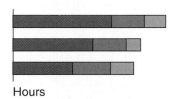

Grouped bar charts compare several aspects of each item, or several items over time.

Segmented, subdivided, or **stacked bars** sum the components of an item.

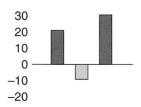

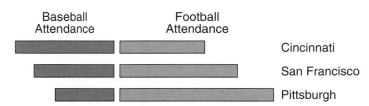

Deviation bar charts identify positive and negative values.

Paired bar charts show the correlation between two items.

Starting Salary

Northeast	$ $ $ $ $ $ $		$ = $5,000
South	$ $ $ $ $ $		
Midwest	$ $ $ $ $		
West	$ $ $ $ $ $ $ $		

Histograms or **pictograms** use images to create the bars.

Line Graphs

Line graphs are also easy to interpret. Use line graphs to compare items over time, to show frequency or distribution, and to show correlations.

- Label both horizontal and vertical axes.
- When time is a variable, put it on the horizontal axis.
- Avoid using more than three different lines on one graph. Even three lines may be too many if they cross each other.
- Avoid using perspective. Perspective makes the values harder to read and can make comparison difficult.

Line graphs with the area below the line filled in are sometimes called **landscape graphs** (Figure 16.1).

Dot Charts

Dot charts show correlations or other large data sets.

- Label both horizontal and vertical axes.
- Keep the dots fairly small. If they get too big, they no longer mark data "points"; some of the detail is lost.

Figure 16.5

Drawings Focus on Details

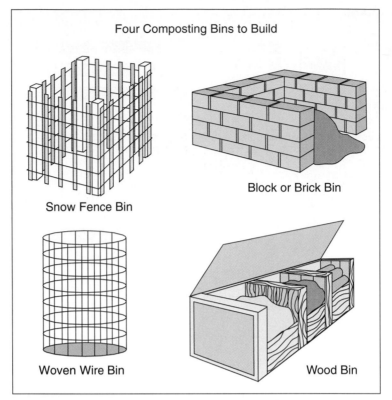

Four Composting Bins to Build

Snow Fence Bin

Block or Brick Bin

Woven Wire Bin

Wood Bin

Source: *The Columbus Dispatch*, May 13, 1991, Advertising Section, 6.

Photographs

Photographs convey a sense of authenticity. The photo of a prototype helps convince investors that a product can be manufactured; the photo of a devastated area can suggest the need for government grants or private donations.

You may need to **crop** a photo for best results. If someone else is doing the production, mark the places for cropping in the margins of the photo or attach non-sticky paper. Never write or mark on the photo or the negative.

A growing problem with photos is that they may be edited or staged, purporting to show something as reality which never occurred. *New York Newsday* combined separate photos of Nancy Kerrigan and Tonya Harding into one picture to make it appear that the two were skating near each other. *USA Today* posed a picture for its "Teens and Drugs" news story in August 1996.[10]

Drawings

The richness of detail in photos makes them less effective than drawings for focusing on details. With a drawing, the artist can provide as much or as little detail as is needed to make the point; different parts of the drawing can show different layers or levels of detail. Drawings are also better for showing structures underground, undersea, or in the atmosphere. (See Figure 16.5.)

Maps

Use maps to emphasize location or to compare items in different locations. Several computer software packages now allow users to generate local, state,

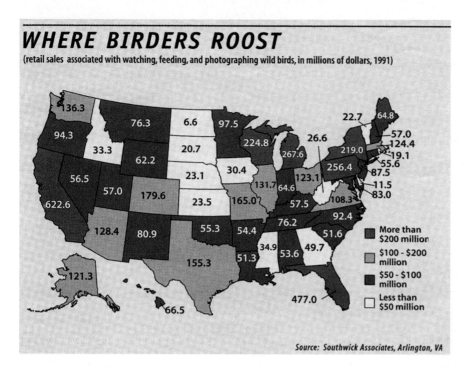

WHERE BIRDERS ROOST

(retail sales associated with watching, feeding, and photographing wild birds, in millions of dollars, 1991)

Legend:
- More than $200 million
- $100 - $200 million
- $50 - $100 million
- Less than $50 million

Source: Southwick Associates, Arlington, VA

Source: *American Demographics*, December 1996, 49.

Figure 16.6

Maps Show Where Potential Customers Are

national, or global maps, adding color or shadings, and labels. (See Figure 16.6.)

- Label states, provinces, or countries if it's important that people be able to identify levels in areas other than their own.
- Avoid using perspective. Perspective makes the values harder to read and can make comparison difficult.

Gannt Charts

Gannt charts are bar charts used to show schedules. They're most commonly used in proposals. (See Figure 16.7.)

- Color-code bars to indicate work planned and work completed.
- Use a red outline to indicate **critical activities,** which must be completed on time if the project is to be completed by the due date.
- Use diamonds to indicate progress reports, major achievements, or other accomplishments.

5. Use Color and Decoration with Restraint.

Color makes visuals more dramatic, but it creates at least two problems. First, readers try to interpret color, an interpretation that may not be appropriate. Perhaps the best use of color occurs in the weather maps printed daily in many newspapers. Blue seems to fit cold; red seems to fit hot temperatures. Second, meanings assigned to colors differ depending on the audience's national background and profession.

As we have seen in Chapter 12, connotations for color vary from culture to culture. Blue suggests masculinity in the United States, criminality in France,

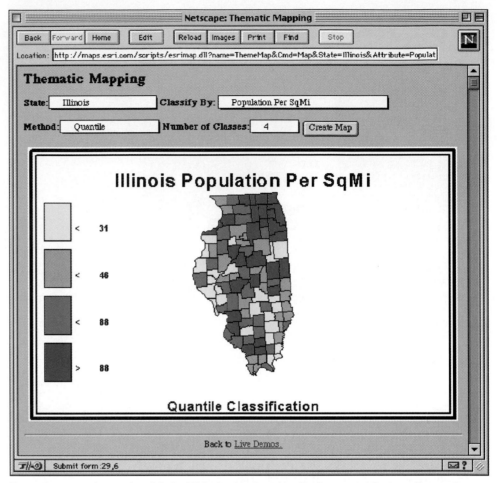

To see how mapping works, visit the Web site developed by Environmental Systems Research Institute (http://maps.esri.com/ESRI/mapobjects/demos.htm). Scroll down to "Make a Thematic Map" and click. Use the boxes to find your state and the variable you want to map: population, rent, and so forth.

strength or fertility in Egypt, and villainy in Japan. Red is sometimes used to suggest danger or *stop* in the United States; it means *go* in China and is associated with festivities. Red suggests masculinity or aristocracy in France, death in Korea, blasphemy in some African countries, and luxury in many parts of the world. Yellow suggests caution or cowardice in the United States, prosperity in Egypt, grace in Japan, and femininity in many parts of the world.[11]

These general cultural associations may be superseded by corporate, national, or professional associations. Some people associate blue with IBM or Hewlett-Packard and red with Coca-Cola, communism, or Japan. People in specific professions learn other meanings for colors. Blue suggests *reliability* to financial managers, *water* or *coldness* to engineers, and *death* to health care professionals. Red means *losing money* to financial managers, *danger* to engineers, but *healthy* to health care professionals. Green usually means *safe* to engineers, but *infected* to health care professionals.[12]

These various associations suggest that color is safest with a homogenous audience that you know well. In an increasingly multicultural workforce, color may send signals you do not intend.

Gann Charts Show the Schedule for Completing a Project   **Figure 16.7**

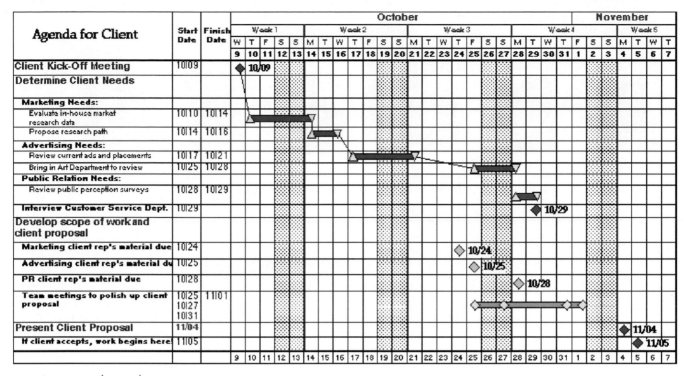

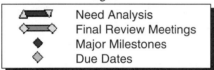

Legend

Need Analysis
Final Review Meetings
Major Milestones
Due Dates

When you do use color in visuals, Thorell and Smith suggest these guidelines:[13]

- Use no more than five colors when colors have meanings.
- Use glossy paper to make colors more vivid.
- Be aware that colors on a computer screen always look brighter than the same colors on paper because the screen sends out light.

In any visual, use as little shading and as few lines as are necessary for clarity. Don't clutter up the visual with extra marks. When you design black and white graphs, use shades of gray rather than stripes, wavy lines, and checks to indicate different segments or items.

Resist the temptation to make your visual "artistic" or "relevant" by turning it into a picture or adding clip art. **Clip art** is predrawn images that you can import into your newsletter, sign, or graph. A small drawing of a car in the corner of a line graph showing the number of miles driven is acceptable in an oral presentation, but out of place in a written report. Turning a line graph into a highway to show miles driven makes it harder to read: it's hard to separate the data line from lines that are merely decorative. Edward Tufte uses the term **chartjunk** for decorations that at best are irrelevant to the visual and at worst mislead the reader.[14] If you use clip art, be sure that the images of people show a good mix of both sexes, various races and ages, and various physical conditions.

Figure 16.8   **Chartjunk and Dimensions Distort Data**

Business travel costs per day: the city vs. suburbia

Boston: $216
North surburbs: $128

Chicago: $226
South surburbs: $110

New York—Manhattan: $338
New York—Conn. surburbs: $148

St. Louis: $162
St Louis County surburbs: $134

San Francisco: $208
North and East surburbs: $129

Washington, D.C.: $260
Washington, D.C.—Virginia surburbs: $156

Source: *America West Airlines Magazine,* May 1995, 64.

6. Be Sure the Visual Is Accurate and Ethical.

Always double-check your visuals to be sure the information is accurate. However, many visuals have accurate labels but misleading visual shapes. Visuals communicate quickly; audiences remember the shape, not the labels. If the reader has to study the labels to get the right picture, the visual is unethical even if the labels are accurate.

Figure 16.8 is distorted by chartjunk and dimensionality. In an effort to make "Bargains in the 'Burbs" interesting, the artist used suitcases instead of bars. The numbers show that the cost of business travel each day in New York is about a third higher than in Chicago. But the New York suitcase appears to be more than twice as big as the Chicago suitcase. Two-dimensional figures distort data by multiplying the apparent value by the width as well as by the height—four times for every doubling in value. Perspective graphs are especially hard for readers to interpret and should be avoided.[15]

Even simple bar and line graphs may be misleading if part of the scale is missing, or **truncated.** Truncated graphs are most acceptable when the audience knows the basic data set well. For example, graphs of the stock market almost never start at zero; they are routinely truncated. This omission is acceptable for audiences who follow the market closely.

Since part of the scale is missing in truncated graphs, small changes seem like major ones. The graph in Figure 16.9, from Philadelphia Suburban's *1994 Annual Report,* seems to show a healthy growth. But a close look at the numbers shows a different story. It turns out that the bottom of the glass is 230,000 customers, not zero. The real growth was 6.4%, not the 300% that the visual shows.[16] Another annual report disguised losses by using a negative base.[17] Because readers expect zero to be the base, they're almost certain to misread the visual. Labels may make the visual literally "accurate," but a visual is unethical if someone who looks at it quickly is likely to misinterpret it.

Data can also be distorted when the context is omitted. As Tufte suggests, a drop may be part of a regular cycle, a correction after an atypical increase, or a permanent drop to a new, lower plateau.

To make your visuals more accurate,

- Differentiate between actual and estimated or projected values.
- When you must truncate a scale, do so clearly with a break in the bars or in the background.

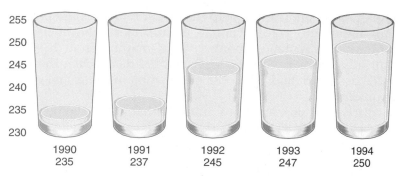

Figure 16.9

**Truncated Scales
Distort Data**

Number of Metered Water Customers (thousands)

Source: *The Wall Street Journal*, May 25, 1995, B1.

- Avoid perspective and three-dimensional graphs.
- Avoid combining graphs with different scales.
- Use images of people carefully in histographs to avoid sexist, racist, or other exclusionary visual statements.

INTEGRATING VISUALS IN YOUR TEXT

Refer to every visual in your text. Normally one gives the table or figure number in the text but not the title. Put the visual as soon after your reference as space and page design permit. If the visual must go on another page, tell the reader where to find it:

> As Figure 3 shows (page 10), . . .

> (See Table 2 on page 14.)

Summarize the main point of a visual *before* you present the visual itself. Then when readers get to it, they'll see it as confirmation of your point.

Weak: Listed below are the results.
Better: As Figure 4 shows, sales doubled in the last decade.

The weak statement mirrors the thought processes that occur as the writer processes data: one first categorizes the data in a very general way ("results"); one next looks at the data; and one finally decides what the data mean. But when this mental process becomes the writer's organizing pattern, the reader is forced to duplicate the whole process by which the writer reached a conclusion. Most readers, understandably, are unwilling to do work which the writer is supposed to do, so they will skim or skip the data presented in this unsatisfactory fashion. When the writer finally comes to the point, readers may be unconvinced because they haven't recognized the significance of the evidence in the table. Remember that you are writing not to reveal how your own mind works but to explain something to your readers and to convince them that your analysis is correct.

How much discussion a visual needs depends on the audience, the complexity of the visual and the importance of the point it makes. If the material is new to the audience, you'll need a fuller explanation than if similar material is presented to this audience every week or month. If the visual is complex, you may want to help the reader find key data points in it. If the point is important, you'll want to discuss its implications in some detail. In contrast, one sentence about a visual may be enough when the audience is already familiar with the topic and the data, when the visual is simple and well designed, and when the information in the visual is a minor part of your proof.

When you discuss visuals, spell out numbers that fall at the beginning of a sentence. If spelling out the number or year is cumbersome, revise the sentence so that it does not begin with a number.

Forty-five percent of the cost goes to pay wages and salaries.
The year 1992 marked the official beginning of the European Economic Community.

Put numbers in parentheses at the end of the clause or sentence to make the sentence easier to read:

Hard to read:	As Table 4 shows, teachers participate (54%) in more community service groups than do members of the other occupations surveyed; dentists (20.8%) participate in more service groups than do members of five of the other occupations.
Better:	As Table 4 shows, teachers participate in more community service groups than do members of the other occupations surveyed (54%); dentists participate in more service groups than do five of the other occupations (20.8%).

USING VISUALS IN YOUR PRESENTATION

Visuals for presentations need to be simpler than visuals the audience reads on paper. The table in Figure 16.3, for example, is too complex for a slide. Depending on the point you needed to make, you might be able to cut out one of the columns, round off the data even more, or present the material in a chart rather than a table.

Visuals for presentations should have titles but don't need figure numbers. Do know where each visual is so that you can return to one if someone asks about it during the question period. Decorative clip art, even though technically chartjunk, is acceptable in oral presentations as long as it does not obscure the story you're telling with the visual.

Rather than reading the visual to the audience, summarize the story and then elaborate on what it means for the audience. If you have copies of all the visuals for your audience, hand them out at the beginning of the talk.

SUMMARY OF KEY POINTS

- Numbers are not "objective." Like words they require interpretation and context to make sense.
- In the rough draft, use visuals to see that ideas are presented completely and to see what relationships exist. In the final report, use visuals to make points vivid, to emphasize material that the reader might skip, and to present material more compactly and with less repetition than words alone would require.
- You'll use more visuals when you want to show relationships and to persuade, when the information is complex or contains extensive numerical data, and when the audience values visuals.
- Pick data to tell a story, to make a point.
- To find stories,

1. Focus on a topic.
2. Simplify the data.
3. Look for relationships and changes.

■ **Paired graphs** juxtapose two simple stories to create a more powerful story.
■ Visuals are not interchangeable. The best visual depends on the kind of data and the point you want to make with the data.
■ Tables are numbers or words arrayed in rows and columns; figures are everything else. Formal visuals have both numbers and titles that indicate what to look for in the visual or why the visual is included and is worth examining.
■ Visuals must present data accurately, both literally and by implication. **Chartjunk** denotes decorations that at best are irrelevant to the visual and at worst mislead the reader. **Truncated scales** omit part of the scale and visually mislead readers. Perspective graphs and graphs with negative bases mislead readers.
■ Summarize the main point of a visual before it appears in the text.
■ Visuals for presentations need to be simpler than visuals on paper.
■ How much discussion a visual needs depends on the audience, the complexity of the visual, and the importance of the point it makes.

Exercises and Problems
For Chapter 16

GETTING STARTED

16–1   Identifying Stories

Of the following, which are stories?

1. Results
2. Computer Use
3. Computer Prices Fall
4. More Single Parents Buy Computers than Do Any Other Group
5. Where Your Tax Dollars Go
6. Sixty Percent of Tax Dollars Pay Entitlements, Interest
7. Percent of Tax Dollars Spent on Entitlements

16–2   Choosing Titles for Stories and Visuals

Which is the best title in each group? Why? Would the other titles ever be acceptable? Why or why not?

1. a. Single Women Are Buying More Computers than Are Single Men.
   b. More Women than Men Will Live Alone with Computers.
   c. What Do Single Women Want? Computers!

2. a. Lawyers in Private Practice Make More than Those in Public Practice.
   b. Lawyers Should Be Private in Choosing Their Salaries.
   c. Private Practice Pays.

3. a. The Poor Give More.
   b. People Making under $11,000 a Year Gave a Larger Percentage of Their Incomes to Churches than Did People Making over $100,000 a Year.
   c. People Making Least Give the Highest Percentage to Church.

16–3   Matching Visuals with Stories

What visual(s) would make it easiest to see each of the following stories?

1. Canada buys 20% of US exports.
2. Undergraduate enrollment rises, but graduate enrollment declines.
3. Population growth will be greatest in the West and South.

4. Open communication ranks Number 1 in reasons to take a job.

5. Companies with fewer than 200 employees created a larger percentage of new jobs than did companies with more than 5,000 employees.

6. Men are more likely than women to see their chances for advancement as good.

7. America's heads of households are getting older.

16–4   Evaluating Visuals

Evaluate each of the following visuals.

- Is visual's message clear?
- Is it the right visual for the story?
- Is the visual designed appropriately? Is color, if any, used appropriately?
- Is the visual free from *chartjunk*?
- Does the visual distort data or mislead the reader in any way?

1.

TRADING PINSTRIPES FOR JEANS

Source: *Business Week,* April 1, 1996, 57.

2. **More Coffee?**

Each symbol equals 200 stores.

Source: *The Wall Street Journal,* January 21, 1997, B1.

3. **How My Time Will Be Used**

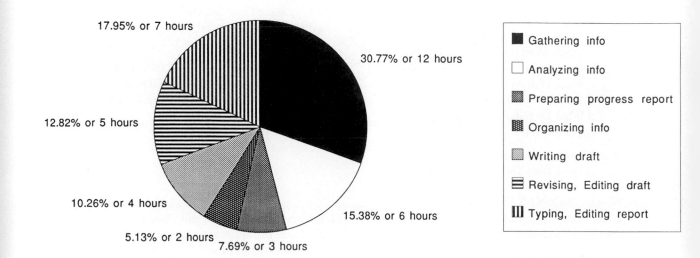

4.

The Spending Pie

The average U.S. metropolitan household devotes half its spending to housing, utilities, transportation, and food.

(percent distribution of estimated average spending by category for households in metropolitan areas, 1993)

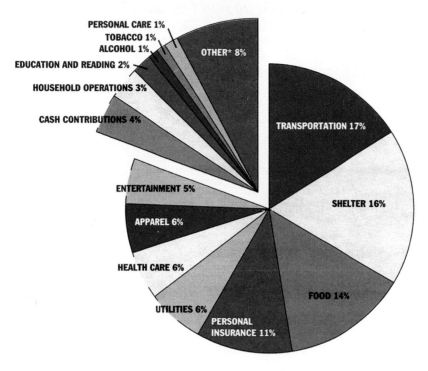

PERSONAL CARE 1%
TOBACCO 1%
ALCOHOL 1%
EDUCATION AND READING 2%
HOUSEHOLD OPERATIONS 3%
CASH CONTRIBUTIONS 4%
ENTERTAINMENT 5%
APPAREL 6%
HEALTH CARE 6%
UTILITIES 6%
PERSONAL INSURANCE 11%
FOOD 14%
SHELTER 16%
TRANSPORTATION 17%
OTHER* 8%

* Housekeeping supplies, furnishing and equipment, and miscellaneous fees such as legal and accounting.
Note: Percentages do not sum to 100 due to rounding.

Source: *American Demographics,* January 1996, 22.

5.

Web Growth Slows

50% April '95   60% Oct '95   43% April '96   36% Oct '96

Source: *PC Magazine,* February 19, 1997, 28.

6.

Pan-American Purchasing Power

About 17 million South-American households have purchasing power of at least 20,000 U.S. dollars a year.

(number of households in millions and percent of households by consumption range, by country, purchasing power parity basis, 1993)

Canada

United States

Mexico

Central America & Caribbean

Colombia, Venezuela, Suriname & Guyana

Brazil

Annual household consumption, 1993 US dollars, purchasing power parity (PPP) basis

< 5,000
5,000 to 10,000
10,000 to 20,000
> 20,000

Ecuador, Peru & Bolivia

Argentina, Chile, Uruguay & Paraguay

Areas are proportional to number of households in each consumption range

country	number of households	less than $5,000	$5,000 to $10,000	$10,000 to $20,000	more than $20,000
Canada	10.4	3.0%	7.1%	21.2%	68.6%
United States	96.4	5.1	7.8	17.1	70.0
Mexico	15.9	14.1	19.7	25.9	40.3
Central America, Caribbean*	14.7	39.4	25.6	20.5	14.5
Colombia, Venezuela, Suriname, Guyana	10.7	12.0	19.3	28.0	40.6
Brazil	34.7	30.1	22.9	23.4	22.8
Ecuador, Peru, Bolivia	9.0	33.9	30.3	23.6	12.2
Argentina, Chile, Uruguay, Paraguay	12.5	3.9	24.2	39.8	32.1

Does not include Cuba

Source: Global Business Opportunities, Pound Ridge, NY

Source: "Pan-American Purchasing Power," *American Demographics,* September 1995, 45.

7.

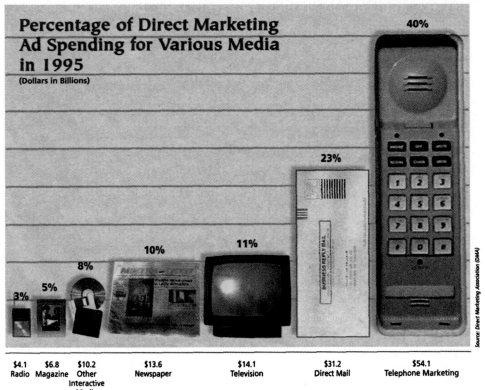

Percentage of Direct Marketing Ad Spending for Various Media in 1995
(Dollars in Billions)

3%	5%	8%	10%	11%	23%	40%
$4.1	$6.8	$10.2	$13.6	$14.1	$31.2	$54.1
Radio	Magazine	Other Interactive Media	Newspaper	Television	Direct Mail	Telephone Marketing

Source: Direct Marketing Association (DMA)

Source: *Direct Marketing*, Special Advertising Section, np.

WEB PAGE

16–5   Creating a Web Guide to Graphs

Create a Web page explaining how to create good visuals. Offer general principles and at least seven links to examples of good and poor visuals. (More is better.) At the top of the page, offer an overview of what the page covers. At the bottom of the page, put the creation/update date and your name and e-mail address.

As Your Instructor Directs,

    a. Turn in two laser copies of your page(s). On another page, give the URLs for each link.

    b. Turn in one laser copy of your page(s) and a disk with the HTML code and .gif files.

    c. Write a memo to your instructor (1) identifying the audience for which the page is designed and explaining (2) the search strategies you used to find material on this topic, (3) why you chose the pages and information you've included, and (4) why you chose the layout and graphics you've used.

    d. Present your page orally to the class.

Hints:

    ▪ Searching for words (*graphs, maps, Gannt charts, data*) will turn up only pages with those words. Also check pages on topics that may use graphs to explain their data: finance, companies' performance, sports, cost of living, exports, and so forth.

    ▪ In addition to finding good and bad visuals on the Web, you can also scan in examples you find in newspapers, magazines, and textbooks.

    ▪ If you have more than nine links, chunk them in small groups under headings.

VISUALS, MEMOS, AND REPORT ASSIGNMENTS

16–6   Creating Visuals

As Your Instructor Directs,

a. Identify visuals that you might use to help analyze each of the following data sets.

b. Identify and create a visual for one or more of the stories in each set.

c. Identify additional information that would be needed for other stories related to these data sets.

1. Projected Number of Jobs to Be Gained or Lost, 1994–2005
   Bank tellers: –152,000
   Bookkeeping, accounting, and auditing clerks: –178,000
   Cashiers: 562,000
   Computer operators (except peripheral equipment): –98,000
   Data entry keyers (except composing): –25,000
   File clerks: –42,000
   General managers and top executives: 466,000
   Home health aides: 428,000
   Personnel clerks (except payroll and timekeeping): –26,000
   Registered nurses: 473,000
   Retail salespeople: 532,000
   Systems analysts: 445,000
   Teachers, secondary school: 386,000
   Typists and word processors: –212,000

   Source: *Employment Outlook: 1994–2005.* Bureau of Labor Statistics, December 1995, in "1997 Career Overview: Where the Jobs Are, and Aren't," *Black Enterprise*, np.

2. Cost of a half-page business letter dictated in 10 minutes:

1930	$ .30	1978	4.77
1935	.52	1980	6.07
1940	.72	1983	7.60
1953	1.17	1985	8.52
1960	1.83	1988	9.69
1964	2.32	1990	10.85
1968	2.54	1993	12.28–18.54
1970	3.05	1995	13.02–19.97
1973	3.31	1996	13.60–20.52
1975	3.79		

   Source: "1996 Cost of a Business Letter," Dartnell Corporation, September 30, 1996, 1, 4.

3. Spending on Sneakers

Spending on Sneakers

(percent distribution of athletic-footwear shoppers, average price per purchase, average number of purchases per year, and percent using money-saving incentives per purchase, by household type and race/ethnicity, October 1994–September 1995)

	percent of buyers	average price per purchase	purchases per year	percent getting deal
Total shoppers	100.0%	$36.32	1.7	47.1%
Singles under age 35	3.7%	$40.75	1.3	52.2
Childless couples under age 35	6.6	40.91	1.7	47.5
Families with children under age 6	66.8	31.67	1.8	47.7
Families with children aged 6 to 17	28.0	34.58	2.0	47.3
Families with children aged 13 to 17	10.5	42.14	2.0	43.8
Singles aged 35 to 54	6.4	39.67	1.4	54.0
Childless couples aged 35 to 54	12.6	37.22	1.7	49.4
Empty nesters aged 55 and older	19.3	34.42	1.5	44.4
Singles aged 55 and older	6.1	33.07	1.4	46.0
Non-Hispanic whites	75.7%	$36.18	1.7	49.0%
Blacks	14.6	37.52	2.0	38.3
Hispanics	7.9	34.72	1.9	48.6
Asian Americans	0.9	38.49	1.8	54.4

Source: A.C. Nielsen

Source: *American Demographics*, March 1996, 10.

16–7   Interpreting Data

As Your Instructor Directs,

a. Identify at least seven stories in one or more of the following data sets.

b. Create visuals for three of the stories.

c. Write a memo to your instructor explaining why you chose these stories and why you chose these visuals to display them.

d. Write a memo to some group that might be interested in your findings, presenting your visuals as part of a short report. Possible groups include career counselors, radio stations, advertising agencies, and Mothers Against Drunk Driving.

e. Brainstorm additional stories you could tell with additional data. Specify the kind of data you would need.

1. Music Preferences

(Percent of adults who like selected types of music by sex, race, age, education, and income, 1992)

	Country/ Western	Mood/ Easy Listening	Rock	Blues/ Rhythm & Blues	Big Band	Jazz	Classical	Show Tunes/ Operettas/ Musicals	Contemporary Folk	Opera
TOTAL	51.7%	48.8%	43.5%	40.4%	35.0%	34.2%	33.6%	27.8%	23.1%	12.6%
SEX										
Men	52	44	48	44	34	38	32	24	23	10
Women	52	53	39	37	36	30	35	31	23	14
RACE										
White	57	50	46	38	37	32	35	30	24	13
Black	19	39	23	59	22	54	18	15	15	8
Other	32	42	38	25	17	26	36	20	18	14
AGE										
18 to 24	39	38	70	39	13	30	24	14	10	5
25 to 34	50	47	59	46	23	41	27	21	19	7
35 to 44	53	52	57	46	30	39	36	25	27	10
45 to 54	61	54	39	40	43	33	39	35	32	16
55 to 64	58	54	14	35	53	30	42	37	26	20
65 to 74	54	55	9	35	61	27	43	42	26	21
75 to 96	46	36	7	23	46	21	29	27	14	17
EDUCATION										
Grade school	48	22	12	14	19	10	12	7	9	6
Some high school	59	31	27	26	24	15	16	12	13	5
High school graduate	57	49	42	36	32	28	25	22	20	9
Some college	50	56	54	50	37	42	39	33	25	14
College graduate	42	56	54	50	43	50	51	39	28	16
Graduate school	46	60	53	59	53	54	65	52	40	26
FAMILY INCOME										
Under $5,000	43	32	36	35	16	27	20	14	11	6
$5,000 to $9,999	52	36	32	30	27	21	23	14	17	7
$10,000 to $14,999	55	35	33	34	30	25	25	19	18	12
$15,000 to $24,999	57	43	39	35	31	29	29	23	19	9
$25,000 to $49,999	54	56	50	43	38	36	35	29	26	13
$50,000 or more	48	62	55	52	45	47	47	44	31	17
Not ascertained	42	46	35	36	37	35	35	29	20	13

Note: In 1992, U.S. population aged 18 and older was 186 million.

Source: Authors' tabulations of National Endowment for the Arts survey, 1992.

Source of data: *American Demographics*, August 1994, 27.

2. Drinking Patterns

WHO DRINKS HOW MUCH HOW OFTEN

PERCENT OF ADULT MALE POPULATION THAT ...	DRINKS AT ALL	DRINKS DAILY	DRINKS 60+ DRINKS A MONTH	DRINKS 5+ DRINKS A DAY AT LEAST ONCE A WEEK	DRINKS 8+ DRINKS A DAY AT LEAST ONCE A WEEK
TOTAL	71%	10%	21%	9%	4%
BY AGE:					
18–29	77%	5%	24%	17%	9%
30–39	73%	9%	19%	7%	2%
40–49	72%	8%	21%	8%	4%
50–59	65%	16%	23%	7%	4%
60 and over	66%	16%	18%	3%	1%
BY EDUCATION:					
Less than high school	65%	13%	23%	15%	6%
High school graduate	70%	7%	21%	10%	5%
Some college	76%	10%	23%	8%	4%
College degree/higher	77%	11%	20%	3%	2%
BY FAMILY INCOME:					
Up to $9,999	68%	9%	30%	19%	10%
$10,000–$19,999	66%	12%	20%	12%	4%
$20,000–$29,999	65%	9%	22%	11%	4%
$30,000–$39,999	72%	8%	18%	7%	5%
$40,000–$59,999	80%	13%	20%	6%	2%
$60,000 and over	79%	10%	26%	6%	3%

Source of data: *Fortune*, March 6, 1995, 168.

3. Projected Drinking Patterns, 1997–2007

HAPPY HOUR IN AMERICA

(projected thousands of adults who drank any alcoholic beverage in the past six months, by sex and age, 1997, 2000, and 2007, and percent change, 1997-2000, and 1997-2007)

	1997	2000	2007	percent change 1997-2000	percent change 1997-2007
MEN					
Total	54,481	54,472	54,419	0.0%	−0.1%
21 to 24	4,579	4,596	4,685	0.4	2.3
25 to 34	13,446	12,273	11,268	−8.7	−16.2
35 to 44	14,182	14,140	12,287	−0.3	−13.4
45 to 54	10,304	11,201	12,558	8.7	21.9
55 to 64	5,465	5,798	7,088	6.1	29.7
65 and older	6,506	6,465	6,534	−0.6	0.4
WOMEN					
Total	47,637	46,890	44,948	−1.6%	−5.6%
21 to 24	3,649	3,573	3,375	−2.1	−7.5
25 to 34	11,315	10,156	8,864	−10.2	−21.7
35 to 44	12,691	12,531	10,746	−1.3	−15.3
45 to 54	8,838	9,466	10,197	7.1	15.4
55 to 64	5,062	5,348	6,486	5.7	28.1
65 and older	6,083	5,815	5,279	−4.4	−13.2

Source: Mediamark Research, Inc., Census Bureau, and American Demographics

SIPPING IN THE 21ST CENTURY

(projected thousands of men and women who drank alcohol in the past six months, by type of alcohol, 1997 and 2007, and percent change 1997-2007)

	1997	2007	percent change 1997-2007
MEN			
Any	54,481	54,419	−0.1%
Wine	24,972	21,751	−12.9
Beer	46,549	46,547	0.0
White goods	18,530	16,829	−9.2
Brown goods	22,603	18,745	−17.1
WOMEN			
Any	47,637	44,948	−5.6%
Wine	32,045	29,061	−9.3
Beer	28,071	25,761	−8.2
White goods	18,410	17,064	−7.3
Brown goods	16,326	10,541	−35.4

Note: White goods are distilled spirits, such as vodka and gin; brown goods include whiskey and cognac.

Source: Mediamark Research Inc, Census Bureau, and American Demographics

Source of data: *American Demographics*, January, 1997, 4, 6.

4. What Americans Earn

■ *What Americans Earn*

Profession	Initial pay	Industry average	Typical top pay
Accounting & Finance			
Public accountant			
Big Six firm	$30,125	$38,625	$69,750
Small firm	$24,750	$36,500	$63,000
Corporate accountant			
Associate accountant	$25,000	$28,400	$31,200
Senior auditor	$37,200	$42,500	$48,600
Senior tax accountant	$46,900	$55,300	$62,800
Controller	$97,900	$147,900	$176,000
Treasurer	$108,000	$160,500	$191,100
CFO	$165,000	$277,200	$345,000
Advertising			
Advertising copywriter	$30,000	$50,000	$90,000
Art director	$27,500	$47,500	$82,500
Account executive	$28,000	$62,500	$375,000
Creative director	$150,000	$300,000	$500,000
Architecture			
Architect	$27,000	$35,000	$43,900
Principal/partner	$35,000	$50,000	$110,000
CEO	$1,131,042	$1,524,057	$2,043,294
Consulting			
Strategic consultant	$47,677	$120,660	$307,667
Human resources consultant	$38,633	$64,218	$139,099
MIS consultant	$39,120	$81,569	$130,156
Corporate Ethics			
Ethics administrator	$35,000	$50,000	$70,000
VP for ethics	$95,000	$140,000	$200,000
Education			
University professor	$39,050	$49,490	$63,450
Elementary teacher	$25,693	$36,357	$50,600
Secondary teacher	$26,077	$37,764	$53,300
Engineering			
Biomedical engineer	$37,750	$72,500	$150,000
Chemical engineer	$39,863	$73,970	$179,700
Civil engineer	$30,690	$62,000	$141,260
Electrical engineer	$33,000	$65,876	$146,000
Mechanical engineer	$36,935	$65,160	$155,734
Industrial engineer	$35,244	$67,000	$215,000
Financial services			
Financial planner	$27,000	$50,000	$200,000
Portfolio manager	$40,000	$100,000	$150,000
Loan officer			
Mortgage	$27,200	$54,600	$67,800
Commercial	$41,500	$71,000	$86,200
Actuary	$25,382	$36,914	$58,432
Life insurance underwriter	$23,500	$37,564	$52,563
Group insurance underwriter	$27,421	$38,883	$56,400
Government jobs			
Economist	$21,486	$46,852	$102,338
Budget analyst	$21,486	$38,885	$102,338
Personnel manager	$18,956	$46,852	$102,338

■ *What Americans Earn* (Cont'd)

Profession	Initial pay	Industry average	Typical top pay
Government jobs (cont'd)			
Agency head	—	—	$148,400
CIA director	—	—	$133,600
Congressman	—	—	$133,600
Cabinet member	—	—	$148,400
Health care			
Family practice physician			
Private	$86,300	$123,700	$169,400
HMO	$96,700	$123,300	$170,000
Neurosurgeon	$158,500	$263,300	$450,400
Cardiothoracic surgeon	$175,900	$312,300	$435,650
Plastic surgeon	$157,500	$181,000	$341,200
Registered nurse	$34,600	$39,800	$45,700
Licensed physical therapist	$35,500	$45,400	$53,800
High technology			
Software engineer	$33,702	$54,470	$75,524
Hardware engineer	$33,592	$54,704	$75,360
CD-ROM producer	$35,000	$60,000	$100,000
Human resources			
Employee-training manager	$49,500	$59,000	$65,700
Benefits manager	$63,800	$85,200	$101,600
Human resources VP	$118,100	$188,700	$235,600
Information services			
Programming trainee	$9,000	$19,500	$28,000
LAN/WAN specialist	$27,900	$41,000	$49,983
Database specialist	$33,228	$45,193	$69,000
Systems analyst	$35,728	$44,026	$49,270
Applications programmer	$25,992	$49,000	$55,000
MIS director	$57,700	$89,000	$210,000
IRS agent			
Tax auditor	$19,500	$34,000	$38,500
Revenue officer	$19,500	$34,000	$66,606
Revenue agent	$19,500	$49,663	$81,013
Law			
Private practice			
Associate	$58,942	$74,318	$103,562
Partner	$114,213	$183,364	$301,611
Public prosecutor	$23,000	$30,000	$38,000
Public defender	$20,000	$28,900	$40,000
Corporate lawyer	$61,932	$79,297	$111,708
Chief legal officer	$169,300	$258,966	$445,000
Paralegal	$30,470	$37,686	$50,544
Lobbying			
Trade association lobbyist			
Small trade group	$35,000	$47,500	$60,000
Large trade group	$100,000	$300,000	$500,000
Corporate lobbyist	$36,000	$60,000	$120,000
Manufacturing			
Foreman	$32,240	$40,300	$48,360
Purchasing agent	$42,240	$52,800	$63,360
Warehouse manager	$41,231	$53,600	$65,969

■ *What Americans Earn* (Cont'd)

Profession	Initial pay	Industry average	Typical top pay
Manufacturing (cont'd)			
Director of engineering	$57,231	$74,400	$91,569
Manager of materials	$57,308	$74,500	$91,692
Plant manager	$77,462	$100,700	$123,938
VP for manufacturing	$106,231	$138,100	$169,969
Marketing			
Marketing assistant	$18,900	$24,000	$30,000
Market research manager	$45,770	$57,000	$103,000
Brand manager	$45,000	$61,000	$109,125
Direct-marketing manager	$40,000	$66,000	$110,000
VP for marketing	$109,250	$146,050	$212,750
Media			
Newspaper reporter	$21,856	$24,127	$37,113
Magazines			
Senior editor	$28,800	$41,900	$76,000
Managing editor	$28,400	$44,000	$210,000
Executive editor	$43,100	$52,800	$443,000
Book editor	$21,000	$44,090	$72,990
TV news reporter	$16,560	$30,400	$92,688
TV news anchor	$25,453	$65,824	$248,183
Movie producer	$400,000	$1,000,000	$5,000,000
Movie director	$50,000	$300,000	$500,000
Middle Management	$50,035	$69,675	$151,165
Public relations			
Publicity agent	$19,210	$49,877	$66,467
In-house publicist	$23,400	$55,480	$62,613
Sales			
Sales trainee	$19,800	$30,700	$35,400
Sales representative	$38,900	$48,400	$59,900
Sales manager	$55,800	$65,300	$80,300
District sales manager	$64,900	$74,800	$88,100
Regional sales manager	$81,400	$95,000	$116,400
VP for sales	$136,100	$178,200	$226,900
Secretaries			
Secretary	$12,480	$28,189	$50,000
Receptionist	$13,000	$22,387	$28,000
Executive secretary	$14,000	$37,485	$70,000
Wall Street			
Investment banker			
Generalist	$95,000	$440,000	$1,250,000
M&A specialist	$95,000	$590,000	$1,750,000
Trader			
General instruments	$60,000	$290,000	$1,000,000
Foreign exchange or derivatives specialist	$60,000	$360,000	$2,000,000
Risk manager	$450,000	$725,000	$1,000,000
Retail stockbroker	$50,000	$150,000	$620,000
Institutional stockbroker	$88,000	$345,000	$1,000,000

Source of data: *Fortune,* June 26, 1995, 82–86.

Making Oral Presentations

Chapter Outline

An Inside Perspective: Making Oral Presentations

Luis E. Lamela, President and CEO
CAC Medical Centers

Luis Lamela makes presentations to a variety of internal and external audiences including medical professionals, providers, clients. CAC Medical Centers, headquartered in Coral Gables, Florida, is a comprehensive medical delivery network comprised of 28 single- and multispecialty medical centers in south Florida. It is a federally qualified health maintenance organization (HMO). Its parent company is United HealthCare Corporation, a national leader in health care management.

The key to a successful oral presentation is to keep things simple. I try to stick to three points. I give an overview of the points, present them to the audience, and summarize them at the end.

My purpose or desired outcome, the type of audience, and the message dictate the formality of the presentation, the kind of visuals, the number of anecdotes, and the jokes or examples that I use. Most of my presentations are designed to sell, to explain, or to motivate. When I plan the presentation, I think about the audience. Are they professionals or nonprofessionals? Purchasers or sellers? Providers or users? Internal or external? My purpose and the audience mix determine the tone and focus of the presentation.

When I make a presentation, I use the visuals as the outline. I will not use notes. I like to select the kind of visual that not only best supports the message but also best fits the audience and the physical location. PowerPoint, slides, overhead transparencies, and flip charts are the four main kinds of visuals I use.

PowerPoint and slide presentations work well when I am selling a product or an idea to large groups (15 people or more). In this format, I like to use examples and graphs and tables to support my message in a general way.

In small presentations, including one-on-ones and presentations where the audience is part of the actual process, I like transparencies or flip charts. They allow me to be closer to the audience and to be more informal.

I get very, very nervous when I speak in public. I handle my nervousness by just trying to look as if, instead of talking to so many people, I'm walking in and talking to a single person. I don't like to speak behind lecterns. Instead, I like to get out and just be open and portray that openness: "I'm here to tell you a story."

I try not to lecture but to use anecdotes, and I think that people find them interesting and relate better to them. For example, our multispecialty medical centers differ according to the demographics of the area. In Hispanic areas, examination rooms need to be bigger because as Hispanics we bring the concept of the extended family right into the examination room. But if we're going to build a center in an Anglo area, exam rooms will be smaller.

I try very hard for people to enjoy my presentations by showing enthusiasm on the subject and by being sincere. I try not to use a hard sell—I just try to report or to explain—and I think that comes across. In addition, it helps that I am speaking about something that I very strongly believe in and something that I really, really enjoy doing.

Luis E. Lamela, February 11, 1997

"I like to get out and just be open and portray that openness: 'I'm here to tell you a story.' "

Luis E. Lamela, CAC Medical Centers

The power to persuade people to care about something you believe in is crucial to business success. Making a good oral presentation is more than just good delivery: it also involves developing a strategy that fits your audience and purpose, having good content, and organizing material effectively. The choices you make in each of these areas are affected by your purposes, the audience, and the situation.

PURPOSES IN ORAL PRESENTATIONS

Oral presentations have the same three basic purposes that written documents have: to inform, to persuade, and to build goodwill. Like written messages, most oral presentations have more than one purpose.

Informative presentations inform or teach the audience. Training sessions in an organization are primarily informative. Secondary purposes may be to persuade new employees to follow organizational procedures, rather than doing something their own way, and to help them appreciate the organizational culture (✖ p. 61).

Persuasive presentations motivate the audience to act or to believe. Giving information and evidence is an important means of persuasion. In addition, the speaker must build goodwill by appearing to be credible and sympathetic to the audience's needs. The goal in many presentations is a favorable vote or decision. For example, speakers making business presentations may try to persuade the audience to approve their proposals, to adopt their ideas, or to buy their products. Sometimes the goal is to change behavior or attitudes or to reinforce existing attitudes. For example, a speaker at a meeting of factory workers may stress the importance of following safety procedures. A speaker at a church meeting may talk about the problem of homelessness in the community and try to build support for community shelters for the homeless.

Goodwill presentations entertain and validate the audience. In an after-dinner speech, the audience wants to be entertained. Presentations at sales meetings may be designed to stroke the audience's egos and to validate their commitment to organizational goals.

Make your purpose as specific as possible.

Weak: The purpose of my presentation is to discuss saving for retirement.
Better: The purpose of my presentation is to persuade my audience to put their
             401K funds in stocks and bonds, not in money market accounts and CDs.
or: The purpose of my presentation is to explain how to calculate how much
             money someone needs to save in order to maintain a specific lifestyle after
             retirement.

Note that the purpose *is not* the introduction of your talk; it is the principle that guides your choice of strategy and content.

COMPARING WRITTEN AND ORAL MESSAGES

Giving a presentation is in many ways very similar to writing a message. All of the chapters up to this point—on using you-attitude and positive emphasis, developing reader benefits, analyzing your audience, designing slides, overcoming objections, doing research, and analyzing data—remain relevant as you plan an oral presentation.

A written message makes it easier to

- Present extensive or complex financial data.
- Present many specific details of a law, policy, or procedure.
- Minimize undesirable emotions.

Oral messages make it easier to

- Use emotion to help persuade the audience.
- Focus the audience's attention on specific points.
- Answer questions, resolve conflicts, and build consensus.
- Modify a proposal that may not be acceptable in its original form.
- Get immediate action or response.

Oral and written messages have many similarities. In both, you should

- Adapt the message to the specific audience.
- Show the audience how they would benefit from the idea, policy, service, or product.
- Overcome any objections the audience may have.
- Use you-attitude and positive emphasis.
- Use visuals to clarify or emphasize material.
- Specify exactly what the audience should do.

PLANNING A STRATEGY FOR YOUR PRESENTATION

A **strategy** is your plan for reaching your specific goals with a specific audience.

In all oral presentations, simplify what you want to say. Identify the one idea you want the audience to take home. Simplify your supporting detail so it's easy to follow. Simplify visuals so they can be taken in at a glance. Simplify your words and sentences so they're easy to understand.

An oral presentation needs to be simpler than a written message to the same audience. If readers forget a point, they can turn back to it and reread the paragraph. Headings, paragraph indentation, and punctuation provide visual cues to help readers understand the message. Listeners, in contrast, must remember what the speaker says. Whatever they don't remember is lost. Even asking questions requires the audience to remember which points they don't understand.

Analyze your audience for an oral presentation just as you do for a written message. If you'll be speaking to co-workers, talk to them about your topic or proposal to find out what questions or objections they have. For audiences inside the organization, the biggest questions are often practical ones: Will it work? How much will it cost? How long will it take?[1]

Think about the physical conditions in which you'll be speaking. Will the audience be tired at the end of a long day of listening? Sleepy after a big meal? Will the group be large or small? The more you know about your audience, the better you can adapt your message to the audience.

For example, Matt Hession knew that his audience of pharmacists didn't want to talk to salespeople. So he devised a one-minute presentation which he offers as entertainment—and as a challenge. Figure 17.1 gives his script. He takes off his watch to drive home the point that he really will take only a minute of the pharmacist's time. He starts off with reader benefits (☞ p. 69) and uses psychological description (☞ p. 223) so that the pharmacists can see themselves enjoying those benefits. Because the commission structure is complicated, that goes in a handout rather than in the presentation itself.

Figure 17.1 **Script for a One-Minute Presentation**

"When I walk into a store, I spot the clerk closest to the pharmacist. Because the pharmacist is behind the counter, I can't get to him directly. So I speak loudly, and I know he is overhearing what's going on. If I walk in looking like a salesman, the pharmacist immediately thinks, `I don't want to buy anything or talk to you.' I nullify that feeling right off the bat. The pharmacist thinks, `He's entertainment. It's only a minute, and it doesn't cost anything.' I'm not threatening anymore. Customers smile; they want to hear what I have to say. I take off my watch to show that I'm serious."

My name is Matt Hession with Key Medical. I know the pharmacist is real busy. But when he has a moment, I have a one-minute presentation. (Start to take off watch.) **And he can leave his wallet in his pocket.**

"As I walk behind the counter, I try to assess how promising a partner this would be. How busy is the place? Is it handling any medical equipment—like walkers—already? Is the back of the store neat, clean, and well organized? I'm also thinking of anything I can quickly add to personalize the presentation. For example, if there is a pediatrician next door, I'll point out that we handle nebulizers—small machines used by kids with asthma—and that we can get same-day approval on Medicaid. I hold up my watch again to emphasize that I'm serious about this taking only one minute."

(The clerk acknowledges and relays the request. But the pharmacist has overheard the conversation. "I'll be with you in a bit," he says. A couple of minutes later, he motions for me to step behind the counter. As we shake hands, I introduce myself again and hold up the watch.)

"I am telling the pharmacists that this is something the chains do not have. This strikes an immediate note. Independent pharmacists, who are usually also the store owners, complain that chains like Wal-Mart have certain advantages. Now, they think, they will have an edge. They have two questions: How much time will it take? How much will it cost me? I answer those right up front."

We're in the home-medical-equipment business. Our company has developed a program just for independently owned community drugstores. Our program costs you nothing and takes up very little of your time.

Here's how it works: a customer walks into your store and sees one of the signs that we provide to you, indicating that you can get customers any type of home-medical equipment. The customer inquires about a home oxygen system that her father needs. You answer, "Let me get our equipment partner on the phone for you." You dial our 800 number and tell us who you are, the name of your store, and its location. Then you give us your customer's name and her question. We either talk to the customer right there or call her at home—your choice. We see if we can answer her questions and help to meet her needs. If it results in a sale or rental, we deliver the equipment, and we teach the customer how to use it. We do the insurance filing or billing. We service the equipment. The whole nine yards. Your job is to educate your customers that they can obtain home-medical equipment through you.

"It would take longer than a minute, obviously, to explain the commission structure. There are three different scenarios—a sale, a rental, or a lease-to-own option—and I can't cover those in under two minutes. And with customers in earshot, we don't have privacy, anyway. But I will give answers on two questions the pharmacists often ask: Where is your home office, and how do you deliver these things? The details are very clearly spelled out in the material I give them."

Here's a copy of our partnership agreement. It spells our your commission structure as well as other important concerns.

Source: Joshua Hyatt, "The 60-Second Sales Pitch," *Inc.*, October 1994, 88–89.

When he calls the next week, he says, "This is Matt. I did the one-minute presentation. . . . They always remember me." And 90% of them eventually sign contracts.

Choosing the Kind of Presentation

Choose one of three basic kinds of presentations: monologue, guided discussion, or interactive.

In a **monologue presentation,** the speaker speaks without interruption; questions are held until the end of the presentation, where the speaker functions as an expert. The speaker plans the presentation in advance and delivers it without deviation. This kind of presentation is the most common in class situations, but it's often boring for the audience. Good delivery skills are crucial, since the audience is comparatively uninvolved.

Linda Driskill suggests that **guided discussions** offer a better way to present material and help an audience find a solution it can "buy into." In a guided discussion, the speaker presents the questions or issues that both speaker and audience have agreed on in advance. Rather than functioning as an expert with all the answers, the speaker serves as a facilitator to help the audience tap its own knowledge. This kind of presentation is excellent for presenting the results of consulting projects, when the speaker has specialized knowledge, but the audience must implement the solution if it is to succeed. Guided discussions need more time than monologue presentations, but produce more audience response, more responses involving analysis, and more commitment to the result.[2]

An **interactive presentation** is a conversation, even if the speaker stands up in front of a group and uses charts and overheads. Most sales presentations are interactive presentations. The sales representative uses questions to determine the buyer's needs, probe objections, and gain provisional and then final commitment to the purchase. Even in a memorized sales presentation, the buyer will talk at least 30% of the time. In a problem-solving sales presentation, top salespeople let the buyer do 70% of the talking up until the action close (p. 281).[3]

Adapting Your Ideas to the Audience

Measure the message you'd like to send against where your audience is now. If your audience is indifferent, skeptical, or hostile, focus on the part of your message the audience will find most interesting and easiest to accept.

Don't seek a major opinion change in a single oral presentation. If the audience has already decided to hire an advertising agency, then a good presentation can convince them that your agency is the one to hire. But if you're talking to a small business that has always done its own ads, limit your purpose. You may be able to prove that an agency can earn its fees by doing things the owner can't do and by freeing the owner's time for other activities. A second presentation may be needed to prove that an ad agency can do a *better* job than the small business could do on its own. Only after the audience is receptive should you try to persuade the audience to hire your agency rather than a competitor.

Make your ideas relevant to your audience by linking what you have to say to their experiences and interests. Showing your audience that the topic affects them directly is the most effective strategy. When you can't do that, at least link the topic to some everyday experience.

Adapting the Presentation to the Audience*

When Jerry Stackhouse turned pro, many companies made presentations designed to sign him to represent their products. Fila won, in part because of a presentation and visuals specifically adapted to Mr. Stackhouse.

During his initial presentation to Mr. Stackhouse, Fila executive Howe Burch placed a poster directly across from where Mr. Stackhouse was sitting. It listed the names of 18 NBA Nike endorsers in fuzzy, hard-to-read type. But there was no mistaking the slogan printed in big letters: "Looks like the Swoosh [Nike's logo] is becoming a blur. At Fila, Stackhouse will be a Standout."

Mr. Burch also brought along a prototype of the Stackhouse shoe, a model that was ready to go into production but just needed a name. At a second meeting, Mr. Burch arrived carrying a paper bag that he placed on a side table. Mr. Stackhouse asked, "Is that my shoe in the bag?"

Fila knew right then that it had Mr. Stackhouse in the bag, too.

*Paragraphs 2–4 quoted from Roger Thurow, "A Rookie Guard Scores Big at Marketing," *The Wall Street Journal*, February 9, 1996, A6.

> When was the last time you were hungry? Maybe you remember being hungry while you were on a diet, or maybe you had to work late at a lab and didn't get back to the dorm in time for dinner.

Speech about world hunger to an audience of college students

Strategy for a Corporate Speech*

Security directors of the 50 most prominent international banks meet periodically to discuss common problems. BankAmerica's Bob Beck wanted to talk to the group about chemical dependency and BankAmerica's approach to the problem.

Audience's initial position: Resistant. Most favored testing, not treatment.

One point to leave with audience: Treatment is a practical alternative that works.

Adapting message to audience: Used terms from sports, banking, and security to make it easy for audience to identify with message. Backed up points with details and statistics. Explained problems of drug testing. Did not ask for action.

Opener: Hard-hitting statistics on how much chemical dependency costs US businesses—$26 billion a year.

Outline: (1) Chemical dependency as a disease; the size of the problem; testing as the usual response. (2) BankAmerica's treatment approach: policy, program design, and education in the workplace. (3) The business advantages of treatment: protects investment in trained people; confines business losses caused by chemical dependency.

*Based on Robin Welling, *No Frills, No Nonsense, No Secrets* (San Francisco: International Association of Business Communicators, 1988), 290–93.

Planning a Strong Opening and Close

The beginning and end of a presentation, like the beginning and end of a written document, are positions of emphasis. Use those key positions to interest the audience and emphasize your key point. You'll sound more natural and more effective if you talk from notes but write out your opener and close in advance and memorize them. (They'll be short: just a sentence or two.)

Consider using one of the four modes for openers that appeared in Chapter 11: startling statement, narration or anecdote, questions, or quotation. The more you can do to personalize your opener for your audience, the better. Recent events are better than things that happened long ago; local events are better than events at a distance; people they know are better than people who are only names.

Startling Statement

> Twelve of our customers have canceled orders in the past month.

This presentation to a company's executive committee went on to show that the company's distribution system was inadequate and to recommend a third warehouse located in the Southwest.

Narration or Anecdote

> A mother was having difficulty getting her son up for school. He pulled the covers over his head.
> "I'm not going to school," he said. "I'm not ever going again."
> "Are you sick?" his mother asked.
> "No," he answered. "I'm sick of school. They hate me. They call me names. They make fun of me. Why should I go?"
> "I can give you two good reasons," the mother replied. "The first is that you're 42 years old. And the second is *you're the school principal.*"[4]

This speech to a seminar for educators went on to discuss "the three knottiest problems in education today." Educators had to face those problems; they couldn't hide under the covers.

Question

> Are you going to have enough money to do the things you want to when you retire?

This presentation to a group of potential clients discusses the value of using the services of a professional financial planner to achieve one's goals for retirement.

Quotation

> According to Towers Perrin, the profits of Fortune 100 companies would be 25% lower—they'd go down $17 billion—if their earnings statements listed the future costs companies are obligated to pay for retirees' health care.

This presentation on options for health care for retired employees urges executives to start now to investigate options to cut the future costs.

Your opener should interest the audience and establish a rapport with them. Some speakers use humor to achieve those goals. However, an inappropriate joke can turn the audience against the speaker. Never use humor that's directed against the audience. In contrast, speakers who can make fun of themselves almost always succeed:

> It's both a privilege and a pressure to be here.[5]

Humor isn't the only way to set an audience at ease. Smile at your audience before you begin; let them see that you're a real person and a nice one.

The end of your presentation should be as strong as the opener. For your close, you could do one or more of the following: (1) restate your main point; (2) refer to your opener to create a frame for your presentation; (3) end with a vivid, positive picture; (4) tell the audience exactly what to do to solve the problem you've discussed. The following close from a fund-raising speech combines a restatement of the main point with a call for action, telling the audience what to do.

> Plain and simple, we need money to run the foundation, just like you need money to develop new products. We need money to make this work. We need money from you. Pick up that pledge card. Fill it out. Turn it in at the door as you leave. Make it a statement about your commitment . . . make it a big statement.[6]

When you write out your opener and close, be sure to use oral rather than written style. As you can see in the example close above, oral style uses shorter sentences and shorter, simpler words than writing does. Oral style can even sound a bit choppy when it is read by eye. Oral style uses more personal pronouns, a less varied vocabulary, and more repetition.

Planning Visuals and Other Devices to Involve the Audience

Visuals can give your presentation a professional image. As more and more businesses buy computer graphics packages, more and more presentations use slides or overhead transparencies, which, confusingly, are often called *slides,* too. You design the graphics on your computer, then give the disk to a service bureau that produces slides. As color printers become more common, business people will be able to produce color overhead transparencies in-house.

One study showed that presenters using overhead transparencies were perceived as "better prepared, more professional, more persuasive, more credible, and more interesting" than speakers who did not use visuals. They were also more likely to persuade a group to adopt their recommendations.[7] A study comparing the use of different kinds of visuals found that presenters using slides appeared more professional, but presenters using overhead

Cultural Styles of Presentations*

When you make an international presentation, be sensitive to your host country's cultural preferences for presentations.

In Japan, speak in a modest, personal, conversational style. Look at the whole group; remember that the oldest person is probably the most important. Plan carefully so that your presentation fits in the available time—and remember that interpretation cuts your actual speaking time in half.

In Sweden, don't save points for a question-and-answer session. Swedes consider it rude to ask questions at the end of a presentation: to do so suggests the speaker has not been clear. Instead, include all your material in the body of the presentation. The best close is a well-crafted question that applies the material from the presentation, leaving the audience something to think about.

*Based on Bronwen Jones, *Doing Business in Japan: An ABC for Better Communications* ([Tokyo:] JETRO, 1991), 16, and H. Ned Seelye and Alan Seelye-James, *Culture Clash* (Lincolnwood, IL: NTC Business Books, 1995), 30–31.

Figure 17.2   **PowerPoint Slides for an Informative Presentation**

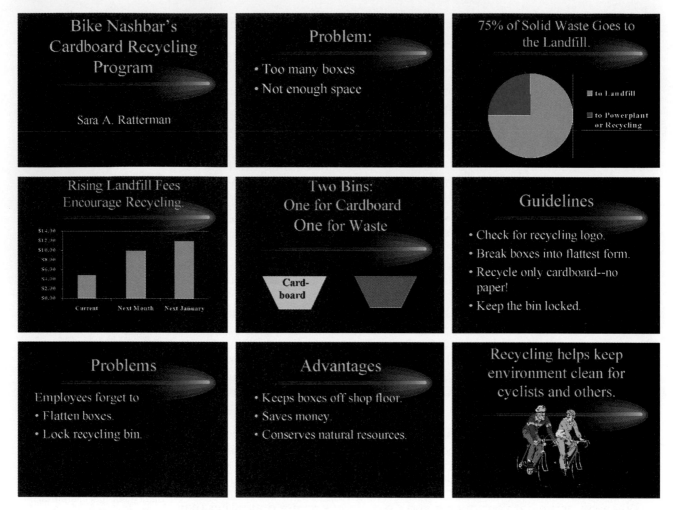

transparencies seemed more interesting. Colored overhead transparencies were most effective in persuading people to act.[8]

Use at least 14-point type for transparencies; 18-point is even better. If possible, use a square area for your text or visual, rather than the whole vertical page, so that your transparency will fit on the screen without your having to move it. For PowerPoint slides, use 44-point type (or larger) for titles and main heads. Your smallest subheading should be no smaller than 28-point type.

Well-designed visuals can serve as an outline for your talk (see Figure 17.2), eliminating the need for additional notes. Plan at most one visual for every minute of your talk, plus two visuals to serve as title and conclusion. Don't try to put your whole talk on visuals. Visuals should highlight your main points, not give every detail.

Use these guidelines to create and show visuals for presentations:

- Make only one point with each visual. Break a complicated point down into several visuals.
- Give each visual a title that makes a point.
- Limit the amount of information on a visual. Use 35 words or less; use simple graphs, not complex ones.
- Don't put your visual up till you're ready to talk about it. Leave it up until your next point; don't turn the projector or overhead off.

See Chapter 6 for information on designing slides and Chapter 16 for information on how to present numerical data through visuals.

Visuals work only if the technology they depend on works. When you give presentations in your own office, check the equipment in advance. When you make a presentation in another location or for another organization, arrive early so that you'll have time not only to check the equipment but also to track down a service worker if the equipment isn't working. Be prepared with a backup plan to use if you're unable to show your slides or videotape.

You can also involve the audience in other ways. A student giving a presentation on English-French Business Communication demonstrated the differences in US and French handshakes by asking a fellow class member to come up to shake hands with her. Another student discussing the need for low-salt products brought in a container of Morton salt, a measuring cup, a measuring spoon, and two plates. As he discussed the body's need for salt, he measured out three teaspoons onto one plate: the amount the body needs in a month. As he discussed the amount of salt the average US diet provides, he continued to measure out salt onto the other plate, stopping only when he had 1¼ pounds of salt—the amount in the average US diet. The demonstration made the discrepancy clear in a way words or even a chart could not have done.[9] To make sure that his employees understood where money went, the CEO of a specialty printing shop in Algoma, Wisconsin, printed up $2 million in play money and handed out big cards to employees marked *Labor, Depreciation, Interest,* and so forth. Then he asked each "category" to come up and take its share of the revenues. The action was more dramatic than a color pie chart could ever have been.[10] Another speaker who was trying to raise funds used the simple act of asking people to stand to involve them, to create emotional appeal, and to make a statistic vivid:

> [A speaker] was talking to a luncheon club about contributing to the relief of an area that had been hit by a tornado. The news report said that 70% of the people had been killed or disabled. The room was set up [with] ten people at each round table. He asked three persons at each table to stand. Then he said, ". . . You people sitting are dead or disabled. You three standing have to take care of the mess. You'd need help, wouldn't you?"[11]

CHOOSING INFORMATION TO INCLUDE IN A PRESENTATION

Choose the information that is most interesting to your audience and that answers the questions your audience will have. Limit your talk to three main points. In a long presentation (20 minutes or more) each main point can have subpoints. Your content will be easier to understand if you clearly show the relationship between each of the main points. Turning your information into a story also helps. For example, a controller might turn charts of financial data into the following story:

> The increase in sales income is offset by an increase in manufacturing costs. Why? Because the cost of material is out of line. Material costs for product #503 tripled last month. An analysis of the three shifts shows that the cost of materials jumped 800% on the second shift. Now, the problem is to find out why the second shift uses so much more material than the other shifts making the same product.[12]

Back up each point with solid support. Statistics and numbers can be convincing if you present them in ways that are easy to hear. Simplify numbers by reducing them to two significant digits.

Get the Story Straight*

How do you persuade investors, bankers, and securities analysts to want to invest in your company? You tell them a story.

Presentation coach Jerry Weissman leads business people through an entire day on identifying the best story. Presentation skills (like building in pauses so listeners can absorb information) come later.

Before coaching, client David Angel described his company like this: "Information Storage Devices provides voice solutions using the company's unique, patented multilevel storage technique. . . ."

After coaching, Angel started his presentation this way: "We make voice chips. They're extremely easy to use. They have unlimited applications. And they last forever."

*Based on Dan Gillmor, "Putting on a Powerful Presentation," *Hemispheres,* March 1996, 31–32.

| Hard to Hear: | If the national debt were in pennies, it would take 17,006,802,720 people, each carrying 100 pounds of pennies, to carry all of our debt. |
| Easier to Hear: | If the national debt were in pennies, it would take 17 billion people, each carrying 100 pounds of pennies, to carry all of our debt.[13] |

In an informative presentation, link the points you make to the knowledge your audience has. Show the audience members that your information answers their questions, solves their problems, or helps them do their jobs. When you explain the effect of a new law or the techniques for using a new machine, use specific examples that apply to the decisions they make and the work they do. If your content is detailed or complicated, give people a written outline or handouts. The written material both helps the audience keep track of your points during the presentation and serves as a reference after the talk is over.

Quotations work well as long as you cite authorities whom your audience genuinely respects. Often you'll need to paraphrase a quote to put it into simple language that's easy to understand. Be sure to tell whom you're citing: "According to Al Gore," "An article in *Business Week* points out that," and so forth.

Demonstrations can prove your points dramatically and quickly. During the investigation of the *Challenger* disaster, the late physicist Richard Feynman asked for a glass of water. When it came, he put a piece of the space shuttle's O-ring into the cold water. After less than a minute, he took it out and pinched it with a small clamp. The material kept the pinched shape when the clamp came off. The material couldn't return to its original shape.[14] A technical explanation could have made the same point: the O-ring couldn't function in the cold. But the demonstration was fast and easy to understand. It didn't require that the audience follow complex chemical or mathematical formulas. In an oral presentation, seeing is believing.

To be convincing, you must answer the audience's questions and objections.

> Some people think that working women are less reliable than men. But the facts show that women take fewer sick days than men do.

However, don't bring up negatives or inconsistencies unless you're sure that the audience will think of them. If you aren't sure, save your evidence for the question phase. If someone does ask, you'll have the answer.

ORGANIZING YOUR INFORMATION

Most presentations use a direct pattern of organization, even when the goal is to persuade a reluctant audience. In a business setting, the audience is in a hurry and knows that you want to persuade them. Be honest about your goal, and then prove that your goal meets the audience's needs too.

In a persuasive presentation, start with your strongest point, your best reason. If time permits, give other reasons as well and respond to possible objections. Put your weakest point in the middle so that you can end on a strong note.

Often one of five standard patterns of organization will work.

- **Chronological.** Start with the past, move to the present, and end by looking ahead.
- **Problem–causes–solution.** Explain the symptoms of the problem, identify its causes, and suggest a solution. This pattern works best when the audience will find your solution easy to accept.

- **Excluding alternatives.** Explain the symptoms of the problem. Explain the obvious solutions first and show why they won't solve the problem. End by discussing a solution that will work. This pattern may be necessary when the audience will find the solution hard to accept.
- **Pro–con.** Give all the reasons in favor of something, then those against it. This pattern works well when you want the audience to see the weaknesses in its position.
- **1-2-3.** Discuss three aspects of a topic. This pattern works well to organize short informative briefings. "Today I'll review our sales, production, and profits for the last quarter."

Make your organization clear to your audience. Written documents can be reread; they can use headings, paragraphs, lists, and indentations to signal levels of detail. In a presentation, you have to provide explicit clues to the structure of your discourse.

Early in your talk—perhaps immediately after your opener—provide an **overview of the main points** you will make.

> First, I'd like to talk about who the homeless in Columbus are. Second, I'll talk about the services The Open Shelter provides. Finally, I'll talk about what you—either individually or as a group—can do to help.

An overview provides a mental peg that hearers can hang each point on. It also can prevent someone missing what you are saying because he or she wonders why you aren't covering a major point that you've saved for later.[15]

Offer a clear signpost as you come to each new point. A **signpost** is an explicit statement of the point you have reached. Choose wording that fits your style. The following statements are four different ways that a speaker could use to introduce the last of three points:

> Now we come to the third point: what you can do as a group or as individuals to help homeless people in Columbus.

> So much for what we're doing. Now let's talk about what you can do to help.

> You may be wondering, what can I do to help?

> As you can see, the Shelter is trying to do many things. We could do more things with your help.

DELIVERING AN EFFECTIVE PRESENTATION

Audiences want the sense that you're talking directly to them and that you care that they understand and are interested. They'll forgive you if you get tangled up in a sentence and end it ungrammatically. They won't forgive you if you seem to have a "canned" talk that you're going to deliver no matter who the audience is or how they respond. You can convey a sense of caring to your audience by making direct eye contact with them and by using a conversational style.

Dealing with Fear

Feeling nervous is normal. But you can harness that nervous energy to help you do your best work. As one student said, you don't need to get rid of your butterflies. All you need to do is make them fly in formation.

Being Interviewed by the Press*

Business people and community leaders are often interviewed by the press. To appear your best on camera, on tape, or in a story,

- Try to find out in advance why you're being interviewed and what information the reporter wants.
- Practice answering possible questions in a single sentence. A long answer is likely to be cut for TV or radio news.
- Talk slowly. You'll have time to think, the audience will have more time to understand what you're saying, and a reporter taking notes will record your words more accurately.
- To reduce the possibility of being misquoted, bring along a cassette recorder to tape the interview. Better still, bring two—and offer to give one tape to the interviewer.

*Based on James L. Graham, "What to Do When a Reporter Calls," *IABC Communication World*, April 1985, 15, and Robert A. Papper, conversation with the author, March 17, 1991.

To calm your nerves as you prepare to give an oral presentation,

- Be prepared. Analyze your audience, organize your thoughts, prepare visual aids, practice your opener and close, check out the arrangements.
- Use only the amount of caffeine you normally use. More or less may make you jumpy.
- Avoid alcoholic beverages.
- Relabel your nerves. Instead of saying, "I'm scared," try saying, "My adrenaline is up." Adrenaline sharpens our reflexes and helps us do our best.

Just before your presentation,

- Consciously contract and then relax your muscles, starting with your feet and calves and going up to your shoulders, arms, and hands.
- Take several deep breaths from your diaphragm.

During your presentation,

- Pause and look at the audience before you begin speaking.
- Concentrate on communicating well.
- Use body energy in strong gestures and movement.

Using Eye Contact

Look directly at the people you're talking to. In one study, speakers who looked more at the audience during a seven-minute informative speech were judged to be better informed, more experienced, more honest, and friendlier than speakers who delivered the same information with less eye contact.[16] An earlier study found that speakers judged sincere looked at the audience 63% of the time, while those judged insincere looked at the audience only 21% of the time.[17]

The point in making eye contact is to establish one-on-one contact with the individual members of your audience. People want to feel that you're talking to them. Looking directly at individuals also enables you to be more conscious of feedback from the audience, so that you can modify your approach if necessary.

Developing a Good Speaking Voice

People will enjoy your presentation more if your voice is easy to listen to. To find out what your voice sounds like, tape record it. Also tape the voices of people on TV or on campus whose voices you like and imitate them. In a few weeks, tape yourself again.

George Fluharty and Harold Ross suggest three ways to find your best speaking voice:

- Close your ears with your fingers and hum up and down the scale until you find the pitch where the hum sounds loudest or most vibrant to you. This pitch will be near your optimum pitch.
- Sing down the scale as far as you can go without forcing. Call this note *do* and sing up the scale to *sol.* This note will be near your optimum pitch.
- If you have a piano, locate the lowest note you can produce and also your highest falsetto note. Your optimum pitch will be approximately one fourth of the distance from your lowest note.[18]

When you speak to a group, talk loudly enough so that people can hear you easily. If you're using a microphone, adjust your volume so you aren't shouting. When you speak in an unfamiliar location, try to get to the room early so you can check the size of the room and the power of the amplification equipment. If you can't do that, ask early in your talk, "Can you hear me in the back of the room?"

The bigger the group is, the more carefully you need to **enunciate,** that is, voice all the sounds of each word. Words starting or ending with *f, t, k, v,* and *d* are especially hard to hear. "Our informed and competent image" can sound like "Our informed, incompetent image."

To enunciate, use your tongue and lips. Researchers have identified 38 different sounds. Of these, you make 31 with your tongue and 7 with your lips. None are made with the jaw, so how wide you open your mouth really doesn't matter. If the tongue isn't active enough, muscles in the throat try to compensate, producing sore throats and strained voices.[19]

Tongue twisters can help you exercise your tongue and enunciate more clearly. Stephen Lucas suggests the following:

- Sid said to tell him that Benny hid the penny many years ago.
- Fetch me the finest French-fried freshest fish that Finney fries.
- Three gray geese in the green grass grazed.
- Shy Sarah saw six Swiss wristwatches.
- One year we had a Christmas brunch with Merry Christmas mush to munch. But I don't think you'd care for such. We didn't like to munch mush much.[20]

You can also reduce pressure on your throat by fitting phrases to your ideas. If you cut your sentences into bits, you'll emphasize words beginning with vowels, making the vocal cords hit each other. Instead, run past words beginning with vowels to emphasize later syllables or later words:[21]

Choppiness hurts vocal cords:	*We* must take more responsibility not *Only* for *Ourselves* *And* *Our* families but for *Our* communities *And* *Our* country.
Smooth phrasing protects throat:	*We* must take more *Responsibility* *Not* only for our *Selves* and our *Families* but for our *Communities* and our *Country.*

You can reduce the number of *uhs* you use by practicing your talk several times. Filler sounds aren't signs of nervousness. Instead, say psychologists at Columbia University, they occur when speakers pause searching for the next word. Searching takes longer when people have big vocabularies or talk about topics where a variety of word choices are possible. Practicing your talk makes your word choices automatic, and you'll use fewer *uhs.*[22]

Vary your volume, pitch, and speed. Speakers who speak quickly and who vary their volume during the talk are more likely to be perceived as competent.[23] Sound energetic and enthusiastic. If your ideas don't excite you, why should your audience find them exciting?

Standing and Gesturing

Stand with your feet far enough apart for good balance, with your knees flexed. Unless the presentation is very formal or you're on camera, you can

Appearing on Camera*

When you make a presentation on video, be informal and friendly. Look at the camera when you talk to create the effect of making eye contact with the audience.

Since the sound reproduction equipment may deaden voices, make a special effort to vary pitch and expression. Don't interrupt another speaker. Two people talking at the same time on camera produce gibberish.

Dress for the camera.

- Don't wear white. Only very expensive cameras can handle pure white.
- Don't wear bold stripes, checks, plaids, or polka dots.
- Don't wear large accessories.
- Red, blue, and green photograph well. If an entire outfit in red seems too bold, consider wearing a red tie or blouse.

*Based on Robert A. Papper, conversation with the author, March 17, 1991.

Handling Questions*

On behalf of Greenpeace USA, Christopher Childs gives more than 100 presentations a year to schools, colleges, and churches.

"For the question-and-answer period, I try to stay in touch with our campaigners to find out what's most important. But I also try to stay aware of my personal motivations. When I'm very clear about what I want to accomplish, the questions take care of themselves. . . .

"Occasionally I get hostile questions, and while I try to deal on a factual level with the issues, I look to see if I can tell what's going on with the person. Oftentimes they're not hostile at all, but very concerned. When it's workable in a public forum, I might suggest to them what I hear them really saying. Often they really appreciate the effort."

*Quoted from Jess Wells, "Stage Presence: Professional Speakers Share Their Techniques," *Publish*, December 1990, 82.

walk if you want to. Some speakers like to come in front of the lectern to remove that barrier between themselves and the audience.

Build on your natural style for gestures. Gestures usually work best when they're big and confident.

Using Notes and Visuals

Unless you're giving a very short presentation, you'll probably want to use notes. Even experts use notes. The more you know about the subject, the greater the temptation to add relevant points that occur to you as you talk. Adding an occasional point can help to clarify something for the audience, but adding too many points will destroy your outline and put you over the time limit.

Put your notes on cards or on sturdy pieces of paper. Most speakers like to use 4-by-6-inch or 5-by-7-inch cards because they hold more information. Your notes need to be complete enough to help you if you go blank, so use long phrases or complete sentences. Under each main point, jot down the evidence or illustration you'll use. Indicate where you'll refer to visuals.

Look at your notes infrequently. Most of your gaze time should be directed to members of the audience. Hold your notes high enough so that your head doesn't bob up and down like a yo-yo as you look from the audience to your notes and back again.

If you have lots of visuals and know your topic well, you won't need notes. If possible, put the screen to the side so that you won't block it. Face the audience, not the screen. With transparencies, you can use color marking pens to call attention to your points as you talk. Show the entire visual at once: don't cover up part of it. If you don't want the audience to read ahead, prepare several visuals that build up. In your overview, for example, the first visual could list your first point, the second the first and second, and the third all three points.

Keep the room lights on if possible; turning them off makes it easier for people to fall asleep and harder for them to concentrate on you.

HANDLING QUESTIONS

Prepare for questions by listing every fact or opinion you can think of that challenges your position. Treat each objection seriously and try to think of a way to deal with it. If you're talking about a controversial issue, you may want to save one point for the question period, rather than making it during the presentation. Speakers who have visuals to answer questions seem especially well prepared.

During your presentation, tell the audience how you'll handle questions. If you have a choice, save questions for the end. In your talk, answer the questions or objections that you expect your audience to have. Don't exaggerate your claims so that you won't have to back down in response to questions later.

During the question period, don't nod your head to indicate that you understand a question as it is asked. Audiences will interpret nods as signs that you agree with the questioner. Instead, look directly at the questioner. As you answer the question, expand your focus to take in the entire group. Don't say, "That's a good question." That response implies that the other questions have been poor ones.

If the audience may not have heard the question or if you want more time to think, repeat the question before you answer it. Link your answers to the points you made in your presentation. Keep the purpose of your presentation in mind, and select information that advances your goals.

If a question is hostile or biased, rephrase it before you answer it. "You're asking whether. . . ." Or suggest an alternative question: "I think there are problems with both the positions you describe. It seems to me that a third solution which is better than either of them is. . . ."

Occasionally someone will ask a question that is really designed to state the speaker's own position. Respond to the question if you want to. Another option is to say, "I'm not sure what you're asking," or even, "That's a clear statement of your position. Let's move to the next question now." If someone asks about something that you already explained in your presentation, simply answer the question without embarrassing the questioner. No audience will understand and remember 100% of what you say.

If you don't know the answer to a question, say so. If your purpose is to inform, write down the question so that you can look up the answer before the next session. If it's a question to which you think there is no answer, ask if anyone in the room knows. When no one does, your "ignorance" is vindicated. If an expert is in the room, you may want to refer questions of fact to him or her. Answer questions of interpretation yourself.

At the end of the question period, take two minutes to summarize your main point once more. (This can be a restatement of your close.) Questions may or may not focus on the key point of your talk. Take advantage of having the floor to repeat your message briefly and forcefully.

MAKING GROUP PRESENTATIONS

Plan carefully to involve as many members of the group as possible in speaking roles.

The easiest way to make a group presentation is to outline the presentation and then divide the topics, giving one to each group member. Another member can be responsible for the opener and the close. During the question period, each member answers questions that relate to his or her topic.

In this kind of divided presentation, be sure to

- Plan transitions.
- Enforce time limits strictly.
- Coordinate your visuals so that the presentation seems a coherent whole.
- Practice the presentation as a group at least once; more is better.

The best group presentations are even more fully integrated: the group writes a very detailed outline, chooses points and examples, and creates visuals together. Then, within each point, voices trade off. This presentation is most effective because each voice speaks only a minute or two before a new voice comes in. However, it works only when all group members know the subject well and when the group plans carefully and practices extensively.

Whatever form of group presentation you use, be sure to introduce each member of the team to the audience and to pay close attention to each other. If other members of the team seem uninterested in the speaker, the audience gets the sense that that speaker isn't worth listening to.

SUMMARY OF KEY POINTS

- **Informative presentations** inform or teach the audience. **Persuasive presentations** motivate the audience to act or to believe. **Goodwill presentations** entertain and validate the audience. Most oral presentations have more than one purpose.
- A written message makes it easier to present extensive or complex information and to minimize undesirable emotions. Oral messages make it easier to use emotion, to focus the audience's attention, to answer questions and resolve conflicts quickly, to modify a proposal that may not be acceptable in its original form, and to get immediate action or response.

- In both oral and written messages, you should

  - Adapt the message to the specific audience.
  - Show the audience how they benefit from the idea, policy, service, or product.
  - Overcome any objections the audience may have.
  - Use you-attitude and positive emphasis.
  - Use visuals to clarify or emphasize material.
  - Specify exactly what the audience should do.

- An oral presentation needs to be simpler than a written message to the same audience.
- In a **monologue presentation,** the speaker plans the presentation in advance and delivers it without deviation. In a **guided discussion,** the speaker presents the questions or issues that both speaker and audience have agreed on in advance. Rather than functioning as an expert with all the answers, the speaker serves as a facilitator to help the audience tap its own knowledge. An **interactive presentation** is a conversation using questions to determine the buyer's needs, probe objections, and gain provisional and then final commitment to the purchase.
- Adapt your message to your audience's beliefs, experience, and interests.
- Use the beginning and end of the presentation to interest the audience and emphasize your key point.
- Using visuals makes a speaker seem more prepared, more interesting, and more persuasive.
- Use a direct pattern of organization. Put your strongest reason first.
- Limit your talk to three main points. Early in your talk—perhaps immediately after your opener—provide an **overview of the main points** you will make. Offer a clear signpost as you come to each new point. A **signpost** is an explicit statement of the point you have reached.
- To calm your nerves as you prepare to give an oral presentation,

  - Be prepared. Analyze your audience, organize your thoughts, prepare visual aids, practice your opener and close, check out the arrangements.
  - Use only the amount of caffeine you normally use.
  - Avoid alcoholic beverages.
  - Relabel your nerves. Instead of saying, "I'm scared," try saying, "My adrenaline is up." Adrenaline sharpens our reflexes and helps us do our best.

    Just before your presentation,
  - Consciously contract and then relax your muscles, starting with your feet and calves and going up to your shoulders, arms, and hands.
  - Take several deep breaths from your diaphragm.

    During your presentation,
  - Pause and look at the audience before you begin speaking.
  - Concentrate on communicating well.
  - Use body energy in strong gestures and movement.

- Convey a sense of caring to your audience by making direct eye contact with them and by using a conversational style.
- Treat questions as opportunities to give more detailed information than you had time to give in your presentation. Link your answers to the points you made in your presentation.
- Repeat the question before you answer it if the audience may not have heard it or if you want more time to think. Rephrase hostile or biased questions before you answer them.
- The best group presentations result when the group writes a very detailed outline, chooses points and examples, and creates visuals together. Then, within each point, voices trade off.

Exercises and Problems
For Chapter 17

GETTING STARTED

17–1 Analyzing Openers and Closes

The following openers and closes came from class presentations on information interviews.

- Does each opener make you interested in hearing the rest of the presentation?
- Does each opener provide a transition to the overview?
- Does the close end the presentation in a satisfying way?

a. Opener: I interviewed Mark Perry at AT&T.
   Close: Well, that's my report.

b. Opener: How many of you know what you want to do when you graduate?
   Close: So, if you like numbers and want to travel, think about being a CPA. Arthur Andersen can take you all over the world.

c. Opener: You don't have to know anything about computer programming to get a job as a technical writer at CompuServe.
   Close: After talking to Raj, I decided technical writing isn't for me. But it is a good career if you work well under pressure and like learning new things all the time.

d. Opener: My report is about what it's like to work in an advertising agency.
   Middle: They keep really tight security; I had to wear a badge and be escorted to Susan's desk.
   Close: Susan gave me samples of the agency's ads and even a sample of a new soft drink she's developing a campaign for. But she didn't let me keep the badge.

PRESENTATION ASSIGNMENTS

17–2 Making a Short Oral Presentation

As Your Instructor Directs,
Make a short (three- to five-minute) presentation, with three to eight PowerPoint slides, on one of the following topics:

a. Explain how what you've learned in classes, in campus activities, or at work will be useful to the employer who hires you after graduation.

b. Profile someone who is successful in the field you hope to enter and explain what makes him or her successful.

c. Describe a specific situation in an organization in which communication was handled well or badly.

d. Make a short presentation based on another problem in this book.
   1–6   Introduce yourself to the class.
   3–11   Analyze your boss.
   3–12   Analyze your co-workers.
   7–5   Explain a "best practice" in your organization.
   7–12   Explain what a new hire in your unit needs to know to be successful.

8–11   Tell your boss about a problem in your unit.

9–12   Recommend a co-worker for a bonus or an award.

10–7   Motivate employees in your unit to do their best work.

10–9   Ask for more resources for your unit.

11–7   Make a sales presentation for a product or service.

14–11 Describe your choices in creating a brochure.

18–2   Tell the class in detail about one of your accomplishments.

19–4   Explain one of the challenges (e.g., technology, ethics, international competition) that the field you hope to enter is facing.

19–5   Profile a company you would like to work for and explain why you think it would be a good employer.

19–6 Share the results of an information interview.

20–2 Share the advice of students currently on the job market.

20–3 Share what you learn when you interview an interviewer.

20–4 Explain your interview strategy.

17–3 Making a Longer Oral Presentation

As Your Instructor Directs,
Make a 5- to 12-minute presentation on one of the following. Use visuals to make your talk effective.

a. Show why your unit is important to the organization and either should be exempt from downsizing or should receive additional resources.

b. Persuade your supervisor to make a change that will benefit the organization.

c. Persuade your organization to make a change that will improve the organization's image in the community.

d. Persuade classmates to donate time or money to a charitable organization. (Read Chapter 11.)

e. Persuade an employer that you are the best person for the job.

f. Use another problem in this book as the basis for your presentation.

   3–13 Analyze an organization's culture.

3–14 Analyze a discourse community.

5–1 Describe the composing process(es) of a writer you've interviewed.

6–5 Evaluate the page design of one or more documents.

6–6 Evaluate the design of a Web page.

7–8 Present a Web page you have designed.

8–19 Analyze rejection letters students on your campus have received.

10–15 Persuade your campus to make a change.

11–3 Analyze one or more sales or fund-raising letters.

12–4 Analyze international messages that your workplace has created or received.

14–15 Summarize the results of a survey you have conducted.

15–10 Summarize the results of your research.

17–4 Making a Group Oral Presentation

As Your Instructor Directs,
Make a 5- to 12-minute presentation on one of the following. Use visuals to make your talk effective.

1–5 Explain the role of communication in one or more organizations.

12–6 Report on another country.

13–10 Recommend whether a mall should hire ethnic Santas.

13–11 Recommend an Internet use policy.

13–18 Present brochures you have designed to the class.

13–19 Describe the listening strategies of workers you have interviewed.

17–5 Evaluating Oral Presentations

Evaluate an oral presentation given by a classmate or given by a speaker on your campus. Use the following categories:

Strategy

1. Choosing an effective kind of presentation for the situation.
2. Adapting ideas to audience's beliefs, experience, and interests.
3. Using a strong opening and close.
4. Using visual aids or other devices to involve audience.

Content

5. Using specific, vivid supporting material and language.
6. Providing rebuttals to counterclaims or objections.

Organization

7. Providing an overview of main points.
8. Signposting main points in body of talk.
9. Providing adequate transitions between points and speakers.

Delivery

10. Making direct eye contact with audience.
11. Using a conversational style.
12. Using voice and gestures effectively.
13. Using notes and visuals effectively.
14. Handling questions effectively.

As Your Instructor Directs,

a. Fill out a form indicating your evaluation in each of the areas.
b. Share your evaluation orally with the speaker.
c. Write a memo to the speaker evaluating the presentation. Send a copy of your memo to your instructor.

17–6   Evaluating Team Presentations

Evaluate team presentations using the following questions:

1. How thoroughly were all group members involved?
2. Did members of the team introduce themselves or each other?
3. Did team members seem interested in what their teammates said?
4. How well was the material organized?
5. How well did the material hold your interest?
6. How clear did the material seem to you?
7. How effective were the visuals?
8. How well did the team handle questions?
9. What could be done to improve the presentation?
10. What were the strong points of the presentation?

As Your Instructor Directs,

a. Fill out a form indicating your evaluation in each of the areas.
b. Share your evaluation orally with the speaker.
c. Write a memo to the speaker evaluating the presentation. Send a copy of your memo to your instructor.

17–7   Evaluating the Way a Speaker Handles Questions

Listen to a speaker talking about a controversial subject. (Go to a talk on campus or in town, or watch a speaker on a TV show like "Face the Nation" or "60 Minutes.") Observe the way he or she handles questions.

■ About how many questions does the speaker answer?
■ What is the format for asking and answering questions?
■ Are the answers clear? responsive to the question? something that could be quoted without embarrassing the speaker and the organization he or she represents?
■ How does the speaker handle hostile questions? Does the speaker avoid getting angry? Does the speaker retain control of the meeting? How?
■ If some questions were not answered well, what (if anything) could the speaker have done to leave a better impression?
■ Did the answers leave the audience with a more or less positive impression of the speaker? Why?

As Your Instructor Directs,

a. Share your evaluation with a small group of students.
b. Present your evaluation formally to the class.
c. Summarize your evaluation in a memo to your instructor.

Job Hunting

Résumés

Chapter Outline

An Inside Perspective:
Résumés

Socorro Kosaka, Human Resources Specialist
North American Aircraft Division of Boeing North American

Socorro Kosaka recruits college graduates for the North American Division of Boeing North American, a subsidiary of The Boeing Company. Headquartered in Seattle, Washington, Boeing is the world's leading manufacturer of commercial airplanes. Boeing's North American Aircraft Division has built more military aircraft than any other airplane builder in the free world.

The first thing I want to see in a résumé submitted by a recent college graduate, after the name, address, and telephone number, is education. I want to see the degree, major/minor, date of graduation, college/university, and grade point average (GPA). Computer proficiency is crucial. Identify computer skills in a separate category (e.g., "computer skills," "software") and list the software, programming languages, and hardware you've used.

Give details about work experience only if it's relevant. Waiting on tables or working at the nearest mall can go on one line: "Worked during college at . . . ." However, give details about internships, co-ops, and projects in companies like those you want to work for. Specify how long the assignment lasted, whom you reported to, and what you did. If you presented your work to management, say so.

Highlight honors, great grades, scholarships, and leadership skills. If you've earned a degree with a lot of personal sacrifice, find a way to explain that to the reader. I once interviewed a student who had been brought to the United States at the age of five by his grandfather, while his immediate family remained in Vietnam. The grandfather died when the student was 15, so the student took a job after high school and paid his way through a technical school. He was awarded the highest honors in his class and became an autocad designer. On the job, he recognized the limitations of his education. He enrolled in an excellent out-of-state college, worked his way through the five years it took him to finish an undergraduate degree, and managed to send money to his mother and younger siblings in Vietnam. He put this information on his résumé under "accomplishments."

In my company, applicants can e-mail résumés to us or fill out applications on our Web page. Résumés submitted electronically go into a central database, which the recruiter can search for key words that meet the requirements for an open position.

Appearance is less important on an electronic résumé since only a computer will be reading it. However, accuracy is still crucial. Résumés that applicants mail or bring to interviews should be well written, visually attractive, and totally free from errors.

Socorro Kosaka, March 7, 1997

Visit Boeing North American's Web site: http://bna.boeing.com/

"Résumés . . . should be well written, visually attractive, and totally free from errors."

Socorro Kosaka, Boeing North American

A **résumé** is a persuasive summary of your qualifications for employment. If you're on the job market, having a résumé makes you look well organized and prepared. When you're employed, having an up-to-date résumé makes it easier to take advantage of opportunities that may come up for an even better job. If you're several years away from job hunting, preparing a résumé now will make you more conscious of what to do in the next two or three years to make yourself an attractive candidate. Writing a résumé is also an ego-building experience: the person who looks so good on paper is **you!**

This chapter covers paper, Web, and scannable résumés. Job application letters (sometimes called "cover letters") are discussed in Chapter 19. Chapter 20 discusses interviews and the communication after the interview. All three chapters focus on job hunting in the United States. Conventions, expectations, and criteria differ from culture to culture: different norms apply in different countries.

All job communications must be tailored to your unique qualifications. Adopt the wording or layout of an example if it's relevant to your own situation, but don't be locked into the forms in this book. You've got different strengths; your résumé will be different, too.

A TIME LINE FOR JOB HUNTING

Informal preparation for job hunting should start soon after you arrive on campus. Join extracurricular organizations on campus and in the community to increase your knowledge and provide a network for learning about jobs. Find a job that gives you experience. Note which courses you like—and why you like them. If you like thinking and learning about a subject, you're more likely to enjoy a job in that field.

Formal preparation for job hunting should begin a full year *before you begin interviewing*. Visit the campus Placement Office to see what services it provides. Ask friends who are on the job market about their experiences in interviews; find out what kinds of job offers they get. Check into the possibility of getting an internship or a co-op job that will give you relevant experience before you interview.

The year you interview, register with your Placement Office early. If you plan to graduate in the spring, prepare your résumé and plan your interview strategy early in the fall. Initial campus interviews occur from October to February for May or June graduation. In January or February, write to any organization you'd like to work for that hasn't interviewed on campus. From February to April, you're likely to visit one or more offices for a second interview.

Try to have a job offer lined up *before* you get the degree. People who don't need jobs immediately are more confident in interviews and usually get better job offers. If you have to job hunt after graduation, plan to spend at least 30 hours a week on your job search. The time will pay off in a better job that you find more quickly.

EVALUATING YOUR STRENGTHS AND INTERESTS

A self-assessment is the first step in producing a good résumé. Each person could do several jobs happily. Personality and aptitude tests can tell you what your strengths are, but they won't say, "You should be a ___." You'll still need to answer questions like these:

- What achievements have given you the most satisfaction? *Why* did you enjoy them?
- Would you rather have firm deadlines or a flexible schedule? Do you prefer working alone or with other people? Do you prefer specific instructions and standards for evaluation or freedom and uncertainty? How comfortable are you with pressure? Are you willing to "pay your dues" for several years before you are promoted? How much challenge do you want?
- Are you willing to take work home? To travel? How important is money to you? Prestige? Time to spend with family and friends?
- Where do you want to live? What features in terms of weather, geography, cultural and social life do you see as ideal?
- Is it important to you that your work achieve certain purposes or values, or do you see work as "just a way to make a living"? Are the organization's culture and ethical standards important to you?

Once you know what is most important to you, analyze the job market to see where you could find what you want. For example, Peter's greatest interest is athletics, but he isn't good enough for the pros. Studying the job market might suggest several alternatives. He could teach sports and physical fitness as a high school coach or a corporate fitness director. He could cover sports for a newspaper, a magazine, or a TV station. He could go into management or sales for a professional sports team, a health club, or a company that sells sports equipment.

How Employers Use Résumés

Understanding how employers use résumés will help you create a résumé that works for you.

1. **Employers use résumés to decide whom to interview.** (The major exceptions are on-campus interviews, where the campus placement office has policies that determine who meets with the interviewer.) Since résumés are used to screen out applicants, omit anything that may create a negative impression.
2. **The search committee skims résumés.** Companies often get 100 or more résumés a day even when they have not advertised positions; a company that advertises an opening may get up to 1,000 applicants for a single position. A résumé gets a quick glance for 8 to 30 seconds. Only the résumés that pass the "skim test" are read more closely. Use layout and visual impact to highlight your credentials.
3. **Employers assume that your letter and résumé represent your best work.** Neatness, accuracy, and freedom from typographical errors are essential.
4. **Interviewers usually reread your résumé before the interview to refresh their memories.** Be ready to offer fuller details about everything on your résumé.
5. **After the search committee has chosen an applicant, it submits the applicant's résumé to people in the organization who must approve the appointment.** These people may have different backgrounds and areas of expertise. Spell out acronyms. Explain Greek-letter honor societies, unusual job titles, or organizations that may be unfamiliar to the reader.

What Employers Want*

In a survey conducted by the National Association of Colleges and Employers, the number one thing employers wanted was communication skills.

Interpersonal skills ranked second.

Technical skills, such as knowledge of accounting or fashion merchandising or engineering, came next, followed by experience working in teams and previous work experience.

*Based on Carol Kleiman, "Web Site Occupations Are Growing by the Gigabyte," *The Columbus Dispatch,* February 9, 1997.

GUIDELINES FOR RÉSUMÉS

Writing a résumé is not an exact science. If your skills are in great demand, you can violate every guideline here and still get a good job. But when you must compete against many applicants, these guidelines will help you look as good on paper as you are in person.

Length

A one-page résumé is sufficient, but do fill the page. Less than a full page suggests that you do not have very much to say for yourself.

The average résumé is now two pages, according to career-planning consultant Marilyn Moats Kennedy. An experiment that mailed one- or two-page résumés to Big Six accounting firms showed that even readers who said they preferred short résumés were more likely to want to interview the candidate with the longer résumé.[1]

If you do use more than one page, the second page should have at least 10 to 12 lines. Use a second sheet and staple it to the first so that readers who skim see the staple and know that there's more. Leave less important information for the second page. Put your name and "Page 2" or "Cont." on the page. If the pages are separated, you want the reader to know who the qualifications belong to and that the second page is not your whole résumé.

Emphasis

Emphasize the things you've done that (a) are most relevant to the position for which you're applying, (b) show your superiority to other applicants, and (c) are recent.

Show that you're qualified by giving details on relevant course projects, activities, and jobs where you've done similar work. Marketing recruiters responded more positively to résumés giving details about course projects, especially when candidates had little relevant work experience.[2] Be brief about low-level jobs that simply show dependability. To prove that you're the best candidate for the job, emphasize items that set you apart from other applicants: promotions, honors and achievements, experience with computers or other relevant equipment, foreign languages, and so on.

You may include high school jobs, activities, and honors to fill the page if you're getting a two- or four-year degree. If you can fill a page without high school activities and honors, omit them. When you're 25 or older, include information about high school only if you need it to show geographical flexibility. Focus on achievements in the last three to five years. Whatever your age at the time you write a résumé, you want to suggest that you are now the best you've ever been.

Include full-time work after high school before you returned to college and work during college to support yourself or to earn expenses. If the jobs you held then were low-level ones, present them briefly or combine them:

1995-98   Part-time and full-time jobs to support family

You can emphasize material by putting it at the top or the bottom of a page, by giving it more space, and by setting it off with white space. The beginning and end—of a document, a page, a list—are positions of emphasis. When you have a choice (e.g., in a list of job duties), put less important material in the middle, not at the end, to avoid the impression of "fading out."

Weak order:	Coordinated weekly schedules, assigned projects to five staff members, evaluated their performance, and submitted weekly time sheets.
Emphatic order:	Coordinated weekly schedules and submitted weekly time sheets. Assigned projects to five staff members and evaluated their performance.

You can also emphasize material by presenting it in a vertical list, by using a phrase in a heading, and by providing details. For example, rather than presenting your internship work in long paragraphs, use bulleted lists to make your accomplishments stand out.

Details

Details provide evidence to support your claims (☞ p. 258), convince the reader, and separate you from other applicants. Tell how many people you trained or supervised, how much money you budgeted or raised. Describe the aspects of the job you did.

Too vague:	Sales Manager, *The Daily Collegian*, University Park, PA, 1997-98. Supervised staff; promoted ad sales.
Good details:	Sales Manager, *The Daily Collegian*, University Park, PA, 1997-98. Supervised 22-member sales staff; helped recruit, interview, and select staff; assigned duties and scheduled work; recommended best performers for promotion. Motivated staff to increase paid ad inches 10% over previous year's sales.

Omit details that add nothing to a title, that are less impressive than the title alone, or that suggest a faulty sense of priorities (e.g., listing minor offices in an organization that tries to give everyone something to do). Either use strong details or just give the office or job title without any details.

Writing Style

Without sacrificing content, be as concise as possible.

Wordy:	Member, Meat Judging Team, 1996-97 Member, Meat Judging Team, 1997-98 Member, Meat Judging Team, 1998-99 Captain, Meat Judging Team, 1998-98
Tight:	Meat Judging Team, 1996-99; Captain 1998-99
Wordy:	Performed foundation load calculations
Tight:	Calculated foundation loads

Résumés normally use phrases and sentence fragments. Complete sentences are acceptable if they are the briefest way to present information. To save space and to avoid sounding arrogant, never use *I* in a résumé. *Me* and *my* are acceptable if they are unavoidable or if using them reduces wordiness.

Verbs or gerunds (the *-ing* form of verbs) create a more dynamic image of you than do nouns, so use them on résumés that will be read by people. (Rules for scannable résumés to be read by computers come later in this chapter.) In the revisions below, nouns, verbs, and gerunds are in bold type.

Résumés for the Big Six*

Carl M. Anderson, a Regional Director of Recruiting for Coopers & Lybrand's office in Columbus, Ohio, says,

"[Students should] use the placement office. Researching employers does two things for them. They can learn more specifics about the companies they're going to talk to and truly be more knowledgeable and interested in the job, and then they can make a more enlightened decision about it. Second, to get through the process successfully, I think students have to do fairly thorough self-assessments. They have to sit down with a pad and pencil and list their strengths and weaknesses.

"[On the résumé,] I want to see some evidence of some involvement and some leadership. I'm looking for evidence of taking on some specific responsibilities, putting forth some effort. I'm looking for doers rather than joiners. Just being a member of eight organizations never impresses me. I want to see some phraseology on there that says 'Took responsibility for annual such-and-such drive as chairman, led successful drive'—quantified in these ways."

*Quoted from phone interview with Kitty Locker, January 25, 1994.

Nouns: Chair, Income Tax Assistance Committee, Winnipeg, MB, 1997-98. Responsibilities: **recruitment** of volunteers; flyer **design, writing,** and **distribution** for **promotion** of program; **speeches** to various community groups and nursing homes to advertise the service.

Verbs: Chair, Income Tax Assistance Committee, Winnipeg, MB, 1997-98. **Recruited** volunteers for the program. **Designed, wrote,** and **distributed** a flyer to promote the program; **spoke** to various community groups and nursing homes to advertise the service.

Gerunds: Chair, Income Tax Assistance Committee, Winnipeg, MB, 1997-98. Responsibilities included **recruiting** volunteers for the program; **designing, writing,** and **distributing** a flyer to promote the program; and **speaking** to various community groups and nursing homes to advertise the service.

Note that the items in the list must be in parallel structure (➤ p. 98).

Layout, Printing, and Paper

Experiment with layout, fonts, and spacing to get an attractive résumé. Consider creating a letterhead that you use for both your résumé and your application letter.

Use enough white space to make your résumé easy to read, but not so much that you look as if you're padding. Even if you pay someone else to produce your résumé, *you* must specify the exact layout: you cannot expect a paid typist to care as much about your résumé as you do.

Print your résumé on a laser printer. Take advantage of different sizes of type and perhaps of rules (thin lines) to make your résumé look professional.

Print your résumé on standard 8½-by-11-inch paper (never legal size). Use 20-lb. bond paper (paper with 20 to 25% cotton content). White paper is standard; a very pale color is also acceptable. If you have a two-page résumé, consider having it printed on the front and left-inside page of a folded 11-by-17-inch page, with your application letter on the right-inside page.

KINDS OF RESUMES

There are two kinds of résumés: chronological and skills. A **chronological résumé** summarizes what you did in a time line (starting with the most recent events, and going backward in **reverse chronology**). It emphasizes degrees, job titles, and dates. It is the traditional résumé format. Figures 18.1 and 18.3 show chronological résumés. Use a chronological résumé when

- Your education and experience are a logical preparation for the position for which you're applying.
- You have impressive job titles, offices, or honors.

A **skills résumé** emphasizes the skills you've used, rather than the job in which or the date when you used them. Figures 18.4 and 18.5 show skills résumés. Use a skills résumé when

- Your education and experience are not the usual route to the position for which you're applying.
- You're changing fields.
- You want to combine experience from paid jobs, activities or volunteer work, and courses to show the extent of your experience in administration, finance, speaking, etc.
- Your recent work history may create the wrong impression (e.g., it has gaps, shows a demotion, shows job-hopping, etc.).

A Chronological Résumé   **Figure 18.1**

A vertical line provides visual variety.

Vary font sizes. The name is in 18-point, the main headings in 12-point, and the text in 11-point type.

Jerry A. Jackson

Campus Address   **Permanent Address**
1636½ Highland Street   45 East Mulberry
Columbus, OH 43201   Huntington, NY 11746
(614) 555-5718   (516) 555-7793
   jackson.2495@osu.edu
   http://www.fisher.osu/students/jackson.2495/home.htm

If you have a professional webpage, include its URL.

Education

B.S. in Family Financial Management, June 1998, The Ohio State University, Columbus, OH
   "B" Average   *List not only major courses but also others*
   Courses Related to Major: *that will enhance your performance*
      Accounting I and II   Business and Professional Writing
      Finance   Computer Programming
      Economics I and II   Statistics
      Family Resource Management   Public Speaking
      Family and Human Development   Interpersonal Communication

Sports Experience

BAAD (Buckeye Athletes Against Drugs)
Intramural Hockey Team (Division Champions, Winter 1997)
Three-year Varsity Letterman, Ohio State University, Columbus, OH
Men's NCAA Division I Lacrosse *(The Lacrosse team did poorly, so he omits its ranking.)*

Experience

Financial Sales Representative, Primerica Company, Columbus, OH, February 1997-present. Work with clients to plan investment strategies; recommend specific investments.

Entrepreneur, Huntington, NY and Columbus OH, September 1996-January 1997. Created a saleable product, secured financial backing, found a manufacturer, supervised production, and sold product—12 dozen T-shirts at a $5.25 profit each—to help pay for school expenses. *How to handle self-employment.*

Landscape Maintenance Supervisor, Huntington, NY, Summers 1988-96. Formed a company to cut lawns, put up fences, fertilize, garden, and paint houses. Hired, fired, trained, motivated, and paid friends to complete jobs.

Collector and Repairman, ACN Inc., Huntington, NY, Summers 1988-95. Collected and counted up to $10,000 a day. Worked with technicians troubleshooting and repairing electronic and coin mechanisms of video and pinball games, cigarette machines, and jukeboxes. Drove company cars and trucks throughout New York metro area to collect cash and move and repair machines.

Specify large sums of money.

Provide details to interest readers, set you apart from other applicants.

Honesty in the Résumé

Never lie in a résumé.

It's OK to omit negative information (like a low grade point average). If you were an officer in an organization, it's OK to list the title even if you didn't do much. It's OK to provide details when you did more than the job title indicates, or to give the job title alone if you had an inflated official title (e.g., Assistant Manager) but didn't really do much.

But it isn't OK to lie.

Interviewers will ask you about items in the résumé. If you have to back down, you destroy your credibility. And if lies are discovered after someone is hired, the person is fired.

The two kinds differ in what information is included and how that information is organized. You may assume that the advice in this chapter applies to both kinds of résumés unless there is an explicit statement that the two kinds of résumés would handle a category differently.

WHAT TO INCLUDE IN A RÉSUMÉ

Although the résumé is a factual document, its purpose is to persuade. In a job application form or an application for graduate or professional school, you answer every question even if the answer is not to your credit. In a résumé, you cannot lie, but you can omit anything that does not work in your favor.

Résumés commonly contain the following information. The categories marked with an asterisk are essential.

> *Name, Address, and Phone Number
> Career Objective
> *Education
> *Experience
> Honors
> Activities
> References

You may choose other titles for these categories and add categories that are relevant for your qualifications: COMPUTER SKILLS, FOREIGN LANGUAGES.

EDUCATION and EXPERIENCE always stand as separate categories, even if you have only one item under each head. Combine other headings so that you have at least two long or three short items under each heading. For example, if you're in one honor society, two social clubs, and on one athletic team, combine them all under ACTIVITIES AND HONORS.

If you have more than seven items under a heading, consider using subheadings. For example, a student who had a great many activities might divide them into STUDENT GOVERNMENT, OTHER CAMPUS ACTIVITIES, and COMMUNITY SERVICE.

Put your strongest categories near the top and at the bottom of the first page. If you have impressive work experience, you might want to put that category first after your name, put EDUCATION in the middle of the page, and put your address at the bottom.

Name, Address, and Phone Number

Use your full name, even if everyone calls you by a nickname. You may use an initial rather than spelling out your first or middle name. Put your name in big type.

If you use only one address, consider centering it under your name. If you use two addresses (office and home, campus and permanent, until _____/ after_____) set them up side by side to balance the page visually. Use a comma after the city before the state. It is OK to use either post office (two letter, full caps, no period) or traditional abbreviations for the state. Be consistent throughout the résumé.

> Urbana, IL 61801
> Wheaton, Illinois 60187
> Morton, Ill. 61550

If you have an e-mail address, give it too.

Give a complete phone number, including the area code. Either put the area code in parentheses, space, then put the number OR separate the area code by a hyphen.

(217) 555-1212 or 217-555-1212

If you don't have a phone, try to make arrangements with someone to take messages for you—employers usually call to schedule interviews and make job offers.

Omit your age, marital status, race, sex, and health. Questions about these topics are illegal.

Career Objective

CAREER OBJECTIVE statements should sound like the job descriptions an employer might use in a job listing. Keep your statement brief—two or three lines at most. Tell what you want to do, what level of responsibility you want to hold.

Ineffective care objective:	To offer a company my excellent academic foundation in hospital technology and my outstanding skills in oral and written communication
Better career objective:	Hospital and medical sales requiring experience with state-of-the-art equipment

Good CAREER OBJECTIVES are hard to write. If you talk about entry-level work, you won't sound ambitious; if you talk about where you hope to be in 5 or 10 years, you won't sound as though you're willing to do entry-level work. When you're applying for a job that is a natural outgrowth of your education and experience, omit this category and specify the job you want in your cover letter.

Often you can avoid writing a CAREER OBJECTIVE statement by putting the job title or field under your name.

Joan Larson Ooyen	Terence Edward Garvey	David R. Lunde
Marketing	Technical Writer	Corporate Fitness Director

Note that you can use the field you're in even if you're a new college graduate. To use a job title, you should have some relevant work experience.

If you use a separate heading for CAREER OBJECTIVE, put it immediately after your address, before the first major heading.

Education

EDUCATION can be your first major category if you've just earned (or are about to earn) a degree, if you have a degree that is essential or desirable for the position you're seeking, or if you can present the information briefly. Put EDUCATION later if you need all of page 1 for another category or if you lack a degree that other applicants may have (see Figure 18.3).

Under EDUCATION, include information about your undergraduate and graduate degrees. You may set up the information in one of three ways. In all of them, use commas to separate elements:

Bachelor of Science in Business Administration, May 2001, University of Illinois at Urbana–Champaign
Options: University of Illinois, Urbana, IL
University of Illinois (Urbana, Illinois)

Objectional Objectives*

The following quotations show how bad a poor objective can be.

Objective: Easy work, pleasant surroundings, large expense account, high wages, and close to home.

Objective: To work with real people again.

Objective: To have something to do.

Objective: To get out of a rut.

Objective: Cash for talent.

Objective: A management position in which I can make order out of chaos and evil.

Objective: To have fun and live large.

*Quoted from "Robert Half's Resumania," in Taunee Besson, *The Wall Street Journal National Employment Business Weekly: Resumes* (New York: John Wiley and Sons, 1994), 64; and Web sites that will remain unidentified.

Use the same form for city, state of all schools. If you continue information about education on the same line, put a period after the state. Otherwise, use no punctuation.

> B.S. in Education, June, 1998, The Ohio State University, Columbus, OH.
>   Undeclared minor in business.

But . . .

> B.S. in Education, June, 1998, The Ohio State University, Columbus, OH

When you're getting a four-year degree, include junior college if it gave you an area of expertise different from the area of your major. Include summer school if you took courses to fit in extra electives or to graduate early but not if you were making up a course you flunked during the year. Include study abroad, even if you didn't earn college credits. If you got a certificate for international study, give the name and explain the significance of the certificate.

To punctuate your degrees, do not space between letters and periods:

A.S. in Office Administration
B.S. in Accountancy
Ed.D. in Business Education

Current usage also permits you to omit the periods.

MBA
PhD in Finance

Highlight proficiency in foreign or computer languages by using a separate category.

Professional certifications can be listed under EDUCATION or in a separate category.

If your GPA is good, include it. Because grade point systems vary, specify what your GPA is based on: "3.4/4.0" means 3.4 on a 4.0 scale. If your GPA is under 3.0 on a 4.0 scale, use words rather than numbers: "B– average." If your GPA isn't impressive, calculate your average in your major and your average for your last 60 hours. If these are higher than your overall GPA, consider using them.

There are two basic options for presenting your educational information. Option I just gives degrees, dates, school, and city; option II also tells about your course work.

Option I: List in reverse chronological order (most recent first) each degree earned, field of study, date, school, city, state of any graduate work, short courses and professional certification courses, college, junior college, or school from which you transferred.

> Master of Accounting Science, May 1999, Arizona State University,
>   Tempe, AZ
> Bachelor of Arts in Finance, May 1997, New Mexico State University,
>   Las Cruces, NM
>
> Plan to sit for the CPA exam November 1999

> BS in Personnel Management, June 1998, Georgia State University,
>   Milledgeville, GA
> AS in Office Management, June 1995, Georgia Community College,
>   Atlanta, GA

Option II: After giving the basic information (degree, field of study, date, school, city, state) about your degree, list courses, using short descriptive titles rather than course numbers. Use a subhead like "Courses Related to Major" or "Courses Related to Financial Management" that will allow you to list all the courses (including psychology, speech, and business communication) that will help you in the job for which you're applying. Don't say "Relevant Courses," as that implies your other courses were irrelevant.

Bachelor of Science in Management, May 1999, Illinois State University,
    Normal, IL
GPA: 3.8/4.0
Courses Related to Management:
     Personnel Administration   Business Decision-Making
     Finance   International Business
     Management I and II   Marketing
     Accounting I and II   Legal Environment of Business
     Business Report Writing   Business Speaking
Salutatorian, Niles Township East High School, June 1995,
    Niles, IL

Listing courses is an unobtrusive way to fill a page. You may also want to list courses or the number of hours in various subjects if you've taken an unusual combination of courses that uniquely qualify you for the position for which you're applying.

BS in Marketing, May 2000, California State University at Northridge
     30 hours in marketing
     15 hours in Spanish
      9 hours in Chicano studies

Honors and Awards

It's nice to have the word HONORS in a heading where it will be obvious even when the reader skims the résumé. If you have fewer than three and therefore cannot justify a separate heading, consider a heading ACTIVITIES AND HONORS to get that important word in a position of emphasis.

Include the following kinds of entries in this category:

- Listings in recognition books (e.g., *Who's Who in the Southwest*).
- Academic honor societies. Specify the nature of Greek-letter honor societies so the reader doesn't think they're just social clubs.
- Fellowships and scholarships, including honorary scholarships for which you received no money and fellowships you could not hold because you received another fellowship at the same time.
- Awards given by professional societies.
- Major awards given by civic groups.
- Varsity letters; selection to all-state or all-America teams; finishes in state, national, or Olympic meets. (These could also go under ACTIVITIES but may look more impressive under HONORS. Put them under one category or the other—not both.)

Omit honors like "Miss Congeniality" that work against the professional image you want your résumé to create.

Figure 18.2

Action Verbs for Résumés

analyzed	directed	led	reviewed
budgeted	earned	managed	revised
built	edited	motivated	saved
chaired	established	negotiated	scheduled
coached	examined	observed	simplified
collected	evaluated	organized	sold
conducted	helped	persuaded	solved
coordinated	hired	planned	spoke
counseled	improved	presented	started
created	increased	produced	supervised
demonstrated	interviewed	recruited	trained
designed	introduced	reported	translated
developed	investigated	researched	wrote

As a new college graduate, try to put HONORS on page 1. In a skills résumé, put HONORS on page 1 if they're major (e.g., Phi Beta Kappa, Phi Kappa Phi). Otherwise, save them till page 2—EXPERIENCE will probably take the whole first page.

Experience

You may use other headings if they work better: WORK EXPERIENCE, SUMMER AND PART-TIME JOBS, MILITARY EXPERIENCE, MARKETING EXPERIENCE, ACHIEVEMENTS RELATED TO CAREER OBJECTIVE.

What to Include

Under this section, include the following information for each job you list: position or job title, organization, city and state (no ZIP code), dates of employment, and other details, such as full- or part-time status, job duties, special responsibilities, or the fact that you started at an entry-level position and were promoted. Include unpaid jobs and self-employment if they provided relevant skills (e.g., supervising people, budgeting, planning, persuading).

Normally, go back as far as the summer after high school. Include earlier jobs if you started working someplace before graduating from high school but continued working there after graduation. However, give minimal detail about high school jobs. If you worked full-time after high school, make that clear. Give details of relevant skills, such as those listed in Figure 18.2.

If as an undergraduate you've earned a substantial portion of your college expenses, say so in a separate sentence either under EXPERIENCE or in the section on personal data. (Graduate students are expected to support themselves.)

These jobs paid 40% of my college expenses.
Paid for 65% of expenses with jobs, scholarships, and loans.

Note that a complete sentence is acceptable if it does not use *I*.

Formats for Setting Up Experience

There are two basic ways to set up the EXPERIENCE section of your résumé. In **indented format,** items that are logically equivalent begin at the same space, with carryover lines indented three spaces or a quarter of an inch. Indented format emphasizes job titles. Figure 18.3 uses indented format. Use

A Community College Student's Chronological Résumé   **Figure 18.3**

Steven W. Zajano

921 South Seventh Street
Cambridge, Ohio 43725
(614) 555-4715

Vertical lists of duties emphasize experience when reader skims.

WORK EXPERIENCE

Use present tense when you're doing the job now.

Groundskeeper, Muskingum College, New Concord, Ohio, 1989-present.
Duties include
* Maintaining campus grounds, athletic fields, and equipment
* Performing electrical, plumbing, and carpentry as needed

How to present a job where you've been promoted.

Crew Leader, Seneca National Fish Hatchery, Senecaville, Ohio, 1988-89.
Started as Young Adult Conservation Corps (YACC) member;
promoted to crew leader after five months.
Duties as crew leader included
* Maintaining hatchery facilities
* Planning work activities and schedules for 12 YACC workers

Be specific about number of people you've supervised.

Puts this duty second so the space below it emphasizes it.

Landscaper, R.G.'s Landscaping Service, Canton, Ohio, Summer 1988.
Duties included
* Maintaining existing lawns
* Landscaping and establishing new lawns

Farm Worker, Hanover Stud Horse Farm, Canal Fulton, Ohio, 1986-88.
Duties included
* Maintaining tractors and mending fences
* Baling hay and straw
* Caring for thoroughbred racing horses

Use parallel structure for all duties.

Puts most interesting duty last where it stands out.

ACTIVITIES AND INTERESTS

Boy Scout Troop, Cambridge, Ohio (Leader)
Bus Ministry, Cambridge United Christian Church
Hunting, fishing, camping, swimming, hiking

Some readers may respond negatively. But this ministry is an important part of Steve's life, and he wants to suggest that he isn't just interested in outdoor recreational pursuits.

EDUCATION

Associate of Applied Sciences, June 1995, Hocking Technical College,
Nelsonville, Ohio
Specialization: Recreation and Wildlife Management

REFERENCES

James Heidler, Grounds Supervisor, Muskingum College, New Concord, Ohio
43725 (614) 555-5024

Richard Jordet, YACC Program Director, Seneca National Fish Hatchery,
Bytesville, Ohio 43723 (614) 555-5541

Gerald Sagan, Professor of Recreation and Wildlife Management, Hocking
Technical College, Nelsonville, Ohio 43765 (614) 555-3492

But I Haven't Done Anything!*

Some students have trouble coming up with details. "I've never really done anything." That's too negative. *Everybody* has done *something*. How have you spent the last five years?

One woman's only job was as a part-time salesclerk in the lighting department of a department store. Her official duties weren't important. But when she focused on what she'd actually done, she had evidence of skills employers want.

She had done research. To answer customers' questions, she read about lighting, vision, and energy consumption. She visited competitors and noticed their products and displays.

She had demonstrated creativity. In August, she rigged up a mannequin to look like a student—slouched in a chair, holding textbook and pop bottle, surrounded by clothes, a football, and a guitar. On the table was a lamp positioned to provide good study light with a sign, "At least he won't ruin his eyes."

Her display worked. The store sold four times as many lamps that August as it ever had, including the month before Christmas.

A résumé entry could give these details to support claims for experience in research and persuading. And she had increased sales in her unit 400%.

*Based on John L. Munschauer, *Jobs for English Majors and Other Smart People* (Princeton, NJ: Peterson's Guides, 1986), 36–37.

commas to separate items. Put a period after the date, before other details about the job (responsibilities, etc.):

Job title, name of organization, city, state, dates. Other information.

EXPERIENCE

Engineering Assistant, Sohio Chemical Company, Lima, Ohio, Summer 1999. Originally hired as a laboratory technician, Summer 1998; promoted following year. As laboratory technician, tested waste water effluents for compliance with Federal EPA standards. As engineering assistant, helped chemists design a test to analyze groundwater quality and seepage around landfills. Presented weekly oral and written progress reports to Director of Research and Development.

Animal Caretaker, Animalcare, Worthington, Ohio, June 1995– September 1997. Full-time during summers; part-time during senior year of high school.

Two-margin or **block format** emphasizes *when* you worked. Don't use two-margin format if your work history has gaps. Figure 18.5 uses two-margin format for EXPERIENCE.

EXPERIENCE	
Summers, 1996–98	Repair worker, Bryant Heating and Cooling, Providence, RI.
1997–98	Library Clerk, Boston University Library, Boston, MA. Part-time during school year.
1995–97	Food Service Worker, Boston University, Boston, MA. Part-time during school year.
Summer, 1995	Delivery person, Domino's Pizza, Providence, RI.

Use a hyphen to join inclusive dates:

March-August, 1998 or write out March to August, 1998
1997-99
'97-'99

If you use numbers for dates, do not space before or after the slash: 10/98–5/99.

Choosing Headings for Skills Résumés

In a skills résumé the subheadings under EXPERIENCE will be the *skills* used in or the *aspects* of the job you are applying for, rather than the title or the dates of the jobs you've held (as in a chronological résumé). For entries under each skill, combine experience from paid jobs, unpaid work, classes, activities, and community service.

Use headings that reflect jargon of the job for which you're applying: *logistics* rather than *planning* for a technical job; *procurement* rather than *purchasing* for a job with the military. Figure 18.4 shows a skills résumé for someone who is changing fields. Marcella suggests that she already knows a lot about the field she hopes to enter by using its jargon for the headings.

A job description can give you ideas for headings. Possible headings and subheadings for skills résumés include

Administration
  Alternates or Subheadings:
    Budgeting
    Coordinating
    Evaluating
    Implementing
    Negotiating
    Planning
    Keeping Records
    Scheduling
    Solving Problems
    Supervising

Communication
  Alternates or Subheadings:
    Conducting Meetings
    Editing
    Fund-Raising
    Interviewing
    Oral Skills
    Negotiating
    Persuasion
    Proposal Writing
    Report Writing

Many jobs require a mix of skills. Try to include the skills that you know will be needed in the job you want. For example, one study identified the six top communication skills for jobs in finance and in management.[3] Applicants who had experience in some of these areas could list them as well as subject-related skills and knowledge.

Finance
  Listening
  Advising
  Building Relationships
  Exchanging Routine Information
  Giving Feedback
  Persuading

Management
  Listening
  Motivating
  Advising
  Building Relationships
  Persuading
  Instructing

You need at least three subheadings in a skills résumé; six or seven is not uncommon. Give enough detail under each subheading so the reader will know what you did. Put the most important category from the reader's point of view first.

In a skills résumé, list your paid jobs under WORK HISTORY or EMPLOY-MENT RECORD near the end of the résumé (see Figures 18.4 and 18.5). List only job title, employer, city, state, and dates. Omit details about what you did, since you will have already used them under EXPERIENCE.

Activities

Employers are very interested in your activities if you're a new college graduate. If you've worked for several years after college or have an advanced degree (MBA, JD), you can omit ACTIVITIES and include PROFES-SIONAL ACTIVITIES AND AFFILIATIONS or COMMUNITY AND PUBLIC SERVICE. If you went straight from college to graduate school but have an unusually strong record under ACTIVITIES, include this category even if all the entries are from your undergraduate days.

Include the following kinds of items under ACTIVITIES:

- Volunteer work. Include important committees and leadership roles.
- Membership in organized student activities. Include important subcommittees, leadership roles. Include minor offices only if they're directly related to the job for which you're applying or if they show growing responsibility (you held a minor office one year, a bigger office the following year). Include so-called major offices (e.g., vice president) even if you did very little. Provide descriptive details if (but only if) they help the reader realize how much you did and the importance of your work.

Figure 18.4 **A Skills Résumé for Someone Changing Fields**

On the first page of a skills résumé, put skills directly related to job for which you're applying.

Marcella G. Cope

370 Monahan Lane
Dublin, OH 43016
614-555-1997
mcope@postbox.acs.ohio-state.edu

Centered format is eye-catching but can be hard to read. Here, action verbs in bold draw the reader's eye.

Objective

Put company's name in objective.

To help create high quality CD-ROM products in Metatec's New Media Solutions Division

Editing and Proofreading Experience

Edited a textbook published by Simon and Schuster, revising with attention to format, consistency, coherence, document integrity, and document design.
Proofed training and instructor's manuals, policy statements, student essays and research papers, internal documents, and promotional materials.
Worked with authors in a variety of fields including English, communication, business, marketing, economics, education, history, sociology, biology, agriculture, computer science, law, and medicine to revise their prose and improve their writing skills by giving them oral and written feedback.

Writing Experience

Wrote training and instructor's manuals, professional papers, and letters, memos, and reports.
Co-authored the forword to a forthcoming textbook (Fall 1996) from NCTE press.
Contributed to a textbook forthcoming (Fall 1996) from Bedford Books/St. Martin's press.

Computer Experience

Center headings only when you use a large font. Here, 14 pt. is used.

Designed a Web page using Microsoft Front Page
(http://www.cohums.ohio-state.edu/english/People/Bracken.1/Sedgwick/)
Learned and used a variety of programs on both Macintosh and PC platforms:

Computer experience is crucial for almost every job. Specify the software and hardware you've worked with.

Word Processing and Spreadsheets
Microsoft Project
Front Page
Pagemaker
Aspects (a form for online synchronous discussion)
Storyspace (a hypertext writing environment)
PowerPoint
E-Mail

Other Business and Management Experience

Developed policies, procedures, and vision statements.
Supervised new staff members in a mentoring program.
Coordinated program and individual schedules, planned work and estimated costs, set goals, and evaluated progress and results.

A Skills Résumé   **Figure 18.5**

Marcella G. Cope

Page 2

Employment History

Graduate Teaching Associate, Department of English, The Ohio State University,
September 1993-Present. Taught Intermediate and First-Year Composition.
Writing Consultant, University Writing Center, The Ohio State University,
January-April 1996
Program Administrator, First-Year Writing Program, The Ohio State University,
September 1994-January 1996

Honors

Phi Kappa Phi Honor Society, inducted 1994. Membership based upon performance
in top ten percent of graduate students nationwide.
Letter of Commendation, 1993, 1994, 1995, 1996. Issued by the Director of
Graduate Studies in recognition of outstanding achievement.
Dean's List, Northwestern University, Evanston, IL

Education

Master of Arts, June 1995, The Ohio State University, Columbus, OH.
Cumulative GPA: 4.0/4.0
Bachelor of Arts, June 1993, Northwestern University, Evanston, IL.
Graduated with Honors.

References

Kitty O. Locker
Associate Professor, Business and Administrative Communication
The Ohio State University
421 Denney Hall, 164 W. 17th Ave.
Columbus, OH 43210
614-555-6556
locker.1@osu.edu

*Choose references
who can speak about
your skills for
the job for which
you're applying.*

Suellynn Duffey
Director, Ohio University Writing Program
Ohio University
140 Chubb Hall
Athens, OH 45701
614-555-9443
duffey@ohiou.edu

James Bracken
Associate Professor, English and Library Science
The Ohio State University
224 Main Library, 1858 Neil Avenue Mall
Columbus, OH 43210
614-555-2786
bracken@osu.edu

- Membership in professional associations. To find out about the association(s) in your field, ask your professors or check scholarly journals.
- Participation in organized activities that require talent or responsibility (e.g., choir, freshman orientation).
- Participation in varsity, intramural, or independent athletics. However, don't list so many sports that you appear not to have had any time to study.
- Social clubs, if you held a major leadership role or if social skills are important for the job for which you're applying.
- Religious organizations if you held a major leadership role or if you're applying for a church-related job.

Major leadership roles may look more impressive if they're listed under EXPERIENCE instead of under ACTIVITIES.

References

Including references anticipates the employer's needs and removes a potential barrier to your getting the job. To make your résumé fit on one page, you can omit this category. However, include REFERENCES if you're having trouble filling the page. Don't say "References Available on Request" since no job applicant is going to refuse to supply references. If you don't want your current employer to know you're job hunting, omit the category in the résumé and say in the letter, "If I become a finalist for the job, I will supply the names of current references."

When you list references, include at least three, usually no more than five, never more than six. As a college student or a new graduate, include at least one professor and at least one employer or advisor—someone who can comment on your work habits and leadership skills. Don't use relatives or roommates, even if you've worked for them. Omit personal or character references who can say nothing about your work. If you're changing jobs, include your current superior.

Always ask the person's permission to list him or her as a reference. Don't say, "May I list you as a reference?" Instead, say, "Can you speak specifically about my work?" Jog the person's mind by taking along copies of work you did for him or her and a copy of your current résumé. Tell the person what points you'd like him or her to stress in a letter. Keep your list of references up to date. If it's been a year or more since you asked someone, ask again—and tell the person about your recent achievements.

For each reference, list name, title or position, organization, city and state, and phone number. You could also give the full mailing address if you think people are more likely to write than to call. Use courtesy titles (*Dr., Mr., Ms.*) for all or for none. By convention, all faculty with the rank of assistant professor or above may be called *Professor*. If you want to list teaching assistants, omit titles for all references.

References whom the reader knows are by far the most impressive. In a skills résumé, choose references who can testify to your abilities in the most important skills areas.

Include the name and address of your placement office if you have written recommendations on file there.

Ways to Set Up References

To save space, present references in indented line format (see Figures 18.1 and 18.3). If you have slightly more room, double space between the names of references. (See Figure 18.3.) In indented line format, use a comma to separate lines. Do not put any punctuation after the ZIP code.

REFERENCES
Thomas Elgee, Professor of Community Health, University of Northern Colorado, Greeley, CO 80639 (302) 351-1111
Elizabeth Tormei, Professor of Women's Studies, University of Northern Colorado, Greeley, CO 80639 (302) 351-2222
Amy Wilson, Director, Rape Crisis Center, Denver, CO 80203 (303) 555-3333
Matthew J. Kohl, Director, Brethren Community Services, Eugene, CO 80689 (302) 726-4444

When you list references vertically, omit punctuation at the end of a line, just as you would in the lines of an address on an envelope. Two-margin format takes up more space and can help you fill a page.

REFERENCES

Thomas Elgee	Elizabeth Tormei
Professor of Community Health	Professor of Women's Studies
University of Northern Colorado	University of Northern Colorado
321 Blevins Building	100 Humanities Building
Greeley, CO 80639	Greeley, CO 80639
(302) 351-1111	(302) 351-2222
Amy Wilson	Matthew J. Kohl
Director	Director
Rape Crisis Center	Brethren Community Services
100 Main Street	4835 Goodale Blvd.
Denver, CO 80203	Eugene, CO 80689
(303) 351-3333	(302) 726-4444

DEALING WITH DIFFICULTIES

Some job hunters face special problems. This section gives advice for five common problems.

"All My Experience Is in My Family's Business."

In your résumé, simply list the company you worked for. For a reference, instead of a family member, list a supervisor, client, or vendor who can talk about your work. Since the reader may wonder whether "Jim Clarke" is any relation to "Clarke Construction Company," be ready to answer interview questions about why you're looking at other companies. Prepare an answer that stresses the broader opportunities you seek but doesn't criticize your family or the family business.

"I've Been Out of the Job Market for a While."

You need to prove to a potential employer that you're up-to-date and motivated. Carl Quintanilla suggests the following ways to do that:

■ Be active in professional organizations. Attend meetings; read trade journals.

- Learn the computer programs that professionals in your field use.
- Find out your prospective employer's immediate priorities. If you can show you'll contribute from day one, you'll have a much easier sell. But to do that, you need to know what skills the employer is looking for, what needs the employer has.
- Show how your at-home experience relates to the workplace. Dealing with unpredictable situations, building consensus, listening, raising money, and making presentations are transferrable skills.
- Create a portfolio of your work—even if it's for imaginary clients—to demonstrate your expertise.[4]

"I Want to Change Fields."

Have a good reason for choosing the field in which you're looking for work. "I want a change" or "I need to get out of a bad situation" does not convince an employer that you know what you're doing.

Think about how your experience relates to the job you want. Jack is an older-than-average student who wants to be a pharmaceutical sales representative. He has sold woodstoves, served subpoenas, and worked on an oil rig. A chronological résumé makes his work history look directionless. But a skills résumé could focus on persuasive ability (selling stoves), initiative and persistence (serving subpoenas), and technical knowledge (courses in biology and chemistry).[5]

Learn about the skills needed in the job you want: learn the buzzwords of the industry. (Chapter 19 has suggestions for ways to find these things out.) Figure 18.4 shows a skills résumé of someone changing fields.

"I Was Fired."

First, deal with the emotional baggage. You need to reduce negative feelings to a manageable level before you're ready to job hunt.

Second, try to learn from the experience. You'll be a much more attractive job candidate if you can show that you've learned from the experience—whether your lesson is improved work habits or that you need to choose a job where you can do work you can point to with pride.

Third, suggests Phil Elder, an interviewer for an insurance company, call the person who fired you and say something like this: "Look, I know you weren't pleased with the job I did at _____. I'm applying for a job at _____ now and the personnel director may call you to ask about me. Would you be willing to give me the chance to get this job so that I can try to do things right this time?" All but the hardest of heart, says Elder, will give you one more chance. You won't get a glowing reference, but neither will the statement be so damning that no one is willing to hire you.[6]

"I Don't Have Any Experience."

If you have a year or more before you job hunt, you can get experience in several ways:

- Take a fast-food job—and keep it. If you do well, you'll be promoted to a supervisor within a year. Use every opportunity to learn about the management and financial aspects of the business.
- Join a volunteer organization that interests you. If you work hard, you'll quickly get an opportunity to do more: manage a budget, write fund-raising materials, and supervise other volunteers.

- Freelance. Design brochures, create Web pages, do tax returns for small businesses. Use your skills—for free, if you have to at first.
- Write. Create a portfolio of ads, instructions, or whatever documents are relevant for the field you want to enter. Ask a professional—an instructor, a local business person, someone from a professional organization—to critique them. Volunteer your services to local fund-raising organizations and small businesses.

Getting experience is particularly important for students with good grades. Pick something where you interact with other people, so that you can show that you can work well in an organization.

If you're on the job market now, think carefully about what you've really done. Complete sentences using the action verbs in Figure 18.2. Think about what you've done in courses, in volunteer work, in unpaid activities. Especially focus on skills in problem-solving, critical thinking, teamwork, and communication. Solving a problem for a hypothetical firm in an accounting class, thinking critically about a report problem in business communication, working with a group in a marketing class, and communicating with people at the senior center where you volunteer are experience, even if no one paid you.

If you're not actually looking for a job but just need to create a résumé for this course, ask your instructor whether you may assume that you're a senior and add the things you hope to do between now and your senior year.

How an Average Student Created an Excellent Résumé

Allyson was convinced that she had nothing to put on her résumé. In a conference, her instructor asked Allyson to describe exactly what she'd done. Allyson's "baby-sitting" was actually house management and child care. But a summer job at Harvard had consisted of changing beds and cleaning rooms for conference guests.

Her five summers of work at a law firm sounded more promising. She went to the library, formulated medical and legal questions, and searched for answers. The information she found helped the firm win a $7 million out-of-court settlement. Not bad for a sophomore in college. But Allyson was in advertising and wanted to go into copywriting, not market research. The experience was certainly worth putting on her résumé, but the kind of thinking she'd done as a law clerk wasn't the kind of thinking she needed to demonstrate to an ad agency.

Some of the items under ACHIEVEMENTS were interesting. The Locker Room was a new restaurant in town where Allyson had had dinner. Its menu said the restaurant "had a long history." In fact, the restaurant was new: the *building* was old. Allyson went up to the owner, told him several of the things that were wrong with the menu, and offered to rewrite it. The owner told her he'd pay her for doing that and also invited her to submit ideas for ads.

The instructor was impressed. The whole anecdote might work in a job application letter, while the résumé could highlight the fact that Allyson had written menu and advertising copy for a real business (not just a class). "What you need," the instructor said, "is a skills résumé."

"Are skills résumés very common?"

"Not as common as chronological résumés. And they're a little harder to write. You can write a chronological résumé just by going through the list and remembering what you've done under EDUCATION, under EXPERI-ENCE, and so on. You can almost fill in the blanks: the job title, the

Résumé Goofs*

Flunked my CPA exam with high grades.

Typing speed: 756 wpm.

Statistics mayor.

My GPA at night is 3.0.

Cities of preference: Mexico City. Languages Spoken: French.

Exposure to German for two years, but many words are not appropriate for business.

Married girls 16 and 18 years.

Delivered papers at age 12 like many other great Americans. The only difference is that they became great.

I am not smart, but I am not stupid.

I am considered charming. References available.

*Quoted from Robert Half, "Rseume goofs," *Managing Your Career,* Spring 1989, 37, 39; Selwyn Feinstein, "Labor Letter," *The Wall Street Journal,* April 5, 1989, A1; Geoff Martz, *How to Survive without Your Parents' Money: Making It from College to the Real World* (New York, Villard Books, 1993), 112; and Web sites that will remain unidentified.

organization, the city and state, the dates. With a skills résumé, you think about the skills you'd need in the job you want to have, the skills the employer is looking for, and show how you've used those skills in what you've already done. A skills résumé lets you take things from classes, from paid jobs, from volunteer work and put them all together.

"How do employers feel about skills résumés?"

"There isn't any good research. One survey asked employers which they'd rather get, and more people said 'the traditional résumé.' But that's just because they know where to look for things on the traditional résumé. Nobody's ever done research taking the same qualifications, presenting them in two different ways, and seeing which way got more interviews or more job offers. I know people who've gotten jobs using skills résumés.

"You want a résumé that immediately says 'WOW' to the employer. People always get more résumés than they want to deal with. To survive the cut, a résumé has to stand out. You want the résumé to have the same punch that you have in person."

The next step was to answer two questions: "What do you want to do? What do you think the employer is looking for?" Allyson replied, "I want to get a job as a copywriter in Cleveland. It's the 10th biggest market, and I'd rather work as a copywriter in a smaller market than have to start as a secretary at a New York agency. I think the agencies want someone who shows creativity, who has a strong personality, who isn't afraid to take risks."

"Then your résumé needs to do that. And it can. You're coming across as a self-starter, a problem-solver. When you actually write your résumé, use the language of your field. *Problem-solver* is a positive term in most fields, but it may or may not be right for advertising. Given what you've done, you could have headings for WRITING EXPERIENCE, CREATING ADS, PLANNING PROMOTIONAL CAMPAIGNS, RESEARCH, and SPEAKING, with a list of items under each one.

"Your résumé is going to make you look qualified. Highly qualified. Other students are going to read it and say, 'But she has done so much. *I* haven't done anything. They're going to feel just the way you felt when you said you hadn't done much in the last four years. But you *have* done a lot. You'll look great in your résumé. Anyone can, who understands the options and who puts in the time and energy."

Allyson still had to tinker with headings, decide what details to use, and experiment with layout and spacing. The final product (Figure 18.6) is worth the work.

ONLINE RÉSUMÉS

Research in 1996 showed that only 2 of the 28 Fortune 500 companies responding to a survey checked the Web for résumés. However, a larger number of companies scan résumés into an electronic job-applicant tracking system.[7] Creating a Web résumé is optional, but prepare a scannable version of your résumé to send any company that asks for it.

Creating a Web Résumé

Post a résumé on the Web only if you can do so for free and if you already know HTML. The chance of an employer finding your résumé is too low to justify the cost of paying to post or taking the time to learn HTML if you don't already know it.

Figure 18.6

Allyson Karnes

A border creates visual variety.

195 W. Ninth
Columbus, OH 43210
(614) 555-3498
karnes.173@osu.edu

6782 Fenwick Drive
Solon, OH 44121
(216) 555-6182

*This really is Allyson's philosophy—
and it's one an agency will appreciate.*

Career Objective

To write creative headlines and print ads that make people remember the product

Education

She presents herself as a fellow professional.

B.A. in Advertising, June 1998, The Ohio State University, Columbus, OH
  Core courses: Copywriting, promotional strategies, magazine writing, graphics, media planning
  Harvard University Writing Program, Summer 1996, Boston, MA

Experience Creating Ads

*Skills résumé allows her to combine
experience from classes and life.*

Led the team that developed the winning promotional strategy for Max & Erma's Restaurants.
- Developed idea for theme for a year's campaign of ads.
- Wrote copy for radio spots, magazine ads, and billboards. One billboard ad had the headline "Multiple Choice" and boxes for burgers, chicken, and salads—with all the boxes checked.
- Presented creative strategy to Max & Erma's CEO and the Head of Advertising.
- Strategy won first place from among 17 proposals.

*Details, wording
demonstrate
her creativity.*

Wrote more than 15 ads for Copywriting class, including
- Ad for cordless phone: "Isn't It Time to Cut the Cord?"
- Slogan for Ohio University's Springfest Jamboree: "In Short, It Jams"
- Billboard for Columbus Boys' School: "Who Said It's Lonely at the Top?"

Wrote ads and revised menu for The Locker Room (restaurant).

Other Writing Experience

Wrote profile on Charlotte Witkind, part owner of the New York Yankees.
Wrote "Commuter Flights" (humor).
Wrote more than 30 magazine articles as part of courses at Harvard University and Ohio State.
Wrote legal briefs as part of course at Harvard.
Wrote summary of research on $7 million medical malpractice case for Garson and Associates.

Employment History

1997-98	Child care and house management, Worthington, OH. Part-time daily during school year.
Summer 1997	Mother's Helper, Princeton, NJ. Cared for six-month-old baby; cared for all three children when parents were away on weekends.
Summer 1996	Maid, Harvard Student Agency, Boston, MA. Part-time while attending Harvard University Writing Program.
Summers 1991-95	Law Clerk, Garson and Associates, Cleveland, OH. Did independent case research used by the firm to win $7 million malpractice out-of-court

Reverse chronology.

A position of emphasis.

Portfolio Available on Request

If you create a Web résumé,

- Include an e-mail link at the top of the résumé under your name.
- Omit your street addresses and phone numbers. (A post office box is OK.) Employers who find your résumé on the Web will have the technology to e-mail you.
- Consider having links under your name and e-mail address to the various parts of your résumé. Use phrases that give the viewer some idea of what you offer: e.g., *Marketing Experience.*
- Link to other pages that provide more information about you (a list of courses, a document you've written), but not to organizations (your university, an employer) that shift emphasis away from your credentials.
- Don't be cute. Do be professional. Link to other pages you've created only if they convey the same professional image as your résumé.
- Put your strongest qualification immediately after your name and e-mail address. If the first screen doesn't interest readers, they won't scroll through the rest of the résumé.
- Specify the job you want. Recruiters respond negatively to scrolling through an entire résumé only to find that the candidate is in another field.[8]
- Specify city and state for educational institutions and employers.
- Use lists, indentations, and white space to create visual variety.
- Most commercial and many university sites offer lists of applicants, with a short phrase after each name. Craft this phrase to convince the recruiter to click on your résumé.
- Proofread the résumé carefully.

Be prepared during the job interview to create HTML text or provide an in-office writing sample. Firms know that candidates can get help with Web pages and online portfolios and may want confirmation that the skills they represent indeed belong to the candidate.[9]

Creating a Scannable Résumé

Increasingly, large companies such as Bank of America, Ford Motor Company, Walt Disney, and The Clorox Company use electronic job-applicant-tracking systems like Resumix and Res-Track. After paper résumés are scanned in, the systems can search them by keyword to match job descriptions. Advanced systems take care of the paperwork throughout the hiring process, notifying each applicant when the résumé has been scanned in, saving interview notes and results of pre-employment testing, automatically generating an "offer" letter, and updating the candidate's file to "hired" and the job requisition to "filled" after the candidate accepts.

Figure 18.7 is an example of a scannable résumé.

To increase the chances that the résumé is scanned correctly,

- Use a standard typeface. Beverly Nelson, William Gallé, and Donna Luse recommend Helvetica, Futura, Optima, Times Roman, New Century Schoolbook, Courier, Univers, and Bookman.[10]
- Use 12- or 14-point type.
- Use a ragged right margin rather than full justification. Scanners can't always handle the extra spaces between words and letters that full justification creates.
- Don't italicize or underline words—even titles of books or newspapers that grammatically require such treatment.
- Check text in full caps or bold to make sure letters don't touch each other.

- Don't use lines, boxes, script, leader dots, or borders.
- Don't use two-column formats or vertical text.
- Print the résumé using portrait (standard page) rather than landscape orientation.
- Put each phone number on a separate line.
- Use plenty of white space.
- Don't fold or staple the pages.
- Don't write anything by hand on your résumé.
- Send a laser copy or a high-quality photocopy. Stray marks defeat scanners.

To increase the number of matches or "hits,"

- Prepare a traditional chronological résumé. Don't be "creative." It doesn't matter where information is: the system can find it anywhere.
- Use a *Keywords* section under your name, address, and phone. In it, put not only degrees, job field or title, and accomplishments but also personality traits and attitude: *dependable, skill in time management, leadership, sense of responsibility.*[11]
- Use industry buzzwords and jargon, even if you're redundant. For example, "Web page design and HTML coding" will "match" either "Web" or "HTML" as a keyword.
- Use conventional terms, even if they're a bit wordy.
- Use nouns. Some systems don't handle verbs well.
- Use common headings such as *Summary of Qualifications, Strengths, Certifications,* and so forth as well as *Education, Experience,* and so on.
- Use as many pages as necessary.
- Mention specific software programs (e.g, *Lotus 1-2-3*) you've used.
- Be specific and quantifiable. "Managed $2 million building materials account" will generate more hits than "manager" or "managerial experience." Listing Microsoft Front Page as a skill won't help as much as "Used Microsoft Front Page to design an interactive Web page for a national fashion retailer, with links to information about style trends, current store promotions, employment opportunities, and an online video fashion show."
- Join honor societies, professional and trade organizations, since they're often used as keywords.[12] Spell out Greek letter societies (the scanner will mangle Greek characters, even if your computer has them): "Pi Sigma Alpha Honor Society." For English words, spell out the organization name; follow it with the abbreviation in parentheses: "College Newspaper Business and Advertising Managers Association (CNBAM)." That way, the résumé will be tagged whether the recruiter searches for the full name or the acronym.
- Put everything in the résumé, rather than "saving" some material for the cover letter. While some applicant-tracking systems can search for keywords in cover letters and other application materials, most extract information only from the résumé, even though they store the other papers. The length of the résumé doesn't matter.

Send only one résumé, even if the firm has more than one position for which you qualify. Most recruiters have negative reactions to multiple résumés, and the tracking system allows the applicant to be coded "NH" (never hire), a coding that persists even if the original recruiter leaves the company. Do, however, bring a separate résumé (designed to be read by humans) to the interview.

Figure 18.7

Jerry A. Jackson

Use 12 or 14-point type in a standard typeface. Here, Times Roman is used.

Keywords: family financial management; investment sales; computer modeling; competitive; self-starter; hard worker; responsible; collegiate athletics; sales experience

In keywords, use labels and terms that employer might include in job listing.

Campus Address
1636¹/₂ Highland Street
Columbus, OH 43201
(614) 555-5718
E-mail address: jackson.2495@osu.edu
Created a Web page on saving for life goals, such as a home, children's education, and retirement: http://www.fisher.osu/students/jackson.2495/home.htm

Give as much information as you like. The computer doesn't care how long the document is.

Permanent Address
45 East Mulberry
Huntington, NY 11746
(516) 555-7793

Education
B.S. in Family Financial Management, June 1998, The Ohio State University, Columbus, OH
"B" Grade Point Average
Comprehensive courses related to major provide not only the basics of family financial management but also skills in communication, writing, speaking, small groups, and computer modeling
Accounting I and II
Business and Professional Writing
Computer Programming
Finance
Economics I and II
Family Resource Management
Family and Human Development
Statistics
Public Speaking
Interpersonal Communication

Don't use columns. Scanners can't handle them.

Sports Experience
BAAD (Buckeye Athletes Against Drugs)
Intramural Hockey Team (Division Champions, Winter 1997)
Three-year Varsity Letterman, Ohio State University, Columbus, OH
Men's NCAA Division I Lacrosse

Experience
Financial Sales Representative, Primerica Company, Columbus, OH, February 1997-present. Work with clients to plan investment strategies; recommend specific investments, including stocks, bonds, mutual funds, and annuities.

Continued   **Figure 18.7**

Entrepreneur, Huntington, NY and Columbus OH, September 1996-January 1997. Created a saleable product, secured financial backing, found a manufacturer, supervised production, and sold product—12 dozen T-shirts at a $5.25 profit each—to help pay for school expenses.

Landscape Maintenance Supervisor, Huntington, NY, Summers 1988-96. Formed a company to cut lawns, put up fences, fertilize, garden, and paint houses. Hired, fired, trained, motivated, and paid friends to complete jobs.

Collector and Repairman, ACN Inc., Huntington, NY, Summers 1988-95. Collected and counted up to $10,000 a day. Worked with technicians troubleshooting and repairing electronic and coin mechanisms of video and pinball games, cigarette machines, and jukeboxes. Drove company cars and trucks throughout New York metro area to collect cash and move and repair machines.

Willing to relocate   *Don't justify margins.*
U.S. citizen   *Doing so creates extra spaces*
                               which confuse scanners.

Experts differ on whether candidates should phone to follow up. Taunee Besson advises phoning the administrator or verifier of the tracking system to ask, "Did you receive my résumé? Was I a match anywhere? Has my résumé been routed? To whom? Which department?" and then calling the manager to whom the résumé has been routed. But Besson admits that some recruiters say that they code "unsolicited phone calls" and see people who make too many as pests.[13]

SUMMARY OF KEY POINTS

- Informal preparation for job hunting should start soon after you arrive on campus. Formal preparation for job hunting should begin a full year before you begin interviewing. The year you interview, register with your Placement Office early.
- Employers skim résumés to decide whom to interview. Employers assume that the letter and résumé represent your best work. Interviewers normally reread the résumé before the interview. After the search committee has chosen an applicant, it submits the résumé to people in the organization who must approve the appointment.
- A résumé must fill at least one page. Use two pages if you have extensive activities and experience.
- Emphasize information that is relevant to the job you want, is recent (last three years), and shows your superiority to other applicants.

- To emphasize key points, put them in headings, list them vertically, and provide details.
- Résumés use sentence fragments punctuated like complete sentences. Items in the résumé must be concise and parallel. Verbs and gerunds create a dynamic image of you.
- A **chronological résumé** summarizes what you did in a time line (starting with the most recent events, and going backward in **reverse chronology**). It emphasizes degrees, job titles, and dates. Use a chronological résumé when
  - Your education and experience are a logical preparation for the position for which you're applying.
  - You have impressive job titles, offices, or honors.
- A **skills résumé** emphasizes the skills you've used, rather than the job in which or the date when you used them. Use a skills résumé when
  - Your education and experience are not the usual route to the position for which you're applying.
  - You're changing fields.
  - You want to combine experience from paid jobs, activities or volunteer work, and courses to show the extent of your experience in administration, finance, speaking, etc.
  - Your recent work history may create the wrong impression (e.g., it has gaps, shows a demotion, shows job-hopping, etc.).
- Résumés commonly contain the applicant's name, address, and phone number, education, and experience. Activities, honors, and references should be included if possible.
- To fill the page, list courses or list references vertically.
- Using a laser printer, print your résumé on quality paper.
- To create a scannable résumé, create a "plain vanilla" text using industry jargon, buzzwords, and acronyms.

Exercises and Problems
For Chapter 18

GETTING STARTED

18–1   Analyzing Your Accomplishments

List the 10 accomplishments that give you the most personal satisfaction. These could be things that other people wouldn't notice. They can be things you've done recently or things you did years ago.

Answer the following question for each accomplishment:

1. What skills or knowledge did you use?
2. What personal traits did you exhibit?

3. What about this accomplishment makes it personally satisfying to you?

As Your Instructor Directs,
a. Share your answers with a small group of other students.
b. Summarize your answers in a memo to your instructor.
c. Present your answers orally to the class.

18–2   Remembering What You've Done

Use the following list to jog your memory about what you've done. For each, give three or four details as well as a general statement.

Describe a time when you

1. Used facts and figures to gain agreement on an important point.

2. Identified a problem that a group or organization faced and developed a plan for solving the problem.
3. Made a presentation or a speech to a group.
4. Won the goodwill of people whose continued support was necessary for the success of some long-term project or activity.
5. Interested other people in something that was important to you and persuaded them to take the actions you wanted.

6. Helped a group deal constructively with conflict.
7. Demonstrated creativity.

As Your Instructor Directs,
 a. Identify which job(s) each detail is relevant for.
 b. Identify which details would work well on a résumé.
 c. Identify which details, further developed, would work well in a job letter.

18–3   Developing Action Statements

Use 10 of the verbs from Figure 18.2 to write action statements describing what you've done in paid or volunteer work, in classes, in extracurricular activities, or in community service.

18–4   Evaluating Career Objective Statements

None of the following career objective statements is effective. What is wrong with each statement as it stands? Which statements could be revised to be satisfactory? Which should be dropped?

1. To use my acquired knowledge of accounting to eventually own my own business.
2. A progressively responsible position as a MARKETING MANAGER where education and ability would have valuable application and lead to advancement.

3. To work with people responsibly and creatively, helping them develop personal and professional skills.
4. A position in international marketing which makes use of my specialization in marketing and my knowledge of foreign markets.
5. To bring Faith, Hope, and Charity to the American workplace.
6. To succeed in sales.
7. To design and maintain Web pages.

18–5   Deciding How Much Detail to Use

In each of the following situations, how detailed should the applicant be? Why?

1. Ron Oliver has been steadily employed for the last six years while getting his college degree, but the jobs have been low-level ones, whose prime benefit was that they paid well and fit around his class schedule.
2. Adrienne Barcus was an assistant department manager at a clothing boutique. As assistant manager, she was authorized to approve checks in the absence of the manager. Her other duties were ringing up sales, cleaning the area, and helping mark items for sales.

3. Lois Heilman has been a clerk-typist in the Alumni Office. As part of her job, she developed a schedule for mailings to alumni, set up a merge system, and wrote two of the letters that go out to alumni. The merge system she set up has cut in half the time needed to produce letters.
4. As a co-op student, Stanley Greene spends every other term in a paid job. He now has six semesters of job experience in television broadcasting. During his last co-op he was the assistant producer for a daily "morning magazine" show.

RÉSUMÉ ASSIGNMENTS

For problems 18–6 through 18–8, write the kind of résumé (chronological, skills, a combination, or a new creation) that best represents your qualifications.

18–6   Writing a Web Résumé

Create a set of Web pages to present your qualifications to an employer. Provide links to course projects and other documents that support your claims.

18–7   Writing a Paper Résumé

Write a résumé on paper that you could mail to an employer or hand to an interviewer at an interview.

As Your Instructor Directs,
   a. Write a résumé for the field in which you hope to find a job.
   b. Write two different résumés for two different job paths you are interested in pursuing.
   c. Adapt your résumé to a specific company you hope to work for.

18–8   Writing a Scannable Résumé

Take the résumé you like best from problem 18–7, and create a scannable version of it.

CHAPTER 19

Job Application Letters

Chapter Outline

Chapter Outline

Job Application Letters

Sapna K. Welsh, Human Resources Representative
Deloitte & Touche LLP

As a Human Resources Representative, Sapna Welsh is responsible for managing and maximizing the effectiveness of the Firm's most important asset, its people. One of her key responsibilities is recruiting. Sapna reviews hundreds of résumés annually. Deloitte & Touche Tomahtsu, one of the Big Six accounting firms, consists of over 59,000 people in more than 120 countries. Headquartered in Wilton, Connecticut, Deloitte & Touche LLP provides accounting, auditing, tax consulting, and computer assurance services. Its mission is to consistently exceed the expectations of its clients and its people.

The cover letter allows you to adapt the skills on your résumé to a specific company and position. The more you know about the company, the easier it will be to write a good letter. You can get information on companies from libraries, annual reports, informational interviews, industry organizations, and the Internet. Also check articles in business periodicals, newspapers, and company literature from the placement office.

Always address the letter to a specific individual, and make sure that the title is correct. Before you write, call the receptionist to ask for the name, proper spelling, and preferred courtesy title. If you have a contact at the company, send your letter to that person, requesting that he or she forward it to the appropriate hiring authority.

An application letter must be succinct, accurate, and persuasive. Most readers will briefly scan a cover letter to determine the purpose of the résumé. Start by informing the reader what you can do and what position you want to be considered for. Brevity and clarity create good visual impact and prompt the reader to read the letter. Use bullet points to highlight skills which directly fulfill the requirements of the position.

Don't provide superfluous personal information (e.g., "I'm married and have two kids and a dog. I've lived in this city for 15 years").

Be concise. Use specific terms to tell the reader exactly what you mean. As a general rule, if you would be uncomfortable saying it, don't write it. Be simple and powerful! As Enrique Jardiel Poncela says, "When something can be read without effort, great effort has gone into its writing."

Adapt the style to the company. For example, colorful, creative letters may be well suited for marketing or sales, but not for accounting or finance. Organizations want to hire people who fit the corporate culture. If you research a company and a position, you can show that you are a good fit for the culture.

Proofread the letter carefully to avoid any errors. Proof for typos, misspellings, and grammatical errors; check for proper business format. Inaccuracies undercut your ability to sell yourself. Remember, this is your first opportunity to make a good impression on the organization.

Sapna K. Welsh, March 20, 1997

Visit Deloitte & Touche's Web site: http://www.dttus.com

"An application letter must be succinct, accurate, and persuasive."

Sapna Welsh, Deloitte & Touche LLP

The purpose of a job application letter is to get an interview. If you get a job through interviews arranged by your campus placement office or through contacts, you may not need to write a letter. However, if you want to work for an organization that isn't interviewing on campus, or later when you change jobs, you will. Writing a letter is also a good preparation for a job interview, since the letter is your first step in showing a specific company what you can do for it.

How Job Letters Differ from Résumés

Enclose a copy of your résumé with your application letter. Although the two documents overlap slightly, they differ in several ways:

- A résumé is adapted to a position. The letter is adapted to the needs of a particular organization.
- The résumé summarizes all your qualifications. The letter shows how your qualifications can help the organization meet its needs, how you differ from other applicants, and that you have some knowledge of the organization.
- The résumé uses short, parallel phrases (✘ p. 98) and sentence fragments. The letter uses complete sentences in well-written paragraphs.

How to Find Out about Employers and Jobs

To adapt your letter to a specific organization, you need information both about the employer and about the job itself. You'll need to know

- The name and address of the person who should receive the letter.

  To get this information, check the ad, call the organization, or consult the directories listed in Figure 19.1. An advantage of calling is that you can find out what courtesy title (✘ p. 47) a woman prefers and get current information. A directory that went to press months ago will not include recent promotions.
- What the organization does and at least four or five facts about it.

  Knowing the organization's larger goals enables you to show how your specific work will help the company meet its goals. Useful facts can include market share, new products or promotions, the kind of computer or manufacturing equipment it uses, plans for growth or downsizing, competitive position, challenges the organization faces, the corporate culture (✘ p. 61), and so forth.

  The directories listed in Figure 19.1 provide information ranging from net worth, market share, and principal products to the names of officers and directors. To get specific financial data (and to see how the organization presents itself to the public), get the company's annual report from your library, or write directly to the company to request a copy. (Note: Only companies whose stock is publicly traded are required to issue annual reports. In this day of mergers and buyouts, many companies are

Is That Job Real?*

Some newspaper ads do not represent real jobs. **Blind ads,** which do not list the company's name, are especially likely to be misleading. One job hunter responded to an ad for "Public Relations/ Counseling." The job was for someone to market prepaid funeral arrangements.

For a free copy of *Job Ads, Job Scams,* call or write

    Federal Trade
       Commission
    Public Reference Branch
    6th and Pennsylvania
       Avenues NW
    Washington, DC 20580
    (202) 326-2222

*Based on Allen Fishman, "Misleading Ads Anger Applicants," *The Columbus Dispatch*, September 6, 1987, 4C, and Matthew Lesko, "Uncle Sam Can Help Folks Starting, Changing Careers," *The Columbus Dispatch*, December 7, 1993, 2D.

Check the job listings and information about companies at the placement office in your community college, college, or university.

Figure 19.1

Where to Get Addresses and Facts about Companies

General Directories
Directory of Corporate Affiliations
Dun's *Million Dollar Directory*
Standard & Poor's Register of Corporations, Directors, and Executives
Thomas Register of American Manufacturers

Specialized Directories and Resource Books
Accounting Firms and Practitioners
California Manufacturers Register
Directory of American Firms Operating in Foreign Countries
Directory of Hotel and Motel Systems
Directory of Management Consultants
Directory of New England Manufacturers
Franchise Annual: Handbook and Directory
O'Dwyer's Directory of Public Relations Firms
The Rand McNally Banker's Directory
Thomas Grocery Register
Standard Directory of Advertisers ("Red Book")
Who's Who in Direct Marketing Creative Services
Television Factbook

owned by other companies. The parent company may be the only one to issue an annual report.) Recruiting notebooks at your campus placement office may provide information about training programs and career paths for new hires. To learn about new products, plans for growth, or solutions to industry challenges, read business newspapers such as *The Wall Street Journal* or *The Financial Post,* business magazines such as *Fortune, Business Week, Forbes,* and trade journals. Each of these has indexes listing which companies are discussed in a specific issue. A few of the trade journals available are listed in Figure 19.2.

■ What the job itself involves.

Notebooks at campus placement offices often have fuller job descriptions than appear in ads. Talk to friends who have graduated recently to learn what their jobs involve. Conduct information interviews to learn more about opportunities that interest you.

Figure 19.2

Examples of Trade Journals

Advertising Age	Discount Store News	The Practical Accountant
American Banker	Electric Power Monthly	Real Estate Today
Automotive News	Financial Analysts Journal	Sales and Marketing
Aviation Week	Graphic Arts Monthly	Management in Canada
Beverage Industry	Grocery Marketing	Software Canada
Benefits Canada	Health Care	Small Business News
Cable Communication	Internal Auditor	Television/Radio Age
Magazine	International Advertiser	Training and Development
CA Magazine	Logging and Sawmill Journal	Journal
Canadian Business	National Electronics	Travel Agent
CPA Practitioner	Nation's Restaurants	Women's Wear Daily
Direct Marketing	Personnel	Variety

Using the Internet in Your Job Search

Every candidate should check the Internet as part of a job search. As Figure 19.3 shows, some job listings are on the Web. The Riley Guide and KMPG Campus, listed in Figure 19.3, provide good advice and links to many job-related Web pages.

Even better, the Web can be a fast way to learn about the company you hope to join.

Check professional listservs and electronic bulletin boards. Employers sometimes post specialized jobs on them: they're always a good way to get information about the industry you hope to enter.

Information Interviews

In an **information interview** you talk to someone who works in the area you hope to enter to find out what the day-to-day work involves and how you can best prepare to enter that field. An information interview can let you know whether or not you'd like the job, give you specific information that you can use to present yourself effectively in your résumé and application letter, and create a good image of you in the mind of the interviewer. If you present yourself positively, the interviewer may remember you when openings arise.

In an information interview, you might ask the following questions:

- Tell me about the papers on your desk. What are you working on right now?
- How do you spend your typical day?
- Have your duties changed a lot since you first started working here?
- What do you like best about your job? What do you like least?
- What do you think the future holds for this kind of work?
- How did you get this job?
- What courses, activities, or jobs would you recommend to someone who wanted to do this kind of work?

To set up an information interview, you can phone or write a letter like the one in Figure 19.4. If you do write, phone the following week to set up a specific time.

Tapping into the Hidden Job Market

Many jobs are never advertised—and the number rises the higher on the job ladder you go. Over 60% of all new jobs come not from responding to an ad but from networking with personal contacts.[1] Some of these jobs are created

Figure 19.3

Job-Hunting Resources on the Web

Job Listings

Career Path Online
  http://www.careerpath.com/
  Job listings from 19 papers, including the *Boston Globe, Chicago Tribune, Los Angeles Times, New York Times, San Jose Mercury News,* and *Washington Post.*
CareerMosaic
  http://www.careermosaic.com/
  Searches its own database and Internet newsgroups. Includes jobs in Canada, Britain, and Asia as well as in the United States.
Monster Board
  http://www.monster.com/
  More than 50,000 job postings.
E-Span
  http://www.espan.com/
  Especially good for technical jobs.
Internet Sites for Job Seekers and Employers (Purdue University Placement Service)
  http://www.ups.purdue.edu/student/jobsites.htm
  Comprehensive lists of current listings, divided by field.
America's Job Bank
  http://www.ajb.dni.us/index.html
CareerNet
  http://www.careers.org/
CareerMagazine
  http://www.careermag.com/
CareerSite
  http://www.careersite.com/
CareerWEB
  http://www.cweb.com
Job Search and Employment Opportunities: Best Bets from the Net
    http://lib.umich.edu/chdocs/employment/
JobTrak
  http://www.jobtrak.com/
  Search listings by region or job type (e.g., internship).
JobWeb
  http://www.jobweb.org/catapult/catapult.htm
Ohio State Business Job Finder
  http://www.cob.ohio-state.edu/dept/fin/osujobs.htm
ProMatch
  http://www.promatch.org/
SkillSearch
  http://www.skillsearch.com/

General Job-Hunting Resources

The Riley Guide: Incorporating the Internet into Your Job Search
  http://www.jobtrak.com/jobguide/what-now.html
  Good information about what to search for and where to look, with links to resources.
KPMG Campus
  http://www.kpmgcampus.com/
  Walks people through the application process for entry-level jobs at KPMG.
Online Career Center
  http://www.occ.com/
  One-page profiles of many companies. Not as much information as the company's own home page, but a good starting point. Especially useful for companies that don't yet have their own Web pages.
Good Employers for Moms and Dads
  http://www.women.com/work/best/
  Rates firms as "family friendly."
Cost of Living in US Cities
  http://www.homefair.com/homefair/cmr/salcalc.html
  Lets job applicants see what salaries will actually buy in various cities.
Kitty Locker's Job Hunting Page
  http://www.cohums.ohio-state.edu/english/People/Locker.1/job.htm
  Links to the job sites listed here and more.

Figure 19.4   **Letter Requesting an Information Interview**

72 E. 13th Avenue
Columbus, OH 43210
November 4, 1997

Mrs. Kam Yuricich   *Use the courtesy*
Clary Communications   *title the reader*
1372 Grandview Avenue *prefers.*
Suite 230
Columbus, OH 43212

Dear Mrs. Yuricich: *If starting with the request seems too*
                             abrupt, work up to it more gradually.

Could I schedule an information interview with you to learn more about how public relations consultants interact with their clients?

Refer to any   I was very interested in your talk to OSU's PRSSA Chapter last month about the
previous   differences between working for a PR firm and being a PR staff person within an
contact   organization. Last summer I had the chance to work as an intern at Management
with   Horizons. While many of my assignments were "go-fer" jobs, my supervisor gave me the
reader.   chance to work on several brochures and to draft two speeches for managers. I enjoyed
                  this variety and would like to learn more about the possibility of working in a PR firm.

Ask about   Perhaps we could also talk about courses that would best prepare me for PR work.
ways to   I have a year and a half left before I graduate, and I have room for several free electives
enter   in my schedule. I'd like to use them as productively as possible.
the field.

I'll call you early next week to set up an appointment. I look forward to your advice as I attempt to find my niche in the work force.

Sincerely,

Mentioning your qualifications
and including a sample of your   *Lee Tan*
work may help persuade the
reader to take time to see you.   Lee Tan
                                           555-5932

                                           Even though you shouldn't
                                           depend on the reader to call
                                           you, it's polite to give your
Encl.: Marketing Brochure for Riverside Hospitals   *phone number under your name.*

especially for a specific person. These unadvertised jobs are called the **hidden job market.** Referral interviews, an organized method of networking, offer the most systematic way to tap into these jobs. **Referral interviews** are interviews you schedule to learn about current job opportunities in your field. Sometimes an interview that starts out as an information interview turns into a referral interview.

A referral interview should give you information about the opportunities currently available in this town in the area you're interested in, refer you to other people who can tell you about job opportunities, and enable the interviewer to see that you could make a contribution to his or her organization. Therefore, the goal of a referral interview is to put you face-to-face with someone who has the power to hire you: the president of a small company, the division vice president or branch manager of a big company, the director of the local office of a state or federal agency.

Start by scheduling interviews with people you know who may know something about that field—professors, co-workers, neighbors, friends. Call your alumni office to get the names and phone numbers of alumni who now work where you would like to work. Your purpose in talking to them is (ostensibly) to get advice about improving your résumé and about general job-hunting strategy and (really) to get **referrals** to other people. In fact, go into the interview with the names of people you'd like to talk to. If the interviewee doesn't suggest anyone, say, "Do you think it would be a good idea for me to talk to _____?"

Then, armed with a referral from someone you know, you call Mr. or Ms. Big and say, "So-and-so suggested I talk with you about job-hunting strategy." If the person says, "We aren't hiring," you say, "Oh, I'm not asking *you* for a job. I'd just like some advice from a knowledgeable person about the opportunities in banking [or desktop publishing, or whatever] in this city." If this person doesn't have the power to create a position, you seek more referrals at the end of *this* interview. (You can also polish your résumé, if you get good suggestions.)

Even when you talk to the person who could create a job for you, you *do not ask for a job.* But to give you advice about your résumé, the person has to look at it. When a powerful person focuses on your skills, he or she will naturally think about the problems and needs in that organization. When there's a match between what you can do and what the organization needs, that person has the power to create a position for you.

Some business people are cynical about information and referral interviewing. Prepare as carefully for these interviews as you would for an interview when you know the organization is hiring. Think in advance of good questions; know something about the general field or industry; try to learn at least a little bit about the specific company.

Always follow up information and referral interviews with personal thank-you letters. Use specifics to show that you paid attention during the interview, and enclose a copy of your revised résumé.

CONTENT AND ORGANIZATION FOR JOB APPLICATION LETTERS

In your letter, focus on

- Major requirements of the job for which you're applying.
- Points that separate you from other applicants.
- Points that show your knowledge of the organization.
- Qualities that every employer is likely to value: the ability to write and speak effectively, to solve problems, to get along with people.

Be a Successful Job Hunter!*

A degree alone doesn't guarantee you a good job. A study by the Administrative Management Society revealed that successful job hunters were more likely to

- **Make lots of contacts; schedule lots of interviews.** Increasing the number of contacts and interviews increases the number of job offers.
- **Adapt your approach to the individual employer.** Many students use the same approach for all potential employers. Adapting the strategy to the employer sets you apart from other applicants and increases the chances of a job offer.
- **Take control of the process.** Employers prefer motivated, active, aggressive candidates.
- **Polish your communication and interpersonal skills.** These skills are needed both to present your qualifications effectively and to make you competitive for the many jobs that require communicating and working with people in addition to specific technical skills.
- **Investigate the hidden job market.** Don't rely just on advertised openings. Use the techniques in this chapter to tap into the "hidden job market."

*Based on Steven R. Dzubow, "Entering the Job Market," *Journal of College Placement* 45, no. 3 (Spring 1985): 49–50.

Creating a Job for Yourself*

David made friends with Lee's receptionist and secretary. Candidates who keep calling and trying to reach potential employers in a pleasant fashion create an obligation on the part of a conscientious support person to determine a time for the hiring manager and candidate to connect by phone. People who leave numerous, pesty voice mail messages, by contrast, seldom get a return call.

When David got a chance to speak to Lee, he said, "I would just like a chance to meet you; I promise I won't take more than 15 minutes." . . . Few hiring managers want to spend more than a few minutes with a borderline "fit." . . . [People] whose résumés don't fit the job profile or posted requirements must ask for a few minutes—not an interview. . . .

David . . . asked about possible areas [in Lee's company] that could be improved or opportunities that Lee's people hadn't had a chance to pursue. Once Lee began thinking about the areas where he needed help, he realized that David did have skills to offer, and he was hired on a contract contingency basis soon after. David's position has since become permanent.

*Quoted from Jackie Larson, "To Get a Job, Be a Pest," *The Wall Street Journal*, April 17, 1995, A12.

Two different hiring situations call for two different kinds of application letters. Write a **solicited letter** when you know that the company is hiring: you've seen an ad, you've been advised to apply by a professor or friend, you've read in a trade publication that the company is expanding. This situation is analogous to a direct request in persuasion (⬤ p. 215): you can indicate immediately that you are applying for the position. Sometimes, however, the advertised positions may not be what you want, or you may want to work for an organization that has not announced openings in your area. Then you write a **prospecting letter.** (The metaphor is drawn from prospecting for gold.)

Prospecting letters help you tap into the hidden job market. In some cases, your prospecting letter may arrive at a company that has decided to hire but has not yet announced the job. In other cases, companies create positions to get a good person who is on the market. Even in a hiring freeze, jobs are sometimes created for specific individuals.

In both solicited and prospecting letters you should

- Address the letter to a specific person.
- Indicate the specific position for which you're applying.
- Be specific about your qualifications.
- Show what separates you from other applicants.
- Show a knowledge of the company and the position.
- Refer to your résumé (which you would enclose with the letter).
- Ask for an interview.

The following discussion follows the job letter from beginning to end. The two kinds of letters are discussed separately where they differ and together where they are the same.

How to Organize Solicited Letters

When you know the company is hiring, organize your letter in this way:

1. State that you're applying for the job (phrase the job title as your source phrased it). Tell where you learned about the job (ad, referral, etc.). Briefly show that you have the major qualifications required by the ad: a college degree, professional certification, job experience, etc. Summarize your other qualifications briefly in the same order in which you plan to discuss them in the letter. This **summary sentence** or **paragraph** then covers everything you will talk about and serves as an organizing device for your letter.

> I have a good background in standard accounting principles and procedures and a working knowledge of some of the special accounting practices of the oil industry. This working knowledge is based on practical experience in the oil fields: I've pumped, tailed rods, and worked as a roustabout.

> My business experience, experience using DeVilbiss equipment, and communication skills qualify me to be an effective part of the sales staff at DeVilbiss.

> Let me put my creative eye, artistic ability, and experience to work for McLean design.

Good letters of application give specifics about your qualifications, show a knowledge of the company and the position for which you're applying, mention the résumé, and ask for an interview.

2. Develop your major qualifications in detail. Be specific about what you've done; relate your achievements to the work you'd be doing in this new job. Remember that readers know only what you tell them. This is not the place for modesty!
3. Develop your other qualifications, even if the ad doesn't ask for them. (If the ad asks for a lot of qualifications, pick the most important three or four.) Show what separates you from the other applicants who will also answer the ad. Demonstrate your knowledge of the organization.
4. Ask for an interview; tell when you'll be available to be interviewed and to begin work. End on a positive, forward-looking note.

Figure 19.5 is an example of a solicited letter.

How to Organize Prospecting Letters

When you don't have any evidence that the company is hiring, you cannot use the pattern for solicited letters. Instead, organize your letter this way:

1. Catch the reader's interest.
2. Create a **bridge** between the attention-getter and your qualifications. Focus on what you know and can do. Since the employer is not planning to hire, he or she won't be impressed with the fact that you're graduating. Summarize your qualifications briefly in the same order in which you plan to discuss them in the letter. This **summary sentence** or **paragraph** then covers everything you will talk about and serves as an organizing device for your letter.
3. Develop your strong points in detail. Be specific. Relate what you've done in the past to what you could do for this company. Show that you know something about the company. Identify the specific niche you want to fill.
4. Ask for an interview and tell when you'll be available for interviews. (Don't tell when you can begin work.) End on a positive, forward-looking note.

Figure 19.6 shows a prospecting letter.

Figure 19.5   **A Solicited Letter**

Tracey has only course work and one part-time job. But by being specific about what she's done in class and on the job, she creates a positive impression.

1072 Adams Street, Apt. 23
Waltham, MA 02254
April 17, 1997

Modified block format is good for letters of application.

Robert H. Catanga, Senior Accountant
IBM Corporation
1717 Central
New York, NY 10021

Dear Mr. Catanga:

Tell where you learned about the job. If the job has a number, provide it.

I am applying for the Accounting position announced on IBM's Web site (jof17747). I will receive a Bachelor of Science degree in accountancy from Bentley this August and plan to take the CPA exam in December. *In paragraph 1, show you have the qualifications the ad lists.*

These terms come from the job listing.

My courses in the accountancy curriculum at Bentley have given me not only the necessary theoretical background but also extensive practical experience in General Ledgers, Accounts Payable, and Travel Expenses. I have worked many cases and problems using computer data, including preparing simulated accounting records for hypothetical firms.

Many courses provide paractice with simulated cases—you may be able to use Tracey's strategy, too.

These true-to-life cases gave me the opportunity to interpret all sorts of data in order to prepare accurate financial statements. For instance, I've learned the best measures for fixed assets and property controls, howto figure inter/intra-company and travel expenses, and the best methods of matching revenues with expenditures. These I could then analyze and compare to past statements in order to identify trends and recommend ways that costs could be reduced so that the business could be run even more efficiently.

The ad asked for experience with spreadsheets and computer graphics.

Courses in speech communication and business writing have taught me how to communicate with various business audiences. This means that I would be able to provide reports, financial statements, and visuals to show how accounting information is related to management needs. I can use Lotus 1-2-3 and create computer graphics to provide the reliable accounting data that IBM needs to continue growing each year.

Relates what she has done to what she could do for the company.

Phrase from the CEO's letter in the 1996 annual report, which Tracey read on the Web.

My three years of experience working for Allstate Insurance Company have also given me the opportunity to take leadership and show responsibility. Although I was hired merely as a part-time typist, my supervisor frequently asked for my recommendations of ways to get work done more efficiently. In fact, I developed a procedure for making out arbitration reports which saved so much time that I was asked to teach it to the other employees in my department.

She gets a lot of mileage out of her part-time job by being specific.

One way to refer to résumé.

The enclosed résumé summarizes my qualifications. I can come to New York for an interview any Tuesday or Thursday afternoon. I can begin work in September and look forward to discussing with you ways in which I can help IBM carry its tradition of excellence into the next century.

Nice allusion to inclusion of IBM in In Search of Excellence.

Sincerely,

Tracey McKenna

Tracey McKenna

You don't have to note the enclosure, but doing so is a nice touch if you have room at the bottom of the page.

First Paragraphs of Solicited Letters

When you know that the firm is hiring, announcing that you are applying for a specific position enables the firm to route your letter to the appropriate person, thus speeding consideration of your application. Identify where you learned about the job: "the position of junior accountant announced in Sunday's *Dispatch*," "William Paquette, our placement director, told me that you are looking for. . . ."

Note how the following paragraph picks up several of the characteristics of the ad:

Ad: Business Education Instructor at Shelby Adult Education. Candidate must possess a Bachelor's degree in Business Education. Will be responsible for providing in-house training to business and government leaders. . . . Candidate should have at least six months' office experience. Prior teaching experience not required.

Letter: I am interested in your position in Business Education. I will receive a Bachelor of Science degree from North Carolina A & T University in December. I have two years' experience teaching word processing and computer accounting courses to adults and have developed leadership skills in the North Carolina National Guard.

Good word choices can help set your letter apart from the scores or even hundreds of letters the company is likely to get in response to an ad. The following first paragraph of a letter in response to an ad by Allstate Insurance Company shows a knowledge of the firm's advertising slogan and sets itself apart from the dozens of letters that start with "I would like to apply for. . . ."

The Allstate Insurance Company is famous across the nation for its "Good Hands Policy." I would like to lend a helping hand to many Americans as a financial analyst for Allstate, as advertised in the *Chicago Tribune*. I have a Bachelor of Science degree in Accounting from Iowa State University and I have worked with figures, computers, and people.

Note that the last sentence forecasts the organization of the letter, preparing for paragraphs about the student's academic background and (in this order) experience with "figures, computers, and people."

First Paragraphs of Prospecting Letters

In a prospecting letter, asking for a job in the first paragraph is dangerous: unless the company plans to hire but has not yet announced openings, the reader is likely to throw the letter away. Instead, catch the reader's interest. Then in the second paragraph you can shift the focus to your skills and experience, showing how they can be useful to the employer. Figure 19.6 is an example of a prospecting letter.

Here are some effective first paragraphs and the second paragraphs that provide a transition to the writer's discussion of his or her qualifications:

- First two paragraphs of a letter to the Director of Publications of Standard Oil:

Americans are so concerned about the preservation of oil reserves that some are even beginning to walk instead of riding. If scarcity of resources makes us use them more carefully, perhaps it would be a good idea to announce that words are in short supply. If people used them more carefully, internal communications specialists like you would have fewer headaches because communications jobs would be done right the first time.

Relating What You've Done to the Job*

The letter continued . . .

As I looked into publishing, it occurred to me that of all the things I have done, the one I could most closely relate to the field was, strangely enough, an experience I had as a baby-sitter.

Immediately, he had the editor's full attention. How could baby-sitting fit in with publishing? During the summer of his junior year in college he had taken a job as a sailing instructor, tutor, and companion for the children of a wealthy family. . . . While the parents were on a cruise, the governess suffered a stroke, sending the cook into a tizzy, the maid into tears, and the chauffeur and gardener into the local bar. Only the student could cope, and he took charge and managed the estate for the rest of the summer.

In his letter of application he described the crisis, and subsequent problems he had faced, and told how he had met them. Then he related those experiences to the problems that he had learned editors, advertisers, printers, and others encounter in the publishing industry.

*Quoted from John L. Munschauer, *Jobs for English Majors and Other Smart People* (Princeton, NJ: Peterson's Guides, 1986), 75–76.

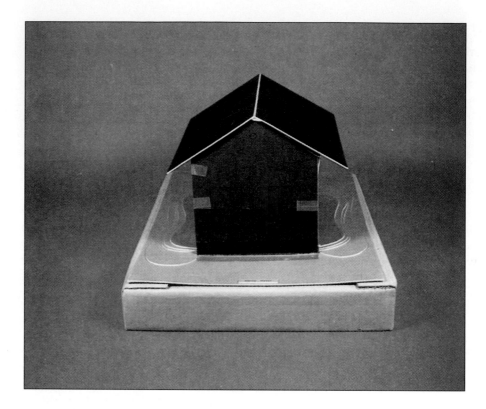

An architecture student's job letter was hand-delivered to the president of the firm he hoped to join. When the box was opened, a cardboard house popped up. The letter started out, "I can design larger buildings, using other materials."

I have worked for the last six years improving my communications skills, learning to use words more carefully and effectively. I have taught Business Communication at a major university, worked for two newspapers, completed a Master's Degree in English, and would like to contribute my skills to your internal communications staff.

■ First two paragraphs of a letter applying to be a computer programmer for an insurance company:

Computers alone aren't the answer to demands for higher productivity in the competitive insurance business. Merging a poorly written letter with a data base of customers just sends out bad letters more quickly. But you know how hard it is to find people who can both program computers and write well.

My education and training have given me this useful combination. I'd like to put my associate's degree in computer technology and my business experience writing to customers to work in State Farm's service approach to insurance.

Questions work well only if the answers aren't obvious. One student used the following paragraph in his first draft:

Do you think that training competent and motivated operating personnel is a serious concern in the nuclear power industry?

If the reader says *yes,* the question will seem dumb. If the reader says *no,* the student has destroyed his common ground. In the next draft, the student revised the first paragraph to read:

> Competent and motivated operating personnel are just as important to the safe and efficient operation of a nuclear power plant as is high quality equipment.

This paragraph gave him an easy transition into talking about himself as a competent, motivated person.

Showing a Knowledge of the Position and the Company

If you could substitute another inside address and salutation and send out the letter without any further changes, it isn't specific enough. A job application letter is basically a claim that you could do a job. Use your knowledge of the position and the company to choose relevant evidence (✖ p. 258) from what you've done to support your claims (✖ p. 258) that you could help the company. (See Figures 19.5 and 19.6.)

The following paragraphs also use the writer's knowledge of the company.

- A letter to Bendix Home Appliances uses information that the student got from information in the campus placement office about the job duties and market share.

> Coursework in business communication has taught me how to write reports that meet the needs of readers. I can use this knowledge to summarize the trends that show up in the Saturday Night Reports that your dealers submit. . . .
>
> A minor in personnel management plus public-relations study has taught me that trends are manifestations of human motives and human feelings, and not just cold numbers. My attention to this fact will enable me to interpret retailers' reports concretely—to keep that thirty cents of every washing machine dollar clinking into Bendix tills.

- A letter to Coopers and Lybrand's Minneapolis office uses information the student learned in a referral interview with a partner in an accounting firm. Because the reader will know that Herr Wollner is a partner in the Berlin office, the student does not need to identify him.

> While I was studying in Berlin last spring, I had the opportunity to discuss accounting methods for multinational clients of Coopers and Lybrand with Herr Fritz Wollner. We also talked about communication among Coopers and Lybrand's international offices.
>
> Herr Wollner mentioned that the increasing flow of accounting information between the European offices—especially those located in Germany, Switzerland, and Austria—and the US offices of Coopers and Lybrand make accurate translations essential. My fluency in German enables me to translate accurately; and my study of communication problems in Speech Communication, Business and Professional Speaking, and Business and Technical Writing will help me see where messages might be misunderstood and choose words which are more likely to communicate clearly.

Figure 19.6   **A Prospecting Letter**

Marcella G. Cope
370 Monahan Lane
Dublin, OH 43016
614-555-1997
mcope@postbox.acs.ohio-state.edu

Marcella creates a "letterhead" that harmonizes with her résumé (see Figure 18.4)

August 23, 1996

Mr. John Harrobin
New Media Solutions
Metatec Corporation
7001 Metatec Boulevard
Dublin, OH 43017

Block format with justified margins lets Marcella get this letter on one page.

Dear Mr. Harrobin:

In a prospecting letter, open with a sentence which (1) will seem interesting and true to the reader and (2) provides a natural bridge to talking about yourself.

One way to refer to the enclosed résumé.

Putting a textbook on a CD-ROM saves paper but does nothing to take advantage of the many possibilities the CD-ROM environment provides. Yet it can be a real challenge to find people who not only write well and proof carefully but also understand multimedia design. You will see from my enclosed resume that I have this useful combination of skills.

Shows knowledge of the company.

Rita Haralabidis tells me that Metatec needs people to design and develop high-quality CD-ROM products to meet business and consumer deadlines. Most of the writing and editing that I do is subject to strict standards and even stricter deadlines, and I know information is useful only if it is available when clients need it.

Shows she can meet company needs.

When I toured Metatec this spring, members of the New Media Solutions Group shared some of their work from a series of interactive CD-ROM textbooks they were developing in tandem with Harcourt Brace. This project sparked my interest in Metatec because of my own experience with evaluating, contributing to, and editing college-level textbooks.

Relates, what she's done to what she could do for this company.

As a program administrator at The Ohio State University, I examined dozens of textbooks from publishers interested in having their books adopted by the nation's largest First-Year Writing Program. This experience taught me which elements of a textbook--both content and design--were successful, and which failed to generate interest. Often, I worked closely with sales representatives to suggest changes for future editions. My own contributions to two nationally-distributed textbooks further familiarized me with production processes and the needs of multiple audiences. My close contact with students convinces me of the need to produce educational materials that excite students, keep their attention, and allow them to learn through words, pictures, and sounds.

All of these terms fit Metatec's production of multi-media educational materials.

My communication and technology skills would enable me to adapt quickly to work with both individual clients and major corporations like CompuServe and The American Medical Association. I am a flexible thinker, a careful editor, a fluent writer, and, most importantly, a quick study. I look forward to meeting you to discuss putting my talents to work for Metatec.

Names specific clients, showing more knowledge of the company.

Sincerely,

Marcella G. Cope

Marcella G. Cope

When you're changing fields, learning quickly is a real plus.

Enclosed: Résumé

■ A letter to KMPG uses information the student learned in a summer job.

> As an assistant accountant for Pacific Bell during this past summer, I worked with its computerized billing and record-keeping system, BARK. I had the opportunity to help the controller revise portions of the system, particularly the procedures for handling delinquent accounts. When the KMPG audit team reviewed Pacific Bell's transactions completed for July, I had the opportunity to observe your System 2170. Several courses in computer science allow me to appreciate the simplicity of your system and its objective of reducing audit work, time, and costs.

One or two specific details usually are enough to demonstrate your knowledge. Be sure to use the knowledge, not just repeat it. Never present the information as though it will be news to the reader. After all, the reader works for the company and presumably knows much more about it than you do.

Showing What Separates You from Other Applicants

Your knowledge of the company separates you from other applicants. You can also use coursework, an understanding of the field, and experience in jobs and extracurricular events to show that you're unique.

■ This student uses both coursework and summer jobs to set herself apart from other applicants:

> My college courses have taught me the essential accounting skills required to contribute to the growth of Monsanto. Since you recently adopted new accounting methods for fluctuations in foreign currencies, you will need people knowledgeable in foreign currency translation to convert currency exchange rates. In two courses in international accounting, I compiled simulated accounting statements of hypothetical multinational firms in countries experiencing different rates of currency devaluation. Through these classes, I acquired the skills needed to work with the daily fluctuations of exchange rates and at the same time formulate an accurate and favorable representation of Monsanto.

> A company as diverse as Monsanto requires extensive record-keeping as well as numerous internal and external communications. Both my summer jobs and my coursework prepare me to do this. As Office Manager for the steamboat *Julia Belle Swain,* I was in charge of most of the bookkeeping and letter writing for the company. I kept accurate records for each workday, and I often entered over 100 transactions in a single day. In business and technical writing I learned how to write persuasive letters and memos and how to present extensive data in reports in a simplified style that is clear and easy to understand.

■ This student uses her sorority experience and knowledge of the company to set herself apart from other applicants in a letter applying to be Assistant Personnel Manager of a multinational firm:

> As a counselor for sorority rush, I was also able to work behind the scenes as well as with the prospective rushees. I was able to use my leadership and communication skills for group activities for 70 young women by planning numerous activities to make my group a cohesive unit. Helping the women deal with rejection was also part of my job. Not all of the rushees made final cuts, and it was the rush counselor who helped put the rejection into perspective.

> This skill could be helpful in speaking to prospective employees wishing to travel to Saudi Arabia. Not all will pass the medical exams or make the visa application deadlines in time, and the Assistant Manager tells these people the news. An even more delicate subject to handle is conveying news of a death of a relative or employee to those concerned. My experience with helping people deal with small losses gives me a foundation to help others deal with more severe losses and deeper grief.

In your résumé, you may list activities, offices, and courses. In your letter, give more detail about what you did and show how that experience will help you contribute to the employer's organization more quickly.

When you discuss your strengths, don't exaggerate. No employer will believe that a new graduate has a "comprehensive" knowledge of a field. Indeed, most employers believe that six months to a year of on-the-job training is necessary before most new hires are really earning their pay. Specifics about what you've done will make your claims about what you can do more believable and ground them in reality.

The Last Paragraph

In the last paragraph, indicate when you'd be available for an interview. If you're free any time, you can say so. But it's likely that you have responsibilities in class and work. If you'd have to go out of town, there may be only certain days of the week or certain weeks that you could leave town for several days. Use a sentence that fits your situation.

> I could come to Albany for an interview any Wednesday or Friday.

> I'll be attending the Oregon Forestry Association's November meeting and will be available for interviews there.

> I could come to Memphis for an interview March 17–21.

Should you wait for the employer to call you, or should you call the employer to request an interview? In a solicited letter, it's safe to wait to be contacted: you know the employer wants to hire someone, and if your letter and résumé show that you're one of the top applicants, you'll get an interview. In a prospecting letter, call the employer. Because the employer is not planning to hire, you'll get a higher percentage of interviews if you're aggressive.

If you're writing a prospecting letter to a firm that's more than a few hours away by car, say that you'll be in the area the week of such-and-such and could stop by for an interview. Companies pay for follow-up visits, but not for first interviews. A company may be reluctant to ask you to make an expensive trip when it isn't yet sure it wants to hire you.

End the letter on a positive note that suggests you look forward to the interview and that you see yourself as a person who has something to contribute, not as someone who just needs a job.

> I look forward to discussing with you ways in which I could contribute to The Limited's continued growth.

Getting a Job with an Inc. 500 Company*

Paul Moran decided he wanted to work for a small company. So he got the *Inc.* 500 list (the list of the 500 fastest-growing small companies, published each year by *Inc.* magazine). He sent letters to all 17 companies in the Los Angeles area, offering to work for free. "I am confident that any financial rewards will come later."

He included a reply coupon, asking employers to fill in a "preliminary job description" and check one of two boxes:

☐ Yes, we are interested in interviewing you for an UNPAID POSITION.

☐ Sorry, we are not interested in having you work for us WITHOUT PAY.

The coupon noted that Moran would call three finalists to set up interviews.

Paul Moran got a job with Collectech Systems. He's now regional president, and the firm is still on the *Inc.* 500 list.

*Based on George Gendron, "FYI," *Inc.*, October 1995, 13.

Writing Style, Tone, and Length

In a letter of application, use a smooth, tight writing style (▶ p. 93). Use the technical jargon of the field, but avoid businessese and stuffy words like *utilize, commence,* and *transpire* (for *happen*).

Unless you're applying for a creative job in advertising, use a conservative style: few contractions, no sentence fragments, cliches, or slang. However, you still want a lively, energetic style that makes you sound like a real person.

Word Choice

Use vivid word choices and details.

Avoid words that can be interpreted sexually. A model letter distributed by the Placement Office at a midwestern university included the following sentence:

> I have been active in campus activities and have enjoyed good relations with my classmates and professors.

One young woman incorporated this sentence in a letter she mailed. The recipient circled the sentence and then passed the letter around the office (and did not invite the woman for an interview). That's not the kind of attention you want your letter to get!

Positive Emphasis

Be positive. Don't plead ("Please give me a chance") or apologize ("I cannot promise that I am substantially different from the lot"). Most negatives should be omitted in the letter.

Avoid word choices with negative connotations (▶ p. 88). Note how the following revisions make the writer sound more confident.

Negative:	I have learned an excessive amount about writing through courses in journalism and advertising.
Positive:	Courses in journalism and advertising have taught me to recognize and to write good copy. My profile of a professor was published in the campus newspaper; I earned an "A+" on my direct mail campaign for the American Dental Association to persuade young adults to see their dentist more often.

Excessive suggests that you think the courses covered too much—hardly an opinion likely to endear you to an employer.

Negative:	You can check with my references to verify what I've said.
Positive:	Professor Hill can give you more information about the program in Industrial Distribution Management.

Verify suggests that you expect the employer to distrust what you've said.

Negative:	I am anxious to talk with you about the opportunities for employment with Arthur Andersen.
Positive:	I look forward to talking with you about opportunities at Arthur Andersen.

Anxious suggests that you're worried about the interview.

You-Attitude

Unsupported claims may sound overconfident, selfish, or arrogant. Create you-attitude (▶ p. 34) by describing exactly what you have done and by showing how that relates to what you could do for this employer.

Getting a Job Overseas*

The Council on International Educational Exchange in New York City can provide information about work permits in Europe. Call 212-822-2600.
  Useful books include *Directory of Jobs and Careers Abroad* (Peterson's Guides).
  How to Get a Job in Europe (Surrey Books).
  How to Get a Job in the Pacific Rim (Surrey Books).

*Based on "Ask Annie," *Fortune,* December 9, 1996, 221

Application Bloopers*

The following sentences came from separate application letters.

Thank you for accepting me recent phone call.

My position has been recently has been eliminated.

I am seeking a position on the Eat Coast.

Attached is a one-page summery.

Please disregard my attached resume as it is woefully out of date.

My talent is at an inordinately high level and my ability to maintain accurate figures and meet deadlines is unspeakable.

In closing, let me outline the previous bookkeeping experience I've been able to endure.

I'd like to discuss how I might compliment the right organization.

P.S. If you hire me away from this nightmare, you'll also save me thousands in therapy.

*Sentences quoted from Tom Burke, "How Do You Spell Quality?" *The Wall Street Journal*, April 8, 1996, A18; and Robert Half's Resumania, quoted in Taunee Besson, *Cover Letters: Proven Techniques for Writing Letters That Will Help You Get the Job You Want* (New York: John Wiley and Sons, 1995), 96–97 and in Rochelle Sharp, "Work Week," *The Wall Street Journal*, February 27, 1996.

Lacks you-attitude:	An inventive and improvising individual like me is a necessity in your business.
You-attitude:	Building a summer house-painting business gave me the opportunity to find creative solutions to challenges. At the end of the first summer, for example, I had nearly 10 gallons of exterior latex left, but no more jobs. I contacted the home economics teacher at my high school. She agreed to give course credit to students who were willing to give up two Saturdays to paint a house being renovated by Habitat for Humanity. I donated the paint and supervised the students. I got a charitable deduction for the paint, and hired the three best students to work for me the following summer. I could put these skills in problem-solving and supervising to work as a personnel manager for Burroughs.
Lacks you-attitude:	A company of your standing could offer the challenging and demanding kind of position in which my abilities could flourish.
You-attitude:	Omit.
Lacks you-attitude:	I want a job with your company.
You-attitude:	I would like to apply for Procter & Gamble's management trainee program.

Remember that the word *you* refers to your reader. Using *you* when you really mean yourself or "all people" can insult your reader by implying that he or she still has a lot to learn about business:

Lacks you-attitude:	Running my own business taught me that you need to learn to manage your time.
You-attitude:	Running my own business taught me to manage my time.

Since you're talking about yourself, you'll use *I* in your letter. Reduce the number of *I*'s by revising some sentences to use *me* or *my*.

Under my presidency, the Agronomy Club . . .
Courses in media and advertising management gave me a chance to . . .
My responsibilities as a summer intern included . . .

In particular, avoid beginning every paragraph with *I*. Begin sentences with prepositional phrases or introductory clauses:

As my résumé shows, I . . .
In my coursework in media and advertising management, I . . .
As a summer intern, I . . .

Paragraph Length and Unity

Keep your first and last paragraphs fairly short—preferably no more than four or five typed lines. Vary paragraph length within the letter; it's OK to have one long paragraph, but don't use a series of eight-line paragraphs.

When you have a long paragraph, check to be sure that it covers only one subject. If it covers two or more subjects, divide it into two or more paragraphs. If a short paragraph covers several subjects, consider adding a topic sentence (p. 99) to provide paragraph unity.

Length

Always use at least a full page. A short letter throws away an opportunity to be persuasive; it may also suggest that you have little to say for yourself or that you aren't very interested in the job.

Without eliminating content, tighten each sentence (p. 93) to be sure that you're using space as efficiently as possible. If your letter is still a bit over a page, use slightly smaller margins, a type size that's one point smaller, or justified proportional type to get more on the page.

However, if you need more than a page, use it. The extra space gives you room to be more specific about what you've done and to add details about your experience that will separate you from other applicants. Employers don't *want* longer letters, but they will read them *if* the letter is well written and *if* the applicant establishes early in the letter that he or she has the credentials the company needs.

SUMMARY OF KEY POINTS

- Résumés differ from letters of application in the following ways:
  - A résumé is adapted to a position. The letter is adapted to the needs of a particular organization.
  - The résumé summarizes all your qualifications. The letter shows how your qualifications can help the organization meet its needs, how you differ from other applicants, and that you have some knowledge of the organization.
  - The résumé uses short, parallel phrases and sentence fragments. The letter uses complete sentences in well-written paragraphs.
- Use directories, annual reports, recruiting literature, business periodicals, and trade journals to get information about employers and jobs to use in your letter.
- Information and referral interviews can help you tap into the **hidden job market**—jobs that are not advertised. In an **information interview** you find out what the day-to-day work involves and how you can best prepare to enter that field. **Referral interviews** are interviews you schedule to learn about current job opportunities in your field.
- When you know that a company is hiring, send a **solicited job letter.** When you want a job with a company that has not announced openings, send a **prospecting job letter.** In both letters, you should
  - Address the letter to a specific person.
  - Indicate the specific position for which you're applying.
  - Be specific about your qualifications.
  - Show what separates you from other applicants.
  - Show a knowledge of the company and the position.
  - Refer to your résumé (which you would enclose with the letter).
  - Ask for an interview.
- Organize a solicited letter in this way:
  1. State that you're applying for the job and tell where you learned about the job (ad, referral, etc.). Briefly show that you have the major qualifications required by the ad. Summarize your qualifications in the order in which you plan to discuss them in the letter.
  2. Develop your major qualifications in detail.
  3. Develop your other qualifications. Show what separates you from the other applicants who will also answer the ad. Demonstrate your knowledge of the organization.
  4. Ask for an interview; tell when you'll be available to be interviewed and to begin work. End on a positive, forward-looking note.
- Organize a prospecting letter in this way:
  1. Catch the reader's interest.
  2. Create a bridge between the attention-getter and your qualifications. Summarize your qualifications in the order in which you plan to discuss them in the letter.

Getting a Job in Tough Times*

When the job market is tight, the following will help set you apart from other applicants:

- **Computer literacy.** Be able to use word processing programs, spreadsheets, and databases. Graphics and page layout programs are a plus.
- **Foreign languages and international experience.** Be able to speak at least one language other than English fluently. If funds permit, travel or study abroad. Cultivate the international students on your campus to gain experience interacting with people from other cultures.
- **Experience.** Put your knowledge and skills to work in internships, volunteer work, and campus or community activities. Take a part-time or full-time job that's related to your field—both to earn money for college and to get experience to land a job after graduation.
- **The ability to sell yourself.** Know about the product (you) and the customer (the employer).

*Based on Joan E. Rigdon, "Glut of Graduates Lets Recruiters Pick Only the Best," *The Wall Street Journal*, May 20, 1993, B1.

3. Develop your strong points in detail. Relate what you've done in the past to what you could do for this company. Show that you know something about the company. Identify the specific niche you want to fill.

4. Ask for an interview and tell when you'll be available for interviews. End on a positive, forward-looking note.

- Use your knowledge of the company, your coursework, your understanding of the field, and your experience in jobs and extracurricular activities to show that you're unique.
- Don't repeat information that the reader already knows; don't seem to be lecturing the reader on his or her business.
- Never use relatives' names in a job letter. Using other names is OK if the reader knows them and thinks well of them, if they think well of you and will say good things about you, and if you have permission to use their names.
- Use positive emphasis to sound confident. Use you-attitude by supporting general claims with specific examples and by relating what you've done to what the employer needs.
- Use at least a full page. It's desirable to limit your letter to one page, but use up to two pages if you need them to showcase all your credentials.

Exercises and Problems
For Chapter 19

GETTING STARTED

19–1   Analyzing First Paragraphs of Prospecting Letters

All of the following are first paragraphs in prospecting letters written by new college graduates. Evaluate the paragraphs on these criteria:

- Is the paragraph likely to interest the reader and motivate him or her to read the rest of the letter?
- Does the paragraph have some content that the student can use to create a transition to talking about his or her qualifications?
- Does the paragraph avoid asking for a job?

1. For the past two and one-half years I have been studying turf management. On August 1, 19___, I will graduate from _____ University with a BA in Ornamental Horticulture. The type of job I will seek will deal with golf course maintenance as an assistant superintendent.

2. Ann Gibbs suggested that I contact you.

3. Each year, the Christmas shopping rush makes more work for everyone at Wieboldt's, especially for the Credit Department. While working for Wieboldt's Credit Department for three Christmas and summer vacations, the Christmas sales increase is just one of the credit situations I became aware of.

4. Whether to plate a two-inch eyebolt with cadmium for a tough, brilliant shine or with zinc for a rust-resistant, less expensive finish is a tough question. But similar questions must be answered daily by your salespeople. With my experience in the electro-plating industry, I can contribute greatly to your constant need of getting customers.

5. What a set of tractors! The new 9430 and 9630 diesels are just what is needed by today's farmer with his ever-increasing acreage. John Deere has truly done it again.

6. Prudential Insurance Company did much to help my college career, as the sponsor of my National Merit Scholarship. Now I think I can give

something back to Prudential. I'd like to put my education, including a B.S. degree in finance from _____University, to work in your investment department.

7. Since the beginning of Delta Electric Construction Co. in 1993, the size and profits have grown steadily. My father, being a stockholder and vice president, often discusses company dealings with me. Although the company has prospered, I understand there have been a few problems of mismanagement. I feel with my present and future qualifications, I could help ease these problems.

19–2   Improving You-Attitude and Positive Emphasis in Job Letters

Revise each of these sentences to improve you-attitude and positive emphasis. You may need to add information.

1. I understand that your company has had problems due to the mistranslation of documents during international ad campaigns.

2. Included in my résumé are the courses in Finance that earned me a fairly attractive grade average.

3. I am looking for a position that gives me a chance to advance quickly.

4. Although short on experience, I am long on effort and enthusiasm.

5. I have been with the company from its beginning to its present unfortunate state of bankruptcy.

19–3   Using Knowledge of the Company

Identify how the following information from business periodicals and trade journals could be used in a job application letter.

1. Tomi Huang rents out tour buses—complete with drivers who speak Spanish, English, or Chinese—to travel agents who book international clients to Disneyland, Las Vegas, and other West Coast attractions. (Source: "Is Immigration Hurting the U.S.?" *Fortune,* August 9, 1993, 79.)

2. "Our business is communicating to the customers of our clients, and more and more of those customers are of all colors and dimensions," says Don Richards, Leo Burnett's Senior VP—Resource Development. (Source: Laurie Freeman, "Burnett Striving for Relevance in Communications," *Advertising Age,* February 17, 1997, S14.)

3. State parks are trying to increase visitorship and income. Ohio parks sell camping gear and rent recreational vehicles. Clint Eastwood has filmed TV ads for California's parks. Texas has a glossy mail-order catalog with Stetson hats, silver earrings, and limestone paperweights. The new revenues help to offset falling state budget allocations. Overall allocations for parks have fallen 22% since 1980, while funds for capital improvements and maintenance have fallen 68%. (Source: Terzah Ewing, "Meet the New Entrepreneurs: State Parks," *The Wall Street Journal,* February 11, 1997, B1.)

4. An ad for the Hyundai S coupe failed because the layout was poor. In this two-page spread, the left-hand page contained the headline and copy; the right-hand page contained a full-page photo of the car in an eye-catching red. Interviewers found that readers' eyes went to the picture on the right; they didn't go back to the left to read the copy. As a result, they learned nothing about the car and were not persuaded to buy it. (Source: Raymond Serafin, "Harkening Back to 'Advertising 101,'" *Advertising Age,* March 23, 1993, S18.)

5. House of Blues is an "entertainment emporium" built around live music. It's the first theme restaurant with a concert hall used as a production studio. HOB restaurants showcase African-American folk art and blues artifacts. (Source: Kathleen Morris, "Oh Yeah, They Also Serve Food," *Business Week,* February 24, 1997, 60.)

As Your Instructor Directs,

a. In a small group of students, answer the following questions:
■ For what specific jobs would the information be most useful?

- What needs does the employer have?
- What kind of details could an applicant use to show that he or she could meet that need?
- Would you use the information in the same way in a letter to a competitor as to the company named in the source?

b. Write a paragraph using (directly or indirectly) the information in the statement.

19–4   Gathering Information about an Industry

Use six recent issues of a trade journal to report on three to five trends, developments, or issues that are important in an industry.

As Your Instructor Directs,
   a. Share your findings with a small group of other students.

b. Summarize your findings in a memo to your instructor.
c. Present your findings to the class.
d. Join with a small group of other students to write a report summarizing the results of this research.

19–5   Gathering Information about a Specific Organization

Gather printed information about a specific organization, using several of the following methods:

- Read the company's annual report.
- Pick up relevant information at the Chamber of Commerce.
- Read articles in trade publications and *The Wall Street Journal* or *The Financial Post* that mention the organization (check the indexes).
- Get the names and addresses of its officers from a directory.

- Read recruiting literature provided by the company.

As Your Instructor Directs,
   a. Share your findings with a small group of other students.
   b. Summarize your findings in a memo to your instructor.
   c. Present your findings orally to the class.
   d. Join with a small group of other students to write a report summarizing the results of this research.

19–6   Conducting an Information Interview

Interview someone working in a field you're interested in. Use the questions listed on page 532 or the shorter list here:

- How did you get started in this field?
- What do you like about your job?
- What do you dislike about your job?
- Can you give me names of three other people who could also give me information about this job?

As Your Instructor Directs,
   a. Share the results of your interview with a small group of other students.
   b. Write up your interview in a memo to your instructor.
   c. Present the results of your interview orally to the class.
   d. Write to the interviewee thanking him or her for taking the time to talk to you.

COMMUNICATING AT WORK

As Your Instructor Directs in problems 19–7 and 19–8,
   a. Create a document or presentation to achieve the goal.
   b. Write a memo to your instructor describing the situation at your

workplace and explaining your rhetorical choices (medium, strategy, tone, wording, graphics or document design, and so forth).

19–7   Applying for an Open Position

Many companies post open positions. Apply for one that interests you.

19–8   Creating a Position for Yourself

Identify a need that your employer has, and propose that you be hired (or promoted) to a full-time position working in this area.

LETTER ASSIGNMENTS

19–9   Writing a Solicited Letter

Write a letter of application in response to an announced opening for a full-time job (not an internship) which a new college graduate could hold.

Turn in a copy of the listing. If you use option (a), (b), or (d) below, your listing will be a copy. If you choose option (c), you will write the listing and can design your ideal job.

a. Respond to an ad in a newspaper, a professional journal, in the placement office, or on the Web. Use an ad that specifies the company, not a blind ad. Be sure that you are fully qualified for the job.

b. Take a job description and assume that it represents a current opening. Use a directory to get the name of the person to whom the letter should be addressed.

c. If you have already worked somewhere, you may assume that your employer is asking you to apply for full-time work after graduation. Be sure to write a fully persuasive letter.

d. Respond to one of the listings below. Use a directory to get the name and address of the person to whom you should write.

1. Pepsi-Cola is hiring an **assistant auditor.** Minimum 12 hours of accounting. Work includes analysis and evaluation of operating and financial controls and requires contact with many levels of Company management. Extensive travel (50%) required through the United States, along with some international work. Effective written and oral communication skills a must, along with sound decision-making abilities. Locations: Los Angeles, Dallas, Atlanta, Philadelphia, Denver, Chicago.

2. A member of Congress in your state wants an **office manager** for a local office in your state and a **staff member** for the Washington, DC office. The office manager will answer constituent questions, write press releases, assist with travel appearances, record contributions, and recruit and supervise volunteer staff. Good oral and interpersonal skills a must; political and financial skills helpful. The staff member in Washington will answer mail, help with political research, and draft bills and reports. Good writing and research skills a must; interpersonal skills and political savvy helpful.

3. The Extension Service in your state wants an **Extension and 4-H Youth Leader** to provide overall leadership in the development of an effective long-range educational program for all youth. Duties include recruiting, training, and motivating volunteer leaders.

4. The Federal Trade Commission wants a **computer specialist** to provide end-user support to FTC staff and to maintain the commission's Web site. Must be familiar with IBM-compatible personal computers and HTML. Ability to write programs and patches a plus.

5. Arthur Andersen is hiring **consultants.** Travel to client locations to solve client problems. Need someone with good research, problem-solving, and communication skills. Jobs at all locations; write directly to office you wish to join.

6. The Limited is hiring **executive development program trainees.** After completing 10-week training programs, trainees will become assistant buyers. Prefer people with strong interest and experience in retailing. Apply directly to the store for which you want to work.

7. Procter & Gamble is looking for **sales management trainees**—any major. An intensive sales training program leading to sales management. After training will have personal selling responsibility for major accounts, will manage sales plans and presentations, will analyze business results and recommend action.

8. Tenneco has openings for **employee relations personnel.** All majors. Responsible for a broad range of areas, such as compensation and benefits, manpower training, training and development, employee selection and placement, and EEO (Equal Employment Opportunities). Overseas placement possible.

9. Your state wants **assistant international trade managers** for offices in London, Paris, Tokyo, Hong Kong, and Buenos Aires. Duties include promoting state exports, promoting the state as a site for foreign business investment and branch plants, and representing the state to government officials. Candidate should know language and culture of target country.

10. Ogilvie & Mather is hiring **assistant account executives.** You will be assigned to a major client account, and will help develop strategies for marketing and advertising, with specific assignments in one of the following: creative, media, research, or production.

19–10   Writing a Prospecting Letter

Pick a company you'd like to work for and apply for a specific position. The position can be one that already exists or one that you would create if you could to match your unique blend of talents. Give your instructor a copy of the job description with your letter.

Address your letter to the president of a small company, the area vice president or branch manager of a large company. Use directories to get the name and address of the person with the power to create a job for you.

CHAPTER 20

Job Interviews, Follow-Up Letters and Calls, and Job Offers

Chapter Outline

An Inside Perspective: Job Interviews

Frederick B. Lamster, Vice President, Human Resources Cacique

Frederick B. Lamster interviews job applicants at all levels, from interns and entry-level workers to vice presidents. Headquartered in Columbus, Ohio, Cacique is a division of Intimate Brands, Inc. Cacique is a $50 million specialty retailer of intimate apparel.

From my perspective, the best interviewees are thoughtful, answer questions, and give me a full picture of themselves. I want to know that they know what Cacique is, that they know we are part of The Limited, that they've been in the stores and have something to say about them. To be successful, prepare for the interview. Know the company and its parent. Know its history. Know why you are there and what your career goals are.

I don't come into the interview with set questions. But there are questions I *like* to ask: What made you successful in a position? What was your last superviser like? How did you work with him or her? These questions usually come up.

The best answers depend on the position I'm interviewing for. If I'm interviewing candidates for a merchandising position, I want to see creativity. If I'm looking for someone for a human resources function, I want to know how a person will fit into an organization.

Behavioral and situational interviews invite applicants to talk about their experiences. We're trying to find out why someone acted in a certain way in the past—it's an indication of the future. And we want to see how achievements occurred.

Not every interview goes well. Not every candidate interviews effectively. If an interview isn't going well, ask the interviewer why this is so. Then, start your answer over and be clear and precise. Being assertive is better than letting the interview "die."

After the initial interview, send a note. Call if you don't hear anything within a week. If you're interested in the job, some kind of follow-up is a necessity. Even if you aren't interested, it's a courtesy.

In a second, office interview, the candidate talks to people who would be direct supervisors and some of the function staff. These interviews focus even more on skills and experience.

Sometimes, phone interviews are used to screen candidates before a visit. We use video interviews if a candidate is in another city and can't get to the home office quickly enough.

My advice to students on the job market is this: Do your homework. Put your best foot forward. Dress the part. And if you are as intelligent as you think you are, show it.

Frederick B. Lamster, April 11, 1997

Visit Cacique's Web site: http://www.limited.net/cacique/

"Do your homework. Put your best foot forward. Dress the part. And if you are as intelligent as you think you are, show it."

Frederick B. Lamster, Cacique

Job interviews are scary, even when you've prepared thoroughly. But when you are prepared, you can harness the adrenaline to work for you, so that you put your best foot forward and get the job you want.

INTERVIEWING AT THE TURN OF THE CENTURY

Interviews are changing as interviewers respond to interviewees who are prepared to answer the standard questions. In the late 90s, many employers expect you to

- Be more aggressive. One employer says he deliberately tells the company receptionist to brush off callers who ask about advertised openings. He interviews only those who keep calling and offer the receptionist reasons why they should be interviewed.
- Follow instructions to the letter. The owner of a delivery company tells candidates to phone at a precise hour. Failing to do so means that the person couldn't be trusted to deliver packages on time.[1]
- Participate in many interviews. In 1996, Xerox outsourced preliminary interviews. Applicants went through six interviews with a separate company before they actually met someone from Xerox. High-level jobs may require even more preliminary interviews. A senior vice president in a high-tech company went through 17 interviews before she was offered the job.[2]
- Have one or more interviews by phone, computer, or video.
- Take one or more tests, including drug tests, aptitude tests, computer simulations, and essay exams where you're asked to explain what you'd do in a specific situation.
- Be approved by the team you'll be joining. In companies with self-managed work teams, the team has a say in who is hired.
- Provide—at the interview or right after it—a sample of the work you're applying to do. You may be asked to write a memo or a proposal, calculate a budget on a spreadsheet, or make a presentation.

All the phoning required in 90s interviews places a special emphasis on phone skills.

If you speak to a secretary, be nice to him or her. Find out the person's name on your first call and use it on subsequent calls. "Thank you for being so patient. Can you tell me when a better time might be to try to get Mr. or Ms. X? I'll try again on [date]." Sometimes, if you call after 5 PM, executives answer their own phones since clerical staff have gone home.

If you get someone's voice mail, leave a concise message—complete with your name and phone number. Even if you've called 10 times, keep your voice pleasant.

If you get voice mail repeatedly, call the main company number to speak with a receptionist. Ask whether the person you're trying to reach is in the building. If he or she is on the road, ask when the person is due in.

Applicants for teller's positions at the Great Western Bank in Chatsworth, California, start with computer simulations greeting customers, making change, or dealing with angry customers. Other computer screens feature real tellers talking about their jobs.

DEVELOPING AN INTERVIEW STRATEGY

Develop an overall strategy based on your answers to these three questions:

1. **What about yourself do you want the interviewer to know?** Pick two to five points that represent your strengths for that particular job. These facts may be achievements, character traits (such as enthusiasm), experiences that qualify you for the job and separate you from other applicants, the fact that you really want to work for this company, and so on. For each strength, think of a specific action or accomplishment to support it. For example, be ready to give an example to prove that you're "hard working." Be ready to show how you helped an organization save money or serve customers better.

   Then at the interview, listen to every question to see if you could make one of your key points as part of your answer. If the questions don't allow you to make your points, bring them up at the end of the interview.

2. **What disadvantages or weaknesses do you need to minimize?** Expect that you may be asked to explain weaknesses or apparent weaknesses in your record: age, sex, physical disabilities, lack of experience, so-so grades, and gaps in your record.

Plan how to deal with these issues if they arise. See the suggestions later in this chapter under "Kinds of Interviews" and "Traditional Questions."

3. **What do you need to know about the job and the organization to decide whether or not you want to accept this job if it is offered to you?** Plan *in advance* the criteria on which you will base your decision (you can always change the criteria). Use "Deciding Which Offer to Accept" below to plan questions to elicit the information you'll need to rank each offer.

TAKING CARE OF THE DETAILS

Inappropriate clothing or being late can cost you a job. Put enough time into planning details so that you can move on to substantive planning.

What to Wear

If you're interviewing for a management or office job, wear a business suit. What kind of suit? If you've got good taste and a good eye for color, follow your instincts. If fashion isn't your strong point, read John Molloy's *Dress for Success* (men's clothes) and *The New Woman's Dress for Success Book*. Perhaps the best suggestion in the books is his advice to visit expensive stores, noting details—the exact shade of blue in a suit, the number of buttons on the sleeve, the placement of pockets, the width of lapels—and then go to stores in your price range and buy a suit that has the details found on more expensive clothing.

If you're interviewing for a position that involves working, visiting, or supervising muddy or dirty sites, wear sturdy clothes that suggest you're willing to wear flannel shirts and get your shoes dirty.[3] In this case, looking "good" is less important than looking businesslike.

Consider the corporate culture. A woman who was interviewing for a job at The Gap wore a matching linen skirt and blouse that were similar to Gap clothing. Her clothing was evidence that she'd researched the job.[4]

Choose comfortable shoes. You may do a fair amount of walking during the office visit or plant trip.

Take care of all the details. Check your heels to make sure they aren't run down; make sure your shoes are shined. Have your hair cut or styled conservatively. Jewelry and makeup should be understated. Personal hygiene must be impeccable. Avoid cologne and perfumed aftershave lotions.

What to Bring to the Interview

Bring extra copies of your résumé. If your campus placement office has already given the interviewer a data sheet, present the résumé at the beginning of the interview: "I thought you might like a little more information about me."

Bring something to write on and something to write with. It's OK to bring in a small notepad with the questions you want to ask on it.

Bring copies of your work or a portfolio: an engineering design, a copy of a memo you wrote on a job or in a business writing class, an article you wrote for the campus paper. You don't need to present these unless the interview calls for them, but they can be very effective: "Yes, I have done a media plan. Here's a copy of a plan I put together in my advertising seminar last year. We had a fixed budget and used real figures for cost and rating points, just as I'd do if I joined Foote, Cone & Belding."

Video Interviews*

Two kinds of video interviews exist. In the first, the company sends a list of questions, asking the applicant to tape the responses. The second kind is a live interview using videoconferencing equipment.

If you're asked to prepare a videotape,

- Practice your answers.
- Tape the interview as many times as necessary to get a tape that presents you at your best.
- Be specific. Since the employer can't ask follow-up questions, you need to be detailed about how your credentials could help the employer.

If you have an interview by videoconference,

- Tape yourself so you can make any adjustments in pronunciation, voice qualities, posture, and clothing.
- Keep your answers short. Then say, "Would you like more information?" People are more reluctant to interrupt a speaker in another location, and body language is limited.

*Based on Raju Narisetti, "Work Week," *The Wall Street Journal*, November 21, 1995, A1; Steve Ralston, "Advances in Employment Interviewing Technology," and Jan Harding, Comments, both in Mini-Conference on Emerging Technologies: Focus on the World Wide Web and Its Uses in Business Communication, Columbus, OH, July 28–29, 1995.

Bring the names, addresses, and phone numbers of references if you didn't put them on your résumé. Bring complete details about your work history and education, including dates and street addresses, in case you're asked to fill out an application form.

If you can afford it, buy a briefcase to carry these items. At this point in your life, an inexpensive vinyl briefcase is acceptable.

Note-Taking

During or immediately after the interview, write down

- The name of the interviewer (or all the people you talked to, if it's a group interview or an office visit).
- What the interviewer seemed to like best about you.
- Any negative points or weaknesses that came up that you need to counter in your follow-up letter or phone calls.
- Answers to your questions about the company.
- When you'll hear from the company.

The easiest way to get the interviewer's name is to ask for his or her card. You may be able to make all the notes you need on the back of the card.

Some interviewers say that they respond negatively to applicants who take notes during the interview. However, if you have several interviews back-to-back or if you know your memory is terrible, do take brief notes during the interview. That's better than forgetting which company said you'd be on the road every other week and which interviewer asked that *you* get in touch with him or her.

PRACTICING FOR THE INTERVIEW

Rehearse everything you can: put on the clothes you'll wear and practice entering a room, shaking hands, sitting down, and answering questions. Ask a friend to interview you. Saying answers out loud is surprisingly harder than saying them in your head.

Some campuses have videotaping facilities so that you can watch your own sample interview. Videotaping is more valuable if you can do it at least twice, so you can modify behavior the second time and check the tape to see whether the modification works.

DURING THE INTERVIEW

Your interviewing skills will improve with practice. If possible, schedule a few interviews with other companies before your interview with the company that is your first choice. However, even if you're just interviewing for practice, you must still do all the research on that company. If interviewers sense that you aren't interested, they won't take you seriously and you won't learn much from the process.

How to Act

Should you "be yourself"? There's no point in assuming a radically different persona. If you do, you run the risk of getting into a job that you'll hate (though the persona you assumed might have loved it). Furthermore, as interviewers point out, you have to be a pretty good actor to come across convincingly if you try to be someone other than yourself. On the other hand, all of us have several selves: we can be lazy, insensitive, bored, slow-witted, and tongue-tied, but we can also be energetic, perceptive, interested, intelligent, and articulate. Be your best self at the interview.

Interviews can make you feel vulnerable and defensive; to counter this, review your accomplishments—the things you're especially proud of having done. You'll make a better impression if you have a firm sense of your own self-worth.

Every interviewer repeats the advice that your mother probably gave you: sit up straight, don't mumble, look at people when you talk. It's good advice for interviews. Be aware that many people respond negatively to smoking.

Office visits that involve meals and semisocial occasions call for sensible choices. When you order, choose something that's easy and unmessy to eat. Watch your table manners. Eat a light lunch, with no alcohol, so that you'll be alert during the afternoon. At dinner or an evening party, decline alcohol if you don't drink. If you do drink, accept just one drink—you're still being evaluated, and you can't afford to have your guard down. Be aware that some people respond negatively to applicants who drink hard liquor.

Parts of the Interview

Every interview has an opening, a body, and a close.

In the **opening** (two to five minutes), good interviewers will try to set you at ease. Some interviewers will open with easy questions about your major or interests. Others open by telling you about the job or the company. If this happens, listen so you can answer later questions to show that you can do the job or contribute to the company that's being described.

The **body** of the interview (10 to 25 minutes) is an all-too-brief time for you to highlight your qualifications and find out what you need to know to decide if you want to accept a plant trip. Expect questions that give you an opportunity to showcase your strong points and questions that probe any weaknesses evident from your résumé. (You were neither in school nor working last fall. What were you doing?) Normally the interviewer will also try to sell you on the company and give you an opportunity to raise questions.

You need to be aware of time so that you can make sure to get in your key points and questions: "We haven't covered it yet, but I want you to know that I . . . ." "I'm aware that it's almost 10:30. I do have some more questions that I'd like to ask about the company."

In the **close** of the interview (two to five minutes), the interviewer will usually tell you what happens next: "We'll be bringing our top candidates to the office in February. You should hear from us in three weeks." One interviewer reports that he gives applicants his card and tells them to call him. "It's a test to see if they are committed, how long it takes for them to call, and whether they even call at all."[5]

Close with an assertive statement. Depending on the circumstances, you could say: "I've certainly enjoyed learning more about General Electric." "I hope I get a chance to visit your Phoenix office. I'd really like to see the new computer system you talked about." "This job seems to be a good match between what you're looking for and what I'd like to do."

Stress Interviews

A **stress interview** deliberately puts the applicant under stress. If the stress is physical (for example, you're given a chair where the light is in your eyes), be assertive: move to another chair or tell the interviewer that the behavior bothers you.

Stress Interviews for Salespeople at Dataflex*

Rick Rose, CEO of Dataflex, is "deliberately adversarial" at a first interview. After about five minutes, he tells interviewees they aren't very good—even if they are. He wants applicants who believe in themselves and will try to persuade him that he's wrong.

He challenges canned answers. If an applicant says he or she wants to be in sales "to help people," Rose responds, "You want to help people? Go be a nurse."

Rick tells candidates to call him after the interview. Those who do call back get second interviews with all the current salespeople.

And when all of that goes positively, the interviewee is invited to participate in a week's worth of sales meetings, which start at 7 AM four times a week. The people who do participate—not merely attend—are the people who get hired.

*Based on Richard C. Rose and Echo Montgomery Garrett, "Guerrilla Interviewing," *Inc.*, December 1992, 145–47.

Usually the stress is psychological. A group of interviewers fire rapid questions. A single interviewer probes every weak spot in the applicant's record and asks questions that elicit negatives. If you get questions that put you on the defensive, **rephrase** them in less inflammatory terms, if necessary, and then **treat them as requests for information.**

Q: Why did you major in physical education? That sounds like a pretty Mickey Mouse major.

A: You're asking whether I have the academic preparation for this job. I started out in physical education because I've always loved sports. I learned that I couldn't graduate in four years if I officially switched my major to business administration because the requirements were different in the two programs. But I do have 21 hours in business administration and 9 hours in accounting. And my sports experience gives me practical training in teamwork, motivating people, and management.

Respond assertively. The candidates who survive are those who stand up for themselves and who explain why indeed they *are* worth hiring.

Silence can also create stress. One woman walked into her scheduled interview to find a male interviewer with his feet up on the desk. He said, "It's been a long day. I'm tired and I want to go home. You have five minutes to sell yourself." Since she had planned the points she wanted to be sure interviewers knew, she was able to do this. "Your recruiting brochure said that you're looking for someone with a major in accounting and a minor in finance. As you may remember from my résumé, I'm majoring in Accountancy and have had 12 hours in finance. I've also served as treasurer of a local campaign committee and have worked as a volunteer tax preparer through the Accounting Club." When she finished, the interviewer told her it was a test: "I wanted to see how you'd handle it."

Increasingly common is the variety of stress interview that asks you to do—on the spot—the kind of thing the job would require. An interviewer for a sales job handed applicants a ballpoint pen and said, "Sell me this pen." (It's OK to ask who the target market is and whether this is a repeat or a new customer.) AT&T asks some applicants to deliver presentations or lead meetings. Massachusetts Mutual Life asked the finalists for a vice presidency to process memos and reports in a two-hour in-basket exercise and participate in several role plays.[6]

Sexist interviews are a special variety of stress interviews. Although questions about marriage and children are illegal, they occasionally are asked. An interview can also be categorized as sexist if the interviewer implies that an applicant can't do the job because she's female: "You're a woman and you're short. You'd be working with tall men in this job. How would you handle them?"

Although you're within your rights to say "I don't think that question is legal," a low-key response is more likely to lead to a job offer. Respond as you would to a stress question: **rephrase the question and treat it as a legitimate request for information.**

Q: Aren't you just looking for a husband?

A: You may be asking whether I'll stay with you long enough to justify the expense of training me as a staff accountant. Well, I'm not promising to work for you the rest of my life, just as you're not promising to employ me for the rest of my life. How long I stay will depend upon whether my assignments continue to be interesting and challenging and whether I can advance.

Sometimes interviewers who do not ask sexist questions still have reservations about offering jobs to women. You may want to set at rest the

Testing the Intangibles*

A growing number of companies, including General Motors and American Express, are no longer satisfied with traditional job interviews.

They are making applicants for many white-collar jobs run a gauntlet of paper-and-pencil tests, role-playing exercises, decision-making simulations, and brain teasers. Others put candidates through a long series of interviews by psychologists or trained interviewers. . . .

[E]mployers want to grade upper-echelon job candidates on intangible qualities. Is she creative and entrepreneurial? Can she lead and coach? Can he work in teams? Is he flexible and capable of learning? Does she have passion and a sense of urgency? How will he function under pressure?

Most important, will the potential recruit fit the corporate culture?

These tests . . . can take from an hour to two days.

*Quoted from Judith H. Dobrzynski, "Applicants Find It Takes More Than a Resume to Land a Job in the '90s," *The Columbus Dispatch*, September 8, 1996, 8I.

Amy's Ice Creams' stores sell entertainment. To find creative, zany employees, Amy Miller gives applicants a white paper bag and a week to do something with it. People who produce something unusual are hired.

interviewer's fears by bringing up the subject yourself: "You may have noticed that I'm married. My husband is a dentist and could relocate if the company wanted to transfer me."

ANSWERING TRADITIONAL INTERVIEW QUESTIONS

First interviews seek to screen out less qualified candidates rather than to find someone to hire. Negative information will hurt you less if it comes out in the middle of the interview and is preceded and followed by positive information. If the interviewer asks a question as you're on your way out which you blow, don't leave until you've said something positive—perhaps restating one of the points you want the interviewer to know about you.

As Figure 20.1 shows, successful applicants use different communication behaviors than do unsuccessful applicants. Successful applicants are more likely to use the company name during the interview, support their claims with specific details, and ask specific questions about the company and the industry. In addition to practicing the content of questions, try to incorporate these tactics.

The following questions frequently come up at interviews. Do some unpressured thinking before the interview so that you'll be able to come up with answers that are responsive, honest, and paint a good picture of you. Choose answers that fit your qualifications and your interview strategy.

1. Tell me about yourself.
   Don't launch into an autobiography. Instead, state the things about yourself that you want the interviewer to know. Give specifics to prove each of your strengths.

2. What makes you think you're qualified to work for this company? Or, I'm interviewing 120 people for two jobs. Why should I hire you?
   This question may feel like an attack. Use it as an opportunity to state your strong points: your qualifications for the job, the things that separate you from other applicants.

3. What two or three accomplishments have given you the greatest satisfaction?

The Communication Behaviors of Successful Interviewees   **Figure 20.1**

	Unsuccessful Interviewees	Successful Interviewees
Statements about the position	Had only vague ideas of what they wanted to do; changed "ideal job" up to six times during the interview.	Specific and consistent about the position they wanted; were able to tell why they wanted the position.
Use of company name	Rarely used the company name.	Referred to the company by name four times as often as unsuccessful interviewees.
Knowledge about company and position	Made it clear that they were using the interview to learn about the company and what it offered.	Made it clear that they had researched the company; referred to specific brochures, journals, or people who had given them information.
Level of interest, enthusiasm	Responded neutrally to interviewer's statements: "OK," "I see." Indicated reservations about company or location.	Expressed approval of information provided by the interviewer nonverbally and verbally; "That's great!" Explicitly indicated desire to work for this particular company.
Picking up on interviewer's cues	Gave vague or negative answers even when a positive answer was clearly desired ("How are your math skills?").	Answered positively and confidently—and backed up the claim with a specific example of "problem solving" or "toughness."
Use of industry terms and technical jargon	Used almost no technical jargon.	Used technical jargon: "point of purchase display," "NCR charge," "two-column approach," "direct mail."
Use of specifics in answers	Gave short answers—10 words or less, sometimes only one word; did not elaborate. Gave general responses: "fairly well."	Supported claims with specific personal experiences, comparisons, statistics, statements of teachers and employers.
Questions asked by interviewee	Asked a small number of general questions.	Asked specific questions based on knowledge of the industry and the company. Personalized questions: "What would my duties be?"
Control of time and topics	Interviewee talked 37% of the interview time, initiated 36% of the comments.	Interviewee talked 55% of the total time, initiated subjects 56% of the time.

Based on research reported by Lois J. Einhorn, "An Inner View of the Job Interview: An Investigation of Successful Communicative Behaviors," *Communication Education* 30 (July 1981): 217–28.

Pick accomplishments that you're proud of, that create the image you want to project, and that enable you to share one of the things you want the interviewer to know about you. Focus not just on the end result, but on the problem-solving and thinking skills that made the achievement possible.

4. Why do you want to work for us? What is your ideal job?
Even if you're interviewing just for practice, make sure you have a good answer—preferably two or three reasons you'd like to work for that company. If you don't seem to be taking the interview seriously, the interviewer won't take you seriously, and you won't even get good practice.

If your ideal job is very different from the ones the company has available, the interviewer may simply say there isn't a good match and end the interview. If you're interested in this company, do some research so that what you ask for is in the general ballpark of the kind of work the company offers.

Persistence Pays Off*

The interview was a disaster. She was awkward and inarticulate. All she could say was that she really wanted to work for the company, but she could not say what she could offer in return. She was turned down flat.

As she interviewed more, she got the hang of it and began to get some job offers, but her first interview gnawed at her. It had been for the job she really wanted. Figuring that she had one zero from that company and that two zeroes would not be worse than one, she called on the employer again, explained that when she had been there before it had been her first interview and that she had really not known how to handle herself. She told the employer that she really felt she had something to offer and asked if she could have another interview.

The employer was impressed. He liked persistence. The fact that the candidate had come back demonstrated a real interest in the company. A second interview was granted, and the young woman got the job.

*Quoted from John L. Munschauer, *Jobs for English Majors and Other Smart People* (Princeton, NJ: Peterson's Guides, 1986), 159–60.

5. What college subjects did you like best and least? Why?

This question may be an icebreaker; it may be designed to discover the kind of applicant they're looking for. If your favorite class was something outside your major, prepare an answer that shows that you have qualities that can help you in the job you're applying for: "My favorite class was a seminar in the American novel. We got a chance to think on our own, rather than just regurgitate facts; we made presentations to the class every week. I found I really like sharing my ideas with other people and presenting reasons for my conclusions about something."

6. What is your class rank? Your grade point? Why are your grades so low?

If your grades aren't great, be ready with a nondefensive explanation. If possible, show that the cause of low grades now has been solved or isn't relevant to the job you're applying for: "My father almost died last year, and my schoolwork really suffered." "When I started, I didn't have any firm goals. Once I discovered the field that was right for me, my grades have all been 'Bs' or better." "I'm not good at multiple-choice tests. But you need someone who can work with people, not someone who can take tests."

7. What have you read recently? What movies have you seen recently?

These questions may be icebreakers; they may be designed to probe your intellectual depth. The term you're interviewing, read at least one book or magazine (regularly) and see at least one movie that you could discuss at an interview.

8. Show me some samples of your writing.

Many jobs require the ability to write well. Employers no longer take mastery of basic English for granted, even if the applicant has a degree from a prestigious university.

The year you're interviewing, go through your old papers and select the best ones, retyping them if necessary, so that you'll have samples if you're asked for them. If you don't have samples at the interview, mail them to the interviewer immediately after the interview.

9. Where do you see yourself in five years?

Employers ask this question to find out if you are a self-starter or if you passively respond to what happens. You may want to have several scenarios for five years from now to use in different kinds of interviews. Or you may want to say, "Well, my goals may change as opportunities arise. But right now, I want to. . . ."

10. What are your interests outside work? What campus or community activities have you been involved in?

While it's desirable to be well-rounded, naming 10 interests is a mistake: the interviewer may wonder when you'll have time to work.

If you mention your fiancé, spouse, or children in response to this question ("Well, my fiancé and I like to go sailing"), it is perfectly legal for the interviewer to ask follow-up questions ("What would you do if your spouse got a job offer in another town?"), even though the same question would be illegal if the interviewer brought up the subject first.

11. What have you done to learn about this company?

An employer may ask this to see what you already know about the company (if you've read the recruiting literature, the interviewer doesn't need to repeat it). This question may also be used to see how active a role you're taking in the job search process and how interested you are in this job.

12. What adjectives would you use to describe yourself?

Use only positive ones. Be ready to illustrate each with a specific example of something you've done.

13. What is your greatest strength?

Employers ask this question to give you a chance to sell yourself and to learn something about your values. Pick a strength related to work, school, or activities: "I'm good at working with people." "I really can sell things." "I'm good at solving problems." "I learn quickly." "I'm reliable. When I say I'll do something, I do it." Be ready to illustrate each with a specific example of something you've done.

14. What is your greatest weakness?

Use a work-related negative, even if something in your personal life really is your greatest weakness. Interviewers won't let you get away with a "weakness" like being a workaholic or just not having any experience yet. Instead, use one of the following three strategies:

a. Discuss a weakness that is not related to the job you're being considered for and will not be needed even when you're promoted. (Even if you won't work with people or give speeches in your first job, you'll need those skills later in your career, so don't use them for this question.) End your answer with a positive that *is* related to the job:

> [For a creative job in advertising:] I don't like accounting. I know it's important, but I don't like it. I even hire someone to do my taxes. I'm much more interested in being creative and working with people, which is why I find this position interesting.

> [For a job in administration:] I don't like selling products. I hated selling cookies when I was a Girl Scout. I'd much rather work with ideas—and I really like selling the ideas that I believe in.

> [For a job in architecture:] I hate fund-raising. It always seemed to me if people wanted to give, they would anyway. I'd much rather have something to offer people which will help them solve their own problems and meet their own needs.

b. Discuss a weakness that you are working to improve:

> In the past, I wasn't a good writer. But last term I took a course in business writing that taught me how to organize my ideas and how to revise. I may never win a Pulitzer Prize, but now I'm a lot more confident that I can write effective reports and memos.

c. Discuss a work-related weakness:

> I procrastinate. Fortunately, I work well under pressure, but a couple of times I've really put myself in a bind.

15. Why are you looking for another job?

Stress what you're looking for in a new job, not why you want to get away from your old one.

If you were fired, say so. There are three acceptable ways to explain why you were fired:

a. It wasn't a good match. Add what you now know you need in a job, and ask what the employer can offer in this area.

b. You and your supervisor had a personality conflict. Make sure you show that this was an isolated incident, and that you normally get along well with people.

The Same Answer Can Get Different Responses*

One job hunter I knew named O'Brian looked a recruiter straight in the eye and said, "As for my goals, they are to become president of your company in not too many years." The recruiter called him arrogant and told him to see a counselor. That same day O'Brian was asked again about his vocational plans by another recruiter and gave the same self-assured answer. This recruiter was delighted. As he said later, "All day long, I'd been asking students what they wanted to be in our company some day, and I'd been getting evasive or self-effacing answers. Then O'Brian came along. He is smart and knows what he is after. He is the candidate I want."

A friend of mine was once asked the hackneyed old saw, "And where do you expect to be in three years?" The friend, who should have known better (and does now), replied with the also hackneyed but dangerous, "I expect to be sitting in your chair." . . . The interviewer was shocked. His face got white, and he asked my friend, "Where will I be if you get my job?" The guy was dead serious; he planned to be in the job for a long time and had never thought of moving anywhere. We all laughed when we heard the story, but my friend didn't ever hear from them again.

*Quoted from John L. Munschauer, *Jobs for English Majors and Other Smart People* (Princeton, NJ: Peterson's Guides, 1986), 28–29, and William Lareau, *Inside Track: A Successful Job Search Method* (Piscataway, NJ: New Century, 1985), 157.

Is There Life After Work?*

Questions about work-life balance—which in the past were saved for the final round of interviews or never asked at all—are surfacing in job candidates' first-round talks with employers.

A sampling of questions asked by undergraduate recruits . . . :

1. Do people who work for you have a life off the job?
2. Do your employees get to see their families?
3. What support can you offer my significant other?
4. Do you offer flextime?
5. If my job requires too much travel, can I change without doing serious damage to my career? . . .

[S]everal [recruiters] say many of the candidates who asked these questions in the past ended up being top performers in their jobs. "The thing I found is that these folks can set their priorities within time limits," says Faye Ambrefe Omasta, who recruits management trainees for GTE. Gordon Welton, placement manager for Principal Financial Group, adds, . . . "They know what's important to them. They're passionate not just about their work, but about themselves."

*Quoted from Sue Shellenbarger, "New Job Hunters Ask Recruiters, 'Is There Life After Work?' " The Wall Street Journal, January 29, 1996, B1.

c. You made mistakes, but you've learned from them and are now ready to work well. Be ready to offer a specific anecdote proving that you have indeed changed.

16. What questions do you have?

This question gives you a chance to cover things the interviewer hasn't brought up; it also gives the interviewer a sense of your priorities and values. Don't focus on salary or fringe benefits. Better questions are

- What would I be doing on a day-to-day basis?
- What kind of training program do you have? If, as I'm rotating among departments, I find that I prefer one area, can I specialize in it when the training program is over?
- How do you evaluate employees? How often do you review them? Where would you expect a new trainee (banker, staff accountant) to be three years from now?
- What happened to the last person who had this job?
- How are interest rates (a new product from competitors, imports, demographic trends, government regulations, etc.) affecting your company?
- How would you describe the company's culture?
- This sounds like a great job. What are the drawbacks?

You won't be able to anticipate every question you may get. (One interviewer asked students, "What vegetable would you like to be?" Another asked, "If you were a cookie, what kind of cookie would you be?"[7]) Check with other people at your college or university who have interviewed recently to find out what questions are being asked in your field.

BEHAVIORAL AND SITUATIONAL INTERVIEWS

Many companies, dissatisfied with hires based on responses to traditional questions, are now using behavioral or situational interviews. **Behavioral interviews** ask the applicant to describe actual behaviors, rather than plans or general principles. Thus instead of asking "How would you motivate people?" the interviewer might ask, "Tell me what happened the last time you wanted to get other people to do something." Follow-up questions might include, "What exactly did you do to handle the situation? How did you feel about the results? How did the other people feel? How did your superior feel about the results?" Since behavioral questions require applicants to tell what they actually did—rather than to say what ought to be done—interviewers feel they offer better insight into how someone will actually function as an employee.

Situational interviews put you in a situation that allows the interviewer to see whether you have the qualities the company is seeking. For example, Southwest Airlines found that 95% of the complaints it received were provoked by only 5% of its personnel. When managers explored further, they found that these 5% of employees were self-centered. To weed out self-centered applicants, Southwest now puts several candidates into a room and asks each to give a five-minute speech on "Why I Want to Work with Southwest Airlines." But the interviewers watch the *audience* to hire the people who are pulling for other speakers to do well, as opposed to those who are only thinking about their own performance.[8]

Situational interviews may also be conducted using traditional questions but evaluating behaviors other than the answers. Greyhound hired applicants for its customer-assistance center who made eye contact with the interviewer and smiled at least five times during a 15-minute interview.[9]

AFTER THE INTERVIEW

What you do after the interview can determine whether you get the job. One woman wanted to switch from banking, where she was working in corporate relations, to advertising. The ad agency interviewer expressed doubts about her qualifications. Immediately after leaving the agency, she tracked down a particular book the interviewer had mentioned he was looking for but had been unable to find. She presented it to him—and was hired.[10]

Xerox expects applicants for sales and repair positions to follow up within 10 days. If they don't, the company assumes that the person wouldn't follow up with clients.[11]

If the employer sends you an e-mail query, answer it promptly. You're being judged not only on what you say but on how quickly you respond.

Follow-Up Phone Calls and Letters

After a first interview, make follow-up phone calls to reinforce positives from the first interview, to overcome any negatives, and to get information you can use to persuade the interviewer to hire you. Career coach Kate Weldon suggests asking the following questions:

- "Is there more information I can give you?"
- "I've been giving a lot of thought to your project and have some new ideas. Can we meet to go over them?"
- "Where do I stand? How does my work compare with the work others presented?"[12]

A letter after an office visit is essential to thank your hosts for their hospitality as well as to send in receipts for your expenses. The letter should

- Remind the interviewer of what he or she liked in you.
- Counter any negative impressions that may have come up at the interview.
- Use the jargon of the company and refer to specific things you learned during your interview or saw during your visit.
- Be enthusiastic.
- Refer to the next move, whether you'll wait to hear from the employer or whether you want to call to learn about the status of your application.

Be sure the letter is well written and error-free. One employer reports,

I often interviewed people whom I liked, . . . but their follow-up letters were filled with misspelled words and names and other inaccuracies. They blew their chance with the follow-up letter.[13]

Figure 20.2 is an example of a follow-up letter after an office visit.

Negotiating for Salary and Benefits

The best time to negotiate for salary and benefits is after you have the job offer. Try to delay discussing salary early in the interview process, when you're still competing against other applicants.

Prepare for salary negotiations by finding out what the going rate is for the kind of work you hope to do. Cultivate friends who are now in the work force to find out what they're making. Ask the campus placement office for figures on what last year's graduates got. Check trade journals. For example, *Advertising Age* publishes an annual salary survey segmented by agency size and region of the country. The survey gives figures for managers and

Figure 20.2   **Follow-Up Letter after an Office Visit**

405 West College, Apt. 201   *Single-space your address, date*
Thibodaux, LA 70301   *when you don't use letterhead.*
April 2, 1998

Mr. Robert Land, Account Manager
Sive Associates
378 Norman Boulevard
Cincinnati, OH 48528

Dear Mr. Land:

After visiting Sive Associates last week, I'm even more sure that writing direct mail is the career for me.

Refers to things she saw and learned during the interview.

I've always been able to brainstorm ideas, but sometimes, when I had to focus on one idea for a class project, I wasn't sure which idea was best. It was fascinating to see how you make direct mail scientific as well as creative by testing each new creative package against the control. I can understand how pleased Linda Hayes was when she learned that her new package for *Smithsonian* beat the control.

Seeing Kelly, Luke, and Gene collaborating on the Sesame Street package gave me some sense of the tight deadlines you're under. As you know, I've learned to meet deadlines, not only for my class assignments, but also in working on Nicholls' newspaper. The award I won for my feature on the primary election suggests that my quality holds up even when the deadline is tight!

Reminds interviewer of her strong points.

Thank you for your hospitality while I was in Cincinnati. You and your wife made my stay very pleasant. I especially appreciate the time the two of you took to help me find information about apartments that are accessible to wheelchairs. Cincinnati seems like a very liveable city.

I'm excited about a career in direct mail and about the (possibility) of joining Sive Associates. I look forward to hearing from you soon!

Be positive, not pushy. She doesn't assume she has the job.

Refers to what will happen next.

Sincerely,

Gina Focasio

Gina Focasio
(504) 555-2948

Writer's phone number.

Puts request for reimbursement in P.S. to de-emphasize it, focuses on the job, not the cost of the trip.

P.S. My expenses totalled $454. Enclosed are receipts for my plane fare from New Orleans to Cincinnati ($367), the taxi to the airport in Cincinnati ($30), and the bus from Thibodaux to New Orleans ($57).

Encl.: Receipts for Expenses

officers, not entry-level workers, but the numbers still give you an upper limit: you can figure that an entry-level copywriter will make less than the chief copywriter. *Working Woman* publishes a salary survey every July that gives figures for a variety of jobs. Specialized books can also help, such as the annual *Direct Marketing and Telemarketing Guide* or the *Robert Half and Accountemps Salary Guide.*

This research is crucial. One study showed that male BA and MBA candidates expected to start at salaries 16.5% higher than the salaries women BA and MBA candidates expected.[14] Knowing what a job is worth will give you the confidence to negotiate more effectively.

If the interviewer asks you about your salary requirements before a job offer has been made, try this response: "I'm sure your firm can pay me what I'm worth." Then either ask about pay ranges or go back to your qualifications for the job. If the interviewer demands a response, give a range using odd increments: "I'd expect to make between $32,300 and $36,900." As you say this, *watch the interviewer.* If he or she has that blank look we use to hide dismay, you may have asked for much more than the company was planning to offer. Quickly continue, ". . . depending, of course, on fringe benefits and how quickly I could be promoted. However, salary isn't the most important criterion for me in choosing a job, and I won't necessarily accept the highest offer I get. I'm interested in going somewhere where I can get good experience and use my talents to make a real contribution."

The best way to get more money is to convince the employer that you're worth it. During the interview process, show what you can do that the competition can't. Work to redefine the position in the employer's eyes from a low-level, anybody-could-do-it job to a complex combination of duties that only someone with your particular mix of talents could do.

After you have the offer, you can begin negotiating salary and benefits. You're in the strongest position when (1) you've done your homework and know what the usual salary and benefits are and (2) you can walk away from this offer if it doesn't meet your needs. Again, avoid naming a specific salary. Don't say you can't accept less. Instead, Kate Wendleton suggests, say you "would find it difficult to accept the offer" under the terms first offered.[15]

Remember that you're negotiating a package, not just a starting salary. A company that truly can't pay any more money now might be able to review you for promotion sooner than usual, or pay your moving costs, or give you a better job title. Some companies offer fringe benefits that may compensate for lower taxable income: use of a company car, reimbursements for education, child care or elder care subsidies, or help in finding a job for your spouse or partner. And think about your career, not just the initial salary. Sometimes a low-paying job at a company that will provide superb experience will do more for your career (and your long-term earning prospects) than a high salary now with no room to grow.

Work toward a win-win solution. You want the employer to be happy that you're coming on board and to feel that you've behaved maturely and professionally.

Deciding Which Offer to Accept

The problem with choosing among job offers is that you're comparing apples and oranges. The job with the most interesting work pays peanuts. The job that pays best is in a city where you really don't want to live. It's your life. The secret of professional happiness is taking a job where the positives are things you want and the negatives are things that don't matter much to you.

Finding Rewarding Work*

In the last nine years, a group of 22 business school graduates have averaged 4.3 jobs per person, with a few in their seventh job. Eight have had "involuntary departures." Their careers would have been more efficient and less painful if they had known more about themselves and about the world they were entering.

They didn't understand the changing nature of work.

They didn't expect business cycles and politics to affect them.

They didn't know people were irrational, driven by fear, greed and jealousy.

They hadn't thought about the nonfinancial sources of satisfaction they needed.

They hadn't realized that they had moral values.

The lesson their experience teaches is that the more you know about yourself, about the economy, and about the company you're considering joining, the more likely it is that your job will give you a sense of reward that goes beyond a paycheck.

*Based on Jan Harding, "Closing the Circle: Collaboration with Recent Graduates," Mini-Conference on Accounting and Business Communication, Columbus, OH, July 26–27, 1996.

Figure 20.3

Forced Choice Chart

When you're not sure which job to accept, use this table of fractions. See instructions in the last paragraph on this page.

$\frac{1}{2}$ $\frac{1}{3}$ $\frac{1}{4}$ $\frac{1}{5}$ $\frac{1}{6}$ $\frac{1}{7}$ $\frac{1}{8}$ $\frac{1}{9}$ $\frac{1}{10}$ $\frac{1}{11}$ $\frac{1}{12}$ $\frac{1}{13}$ $\frac{1}{14}$ $\frac{1}{15}$ $\frac{1}{16}$ $\frac{1}{17}$ $\frac{1}{18}$ $\frac{1}{19}$ $\frac{1}{20}$

$\frac{2}{3}$ $\frac{2}{4}$ $\frac{2}{5}$ $\frac{2}{6}$ $\frac{2}{7}$ $\frac{2}{8}$ $\frac{2}{9}$ $\frac{2}{10}$ $\frac{2}{11}$ $\frac{2}{12}$ $\frac{2}{13}$ $\frac{2}{14}$ $\frac{2}{15}$ $\frac{2}{16}$ $\frac{2}{17}$ $\frac{2}{18}$ $\frac{2}{19}$ $\frac{2}{20}$

$\frac{3}{4}$ $\frac{3}{5}$ $\frac{3}{6}$ $\frac{3}{7}$ $\frac{3}{8}$ $\frac{3}{9}$ $\frac{3}{10}$ $\frac{3}{11}$ $\frac{3}{12}$ $\frac{3}{13}$ $\frac{3}{14}$ $\frac{3}{15}$ $\frac{3}{16}$ $\frac{3}{17}$ $\frac{3}{18}$ $\frac{3}{19}$ $\frac{3}{20}$

$\frac{4}{5}$ $\frac{4}{6}$ $\frac{4}{7}$ $\frac{4}{8}$ $\frac{4}{9}$ $\frac{4}{10}$ $\frac{4}{11}$ $\frac{4}{12}$ $\frac{4}{13}$ $\frac{4}{14}$ $\frac{4}{15}$ $\frac{4}{16}$ $\frac{4}{17}$ $\frac{4}{18}$ $\frac{4}{19}$ $\frac{4}{20}$

$\frac{5}{6}$ $\frac{5}{7}$ $\frac{5}{8}$ $\frac{5}{9}$ $\frac{5}{10}$ $\frac{5}{11}$ $\frac{5}{12}$ $\frac{5}{13}$ $\frac{5}{14}$ $\frac{5}{15}$ $\frac{5}{16}$ $\frac{5}{17}$ $\frac{5}{18}$ $\frac{5}{19}$ $\frac{5}{20}$

$\frac{6}{7}$ $\frac{6}{8}$ $\frac{6}{9}$ $\frac{6}{10}$ $\frac{6}{11}$ $\frac{6}{12}$ $\frac{6}{13}$ $\frac{6}{14}$ $\frac{6}{15}$ $\frac{6}{16}$ $\frac{6}{17}$ $\frac{6}{18}$ $\frac{6}{19}$ $\frac{6}{20}$

$\frac{7}{8}$ $\frac{7}{9}$ $\frac{7}{10}$ $\frac{7}{11}$ $\frac{7}{12}$ $\frac{7}{13}$ $\frac{7}{14}$ $\frac{7}{15}$ $\frac{7}{16}$ $\frac{7}{17}$ $\frac{7}{18}$ $\frac{7}{19}$ $\frac{7}{20}$

$\frac{8}{9}$ $\frac{8}{10}$ $\frac{8}{11}$ $\frac{8}{12}$ $\frac{8}{13}$ $\frac{8}{14}$ $\frac{8}{15}$ $\frac{8}{16}$ $\frac{8}{17}$ $\frac{8}{18}$ $\frac{8}{19}$ $\frac{8}{20}$

$\frac{9}{10}$ $\frac{9}{11}$ $\frac{9}{12}$ $\frac{9}{13}$ $\frac{9}{14}$ $\frac{9}{15}$ $\frac{9}{16}$ $\frac{9}{17}$ $\frac{9}{18}$ $\frac{9}{19}$ $\frac{9}{20}$

$\frac{10}{11}$ $\frac{10}{12}$ $\frac{10}{13}$ $\frac{10}{14}$ $\frac{10}{15}$ $\frac{10}{16}$ $\frac{10}{17}$ $\frac{10}{18}$ $\frac{10}{19}$ $\frac{10}{20}$

$\frac{11}{12}$ $\frac{11}{13}$ $\frac{11}{14}$ $\frac{11}{15}$ $\frac{11}{16}$ $\frac{11}{17}$ $\frac{11}{18}$ $\frac{11}{19}$ $\frac{11}{20}$

$\frac{12}{13}$ $\frac{12}{14}$ $\frac{12}{15}$ $\frac{12}{16}$ $\frac{12}{17}$ $\frac{12}{18}$ $\frac{12}{19}$ $\frac{12}{20}$

$\frac{13}{14}$ $\frac{13}{15}$ $\frac{13}{16}$ $\frac{13}{17}$ $\frac{13}{18}$ $\frac{13}{19}$ $\frac{13}{20}$

$\frac{14}{15}$ $\frac{14}{16}$ $\frac{14}{17}$ $\frac{14}{18}$ $\frac{14}{19}$ $\frac{14}{20}$

$\frac{15}{16}$ $\frac{15}{17}$ $\frac{15}{18}$ $\frac{15}{19}$ $\frac{15}{20}$

$\frac{16}{17}$ $\frac{16}{18}$ $\frac{16}{19}$ $\frac{16}{20}$

$\frac{17}{18}$ $\frac{17}{19}$ $\frac{17}{20}$

$\frac{18}{19}$ $\frac{18}{20}$

$\frac{19}{20}$

Number of times I've chosen

1 _____ 5 _____ 9 _____ 13 _____ 17 _____
2 _____ 6 _____ 10 _____ 14 _____ 18 _____
3 _____ 7 _____ 11 _____ 15 _____ 19 _____
4 _____ 8 _____ 12 _____ 16 _____ 20 _____

To choose among job offers, you need to know what is truly important to *you.* Start by answering questions like the following:

- Are you willing to take work home? To travel? How important is money to you? Prestige? Time to spend with family and friends?
- Would you rather have firm deadlines or a flexible schedule? Do you prefer working alone or with other people? Do you prefer specific instructions and standards for evaluation or freedom and uncertainty? How comfortable are you with pressure? How much challenge do you want?
- Where do you want to live? What features in terms of weather, geography, cultural and social life do you see as ideal?
- Is it important to you that your work achieve certain purposes or values, or do you see work as "just a way to make a living"? Are the organization's culture and ethical standards ones you find comfortable?
- Can you picture yourself doing this job 40 hours a week?
- Will you be able to do work you can point to with pride?

After you've done this brainstorming, make a list of *everything you'd like in your ideal job.* Then, to see which points are really important to you, do a forced choice. In a **forced choice,** you compare each item against every other one. Number the items in the order in which they happened to occur to you. Then, using the table of fractions in Figure 20.3, rank each pair. For "½" compare item 1 and item 2. If you could only have one of the two, which would you prefer. Circle that number. For "⅓," compare item 1 with item 3. Again, circle the item that's more important. Repeat until you've made a choice between each of the possible pairs. Then count the number of times you've chosen each item. The things you've chosen most often are the ones that matter: they're the ones you should look for in your job.

1. High income
2. Time to spend with my family
3. Near mountains
4. Job opportunities for Linda
5. Opportunity for advancement
6. Nonracist environment
7. Company with other African Americans in leadership roles
8. Socially responsible company
9. Lots of open land near by
10. Challenging work
11. Minimal travel as part of job
12. Good college or pro sports teams in town
13. Cost of living not too high
14. Good schools
15. Town with large African-American community
16. Town with parks, civic services
17. Lots of interaction with other people
18. Company that will encourage me to get a master's degree and even pay for it
19. Company with good fringe benefits
20. Not have to work weekends

Figure 20.4

Jim's List for a Forced Choice

You can list more items or fewer, in any order. Then use the Forced Choice Chart to see which really matter to you.

Figure 20.4 is the list that one man produced. The items are numbered in the order in which they occurred to him. To find out what's truly important and what's nice but not necessary, Jim can do a forced choice. If he had to choose between a high income and having time for his family, which would he prefer? Counting up the number of times he chooses each factor will tell him what he really wants.

Some employers offer jobs at the end of the office visit. In other cases, you may wait for weeks or even months to hear. Employers almost always offer jobs orally. You must say something in response immediately, so it's good to plan some strategies in advance.

If your first offer is not from your first choice, express your pleasure at being offered the job, but do not accept it on the phone. "That's great! I assume I have two weeks to let you know?" Then *call* the other companies you're interested in. Explain, "I've just got a job offer, but I'd rather work for you. Can you tell me what the status of my application is?" Nobody will put that information in writing, but almost everyone will tell you over the phone. With this information, you're in a better position to decide whether to accept the original offer.

Companies routinely give applicants two weeks to accept or reject offers. Some students have been successful in getting those two weeks extended to several weeks or even months. Certainly if you cannot decide by the deadline, it is worth asking for more time: the worst the company can do is say *no*. If you do try to keep a company hanging for a long time, be prepared for weekly phone calls asking you if you've decided yet.

Make your acceptance contingent upon a written job offer confirming the terms. That letter should spell out not only salary but also fringe benefits and any special provisions you have negotiated. If something is missing, call the interviewer for clarification: "You said that I'd be reviewed for a promotion and higher salary in six months, but that isn't in the letter." You have more power to resolve misunderstandings now than you will after six months or a year on the job.

Behind the Scenes with a CPA Recruiter*

Every half hour [Don Kipper] will interview a different candidate. . . . What he looks for is "persistence, self-confidence, verbal skills, an ability to answer questions clearly and concisely. Can you think on your feet?" . . .

He's always on campus, officially and unofficially at the honor societies, cocktail parties and the like. He takes an active interest in student affairs and uses it to scoop his rivals on the best potential executives. Once identified, they are invited straight into the corporate office. . . .

Kipper is active in campus workshops, helping students improve their interviewing skills. . . . One unfortunate recently got Kipper's face three inches from his, demanding, "You were drunk last night. After that, why should I waste my time talking to you?" . . .

His advice? "Get involved with the extracurricular campus activities. That's where you'll get discovered."

*Quoted from Martin John Yate, "The Life of a Recruiter," *The Columbus Dispatch*, November 18, 1986, F1.

When you've accepted one job, let the other places you visited know that you're no longer interested. Then they can go to their second choices. If you're second on someone else's list, you'll appreciate other candidates' removing themselves so the way is clear for you.

SUMMARY OF KEY POINTS

- Develop an overall strategy based on your answers to these three questions:
  1. What two to five facts about yourself do you want the interviewer to know?
  2. What disadvantages or weaknesses do you need to overcome or minimize?
  3. What do you need to know about the job and the organization to decide whether or not you want to accept this job if it is offered to you?
- Wear a conservative business suit to the interview.
- Bring an extra copy of your résumé, something to write on and write with, and copies of your work to the interview.
- Record the name of the interviewer, what the interviewer liked about you, any negative points that came up, answers to your questions about the company, and when you'll hear from the company.
- Rehearse everything you can. Ask a friend to interview you. If your campus has videotaping facilities, watch yourself on tape so that you can evaluate and modify your interview behavior.
- Be your best self at the interview.
- In a **stress** interview, the interviewer deliberately creates physical or psychological stress. Change the conditions that create physical stress. Meet psychological stress by rephrasing questions in less inflammatory terms and treating them as requests for information.
- Successful applicants know what they want to do, use the company name in the interview, have researched the company in advance, back up claims with specifics, use technical jargon, ask specific questions, and talk more of the time.
- As you practice answers to questions you may be asked, choose answers that fit your qualifications and your interview strategy.
- **Behavioral interviews** ask the applicant to describe actual behaviors, rather than plans or general principles. **Situational interviews** put you in a situation that allows the interviewer to see whether you have the qualities the company is seeking.
- Use follow-up phone calls to reinforce positives from the first interview, to overcome any negatives, and to get information you can use to persuade the interviewer to hire you.
- A follow-up letter should
  - Remind the interviewer of what he or she liked in you.
  - Allay any negative impressions that may have come up at the interview.
  - Use the jargon of the company and refer to specific things you learned during your interview or saw during your visit.
  - Be enthusiastic.
  - Refer to the next move you'll make.
- In a **forced choice,** you compare each item against every other one to learn which points are most important to you.
- If your first offer isn't from your first choice, call the other companies you're interested in to ask the status of your application.

Exercises and Problems
For Chapter 20

GETTING STARTED

20–1   Making a Forced Choice

On another sheet of paper, list the criteria you'd like in a job. Number each item. Then compare each pair.

If you have 20 items or fewer, you can use the Forced Choice Chart in Figure 20.3 to record your preferences. If you have more than 20 items, make a new chart so that each number will be compared with every other number.

On the chart, mark the number in each pair that corresponds with the item you'd choose if you could have only one of them. Then count how many times you've marked "1", how many times you've marked "2", etc. The items that you mark most often are the features you should try to find in a job.

As Your Instructor Directs,
a. Share your answers with a small group of other students.
b. Summarize your answers in a memo to your instructor.
c. Present your answers orally to the class.

20–2   Interviewing Job Hunters

Talk to students at your school who are interviewing for jobs this term. Possible questions to ask them include

- What field are you in? How good is the job market in that field this year?
- How long is the first interview with a company, usually?
- What questions have you been asked at job interviews? Were you asked any stress or sexist questions? Any really oddball questions?
- What answers seemed to go over well? What answers bombed?
- At an office visit or plant trip, how many people did you talk to? What were their job titles?
- Were you asked to take any tests (skills, physical, drugs)?

- How long did you have to wait after a first interview to learn whether you were being invited for an office visit? How long after an office visit did it take to learn whether you were being offered a job? How much time did the company give you to decide?
- What advice would you have for someone who will be interviewing next term or next year?

As Your Instructor Directs,
a. Summarize your findings in a memo to your instructor.
b. Report your findings orally to the class.
c. Join with a small group of students to write a group report describing the results of your survey.

20–3   Interviewing an Interviewer

Talk to someone who regularly interviews candidates for entry-level jobs. Possible questions to ask include the following:

- How long have you been interviewing for your organization? Does everyone on the management ladder at your company do some interviewing, or do people specialize in it?
- Do you follow a set structure for interviews? What are some of the standard questions you ask?

- What are you looking for? How important are (1) good grades, (2) leadership roles in extracurricular groups, or (3) relevant work experience? What advice would you give to someone who lacks one or more of these?
- What are the things you see students do that create a poor impression? Think about the worst candidate you've interviewed. What did he or she do (or not do) to create such a negative impression?

- What are the things that make a good impression? Recall the best student you've ever interviewed. Why did he or she impress you so much?
- How does your employer evaluate and reward your success as an interviewer?
- What advice would you have for someone who still has a year or so before the job hunt begins?

As Your Instructor Directs,
- a. Summarize your findings in a memo to your instructor.
- b. Report your findings orally to the class.
- c. Join with a small group of students to write a group report describing the results of your survey.
- d. Write to the interviewer thanking him or her for taking the time to talk to you.

20–4 Preparing an Interview Strategy

Based on your analysis in problems 18–1, 18–2, and 20–1, prepare an interview strategy.

1. List two to five things about yourself that you want the interviewer to know before you leave the interview.
2. Identify any weaknesses or apparent weaknesses in your record and plan ways to explain them or minimize them.

3. List the points you need to learn about an employer to decide whether to accept an office visit or plant trip.

As Your Instructor Directs,
- a. Share your strategy with a small group of other students.
- b. Describe your strategy in a memo to your instructor.
- c. Present your strategy orally to the class.

20–5 Preparing Questions to Ask Employers

Prepare a list of questions to ask at job interviews.

1. Prepare a list of three to five general questions that apply to most employers in your field.
2. Prepare two to five specific questions for the three companies you are most interested in.

As Your Instructor Directs,
- a. Share the questions with a small group of other students.
- b. List the questions in a memo to your instructor.
- c. Present your questions orally to the class.

20–6 Preparing Answers to Questions You May Be Asked

Prepare answers to each of the interview questions listed in this chapter and to any other questions that you know are likely to be asked of job hunters in your field or on your campus.

As Your Instructor Directs,
- a. Write down the answers to your questions and turn them in.
- b. Conduct mini-interviews in a small group of students. In the group, let student A be the interviewer and ask five questions from the list. Student B will play the job candidate and answer the questions, using real information about student B's field and qualifications. Student C will evaluate the content of the answer. Student D will observe the nonverbal behavior of the interviewer (A); student E will observe the nonverbal behavior of the interviewee (B).

After the mini-interview, let students C, D, and E share their observations and recommend ways that B could be even more effective. Then switch roles. Let another student be the interviewer and ask five questions of another interviewee, while new observers note content and nonverbal behavior. Continue the process until everyone in the group has had a chance to be "interviewed."

- c. Assume that you are an independent behavioral psychologist hired to conduct screening interviews and interview yourself (silently, if you like). Then write a report to the organization considering the applicant, identifying each strength, weakness, and other characteristics. Support each claim with one or more behavioral examples. Write about yourself in the third person.

(Option c based on a problem written by William J. Allen, University of La Verne and University of Phoenix.)

E-MAIL AND LETTER ASSIGNMENTS

20–7   Writing a Follow-Up Letter after an Office Visit or Plant Trip _____

Write a follow-up e-mail message or letter after an office visit or plant trip. Thank your hosts for their hospitality; relate your strong points to things you learned about the company during the visit; allay any negatives that may remain; be enthusiastic about the company; and submit receipts for your expenses so you can be reimbursed.

20–8   Clarifying the Terms of a Job Offer _____

Last week, you got a job offer from your first choice company, and you accepted it over the phone. Today, the written confirmation arrived. The letter specifies the starting salary and fringe benefits you had negotiated. However, during the office visit, you were promised a 5% raise in six months. The job offer says nothing about the raise. You do want the job, but you want it on the terms you thought you had negotiated.

Write to your contact at the company, Damon Winters.

Formats for Letters and Memos

Appendix Outline

Formats for Letters

Alternate Format for Letters That Are Not Individually Typed

Typing Envelopes

Format for Memos

State and Province Abbreviations

An Inside Perspective:
Formats for Letters and Memos

William A. Anthony, Jr., Staff Representative
Ohio Civil Service Employees Association

Bill Anthony writes memos and announcements to union members and letters to a variety of audiences, including government officials and political candidates. The Ohio Civil Service Employees Association (OCSEA), headquartered in Columbus, Ohio, is a union representing the majority of the 65,000 employees who work for the state of Ohio.

When I write letters on behalf of OCSEA, I want our readers to perceive us as a professional organization. Using letterhead stationery for the first page of a letter helps create a professional image. Our letterhead tells the reader who we are, gives our address and our 1-800, local phone, and fax numbers. It also lists the names and titles of our officers. The second or subsequent pages use plain paper.

In the salutation, I use the name I use in conversation. For example, in a letter summarizing a recent conversation, I used "Dear Sue." It would seem odd to say "Dear Ms. Smith" if I called her "Sue" during the conversation. If I am attempting to build unity and encourage solidarity, I might use "Dear Sister" instead of "Dear Sue."

When I don't know the reader personally, I am more formal. For example, I use "Dear Ms. Smith" if the person is a nonmember or a fair share fee payer. (Fair share fee payers have no voting rights and are not card-carrying members. They still must pay dues, and they are entitled to fair representation by the union.)

Even form letters can be personalized. For example, if I'm asking candidates to appear before our screening committee, then I personalize each of those letters by using the computer's merge function to put in the reader's name and even references to something I had talked to that person about.

I use the close "In Solidarity" in my letters to union members in good standing. This close helps solidify the goodwill, unity, and trust union members must have towards each other.

Even though people call me "Bill," I sign my letters "William A. Anthony, Jr." The only exceptions are to close friends and some staff.

We use letterhead for memos, too. (Again, I use a plain sheet of paper if a second page is required.) I have also created a memo format on my computer to use for memos within the office and to members I know very well. I initial memos either "BA" or "WAA." I use "BA" to other staff and friends and "WAA" for everyone else.

In addition to letters and memos, I also create flyers and announcements. I try to make these unique and easy to read. I design them so that the reader's eye is drawn to the most important information on the page. Desktop publishing lets me take a headline like, "Your Vote Does Count," and put a rectangle or a circle or ellipse around the words. Making the type black and the rectangle, circle, or ellipse white with a shadow underneath is one way to draw attention to what we want to say.

William A. Anthony, Jr., March 26, 1997

Call OCSEA at 1-800-969-4702

"Using letterhead stationery for the first page of a letter helps create a professional image."

William A. Anthony, Jr., Ohio Civil Service Employees Association

Letters normally go to people outside your organization; **memos** go to other people in your organization. In very large organizations, corporate culture determines whether people in different divisions or different locations feel close enough to each other to write memos. Letters and memos do not necessarily differ in length, formality, writing style, or pattern of organization. However, letters and memos do differ in format. **Format** means the parts of a document and the way they are arranged on the page.

FORMATS FOR LETTERS

Many organizations adopt a single format that all writers must use. If your organization has a standard format, use it.

Many organizations and writers choose one of three letter formats: **block** (see Figure A.2) **modified block** (see Figure A.3), or the **Administrative Management Society Simplified** format, also called **AMS Simplified** (see Figure A.4). Your organization may make minor changes from the diagrams in margins or spacing.

Figure A.1 shows how the three formats differ.

Use the same level of formality in the **salutation,** or greeting, as you would in talking to someone on the phone: *Dear Glenn* if you're on a first-name basis, *Dear Mr. Helms* if you don't know the reader well enough to use the first name.

Some writers feel that the AMS Simplified format is better since the reader is not *Dear.* Omitting the salutation is particularly good when you do not know the reader's name or do not know which courtesy title (➤ p. 47) to use. (For a full discussion on nonsexist salutations and salutations when you don't know the reader's name, see Chapter 2.) However, readers like to see their names. Since the AMS Simplified omits the reader's name in the salutation, writers who use this format but who also want to be friendly often try to use the reader's name early in the body of the letter.

The Simplified letter format is good in business-to-business mail, or in letters where you are writing to anyone who holds a job (admissions officer,

Figure A.1   **Comparing and Contrasting Letter Formats**

	Block	Modified Block	AMS Simplified
Date and signature block	Lined up at left margin	Lined up ½ or ⅔ over to the right	Lined up at left margin
Paragraph indentation	None	Optional	None
Salutation and complimentary close	Yes	Yes	None
Subject line	Optional	Rare	Yes
Lists, if any	Indented	Indented	At left margin
Writer's signature	Yes	Yes	None
Writer's typed name	Upper- and lower-case	Upper- and lower-case	Full capital letters
Paragraph spacing	Single-spaced, double-space between	Single-spaced, double-space between	Single-spaced, double-space between

Block Format on Letterhead (mixed punctuation)   **Figure A.2**

Northwest Hardware Warehouse

100 Freeway Exchange   Provo, UT 84610   (801) 555-4683

Line up everything at left margin

↕ 2–6 spaces depending on length of letters

June 20, 1997

1"–1 1/2"

Mr. James E. Murphy, Accounts Payable   *Title could be on a separate line*
Salt Lake Equipment Rentals
5600 Wasatch Boulevard
Salt Lake City, Utah 84121

Dear Jim: *Colon in mixed punctuation*

Use first name in salutation if you'd use it on the phone

The following items totaling $393.09 are still open on your account.   *¶ 1 never has a heading*

Invoice #01R-784391 *Bold or underline heading*

After the bill for this invoice arrived on May 14, you wrote saying that the material had not been delivered to you. On May 29, our Claims Department sent you a copy of the delivery receipt signed by an employee of Salt Lake Equipment. You have had proof of delivery for over three weeks, but your payment has not yet arrived.   *5/8" – 1"*

Single-space paragraphs
Double-space between paragraphs

Please send a check for $78.42.

Triple-space before new heading

Voucher #59351

The reference line on your voucher #59351, dated June 11, indicates that it is the gross payment for invoice #01G-002345. However, the voucher was only for $1171.25, while the invoice amount was $1246.37. Please send a check for $75.12 to clear this item.

Do not indent paragraphs

Voucher #55032

Voucher #55032, dated June 15, subtracts a credit for $239.55 from the amount due. Our records do not show that any credit is due on this voucher. Please send either an explanation or a check to cover the $239.55 immediately.

Total Amount Due   *Headings are optional in letters*

Please send a check for $393.09 to cover these three items and to bring your account up to date.

↕ 2–3 spaces
Sincerely,

3–4 spaces

Neil Hutchinson
Credit Representative

cc: Joan Stottlemyer, Credit Manager

Leave bottom margin of 3–6 spaces— more if letter is short

Figure A.3   **Modified Block Format on Letterhead (mixed punctuation)**

Bay City Information Systems

2–6 spaces

September 14, 1998
Line up date with signature block 1/2 or 2/3 of the way over

2–4 spaces

1"–1 1/2"

Ms. Mary E. Arcas
Personnel Director
Cyclops Communication Technologies
1050 South Sierra Bonita Avenue
Los Angeles, CA 90019   *Zip code on same line*

Dear Ms. Arcas: *Colon in mixed punctuation*

5/8" - 1"

Indenting ¶ is optional in modified block

    Colleen Kangas was hired as a clerk-typist by Bay City Information Systems on April 4, 1996, and was promoted to Administrative Assistant on August 1, 1991. At her review in June, I recommended that she be promoted again. She is an intelligent young woman with good work habits and a good knowledge of computer software.

Single-space paragraphs

    As an Adminstrative Assistant, Colleen not only handles routine duties such as processing time cards, ordering supplies, and entering data, but also screens calls for two marketing specialists, answers basic questions about Bay City Information Systems, compiles the statistics I need for my monthly reports, and investigates special assignments for me. In the past eight months, she has investigated freight charges, inventory department hardware, and microfiche files. I need only to give her general directions: she has a knack for tracking down information quickly and summarizing it accurately.

Double-space between paragraphs

    Although the department's workload has increased during the year, Colleen manages her time so that everything gets done on schedule. She is consistently poised and friendly under pressure. Her willingness to work overtime on occasion is particularly remarkable considering that she has been going to college part-time ever since she joined our firm.

    At Bay City Information Systems, Colleen uses Microsoft Word and Access software. She tells me that she has also used WordPerfect and PowerPoint in her college classes.

    If Colleen were staying in San Francisco, we would want to keep her. She has the potential either to become an Executive Secretary or to move into line or staff work, especially once she completes her degree. I recommend her highly.

2–3 spaces

Sincerely,   *Comma in mixed punctuation*

3–4 spaces

Jeanne Cederlind

Headings are optional in letters

Jeanne Cederlind
Vice President, Marketing

Line up signature block with date

2–4 spaces

Encl.: Evaluation Form for Colleen Kangas

Leave at least 3–6 spaces at bottom of page—more if letter is short

AMS Simplified Format on Letterhead   **Figure A.4**

McFarlane Memorial HOSPITAL

1500 Main Street ◆ Iowa City, IA 52232 ◆ (319) 555-3113

2 – 4 spaces

Line up everything at left margin

August 24, 1998

2 – 4 spaces

1"–1½"

Melinda Hamilton
Medical Services Division
Health Management Services, Inc.
4333 Edgewood Road, NE
Cedar Rapids, IA 52401

Triple space   *Subject line in full capital letters*

REQUEST FOR INFORMATION ABOUT COMPUTER SYSTEMS

← No salutation

We're interested in upgrading our computer system and would like to talk to one of your marketing representatives to see what would best meet our needs. We will use the following criteria to choose a system:

1. Ability to use our current software and data files.   *Double-space between items in list if any items are more than one line long*

2. Price, prorated on a three-year expected life.

3. Ability to provide auxiliary services, e.g., controlling inventory of drugs and supplies, monitoring patients' vital signs, and faster processing of insurance forms.

4. Freedom from downtime.

Triple-space between list, next paragraph

Do not indent paragraphs

McFarlane Memorial Hospital has 50 beds for acute care and 75 beds for long-term care. In the next five years, we expect the number of beds to remain the same while outpatient care and emergency room care increase.

Could we meet the first or the third week in September? We are eager to have the new system installed by Christmas if possible.

Please call me to schedule an appointment.   *Headings are optional in letters*

No close. No signature.

HUGH PORTERFIELD   *Writer's name in full capital letters*
Controller

2–4 spaces

Encl.: Specifications of Current System
        Data Bases Currently in Use

cc: Rene Seaburg

Leave 3–6 spaces at bottom of page — more if letter is short customer service representative) rather than to a specific person. It is too cold and distancing for cultures that place a premium on relationships, such as in Puerto Rico.[1]

Sincerely and *Yours truly* are standard **complimentary closes.** When you are writing to people in special groups or to someone who is a friend as well as a business acquaintance, you may want to use a less formal close. Depending on the circumstances, the following informal closes might be acceptable: *Yours for a better environment, Cordially, Thank you!,* or even *Ciao.*

In **mixed punctuation,** a colon follows the salutation and a comma follows the close. In a sales or fund-raising letter, it is acceptable to use a comma after the salutation to make the letter look like a personal letter rather than like a business letter. In **open punctuation,** omit all punctuation after the salutation and the close. Mixed punctuation is traditional. Open punctuation is faster to type.

A **subject line** tells what the letter is about. Subject lines are required in memos; they are optional in letters. Good subject lines are specific, concise, and appropriate for your purposes and the response you expect from your reader.

- When you have good news, put it in the subject line.
- When your information is neutral, summarize it concisely in the subject line.
- When your information is negative, use a negative subject line if the reader may not read the message or needs the information to act, or if the negative is your error.
- When you have a request that will be easy for the reader to grant, put either the subject of the request or a direct question in the subject line.
- When you must persuade a reluctant reader, use a common ground, a reader benefit, or a directed subject line that makes your stance on the issue clear.

For examples of subject lines in each of these situations, see Chapters 7, 8, and 9.

A **reference line** refers the reader to the number used on the previous correspondence this letter replies to, or the order or invoice number this letter is about. Very large organizations, like the IRS, use numbers on every piece of correspondence they send out so that it is possible quickly to find the earlier document to which an incoming letter refers.

Although not every example uses the same devices to provide visual impact, all three formats can use headings, lists, and indented sections for emphasis.

Each of the three formats has advantages. Both block and AMS Simplified can be typed quickly since everything is lined up at the left margin. Block format is the format most frequently used for business letters; readers expect it. Modified block format creates a visually attractive page by moving the date and signature block over into what would otherwise be empty white space. Modified block is a traditional format; readers are comfortable with it.

The examples of the three formats in Figures A.2–A.4 show one-page letters on company letterhead. **Letterhead** is preprinted stationery with the organization's name, logo, address, and phone number. Figure A.5 shows how to set up modified block format when you do not have letterhead. (It is also acceptable to use block format without letterhead.)

When your letter runs two or more pages, use a heading on the second page to identify it. Using the reader's name helps the writer, who may be printing out many letters at a time, to make sure the right second page gets in the envelope. The two most common formats are shown in Figures A.6,

Modified Block Format without Letterhead (open punctuation)   **Figure A.5**

6 – 12 spaces

Single space   11408 Brussels Ave. NE
Albuquerque, NM 87111
November 5, 1994

1"–1 1/2"   *2 – 6 spaces*

Mr. Tom Miller, President
Miller Office Supplies Corporation
P.O. Box 2900
Lincolnshire, IL 60197-2900

Subject: Invoice No. 664907, 10/29/94   *Subject line is optional in block & modified block*

Indenting paragraphs is optional in modified block   Dear Mr. Miller   *No punctuation in open punctuation*

My wife, Caroline Lehman, ordered and received the briefcase listed on page 71 of your catalog (881-CD-L-9Q-4). The catalog said that the Leatherizer, 881-P-4, was free. On the order blank she indicated that she did want the Leatherizer and marked "Free" in the space for price. Nevertheless, the bill charged us for the Leatherizer.   *5/8" – 1"*

Please remove the $3.19 charge for the Leatherizer from our bill. The total bill was for $107.53, and with the $3.19 deducted, I assume the correct amount for the bill should be $104.34. I have enclosed a check for $104.34.

Please confirm that the charge has been removed and that our account for this order is now paid in full.

Sincerely   *No punctuation in open punctuation*

3 – 4 spaces

William T. Mozing

2 – 4 spaces

Encl.: Check for $104.34   *Line up signature block with date*

A.7, A.8, and below. Note even when the signature block is on the second page, it is still lined up with the date.

Reader's Name
Date
Page Number

or

| Reader's Name | Page Number | Date |

When a letter runs two or more pages, use letterhead only for page 1. (See Figures A.6, A.7, and A.8.) For the remaining pages, use plain paper that matches the letterhead in weight, texture, and color.

Set side margins of 1 inch to 1½ inches on the left and ¾ inch to 1 inch on the right. If your letterhead extends all the way across the top of the page, set your margins even with the ends of the letterhead for the most visually pleasing page. The top margin should be three to six lines under the letterhead, or 2 inches down from the top of the page if you aren't using letterhead. If your letter is very short, you may want to use bigger side and top margins so that the letter is centered on the page.

To eliminate typing the reader's name and address on an envelope, some organizations use envelopes with cut-outs or windows so that the **inside address** (the reader's name and address) on the letter shows through and can be used for delivery. If your organization does this, adjust your margins, if necessary, so that the whole inside address is visible.

Many letters are accompanied by other documents. Whatever these documents may be—a multi-page report or a two-line note—they are called **enclosures,** since they are enclosed in the envelope. The writer should refer to the enclosures in the body of the letter: "As you can see from my résumé, ..." The enclosure line reminds the person who seals the letter to include the enclosures.

Sometimes you write to one person but send copies of your letter to other people. If you want the reader to know that other people are getting copies, list their names on the last page. The abbreviation *cc* originally meant *carbon copy* but now means *computer copy.* Other acceptable abbreviations include *pc* for *photocopy* or simply *c* for *copy.* You can also send copies to other people without telling the reader. Such copies are called **blind copies.** Blind copies are not mentioned on the original; they are listed on the copy saved for the file with the abbreviation *bc* preceding the names of people getting these copies.

You do not need to indicate that you have shown a letter to your superior or that you are saving a copy of the letter for your own files. These are standard practices.

ALTERNATE FORMAT FOR LETTERS THAT ARE NOT INDIVIDUALLY TYPED

Merge functions in word processing programs allow you to put in a reader's name and address even in a form letter. *If you use a specific name in the salutation,* also use the reader's name and address in the inside address.

If you cannot afford to type each reader's name and address individually on the page, you have two options. The first option is to omit the inside address and use a generic salutation: "Dear Voter." The second option is to omit the salutation and use the space where it and the inside address normally go for a benefit or attention-getter. Figure A.9 illustrates this option.

Second Page of a Two-Page Letter, Block Format (mixed punctuation)   **Figure A.6**

State
University

4300 Gateway Boulevard
Midland, TX 78603

August 10, 1994

Ms. Stephanie Voght
Stephen F. Austin High School
1200 Southwest Blvd.
San Antonio, TX 78214

1″–1 1/2″

2 – 3 spaces

Dear Ms. Voght: *Colon in mixed punctuation.*

Enclosed are 100 brochures about State University to distribute to your students. The brochures describe the academic programs and financial aid available. When you need additional brochures, just let me know.

5/8″ – 1″

Videotape about State University

You may also want to show your students the videotape "Life at State University." This 45-minute tape gives a view of classes, dorm life, and extracurricular activities. The

*Plain paper
for page 2.*

1/2″ – 1″

Center

Stephanie Voght ← *Reader's
name*   2   August 10, 1997

*Also OK to line up page number
date at left under reader's name.*

campus life, including football and basketball games, fraternities and sororities, clubs and organizations, and opportunities for volunteer work. The tape stresses the diversity of the student body and the very different lifestyles that are available at State.

*Triple space before
each new heading.*

Scheduling the Videotape   *Bold or underline headings.*

To schedule your free showing, just fill out the enclosed card with your first, second, and third choices for dates, and return it in the stamped, self-addressed envelope. Dates are reserved in the order that requests arrive. Send in your request early to increase the chances of getting the date you want.

*Same
margins
as p 1.*

"Life at State University" will be on its way to give your high school students a preview of the college experience.

Sincerely, *Comma in mixed punctuation.*

*3 – 4
spaces*

Michael L. Mahler
Director of Admissions

*Headings are
optional in
letters.*

2 – 4 spaces

Encl.: Brochures, Reservation Form

cc: R. J. Holland, School Superintendent
     Jose Lavilla, President, PTS Association

Figure A.7   **Second Page of a Two-Page Letter, Modified Block Format (mixed punctuation)**

Glenarvon Carpets

1500 Summit Avenue   (612) 555-1002
Minneapolis, MN   Fax (612) 555-4032

November 8, 1997
Line up date with signature block.

↕ *2 – 4 spaces*

Mr. Roger B. Castino
Castino Floors and Carpets
418 E. North Street
Brockton, MA 02410

Dear Mr. Castino:

Indenting paragraphs is optional in modified block.

Welcome to the team of Glenarvon Carpet dealers!

Your first shipment of Glenarvon samples should reach you within ten days. The samples include new shades for the nineties in a variety of weights. With Glenarvon Carpets, your customers can choose matching colors in heavy-duty weights for high-traffic areas and lighter, less expensive weights for less-used rooms.

Plain paper for page 2

↕ *1/2" – 1"*

Roger B. Castino ← *Reader's name*

Center
2

November 8, 1997

territory. In addition, as a dealer you receive

* Sales kit highlighting product features
* Samples to distribute to customers
* Advertising copy to run in local newspapers
* Display units to place in your store.

Indent or center list to emphasize it.

Use same margins as p 1.

The Annual Sales Meeting each January keeps you up-to-date on new products while you get to know other dealers and Glenarvon executives and relax at a resort hotel.

Make your reservations now for Monterey January 10-13 for your first Glenarvon Sales Meeting!

Cordially, *Comma in mixed punctuation.*

3 – 4 spaces ↕

Barbara S. Charbonneau

Barbara S. Charbonneau
Vice President, Marketing

Line up signature block with date in heading and on p 1.

↕ *1 – 4 spaces*

Encl.: Organization Chart
Product List
National Advertising Campaigns in 1996

1 – 4 spaces

cc: Nancy Magill, Northeast Sales Manager
Edward Spaulding, Sales Representative

↕ *3 – 6 spaces — more if second page isn't a full page.*

Second Page of a Two-Page Letter, AMS Simplified Format   **Figure A.8**

&ptions
for
Living

2 – 4 spaces

January 20, 1998

2 – 3 spaces

Gary Sammons, Editor
<u>Southeastern Home</u> Magazine
253 North Lake Street
Newport News, VA 23612

Triple space   *Subject line in full caps*

MATERIAL FOR YOUR STORY ON HOMES FOR PEOPLE WITH DISABILITIES

No salutation

Apartments and houses can easily be designed to accommodate people with
disabilities. From the outside, the building is indistinguishable from conventional
housing. But the modifications inside permit people who use wheelchairs or whose
sight or hearing is impaired to do everyday things like shower, cook, and do laundry.

Plain paper for page 2

1/2" – 1"

Gary Sammons   ← *Reader's*
January 20, 1998   *name*

Everything   Page 2   in hallways and showers and adjustable cabinets that can be raised or
lined up   lowered. Cardinal says that the adaptations can run from a few dollars to $5000,
at left   depending on what the customer selects.
margin

The Builders Association of South Florida will install many features at no extra cost:
36—inch doorways—eight inches wider than standard—to accommodate
wheelchairs and extra wiring for electronic items for people whose sight or hearing
Same   is impaired.
margins
as page 1   If you'd like pictures to accompany your story, just let me know.

No close, no signature
MARILYN TILLOTSON   *Writer's name in full caps*
Executive Director

Encl.: Blueprints for Housing for People with Disabilities

cc: Douglas Stringfellow, President, BASF
     Thomas R. Galliher, President, Cardinal Industries

at least 3 – 6 spaces — more if page 2 is not a full page

Figure A.9   **A Form Letter Whose Attention-Getter Mimics an Inside Address**

**COMPUTER
SUPPORT
CORPORATION**

2215 Midway Road
Carrollton, Texas 75006
(214) 661-8960
Telex: 284831 CSCTX UR
Fax: (214) 661-1096

*"Johnson Box" used for emphasis,
visual variety*

```
* * * * * * * * * * *
* Five FREE Libraries *
* Worth Up to $615!   *
* * * * * * * * * * *
```

*Date omitted so letter can be sent
out unchanged
Johnson Box visually substitutes
for date*

*Attention–getter
visually
substitutes
for inside
address,
salutation*

```
No Other Business
Graphics Software Can
Match the Versatility &
Flexibility of Diagraph!
```

Let us prove to you that Diagraph is a breakthrough in business
graphics software.

Use Diagraph to turn your ideas, concepts, plans, and data into
organization charts, signs, flow charts, diagrams, forms, and maps.
Diagraph comes with a money-back guarantee. Use it for 30 days and
we're certain that you will have discovered so many uses for
Diagraph that you won't want to part with it.

And now you have two choices: Diagraph/500 for only $99 or
Diagraph/2000 for $395.

Diagraph/500 files are fully compatible with Diagraph/2000 so you
can upgrade to Diagraph/2000 at any time. What's more, the cost of
Diagraph/500 is credited towards your purchase of Diagraph/2000.

See the enclosed data sheet for additional information or call us
today to see how the power of Diagraph can enhance everything you
write!

                              Sincerely,

4 sp.   Gail McCannon

                              Gail McCannon
                              Director, Customer Services

Initials of writer

GM:ec *← Initials of typist*

*Signature block lined up with
Johnson Box*

Encl.

P.S. As an added incentive, if you purchase Diagraph/2000 before
November 30, you can select five Diagraph libraries, worth up to
$615, absolutely free. Call for more details.

*Reader benefit saved for a P.S.
People's eyes go to P.S., which they may
read before returning to rest of letter.*

TYPING ENVELOPES

Business envelopes need to put the reader's name and address in the area that is picked up by the Post Office's Optical Character Readers (OCRs). Use side margins of at least 1 inch. Your bottom margin must be at least ⅝ inch but no bigger than 2¼ inches.

Most businesses use envelopes that already have the return address printed in the upper left-hand corner. When you don't have printed envelopes, type your name (optional), your street address, and your city, state, and zip code in the upper left-hand corner. Since the OCR doesn't need this information to route your letter, exact margins don't matter. Use whatever is convenient and looks good to you.

FORMAT FOR MEMOS

Memos omit both the salutation and the close entirely. Memos never use indented paragraphs. Subject lines are required; headings are optional. Each heading must cover all the information until the next heading. Never use a separate heading for the first paragraph.

Figure A.10 illustrates the standard memo format typed on a plain sheet of paper. Note that the first letters of the reader's name, the writer's name, and the subject phrase are lined up vertically. Note also that memos are usually initialed by the To/From block. Initialing tells the reader that you have proofread the memo and prevents someone sending out your name on a memo you did not in fact write.

Some organizations have special letterhead for memos. When *Date/To/From/Subject* are already printed on the form, the date, writer's and reader's names, and subject are set at the main margin to save typing time. (See Figure A.11.)

Some organizations alter the order of items in the Date/To/From/Subject block. Some organizations ask employees to sign memos rather than simply initialing them. The signature goes below the last line of the memo, starting halfway over on the page, and prevents anyone's adding unauthorized information.

If the memo runs two pages or more, set up the second and subsequent pages just as you do for the second page of a letter. When you write frequently to the same people, putting a brief version of the subject line will be more helpful than just using "All Employees." See Figure A.12.

Brief Subject Line		
Date		
Page Number		

or

Brief Subject Line	Page Number	Date

STATE AND PROVINCE ABBREVIATIONS

States with names of more than five letters are frequently abbreviated in letters and memos. The Post Office abbreviations use two capital letters with no punctuation. See Figure A.13.

Figure A.10   **Memo Format (on Plain Paper)**

Everything lined up at left   *Plain paper*

2 – 4 spaces ↕   October 7, 1997

Line up

To: Annette T. Califero

Double space

From: Kyle B. Abrams **KBA** *Writer's initials added in ink*

1" – 1 1/2"

←————————→ Subject: A Low-Cost Way to Reduce Energy Use   *Capitalize first letter of each major word in subject line*

No heading for ¶ 1   As you requested, I've investigated low-cost ways to reduce our energy use. Reducing the building temperature on weekends is a change that we could make immediately, that would cost nothing, and that would cut our energy use by about 6%.

←——→ *5/8" – 1"*

Triple space before each new heading

The Energy Savings from a Lower Weekend Temperature *Bold or underline headings*

Single-space paragraphs; double-space between paragraphs   Lowering the temperature from 68° to 60° from 8 p.m. Friday evening to 4 a.m. Monday morning could cut our total consumption by 6%. It is not feasible to lower the temperature on weeknights because a great many staff members work late; the cleaning crew also is on duty from 6 p.m. to midnight. Turning the temperature down for only four hours would not result in a significant heat saving.

Turning the heat back up at 4 a.m. will allow the building temperature to be back to 68° by 9 a.m. Our furnace already has computerized controls which can be set to automatically lower and raise the temperature.

Triple sp

How a Lower Temperature Would Affect Employees *Capitalize first letter of each major word of heading*

Do not indent paragraphs   A survey of employees shows that only 7 people use the building every weekend or almost every weekend. Eighteen percent of our staff have worked at least one weekend day in the last two months; 52% say they "occasionally" come in on weekends.

People who come in for an hour or less on weekends could cope with the lower temperature just by wearing warm clothes. However, most people would find 60° too cool for extended work. Employees who work regularly on weekends might want to install space heaters.

Action Needed to Implement the Change

Would you also like me to check into the cost of buying a dozen portable space heaters? Providing them would allow us to choose units that our wiring can handle and would be a nice gesture towards employees who give up their weekends to work. I could have a report to you in two weeks.

We can begin saving energy immediately. Just authorize the lower temperature, and I'll see that the controls are reset for this weekend.

Memos are initialed by To/From/Subject block — no signature   *Headings are optional in memos*

Memo Format (on memo letterhead)   **Figure A.11**

**Kimball,
Walls, and
Morganstern**

Date: March 15, 1998 *Line up with printed Date/To/From/Subject*

To: Annette T. Califero

From: Kyle B. Abrams *KBA* *Writer's initials added in ink*   *Capitalize first
letter of each major
word in subject line*

Subject: The Effectiveness of Reducing Building Temperatures on Weekends

Triple space

*Margin lined up
with items in
To/From/Subject
block to save
typing time*

Reducing the building temperature to 60° on weekends has cut energy use by 4% compared to last year's use from December to February and has saved our firm $22,000.

This savings is particularly remarkable when you consider that this winter has been colder than last year's, so that more heat would be needed to maintain the same temperature.   *5/8" – 1"*

Fewer people have worked weekends during the past three months than during the preceding three months, but snow and bad driving conditions may have had more to do with keeping people home than the fear of being cold. Five of the 12 space heaters we bought have been checked out on an average weekend. On one weekend, all 12 were in use and some people shared their offices so that everyone could be in a room with a space heater.

Fully 92% of our employees support the lower temperature. I recommend that we continue turning down the heat on weekends through the remainder of the heating season and that we resume the practice when the heat is turned on next fall.

Headings are optional in memos

Figure A.12   **Option 2 for Page 2 of a Memo**

1"–1 1/2"

February 18, 1998

To: Dorothy N. Blasingham

Writer's initials added in ink

Double- From: Roger L. Trout **R.L.T.**
space

Subject: Request for Third-Quarter Computer Training Sessions *Capitalize first letter of all major words in subject line*

¶ I never *Triple space*
has a
heading Could you please run advanced training sessions on using Lotus 1-2-3 and WordPerfect in   *5/8" – 1"*
April and May and basic training sessions for new hires in June?

Triple-space before a heading

Advanced Sessions on Lotus 1-2-3
Bold or underline headings
Once the tax season is over, Jose Cisneros wants to have his first- and second-year people take your advanced course on Lotus 1-2-3. Plan on about 45-50 people in three sessions. The *Double-* people in the course already use Lotus 1-2-3 for basic spreadsheets but need to learn the fine *space* points of macros and charting.
between
paragraphs
If possible, it would be most convenient to have the sessions run for four afternoons rather than for two full days.

Plain paper
for page 2   *1/2" – 1"*

Brief   *Page*
subject line or   *number*
Dorothy N. Blasingham ← *reader's name*   2   February 18, 1998

Also OK to line up page number, date at left under reader's

Same margins before the summer vacation season begins.
as p 1.

Orientation for New Hires *Capitalize first letter of all major words in heading*

With a total of 16 full-time and 34 part-time people being hired either for summer or permanent work, we'll need at least two and perhaps three orientation sessions. We'd like to hold these the first, second, and third weeks in June. By May 1, we should know how many people will be in each training session.

Would you be free to conduct training sessions on how to use our computers on June 8, June 15, and June 22? If we need only two dates, we'll use June 8 and June 15, but please block off the 22nd too in case we need a third session.

Triple-space before a heading
Request for Confirmation

Let me know whether you're free on these dates in June, and which dates you'd prefer for the sessions on Lotus 1-2-3 and WordPerfect. If you'll let me know by February 25, we can get information out to participants in plenty of time for the sessions.

Thanks!

Memos are initialed by   *Headings are optional*
To/From/Subject block   *in memos*

Post Office Abbreviations for States, Territories, and Provinces   **Figure A.13**

State Name	Post Office Abbreviation	State Name	Post Office Abbreviation	Territory	Post Office Abbreviation
Alabama	AL	Missouri	MO	Guam	GU
Alaska	AK	Montana	MT	Puerto Rico	PR
Arizona	AZ	Nebraska	NE	Virgin Islands	VI
Arkansas	AR	Nevada	NV		
California	CA	New Hampshire	NH		

State Name	Post Office Abbreviation	State Name	Post Office Abbreviation	Province Name	Post Office Abbreviation
Colorado	CO	New Jersey	NJ	Alberta	AB
Connecticut	CT	New Mexico	NM	British Columbia	BC
Delaware	DE	New York	NY	Labrador	LB
District of Columbia	DC	North Carolina	NC	Manitoba	MB
Florida	FL	North Dakota	ND	New Brunswick	NB
Georgia	GA	Ohio	OH	Newfoundland	NF
Hawaii	HI	Oklahoma	OK	Northwest Territories	NT
Idaho	ID	Oregon	OR	Nova Scotia	NS
Illinois	IL	Pennsylvania	PA	Ontario	ON
Indiana	IN	Rhode Island	RI	Prince Edward Island	PE
Iowa	IA	South Carolina	SC	Quebec	PQ
Kansas	KS	South Dakota	SD	Saskatchewan	SK
Kentucky	KY	Tennessee	TN	Yukon Territory	YT
Louisiana	LA	Texas	TX		
Maine	ME	Utah	UT		
Maryland	MD	Vermont	VT		
Massachusetts	MA	Virginia	VA		
Michigan	MI	Washington	WA		
Minnesota	MN	West Virginia	WV		
Mississippi	MS	Wisconsin	WI		
		Wyoming	WY		

Writing Correctly

Appendix Outline

Using Grammar
Agreement
Case
Dangling Modifier
Misplaced Modifier
Parallel Structure
Predication Errors

Understanding Punctuation

Punctuating Sentences
Comma Splices
Run-on Sentences (RO)
Sentence Fragments (Frag)

Punctuation within Sentences
Apostrophe
Colon

Comma
Dash
Hyphen
Parentheses
Period
Semicolon

Special Punctuation Marks
Quotation Marks
Square Brackets
Ellipses
Underlining and Italics

Writing Numbers and Dates

Words That Are Often Confused

Proofreading Symbols

An Inside Perspective:
Writing Correctly

Caroline Sanchez Crozier, President/CEO
Computer Services & Consulting, Inc.

Caroline Sanchez Crozier was named "Small Business Person of the Year" in 1993 by the State of Illinois. Computer Services & Consulting, in Chicago, Illinois, provides computer hardware and software sales, services, and support throughout the Midwest. The company's interactive software programs help children and adults improve reading, punctuation and grammar, usage, and spelling.

Communicating clearly with your clients is an important part of any business's success. Effective writing, presentation, and communication skills are essential. These skills are especially important to individuals running their own businesses. Your writing and grammar skills speak volumes about you.

Clients view clear, precise communication skills as a sign of the company being confident, knowledgeable, and caring. A company that takes the time to present well-written material to a customer or client is showing responsibility. A company that presents material filled with grammatical errors looks sloppy. To a consumer, sloppiness denotes a poorly run business. Clients will look instead to a company that takes care of details and can be relied upon to do quality work.

Technology, especially e-mail and the Internet, focuses on writing. Communicating through writing is replacing much of what used to be oral communication. Many employees and students rely on spelling and grammar checkers on their computers. These tools will not always save you. If an employer sees a mistake even after your work has been through a spell checker, you look careless. You did not take the time or did not care enough about your work to read through it.

Our company designs educational software with a focus on children who learn English as their second language (ESL). As an ESL student myself, I understand the importance of learning good grammar skills early on. Students need to overcome their fears of learning grammar. Be committed that you're just going to do it, and find a way to learn. You may want to find someone that you're comfortable with to read your material and critique it. Before you know it, you've improved. Or you may want to take courses on your own, such as the reading or grammar programs that I have. Computer learning is private: it's just between you and the computer.

There is only one way to become a better writer and that is to practice. Students should write often and constantly strive to strengthen their grammar skills.

Look at writing as a way to document the good things you do throughout your job. Keep a diary of your work habits, of your strengths, of the successes that only you know. Then when it's time for a review or time to talk about a promotion, you can provide this information. You are your best spokesperson.

Caroline Sanchez Crozier, February 19, 1997

Visit Computer Services & Consulting's Web site: http://www.julex.com

"Your writing and grammar skills speak volumes about you."

Carolyn Sanchez Crozier, Computer Services & Consulting, Inc.

Too much concern for correctness at the wrong stage of the writing process can backfire: writers who worry about grammar and punctuation when they're writing a first or second draft are more likely to get writer's block. Wait till you have your ideas on paper to check your draft for correct grammar, punctuation, typing of numbers and dates, and word use. Use the proofreading symbols at the end of the chapter to indicate changes needed in a typed copy.

Most writers make a small number of grammatical errors repeatedly. Most readers care deeply about only a few grammatical points. Keep track of the feedback you get (from your instructors now, from your supervisor later) and put your energy into correcting the errors that bother the people who read what you write. A command of standard grammar will help you build the credible, professional image you want to create with everything you write.

This appendix begins with a discussion of six grammatical issues: agreement, case, dangling and misplaced modifiers, parallel structure, and predication errors. The section on punctuating sentences shows you how to use periods, semicolons, and commas to avoid comma splices, run-on sentences, and sentence fragments. The section on punctuation within sentences covers apostrophes, colons, commas, dashes, hyphens, parentheses, and periods. The section on special punctuation covers marks used to quote material or for emphasis: quotation marks, square brackets, ellipses, and underlining and italics. Next, the appendix defines 50 pairs of words that are often confused and shows how to use them correctly. The last section shows you how to make changes in a typed draft when you proofread.

USING GRAMMAR

With the possible exception of spelling, grammar is the aspect of writing that writers seem to find most troublesome. Faulty grammar is often what executives are objecting to when they complain that college graduates or MBAs "can't write."

Agreement

Subjects and verbs agree when they are both singular or both plural.

Incorrect:	The accountants who conducted the audit was recommended highly.
Correct:	The accountants who conducted the audit were recommended highly.

Subject–verb agreement errors often occur when other words come between the subject and the verb. Edit your draft by finding the subject and the verb of each sentence.

American usage treats company names and the words *company* and *government* as singular nouns. British usage treats them as plural:

Correct (U.S.):	State Farm Insurance trains its agents well.

Correct
(Great
Britain):   Lloyds of London train their agents well.

Use a plural verb when two or more singular subjects are joined by *and*.

Correct: Larry McGreevy and I are planning to visit the client.

Use a singular verb when two or more singular subjects are joined by *or, nor,* or *but*.

Correct: Either the shipping clerk or the superintendent has to sign the order.

When the sentence begins with *Here* or *There,* make the verb agree with the subject that follows the verb.

Correct: Here is the booklet you asked for.

Correct: There are the blueprints I wanted.

Note that some words that end in *s* are considered to be singular and require singular verbs.

Correct: A series of meetings is planned.

When a situation doesn't seem to fit the rules, or when following a rule produces an awkward sentence, revise the sentence to avoid the problem.

Problematic: The Plant Manager in addition to the sales representative (was, were?) pleased with the new system.
Better: The Plant Manager and the sales representative were pleased with the new system.

Problematic: None of us (is, are?) perfect.
Better: All of us have faults.

Errors in **noun–pronoun agreement** occur if a pronoun is of a different number or person than the word it refers to.

Incorrect: All drivers of leased automobiles are billed $100 if damages to his automobile are caused by a collision.
Correct: All drivers of leased automobiles are billed $100 if damages to their automobiles are caused by collisions.

Incorrect: A manager has only yourself to blame if things go wrong.
Correct: As a manager, you have only yourself to blame if things go wrong.

The following words require a singular pronoun:

everybody	neither
each	nobody
either	a person
everyone	

Correct: Everyone should bring his or her copy of the manual to the next session on changes in the law.

If the pronoun pairs necessary to avoid sexism seem cumbersome, avoid the terms in this list. Instead, use words that take plural pronouns or use second-person *you*.

Each pronoun must refer to a specific word. If a pronoun does not refer to a specific term, add a word to correct the error.

The Errors That Bother People in Organizations*

Professor Maxine Hairston constructed a questionnaire with 65 sentences, each with one grammatical error. The administrators, executives, and business people who responded were most bothered by the following:

- Wrong verb forms ("he brung his secretary with him")
- Double negatives
- Objective pronoun used for subject of sentence ("Him and Richards were the last ones hired.")
- Sentence fragments
- Run-on sentences
- Failure to capitalize proper names
- "Would of" for "would have"
- Lack of subject–verb agreement
- Comma between verb and complement ("Cox cannot predict, that street crime will diminish.")
- Lack of parallelism
- Adverb errors ("He treats his men bad.") "Set" for "sit."

They also disliked

- Errors in word meaning
- Dangling modifiers
- "I" as objective pronoun ("The army moved my husband and I")
- Not setting off interrupters (e.g., "However") with commas
- Tense switching
- Plural modifiers with singular nouns.

*Based on Maxine Hairston, "Not All Errors Are Created Equal: Nonacademic Readers in the Professions Respond to Lapses in Usage," *College English* 43, no. 8 (December 1981):794–806.

Figure B.1

The Case of the Personal Pronoun

	Nominative (Subject of Clause)	Possessive	Objective	Reflexive/ Intensive
Singular				
1st person	I	my, mine	me	myself
2nd person	you	your, yours	you	yourself
3rd person	he/she/it	his/her(s)/its	him/her/it	himself/herself/itself
	one/who	one's/whose	one/whom	oneself/(no form)
Plural				
1st person	we	our, ours	us	ourselves
2nd person	you	your, yours	you	yourselves
3rd person	they	their, theirs	them	themselves

Incorrect: We will open three new stores in the suburbs. This will bring us closer to our customers.

Correct: We will open three new stores in the suburbs. This strategy will bring us closer to our customers.

Hint: Make sure *this* and *it* refer to a specific noun in the previous sentence. If either refers to an idea, add a noun ("this strategy") to make the sentence grammatically correct.

Use *who* and *whom* to refer to people and *which* to refer to objects. *That* can refer to anything: people, animals, organizations, and objects.

Correct: The new Executive Director, who moved here from Boston, is already making friends.

Correct: The information which she wants will be available tomorrow.

Correct: This confirms the price that I quoted you this morning.

Case

Case refers to the grammatical role a noun or pronoun plays in a sentence. Figure B.1 identifies the case of each personal pronoun.

Use **nominative** pronouns for the **subject** of a clause.

Correct: Shannon Weaver and I talked to the customer, who was interested in learning more about integrated software.

Use **possessive** pronouns to show who or what something belongs to.

Correct: Microsoft Office 97 will exactly meet her needs.

Use **objective** pronouns as **objects** of verbs or prepositions.

Correct: When you send in the quote, thank her for the courtesy she showed Shannon and me.

Hint: Use *whom* when *him* would fit grammatically in the same place in your sentence.

I am writing this letter to (who/whom?) it may concern.
I am writing this letter to him.
Whom is correct.

Have we decided (who, whom?) will take notes?
Have we decided he will take notes?
Who is correct.

Use **reflexive** and **intensive** pronouns to refer to or emphasize a noun or pronoun that has already appeared in the sentence.

Correct: I myself think the call was a very productive one.

Do not use reflexive pronouns as subjects of clauses or as objects of verbs or propositions.

Incorrect: Elaine and myself will follow up on this order.
Correct: Elaine and I will follow up on this order.

Incorrect: He gave the order to Dan and myself.
Correct: He gave the order to Dan and me.

Note that the first-person pronoun comes after names or pronouns that refer to other people.

Dangling Modifier (DM)

Modifiers are words or phrases that give more information about the subject, verb, or object in a clause. A modifier **dangles** when the word it modifies is not actually in the sentence. The solution is to reword the modifier so that it is grammatically correct.

Incorrect: Confirming our conversation, the truck will leave Monday.
               [The speaker is doing the confirming. But the speaker isn't in the sentence.]

Incorrect: At the age of eight, I began teaching my children about American business.
               [This sentence says that the author was eight when he or she had children who could understand business.]

Correct a dangling modifier in one of these ways:

■ Recast the modifier as a subordinate clause.

Correct: As I told you, the truck will leave Monday.

Correct: When they were eight, I began teaching my children about American business.

■ Revise the main clause so its subject or object can be modified by the now-dangling phrase.

Correct: Confirming our conversation, I have scheduled the truck to leave Monday.

Correct: At the age of eight, my children began learning about American business.

Hint: Whenever you use a verb or adjective that ends in *-ing*, make sure it modifies the grammatical subject of your sentence. If it doesn't, reword the sentence.

Misplaced Modifier (MM)

A **misplaced modifier** appears to modify another element of the sentence than the writer intended.

Anguished English*

Richard Lederer recorded the following howlers:

■ CEMETERY ALLOWS PEOPLE TO BE BURIED BY THEIR PETS.
■ KICKING BABY CONSIDERED TO BE HEALTHY
■ DIRECTOR OF TRUMAN LIBRARY KNOWS NEWSMAN'S PROBLEMS—HE WAS ONE.
■ MAN FOUND BEATEN, ROBBED BY POLICE

*Quoted from Richard Lederer, *More Anguished English* (New York: Delacorte Press, 1993), 166–67.

What Bothers Your Boss?

Most bosses care deeply about only a few points of grammar. Find out which errors are your supervisor's pet peeves, and avoid them.

Any living language changes. New usages appear first in speaking. Here are four issues on which experts currently disagree:

1. Plural pronouns to refer to *everybody, everyone,* and *each.* Standard grammar says these words require singular pronouns.
2. Split infinitives. An infinitive is the form of a verb that contains *to: to understand.* An infinitive is **split** when another word separates the *to* from the rest of an infinitive: *to easily understand.*
3. *Hopefully* to mean *I hope that. Hopefully* means "in a hopeful manner." However, a speaker who says "Hopefully, the rain will stop" is talking about the speaker's hope, not the rain's.
4. *Verbal* to mean *oral. Verbal* means "using words." Both writing and speaking are verbal communication. Nonverbal communication (for example, body language) does not use words.

Ask your instructor and your boss whether they are willing to accept the less formal usage. When you write to someone you don't know, use standard grammar and usage.

Incorrect: Customers who complain often alert us to changes we need to make. [Does the sentence mean that customers must complain frequently to teach us something? Or is the meaning that frequently we learn from complaints?]

Correct a misplaced modifier by moving it closer to the word it modifies or by adding punctuation to clarify your meaning. If a modifier modifies the whole sentence, use it as an introductory phrase or clause; follow it with a comma.

Correct: Often, customers who complain alert us to changes we need to make.

Parallel Structure

Items in a series or list must have the same grammatical structure.

Not parallel: In the second month of your internship, you will
                  1. Learn how to resolve customers' complaints.
                  2. Supervision of desk staff.
                  3. Interns will help plan store displays.

Parallel: In the second month of your internship, you will
                  1. Learn how to resolve customers' complaints.
                  2. Supervise desk staff.
                  3. Plan store displays.

Also parallel: Duties in the second month of your internship include resolving customers' complaints, supervising desk staff, and planning store displays.

Hint: When you have two or three items in a list (whether the list is horizontal or vertical) make sure the items are in the same grammatical form. Put lists vertically to make them easier to see.

Predication Errors

The predicate of a sentence must fit grammatically and logically with the subject.

In sentences using *is* and other linking verbs, the complement must be a noun, an adjective, or a noun clause.

Incorrect: The reason for this change is because the SEC now requires fuller disclosure.
Correct: The reason for this change is that the SEC now requires fuller disclosure.

Make sure that the verb describes the action done by or done to the subject.

Incorrect: Our goals should begin immediately.
Correct: Implementing our goals should begin immediately.

Understanding Punctuation

Punctuation marks are road signs to help readers predict what comes next.

When you move from the subject to the verb, you're going in a straight line; no comma is needed. When you end an introductory phrase or clause, the comma tells readers the introduction is over and you're turning to the main clause. When words interrupt the main clause, like this, commas tell

Mark	Tells the Reader
Period	We're stopping.
Semicolon	What comes next is closely related to what I just said.
Colon	What comes next is an example of what I just said.
Dash	What comes next is a dramatic example of or a shift from what I just said.
Comma	What comes next is a slight turn, but we're going in the same basic direction.

Figure B.2

What Punctuation Tells the Reader

the reader when to turn off the main clause for a short side route and when to return.

Some people have been told to put commas where they'd take breaths. That's bad advice. How often you'd take a breath depends on how big your lung capacity is, how fast and how loud you're speaking, and the emphasis you want. Commas aren't breaths. Instead, like other punctuation, they're road signs.

PUNCTUATING SENTENCES

A **sentence** contains at least one main clause. A **main clause** is a complete statement. A **subordinate** or **dependent clause** contains both a subject and verb but is not a complete statement and cannot stand by itself. A phrase is a group of words that do not contain both a subject and a verb.

Main clauses
  Your order will arrive Thursday.
  He dreaded talking to his supplier.
  I plan to enroll for summer school classes.
Subordinate clauses
  if you place your order by Monday
  because he was afraid the product would be out of stock
  since I want to graduate next spring
Phrases
  With our current schedule
  As a result
  After talking to my advisor

A clause with one of the following words will be subordinate:

after
although, though
because, since
before, until
if
when, whenever
while, as

Using the correct punctuation will enable you to avoid three major sentence errors: comma splices, run-on sentences, and sentence fragments.

Comma Splices (CS)

A **comma splice** or **comma fault** occurs when two main clauses are joined only by a comma (instead of by a comma and a coordinating conjunction).

The Most Common Errors in First-Year Composition Papers*

A survey of hundreds of student papers found that the following errors were most common:

1. No comma after introductory element
2. Vague pronoun reference
3. No comma in compound sentence
4. Wrong word
5. No comma in nonrestrictive clause
6. Wrong/missing inflected endings
7. Wrong or missing preposition
8. Comma splice
9. Possessive apostrophe error
10. Tense shift
11. Unnecessary shift in person
12. Sentence fragment
13. Wrong tense or verb form
14. Subject–verb agreement error
15. Lack of comma in series
16. Pronoun agreement error
17. Unnecessary comma with restrictive clause
18. Run-on or fused sentence
19. Dangling or misplaced modifier
20. Its/it's error

*Based on Robert J. Connors and Andrea A. Lunsford, "Frequency of Formal Errors in Current College Writing, or Ma and Pa Kettle Do Research," *College Composition and Communication* 39, no. 4 (December 1988): 403.

| Incorrect: | The contest will start in June, the date has not been set. |

Correct a comma splice in one of the following ways:

- If the ideas are closely related, use a semicolon rather than a comma. If they aren't closely related, start a new sentence.

| Correct: | The contest will start in June; the exact date has not been set. |

- Add a coordinating conjunction.

| Correct: | The contest will start in June, but the exact date has not been set. |

- Subordinate one of the clauses.

| Correct: | Although the contest will start in June, the date has not been set. |

Remember that you cannot use just a comma with the following transitions.

however
therefore
nevertheless
moreover

Instead, use a semicolon to separate the clauses or start a new sentence.

| Incorrect: | Computerized grammar checkers do not catch every error, however, they may be useful as a first check before an editor reads the material. |
| Correct: | Computerized grammar checkers do not catch every error. However, they may be useful as a first check before an editor reads the material. |

Run-on Sentences (RO)

A **run-on sentence** strings together several main clauses using *and, but, or, so,* and *for*. Run-on sentences and comma splices are "mirror faults." A comma splice uses *only* the comma and omits the coordinating conjunction, while a run-on sentence uses *only* the conjunction and omits the comma. Correct a short run-on sentence by adding a comma. Separate a long run-on sentence into two or more sentences. Consider subordinating one or more of the clauses.

| Incorrect: | We will end up with a much smaller markup but they use a lot of this material so the volume would be high so try to sell them on fast delivery and tell them our quality is very high. |
| Correct: | Although we will end up with a much smaller markup, volume would be high since they use a lot of this material. Try to sell them on fast delivery and high quality. |

Sentence Fragments (Frag)

In a **sentence fragment,** a group of words that is not a complete sentence is punctuated as if it were a complete sentence.

| Incorrect: | Observing these people, I have learned two things about the program. The time it takes. The rewards it brings. |

To fix a sentence fragment, either add whatever parts of the sentence are missing or incorporate the fragment into the sentence before it or after it.

| Correct: | Observing these people, I have learned that the program is time-consuming but rewarding. |

Remember that clauses with the following words are not complete sentences. Join them to a main clause.

after
although, though
because, since
before, until
if
when, whenever
while, as

Incorrect: We need to buy a new computer system. Because our current system is obsolete.

Correct: We need to buy a new computer system because our current system is obsolete.

PUNCTUATION WITHIN SENTENCES

The good business and administrative writer knows how to use the following punctuation marks: apostrophes, colons, commas, dashes, hyphens, parentheses, periods, and semicolons.

Apostrophe

1. Use an apostrophe in a contraction to indicate that a letter has been omitted.

   We're trying to renegotiate the contract.
   The '90s have been years of restructuring for our company.

2. To indicate possession, add an apostrophe and an *s* to the word.

   The corporation's home office is in Houston, Texas.

   Apostrophes to indicate possession are especially essential when one noun in a comparison is omitted.

   This year's sales will be higher than last year's.

   When a word already ends in an *s*, add only an apostrophe to make it possessive.

   The meeting will be held at New Orleans' convention center.

   With many terms, the placement of the apostrophe indicates whether the noun is singular or plural.

   Incorrect: The program should increase the participant's knowledge.
   [Implies that only one participant is in the program.]

   Correct: The program should increase the participants' knowledge.
   [Many participants are in the program.]

Hint: Use "of" in the sentence to see where the apostrophe goes.

   The figures of last year = last year's figures
   The needs of our customers = our customers' needs

Note that possessive pronouns (e.g., *his, ours*) usually do not have apostrophes. The only exception is *one's*.

The Fumblerules of Grammar*

1. Avoid run-on sentences they are hard to read.
2. A writer must not shift your point of view.
3. Verbs has to agree with their subjects.
4. No sentence fragments.
5. Reserve the apostrophe for it's proper use and omit it when its not needed.
6. Proofread carefully to see if you any words out.
7. Avoid commas, that are unnecessary.
8. Steer clear of incorrect forms of verbs that have snuck in the language.
9. In statements involving two word phrases make an all out effort to use hyphens.
10. Last but not least, avoid clichés like the plague; seek viable alternatives.

*Quoted from William Safire, "On Language: The Fumblerules of Grammar," *New York Times Magazine*, November 11, 1979, 16, and "On Language: Fumblerule Follow-up," *New York Times Magazine*, November 25, 1979, 14.

The company needs the goodwill of its stockholders.
His promotion was announced yesterday.
One's greatest asset is the willingness to work hard.

3. Use an apostrophe to make plurals that could be confused for other words.

I earned A's in all my business courses.

However, other plurals do not use apostrophes.

Colon

1. Use a colon to separate a main clause and a list that explains the last element in the clause. The items in the list are specific examples of the word that appears immediately before the colon.

Please order the following supplies:
Printer ribbons
Computer paper (20-lb. white bond)
Bond paper (25-lb., white, 25% cotton)
Company letterhead
Company envelopes.

When the list is presented vertically, capitalize the first letter of each item in the list. When the list is run in with the sentence, you don't need to capitalize the first letter after the colon.

Please order the following supplies: printer ribbons, computer paper (20-lb. white bond), bond paper (25-lb., white, 25% cotton), company letterhead, and company envelopes.

Do not use a colon when the list is grammatically part of the main clause.

Incorrect:	The rooms will have coordinated decors in natural colors such as: eggplant, moss, and mushroom.
Correct:	The rooms will have coordinated decors in natural colors such as eggplant, moss, and mushroom.
	or
Correct:	The rooms will have coordinated decors in a variety of natural colors: eggplant, moss, and mushroom.

If the list is presented vertically, some authorities suggest introducing the list with a colon even though the words preceding the colon are not a complete sentence.

2. Use a colon to join two independent clauses when the second clause explains or restates the first clause.

Selling is simple: give people the service they need, and they'll come back with more orders.

Comma

1. Use commas to separate the main clause from an introductory clause, the reader's name, or words that interrupt the main clause. Note that commas both precede and follow the interrupting information.

R. J. Garcia, the new Sales Manager, comes to us from the Des Moines office.

A **nonessential clause** gives extra information that is not needed to identify the noun it modifies. Because nonessential clauses give extra information, they need extra commas.

THE HISTORY OF PUNCTUATION*

WHEN WRITING BEGAN THERE WERE NO BREAKS BETWEEN WORDS
In inscriptions on monuments in ancient Greece, breaks were chosen to create balance and proportion.
WHEN WRITI
NG BEGAN TH
ERE WERE NO
BREAKS BET
WEEN WORDS
In the third century BC, Aristophanes added a dot high in the line (like this ·), after a complete thought, or *periodos*. For part of a complete thought, or *colon,* he used a dot on the line (like this .). For a comma, or subdivision of a colon, he used a dot halfway up (like this ·).
The monks in the Middle Ages substituted a strong slash for the midway dot. As time went on, the strong slash was shortened and acquired a curl—becoming our comma today.

*Based on Lionel Casson, "how and why punctuation ever came to be invented," *Smithsonian* 19, no. 7 (October 1988), 216.

Sue Decker, who wants to advance in the organization, has signed up for the company training program in sales techniques.

Do not use commas to set off information that restricts the meaning of a noun or pronoun. **Essential clauses** give essential, not extra, information.

Anyone ☐ who wants to advance in the organization ☐ should take advantage ofon-the-job training.

Do not use commas to separate the subject from the verb, even if you would take a breath after a long subject.

Incorrect:	Laws requiring anyone collecting $5,000 or more on behalf of another person, apply to schools and private individuals as well to charitable groups and professional fund-raisers.
Correct:	Laws requiring anyone collecting $5000 or more on behalf of another person ☐ apply to schools and private individuals as well to charitable groups and professional fund-raisers.

2. Use a comma after the first clause in a compound sentence if the clauses are long or if they have different subjects.

This policy eliminates all sick leave credit of the employee at the time of retirement, and payment will be made only once to any individual.

Do not use commas to join independent clauses without a conjunction. Doing so produces comma splices.

3. Use commas to separate items in a series. Using a comma before the *and* or *or* is not required by some authorities, but using a comma always adds clarity. The comma is essential if any of the items in the series themselves contain the word *and*.

The company pays the full cost of hospitalization insurance for eligible employees, spouses, and unmarried dependent children under age 23.

Dash

Use dashes to emphasize a break in thought.

Ryertex comes in 30 grades—each with a special use.

To type a dash, use two hyphens with no space before or after.

Hyphen

1. Use a hyphen to indicate that a word has been divided between two lines.

Attach the original receipts for lodging, meals, tips, transportation, and registration fees.

Divide words at syllable breaks. If you aren't sure where the syllables divide, look up the word in a dictionary. When a word has several syllables, divide it after a vowel or between two consonants. Don't divide words of one syllable (e.g., *used*); don't divide a two-syllable word if one of the syllables is only one letter long (e.g., *acre*).

2. Use hyphens to join two or more words used as a single adjective.

Order five 10- or 12-foot lengths.
The computer-prepared Income and Expense statements will be ready next Friday.

The hyphen prevents misreading. In the first example, five lengths are
needed, not lengths of 5, 10, or 12 feet. In the second example, without
the hyphen, the reader might think that *computer* was the subject and
prepared was the verb.

Parentheses

1. Use parentheses to set off words, phrases, or sentences used to explain or
   comment on the main idea.

   > For the thinnest Ryertex (.015″) only a single layer of the base material may be
   > used, while the thickest (10″) may contain over 600 greatly compressed layers
   > of fabric or paper. By varying the fabric used (cotton, asbestos, glass, or nylon)
   > or the type of paper, and by changing the kind of resin (phenolic, melamine,
   > silicone, or epoxy), we can produce 30 different grades.

   Any additional punctuation goes outside the second parenthesis when
   the punctuation applies to the whole sentence. It goes inside when it
   applies only to the words in the parentheses.

   > Please check the invoice to see if credit should be issued. (A copy of the invoice
   > is attached.)

2. Use parentheses for the second of two numbers presented both in words
   and in figures.

   > Construction must be completed within two (2) years of the date of the contract.

Period

1. Use a period at the end of a sentence. Leave two spaces before the next
   sentence.

2. Use a period after some abbreviations. When a period replaces a person's
   name, leave one space after the period before the next word. In other
   abbreviations, no space is necessary.

   > R. J. Tebeaux has been named Vice President for Marketing.
   > The U.S. division plans to hire 300 new M.B.A.s in the next year.

   The tendency is to reduce the use of punctuation. It would also be correct
   to write

   > The US division plans to hire 300 new MBAs in the next year.

Semicolon

1. Use semicolons to join two independent clauses when they are closely
   related.

   > We'll do our best to fill your order promptly; however, we cannot guarantee a
   > delivery date.

   Using a semicolon suggests that the two ideas are very closely connected.
   Using a period and a new sentence is also correct but implies nothing
   about how closely related the two sentences are.

2. Use semicolons to separate items in a series when the items themselves
   contain commas.

   > The final choices for the new plant are El Paso, Texas; Albuquerque, New
   > Mexico; Salt Lake City, Utah; Eureka, California; and Eugene, Oregon.

Hospital benefits are also provided for certain specialized care services such as diagnostic admissions directed toward a definite disease or injury; normal maternity delivery, Caesarean section delivery, or complications of pregnancy; and in-patient admissions for dental procedures necessary to safeguard the patient's life or health.

Hint: A semicolon could be replaced by a period and a capital letter. It has a sentence on both sides.

SPECIAL PUNCTUATION MARKS

Quotation marks, square brackets, ellipses, and underlining are necessary when you use quoted material.

Quotation Marks

1. Use quotation marks around the names of brochures, pamphlets, and magazine articles.

    Enclosed are 30 copies of our pamphlet "Saving Energy."

    You'll find articles like "How to Improve Your Golf Game" and "Can You Keep Your Eye on the Ball?" in every issue.

    In US punctuation, periods and commas go inside quotation marks. Colons and semicolons go outside. Question marks go inside if they are part of the material being quoted.

2. Use quotation marks around words to indicate that you think the term is misleading.

    These "pro-business" policies actually increase corporate taxes.

3. Use quotation marks around words that you are discussing as words.

    Forty percent of the respondents answered "yes" to the first question.
    Use "Ms." as a courtesy title for a woman unless you know she prefers another title.

    It is also acceptable to use underlining or italicize words instead of using quotation marks.

4. Use quotation marks around words or sentences that you quote from someone else.

    "The Fog Index," says its inventor, Robert Gunning, is "an effective warning system against drifting into needless complexity."

Square Brackets

Use square brackets to add your own additions to or changes in quoted material.

Senator Smith's statement: "These measures will increase the deficit."

Your use of Smith's statement:	According to Senator Smith, "These measures [in the new tax bill] will increase the deficit."

The square brackets show that Smith did not say these words; you add them to make the quote make sense in your document.

Ellipses

Ellipses are spaced dots. In typing, use three spaced periods for an ellipsis. When an ellipsis comes at the end of a sentence, use a dot immediately after the last letter of the sentence for a period. Then add three spaced dots. Two spaces follow the last of the four dots.

1. Use ellipses to indicate that one or more words have been omitted in the middle of quoted material. You do not need ellipses at the beginning or end of a quote.

   The Wall Street Journal notes that Japanese magazines and newspapers include advertisements for a "$2.1 million home in New York's posh Riverdale section . . . 185 acres of farmland [and] . . . luxury condos on Manhattan's Upper East Side."

2. In advertising and direct mail, use ellipses to imply the pace of spoken comments.

   If you've ever wanted to live on a tropical island . . . cruise to the Bahamas . . . or live in a castle in Spain . . .
   . . . you can make your dreams come true with Vacations Extraordinaire.

Underlining and Italics

1. Underline or italicize the names of newspapers, magazines, and books.

   The Wall Street Journal   *The Wall Street Journal*
   Fortune   *Fortune*
   The Wealth of Nations   *The Wealth of Nations*

   Titles of brochures and pamphlets are put in quotation marks.

2. Underline or italicize words to emphasize them.

   Here's a bulletin that gives you, in handy chart form, workable data on over 50 different types of tubing and pipe.

   If you have a printer that has a bold typeface, you may use bold to emphasize words.

WRITING NUMBERS AND DATES

Spell out **numbers** from one to nine. Use figures for numbers 10 and over in most cases. Always use figures for amounts of money.

Spell out any number that appears at the beginning of a sentence. If spelling it out is impractical, revise the sentence so that it does not begin with a number.

Fifty students filled out the survey.
The year 1992 marked the official beginning of the European Economic Community.

When two numbers follow each other, use words for the smaller number and figures for the larger number.

In **dates,** use figures for the day and year. The month is normally spelled out. Be sure to spell out the month in international business communication. American usage puts the month first, so that *1/10/97* means *January 10, 1997.* European usage puts the day first, so that *1/10/97* means *October 1, 1997.* Modern punctuation uses a comma before the year only when you give both the month and the day of the month:

May 1, 1998
but
Summers 1997–90
August 1998
Fall 1997

No punctuation is needed in military or European usage, which puts the day of the month first: 13 July 1998. Do not space before or after the slash used to separate parts of the date: 5/97-10/98.

Use a hyphen to join inclusive dates.

March-August 1997 **(or write out:** March to August 1997**)**
'98-'99
1996-2000

Note that you do not need to repeat the century in the date that follows the hyphen: 1998-99.

WORDS THAT ARE OFTEN CONFUSED

Here's a list of words that are frequently confused. Master them, and you'll be well on the way to using words correctly.

1. accede/exceed
   accede: to yield
   exceed: to go beyond, surpass
   I accede to your demand that we not exceed the budget.
2. accept/except
   accept: to receive
   except: to leave out or exclude; but
   I accept your proposal except for point 3.
3. access/excess
   access: the right to use; admission to
   excess: surplus
   As supply clerk, he had access to any excess materials.
4. adept/adopt
   adept: skilled
   adopt: to take as one's own
   She was adept at getting people to adopt her ideas.
5. advice/advise
   advice: (noun) counsel
   advise: (verb) to give counsel or advice to someone
   I asked him to advise me but I didn't like the advice I got.
6. affect/effect
   affect: (verb) to influence or modify
   effect: (verb) to produce or cause; (noun) result
   He hoped that his argument would affect his boss' decision, but so far as he could see, it had no effect.
   The tax relief effected some improvement for the citizens whose incomes had been affected by inflation.
7. affluent/effluent
   affluent: (adjective) rich, possessing in abundance
   effluent: (noun) something that flows out
   Affluent companies can afford the cost of removing pollutants from the effluents their factories produce.

More Anguished English*

- Family Physician. Hours: 10:30-12:20-3:30-4:45 Monday-Friday, 10:30-11:45 Saturday. Limited Amount of Patience.
- Aunt and Roach Killer—1.29.
- He is recovering from a near-fatal accident that sent him into a comma.
- The board voted by telephone pole.
- I found a liter of pups.

*Quoted from Richard Lederer, *More Anguished English* (New York: Delacorte Press, 1993), 166–67.

8. a lot/allot

a lot: many (informal)

allot: divide or give to

A lot of players signed up for this year's draft. We allotted one first-round draft choice to each team.

9. amount/number

amount: (use with concepts that cannot be counted individually but can only be measured)

number: (use when items can be counted individually)

It's a mistake to try to gauge the amount of interest he has by the number of questions he asks.

10. are/our

are: (plural linking verb)

our: belonging to us

Are we ready to go ahead with our proposal?

11. attributed/contributed

attributed: was said to be caused by

contributed: gave something to

The rain probably contributed to the accident, but the police officer attributed the accident to driver error.

12. between/among

between: (use with only two choices)

among: (use with more than two choices)

This year the differences between the two candidates for president are unusually clear.

I don't see any major differences among the candidates for city council.

13. cite/sight/site

cite: (verb) to quote

sight: (noun) vision, something to be seen

site: (noun) location, place where a building is or will be built

She cited the old story of the building inspector who was depressed by the very sight of the site for the new factory.

14. complement/compliment

complement: (verb) to complete, finish; (noun) something that completes

compliment: (verb) to praise; (noun) praise

The compliment she gave me complemented my happiness.

15. compose/comprise

compose: make up, create

comprise: consist of, be made up of, be composed of

The city council is composed of 12 members. Each district comprises an area 50 blocks square.

16. confuse/complicate/exacerbate

confuse: to bewilder

complicate: to make more complex or detailed

exacerbate: to make worse

Because I missed the first 20 minutes of the movie, I didn't understand what was going on. The complicated plot exacerbated my confusion.

17. dependant/dependent

dependant: (noun) someone for whom one is financially responsible

dependent: (adjective) relying on someone else

IRS regulations don't let us count our 25-year-old son as a dependant, but he is still financially dependent on us.

18. describe/prescribe

    describe: list the features of something, tell what something looks like

    prescribe: specify the features something must contain

    > The law prescribes the priorities for making repairs. This report describes our plans to comply with the law.

19. discreet/discrete

    discreet: tactful, careful not to reveal secrets

    discrete: separate, distinct

    > I have known him to be discreet on two discrete occasions.

20. do/due

    do: (verb) act or make

    due: (adjective) scheduled, caused by

    > The banker said she would do her best to change the due date.

    > Due to the computer system, the payroll can be produced in only two days for all 453 employees.

21. elicit/illicit

    elicit: (verb) to draw out

    illicit: (adjective) not permitted, unlawful

    > The reporter could elicit no information from the Senator about his illicit love affair.

22. eminent/immanent/imminent

    eminent: distinguished

    immanent: dwelling within tangible objects

    imminent: about to happen

    > The eminent doctor believed that death was imminent. The eminent minister believed that God was immanent.

23. fewer/less

    fewer: (use for objects that can be counted individually)

    less: (use for objects that can be measured but not counted individually)

    > There is less sand in this bucket; there are probably fewer grains of sand, too.

24. forward/foreword

    forward: ahead

    foreword: preface, introduction

    > The author looked forward to writing the foreword to the book.

25. good/well

    good: (adjective, used to modify nouns; as a noun, means something that is good)

    well: (adverb, used to modify verbs, adjectives, and other adverbs)

    > Her words "Good work!" told him that he was doing well.

    > He spent a great deal of time doing volunteer work because he believed that doing good was just as important as doing well.

26. i.e./e.g.

    i.e.: (*id est*—that is) introduces a restatement or explanation of the preceding word or phrase

    e.g.: (*exempli gratia*—for the sake of an example; for example) introduces one or more examples

    > Although he had never studied Latin, he rarely made a mistake in using Latin abbreviations, e.g., i.e., etc., because he associated each with a mnemonic device (i.e., a word or image used to help one remember something). He remembered *i.e.* as *in effect*, pretended that *e.g.* meant *example given*, and used *etc.* only when *examples to continue* would fit.

The Knead for Approve Reed Her with a Spell Chequer

Who wood have guest
The Spell Chequer would
super seed
The assent of the editor
Who was once a mane
figure? . . .
Once, awl sought his council;
Now nun prophet from him.
How suite the job was;
It was all sew fine. . . .
Never once was he board
As he edited each claws,
Going strait to his deer work
Where he'd in cyst on clarity.
Now he's holy unacceptable,
Useless and knot
kneaded. . . .
This is know miner issue,
Fore he cannot urn a wage.
Two this he takes a fence,
Butt nose naught watt too
due.
He's wade each option
Of jobs he mite dew,
But nothing peaks his interest
Like making pros clear.
Sum will see him silly
For being sew upset,
But doesn't good righting
Go beyond the write spelling?

*Quoted from Jeff Lovill, "On the Uselessness of an Editor in the Presents of a Spell Chequer," *Technical Communication* 35, no. 4 (1988), 267, and Edward M. Chilton, "Various Comments on 4Q88," *Technical Communication* 36, no. 2 (1989), 173.

27. imply/infer
    imply: suggest, put an idea into someone's head
    infer: deduce, get an idea out from something
    > She implied that an announcement would be made soon. I inferred from her smile that it would be an announcement of her promotion.
28. it's/its
    it's: it is, it has
    its: belonging to it
    > It's clear that a company must satisfy its customers to stay in business.
29. lectern/podium
    lectern: raised stand with a slanted top that holds a manuscript for a reader or notes for a speaker
    podium: platform for a speaker or conductor to stand on
    > I left my notes on the lectern when I left the podium at the end of my talk.
30. lie/lay
    lie: to recline; to tell a falsehood (never takes an object)
    lay: to put an object on something (always takes an object)
    > He was laying the papers on the desk when I came in, but they aren't lying there now.
31. loose/lose
    loose: not tight
    lose: to have something disappear
    > If I lose weight, this suit will be loose.
32. moral/morale
    moral: (adjective) virtuous, good; (noun: morals) ethics, sense of right and wrong
    morale: (noun) spirit, attitude, mental outlook
    > Studies have shown that coed dormitories improve student morale without harming student morals.
33. objective/rationale
    objective: goal
    rationale: reason, justification
    > The objective of the meeting was to explain the rationale behind the decision.
34. personal/personnel
    personal: individual, to be used by one person
    personnel: staff, employees
    > All personnel will get personal computers by the end of the year.
35. possible/possibly
    possible: (adjective) something that can be done
    possibly: (adverb) perhaps
    > It is possible that we will be able to hire this spring. We can choose from possibly the best graduating class in the past five years.
36. precede/proceed
    precede: (verb) to go before
    proceed: (verb) to continue; (noun: proceeds) money
    > Raising the money must precede spending it. Only after we obtain the funds can we proceed to spend the proceeds.
37. principal/principle
    principal: (adjective) main; (noun) person in charge; money lent out at interest
    principle: (noun) basic truth or rule, code of conduct
    > *The Prince*, Machiavelli's principal work, describes his principles for ruling a state.

38. quiet/quite
    quiet: not noisy
    quite: very
    > It was quite difficult to find a quiet spot anywhere near the floor of the stock exchange.

39. regulate/relegate
    regulate: control
    relegate: put (usually in an inferior position)
    > If the federal government regulates the size of lettering on country road signs, we may as well relegate the current signs to the garbage bin.

40. residence/residents
    residence: home
    residents: people who live in a building
    > The residents had different reactions when they learned that a shopping mall would be built next to their residence.

41. respectfully/respectively
    respectfully: with respect
    respectively: to each in the order listed
    > When I was introduced to the Queen, the Prime Minister, and the court jester, I bowed respectfully, shook hands politely, and winked, respectively.

42. role/roll
    role: part in a play or script, function (in a group)
    roll: (noun) list of students, voters, or other members; round piece of bread; (verb) move by turning over and over
    > While the teacher called the roll, George—in his role as class clown—threw a roll he had saved from lunch.

43. simple/simplistic
    simple: not complicated
    simplistic: watered down, oversimplified
    > She was able to explain the proposal in simple terms without making the explanation sound simplistic.

44. stationary/stationery
    stationary: not moving, fixed
    stationery: paper
    > During the earthquake, even the stationery was not stationary.

45. their/there/they're
    their: belonging to them
    there: in that place
    they're: they are
    > There are plans, designed to their specifications, for the house they're building.

46. to/too/two
    to: (preposition) function word indicating proximity, purpose, time, etc.
    too: (adverb) also, very, excessively
    two: (adjective) the number 2
    > The formula is too secret to entrust to two people.

47. unique/unusual
    unique: sole, only, alone
    unusual: not common
    > I believed that I was unique in my ability to memorize long strings of numbers until I consulted the *Guinness Book of World Records* and found that I was merely unusual: someone else had equalled my feat in 1993.

Spelling Demons

The words listed below (in order of increasing difficulty) are among the most frequently misspelled words in English. How many of them do you spell correctly?

1. Grammar
2. Argument
3. Surprise
4. Achieve
5. Definitely
6. Separate
7. Desirable
8. Development
9. Existence
10. Occasion
11. Assistant
12. Repetition
13. Privilege
14. Dependent
15. Consensus
16. Accommodate
17. Occurrence
18. Commitment
19. Allotted
20. Liaison
21. Proceed
22. Harass
23. Dissention
24. Prerogative
25. Inadvertent

*Based on Bruce O. Boston, ed., *Stet!* (Alexandria, VA: Editorial Experts, 1986), 267–68.

48. verbal/oral
    verbal: using words
    oral: spoken, not written
       His verbal skills were uneven: his oral communication was excellent,
       but he didn't write well. His sensitivity to nonverbal cues was acute:
       he could tell what kind of day I had just by looking at my face.
    Hint: Oral comes from the Latin word for mouth, **os.** Think of Oral-B
    Toothbrushes: For the mouth. Verbal comes from the Latin word for
    word, **verba.** Nonverbal language is language that does not use words
    (e.g., body language, gestures).
49. whether/weather
    whether: (conjunction) used to introduce possible alternatives
    weather: (noun) state of the atmosphere: wet or dry, hot or cold, calm or
    storm
       We will have to see what the weather is before we decide whether to
       hold the picnic indoors or out.
50. your/you're
    your: belonging to you
    you're: you are
       You're the top candidate for promotion in your division.

PROOFREADING SYMBOLS

Use the proofreading symbols in Figure B.3 to make corrections when you no
longer have access to a typewriter. Figure B.4 shows how the symbols can be
used to correct a typed text.

Figure B.3

Proofreading Symbols

✐	delete
ⸯ	insert a letter
⁋	start a new paragraph here
(stet)	stet (leave as it was before the marked change)
(tr) ⌐	transpose (reverse)
(lc)	lower case (don't capitalize)
≡	capitalize
[	move to left
]	move to right
⌐	move up
⌐	move down
#	leave a space
⌢	close up
‖	align vertically

Figure B.4

Marked Text

We could cut our travel bill by reimbursing employees only for the cost of a budget hotel or motel room.

A recent article from *The Wall Street Journal* suggests that many low-cost hotles and motels are tring to appeal to business travelers. chains that are actively competing for the business market include

Motel 6
Hampton Inns
   Fairfield Inns
Econologde
Super 8

Comfort Inn
Travelodge.

To attract business travelers, some budget chains now offer free local phone calls, free in-room movies, free continental breakfasts and free Computer hookups.

By staying in a budget hotel, the business travelers can save at least $10 to $20 a night--often much more. For a company whose employees travel frequently, the savings can be considerable. Last year Megacorp reimbursed employees for a total of 4,392 nights in hotels. If each employee had stayed in a budget hotel, our expenses for travel would be en $44,000 to $88,000 lower. Budget hotels would not be appropriate for sales meetings since they lack photocopying facilities or meeting rooms. However, we could and should use budget hotels and motels for ordinary on-the-road travel.

Exercises and Problems
For Appendix B

B–1 Diagnostic Test on Punctuation and Grammar

Identify and correct the errors in the following passages.

a. | Company's are finding it to their advantage to cultivate their suppliers. Partnerships between a company and it's suppliers can yield hefty payoffs for both company and supplier. One example is Bailey Controls, an Ohio headquartered company. Bailey make control systems for big factories. They treat suppliers almost like departments of their own company. When a Bailey employee passes a laser scanner over a bins bar code the supplier is instantly alerted to send more parts.

b. | Entrepreneur Trip Hawkins appears in Japanese ads for the video game system his company designed. "It plugs into the future! he says in one ad, in a cameo spliced into shots of U.S kids playing the games. Hawkins is one of several US celebrieties and business people whom plug products on Japanese TV. Jodie Foster, harrison ford, and Charlie Sheen adverstises canned coffee beer and cigarettes respectively.

c. | Mid size firms employing between 100 and 1000 peopole represent only 4% of companies in the U.S.; but create 33% of all new jobs. One observe attributes their success to their being small enough to take advantage of economic opportunity's agilely, but big enough to have access to credit and to operate on a national or even international scale. The biggest hiring area for midsize company's is wholesale and retail sales (38% of jobs), construction (20% of jobs, manufacturing (19% of jobs), and services (18 of jobs).

B–2 Providing Punctuation

Provide the necessary punctuation in the following sentences. Note that not every box requires punctuation.

1. The system □ s □ user □ friendly design □ provides screen displays of work codes □ rates □ and client information.
2. Many other factors also shape the organization □ s □ image □ advertising □ brochures □ proposals □ stationery □ calling cards □ etc.
3. Charlotte Ford □ author of □ Charlotte Ford □ s □ Book of Modern Manners □ □ says □ □ Try to mention specifics of the conversation to fix the interview permanently in the interviewer □ s □ mind and be sure to mail the letter the same day □ before the hiring decision is made □ □
4. What are your room rates and charges for food service □
5. We will need accommodations for 150 people □ five meeting rooms □ one large room and four small ones □ □ coffee served during morning and afternoon breaks □ and lunches and dinners.
6. The Operational Readiness Inspection □ which occurs once every three years □ is a realistic exercise □ which evaluates the National Guard □ s □ ability to mobilize □ deploy □ and fight.
7. Most computer packages will calculate three different sets of percentages □ row percentages □ column percentages □ and table percentages □
8. In today □ s □ economy □ it □ s almost impossible for a firm to extend credit beyond it □ s regular terms.
9. The Department of Transportation does not have statutory authority to grant easements □ however □ we do have authority to lease unused areas of highway right □ of □ way.
10. The program has two goals □ to identify employees with promise □ and to see that they get the training they need to advance.

B–3   Providing Punctuation

Provide the necessary punctuation in the following sentences. Note that not every box requires punctuation.

1. To reduce secretaries ☐ overtime hours ☐ the office should hire part ☐ time secretaries to work from 5 to 9 p.m.
2. Since memberships can begin at any time during the year ☐ all member ☐ s ☐ dues are recognized on a cash basis when they are received.
3. I would be interested in working on the committee ☐ however ☐ I have decided to do less community work so that I have more time to spend with my family.
4. One of the insurance companies ☐ American Family Corp ☐ ☐ Columbus ☐ GA ☐ said it hopes to persuade the FASB to reconsider the rule.
5. The city already has five ☐ two ☐ hundred ☐ bed hospitals.
6. Students run the whole organization ☐ and are advised by a Board of Directors from the community.
7. I suggest putting a bulletin board in the rear hallway with all the interviewer ☐ s ☐ pictures on it.
8. ☐ Most African-American businesses just get enough money to open the doors ☐ ☐ says Mr. Quinn ☐ adding ☐ that the $10,000 or so of savings he used to start up simply wasn ☐ t enough ☐ ☐
9. Otis Conward, Jr ☐ ☐ who grew up in this area ☐ now heads the Council for Economic development.
10. Volunteers also participate in a one ☐ on ☐ one pal program.

B–4   Editing for Grammar and Usage

Revise these sentences to correct errors in grammar and usage.

1. As one of the students in a good program, our company is interested in interviewing you.
2. By making an early reservation, it will give us more time to coordinate our trucks to better serve your needs.
3. Videoconferencing can be frustrating. Simply because little time is available for casual conversation.
4. Often documents end up in files that aren't especially good.
5. Pay yourself with the Automatic Savings Account, with this account any amount your choose will be transferred automatically from your checking account to your savings account each month.
6. We help clients
   - Manage change
   - Marketing/promotion
   - Developing better billing systems.
7. My education and training has prepared me to contribute to your company.
8. Employees which lack experience in dealing with people from other cultures may benefit from seminars in international business communication.
9. A team of people from marketing, finance, and production are preparing the proposal.
10. A new employee should try to read verbal and nonverbal signals to see which aspects of your job are most important.

B–5   Editing for Grammar and Usage

Revise the following sentences to eliminate errors in grammar and usage.

1. The number of students surveyed that worked more than 20 hours a week was 60%.
2. Not everyone is promoted after six months some people might remain in the training program a year before being moved to a permanent assignment.
3. The present solutions that has been suggested are not adequate.
4. At times while typing and editing, the text on your screen may not look correct.

5. All employees are asked to cut back on energy waste by the manager.
6. The benefits of an on-line catalog are
   1. We will be able to keep records up-to-date;
   2. Broad access to the catalog system from any networked terminal on campus;
   3. The consolidation of the main catalog and the catalogs in the departmental and branch libraries;
   4. Cost savings.

7. You can take advantage of several banking services. Such as automatic withdrawal of a house or car payment and direct deposit of your pay check.
8. As a freshman, business administration was intriguing to me.
9. Thank you for the help you gave Joanne Jackson and myself.
10. I know from my business experience that good communication among people and departments are essential in running a successful corporation.

B–6   Editing for Grammar and Usage

Revise the following sentences to eliminate errors in grammar and usage.

1. If a group member doesn't complete their assigned work, it slows the whole project down.
2. Our phones are constantly being used. Not only for business calls, but also for personal calls.
3. Todd drew the graphs after him and I discussed the ideas for them.
4. Originally a group of four, a member dropped out after the first meeting due to a death in the family.
5. Our group met seven times outside of class, we would have met even more if we could have found times when we could all get together.

6. There has also been suggestions for improving the airflow in the building.
7. I didn't appreciate him assuming that he would be the group's leader.
8. With people like yourself giving gifts, the 4-H program will be able to survive and grow.
9. Volunteers need a better orientation to Planned Parenthood as a whole, to the overall clinic function, and to the staff there is also a need to clarify volunteer responsibilities.
10. Children are referred to the Big Brother/Big Sister program by their school social workers, often from underprivileged homes.

B–7   Using Plurals and Possessives

Choose the right word for each sentence.

1. Many Canadian (companies, company's) are competing effectively in the global market.
2. We can move your (families, family's) furniture safely and efficiently.
3. The (managers, manager's) ability to listen is just as important as his or her technical knowledge.
4. A (memos, memo's) style can build goodwill.
5. (Social workers, social worker's) should tell clients about services available in the community.

6. The (companies, company's) benefits plan should be checked periodically to make sure it continues to serve the needs of employees.
7. Information about the new community makes the (families, family's) move easier.
8. The (managers, manager's) all have open-door policies.
9. (Memos, memo's) are sent to other workers in the same organization.
10. Burnout affects a (social workers, social worker's) productivity as well as his or her morale.

B–8   Choosing the Right Word

Choose the right word for each sentence.

1. Exercise is (good, well) for patients who have had open-heart surgery.

2. This response is atypical, but it is not (unique, unusual).

3. The personnel department continues its (roll, role) of compiling reports for the federal government.
4. The Accounting Club expects (its, it's) members to come to meetings and participate in activities.
5. Part of the fun of any vacation is (cite, sight, site)-seeing.
6. The (lectern, podium) was too high for the short speaker.
7. The (residence, residents) of the complex have asked for more parking spaces.

8. Please order more letterhead (stationary, stationery).
9. The closing of the plant will (affect, effect) house prices in the area.
10. Better communication (among, between) design and production could enable us to produce products more efficiently.

B–9 Choosing the Right Word

Choose the right word for each sentence.

1. The audit revealed a small (amount, number) of errors.
2. Diet beverages have (fewer, less) calories than regular drinks.
3. In her speech, she (implied, inferred) that the vote would be close.
4. We need to redesign the stand so that the catalog is eye-level instead of (laying, lying) on the desk.
5. (Their, There, They're) is some evidence that (their, there, they're) thinking of changing (their, there, they're) policy.
6. The settlement isn't yet in writing; if one side wanted to back out of the (oral, verbal) agreement, it could.

7. In (affect, effect), we're creating a new department.
8. The firm will be hiring new (personal, personnel) in three departments this year.
9. Several customers have asked that we carry more campus merchandise, (i.e., e.g.,) pillows and mugs with the college seal.
10. We have investigated all of the possible solutions (accept, except) adding a turning lane.

B–10 Choosing the Right Word

Choose the right word for each sentence.

1. The author (cites, sights, sites) four reasons for computer phobia.
2. The error was (do, due) to inexperience.
3. (Your, you're) doing a good job motivating (your, you're) subordinates.
4. One of the basic (principals, principles) of business communication is "Consider the reader."
5. I (implied, inferred) from the article that interest rates would go up.
6. Working papers generally are (composed, comprised) of working

trial balance, assembly sheets, adjusting entries, audit schedules, and audit memos.
7. Eliminating time clocks will improve employee (moral, morale).
8. The (principal, principle) variable is the trigger price mechanism.
9. (Its, It's) (to, too, two) soon (to, too, two) tell whether the conversion (to, too, two) computerized billing will save as much time as we hope.
10. Formal training programs (complement, compliment) on-the-job opportunities for professional growth.

B–11 Tracking Your Own Mechanical Errors

Analyze the mechanical errors (grammar, punctuation, word use, and typos) in each of your papers.

■ How many different errors are marked on each paper?

■ Which three errors do you make most often?

■ Is the number of errors constant in each paper, or does the number increase or decrease during the term?

As Your Instructor Directs,

a. Correct each of the mechanical errors in one or more papers.

b. Deliberately write two new sentences in which you make each of your three most common errors. Then write the correct version of each sentence.

c. Write a memo to your instructor discussing your increasing mastery of mechanical correctness during the semester or quarter.

d. Briefly explain to the class how to avoid one kind of error in grammar, punctuation, or word use.

Making and Communicating Meaning

Appendix Outline

An Inside Perspective:
Making and Communicating Meaning

Ruth Ann Hendrickson, Research Scientist
Battelle Memorial Institute

Ruth Ann Hendrickson prepares reports for Congress and federal agencies which will be used to make public policy. Headquartered in Columbus, Ohio, Battelle is a not-for-profit organization that develops, manages and commercializes technology. Battelle develops products for industry, specializing in energy, the environment, national security, and transportation.

Our projects start out as brainstorming around a table. We bring in government representatives, policy analysts, economists, subject-matter experts from Battelle, industry representatives, and state and local planning officials. Everyone has something to say, since the decision will affect their organizations and their lives. Sometimes the same idea comes up from several different perspectives. It's like a game of "telephone." As information goes from one person to another, it can be distorted, lost, or embroidered. Our job is to try to verify and organize what people have said into an objective document that can be reviewed by, for example, the Secretary of the US Department of Transportation. Reports are our products.

The scientific method drives what we do. Policy analysis and development should be based on facts and inferences—which can be verified—not on judgments and opinions. Business people often are very emotional. Sometimes, emotion is wrapped up in money—people want to do things that will benefit them financially. But emotions come from other sources as well. Sometimes someone will argue passionately about a safety or an environmental issue, but the passion is based on emotions, not facts. We define facts as results that can be replicated—so that whoever collects the data, the results stay the same. When the results change, you have a specific observation, perhaps, but not a fact.

Right now, we're working on a report that will be used to determine regulations for truck size and weight. The federal government will use the information to decide whether to change regulations for interstate highways; some states may also base decisions on the report. These decisions have to be based on factual analysis, not an emotional response. We gather information, check to make sure that the data come from a reliable source, and screen out opinions and judgments, which cannot be verified.

The biggest challenge in my job is to ensure that we see the nuances of an issue. It's important that we not polarize an issue, seeing only black and white. Instead, with public policy, it's important to see many possible alternatives and to think outside the box. If you don't do that, policy will never change.

Ruth Ann Hendrickson, June 4, 1997

Visit Battelle Memorial Institute's Web site:
http://estd/battelle.org/battelle.html

"The biggest challenge of my job is to ensure that we see the nuances of an issue."

Ruth Ann Hendrickson, Battelle Memorial Institute

Many miscommunications arise not because people genuinely disagree but because they use symbols to mean different things and make different assumptions. **Communication theory** attempts to explain what happens when we communicate. **Semantics** is the study of the way our behavior is influenced by the words and other symbols we use to communicate. (Sometimes it is called *general semantics* to distinguish it from more narrow meanings of *semantics*.) Because semantics deals with the way we perceive and process information, conflicts that "are just a matter of semantics" may be serious. Depending on the situation, it may or may not be possible to find words that everyone can endorse.

Communication theory and semantics both show why and where communication can break down. They are most useful for persuasion in difficult situations, working and writing in groups, and writing reports. This appendix suggests what we can do—as writers and speakers—to get more of our meaning across to other people and—as readers and listeners—to more accurately understand the messages that we receive.

COMMUNICATION CHANNELS IN ORGANIZATIONS

Channels vary in speed, accuracy of transmission, cost, number of messages carried, number of people reached, efficiency, and ability to promote goodwill. Depending on the audience, your purposes, and the situation, one channel may be better than another.

Oral channels are better for group decision making, allow misunderstandings to be cleared up more quickly, and seem more personal. Shorter communication channels are more accurate than longer chains. And all-channel patterns, where everyone can communicate with everyone else, produce better group decisions and more satisfaction. Figure C.1 illustrates some of the communication channels that exist in organizations.

Managers choose channels based on their familiarity with the channel and on the situation. Lamar Reinsch and Raymond Beswick found that voice mail was the preferred channel when employees on one shift needed to communicate with those on another. Administrative, professional, and technical workers were less likely to use voice mail for complex or negative messages or for messages that needed to be documented in writing. In fact, for important messages when the cost of miscommunication was high, managers usually used two different channels, for example, talking to someone about a written memo.[1]

Channel choice may also be influenced by organizational culture. At Microsoft, e-mail is the preferred channel, and new employees have to learn to use it effectively.

A MODEL OF THE COMMUNICATION PROCESS

The following model of the communication process drastically simplifies what is perhaps the most complex human activity. However, even a simplified model can give us a sense of the complexity of the communication

He Sounds Older than He Looks*

Low-tech communication can have advantages. Michael G. Rubin makes most of his deals by phone, thus avoiding questions about his age.

At the age of 13, with $2,500 in bar mitzvah money, he opened a ski-repair shop in the basement of his parents' home. The next year, he opened his first retail store. By the time he was 16, the single store had expanded into a small chain.

When he was 17, he founded KPR Sports International. Within five years, the company was earning $5 million on sales of $50 million. Mr. Rubin was 22.

*Based on Stephanie N. Mehta, "Man in a Hurry: A Mogul in Sporting Goods at Age 22," *The Wall Street Journal*, June 5, 1995, B1.

Figure C.1

Examples of Communication Patterns in Organizations

Direct channel from A to B

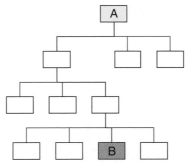

A must go through other people to get to B.

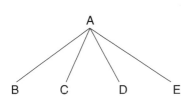

A can send messages to four people simultaneously. They must go through A to send messages to each other.

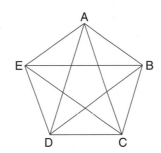

A can send messages to four people simultaneously. They can send messages directly to each other.

process. And the model is useful in helping us see where and why miscommunication occurs. Figure C.2 shows the basic process that occurs when one person tries to communicate ideas to someone else.

The process begins when Person A (let's call him Alex) **perceives** some stimulus. Here we are talking about literal perception: the ability to see, to hear, to taste, to smell, to touch. Next, Alex **interprets** what he has perceived. Is it important? Unusual? The next step is for Alex to **choose** or **select** the information he wishes to send to Person B (whom we'll call Barbara). Now Alex is ready to put his ideas into words. (Some people argue that we can think only in words and would put this stage before interpretation and choice.) Words are not the only way to convey ideas; gestures, clothing, and pictures can carry meaning nonverbally. The stage of putting ideas into any of these symbols is called **encoding.** Then Alex must **transmit** the message to Barbara using some **channel.** Channels include memos, phone calls, meetings, billboards, TV ads, and e-mail, to name just a few.

To receive the message, Barbara must first **perceive** it. Then she must **decode** it, that is, extract meaning from the symbols. Barbara then repeats the steps Alex has gone through: interpreting the information, choosing a response, and encoding it. The response Barbara sends to Alex is called **feedback.** Feedback may be direct and immediate or indirect and delayed; it may be verbal or nonverbal.

Noise can interfere with every aspect of the communication process. Noise may be physical or psychological. Physical noise could be a phone line with static, a lawn mower roaring outside a classroom, or handwriting that is hard to read. Psychological noise could include not liking a speaker, being concerned about something other than the message, or already having one's mind made up on an issue.

Figure C.2

**A Model of
Two-Person
Communication with
Feedback**

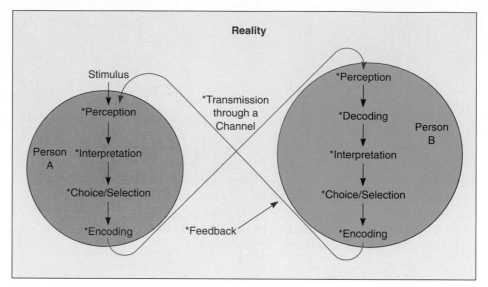

*Noise (and miscommunication) can occur here.

Channel overload occurs when the channel cannot handle all the messages that are being sent. A small business may have only two phone lines; no one else can get through if both lines are in use. **Information overload** occurs when more messages are transmitted than the human receiver can handle. Some receivers process information "first come, first served." Some may try to select the most important messages and ignore others. A third way is to depend on abstracts or summaries prepared by other people. None of these ways is completely satisfactory.

Here's how the process might work in an organizational situation.

Alex is an inspector for a state Department of Public Health who inspects nursing homes to be sure that they meet state standards. Answering some of the questions on the form calls only for **perception** (Does each resident have a separate bed?). Others depend on **interpretation** as well as perception (Do residents receive appropriate care?). Today Alex is appalled at the condition of the Olde Folks Inne. He must **choose** details to put in his report to document his judgment that Olde Folks violates state standards.

Alex **encodes** his information in words only; he didn't think to bring a camera along, and he doesn't think a drawing or a table is necessary. The **channel** he chooses is the standard format for inspection reports in his office. He **transmits** his report to his boss, who may forward it to the Attorney General's office if the violations are sufficiently severe.

Barbara is a lawyer in the Attorney General's office. She gets Alex's report about three weeks after he wrote it (the **channel** isn't very fast) but doesn't read the report for another two weeks because she's so busy. Barbara is experiencing **information overload:** she cannot deal with messages as fast as they arrive.

When Barbara finally reads Alex's report, she **perceives** the typed document and **decodes** it. There are some technical terms in the report (Alex has talked about § 302.1.a of the State Code for Nursing Homes), which she understands since she's an expert in this area. She must **interpret** Alex's information. Are the violations severe enough to warrant filing a case against Olde Folks? She thinks they are. Furthermore, the governor made a speech three months ago promising to curb abuses in nursing homes, so clearing up this case will make her and her office look good.

Barbara **chooses** points that she wants to check on; she **encodes** her questions in simple, direct language and **transmits** her message to Alex by a phone call. Her questions serve as **feedback.** Alex learns that his report is on target, but that at several points Barbara needs more information. (It isn't enough to say that residents are *neglected;* Barbara needs measurable, objective data to prove her case.)

The initial communication circuit expands. Barbara makes an appointment to visit the nursing home with Alex to collect the evidence she needs and interview some of the residents. She adds these **perceptions** to the information Alex has already given her. In her office after the visit, Barbara will **interpret** the evidence, **choose** the strongest arguments, and **encode** and **transmit** messages designed to make the nursing home make the necessary improvements voluntarily. She'll try persuasion and negotiation first; if they fail, she'll **encode** and **transmit** the documents necessary to file a suit against the nursing home.

The example above represents successful communication. But things don't always work so well. At every stage, both Alex and Barbara could misperceive, misinterpret, choose badly, encode poorly, and choose inappropriate channels. Miscommunication can also occur because different people have different frames of reference. We always interpret messages in light of our personal experiences, our cultures (➤ p. 309) and subcultures, and even the point in history at which we live.

Principles of Semantics

Semantic principles offer guidelines for improving communication. The basic principles of semantics may be expressed in eight statements. In the list below, the principles are linked to the parts of the communication model they explain.

Perception

1. Perception involves the perceiver as well as what is perceived.

Interpretation

2. Observations, inferences, and judgments are not the same thing.
3. No two things are ever exactly alike.
4. Things change significantly with time.
5. Most *either-or* classifications are not legitimate.

Choice

6. A statement is never the whole story.

Encoding and Decoding

7. Words are not identical to the objects they represent.
8. The symbols used in communication must stand for essentially the same thing in the minds of the sender and the receiver.

Let's look at each of these principles.

1. Perception Involves the Perceiver as Well as What Is Perceived.

What we see is conditioned by what we are able to see, what we have seen in the past, what we are prepared to see, and what we want to see.

Freshness Is in the Eye of the Beholder*

Stew Leonard's food store in Norwalk, Connecticut, is one of the most successful supermarkets in the United States. Part of the success comes from listening to customers—and giving them what they ask for.

At a focus group meeting, a woman complained that the store didn't sell fresh fish. The fish sales rep, who was also at the meeting, protested: the fish came fresh every morning, some from the Fulton Fish Market, some from the Boston Piers. But the customer held her ground. To her, fish on a styrofoam plate in plastic wrap didn't look fresh.

What did the Leonards do? "We set up a fish bar with ice in it . . . it's the same price as over in the package. Our packaged fish didn't decrease at all, but we doubled our fish sales. We were doing about 15,000 pounds a week; now we're doing 30,000 pounds a week."

*Based on "In Search of Excellence: The Film," transcript by John Nathan (Waltham, MA: Nathan-Tyler Productions, 1985), 6–8, and Joanne Kaufman, "In the Moo: Shopping at Stew Leonard's," *The Wall Street Journal*, September 17, 1987, 28.

Figure C.3

**How Context Affects
Perception**

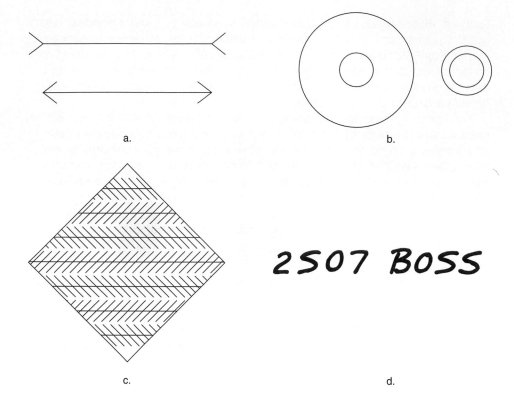

Our ability to perceive is limited first of all by our senses. Some people cannot distinguish between red and green; some people need glasses to see or hearing aids to hear. Perception is also affected by context. A line may appear longer or shorter depending on arrows at its ends (Figure C.3a). A circle may appear bigger or smaller depending on the circle around it (Figure C.3b). Parallel lines may appear slanted when other lines cross them (Figure C.3c). A symbol may appear to be the letter *S* or the number *5* depending on whether it's part of a word or a number (Figure C.3d).

Perceptions can even shape reality. In one school, a group of researchers gave teachers their students' aptitude scores, telling the teachers that they wanted to see whether high-scoring children really learned more quickly. At the end of the term, the high-aptitude children indeed scored higher on achievement tests than their classmates did. At this point, the researchers revealed the truth: the aptitude scores they had given the teachers had no relation to the students' real scores. The children who learned the most were not the smartest ones, but rather those the teachers *perceived* to be the smartest—those they expected to learn most easily. Evidently, by nonverbal feedback, extra attention, or some other means, the teachers enabled these children to learn more, whether or not they really were "smart."[2]

This experiment has implications for supervisors as well as teachers, for it suggests that our own expectations may shape the performances we get from those we evaluate.

Perception is also affected by what we want to see. Most people have a tendency to attribute their own feelings to other people as well; we tend to repress ideas that are unpleasant or threatening. We may tune out messages we think will challenge our own positions; we seek messages that support the positions we have taken. The most avid readers of car ads are people who have just bought that make of car and who want to be reassured that they made the right choice.[3]

1-800-305-2185

Nike's "swoosh" is such a powerful symbol that ads don't need to carry the brand name.

Use these correctives to check the accuracy of your perceptions:

1. Recognize that everyone's perception will be in some measure biased; the person who sees only reality does not exist.
2. Recognize that different positions cause us to view reality differently and to make different inferences from what we observe. When you disagree with someone, try to go back to the original observation to see if a difference in perception is at the root of the conflict.
3. If a new idea comes along that does not fit neatly into your worldview, recognize that your worldview, not the challenging idea, may need rethinking.

2. Observations, Inferences, and Judgments Are Not the Same Thing.

> Ten minutes before lunchtime, Jan is talking on the phone. Her manager thinks, "I don't believe it! She's talking again. Doesn't she ever work?" Jan is talking to a potential customer; she sees the call as part of her job, since it may eventually lead to a sale. She can't understand why her manager doesn't think she's serious about her career.

Jan's manager sees a woman talking on the phone; he assumes that she's wasting time. He has jumped to the wrong conclusion about the meaning of her behavior. But, as Tim R. V. Davis points out, we are usually less interested

General Inference*

Our battalion reported to the recreation-theater for a briefing by the new general. Among the topics he spoke about was safety. "How many of you wore your seat belts on the way over here?" he asked us. Of the 400 soldiers present, only a few raised their hands.

The general, obviously annoyed, began to berate us for not following regulations. Then his aide leaned over to him. "Excuse me, sir," he whispered. "Their battalion area is across the street, so most of them walked."

*Quoted from "Humor in Uniform," Reader's Digest, July 1993, 111.

The Camera Lies*

The truthfulness of photographic images has been vastly overrated. . . . [Cameras] can distort the viewer's interpretation of reality in at least six ways:

■ The angle of view is critical, as football fans know well from instant replays. From one angle of view, the receiver is in bounds; from another, it's no catch.

■ The framing of an image extracts only a portion of a scene. . . . What lies beyond the edge of the frame could lead to a completely different reading of the situation.

■ Timing also removes context, by isolating a fraction of a second in time . . . Was the Congressman truly asleep or just blinking?

■ Under- or overexposure can . . . wash out detail in parts of an image, deleting essential information.

■ The lens itself modifies perspective. A telephoto lens makes foreground and background objects appear much closer to each other than they really are.

■ Reproduction size significantly alters perception of content. . . . [Details can be emphasized by blowing up the photo; patterns can be hidden when the photo doesn't show] "the whole picture."

*Quoted from A. G., "Photographic Truth: Fact or Fiction," *NADTP Journal*, September 1993, 16–18.

in an action than in what we think that action means.[4] And interpretation invariably creates the possibility of error.

Semanticists would say that Jan's boss is confusing observations and inferences. To a semanticist, an **observation** is a statement that you yourself have verified. An **inference** is a statement that you have not personally verified, but whose truth or falsity could be established, either now or in the future. A **judgment** or an **opinion** is a statement that can never be verified, since it includes terms that cannot be measured objectively. Let's look at some examples.

1. The book you are reading is titled *Business and Administrative Communication*.
2. The author teaches at The Ohio State University.
3. The book is the best college text in business communication.

Statement 1 is an observation: you can verify it by checking the cover and title page. Statement 2 is an inference. It seems reasonable, based on what the title page says, but you don't know that of your own knowledge. (Even if the statement was true when the book went to press, is it still true?) However, you could check the truth of the statement if you wanted to take the time and trouble to do so. Statement 3 is a judgment. There is no way to prove that it is true, because people will have different notions of what makes a textbook the "best."

Semanticists claim that only observations are facts. Consider this statement:

Scientists first cloned mammals in 1997.

Is that a fact? Very few people reading this book observed the birth of the cloned sheep in Scotland in person. Most of us saw pictures of the sheep on TV or read about it in newspapers and newsmagazines. We accept statements about the cloning as fact because we trust the TV announcers who reported it then and the books that record it now. But all of us have seen images on TV that were fiction, not fact. Digital imaging allows editors to alter pictures in magazines and books. In the mid-1990s, The Gap removed the cigarettes that jazz trumpeter Miles Davis and actor John Wayne were holding in pictures showing them in khakis.[5] Nor is printed information necessarily true. A widely quoted 1987 report called "Workplace 2000" said that non-Hispanic white males entering the US work force would drop to 15% by the end of the century. A missing word and the word *entering* distorted the meaning: actually, the percentage of white males in the work force is expected to decline only 3 percentage points, from 41% in 1994 to 38% in 2005.[6]

Usually, we call statements *facts* if nearly everyone in our culture accepts them as true. But something is not necessarily true just because large numbers of people believe it. Before Columbus's discovery of America, nearly everyone believed that the world was flat. If one defines *facts* not as widely shared beliefs but as observations, there are almost no facts. Almost everything we know we take on someone else's authority rather than on our own. Even much of what we know by observation may be inference rather than direct observation. Furthermore, observations vary from person to person, since different people will have verified different things.

In everyday life and in business, you have to make decisions based on inferences ("That driver whose right turn signal is blinking intends to turn right." "I will live long enough to need a retirement fund." "The sales figures I've been given are accurate.") and even on judgments ("We have too much money tied up in long-term investments."). What should you as a reader or writer do?

Both as a reader and writer,

1. Check to see whether a statement is an observation, an inference, or a judgment.

As a reader or listener making decisions based on information you get from other people,

2. Estimate the accuracy of the inference by comparing it to your experiences with the source and with this kind of situation. If the cost of making a mistake is high, try to get more information.

As a writer or speaker trying to persuade people,

3. Use measurable statements, not just statements that contain value terms that will mean different things to different people.

Not: Buying a slag grinder would be a good investment.
But: Buying a slag grinder will enable us to save $25,000 on the Moreland order alone.

4. Label your inferences, so that your audience can distinguish between what you know to be the case and what you think, assume, believe, or judge to be true. In the following examples, the italicized words remind readers that the statements are inferences.

> *He predicts* that the stock market *could* move up an additional 10% to 20% during the next 12 to 18 months.
>
> *The results of our survey suggest* that employees will accept the proposed limits on health care benefits only if benefits for top management are also frozen or cut.

3. No Two Things Are Ever Exactly Alike.

We make sense of the world by grouping things into categories. Once we have categories, we do not have to evaluate each new experience independently; instead, we simply assign it to a category and then make the response we find appropriate to that category.

Unfortunately, this convenient lumping can lead to **stereotyping:** putting similar people or events into a single category, even though significant differences exist. A list of the customers whose accounts are overdue, for example, may include several different kinds of people:

- A good customer who is behind on bills because of a temporary setback.
- A marginal risk who won't pay the bill until forced to do so.
- Someone whose record-keeping is poor and who has honestly forgotten to pay.
- Someone who claims that he or she never received the merchandise or that the amount of the bill is in error and who is delaying payment until the dispute is settled.

The approach that would be needed to get a customer in the second category to pay would be unnecessary and even offensive if used with customers in other groups. Different "delinquent" customers need to be treated differently.

Generalizing—faultily—on the basis of experience is a particular problem when our experience is limited to one or two cases. Suppose, for example, that someone has an Asian supervisor who isn't a good boss. If the supervisor is the only Asian boss the employee has ever known, the employee may conclude that Asians don't make good supervisors. If the same employee has an Anglo supervisor who isn't a good boss, he or she is less likely to assume that Anglos can't be good supervisors. Because we see many Anglo supervisors, some of whom are better than others, it is easy to recognize that the weakness of an individual doesn't condemn the whole group.

But Things Are Different Now*

Conventional wisdom is that US companies can't sell unaltered appliances in Japan: Japanese houses are just too small for them. Conventional wisdom is no longer true.

The Japanese discount chain Kojima sells GE appliances. Between June 1995 and June 1996, GE's share of the Japanese refrigerator market went from 1% to 3%.

Why the change? Two factors seem responsible: more Japanese women continue to work after marriage and can't shop daily for food. And Japan's weak economy has made consumers interested in saving money. A GE refrigerator costs about half as much as a smaller Japanese model.

True, the larger model won't fit in small kitchenettes. Buyers solve that problem by putting the US refrigerators in their living rooms.

*Based on Morihiko Shirouzu, "Flouting 'Rules' Sells GE Fridges in Japan," *The Wall Street Journal,* October 31, 1995, B1.

To guard against stereotyping, you should

1. Recognize significant differences as well as similarities. The members of any one group are not identical.
2. Be sure that any analogy you use to make your point clear is accurate at the point of comparison.

4. Things Change Significantly with Time.

If you keep up with the stock market, with commodity prices, or with interest rates, you know that things (especially prices) change significantly with time.

People change too. The sales representative who was once judged too abrasive to make a good supervisor may have mellowed by now; employees who accepted management dictates without question 20 years ago may be more critical; the student who almost flunked out freshman year may have settled down, solved his or her problems, and become an excellent prospect for employment or graduate school.

Someone who does not recognize that prices, situations, and people change is guilty of making a **frozen evaluation.** The following corrections help us remember not to freeze evaluations:

1. Date statements. The price of IBM stock on October 20, 1991, is not the price of IBM stock on January 3, 1998.
2. Provide a frame of reference so your reader has some basis for comparing grades, profits, injuries, percentages, or whatever the relevant criterion may be.
3. Periodically retest your assumptions about people, businesses, products, and services to make sure that your evaluations apply to the present situation.

5. Most *Either-Or* Classifications Are Not Legitimate.

A common logical fallacy is **polarization:** trying to force the reader into a position by arguing that there are only two possible positions, one of which is clearly unacceptable:

> Either the supervisor runs this department with a firm hand, or anarchy will take over and the work will never get done.

Very few areas of life allow only two options. Running a department "with a firm hand" is only one of several possible leadership styles; sharing authority with or even transferring it entirely to subordinates need not result in anarchy.

Even people who admit that there are more than two possible positions may still limit the options unnecessarily. Imposing limits that do not exist in reality is called **blindering,** after the blinders that horses wear. Blindering can lead to polarization.

Sometimes blindering is responsible for bad questions in surveys:

> Do you own _____, rent _____, or live with your parents _____?

At first glance, that may seem to cover the options. But what about someone who lives with a friend or with relatives other than parents? What about a minister who lives in a parsonage or manse furnished by the church as part of the minister's compensation? The minister does not own the house, but neither does he or she rent it. Depending on what the makers of the questionnaire really want to know, better questions would be:

> How much is your housing worth a month?
> How much do you pay a month for your housing?

Polarization sharpens divisions between people and obscures the common ground on which they could forge a decision that everyone could live with. Blindering prevents our seeing creative solutions to the problems we face. Here are some correctives:

1. Recognize the complexities of a situation. Resist the temptation to oversimplify.
2. Whenever you see only two alternatives, consciously search for a third, and maybe even a fourth or fifth, before you make your decision.
3. Redefine the question or problem to get at the real issue.

> Don't ask: How can I as a manager show that I'm in control?
> Ask: How can we improve productivity in this unit?

6. A Statement Is Never the Whole Story.

It is impossible to know everything; it is impossible to tell someone everything. Thinking that we know everything about a subject or can communicate everything about it that is important is the fallacy semanticists call **allness.** When we assume that a statement contains all the important information, or when the context is omitted (deliberately or inadvertently), meanings are inevitably twisted.

For example, you've probably read that US investments suffer because US families save far less than do Japanese families. But, according to several economists, this statement overlooks differences in what counts as savings and as investments. Many US families own their own homes, yet their equity isn't considered "savings." Few Japanese own homes; their "savings" are more likely to be in stocks and bonds. Economist Fumio Hayashi points out that Japanese accounting values depreciation at historical cost figures, thus understating the value of assets and making investment look higher. Furthermore, the US counts government spending—even on schools, roads, and warships—as consumption. The Japanese system considers such expenditures to be investments.[7] When these differences are considered, the alleged gap between the two countries' savings and investment rates disappears.

Since, even with the best intentions, we cannot include everything, what can we do to avoid misstatements by implication?

1. Recognize that the reports you get are filtered; you are not getting all the facts, and you are almost certainly getting inferences as well as observations.
2. Check the correspondence you send out to make sure you have provided the background information the reader needs to interpret your message accurately.

7. Words Are Not Identical to the Objects They Represent.

People perceive objects and think of ideas; they attach labels to those objects and ideas. Other labels could be substituted without changing reality. Indeed, the ability to attach a new label to an object—to attach a different

The Map Is Not the Territory*

Traveling over the United States in a balloon, Huck Finn expects the world to look just like the maps he has seen:

". . . [If] we was going so fast we ought to be past Illinois, oughtn't we?"

"Certainly."

"Well, we ain't."

"What's the reason we ain't?"

"I know by the color. We're right over Illinois yet. And you can see for yourself that Indiana ain't in sight."

"I wonder what's the matter with you, Huck. You know by the *color?*"

"Yes, of course I do."

"What's the color got to do with it?"

"It's got everything to do with it. Illinois is green, Indiana is pink. You show me any pink down here, if you can. No, sir; it's green."

"Indiana *pink?* Why, what a lie!"

"It ain't no lie; I've seen it on the map, and it's pink."

*Quoted from Mark Twain, *Tom Sawyer Abroad*, Chap. 3, *The Family Mark Twain* (New York: Harper, 1935), 1101–02.

Figure C.4

Semantic Triangle

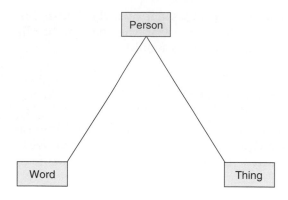

meaning to it—is a key element of creative intelligence. In the **semantic triangle** in Figure C.4, there is no base, no connection between the thing and the word that symbolizes it. People, who name things and use words, provide the only connection.

We often respond to the label rather than to reality. Our degree of distress during a bleak economic period is likely to be as much a product of the label given the period as it is of the rate of unemployment: a *slowdown* doesn't sound as bad as a *recession,* and even that is better than a *depression.* Labeling a book a *best-seller* is sure to increase sales. An album titled "John Denver's Greatest Hits" catapulted Denver to popularity; none of his previous records had been hits. Billy Joel put the song "You're Only Human" on his "Greatest Hits" album before he had even released it as a single.

Because people respond to symbols, organizations choose names carefully. Corporate name changes raise stock prices 2.4% "solely because of name changes."[8] In World War II, a Navy ship changed its call signal from SAPWORTH to HELLCAT—with a marked improvement in morale.[9] Eastman Kodak called its division making cameras in the United States the "US Equipment Division" until someone looked at the acronym and pointed out that people might not want to buy USED cameras.[10]

Responding to the symbol rather than to reality, "confusing the map with the territory," is called **intensionalism.** Advertising works in part because we respond intensionally to symbols. A man working at a flea market noticed that garden supplies went quickly, but no one was buying broom handles. He bought the entire supply of broom handles for a dime each, put up a sign in his own booth advertising "Tomato stakes—25¢ each," and sold all 300 in two hours.[11] The characteristics of the wooden poles hadn't changed, but the symbol had, and people responded differently to the new symbol.

Since we must use symbols to communicate, it's hard to avoid treating symbols as if they were reality. Semanticists suggest these correctives:

1. Support general statements and evaluations with specific evidence or examples.
2. Check your own responses to make sure that your decisions are based not on labels but on valid, logical arguments.

8. The Symbols Used in Communication Must Stand for Essentially the Same Thing in the Minds of the Sender and the Receiver.

Communication depends on symbols; if those symbols mean different things to the people who use them, communication will fail. **Bypassing** occurs when two people use the same symbol to mean different things.

Kraft Foods took its decade-old Crystal Light powered fruit drink, added water, and packaged it in fancy bottles like those used for Evian water. This new look made the product seem more contemporary and upscale; sales soared.

Bypassing creates misunderstandings. A factory employee who had been absent frequently notified his supervisor that he would not be at work the next day. The supervisor said "OK," meaning only that he had heard what the worker had said and was acknowledging having heard it. The worker thought the *OK* signified approval, that is, that his absence was acceptable. When he received a written warning notice for poor attendance, he felt he was being treated unfairly and filed a grievance against management.

Symbols have to be learned. New computer users frequently experience bypassing because they don't yet know the computer meaning of various symbols.

> A man called the support line complaining that his computer wasn't working, though he'd followed the directions to the letter. "I inserted the disk into the drive. It said insert the disk into the drive, OK? Then I got up and closed the door to my office. It said close the door."

> A computer consultant told a customer to send him a copy of his disk. A photocopy of the disk arrived in the mail the next day.

> When the instructor told students to erase their disks, one student took out a pencil eraser and applied it to the oxide.[12]

Until we learn to look into each other's minds, we can't be certain that symbols mean exactly the same things to us as they do to the people with whom we communicate. But there are some measures that will help us avoid bypassing:

1. Be sensitive to contexts.
2. Consider the other person. Given his or her background and situation, what is he or she likely to mean?
3. Mirror what the other person has said by putting it into your own words, and let him or her check it for accuracy. (Note: use different words for the key ideas. If you use exactly the same word, you still won't be able to tell if you and the other person mean the same thing by it.)
4. Ask questions.

SUMMARY OF KEY POINTS

- **Communication theory** attempts to explain what happens when we communicate. **Semantics** is the study of the way our behavior is influenced by the words and other symbols we use to communicate. Communication theory and semantics both show why and where communication can break down and what we can do to communicate more effectively.

What's in a Name? (2)*

Twenty years ago, no one could sell portabella mushrooms. But they weren't called portabellas.

In the 1970s, when exotic cultivated mushrooms became a market segment, growers began to remarket the mature, brown mushrooms that were out of favor. In the 1980s, the name *portabella* emerged.

Now, at the turn of the century, portabellas are featured in chefs' signature dishes. In grocery stores, portabellas cost as much as steak. And growers can't keep up with demand.

It helps to have a beautiful name.

*Based on Kim Pierce, "Meaty Portabella Mushrooms Are Springing Up All Over: Change of Name Promotes Interest in Giant, Unglamorous Fungi," *Columbus Dispatch*, May 31, 1995, 6H.

- Because semantics deals with the way we perceive and process information, conflicts that "are just a matter of semantics" may be serious. Depending on the situation, it may or may not be possible to find words that everyone in the group can endorse.
- The best channel for a message will depend on the audience, the sender's purposes, and the situation. Channel choice may be shaped by the organizational culture.
- **Channel overload** occurs when a channel cannot handle all the messages being sent. **Information overload** occurs when the receiver cannot process all the messages that arrive. Both kinds of overload require some sort of selection to determine which messages will be sent and which ones will be attended to.
- A sender goes through the following steps: **perception, interpretation, choice** or **selection,** encoding, transmitting the message through a **channel.** The receiver perceives the message, **decodes** it, interprets it, chooses a response, encodes the response, and transmits it. The message transmitted to the original sender is called **feedback. Noise** is anything that interferes with communication; it can be both physical and psychological. Miscommunication can occur at every point in the communication process.
- Eight principles of semantics will help us avoid errors in perception, interpretation, choice, and encoding and decoding.

Perception

1. Perception involves the perceiver as well as what is perceived.

Interpretation

2. **Observations** are statements you yourself have verified. **Inferences** are statements that have not yet been verified, but which could be. **Judgments** can never be proven, since they depend not on measurable quantities but on values.
3. No two things are ever exactly alike.
4. Things change significantly with time. Violating this principle produces **frozen evaluations.**
5. Most *either-or* classifications are not legitimate. Seeing only two alternatives is called **polarization.** Assuming limits that do not exist is called **blindering.**

Choice

6. A statement is never the whole story. Thinking that one can know or tell everything is called **allness.**

Encoding and Decoding

7. Words are not identical to the objects they represent. The **semantic triangle** shows that the only link between word and object is the person who uses the word.
8. The symbols used in communication must stand for essentially the same thing in the minds of the sender and the receiver. When the sender and the receiver use the same symbol to mean different things, **bypassing** occurs.

Exercises and Problems
For Appendix C

C–1 Choosing a Channel to Reach a Specific Audience _____

Suppose that your business, government agency, or nonprofit group had a product, service, or program targeted for each of the following audiences. What would be the best channel(s) to reach people in that group in your city? Would that channel reach all group members?

  a. Macintosh users.
  b. People who own mutual funds.
  c. Teenagers who do the family grocery shopping.
  d. People who bowl.
  e. Muslims.
  f. Parents whose children play team sports.
  g. Native Americans/Native Canadians.
  h. Lawyers.
  i. People who have Web sites.
  j. People who use wheelchairs.

C–2 Choosing a Channel to Convey a Specific Message _____

Assume that you're the campaign manager for a campus, local, or state race. (Pick a real candidate and a real race.) What would be the advantages and disadvantages of each of the following channels as media to carry ads for your side?

  a. Ad in the campus newspaper.
  b. Posters around campus.
  c. Ad in the local newspaper.
  d. Ad on a local radio station after midnight.
  e. Ad on the local TV station during the local news show.
  f. Ads on billboards.
  g. Ads on yard signs.
  h. Flyers distributed door-to-door.
  i. Ad on cable TV.

C–3 Dealing with Channel and Information Overload _____

In each of the following situations, identify ways that people could deal with the overloads described. What are the consequences of the methods that might be used?

  a. When a radio station announces a prize for the ninth caller, dozens of people try to phone in.
  b. After Bill Gates' e-mail address is printed in a magazine, he gets 5,000 messages in three days.
  c. A car buyer in the United States can choose from 572 makes and models.
  d. At State University, every accounting senior with a GPA of "B" or better wants to interview for jobs with the Big Six Accounting firms, but each firm will interview only 34 seniors at the school.
  e. A major freeway is closed for repairs.
  f. System capacity allows only two of every five calls on cellular phones to get through.
  g. A student wants to attend a lecture by a prominent speaker the night before a paper is due.
  h. A sales representative's job requires him to be on the road four nights a week, but he wants to spend more time with his family.

C–4 Separating Observations, Inferences, and Judgments _____

Indicate whether each of the following statements is an observation, an inference, or a judgment.

  a. This statement is printed in black ink on a page edged in green.
  b. All the exercises and problems in this book are printed on pages edged in green.

c. Printing the problems on pages with colored edges makes them easier to find.

d. Five years from now, 90% of the college texts designed for business courses will use at least two colors of ink.

e. Color printing makes textbooks more interesting.

C–5   Separating Observations, Inferences, and Judgments

Indicate whether each of the following statements is an observation, an inference, or a judgment.

a. There is a chair in this room.

b. The Dow Jones Industrial Average closed above 7000 for the first time in February 1997.

c. High stock prices are a sign that the economy is healthy.

d. Accounting majors get good jobs.

e. All the people in this room will be employed three years from today.

f. It's better to be 75% right and 100% on time than 100% right and a week late.

g. This statement is a complete sentence.

C–6   Separating Observations, Inferences, and Judgments

Pick a topic and write a statement of observation, a statement of inference, and a statement of judgment about it.

C–7   Explaining Bypassing

1. Show how the following statements could produce bypassing.

   a. The house needs painting badly.

   b. I made reservations for seven.

   c. If you think our servers are rude, you should see the manager.

2. Bypassing is the basis of many jokes. Find a joke that depends on bypassing and share it with the class.

C–8   Identifying Semantic Errors

Match each of the following statements with the semantic error it represents.

1. Allness
2. Frozen evaluation
3. Intensionalism
4. Polarization
5. Stereotyping

a. All Australians are cricket maniacs.

b. We tried that two years ago and it didn't work. There's no point in trying it again.

c. My subordinate isn't looking at me while I talk to him. He must be rebelling against my authority.

d. *The New York Times* prints all the news that's fit to print.

e. Junk mail wastes paper and money.

f. He applied for a job last year, and we hired someone else. There's no reason to consider him for our jobs this year.

g. If we grant pay increases, we will have to raise our cost to customers.

h. I swear to tell the truth, the whole truth, and nothing but the truth.

i. Women are more nurturing than men are.

j. Any man who wears a Brooks Brothers suit will be politically and fiscally conservative.

C–9   Verbal Map-Reality Test

Directions: If a statement is *true under all circumstances*, check the line in the "True" column. If the statement is *ever false* or if its truth *cannot be determined*, put a check in the "False" column.

True   False

____ ____   1. A statement is either true or false.

____ ____   2. $1 + 1 = 2$

____ ____   3. A college education is a good thing to have.

____ ____   4. A person is dead when he or she has no heartbeat.

____ ____   5. No one wants to die.

____ ____   6. Roses are red.

____ ____   7. The sum of the angles of a triangle is 180 degrees.

____ ____   8. All people are born equal.

____ ____   9. Freedom of speech is good.

____ ____   10. Do unto others as you would have them do unto you.

Adapted from "Advertising as Communication: How To Test Your Semantic I.Q.," Harry E. Maynard, *Printer's Ink,* December 11, 1964, 52.

C–10   Inference-Observation Tests

Directions: You will read a brief story. Assume that all the information in the story is *accurate* and *true*. You will then read statements about the story. Answer them in order. You may reread the story as you answer the questions, but DO NOT go back to fill in answers or change answers once you have marked them.

As you read each statement, determine whether the statement is

"T"—on the basis of the information presented in the story, the statement is definitely true.

"F"—on the basis of the information presented in the story, the statement is definitely false.

"?"—the statement may be true (or false) but on the basis of the information presented in the story one cannot be sure. (Mark "?" if any part of the statement is doubtful.)

Sample Story

The only vehicle parked in front of 619 Oak Street is a blue van. The words "Valley Cable TV Plumber" are spelled in large black letters across the side of the van.

Statements about the Sample Story

1. The color of the van in front of 619 Oak Street is blue.   T F ?

2. There is no lettering on the side of the van parked in front of 619 Oak Street.   T F ?

3. The people at 619 Oak Street have cable TV.   T F ?

4. The blue van parked in front of 619 Oak Street belongs to Valley Cable TV.   T F ?

Test Story

Babe Smith has been killed. Police have rounded up six suspects, all of whom are gangsters. All of them are known to have been near the scene of the killing at the approximate time that it occurred. All had substantial motives for wanting Smith killed. However, one of the suspected gangsters, Slinky Sam, has positively been cleared of guilt.

Statements about the Story

1. Slinky Sam is known to have been near the scene of the killing of Babe Smith.   T F ?

2. All six of the rounded-up gangsters were known to have been near the scene of the murder.   T F ?

3. Only Slinky Sam has been cleared of guilt.   T F ?

4. All six of the rounded-up suspects were near the scene of Smith's killing at the approximate time that it took place.   T F ?

5. The police do not know who killed Smith.   T F ?

6. All six suspects are known to have been near the scene of the foul deed.   T F ?

7. Smith's murderer did not confess of his or her own free will.   T F ?

8. Slinky Sam was not cleared of guilt.   T F ?

9. It is known that the six suspects were in the vicinity of the cold-blooded assassination.   T F ?

*Test by William Haney, in Harry E. Maynard, "Advertising as Communication: How to Test Your Semantic I.Q.," *Printer's Ink*, December 11, 1964, 53.

C–11 Removing Blinders

To solve the following problems, you may need to remove some "blinders."

a. How can the following be true:
   A = 3
   B = 4
   But A + B = 5

b. How can you drop an egg six feet through the air over a hard surface without breaking the egg?

c. How can you, with one line, turn VII into the number 8?
   How can you, with one line, turn IX into the number 6?

d. Finish the alphabet, putting each letter above or below the line according to the pattern below:

A	EF	HI
BCD	G	J

e. When men and women are on an elevator and all of them are getting off on the seventh floor, who should get off first?

f. Separate all nine dots into their own individual spaces by drawing two squares.

○   ○   ○

○   ○   ○

○   ○   ○

C–12 Identifying Logos

Find four corporate logos. Do all your classmates recognize all the logos? Which logos seem to be especially effective symbols for their organizations? What makes them so effective?

GLOSSARY

A

Abstract or **Executive Summary.** A summary of a report, specifying the recommendations and the reasons for them.

Acknowledgment Responses. Nods, smiles, frowns, and words that let a speaker know you are listening.

Action Close. The end of a direct mail letter, which tells the reader what to do, makes action sound easy, gives a reason for acting promptly, and ends with a reader benefit or a picture of the reader's money helping to solve the problem.

Active Listening. Feeding back the literal meaning or the emotional content or both so that the speaker knows that the listener has heard and understood.

Active Verb. A verb that describes the action of the grammatical subject of the sentence.

Adjustment. The response to a claim letter. If the company agrees to grant a refund, the amount due will be adjusted.

Alliteration. A sound pattern occurring when several words begin with the same sound.

Allness. The semantic error of assuming it is possible to know or communicate everything that is important about a topic.

Alternating Pattern. Discussing the alternatives first as they relate to the first criterion, then as they relate to the second criterion, and so on: ABC, ABC, ABC.

AMS Simplified Format. A letter format that omits the salutation and complimentary close and lines everything up at the left margin.

Analytical Report. A report that interprets information.

Annual Report. A report distributed to stockholders and other audiences summarizing the firm's financial performance and achievements during the year; a document with informative, persuasive, and goodwill purposes.

Argument. The reasons or logic offered to persuade the audience.

Assumptions. Statements that are not proven in a report, but on which the recommendations are based.

B

Bar Graph. A visual consisting of parallel bars or rectangles that represent specific sets of data.

Behavioral Interviews. Job interviews that ask candidates to describe actual behaviors they have used in the past in specific situations.

Bias-Free Language. Language that does not discriminate against people on the basis of sex, physical condition, race, age, or any other category.

Bibliography. A list of all the books and articles about a topic.

Blind Ads. Job listings that do not list the company's name.

Blind Copies. Copies sent to other recipients that are not listed on the original letter or memo.

Blindering. Imposing limits that do not exist in reality.

Block Format. In letters, a format in which inside address, date, and signature block are lined up at the left margin. In résumés, a format in which dates are listed in one column and job titles and descriptions in another. This format emphasizes work history.

Blocking. Disagreeing with every idea that is proposed in a meeting.

Body. The main part of a letter, memo, or report.

Body Language. Nonverbal communication conveyed by posture and movement, eye contact, facial expressions, and gestures.

Boilerplate. Language from a previous document that a writer includes in a new document. Writers use boilerplate both to save time and energy and to use language that has already been approved by the organization's legal staff.

Boxhead. Used in tables, the boxhead is the variable whose label is at the top.

Brainstorming. A method of generating ideas by recording everything people in a group think of, without judging or evaluating the ideas.

Branching Question. Question that sends respondents who answer differently to different parts of the questionnaire. Allows respondents to answer only those questions that are relevant to their experience.

Bridge (in *prospecting job letters*). A sentence that connects the attention-getter to the body of a letter.

Bridge (in *Toulmin logic*). The general principle that authorizes making the step between the claim and the evidence in an argument.

Buffer. A neutral or positive statement designed to allow the writer to bury, or buffer, the negative message.

Build Goodwill. To create a good image of yourself and of your organization—the kind of image that makes people want to do business with you.

Bullets. Large round dots or squares that set off items in a list. When you are giving examples, but the number is not exact and the order does not matter, use bullets to set off items.

Business Slang. Terms that have technical meaning but are used in more general senses. Used sparingly, these terms are appropriate in job application letters and in messages for people in the same organization, who are likely to share the vocabulary.

Businessese. A kind of jargon including unnecessary words. Some words were common two or three hundred years ago but are no longer part of spoken English. Some have never been used outside of business writing. All of these terms should be omitted.

Buying Time with Limited Agreement. Agreeing with the small part of a criticism that one does accept as true.

Bypassing. Miscommunication that occurs when two people use the same symbol to mean different things.

C

Case. The grammatical role a noun or pronoun plays in a sentence. The nominative case is used for the subject of a clause, the possessive to show who or what something belongs to, the objective case for the object of a verb or a preposition.

Central Selling Point. A super reader benefit, big enough to motivate readers by itself, but also serving as an umbrella to cover other benefits and to unify the message.

Chain. The body of a direct mail letter, providing the logical and emotional links that move readers from interest to the action the writer wants.

Channel. The physical means by which a message is sent. Written channels include memos, letters, and billboards. Oral channels include phone calls, speeches, and face-to-face conversations.

Channel Overload. The inability of a channel to carry all the messages that are being sent.

Chartjunk. Decoration that is irrelevant to a visual and that may be misleading.

Checking for Feelings. Identifying the emotions that the previous speaker seemed to be expressing verbally or nonverbally.

Checking for Inferences. Trying to identify the unspoken content or feelings implied by what the previous speaker has actually said.

Choice or **Selection.** The decision to include or omit information in a message.

Chronological Résumé. A résumé that lists what you did in a time line, starting with the most recent events and going backwards in reverse chronology.

Citation. Attributing a quotation or other idea to a source in the body of the report.

Claim. The part of an argument that the speaker or writer wants the audience to agree with.

Claim Letter. A letter seeking a replacement or refund.

Clear. A message whose audience gets the meaning the writer or speaker intended.

Clip Art. Predrawn images that you can import into your newsletter, sign, or graph.

Close. The ending of a document.

Closed or **Defensive Body Position.** Keeping the arms and legs crossed and close to the body. Suggests physical and psychological discomfort, defending oneself, and shutting the other person out.

Closed Question. Question with a limited number of possible responses.

Closure Report. A report summarizing completed research that does not result in action or recommendation.

Clowning. Making unproductive jokes and diverting the group from its task.

Clustering. A method of thinking up ideas by writing the central topic in the middle of the page, circling it, writing down the ideas that topic suggests, and circling them.

Cognitive Dissonance. A theory which posits that it is psychologically uncomfortable to hold two ideas that are dissonant or conflicting. The theory of cognitive dissonance explains that people will resolve dissonance by deciding that one of the ideas is less important, by rejecting one of the ideas, or by constructing a third idea that has room for both of the conflicting ideas.

Cold List. A list used in marketing of people with no prior connection to your group.

Collaborative Writing. Working with other writers to produce a single document.

Collection Letter. A letter asking a customer to pay for goods and services received.

Collection Series. A series of letters asking customers to pay for goods and services they have already received. Early letters in the series assume that the reader intends to pay but final letters threaten legal action if the bill is not paid.

Comma Splice or **Comma Fault.** Using a comma to join two independent clauses. To correct, use a semicolon, subordinate one of the clauses, or use a period and start a new sentence.

Common Ground. Values and goals that the writer and reader share.

Communication Theory. A theory explaining what happens when we communicate and where miscommunication can occur.

Complaint Letter. A letter that challenges a policy or tries to get a decision changed.

Complete. A message that answers all of the audience's questions. The audience has enough information to evaluate the message and act on it.

Complex Sentence. Sentence with one main clause and one subordinate clause.

Complimentary Close. The words after the body of the letter and before the signature. *Sincerely* and *Cordially* are the most commonly used complimentary closes in business letters.

Compound Sentence. Sentence with two main clauses joined by a conjunction.

Conclusions. Section of a report that restates the main points.

Conflict Resolution. Strategies for getting at the real issue, keeping discussion open, and minimizing hurt feelings so that people can find a solution that feels good to everyone involved.

Connotations. The emotional colorings or associations that accompany a word.

Convenience Sample. A group of subjects to whom the researcher has easy access.

Conversational Style. Conversational patterns such as speed and volume of speaking, pauses between speakers, whether questions are direct or indirect. When different speakers assign different meanings to a specific pattern, miscommunication results.

Coordinating. Planning work, giving directions, fitting together contributions of group members.

Coordination. The third stage in the life of a task group, when the group finds, organizes, and interprets information and examines alternatives and assumptions. This is the longest of the four stages.

Correct. A message whose information is accurate and that is free from errors in punctuation, spelling, grammar, word order, and sentence structure.

Counterclaim. In Toulmin logic, a statement whose truth would negate the truth of the main claim.

Credibility. The audience's response to the source of the message.

Criteria. The standards used to evaluate or weigh the factors in a decision.

Critical Activities. Activities that must be completed on time if a project is to be completed by its due date.

Critical Incident. An important event that illustrates a subordinate's behavior.

Cropping. Cutting a photograph to fit a specific space. Also, photographs are cropped to delete visual information that is unnecessary or unwanted.

Culture. The unconscious patterns of behavior and beliefs that are common to a people, nation, or organization.

Cutaway Drawings or **Schematic Diagrams.** Line drawings that depict the hidden or interior portions of an object.

Cycling. The process of sending a document from writer to superior to writer to yet another superior for several rounds of revisions before the document is approved.

D

Dangling Modifier. A phrase that modifies a word that is not actually in a sentence. To correct a dangling modifier, recast the modifier as a subordinate clause or revise the sentence so its subject or object can be modified by the now-dangling phrase.

Data. Facts or figures from which conclusions can be drawn.

Database. A computer program that organizes data in categories the user can then manipulate to get the information he or she needs.

Decision Trees. A branching chart of sequential questions with different paths depending on the answer to each question, designed to allow user to find the best solution quickly.

Decode. To extract meaning from symbols.

Decorative Visual. A visual that makes the speaker's points more memorable but that does not convey numerical data.

Defensive or **Closed Body Position.** Keeping the arms and legs crossed and close to the body. Suggests physical and psychological discomfort, defending oneself, and shutting the other person out.

Demographic Characteristics. Measurable features of an audience that can be counted objectively: age, sex, race, education level, income, etc.

Denial. A refusal to accept or believe something that is potentially harmful or life-threatening. People deny realities that are too much for them to cope with.

Denotation. A word's literal or "dictionary" meaning. Most common words in English have more than one denotation. Context usually makes it clear which of several meanings is appropriate.

Dependent Clause. A group of words containing a subject and a verb but which cannot stand by itself as a complete sentence.

Descriptive Abstract. A listing of the topics an article or report covers that tells how thoroughly each topic is treated but does not summarize what is said about each topic.

Descriptors. Words describing the content of an article. Used to permit computer searches for information on a topic.

Desktop Publishing. The use of powerful desktop computers and laser printers to produce documents that look typeset.

Dingbats. Small symbols such as arrows, pointing fingers, and so forth that are part of a typeface.

Direct Mail. A form of direct marketing that asks for an order, inquiry, or contribution directly from the reader.

Direct Mail Package. The outer envelope of a direct mail letter and everything that goes in it: the mail letter, brochures, samples, secondary letters, reply card, and reply envelope.

Direct Marketing. All advertisements that ask for an order, inquiry, or contribution directly from the reader. Includes direct mail, catalogs, telemarketing (telephone sales), and newspaper and TV ads with 800 numbers to place an order.

Direct Request. A pattern of organization that makes the request directly in the first and last paragraphs.

Directed Subject Line. A subject line that makes clear the writer's stance on the issue.

Discourse Community. A group of people who share assumptions about what channels, formats, and styles to use for communication, what topics to discuss and how to discuss them, and what constitutes evidence.

Divided Pattern. Discussing each alternative completely before going on to the next alternative: AAA, BBB, CCC.

Document Design. The process of writing, organizing, and laying out a document so that it can be easily used by the intended audience.

Documentation. Providing full bibliographic information so that interested readers can go to the original source of material used in a report.

Dominating. Trying to run a group by ordering, shutting out others, and insisting on one's own way.

Dot Charts. Dot charts show correlations or other large data sets. Dot charts have labeled horizontal and vertical axes.

E

Early Letter. A collection letter that is gentle. An early letter assumes that the reader intends to pay but has forgotten or has met with temporary reverses.

Editing. Checking the draft to see that it satisfies the requirements of good English and the principles of business writing. Unlike revision, which can produce major changes in meaning, editing focuses on the surface of writing.

Ego-Involvement. The emotional commitment the audience has to its position.

Electronic Mail or **E-mail.** A mail system that uses computer terminals to bypass paper. Messages are composed on a computer screen; the recipient reads the message on screen.

Elimination of Alternatives. A pattern of organization for reports that discusses the problem and its causes, the impractical solutions and their weaknesses, and finally the solution the writer favors.

Emotional Appeal. Making the audience want to do what the writer or speaker asks.

Empathy. The ability to put oneself in someone else's shoes, to *feel with* that person.

Encode. To put ideas into symbols.

Enunciate. To voice all the sounds of each word while speaking.

Evaluating. Measuring the draft against your goals and the requirements of the situation and audience. Anything produced during each stage of the writing process can be evaluated, not just the final draft.

Evidence. Facts or data the audience already accepts.

Exaggeration. Making something sound bigger or more important than it really is.

Executive Summary. A summary of a report, specifying the recommendations and the reasons for them.

Expectancy Theory. A theory that argues that motivation is based on the expectation of being rewarded for performance and the importance of the reward.

Extensionalism. Inspecting and responding to reality itself.

External Audiences. Audiences who are not part of the writer's organization.

External Documents. Documents that go to people in another organization.

External Report. Report written by a consultant for an organization of which he or she is not a permanent employee.

Extrinsic Benefits. Benefits that are "added on"; they are not a necessary part of the product or action.

Eye Contact. Looking another person directly in the eye.

F

Facsimile or **Fax Machine.** Machine that can send a copy of a document to another location in less than a minute. Fax machines may be stand-alone machines or part of a computer.

Feasibility Study. A report that evaluates two or more possible alternatives and recommends one of them. Doing nothing is always one alternative.

Feedback. The receiver's response to a message.

Figure. Any visual that is not a table.

Five Ws and H.   Questions that must be answered early in a press release: who, what, when, where, why, and how.

Fixed Typeface.   A typeface in which each letter has the same width on the page. Sometimes called *typewriter typeface.*

Flaming.   Sending out an angry e-mail message before thinking about the implications of venting one's anger.

Flesch "Reading Ease Scale."   A readability formula that determines reading ease (measured on a 0 to 100 scale) by subtracting multiples of average words per sentence and average syllables per word from 206.835.

Flow Chart.   A chart representing each subprocess and decision point in a process.

Focus Groups.   Small groups who come in to talk with a skilled leader about a potential product.

Forced Choice.   A choice in which each item is ranked against every other item. Used to discover which of a large number of criteria are crucial.

Form Letter.   A letter that is sent unchanged or with only minor modifications to a large number of readers.

Formal Meetings.   Meetings run under strict rules, like the rules of parliamentary procedure summarized in *Robert's Rules of Order.*

Formal Report.   A report containing formal elements such as a title page, a transmittal, a table of contents, and an abstract.

Formalization.   The fourth and last stage in the life of a task group, when the group makes and formalizes its decision.

Format.   The parts of a document and the way they are arranged on a page.

Formation.   The second stage in the life of a task group, when members choose a leader and define the problem they must solve.

Foundation.   A statement proving the truth of a bridge.

Freewriting.   A kind of writing uninhibited by any constraints. Freewriting may be useful in overcoming writer's block, among other things.

Frozen Evaluation.   An assessment that does not take into account the possibility of change.

G

Gannt Charts.   Bar charts used to show schedules. Gannt charts are most commonly used in proposals.

Gatekeeper.   The audience with the power to decide whether your message is sent on to other audiences. Some gatekeepers are also initial audiences.

Gathering.   Physically getting the background data you need. It can include informal and formal research or simply getting the letter to which you're responding.

General Semantics.   The study of the ways behavior is influenced by the words and other symbols used to communicate.

General Slang.   Words or phrases such as *awesome, smokin',* or *at the end of my rope* that are sometimes used in conversations and in presentations, but are not appropriate in business and administrative writing since they appear sloppy or imprecise.

Gerund.   The *-ing* form of a verb; grammatically, it is a verb used as a noun.

Getting Feedback.   Asking someone else to evaluate your work. Feedback is useful at every stage of the writing process, not just during composition of the final draft.

Glossary.   A list of terms used in a report with their definitions.

Good Appeal.   An appeal in direct marketing that offers believable descriptions of benefits, links the benefits of the product or service to a need or desire that motivates the reader, makes the reader want to read the letter, and motivates the reader to act.

Good Mailing List.   A mailing list used in direct marketing that has accurate addresses and is a good match to the product.

Good Product.   A product that appeals to a specific segment of people, is not readily available in stores, is mailable, and provides an adequate profit margin.

Good Service or Cause.   A service or cause that fills an identifiable need.

Goodwill.   The value of a business beyond its tangible assets, including its reputation and patronage. Also, a favorable condition and overall atmosphere of trust that can be fostered between parties conducting business.

Goodwill Ending.   Shift of emphasis away from the message to the reader. A goodwill ending is positive, personal, and forward-looking and suggests that serving the reader is the real concern.

Goodwill Presentation.   A presentation that entertains and validates the audience.

Grammar Checker.   Software program that flags errors or doubtful usage.

Grapevine.   The informal informational network in an organization, which carries gossip and rumors as well as accurate information.

Grid System.   A means of designing layout by imposing columns on a page and lining up graphic elements within the columns.

Groupthink.   The tendency for a group to reward agreement and directly or indirectly punish dissent.

Guided Discussion.   A presentation in which the speaker presents the questions or issues that both speaker and audience have agreed on in advance.

Instead of functioning as an expert with all the answers, the speaker serves as a facilitator to help the audience tap its own knowledge.

Gunning "Fog Index." A readability formula that determines level of education necessary for comprehension by multiplying average words per sentence by percentage of difficult words by .4.

H

Hard Copy. The paper copy of what is recorded on a word processor.

Hardware. The computer and other equipment necessary for computer technology.

Headings. Words or short phrases that group points and divide your letter, memo, or report into sections.

Hearing. Perceiving sounds.

Hidden Job Market. Jobs that are never advertised but that may be available or may be created for the right candidate.

Hidden Negatives. Words that are not negative in themselves, but become negative in context.

High-Context Culture. A culture in which most information is inferred from the context, rather than being spelled out explicitly in words.

Histogram. A bar graph using pictures, asterisks, or points to represent a unit of the data.

I

Impersonal Expression. A sentence that attributes actions to inanimate objects, designed to avoid placing blame on a reader.

Indented Format. A format for résumés in which items that are logically equivalent begin at the same horizontal space, with carryover lines indented three spaces. Indented format emphasizes job titles.

Independent Clause. A group of words that can stand by itself as a complete sentence.

Inference. A statement that has not yet been verified, but whose truth or falsity could be established, either now or in the future.

Infinitive. The form of the verb that is preceded by *to*.

Inform. To explain something or tell the audience something.

Informal Meetings. Loosely run meetings in which votes are not taken on every point.

Informal Report. A report using letter or memo format.

Information Interview. An interview in which you talk to someone who works in the area you hope to enter to find out what the day-to-day work involves and how you can best prepare to enter that field.

Information Overload. The inability of a human receiver to process all the messages he or she receives.

Information Report. A report that collects data for the reader but does not recommend action.

Informational Messages. In a group, messages focusing on the problem, data, and possible solutions.

Informative Message. Message to which the reader's basic reaction will be neutral.

Informative Presentation. A presentation that informs or teaches the audience.

Informative Report. A report that provides information.

Informative or **Talking Heads.** Headings that are detailed enough to provide an overview of the material in the sections they introduce.

Inside Address. The reader's name and address; put below the date and above the salutation in most letter formats.

Initial Audience. The audience that assigns the message and routes it to other audiences.

Instructions. Step-by-step information about how to perform actions that a single person does.

Intensionalism. An unconscious response to a symbol rather than reality.

Interactive Presentation. A conversation in which the seller uses questions to determine the buyer's needs, probe objections, and gain provisional and then final commitment to the purchase.

Intercultural Competence. The ability to communicate sensitively with people from other cultures and countries, based on an understanding of cultural differences.

Internal Audiences. Audiences in the writer's organization.

Internal Document. Document written for other employees in the same organization.

Internal Documentation. Providing information about a source in the text itself rather than in footnotes or endnotes.

Internal Report. Reports written by employees for use only in their organization.

Interpersonal Communication. Communication between people.

Interpersonal Messages. In a group, messages promoting friendliness, cooperation, and group loyalty.

Interpret. To determine the significance or importance of a message.

Interview. Structured conversation with someone who is able to give you useful information.

Intrapreneurs.   Innovators who work within organizations.

Intrinsic Benefits.   Benefits that come automatically from using a product or doing something.

Introduction.   The part of a report that states the Purpose and Scope of the Report. The Introduction may also include Limitations, Assumptions, Methods, Criteria, and Definitions.

J

Jargon.   There are two kinds of jargon. The first kind is the specialized terminology of a technical field. The second is Businessese, outdated words that do not have technical meanings and are not used in other forms of English.

Judgment or **Opinion.**   A statement that can never be verified, since it includes terms that cannot be measured objectively.

Judgment Sample.   A group of subjects whose views seem useful.

Justification Report.   Report that justifies the need for a purchase, an investment, a new personnel line, or a change in procedure.

Justified Margins.   Margins that end evenly on the right side of the page.

K

Keywords or **Descriptors.**   Words describing the content of an article used to permit computer searches for information on a topic.

Knot.   The action close of a direct mail letter, which harnesses the motivation you have created and turns it into action.

L

Landscape Graphs.   Line graphs with the area below the line filled in are sometimes called landscape graphs.

Laser Printer.   A computer printer that produces high-resolution, sharp, easy-to-read letters.

Late Letter.   A collection letter that threatens legal action if the bill is not paid.

Lead.   An attention-getting statement opening a press release.

Letter.   Short document using block, modified, or AMS simplified letter format that goes to readers outside your organization.

Letterhead.   Stationery with the organization's name, logo, address, and telephone number printed on the page.

Limit.   Boundary placed on a claim that cannot be made with 100% certainty.

Limitations.   Problems or factors that limit the validity of the recommendations of a report.

Line Graph.   A visual consisting of lines that show trends or allow the viewer to interpolate values between the observed values.

Listening.   Decoding and interpreting sounds correctly.

Low-Context Culture.   A culture in which most information is conveyed explicitly in words rather than being inferred from context.

M

Mailing List.   The list of names and addresses to which a direct mail letter is sent.

Main or **Independent Clause.**   A group of words that can stand by itself as a complete sentence.

Maslow's Hierarchy of Needs.   Five levels of human need posited by Abraham H. Maslow. They include physical needs, the need for safety and security, for love and belonging, for esteem and recognition, and for self-actualization.

Memo.   Document using memo format sent to readers in your organization.

Methods Section.   The section of a report or survey describing how the data were gathered.

Middle Letter.   A collection letter that is more assertive than an early letter. Middle letters may offer to negotiate a schedule for repayment if the reader is not able to pay the whole bill immediately, remind the reader of the importance of good credit, educate the reader about credit, or explain why the creditor must have prompt payment.

Minutes.   Records of a meeting, listing the items discussed, the results of votes, and the person responsible for carrying out follow-up steps.

Mirror Question.   Question that paraphrases the content of the answer an interviewee gave to the last question.

Misplaced Modifier.   A word or phrase that appears to modify another element of the sentence than the writer intended.

Mixed Abstract.   An abstract that has characteristics of both summary and descriptive abstracts: it contains the thesis or recommendation and proof, but also contains statements about the article or report.

Mixed Punctuation.   Using a colon after the salutation and a comma after the complimentary close in a letter.

Modified Block Format.   A letter format in which the inside address, date, and signature block are lined up with each other one-half or one-third of the way over on the page.

Modifier.   A word or phrase giving more information about another word in a sentence.

Monochronic Culture.   Culture in which people do only one important activity at a time.

Monologue Presentation.   A presentation in which the speaker speaks without interruption. The presentation is planned and is delivered without deviation.

Myers-Briggs Type Indicator.   A scale that categorizes people on four dimensions: introvert-extravert; sensing-intuitive; thinking-feeling; and perceiving-judging.

N

Negative Message.   A message in which basic information conveyed is negative; the reader is expected to be disappointed or angry.

News Release.   Messages that package information about a company and that the writer would like announced in local and national media.

Noise.   Any physical or psychological interference in a message.

Nominative Case.   The grammatical form used for the subject of a clause. *I, we, he, she,* and *they* are nominative pronouns.

Nonagist.   Words, images, or behaviors that do not discriminate against people on the basis of age.

Nonracist.   Words, images, or behaviors that do not discriminate against people on the basis of race.

Nonrestrictive Clause.   A clause giving extra but unessential information about a noun or pronoun. Because the information is extra, extra commas separate the clause from the word it modifies.

Nonsexist Language.   Language that treats both sexes neutrally, that does not make assumptions about the proper gender for a job, and that does not imply that men are superior to or take precedence over women.

Nonverbal Communication.   Communication that does not use words.

Normal Interview.   A job interview with some questions that the interviewer expects to be easy, some questions that present an opportunity to showcase strong points, and some questions that probe any weaknesses evident from the résumé.

Noun–Pronoun Agreement.   Having a pronoun be the same number (singular or plural) and the same person (first, second, or third) as the noun it refers to.

O

Objective Case.   The grammatical form used for the object of a verb or preposition. *Me, us, him, her,* and *them* are objective pronouns.

Observation.   In semantics, a statement that you yourself have verified.

Omnibus Motion.   A motion that allows a group to vote on several related items in a single vote. Saves time in formal meetings with long agendas.

Open Body Position.   Keeping the arms and legs uncrossed and away from the body. Suggests physical and psychological comfort and openness.

Open Punctuation.   Using no punctuation after the salutation and the complimentary close.

Open Question.   Question with an unlimited number of possible responses.

Opinion.   A statement that can never be verified, since it includes terms that cannot be measured objectively.

Organization.   The order in which ideas are arranged in a message.

Organizational Culture.   The values, attitudes, and philosophies shared by people in an organization that shape its messages and its reward structure.

Orientation.   The first stage in the life of a task group, when members meet and begin to define their task.

Original or **Primary Research.**   Research that gathers new information.

Outpull.   Bring in a bigger response than another version of the same direct mailing.

Outsourcing.   Going outside the company for products and services that once were made by the company's employees.

P

Package.   The outer envelope and everything that goes in it in a direct mailing.

Paired Graphs.   Two simple stories juxtaposed to create a more powerful story.

Parallel Structure.   Putting words or ideas that share the same role in the sentence's logic in the same grammatical form.

Paraphrase.   To repeat in your own words the verbal content of what the previous speaker said.

Passive Verb.   A verb that describes action done to the grammatical subject of the sentence.

People-First Language.   Language that names the person first, then the condition: "people with mental retardation." Used to avoid implying that the condition defines the person's potential.

Perception.   The ability to see, to hear, to taste, to smell, to touch.

Performance Appraisals.   Supervisors' written evaluations of their subordinates.

Persona.   The "author" or character who allegedly writes a letter; the voice that a writer assumes in creating a document.

Personal Space. The distance someone wants between him- or herself and other people in ordinary, nonintimate interchanges.

Personalized. A form letter that is adapted to the individual reader by including the reader's name and address and perhaps other information.

Persuade. To motivate and convince the audience to act.

Persuasive Presentation. A presentation that motivates the audience to act or to believe.

Pictographs or **Histograms.** A bar graph using pictures, asterisks, or points to represent a unit of the data.

Pie Chart. A circular chart whose sections represent percentages of a given quantity.

Pitch. The highness or lowness of a sound. Low-pitched sounds are closer to the bass notes on a piano; high-pitched sounds are closer to the high notes.

Planning. All the thinking done about a subject and the means of achieving your purposes. Planning takes place not only when devising strategies for the document as a whole, but also when generating "miniplans" that govern sentences or paragraphs.

Polarization. A logical fallacy that argues there are only two possible positions, one of which is clearly unacceptable.

Polychronic Culture. Culture in which people do several things at once.

Population. The group a researcher wants to make statements about.

Positive Emphasis. Focusing on the positive rather than the negative aspects of a situation.

Positive or **Good News Message.** Message to which the reader's reaction will be positive.

Possessive Case. The grammatical form used to indicate possession or ownership. *My, our, his, hers, its,* and *their* are possessive pronouns.

Post Office Abbreviations. Two-letter abbreviations for states and provinces.

Prepositions. Words that indicate relationships, for example, *with, in, under, at.*

Presenting Problem. The problem that surfaces as the subject of disagreement. The presenting problem is often not the real problem.

Primary Audience. The audience who will make a decision or act on the basis of a message.

Primary Research. Research that gathers new information.

Pro and Con Pattern. A pattern of organization for reports that presents all the arguments for an alternative and then all the arguments against it.

Probe Question. A follow-up question designed to get more information about an answer or to get at specific aspects of a topic.

Problem-Solving Persuasion. A pattern of organization that describes a problem that affects the reader before offering a solution to the problem.

Procedural Messages. Messages focusing on a group's methods: how it makes decisions, who does what, when assignments are due.

Procedures. Information about how to perform actions that involve several different people at various stages.

Process of Writing. What people actually do when they write. Most researchers would agree that the writing process can include eight parts: planning, gathering, writing, evaluating, getting feedback, revising, editing, and proofreading.

Product of Writing. The final written document.

Progress Report. A statement of the work done during a period of time and the work proposed for the next period.

Proofreading. Checking the final copy to see that it's free from typographical errors.

Proportional Typeface. A typeface in which some letters are wider than other letters (for example, *w* is wider than *i*).

Proposal. Document that suggests a method for finding information or solving a problem.

Prospecting Letter. A job application letter written to companies that have not announced openings but where you'd like to work.

Psychographic Data. Human characteristics that are qualitative rather than quantitative: values, beliefs, goals, and lifestyles.

Psychological Description. Description of a product or service in terms of reader benefits.

Psychological Reactance. Phenomenon occurring when a reader reacts to a negative message by asserting freedom in some other arena.

Purpose Statement. The statement in a proposal or a report specifying the organizational problem, the technical questions that must be answered to solve the problem, and the rhetorical purpose of the report (to explain, to recommend, to request, to propose).

Q

Questionnaire. List of questions for people to answer in a survey.

R

Ragged Right or **Unjustified Margins.** Margins that do not end evenly on the right side of the page.

Random Cluster Sample.   A random sample of subjects at each of a random sample of locations. This method is faster and cheaper when face-to-face interviews are required.

Random Sample.   A sample for which each person of the population theoretically has an equal chance of being chosen.

Reader Benefits.   Benefits or advantages that the reader gets by using the writer's services, buying the writer's products, following the writer's policies, or adopting the writer's ideas. Reader benefits can exist for policies and ideas as well as for goods and services.

Rebuttal.   The refutation of a counterargument.

Recommendation Report.   A report that recommends action.

Recommendations.   Section of a report that specifies items for action.

Reference Line.   A *subject line* that refers the reader to another document (usually a numbered one, such as an invoice).

Referral Interview.   Interviews you schedule to learn about current job opportunities in your field and to get referrals to other people who may have the power to create a job for you. Useful for tapping into unadvertised jobs and the hidden job market.

Release Date.   Date a report will be made available to the public.

Request.   To ask the audience to take an easy or routine action.

Request for Proposal or **RFP.**   A statement of the service or product that an agency wants; a bid for proposals to provide that service or product.

Reply Card.   A card or form designed to make it easy for the reader to respond to a direct mail letter. A good reply card not only leaves space for the reader to fill in mailing and ordering information but also repeats the central selling point, basic product information, and price.

Respondents.   The people who fill out a questionnaire.

Response Rate.   The percentage of subjects receiving a questionnaire who agree to answer the questions.

Restrictive Clause.   A clause limiting or restricting the meaning of a noun or pronoun. Because its information is essential, no commas separate the clause from the word it restricts.

Résumé.   A persuasive summary of your qualifications for employment.

Reverse Chronology.   Starting with the most recent job or degree and going backward. Pattern of organization used for chronological résumés.

Revising.   Making changes in the draft: adding, deleting, substituting, or rearranging. Revision can be

changes in single words, but more often it means major additions, deletions, or substitutions, as the writer measures the draft against purpose and audience and reshapes the document to make it more effective.

RFP.   A statement of the service or product that an agency wants; a bid for proposals to provide that service or product.

Rhetorical Purpose.   The effect the writer or speaker hopes to have on the audience (to inform, to persuade, to build goodwill).

Rhyme.   Repetition of the final vowel sounds, and if the words end with consonants, the final consonant sounds.

Rhythm.   The repetition of a pattern of accented and unaccented syllables.

Rival Hypotheses.   Alternate factors that might explain observed results.

Roll Out.   To send to the whole list of recipients the version of a direct mail letter that performed better in a test of part of the list.

Rule of Three.   The rule explaining that when a series of three items are logically parallel, the last will receive the most emphasis.

Run-on Sentence.   A sentence containing several main clauses strung together with *and, but, or, so,* or *for.*

S

Salutation.   The greeting in a letter: "Dear Ms. Smith."

Sample.   The portion of the population a researcher actually studies.

Sans Serif.   Literally, *without serifs.* Typeface whose letters lack bases or flicks. Helvetica and Geneva are examples of sans serif typefaces.

Saves the Reader's Time.   A message whose style, organization, and visual impact help the reader to read, understand, and act on the information as quickly as possible.

Scope Statement.   A statement in a proposal or report specifying the subjects the report covers and how broadly or deeply it covers them.

Secondary Audience.   The audience affected by the decision or action. These people may be asked by the primary audience to comment on a message or to implement ideas after they've been approved.

Secondary Letters.   Additional letters in a direct mail package. Often on smaller paper, these letters may be to readers who have decided not to accept the offer, from people who have benefited from the charity in the past, and from recognized people corroborating the claims made in the main letter.

Secondary Research.   Research retrieving data someone else gathered.

Semantic Triangle. A triangle without a base, a graphic portrayal of the idea that people provide the only connection between words and things.

Semantics or **General Semantics.** The study of the ways behavior is influenced by the words and other symbols used to communicate.

Sentence Fragment. A group of words that are not a complete sentence but that are punctuated as if they were a complete sentence.

Sentence Outline. An outline using complete sentences that lists the sentences proving the thesis and the points proving each of those sentences. A sentence outline is the basis for a summary abstract.

Serif. The little extensions from the main strokes on the *r* and *g* and other letters. Times Roman and Courier are examples of serif typefaces.

Sexist Interview. A stress interview in which questions are biased against one sex. Many sexist questions mask a legitimate concern. The best strategy is to respond as you would to a stress question: rephrase it and treat it as a legitimate request for information.

Signpost. An explicit statement of the place that a speaker or writer has reached: "Now we come to the third point."

Simple Random Sample. A random sample generated by using a list of all members of a population and a random digit table.

Simple Sentence. Sentence with one main clause.

Situational Interviews. Job interviews in which candidates are asked to describe what they would do in specific hypothetical situations.

Skills Résumé. A résumé organized around the skills you've used, rather than the date or the job in which you used them.

Software. A computer program, usually sold on a disk, that performs a specific task.

Solicited Letter. A job letter written when you know that the company is hiring.

Spot Visuals. Informal visuals that are inserted directly into text. Spot visuals do not have numbers or titles.

Star. The attention-getting opener of a direct mail letter.

Stereotyping. Putting similar people or events into a single category, even though significant differences exist.

Storyboard. A visual representation of the structure of a document, with a rectangle representing each page or unit. An alternative to outlining as a method of organizing material.

Strategy. A plan for reaching your specific goals with a specific audience.

Stratified Random Sample. A sample generated by first dividing the sample into the same proportion of subgroups as exists in the population and then taking a random sample for each subgroup. This method enables a researcher to be sure that all important subgroups are included in the sample.

Stress. Emphasis given to one or more words in a sentence.

Stress Interview. A job interview that deliberately puts the applicant under stress, physical or psychological. Here it's important to change the conditions that create physical stress and to meet psychological stress by rephrasing questions in less inflammatory terms and treating them as requests for information.

Strong Verbs. Verbs that help to convey information forcefully or more clearly than verb strings or nouns.

Structured Interview. An interview that follows a detailed list of questions prepared in advance.

Stub. Used in tables, the stub is the variable listed on the side.

Subject Line. The title of the document, used to file and retrieve the document. A subject line tells readers why they need to read the document and provides a framework in which to set what you're about to say.

Subjects. The people studied in an experiment, focus group, or survey.

Subordinate or **Dependent Clause.** A group of words containing a subject and a verb but that cannot stand by itself as a complete sentence.

Summarizing. Restating and relating major points, pulling ideas together.

Summary Abstract. The logical skeleton of an article or report, containing the thesis or recommendation and its proof.

Summary Sentence or Paragraph. A sentence or paragraph listing in order the topics that following sentences or paragraphs will discuss.

Survey. A method of getting information from a large group of people.

Systematic Random Sample. A random sample generated by setting up a template for a random entry on a page, choosing a random interval, and then taking the name at that entry on every page at the interval. A systematic random sample is often used when the researcher has a phone book.

T

Table. Numbers or words arrayed in rows and columns.

Talking Heads. Headings that are detailed enough to provide an overview of the material in the sections they introduce.

Target Audience.   The audience one tries to reach with a mailing: people who are likely to be interested in buying the product, using the service, or contributing to the cause.

Teaser Copy.   Words written on the envelope to get the reader's attention and persuade him or her to open the envelope.

Teleconferencing.   Telephone conference calls among three or more people in different locations and videoconferences where one-way or two-way TV supplements the audio channel.

Telephone Tag.   Making and returning telephone calls repeatedly before the two people are on the line at the same time.

Telex.   Messages are keyed in on a special machine that translates the keystrokes into a code. Incoming messages are decoded by the machine and printed on paper. Telex messages are common in international business communication.

10-K Report.   A report filed with the Securities and Exchange Commission summarizing the firm's financial performance; an informative document.

Thank-You Letter.   A letter thanking someone for helping you.

Threat.   A statement, explicit or implied, that someone will be punished if he or she does something.

Tone.   The implied attitude of the author toward the reader and the subject.

Tone of Voice.   The rising or falling inflection that indicates whether a group of words is a question or a statement, whether the speaker is uncertain or confident, whether a statement is sincere or sarcastic.

Topic Outline.   An outline listing the main points and the subpoints under each main point. A topic outline is the basis for the table of contents of a report.

Topic Sentence.   A sentence that introduces or summarizes the main idea in a paragraph. A topic sentence may be either stated or implied, and it may come anywhere in the paragraph.

Toulmin Logic.   A model, developed by Stephen Toulmin, useful in planning and in presenting arguments.

Transmit.   To send a message.

Transitions.   Words, phrases, or sentences that show the connections between ideas.

Transmittal.   A memo or letter explaining why something is being sent.

Truncated Code.   Symbols such as asterisks that turn up other forms of a keyword in a computer search.

Truncated Scales.   Graphs with part of the scale missing.

Two-Margin or **Block Format.**   A format for résumés in which dates are listed in one column and job titles and descriptions in another. This format emphasizes work history.

Typeface.   A unified style of type. Each typeface has a design for each letter, number, and symbol. A single typeface will be available in many sizes; it may also be available in bold or italic.

U

Umbrella Sentence or **Paragraph.**   A sentence or paragraph listing in order the topics that following sentences or paragraphs will discuss.

Understatement.   Downplaying or minimizing the size or features of something.

Unity.   Using only one idea or topic in a paragraph or other piece of writing.

Unjustified Margins.   Margins that do not end evenly on the right side of the page.

Unstructured Interview.   An interview based on three or four main questions prepared in advance and other questions that build on what the interviewee says.

V

Verbal Communication.   Communication that uses words; may be either oral or written.

Vested Interest.   The emotional stake readers have in something if they benefit from keeping things just as they are.

Vicarious Participation.   An emotional strategy in fund-raising letters based on the idea that by donating money, readers participate vicariously in work they are not able to do personally.

Visual Impact.   The visual "first impression" you get when you look at a page.

Volume.   The loudness or softness of a voice or other sound.

W

Watchdog Audience.   An audience that has political, social, or economic power and that may base future actions on its evaluation of your message.

Weak Verbs.   Verbs composed of a form of the verb *to be* plus a noun.

White Space.   The empty space on the page. White space emphasizes material that it separates from the rest of the text.

Wild Card or **Truncated Code.**   Symbols such as asterisks that turn up other forms of a keyword in a computer search.

Withdrawing.   Being silent in meetings, not contributing, not helping with the work, not attending meetings.

Wordiness.   Taking more words than necessary to express an idea.

Works Cited.   The sources specifically referred to in a report.

Works Consulted.   Sources read during the research for a report but not mentioned specifically in the report.

Writing.   The act of putting words on paper or on a screen, or of dictating words to a machine or a secretary.

Y

You-Attitude.   A style of writing that looks at things from the reader's point of view, emphasizes what the reader wants to know, respects the reader's intelligence, and protects the reader's ego. Using *you* probably increases you-attitude in positive situations. In negative situations or conflict, avoid *you* since that word will attack the reader.

NOTES

Chapter 1

1. W. B. Johnson and A. E. Packer, *Workforce 2000* (Indianapolis: Hudson Institute, 1987), 99

2. Quoted in John DiGaetani, "Interviews with Allstate," *The ABCA Bulletin* 45, no. 2 (June 1982): 41.

3. Anne Faircloth, "Really Important Things You Need to Know," *Fortune,* January 15, 1996, 37.

4. Quoted in Barrett J. Mandel and Judith Yellen, "Mastering the Memo," *Working Woman,* September 1989, 134.

5. Elaine Viets, "Voice Mail Converts Boss into a Secretary," *Columbus Dispatch,* August 10, 1995, 3E; Rochelle Sharpe, "Work Week," *The Wall Street Journal,* September 26, 1995, A1.

6. Lynn Griffin and James O'Rourke, discussion during the Mini Conference on Communication in Accounting Curricula, Columbus, OH, July 22–23, 1994.

7. Claire B. May and Susan L. Menelaides, "Good Writing Counts," *Journal of Accountancy* 175, no. 7 (July 1993): 77–79.

8. Harold Gardner, "For Accountants, English Is a Second Language," Conference on College Composition and Communication, San Diego, CA, March 31–April 3, 1993.

9. Nancy G. Wilds, "Writing in the Military: A Different Mission," *Worlds of Writing: Teaching and Learning in Discourse Communities,* ed. Carolyn B. Matalene (New York: Random House, 1989), 189.

10. Margot Northey, "The Need for Writing Skill in Accounting Firms," *Management Communication Quarterly* 3 (1990): 480.

11. "Pagers That Say Who Called," *Inc.,* August 1993, 39.

12. Henry Mintzberg, *The Nature of Managerial Work* (New York: Harper & Row, 1973), 32, 65.

13. Frederick K. Moss, "Perceptions of Communication in the Corporate Community," *Journal of Business and Technical Communication* 9.1 (January 1995): 67.

14. John Kotter, *The General Managers* (1982), summarized in Alan Deutschman, "The CEO's Secret of Managing Time," *Fortune,* June 1, 1992, 140.

15. Review of *Make Your Point: A Guide to Improving Your Business and Technical Writing, Journal of Business Communication* 21, no. 1 (Winter 1984): 113. Augmented by telephone conversation with Donald Skarzenski, July 1987.

16. Rebekah Maupin, "How Relevant Is the Current Business Communication Curriculum for Accounting Students?" *The Mid-Atlantic Journal of Business* 29.2 (June 1993): 249.

17. "1996 Cost of a Business Letter" (Chicago: Dartnell/From 9 to 5, September 30, 1996), 1.

18. Dianna Booker, *Cutting Paperwork in the Corporate Culture* (New York: Facts on File, 1986), 24.

19. Claudia MonPere McIsaac and Mary Ann Aschauer, "Proposal Writing at Atherton Jordan, Inc.: An Ethnographic Study," *Management Communication Quarterly* 3 (1990): 535.

20. Elizabeth Allen, "Excellence in Public Relations & Communication Management," IABC/Dayton Awards Banquet, Dayton, OH, July 12, 1990.

21. Frank Grazian, "Can We Cure Murky Memos?" *Communication Briefings* 5, no. 4 (1986): 3.

22. Teri Lammers, "What's Luck Got to Do with It?" *Inc.,* December 1993, 90, and Michael Selz, "Quick Off the Mark: Small Manufacturers Display the Nimbleness the Times Require," *The Wall Street Journal,* December 29, 1993, A1.

23. Donna Fenn, "Leader of the Pack," *Inc.,* February 1996, 31–36.

24. Joseph M. Juran, "Made in U.S.A.: A Renaissance in Quality," *Harvard Business Review,* July–August 1993, 45.

25. Justin Martin, "Are You as Good as You Think You Are?" *Fortune,* September 30, 1996, 152.

26. Susan Greco, "The Art of Selling," *Inc.,* June 1993, 73.

27. John Case, "The Hype about Home Businesses," *Inc.,* The State of Small Business 1996, 58.

28. L. D. DeSimone, George N. Hatsopoulous, Charles P. Holt, et al., "How Can Big Companies Keep the Entrepreneurial Spirit Alive?" *Harvard Business Review,* November–December 1995, 183–92.

29. Alessandra Bianchi, "Mission Improbable," *Inc.,* September 1996, 68–75.

30. John Hilikirk, "Listening to Workers Pays Off," *USA Today,* April 2, 1993, 1B–2B.

31. "Teams: A Formula for Success," *Inc.,* May 1996, 111.

32. James E. Ellis, "Why Overseas? 'Cause That's Where the Sales Are," *Business Week,* January 10, 1994, 62; Joel Kotkin, "Urban Renewal," *Inc.,* March 1996, 24; and Phaedra Hise, "International: Invoicing in 13 Currencies," *Inc.,* November 1995, 101.

33. David A. Victor, personal communication, January 3, 1994, and Linda Beamer and Iris Varner, *Intercultural Business Communication* (Burr Ridge, IL: Irwin, 1994).

34. John J. Fialka, "Col. Wyly's Corps Uses Military Skills to Rescue a Ballet," *The Wall Street Journal,* September 16, 1996, A1; and Ayumi Wakizaka, "Faxes, E-Mail Help the Deaf Get Office Jobs," *The Wall Street Journal,* October 3, 1995, B1, B5.

35. "Tracking with FedEx," *Selling Power,* September 1996, 72; "Here Comes the IntraNet," *Business Week,* February 26, 1996, 76; William M. Bulkeley, "Advances in Networking and Software Push Firms Closer to

Paperless Office," *The Wall Street Journal*, August 5, 1993, B1; Xerox ad, *The Wall Street Journal*, August 11, 1993, A4; and Jim Bessen, "Riding the Marketing Information Wave," *Harvard Business Review*, September–October 1993, 157–58.

36. "Virtual War and Peace," *Wired*, March 1996, 49, 52.

37. Dawn Blalock, "Study Shows Many Execs Are Quick to Write Off Ethics," *The Wall Street Journal*, March 26, 1996, C1.

38. Thomas Petzinger, Jr., "The Front Lines: This Auditing Team Wants You to Create a Moral Organization," *The Wall Street Journal*, January 19, 1996, B1.

39. Clare Ansberry, "Shock Absorber: Bob Stadler Has Lived All the Business Trends of the Past 50 Years," July 11, 1996, A1.

40. Sue Shellenbarger, "High-Powered Fathers Savor Their Decisions to Scale Back Careers," June 12, 1996, B1; Sue Shellenbarger, "All Work and No Play Can Make Jack a Dull Manager," *The Wall Street Journal*, January 24, 1996, B1; Sue Shellenbarger, "Family-Friendly Jobs Are the First Step to Efficient Workplace," *The Wall Street Journal*, May 15, 1996, B1; and Keith H. Hammonds, "Balancing Work and Family," *Business Week*, September 16, 1996, 74.

41. Lori Lewis, "Critical Issues in Communications: Applications to Business," Panel, Association for Business Communication Western Regional Conference, Boise, ID, April 12, 1996.

42. Bianci, "Mission Improbable," 75.

43. Rahul Jacob, "Why Some Customers Are More Equal Than Others," *Fortune*, September 19, 1994, 222, 224.

44. "A Master Class in Radical Change," *Fortune*, December 13, 1993, 82–83.

45. This process was inspired by a process developed by Francis

W. Weeks, *Principles of Business Communication* (Champaign, IL: Stipes, 1973), 45.

Chapter 2

1. Charles Burck, "Learning from a Master," *Fortune*, December 27, 1993, 144; Kathy Casto, "Assumptions about Audience in Negative Messages," Association for Business Communication Midwest Conference, Kansas City, MO, April 30–May 2, 1987; and John P. Wanous and A. Colella, "Future Directions in Organizational Entry Research," *Research in Personnel/Human Resource Management*, ed. Kenneth Rowland and G. Ferris (Greenwich, CT: JAI Press, 1990).

2. Annette N. Shelby and N. Lamar Reinsch, Jr. "Positive Emphasis and You-Attitude: An Empirical Study," *Journal of Business Communication*, 32, no. 4 (October 1995): 303–27.

3. Alan Farnham, "Are You Smart Enough to Keep Your Job?" *Fortune*, January 15, 1996, 42.

4. Mark A. Sherman, "Adjectival Negation and the Comprehension of Multiply Negated Sentences," *Journal of Verbal Learning and Verbal Behavior* 15 (1976): 143–57.

5. Margaret Baker Graham and Carol David, "Power and Politeness: Administrative Writing in an 'Organized Anarchy,'" *Journal of Business and Technical Communication* 10, no. 1 (January 1996): 5–27.

6. John Hagge and Charles Kostelnick, "Linguistic Politeness in Professional Prose: A Discourse Analysis of Auditors' Suggestion Letters, with Implications for Business Communication Pedagogy," *Written Communication* 6, no. 3 (July 1989): 312–39.

7. Brad Edmondson, "What Do You Call a Dark-Skinned Person?" *American Demographics*, October 1993, 9.

8. Lisa Tyler, "Communicating about People with Disabilities: Does the Language We Use Make a Difference?" *The Bulletin of the Association for Business*

Communication 53, no. 3 (September 1990): 65.

9. Marilyn A. Dyrud, "An Exploration of Gender Bias in Computer Clip Art," Association for Business Communication Convention, Chicago, IL, November 6–9, 1996.

Chapter 3

1. Audiences 1, 3, and 4 are based on J. C. Mathes and Dwight Stevenson, *Designing Technical Reports: Writing for Audiences in Organizations*, 2nd ed. (New York: Macmillan, 1991), 40. The fifth audience is suggested by Vincent J. Brown, "Facing Multiple Audiences in Engineering and R&D Writing: The Social Context of a Technical Report," *Journal of Technical Writing and Communication*, 24, no. 1 (1994): 67–75.

2. Isabel Briggs Myers, *Introduction to Type* (Palo Alto, CA: Consulting Psychologists Press, 1980). The material in this section follows Myers's paper.

3. Isabel Briggs Myers and Mary H. McCaulley, *Manual: A Guide to the Development and Use of the Myers-Briggs Type Indicator* (Palo Alto, CA: Consulting Psychologists Press, 1985), 251, 248, respectively.

4. Kitty O. Locker, "What Makes a Collaborative Writing Team Successful? A Case Study of Lawyers and Social Service Workers in a State Agency," *New Visions of Collaborative Writing*, ed. Janis Forman (Portsmouth, NH: Boynton/Cook, 1991).

5. Daniel Pearl, "UPS Takes On Air-Express Competition," *The Wall Street Journal*, December 20, 1990, A4.

6. Keith Naughton, "How Ford's F-150 Lapped the Competition," *Business Week*, July 29, 1996, 74–76.

7. Gabrielle Sándor, "Attitude (Not Age) Defines the Mature Market," *American Demographics*, January 1994, 18–21.

8. Eric N. Berkowitz, Roger A. Kerin, Steven W. Hartley, and

William Rudelius, *Marketing,* 3rd ed. (Homewood, IL: Irwin, 1992), 126; and Carla Marinucci, "Marketers Have Word for You," *San Francisco Examiner,* in *The Columbus Dispatch,* December 23, 1987, B1–B2.

9. PRIZM Brochure, Claritas, Inc., 1995.

10. Alan W. H. Grant and Leonard A. Schlesinger, "Realize Your Customers' Full Profit Potential," *Harvard Business Review,* September–October 1995, 65–66.

11. Scott Jones, "Writing into the Future: Examining the Professionalization and Training of Business Communicators," Association for Business Communication Canadian/East/Midwest Regional Conference, Toronto, CA, April 18–20, 1996.

12. Linda Driskill, "Negotiating Differences among Readers and Writers" (Paper presented at the Conference on College Composition and Communication, San Diego, CA, March 31–April 3, 1993).

13. John J. Weger reports Herzberg's research in *Motivating Supervisors* (New York: American Management Association, 1971), 53–54.

14. Kenneth Labich, "Kissing Off Corporate America," *Fortune,* February 20, 1995, p. 47, and Glenn Burkins, "Work Week," *The Wall Street Journal,* February 13, 1996.

15. For a summary of this research, see Alfie Kohn, "Why Incentive Plans Cannot Work," *Harvard Business Review,* September–October 1993, 54–63.

16. Kevin Leo, "Effective Copy and Graphics," DADM/DMEF Direct Marketing Institute for Professors, Northbrook, IL, May 31–June 3, 1983.

17. Abraham H. Maslow, *Motivation and Personality* (New York: Harper & Row, 1954).

18. Cf. Tove Helland Hammer and H. Peter Dachler, "A Test of Some Assumptions Underlying the Path-Goal Model of Supervision: Some Suggested Conceptual Modifications," *Organizational Behavior and Human Performance* 14 (1975): 73.

19. Edward E. Lawler, III, *Motivation in Work Organizations* (Monterey, CA: Brooks/Cole, 1973), p. 59. Lawler also notes a third obstacle: people may settle for performance and rewards that are just OK. Offering reader benefits, however, does nothing to affect this obstacle.

20. Rachel Spilka, "Orality and Literacy in the Workplace: Process- and Text-Based Strategies for Multiple Audience Adaptation," *Journal of Business and Technical Communication* 4, no. 1 (January 1990): 44–67.

Chapter 4

1. Robert L. Brown, Jr., and Carl G. Herndl, "An Ethnographic Study of Corporate Writing: Job Status as Reflected in Written Text," *Functional Approaches to Writing: A Research Perspective,* ed. Barbara Couture (Norwood, NJ: Ablex, 1986), 16–19, 22–23.

2. Linda Flower, *Problem-Solving Strategies for Writing* (New York: Harcourt Brace Jovanovich, 1981), 39.

3. James Suchan and Robert Colucci, "An Analysis of Communication Efficiency between High-Impact and Bureaucratic Written Communication," *Management Communication Quarterly* 2, no. 4 (May 1989): 464–73.

4. Gloria Pfeif, interview with the author, January 26, 1994.

5. Caleb Solomon, "Clearing the Air: EPA–Amoco Study of Refinery Finds Pollution Rules Focusing on Wrong Part of It," *The Wall Street Journal,* March 29, 1993, A6.

6. Interoffice memo in a steel company.

7. Quoted by Emery Hutchison, "Things My Mother Never Taught Me about Writing," *Journal of Organizational Communications,* Winter 1972, 20.

8. Sign in front of a Kentucky Fried Chicken franchise in Bloomington, IN, July 13, 1984.

9. Philip B. Crosby, *Quality Is Free: The Art of Making Quality Certain* (New York: New American Library, 1979), 79–84.

10. *News-Gazette,* Champaign-Urbana, IL, January 16, 1979, C-8.

11. D. Rhoads, "Cultural Influences on Negotiations with Latin Americans," cited in Lawrence B. Nadler, Marjorie Keeshan Nadler, and Benjamin J. Broome, "Culture and the Management of Conflict Situations," *Communication, Culture, and Organizational Processes,* ed. William B. Gudykunst, Lea P. Stewart, and Stella Ting-Tommey (Beverly Hills, CA: Sage Publications, 1985), 109.

12. Richard C. Anderson, "Concretization and Sentence Learning," *Journal of Educational Psychology* 66, no. 2 (1974): 179–83.

13. January 31, 1978, quoted in Lynn Ashby, "7, 8, Facilitate," *Houston Post,* February 17, 1978.

14. Harris B. Savin and Ellen Perchonock, "Grammatical Structure and the Immediate Recall of English Sentences," *Journal of Verbal Learning and Verbal Behavior* 4 (1965): 348–53, and Pamela Layton and Adrian J. Simpson, "Deep Structure in Sentence Comprehension," *Journal of Verbal Learning and Verbal Behavior* 14 (1975): 658–64.

15. E. B. Coleman, "The Comprehensibility of Several Grammatical Transformations," *Journal of Applied Psychology* 48, no. 3 (1964): 186–90; Keith Raynor, "Visual Attention in Reading: Eye Movements Reflect Cognitive Processes," *Memory and Cognition* 5 (1977): 443–48.

16. Arn Tibbetts, "Ten Rules for Writing Readably," *Journal of Business Communication* 18, no. 4 (Fall 1981): 55–59.

17. Thomas N. Huckin, "A Cognitive Approach to Readability," *New Essays in Technical and Scientific Communication: Research, Theory,*

Practice, ed. Paul V. Anderson, R. John Brockmann, and Carolyn R. Miller (Farmingdale, NY: Baywood, 1983), 93–98.

18. Janice C. Redish and Jack Selzer, "The Place of Readability Formulas in Technical Communication," *Technical Communication* 32, no. 4 (1985): 46–52.

19. James Suchan and Ronald Dulek, "A Reassessment of Clarity in Written Managerial Communications," *Management Communication Quarterly* 4, no. 1 (August 1990): 93–97.

Chapter 5

1. W. Ross Winterowd, *The Contemporary Writer* (New York: Harcourt Brace Jovanovich, 1975), 61.

2. George H. Jensen and John K. DiTiberio, *Personality and the Teaching of Composition* (Norwood, NJ: Ablex Publishing, 1989), 42.

3. Mike Rose, *Writer's Block: The Cognitive Dimension,* published for Conference on College Composition and Communication (Carbondale, IL: Southern Illinois University Press, 1984), 36.

4. See especially Linda Flower and John R. Hayes, "The Cognition of Discovery: Defining a Rhetorical Problem," *College Composition and Communication* 31 (February 1980): 21–32; Rose, *Writer's Block;* and the essays in two collections: Charles R. Cooper and Lee Odell, *Research on Composing: Points of Departure* (Urbana, IL: National Council of Teachers of English, 1978), and Mike Rose, ed., *When a Writer Can't Write: Studies in Writer's Block and Other Composing-Process Problems* (New York: Guilford Press, 1985).

5. Rebecca E. Burnett, "Content and Commas: How Attitudes Shape a Communication-Across-the-Curriculum Program," Association for Business Communication Convention, Orlando, FL, November 1–4, 1995.

6. Peter Elbow, *Writing with Power: Techniques for Mastering the Writing Process* (New York: Oxford University Press, 1981), 15–20.

7. See Gabriela Lusser Rico, *Writing the Natural Way* (Los Angeles: J. P. Tarcher, 1983), 10.

8. Fred Reynolds, "What Adult Work-World Writers Have Taught Me About Adult Work-World Writing," *Professional Writing in Context: Lessons from Teaching and Consulting in Worlds of Work,* (Hillsdale, NJ: Lawrence Erlbaum Associates, 1995), 18–21.

9. Raymond W. Beswick, "Communicating in the Automated Office," American Business Communication Association International Convention, New Orleans, LA, October 20, 1982.

10. Dianna Booker, *Cutting Paperwork in the Corporate Culture* (New York: Facts on File Publications, 1986), 23.

11. Susan D. Kleimann, "The Complexity of Workplace Review," *Technical Communication* 38, no. 4 (1991): 520–26.

12. This three-step process is modeled on the one suggested by Barbara L. Shwom and Penny L. Hirsch, "Managing the Drafting Process: Creating a New Model for the Workplace," *The Bulletin of the Association for Business Communication,* 57, no. 2 (June 1994): 1–10.

13. Glenn J Broadhead and Richard C. Freed, *The Variables of Composition: Process and Product in a Business Setting,* Conference on College Composition and Communication Studies in Writing and Rhetoric (Carbondale, IL: Southern Illinois University Press, 1986), 57.

14. Christina Haas, "How the Writing Medium Shapes the Writing Process: Effects of Word Processing on Planning," *Research in the Teaching of English* 23, no. 2 (May 1989): 181; and Christina Haas,

" 'Seeing It on the Screen Isn't Really Seeing It': Computer Writers' Reading Problems," *Critical Perspectives on Computers and Composition Instruction,* ed. Gail Hawisher and Cynthia Selfe (New York: Teachers College Press, 1989), 18–23.

15. Sara Kiesler, Jane Siegel, and Timothy W. McGuire, "Social Psychological Aspects of Computer-Mediated Communication," *American Psychologist* 39, no. 10 (October 1984): 1129; also Esther T. Huckaby, telephone conversation with the author, August 3, 1987.

Chapter 6

1. Linda Reynolds, "The Legibility of Printed Scientific and Technical Information," *Information Design,* ed. Ronald Easterby and Harm Zwaga (New York: John Wiley & Sons, 1984), 187–208.

2. George A. Miller, "The Magical Number Seven, Plus or Minus Two: Some Limits on Our Capacity for Processing Information," *Psychological Review* 63, no. 2 (March 1956): 81–97.

3. Once we know how to read English, the brain first looks to see whether an array of letters follows the rules of spelling. If it does, the brain then treats the array as a word (even if it isn't one, such as *tweal*). The shape is processed in individual letters only when the shape is not enough to suggest meaning. Jerry E. Bishop, "Word Processing: Research on Stroke Victims Yields Clues to the Brain's Capacity to Create Language," *The Wall Street Journal,* October 12, 1993, A6.

4. David Matis, "The Graphic Design of Text," *Intercom,* February 1996, 23.

5. M. Gregory and E. C. Poulton, "Even versus Uneven Right-Hand Margins and the Rate of Comprehension of Reading," *Ergonomics* 13 (1970): 427–34.

6. Russell N. Baird, Arthur T. Turnbull, and Duncan

McDonald, *The Graphics of Communication: Typography, Layout, Design, Production,* 5th ed. (New York: Holt, Rinehart & Winston, 1987), 37.

7. Philip M. Rubens, "A Reader's View of Text and Graphics: Implications for Transactional Text," *Journal of Technical Writing and Communication* 16, nos. 1–2 (1986): 78.

8. M. E. Wrolstad, "Adult Preferences in Typography: Exploring the Function of Design," *Journalism Quarterly* 37 (Winter 1960): 211–23; summarized in Rolf F. Rehe, "Typography: How to Make It Most Legible," Design Research International, Carmel, IN, 57.

9. Elizabeth Keyes, "Typography, Color, and Information Structure," *Technical Communication,* 40, no. 4 (November 1993): 652; and Joseph Koncelik, "Design, Aging, Ethics, and the Law" (Paper presented in Columbus, OH, May 6, 1993).

10. Marilyn A. Dyrud, "An Exploration of Gender Bias in Computer Clip Art," Association for Business Communication Annual Convention, Chicago, IL, November 1–9, 1996.

11. Jakob Nielsen, "Top Ten Mistakes in Web Design," May 1996, http://www.useit.com/alertbox/9605.html.

12. For a review of the events and an analysis of the management problems, see J. C. Mathes, "Three Mile Island: The Management Communication Role," *Engineering Management International* 3 (1986): 261–68.

Chapter 7

1. Thomas L. Fernandez and Roger N. Conaway, "Writing Business Letters II: Essential Elements Revisited," *1996 Refereed Proceedings,* Association for Business Communication Southwest Region, ed. Marsha L. Bayless, 65–68.

2. In a study of 483 subject lines written by managers and MBA students, Priscilla S. Rogers found that the average subject line was 5 words; only 10% of the subject lines used 10 or more words ("A Taxonomy for Memorandum Subject Lines," *Journal of Business and Technical Communication* 4, no. 2 [September 1990]: 28–29).

3. Iris I. Varner and Carson H. Varner, "The Press Release to Illustrate Reader Adaptation in Business Report Writing," *ABCA Bulletin* 42, no. 3 (September 1979):3.

4. *Communication Briefings* 1, no. 12 (October 1982): 2.

5. Richard C. Whitely, *The Customer-Driven Company* (Reading, MA: Addison-Wesley, 1991), 39–40.

6. An earlier version of this problem, the sample solutions, and the discussion appeared in Francis W. Weeks and Kitty O. Locker, *Business Writing Cases and Problems* (Champaign, IL: Stipes, 1980), 40–44.

Chapter 8

1. Kitty O. Locker, "Factors in Reader Responses to Negative Messages: Experimental Evidence for Changing What We Teach," unpublished manuscript.

2. Allan Sloan, "The Hit Men," *Newsweek,* February 26, 1996, 48.

3. Locker, "Factors in Reader Reactions."

4. Jack W. Brehm, *A Theory of Psychological Reactance* (New York: Academic Press, 1966).

5. Carol David, "Rereading Bad News: Policy and Procedural Memos and Bad News Lore," Association for Business Communication Annual Convention, Montreal, Canada, October 27–30, 1993.

6. Leslie N. Vreeland, "SEC 'Cop' Has Eye on Mutual Funds," *The Columbus Dispatch,* July 21, 1987, 3F.

7. Frederick M. Jablin and Kathleen Krone, "Characteristics of Rejection Letters and Their Effects on Job Applicants," *Written Communication* 1, no. 4 (October 1984): 387–406.

8. John D. Pettit, "An Analysis of the Effects of Various Message Presentations on Communicatee Responses," Ph.D. diss. Louisiana State University, 1969; and Jack D. Eure, "Applicability of American Written Business Communication Principles Across Cultural Boundaries in Mexico," *Journal of Business Communication* 14 (1976): 51–63.

9. Elizabeth A. McCord, "The Business Writer, the Law, and Routine Business Communication: A Legal and Rhetorical Analysis," *Journal of Business and Technical Communication* 5, no. 2 (1991): 183.

10. Gabriella Stern, "Companies Discover That Some Firings Backfire into Costly Defamation Suits," *The Wall Street Journal,* May 5, 1993, B1.

Chapter 9

1. Art Kleiner, "Flexing Their Mussels, *Garbage,* July/August 1992, 50.

2. Alan Farnham, "You're So Vain," *Fortune,* September 9, 1996, 78–80.

3. John D. Hartigan, "Giving Kids Condoms Won't Work," *The Wall Street Journal,* December 19, 1990, A16.

4. J. C. Mathes and Dwight W. Stevenson, *Designing Technical Reports: Writing for Audiences in Organizations* (Indianapolis: Bobbs-Merrill, 1979), 18–19.

5. James Suchan and Ron Dulek, "Toward a Better Understanding of Reader Analysis," *Journal of Business Communication* 25, no. 2 (Spring 1988): 40.

6. Frances Harrington, "Formulaic Patterns versus Pressures of Circumstances: A Rhetoric of Business Situations," Conference on College Composition and Communication, New Orleans, LA, March 17–19, 1986.

7. Min-Sun Kim and Steven R. Wilson, "A Cross-Cultural

Comparison of Implicit Theories of Requesting," *Communication Monographs* 61, no. 3 (September 1994): 210–35.

8. Priscilla S. Rogers, "A Taxonomy for the Composition of Memorandum Subject Lines: Facilitating Writer Choice in Managerial Contexts," *Journal of Business and Technical Communication* 4, no. 2 (September 1990): 21–43.

9. See John Nathan, "In Search of Excellence: The Film" (Waltham, MA: Nathan/Tyler Productions, 1985), 9–14.

10. Karen Lowry Miller and David Woodruff, "The Man Who's Selling Japan on Jeeps," *Business Week*, July 19, 1993, 56–57.

11. Daniel J. O'Keefe, *Persuasion* (Newbury Park, CA: Sage, 1990), 168; Joanne Martin and Melanie E. Powers, "Truth or Corporate Propaganda," *Organizational Symbolism*, ed. Louis R. Pondy, Thomas C. Dandridge, Gareth Morgan, and Peter J. Frost (Greenwich, CT: JAI Press, 1983), 97–107; and Dean C. Kazoleas, "A Comparison of the Persuasive Effectiveness of Qualitative versus Quantitative Evidence: A Test of Explanatory Hypotheses," *Communication Quarterly*, 41, no. 1 (Winter 1993): 40–50.

12. Daniel Dieterich to Kitty Locker, March 24, 1993.

13. "Phoning Slow Payers Pays Off," *Inc.*, July 1996, 95.

14. An earlier draft of this problem and analysis appeared in Francis W. Weeks and Kitty O. Locker, *Business Writing Problems and Cases* (Champaign, IL: Stipes, 1980), 78–81.

Chapter 10

1. Kathleen J. Krone and John T. Ludlum, "An Organizational Perspective on Interpersonal Influence," in *Seeking Compliance: The Production of Personal Influence Messages*, ed. James Price Dillard (Scottsdale, AZ: Gorsuch Scarisbrick, 1990), 123–42.

2. "Sell Prospects by Using Their Motivational Triggers," *Personal Selling Power*, October 1993, 48.

3. Walter R. Nord, "Beyond the Teaching Machine: The Neglected Area of Operant Conditioning in the Theory and Practice of Management," *Organizational Behavior and Human Performance* 4 (1969): 375–401.

4. Ronald A. Heifetz and Donald L. Laurie, "The Work of Leadership," *Harvard Business Review*, January–February 1997, 124–34.

5. Denise Rousseau, "Corporate Culture Isn't Easy to Change," *The Wall Street Journal*, August 12, 1996, A12.

6. See Stephen Toulmin, *The Uses of Argument* (Cambridge: Cambridge University Press, 1958).

Chapter 11

1. Murray Raphel, "Reviving the Dying Store," *Direct Marketing*, November 1993, 20–21.

2. "Direct Marketing . . . An Aspect of Total Marketing," *Direct Marketing*, July 1996, 3.

3. Ernan Roman, "More for Your Money," *Inc.*, September 1992, 113, and Con Squires, "Using Personalization to Increase Response," *Fund Raising Management*, August 1993, 51.

4. Larry J. Sabato, "Mailing for Dollars," *Psychology Today*, October 1984, 38.

5. This pattern is an adaptation of the Star-Chain-Hook pattern developed by Cy Frailey in the 1930s.

6. Bill Jayme, quoted in John Francis Tighe, "Complete Creative Checklist for Copywriters," *Advertising Age*, February 9, 1987, 24, 69.

7. John D. Beard, David L. Williams, and J. Patrick Kelly, "The Long versus the Short Letter: A Large Sample Study of a Direct-Mail Campaign," *Journal of Direct Marketing* 4, no. 12 (Winter 1990): 13–20.

8. Jack Maguire to Kitty Locker, December 30, 1986.

9. Jane Maas, *Better Brochures, Catalogs and Mailing Pieces* (New York: St. Martin's Press, 1981), 98–99.

10. Maxwell Sackheim, *My First Sixty-Five Years in Advertising* (Blue Ridge Summit, PA: Tab Books, 1975), 97–100.

Chapter 12

1. "All It Takes Is a Little Investigation," *Going Global: Mexico*, brochure published by *Inc.*, October 1993, n.p.

2. Brian O'Reilly, "Your New Global Work Force," *Fortune*, December 14, 1992, 52–66.

3. Joann S. Lublin, "An Overseas Stint Can Be a Ticket to the Top," *The Wall Street Journal*, January 29, 1996, B1.

4. Rob Norton, "Exploding the Myths about Growth," *Fortune*, November 25, 1996, 84.

5. "Amazing Numbers," *Selling Power*, September 1996, 28.

6. "Hispanic Population Up by More than 50%," *The Columbus Dispatch*, March 11, 1991.

7. "Ethnic Mix Gives California Its Youth," *The Wall Street Journal*, July 12, 1990, B1.

8. "Harvard Tracking Religious Diversity," *The Columbus Dispatch*, November 13, 1993, 10H.

9. R. Gustav Niebuhr, "Islam is Growing Fast in the U.S., Fighting Fear and Stereotypes," *The Wall Street Journal*, October 5, 1990, A1.

10. Joel Dreyfuss, "Get Ready for the New Work Force," *Fortune*, April 23, 1990: 165.

11. David A. Victor, *International Business Communication* (New York: HarperCollins, 1992), 148–60.

12. Christina Haas and Jeffrey L. Funk, " 'Shared Information': Some Observations of Communication in Japanese Technical Settings," *Technical Communication* 36, no. 4 (November 1989): 365.

13. Mahund S. Hashmi and Kent L. Foutz, "Marketing in the Islamic Context," Sixth Annual Eastern Michigan University

Conference on Languages and Communication for World Business and the Professions, Ann Arbor, MI, May 7–9, 1987.

14. William Ruch, *Corporate Communication: A Comparison of Japanese and American Practices* (Westport, CT: Quorum Books, 1984), 5–6.

15. Paula J. Pomerenke, "Cultural Influences on Formulating Arguments in Marketing Reports," Modern Language Association Convention, Toronto, Canada, December 27–30, 1993.

16. Laray M. Barna, "Stumbling Blocks in Intercultural Communication, in *Intercultural Communication,* ed. Larry A. Samovar and Richard E. Porter (Belmont, CA: Wadsworth, 1985), 331.

17. Carmen Judith Nine-Curt, "Hispanic-Anglo Conflicts in Nonverbal Communication," in *Perspectivas Pedagogicas,* ed. I. Abino et al. (Universidad de Puerto Rico, 1983), 235.

18. Laurence Wylie, *Beaux Gestes: A Guide to French Body Talk* (Cambridge, MA: Undergraduate Press, 1977), xi.

19. Marjorie Fink Vargas, *Louder than Words* (Ames, IA: Iowa State University Press, 1986), 47.

20. Michael Argyle, *Bodily Communication* (New York: International University Press, 1975), 89.

21. Jerrold J. Merchant, "Korean Interpersonal Patterns: Implications for Korean/American Intercultural Communication," *Communication* 9 (October 1980): 65.

22. Argyle, *Bodily Communication,* 92.

23. Ray L. Birdwhistell, *Kinesics and Context: Essays on Body Motion Communication* (Philadelphia: University of Philadelphia Press, 1970), 30–31.

24. Edward T. Hall and Mildred Reed Hall, *Hidden Differences* (Hamburg, West Germany: Stern Magazine, 1983), 47.

25. Jack Seward, *The Japanese* (New York: Morrow, 1972), 37.

26. Birdwhistell, *Kinesics and Context,* 81.

27. Foseco Minsep, *The Business Traveller's Handbook: How to Get Along with People in 100 Countries* (New York: Prentice-Hall, 1983), 30.

28. Paul Ekman, Wallace V. Friesen, and John Bear, "The International Language of Gestures," *Psychology Today* 18, no. 5 (May 1984): 64.

29. Nine-Curt, "Hispanic-Anglo Conflicts," 234.

30. Baxter, 1970, reported in Marianne LaFrance, "Gender Gestures: Sex, Sex-Role, and Nonverbal Communication," in *Gender and Nonverbal Behavior,* ed. Clara Mayo and Nancy M. Henley (New York: Springer-Verlag, 1981), 130.

31. Nine-Curt, "Hispanic-Anglo Conflicts," 238.

32. Khamdi Amnatvong, interview with the author, Columbus, OH, August 1987.

33. Brenda Major, "Gender Patterns in Touching Behavior," in *Gender and Nonverbal Behavior,* ed. Clara Mayo and Nancy M. Henley (New York: Springer-Verlag, 1981), 26, 28.

34. "Iran Going to Great Lengths to Keep Men, Women Apart," *The Columbus Dispatch,* July 28, 1994, 12A.

35. Natalie Porter and Florence Gies, "Women and Nonverbal Leadership Cues: When Seeing Is Not Believing," in *Gender and Nonverbal Behavior,* ed. Clara Mayo and Nancy M. Henley (New York: Springer-Verlag, 1981), 48–49.

36. Robert C. Christopher, *Second to None: American Companies in Japan* (New York: Crown, 1986), 102–03.

37. Edward Twitchell Hall, *Hidden Differences: Doing Business with the Japanese* (Garden City, NY: Anchor-Doubleday, 1987), 25.

38. Lawrence B. Nadler, Marjorie Keeshan Nadler, and Benjamin J. Broome, "Culture and the Management of Conflict Situations," in *Communication, Culture, and Organizational Processes,* ed. William B. Gudykunst, Lea P. Stewart, and Stella Ting-Toomey (Beverly Hills, CA: Sage, 1985), 103.

39. Argyle, *Bodily Communication,* 90.

40. Carl Quintanilla, "Work Week," *The Wall Street Journal,* August 13, 1996, A1; Mary Ritchie Key, *Paralanguage and Kinesics* (Metuchen, NJ: Scarecrow, 1975), 23; Fred Hitzhusen, conversation with the author, January 31, 1988; and William Horton, "The Almost Universal Language: Graphics for International Documents," *Technical Communication* 40, no. 4(1993): 687.

41. David Stipp, "Mirror, Mirror on the Wall, Who's the Fairest of Them All?" *Fortune,* September 9, 1996, 87.

42. Vincent O'Neill, "Training the Multi-Cultural Manager," Sixth Annual EMU Conference on Languages and Communication for World Business and the Professions, Ann Arbor, MI, May 7–9, 1987.

43. Akihisa Kumayama, comment during discussion, Sixth Annual EMU Conference on Languages and Communication for World Business and the Professions, Ann Arbor, MI, May 7–9, 1987.

44. Muriel Saville-Troike, "An Integrated Theory of Communication," in *Perspectives on Silence,* ed. Deborah Tannen and Muriel Saville-Troike (Norwood, NJ: Ablex, 1985), 10–11.

45. A. Jann Davis, *Listening and Responding* (St. Louis: Mosby, 1984), 43.

46. Edward T. Hall and William Foote Whyte, "Intercultural Communication: A Guide to Men of Action," *Human Organization* 19, no. 1 (Spring 1960): 7.

47. Marcia Sweezey to BizCom, September 14, 1992.

48. Tim Comerford to Kitty Locker, Akron, OH, April 4, 1991.

Chapter 13

1. For a full account of the accident, see Andrew D. Wolvin and Caroline Gwynn Coakely, *Listening,* 2nd ed. (Dubuque, IA: William C. Brown, 1985), 6.

2. Molefi Asante and Alice Davis, "Black and White Communication: Analyzing Work Place Encounters," *Journal of Black Studies* 16, no. 1 (September 1985): 87–90.

3. Thomas Gordon with Judith Gordon Sands, *P.E.T. in Action* (New York: Wyden, 1976), 83.

4. Thomas J. Knutson, "Communication in Small Decision-Making Groups: In Search of Excellence," *Journal for Specialists in Group Work* 10, no. 1 (March 1985): 28–37. The next four paragraphs summarize Knutson's analysis.

5. For a fuller listing of roles in groups, see David W. Johnson and Frank P. Johnson, *Joining Together: Group Theory and Group Skills* (Englewood Cliffs, NJ: Prentice Hall, 1975), 26–27.

6. Beatrice Schultz, "Argumentativeness: Its Effect in Group Decision-Making and Its Role in Leadership Perception," *Communication Quarterly* 30, no. 4 (Fall 1982): 374–75; Dennis S. Gouran and B. Aubrey Fisher, "The Functions of Human Communication in the Formation, Maintenance, and Performance of Small Groups," in *Handbook of Rhetorical and Communication Theory,* ed. Carroll C. Arnold and John Waite Bowers (Boston: Allyn and Bacon, 1984), 640; and Curt Bechler and Scott D. Johnson, "Leadership and Listening: A Study of Member Perceptions," *Small Group Research* 26, no. 1 (February 1995): 77–85.

7. H. Lloyd Goodall, Jr., *Small Group Communications in Organizations* (Dubuque, IA: William C. Brown, 1985), 39–40.

8. Nance L. Harper and Lawrence R. Askling, "Group Communication and Quality of Task Solution in a Media Production Organization," *Communication Monographs* 47, no. 2 (June 1980): 77–100.

9. Rebecca E. Burnett, "Conflict in Collaborative Decision-Making," in *Professional Communication: The Social Perspective,* ed. Nancy Roundy Blyler and Charlotte Thralls (Newbury Park, CA: Sage, 1993), 144–62.

10. Kimberly A. Freeman, "Attitudes Toward Work in Project Groups as Predictors of Academic Performance," *Small Group Research* 27, no. 2 (May 1996): 265–82.

11. Solomon F. Asch, "Opinions and Social Pressure," *Scientific American* 193, no. 5 (November 1955): 31–35. For a review of recent literature on groupthink, see Marc D. Street, "Groupthink: An Examination of Theoretical Issues, Implications, and Future Research Suggestions," *Small Group Research* 28 no. 1 (February 1997): 72–93.

12. Poppy Lauretta McLeod, Sharon Alisa Lobel, and Taylor H. Cox, Jr., "Ethnic Diversity and Creativity in Small Groups," *Small Group Research* 27, no. 2 (May 1996): 248–64.

13. Deborah Tannen, *That's Not What I Meant!* (New York: William Morrow, 1986).

14. Karen Ritchie, "Marketing to Generation X," *American Demographics,* April 1995, 34–36.

15. Thomas Kochman, *Black and White Styles in Conflict* (Chicago: University of Chicago Press, 1981), 103.

16. Daniel N. Maltz and Ruth A. Borker, "A Cultural Approach to Male-Female Miscommunication," in *Language and Social Identity,* ed. John J. Gumperz (Cambridge: Cambridge University Press, 1982), 202.

17. Thomas Kochman, *Black and White Styles in Conflict* (Chicago: University of Chicago Press, 1981), 44–45.

18. David S. Jalajas and Robert I. Sutton, "Feuds in Student Groups: Coping with Whiners, Martyrs, Saboteurs, Bullies, and Deadbeats," *Mastering Management Education: Innovations in Teaching Effectiveness,* ed. Charles M. Vance (Newbury Park, CA: Sage, 1993), 217–27.

19. Jeffrey A. Fadiman, "Intercultural Invisibility: Deciphering the 'Subliminal' Marketing Message in Afro-Asian Commerce," Sixth Annual Conference on Languages and Communication for World Business and the Professions, Ann Arbor, MI, May 8–9, 1987.

20. Raymond L. Gordon, *Living in Latin America* (Skokie, IL: National Textbook, 1974), 41.

21. Philip R. Harris and Robert T. Moran, *Managing Cultural Differences,* 2nd ed. (Houston: Gulf, 1987), 78.

22. Carol Hymowitz, "A Survival Guide to the Office Meeting," *The Wall Street Journal,* June 21, 1988, 33. Middle managers judged 54% of the meetings they attended to be productive; senior managers judged 58% of their meetings productive.

23. Lisa Ede and Andrea Lunsford, *Singular Texts/Plural Authors: Perspectives on Collaborative Writing* (Carbondale, IL: Southern Illinois Press, 1990), 60.

24. Rebecca Burnett, "Characterizing Conflict in Collaborative Relationships: The Nature of Decision-Making During Coauthoring." PhD dissertation, Carnegie-Mellon University, Pittsburgh, PA, 1991.

25. Kitty O. Locker, "What Makes a Collaborative Writing Team Successful? A Case Study of Lawyers and Social Service Workers in a State Agency," in *New Visions in Collaborative Writing,* ed. Janis Forman (Portsmouth, NJ: Boynton, 1991), 37–52.

26. Ede and Lunsford, *Singular Texts/Plural Authors,* 66.

27. Meg Morgan, Nancy Allen, Teresa Moore, Dianne Atkinson, and Craig Snow, "Collaborative Writing in the Classroom," *The Bulletin of the Association for Business Communication* 50, no. 3 (September 1987): 22.

Chapter 14

1. For a useful taxonomy of proposals, see Richard C. Freed and David D. Roberts, "The

Nature, Classification, and Generic Structure of Proposals," *Journal of Technical Writing and Communication* 19, no. 4 (1989): 317–51.

2. Dana Milbank, "Scientists Have to Beat the Bushes for Money to Stay in Business," *The Wall Street Journal*, November 7, 1990, A1.

3. Christine Peterson Barabas, *Technical Writing in a Corporate Culture: A Study of the Nature of Information* (Norwood, NJ: Ablex Publishing, 1990), 327.

4. Terence P. Paré, "How to Find Out What They Want," *Fortune,* Autumn/Winter 1993, 39.

5. Phaedra Hise, "The Camera Doesn't Lie," *Inc.,* October 1993, 35.

6. Brock Brower, "The Pernicious Power of the Polls," *Money,* March 1988, 146.

7. Janice M. Lauer and J. William Asher, *Composition Research: Empirical Designs* (New York: Oxford University Press, 1986), 66.

8. Irving Crespi, quoted in W. Joseph Campbell, "Phone Surveys Becoming Unreliable, Pollsters Say," *The Columbus Dispatch,* February 21, 1988, 8F.

9. Lauer and Asher, *Composition Research,* 67.

10. Wade Leftwich, "Marketer, Market Thyself," *American Demographics,* August 1993, 2.

11. "How Good Are Polls? We Refuse to Answer," *Business Week,* July 6, 1992, 29.

12. Brower, *Pernicious Power,* 145.

13. Earl E. McDowell, Bridget Mrolza, and Emmy Reppe, "An Investigation of the Interviewing Practices of Technical Writers in Their World of Work," in Earl E. McDowell, *Interviewing Practices for Technical Writers* (Amityville, NY: Baywood Publishing, 1991), 207.

14. Robert A. Papper to Kitty Locker, March 17, 1991.

15. Thomas Hunter, "Pulitzer Winner Discusses Interviewing," *IABC Communication World,* April 1985, 13–14.

Chapter 15

1. Ronald B. Lieber, "Storytelling: A New Way to Get Close to Your Customer," *Fortune,* February 3, 1997, 106.

2. Cynthia Crossen, "Margin of Error: Studies Galore Support Products and Positions, but Are They Reliable?" *The Wall Street Journal,* November 14, 1991, A1, A7.

3. "Whirlpool: How to Listen to Consumers," *Fortune,* January 11, 1993, 77.

4. Peter Lynch with John Rothchild, *One Up on Wall Street: How to Use What You Already Know to Make Money in the Market* (New York: Simon and Schuster, 1989), 187.

5. Patricia Sullivan, "Reporting Negative Research Results," and Kitty O. Locker to Pat Sullivan, June 8, 1990.

6. Michael L. Keene, conversation with the author, May 17, 1988.

7. Jeanne H. Halpern, phone interview with the author, January 21, 1994.

8. James Paradis, David Dobrin, and Richard Miller, "Writing at Exxon ITD: Notes on the Writing Environment of an R&D Organization," in *Writing in Nonacademic Settings* (New York: Guilford, 1985), 300–02.

9. George A. Miller, "The Magical Number Seven, Plus or Minus Two: Some Limits on Our Capacity for Processing Information," *Psychological Review* 63, no. 2 (March 1956): 81–97.

10. Dwight W. Stevenson, Business and Technical Writing Teachers' Roundtable, Purdue, West Lafayette, IN, October 19–20, 1986.

11. Frederick Rose, "In Wake of Cost Cuts, Many Firms Sweep Their History Out the Door," *The Wall Street Journal,* December 21, 1987, 21.

12. "How Investors Use Annual Reports," *American Demographics,* May 1996, 18.

13. Geoffrey A. Cross, "A Bakhtinian Exploration of Factors Affecting the Collaborative Writing of an Executive Letter of an Annual Report," *Research in the Teaching of English* 24 (1990): 173–202.

14. Thomas E. Pinelli, Virginia M. Cordle, and Raymond F. Vondran, "The Function of Report Components in the Screening and Reading of Technical Reports," *Journal of Technical Writing and Communication* 14, no. 2 (1984): 92.

Chapter 16

1. Barbara Rosewicz, "Consumer Lobbies Gain Ground on Capitol Hill By Parlaying Tactics, Timing on Banking Bills," *The Wall Street Journal,* October 5, 1987, 46.

2. "GM's $2 Billion Quarterly Loss Biggest Ever," AP, *The Columbus Dispatch,* November 1, 1990, 1B, and Joseph B. White and Paul Ingrassia, "Huge GM Write-Off Positions Automaker To Show New Growth," *The Wall Street Journal,* November 1, 1990, A1.

3. "Taxing Question," *Business Week,* September 30, 1996, 4.

4. Jared Sandberg, "On-Line Services' User Counts Often Aren't What They Seem," *The Wall Street Journal,* October 6, 1995, B1.

5. Cynthia Crossen, "Diaper Debate: A Case Study of Tactical Research," *The Wall Street Journal,* May 17 1994, B8.

6. "The Incredible Shrinking Failure Rate," *Inc.,* October 1993, 58.

7. Gene Zelazny, *Say It with Charts: The Executive's Guide to Successful Presentations,* 2nd ed. (Homewood, IL: Business One Irwin, 1991), 52.

8. Most of these guidelines are given by Zelazny, *Say It With Charts.*

9. W. S. Cleveland and R. McGill, "Graphical Perception: Theory, Experiments, and Application to the Development of Graphic Methods," *Journal of the American Statistical Association* 79, nos. 3 & 7 (1984): 531–53; cited in Jeffry K. Cochran, Sheri A. Albrecht, and Yvonne A. Greene, "Guidelines for

Evaluating Graphical Designs: A Framework Based on Human Perception Skills," *Technical Communication* 36, no. 1 (February 1989): 27.

10. G. Bruce Knecht, "At USA Today, A Staged Photo Isn't Good News," *The Wall Street Journal*, August 22, 1996, B1, B2.

11. L. G. Thorell and W. J. Smith, *Using Computer Color Effectively: An Illustrated Reference* (Englewood Cliffs, NJ: Prentice Hall, 1990), 12–13; William Horton, "The Almost Universal Language: Graphics for International Documents," *Technical Communication* 40, no. 4 (1993): 687; and Thyra Rauch, "IBM Visual Interface Design," *The STC Usability PIC Newsletter*, January 1996, 3.

12. Thorell and Smith, *Using Computer Color Effectively*, 13.

13. Ibid., 49–51, 214–15.

14. Edward R. Tufte, *The Visual Display of Quantitative Information* (Cheshire, CT: Graphics Press, 1983), 113.

15. Thophilus Addo, "The Effects of Dimensionality in Computer Graphics," *Journal of Business Communication* 31, no. 4 (October 1994): 253–65.

16. Kathleen Deveny, "What's Wrong with This Picture? Utility's Glasses Are Never Empty," *The Wall Street Journal*, May 25, 1995, B1.

17. Day Mines *1974 Annual Report*, 1; reproduced in Tufte, *The Visual Display of Quantitative Information*, 54.

Chapter 17

1. Carol Hymowitz, "When You Tell the Boss, Plain Talk Counts," *The Wall Street Journal*, June 16, 1989, B1.

2. Linda Driskill, "How the Language of Presentations Can Encourage or Discourage Audience Participation," paper presented at the Conference on College Composition and Communication, Cincinnati, OH, March 18–21, 1992.

3. Anne Fisher, "Willy Loman Couldn't Cut It," *Fortune*, November 11, 1996, 210.

4. Ray Alexander, *Power Speech: Why It's Vital to You* (New York: AMACOM, 1986), 156.

5. Robert S. Mills, conversation with the author, March 10, 1988.

6. Phil Theibert, "Speechwriters of the World, Get Lost!" *The Wall Street Journal*, August 2, 1993, A10.

7. "A Study of the Effects of the Use of Overhead Transparencies on Business Meetings," Wharton Applied Research Center, reported in Martha Jewett and Rita Margolies, eds., *How to Run Better Business Meetings: A Reference Guide for Managers* (New York: McGraw-Hill, 1987), 109–110.

8. University of Minnesota/3M Study, reported in Martha Jewett and Rita Margolies, eds., *How to Run Better Business Meetings: A Reference Guide for Managers* (New York: McGraw-Hill, 1987), 115.

9. Stephen E. Lucas, *The Art of Public Speaking*, 2nd ed. (New York: Random House, 1986), 248.

10. John Case, "A Company of Businesspeople," *Inc.*, April 1993, 90.

11. Edward J. Hegarty, *Humor and Eloquence in Public Speaking* (West Nyack, NY: Parker, 1976), 204.

12. Based on Jewett and Margolies, *How to Run Better Business Meetings: A Reference Guide for Managers*, 183–85.

13. The comparison is taken from Jim Martin, "National Debt: Pennies to Heaven," *The Wall Street Journal*, February 22, 1988, 18.

14. Andy Rooney, "World Has Lost Mental Magician," Tribune Media Syndicate, *The Columbus Dispatch*, February 22, 1988, 7A.

15. Some studies have shown that previews and reviews increase comprehension; other studies have found no effect. For a summary of the research see Kenneth D. Frandsen and Donald R. Clement, "The Functions of Human Communication in Informing: Communicating and Processing

Information," *Handbook of Rhetorical and Communication Theory*, ed. Carroll C. Arnold and John Waite Bowers (Boston: Allyn and Bacon, 1984), 340–41.

16. S. A. Beebe, "Eye Contact: A Nonverbal Determinant of Speaker Credibility," *Speech Teacher* 23 (1974): 21–25; cited in Marjorie Fink Vargas, *Louder than Words* (Ames, IA: Iowa State University Press, 1986), 61–62.

17. J. Wills, "An Empirical Study of the Behavioral Characteristics of Sincere and Insincere Speakers," Ph.D. diss., University of Southern California, 1961; cited in Vargas, *Louder than Words*, 62.

18. George W. Fluharty and Harold R. Ross, *Public Speaking* (New York: Barnes & Noble, 1981), 162–63.

19. Ralph Proodian, "Mind the Tip of Your Tongue," *The Wall Street Journal*, May 4, 1992, A20.

20. Stephen E. Lucas, *The Art of Public Speaking*, 2nd ed. (New York: Random House, 1986), 243.

21. Ralph Proodian, "Raspy Throat? Read This, Mr. President," *The Wall Street Journal*, January 25, 1993, A14.

22. Michael Waldholz, "Lab Notes," *The Wall Street Journal*, March 19, 1991, B1.

23. George B. Ray, "Vocally Cued Personality Prototypes: An Implicit Personality Theory Approach," *Communication Monographs* 53, no. 3 (1986): 266–76.

Chapter 18

1. Timothy D. Schellhardt, "Managing: Pitfalls to Avoid in Drafting a Résumé," *The Wall Street Journal*, November 28, 1990, B1, and Elizabeth Brockman and Kelly Belanger, "One- or Two-Page Résumés: Does It Make a Difference?" Association for Business Communication Midwest Regional Convention, Akron, OH, April 4–5, 1991.

2. Davida H. Charney, Jack Rayman, and Linda Ferreira-Buckley, "How Writing Quality Influences Readers'

Judgments of Résumés in Business and Engineering," *Journal of Business and Technical Communication* 6, no. 1 (January 1992): 38–74.

3. Vincent S. Di Salvo and Janet K. Larsen, "A Contingency Approach to Communication Skill Importance: The Impact of Occupation, Direction, and Position," *The Journal of Business Communication* 24, no. 3 (Summer 1987): 13.

4. Carl Quintanilla, "Coming Back," *The Wall Street Journal,* February 22, 1996, R10.

5. LeAne Rutherford, "Five Fatal Résumé Mistakes," *Business Week's Guide to Careers* 4, no. 3 (Spring/Summer 1986): 60–62.

6. Phil Elder, "The Trade Secrets of Employment Interviews," Association for Business Communication Midwest Convention, Kansas City, MO, May 2, 1987.

7. Kitty O. Locker, Gianna M. Marsella, Alisha C. Rohde, and Paula C. Weston, "Electronic Résumés: Lessons from *Fortune* 500, *Inc.* 500, and Big Six CPA Firms," Association for Business Communication Annual Convention, Chicago, IL, November 6–9, 1996.

8. Ibid.

9. T. T. Sekine, "Employment Portfolios in the Nineties," Association for Business Communication Midwest Convention, Indianapolis, IN, April 20–22, 1995.

10. Beverly H. Nelson, William P. Gallé, and Donna W. Luse, "Electronic Job Search and Placement," Association for Business Communication Convention, Orlando, FL, November 1–4, 1995.

11. Resumix, "Preparing the Ideal Scannable Resume," [http://www.resumix.com] October 16, 1996.

12. Taunee Besson, *The Wall Street Journal National Employment Business Weekly: Résumés* (New York: John Wiley and Sons, 1994), 245.

13. Besson, *Résumés,* 245–56.

Chapter 19

1. Walter Kiechel III, "Preparing for Your Outplacement," *Fortune,* November 30, 1992, 153.

Chapter 20

1. Thomas Petzinger, Jr., "Lewis Roland's Knack for Finding Truckers Keeps Firm Rolling," *The Wall Street Journal,* December 1, 1995, B1.

2. Claud Dotson, comment, Association for Business Communication Western Regional Conference, Boise, ID, April 13, 1996; and "Choosy Firms Force Job Seekers to Jump through Many Hoops," *The Wall Street Journal,* October 6, 1993, B4.

3. Judith A. Swartley to Kitty Locker, March 20, 1989.

4. Sherri Eng, "Company Culture Dictates Attire for Interviews," *The Columbus Dispatch,* August 25, 1996, 33J.

5. The Catalyst Staff, *Marketing Yourself* (New York: G. P. Putnam's Sons, 1980), 179.

6. Julie Amparano Lopez, "Firms Force Job Seekers to Jump through Hoops," *The Wall Street Journal,* October 6, 1993, B1.

7. Donna Stine Kienzler, letter to Ann Granacki, April 6, 1988.

8. Joel Bowman, "Using NLP to Improve Classroom Communication," Association for Business Communication Regional Conference, Lexington, KY, April 9–11, 1992.

9. Christopher Conte, "Labor Letter," *The Wall Street Journal,* October 19, 1993, A1.

10. *Marketing Yourself,* 101.

11. Claud Dotson, comment at the Association for Business Communication Western Regional Conference, Boise, ID, April 13, 1996.

12. Kate Wendleton, *Through the Brick Wall: How to Job-Hunt in a Tight Market* (New York: Villard Books, 1992), 244.

13. Ray Robinson, quoted by Dick Friedman, "The Interview as Mating Ritual," *Working Woman,* April 1987, 107.

14. Brenda Major and Ellen Konar, "An Investigation of Sex Differences in Pay Expectations and Their Possible Causes," *Academy of Management Journal* 27, no. 4 (1984): 782.

15. Wendleton, *Through the Brick Wall,* 278.

Appendix A

1. Maria Rivera, comment to the author, Association for Business Communication East Regional Convention, San Juan, PR, April 28, 1995.

Appendix C

1. N. L. Reinsch, Jr., and Raymond W. Beswick, "Voice Mail versus Conventional Channels: A Cost Minimization Analysis of Individuals' Preferences," *Academy of Management Journal* 11, no. 4 (1990): 801–16.

2. Robert Rosenthal, *Pygmalion in the Classroom* (New York: Holt, Rinehart, and Winston, 1968).

3. Danuta Ehrlich, Isaiah Guttman, Peter Schonbach, and Judson Mills, "Postdecision Exposure to Relevant Information," *Journal of Abnormal and Social Psychology* 54 (1957): 98–102; summarized in Elliot Aronson, *The Social Animal* (San Francisco: W. H. Freeman, 1972), 101.

4. Tim R. V. Davis, "Managing Culture at the Bottom," in *Gaining Control of the Corporate Culture,* ed. Ralph H. Kilman, Mary J. Saxton, Roy Serpa, and Associates (San Francisco: Jossey-Bass Publishers, 1985), 175.

5. "What's Wrong with This Picture?" *The Columbus Dispatch,* May 9, 1994, 2D.

6. Paulette Thomas, "Work Week," *The Wall Street Journal,* October 29, 1996, B1.

7. Paul Craig Roberts, "America's 'Savings Crisis' Is a Chimera," *Business Week,* February 12, 1990, 20.

8. William M. Bulkeley, "A Firm by Any Other Name Means Likely Rise in Stock, Research Finds," *The Wall Street Journal,* July 10, 1987, 22.

9. Elmo R. Zumwalt, Jr., *On Watch: A Memoir* (New York: Times Books, 1976), 189; cited in Thomas J. Peters and Robert H. Waterman, Jr., *In Search of Excellence: Lessons from America's Best-Run Companies* (New York: Warner, 1982), 263–64.

10. "Kodak Alters Use of Name," Champaign-Urbana *News-Gazette,* April 8, 1983, C-1.

11. Roger Trench, "All in a Day's Work," *Reader's Digest,* September 1989, 138.

12. John C. Dvorak, "Crazy Mistakes, Part 1," *PC Magazine,* March 28, 1989, 71, and "Crazy Mistakes, Part 2," *PC Magazine,* June 13, 1989, 71.

PHOTO CREDITS

COMPANY, ORGANIZATION, AND AGENCY INDEX

SUBJECT INDEX